CRITICAL SURVEY
OF
SHORT FICTION

CRITICAL SURVEY

OF

SHORT FICTION

Second Revised Edition

Volume 1
Lee K. Abbott - Morley Callaghan

Editor, Second Revised Edition
Charles E. May
California State University, Long Beach

Editor, First Edition
Frank N. Magill

SALEM PRESS, INC.
Pasadena, California   Hackensack, New Jersey

Managing Editor: Christina J. Moose
Research Supervisor: Jeffry Jensen
Acquisitions Editor: Mark Rehn
Photograph Editor: Philip Bader
Manuscript Editors: Lauren M. Mitchell
Melanie Watkins
Research Assistant: Jeff Stephens
Production Editor: Cynthia Beres
Layout: Ross Castellano

Library of Congress Cataloging-in-Publication Data

Critical survey of short fiction / editor, Charles E. May.—2nd rev. ed.

    7 v. ; cm.

Includes bibliographical references and index.

    First edition edited by Frank Northen Magill.

    Includes bibliographical references and index.

    ISBN 0-89356-006-5 (set : alk. paper) — ISBN 0-89356-007-3 (v. 1 : alk. paper) —
ISBN 0-89356-008-1 (v. 2 : alk. paper) — ISBN 0-89356-009-X (v. 3 : alk. paper) —
ISBN 0-89356-010-3 (v. 4 : alk. paper) — ISBN 0-89356-011-1 (v. 5 : alk. paper) —
ISBN 0-89356-012-X (v. 6 : alk. paper) — ISBN 0-89356-013-8 (v. 7 : alk. paper)

    1. Short story. 2. Short story—History and criticism. 3. Short story—Bio-bibliography.
I. May, Charles E. (Charles Edward) 1941 -   . II. Magill, Frank Northen, 1907-1997.

Ref PN3321 .C7 2001 V. 1

809.3′1—dc21

00-046384

Second Printing

CONTENTS

PUBLISHER'S NOTE

Introduced in 1981, the *Critical Survey of Short Fiction* was the original member of Salem Press's *Critical Survey* series, which now totals more than fifty volumes that cover major world authors in all genres: Short Fiction, Long Fiction, Poetry, and Drama. This edition, the *Critical Survey of Short Fiction: Second Revised Edition*, is actually the third generation of this publication—and by far the most heavily revised of all. In 1987, the original seven-volume edition was supplemented by a volume covering 49 additional short-story writers, and in 1993 these were combined into a single *Revised Edition*, updated to reflect new titles, secondary sources, and 65 more new authors. This set also takes on a new look, providing pictorial information with more than 350 portraits of the authors covered, along with an improved page design that breaks information into more easily consumed chunks of information.

The current publication retains all but one of the authors from the 1993 revised edition. (The sixteenth century British writer John Lyly, the editors decided, had been miscast as a "short-fiction" writer.) To the original 347 authors it adds 133 authors completely new to the *Short Fiction* series—increasing the set's coverage of authors by more than 38 percent. Many, such as Sherman Alexie, Melissa Bank, Chris Offutt, Mona Simpson, and Rick Bass, are authors (several of them Baby Boomers or Generation X-ers) who are relatively new to the scene and whose work promises great things. Others, such as Sue Miller or E. Annie Proulx, are established authors whose work in this genre has been recently recognized. Some, such as Aldous Huxley, Pär Lagerkvist, Amos Oz, Alain Robbe-Grillet, and Miguel de Unamuno y Jugo, are older or "classic" authors previously not included in the *Short Fiction* series. Many, including Isabelle Allende, Ezekiel Mphahlele, Juan Rulfo, and Italo Svevo, are world authors of international repute whose works have become increasingly available to the student audience through translation. Still others, such as James Agee, Maya Angelou, A. S. Byatt, Ralph Ellison, Louise Erdrich, Gail Godwin, Sylvia Plath, Salman Rushdie, John Sayles, and Susan Sontag, are established writers known primarily for work in other genres. Finally, a few, such as Gina Berriault, have written for some time but until recently have been undervalued.

Author essays vary in length, with none shorter than 2,000 words and many much longer. Each essay provides ready-reference top matter, including full birth and death data, full listings of literary works by genre, and bibliographical sources for further study. Each author essay is broken into the following uniformly headed subdivisions:

Principal short fiction: Lists the author's major short-fiction works (collections and sometimes uncollected stories), including titles and dates of original appearance.

Other literary forms: Describes the author's output in other genres, noting the type of work for which he or she is best known.

Achievements: Honors and awards, as well as less tangible contributions to the history of literature and other achievements.

Biography: A condensed biographical sketch with vital information from birth through death (or, if the author is still living, recent activities).

Analysis: Overview of the themes, techniques, and development of the author's work in short fiction.

Story/collection overviews: Multiple discussions of stories and/or story collections typically anthologized or taught, including both description and analysis; each discussion is headed by the work's title.

Other major works: Lists, by genre, all the author's major works other than short fiction.

Bibliography: Cites secondary sources for additional information and study, suitable for students. All bibliographies throughout the set have been heavily updated to reflect recent scholarship.

Contributor's byline: Signed by the academician who wrote the article; updaters are also named.

Volume 7 contains a plate of 29 overview essays: surveys of broad areas. To the original 12 essays that appeared at the end of the 1993 edition, which provided overviews of the development of short fiction through history, have been added 17 new overview essays ranging in length from 3,000 to 10,000 words. The new overviews, devoted to theory and world cultures (including ethnic groups both within and outside the United States), complement the original historical surveys, which have been thoroughly updated or rewritten. The aggregate result is a compact and complete review of short fiction, which should help students of both individual authors and the genre as a whole to fill gaps and make comparisons and connections that would otherwise be difficult to make if the set were devoted solely to author coverage.

This final volume offers another new set of features: "Research Tools." This section comprises not only heavily revised versions of the 1993 edition's "Terms and Techniques," "Short-Fiction Chronology" (time line of key events in the history of short fiction), and "Bibliography" but also cites the winners of major short-fiction awards in three sections: "Major Awards," listing the recipients of five major literary awards since the awards' inception; "The Best American Short Stories," a lengthy section listing the short stories, with authors, included in every edition of this core short-fiction anthology since it began publication in 1915; and "The O. Henry Awards," nearly as long, which lists stories and authors winning the First Prize, Second Prize, and "Other Selected" honors since 1919.

Several listings and appendices are designed to aid the reader both in locating the book's contents and in organizing the contents in useful ways: A complete list of authors covered in the set appears in the front matter to each volume, and both a geographical index of authors and an index of authors by category appear at the end of each volume. The latter arranges the authors by more than 100 subgenres and subject areas with which they are identified, from Absurdism and Adventure through Westerns and Women's Issues. Finally, a comprehensive Subject Index lists authors, those of their works that receive major discussion, titles, and cross-references from foreign-language titles and other names by which the authors were known, as well as concepts and genres where those receive substantial discussion.

Edging beyond a "revised edition" with more than 40 percent new material, this edition owes much to its editor, Charles E. May of California State University, Long Beach. Professor May was responsible not only for thoroughly updating the table of contents, with a view to the needs of both teachers and students; he also devoted significant time to writing and updating articles for the set, finding experts in difficult-to-assign areas, and scrutinizing the set's appendices for usefulness and accessibility. In addition, the set owes a debt to the many academicians and area experts who contributed both to the original editions and to the current one; their names and affiliations are listed in the front matter to this volume.

CONTRIBUTORS TO THE *SECOND REVISED EDITION*

Charles E. May, Editor
California State University, Long Beach

Michael Adams
City University of New York Graduate Center

Thomas P. Adler
Purdue University

A. Owen Aldridge
University of Illinois

Gerald S. Argetsinger
Rochester Institute of Technology

Karen L. Arnold
Montpelier Cultural Arts Center

Marilyn Arnold
Brigham Young University

Robert W. Artinian
Original Contributor

Leonard R. N. Ashley
Brooklyn College, City University of New York

Stanley S. Atherton
Original Contributor

Bryan Aubrey
Independent Scholar

Edmund August
McKendree College

Jane L. Ball
Wilberforce University

Thomas Banks
Ohio Northern University

Carol M. Barnum
Southern College of Technology

Mary Baron
Original Contributor

David Barratt
Independent Scholar

Melissa E. Barth
Appalachian State University

Ben Befu
University of California, Los Angeles

Bert Bender
Original Contributor

Alvin K. Benson
Brigham Young University

Richard P. Benton
Trinity College

Stephen Benz
Barry University

Dorothy M. Betz
Georgetown University

Cynthia A. Bily
Adrian College

Margaret Boe Birns
New York University

Nicholas Birns
New School University

Carol Bishop
Indiana University, Southeast

Lynn Z. Bloom
Original Contributor

Julia B. Boken
Indiana University, Southeast

Jo-Ellen Lipman Boon
Independent Scholar

Virginia Brackett
Triton Community College

Jerry Bradley
Original Contributor

Harold Branam
Savannah State University

Gerhard Brand
California State University, Los Angeles

Laurence A. Breiner
Original Contributor

J. R. Brink
Arizona State University

Keith H. Brower
Salisbury State University

Alan Brown
Livingston University

Mary Hanford Bruce
Monmouth College

Carl Brucker
Arkansas Tech University

Mitzi M. Brunsdale
Mayville State College

Laurie Buchanan
Original Contributor

Louis J. Budd
Original Contributor

Jeffrey L. Buller
Georgia Southern University

Rebecca R. Butler
Dalton College

Susan Butterworth
Independent Scholar

Edmund J. Campion
University of Tennessee

Larry A. Carlson
Original Contributor

John Carpenter
University of Michigan

John Carr
Original Contributor

Warren J. Carson
Original Contributor

Mary LeDonne Cassidy
South Carolina State University

Thomas Cassidy
South Carolina State University

Hal Charles
Eastern Kentucky University

Balance Chow
San Jose State University

John C. Coleman
*Pennsylvania State University,
The Behrend College*

Julian W. Connolly
University of Virginia

Richard Hauer Costa
Texas A&M University

Natalia Costa-Zalessow
San Francisco State University

Lisa-Anne Culp
Oglethorpe University

Richard H. Dammers
Original Contributor

Mary Virginia Davis
Independent Scholar

Kwame Dawes
University of South Carolina

Frank Day
Clemson University

Bill Delaney
Independent Scholar

Joan DelFattore
University of Delaware

Kathryn Zabelle Derounian
University of Arkansas—Little Rock

John F. Desmond
Original Contributor

James E. Devlin
*State University of New York at
Oneonta*

M. Casey Diana
*University of Illinois at Urbana-
Champaign*

Stefan Dziemianowicz
Independent Scholar

Grace Eckley
Drake University

Wilton Eckley
Colorado School of Mines

Robert P. Ellis
Independent Scholar

Thomas L. Erskine
Salisbury State University

Walter Evans
Augusta College

Howard Faulkner
Original Contributor

James Feast
*Baruch College of the City University
of New York*

John W. Fiero
University of Southwestern Louisiana

Edward Fiorelli
St. John's University

Earl E. Fitz
Pennsylvania State University

James K. Folsom
Original Contributor

Ben Forkner
Original Contributor

David W. Foster
Arizona State University

Dean Franco
*California State University,
Long Beach*

Carol Franks
Portland State University

Timothy C. Frazer
Western Illinois University

Kathy Ruth Frazier
Original Contributor

Tom Frazier
Cumberland College

Terri Frongia
University of California, Riverside

Miriam Fuchs
University of Hawaii—Manoa

Jean C. Fulton
Maharishi University of Management

Kenneth Funsten
Original Contributor

James Gaash
Humboldt State University

Michelle Gadpaille
University of Maribor

Louis Gallo
Radford University

Ann Davison Garbett
Averett College

James W. Garvey
Original Contributor

Marshall Bruce Gentry
University of Indianapolis

Jill B. Gidmark
University of Minnesota

Theodore W. Goossen
York University

Linda S. Gordon
Worcester State College

Peter W. Graham
Virginia Polytechnic Institute and State University

Julian Grajewski
Original Contributor

Charles A. Gramlich
Xavier University of Louisiana

James L. Green
Arizona State University

William E. Grim
Ohio University

David Mike Hamilton
Original Contributor

Todd C. Hanlin
University of Arkansas

Betsy Harfst
Kishwaukee College

Mark Harman
Franklin & Marshall College

Natalie Harper
Simon's Rock College of Bard

David V. Harrington
Original Contributor

Stephen M. Hart
University College London

Zia Hasan
King Faisal University

Peter B. Heller
Manhattan College

Terry Heller
Coe College

Diane Andrews Henningfeld
Adrian College

Cheryl Herr
Original Contributor

Allen Hibbard
Middle Tennessee State University

Cynthia Packard Hill
University of Massachusetts at Amherst

Jane Hill
Independent Scholar

Joseph W. Hinton
Independent Scholar

Wendy Ho
University of California, Davis

Nika Hoffman
Crossroads School for Arts & Sciences

William Hoffman
Independent Scholar

Hal Holladay
Simon's Rock College of Bard

Gregory D. Horn
Southwest Virginia Community College

Naana Banyiwa Horne
Indiana University, Kokomo

Sylvia Huete
Original Contributor

Edward Huffstetler
Bridgewater College

Theodore C. Humphrey
California Polytechnic University, Pomona

Archibald E. Irwin
Indiana University, Southeast

Kimberley L. Jacobs
Miami University—Ohio

Shakuntala Jayaswal
University of New Haven

Clarence O. Johnson
Original Contributor

Ronald L. Johnson
Northern Michigan University

Elizabeth Johnston
Acadia University

Eunice Pedersen Johnston
North Dakota State University

Ralph R. Joly
Asbury College

Jane Anderson Jones
Manatee Community College

Paul Kane
Vassar College

Theresa Kanoza
Lincoln Land Community College

William P. Keen
Washington & Jefferson College

Karen A. Kildahl
South Dakota State University

Sue L. Kimball
Methodist College

Cassandra Kircher
Elon College

Grove Koger
Boise Public Library

Paula Kopacz
Eastern Kentucky University

Margaret Wade Krausse
Linfield College

Marvin Lachman
Independent Scholar

Thomas D. Lane
Original Contributor

John Lang
Emory & Henry College

Carlota Larrea
Pennsylvania State University

Eugene S. Larson
Pierce College

Donald F. Larsson
Mankato State University

William Laskowski
Jamestown College

Norman Lavers
Arkansas State University

Harry Lawton
*University of California, Santa
    Barbara*

David Layton
*University of California,
    Santa Barbara*

Allen Learst
Oklahoma State University

Linda Ledford-Miller
University of Scranton

James Ward Lee
University of North Texas

Trevor Le Gassick
University of Michigan

Leon Lewis
Appalachian State University

Douglas Long
Independent Scholar

Michael Loudon
Eastern Illinois University

Robert M. Luscher
University of Nebraska at Kearney

R. C. Lutz
University of the Pacific

Joanne McCarthy
Tacoma Community College

Andrew F. Macdonald
Loyola University

Gina Macdonald
Loyola University

James MacDonald
Humber College

Richard D. McGhee
Arkansas State University

Hugh McLean
University of California, Berkeley

Victoria E. McLure
Texas Tech University

Robert J. McNutt
Original Contributor

Roger J. McNutt
Original Contributor

Bryant Mangum
Original Contributor

Barry Stewart Mann
Independent Scholar

Patricia Marks
Valdosta State College

Karen M. Cleveland Marwick
Independent Scholar

Paul Marx
University of New Haven

Charles E. May
*California State University, Long
    Beach*

Laurence W. Mazzeno
Alvernia College

Kenneth W. Meadwell
University of Winnipeg

Patrick Meanor
*State University of New York,
    College at Oneonta*

Martha Meek
Original Contributor

Helen Menke
Original Contributor

Ann A. Merrill
Emory University

Walter E. Meyers
North Carolina State University

Jennifer Michaels
Grinnell College

Vasa D. Mihailovich
University of North Carolina

Paula M. Miller
Biola University

Robert W. Millett
Original Contributor

Christian H. Moe
*Southern Illinois University at
    Carbondale*

S. S. Moorty
Southern Utah State College

Robert A. Morace
Daemen College

Sherry Morton-Mollo
California State University, Fullerton

Christina Murphy
Original Contributor

Earl Paulus Murphy
Harris-Stowe State College

Brian Murray
Youngstown State University

John M. Muste
Ohio State University

Susan Nayel
Original Contributor

Keith Neilson
California State University, Fullerton

William Nelles
*University of Massachusetts,
    Dartmouth*

Keith Nelson
Original Contributor

Evelyn Newlyn
*Virginia Polytechnic Institute and
State University*

John Nizalowski
Mesa State College

Martha Nochimson
Original Contributor

Emma Coburn Norris
Troy State University

George O'Brien
Georgetown University

Bruce Olsen
Austin Peay State University

James Norman O'Neill
Independent Scholar

Robert M. Otten
Marymount University

Keri L. Overall
University of South Carolina

Cóilín Owens
George Mason University

Janet Taylor Palmer
*Caldwell Community College &
Technical Institute*

Robert J. Paradowski
*Rochester Institute of
Technology*

David J. Parent
Independent Scholar

David B. Parsell
Furman University

Leslie A. Pearl
Independent Scholar

David Peck
*California State University,
Long Beach*

William Peden
University of Missouri—Columbia

William E. Pemberton
University of Wisconsin, LaCrosse

Chapel Louise Petty
Original Contributor

R. Craig Philips
Michigan State University

Allene Phy-Olsen
Austin Peay State University

Susan L. Piepke
Bridgewater College

Constance Pierce
Original Contributor

Adrienne Pilon
*California State University,
Long Beach*

Rosaria Pipia
New York University

Mary Ellen Pitts
Rhodes College

Scott D. Vander Ploeg
Madisonville Community College

Victoria Price
Lamar University

Karen Priest
Lamar University at Orange

Norman Prinsky
Augusta State University

Charles Pullen
Queens University

Jere Real
Lynchburg College

Peter J. Reed
University of Minnesota

Rosemary M. Canfield Reisman
Charleston Southern University

Martha E. Rhynes
Oklahoma East Central University

Richard Rice
James Madison University

James Curry Robison
University of South Florida

Mary Rohrberger
University of Northern Iowa

Douglas Rollins
Dawson College

Jill Rollins
Dawson College

Carl Rollyson
*Baruch College of the City University
of New York*

Paul Rosefeldt
Delgado Community College

Ruth Rosenberg
Original Contributor

Joseph Rosenblum
*University of North Carolina,
Greensboro*

Stella P. Rosenfeld
Cleveland State University

Harry L. Rosser
Boston College

Gabrielle Rowe
McKendree College

Irene Struthers Rush
Independent Scholar

Amelia A. Rutledge
Original Contributor

Murray Sachs
Brandeis University

David Sadkin
Niagara University

Chaman L. Sahni
Boise State University

Selina Samuels
University of New South Wales

David N. Samuelson
Original Contributor

Victor A. Santi
University of New Orleans

Barry Scherr
Dartmouth College

Marilyn Schultz
*California State University,
    Fullerton*

Barbara Kitt Seidman
Linfield College

D. Dean Shackelford
Concord College

Chenliang Sheng
Northern Kentucky University

Allen Shepherd
Original Contributor

Nancy E. Sherrod
Armstrong Atlantic State University

Thelma J. Shinn
Arizona State University

R. Baird Shuman
*University of Illinois at Urbana-
    Champaign*

Charles L. P. Silet
Iowa State University

Karin A. Silet
Iowa State University

Jan Sjåvik
University of Washington

Genevieve Slomski
Independent Scholar

Clyde Curry Smith
University of Wisconsin—River Falls

Roger Smith
Independent Scholar

Ira Smolensky
Monmouth College

Katherine Snipes
Eastern Washington University

Jean M. Snook
*Memorial University of
    Newfoundland*

George Soule
Carleton College

Madison V. Sowell
Brigham Young University

Sandra Whipple Spanier
Original Contributor

Sharon Spencer
Original Contributor

Brian Stableford
Independent Scholar

John Stark
Original Contributor

Joshua Stein
University of California, Riverside

Karen F. Stein
University of Rhode Island

Judith L. Steininger
Milwaukee School of Engineering

Louise M. Stone
Bloomsburg University

William B. Stone
Original Contributor

Gerald H. Strauss
Bloomsburg University

W. J. Stuckey
Purdue University

Mary J. Sturm
Independent Scholar

Alvin Sullivan
*Southern Illinois University at
    Edwardsville*

Eileen A. Sullivan
Original Contributor

James Sullivan
*California State University,
    Los Angeles*

Catherine Swanson
Independent Scholar

Roy Arthur Swanson
University of Milwaukee, Wisconsin

Philip A. Tapley
Louisiana College

James D. Tedder
George Mason University

Christopher J. Thaiss
George Mason University

Terry Theodore
*University of North Carolina at
    Wilmington*

Maxine S. Theodoulou
The Union Institute

David J. Thieneman
University of Louisville

Lou Thompson
Texas Woman's University

Rosemary Barton Tobin
Original Contributor

Evelyn Toft
Fort Hays State University

Christine D. Tomei
Columbia University

Michael Trussler
University of Regina

Richard Tuerk
Texas A&M University—Commerce

Scott D. Vander Ploeg
Madisonville Community College

Dennis Vannatta
University of Arkansas at Little Rock

Jon S. Vincent
University of Kansas

Gary F. Waller
Wilfrid Launer University

Jaquelyn W. Walsh
McNeese State University

Mark A. Weinstein
*University of Nevada—
Las Vegas*

James Michael Welsh
Salisbury State University

James Whitlark
Texas Tech University

Barbara Wiedemann
Auburn University at Montgomery

Albert Wilhelm
*Tennessee Technological
University*

Donna Glee Williams
*North Carolina Center for the
Advancement of Teaching*

Patricia A. R. Williams
Texas Southern University

Judith Barton Williamson
Sauk Valley Community College

Michael Witkoski
Independent Scholar

Anna M. Wittman
University of Alberta

Qingyun Wu
*California State University,
Los Angeles*

Jennifer L. Wyatt
Civic Memorial High School

Mary F. Yudin
Penn State University

Gay Annette Zieger
Independent Scholar

COMPLETE LIST OF AUTHORS

Volume I

Volume II

Volume III

Volume IV

Volume V

Volume VI

CRITICAL SURVEY
OF
SHORT FICTION

A

LEE K. ABBOTT

Born: Panama Canal Zone; October 17, 1947

PRINCIPAL SHORT FICTION
The Heart Never Fits Its Wanting, 1980
Love Is the Crooked Thing, 1986
Strangers in Paradise, 1986
Dreams of Distant Lives, 1989
Living After Midnight, 1991
Wet Places at Noon, 1997

OTHER LITERARY FORMS
Insisting that he lacks the energy to write a novel, Lee K. Abbott sticks to the short story as his genre of choice. He wrote a chapter of the novel *The Putt at the End of the World* (2000).

ACHIEVEMENTS
Lee K. Abbott's stories have been selected to appear in *The Best American Short Stories* ("The Final Proof of Fate and Circumstances," 1984, and "Dreams of Distant Lives," 1987), *Prize Stories: The O. Henry Awards* ("The Final Proof of Fate and Circumstances," 1984 and "Living Alone in Iota," 1984), and *The Pushcart Prize* (1984, 1987, and 1989). He has twice received a National Endowment for the Arts Fellowship (1979 and 1985), the St. Lawrence Award for Fiction (1981), the Editors Choice Award from Wampeter-Doubleday (1986), the National Magazine Award for Fiction (1986), a Major Artist Fellowship from the Ohio Arts Council (1991-1992), a Governor's Award for the Arts from the Ohio Arts Council (1993), and the Syndicated Fiction Award (1995).

BIOGRAPHY
Lee Kittredge Abbott was born in the Panama Canal Zone on October 17, 1947, to a military father and an alcoholic mother, whom he has fictionalized

in such stories as "The End of Grief" and "Time and Fear and Somehow Love." He received his bachelor's degree in English from New Mexico State University in 1970. He married Pamela Jo Dennis in 1969, after which he and his new wife moved to New York City, where he attended Columbia University. He returned to New Mexico State University, where he received an M.A. degree in English in 1973. He went on to earn an M.F.A. from the University of Arkansas in 1977.

Abbott published a number of stories in various literary magazines while working on his M.A. and M.F.A. After accepting a position as an assistant professor of English at Case Western Reserve University, he published his first collection of stories, *The Heart Never Fits Its Wanting*. In 1990, Abbott began teaching writing as a professor at Ohio State University. He has held visiting professor positions at Wichita State University, Southwest Texas State University, and Yale University. He has also taught writing at Rice University, Colorado College, and the Iowa Writer's Workshop.

ANALYSIS
When asked to comment on minimalism for a special issue of *The Mississippi Review*, Abbott disavowed any relationship to that group, insisting he was a "mossback prose-writer who prefers stories with all the parts hanging out and whirling." Abbott once said, "I ride with the Wild Bunch," identifying himself with John Cheever, Peter Taylor, and Eudora Welty. However, he is most clearly connected to the wild bunch of prose writers of the 1970's and 1980's that includes Barry Hannah, Richard Bausch, and Larry Brown—writers who create the voice of a down-and-out rural male from the South or the West who chases liquor, women, and enough money to get

by. In the game of creating rough, redneck lyrical narrative, Abbott is self-consciously one of the best.

"LIVING ALONE IN IOTA"

Reese, the protagonist in this story, has been dumped by his girlfriend and feels desolate: "She makes my ears bleed," he tells the boys where he works. "I mean when she starts kissing my neck, I go off into a dark land. It's like death, only welcome." As a result of his loss, the protagonist is "love-sawed." If the story has any specific statement of theme, it is when Reese tells the members of his crew, "Boys, I am being sand-bagged by memory." He goes to Deming, New Mexico, a small town featured in a number of Abbott's stories, to find his girlfriend. Drinking two six-packs of beer on the way, he arrives "his face yellow with hope," and in a "state as pure and unbecoming as loneliness."

In this wonderfully comic, laugh-out-loud story, Reese tries desperately to win Billy Jean La Took back, but she will have none of it, granting him only one chaste kiss. However, as Abbott says in his typical rural romanticism, "You could tell that kiss really ripped the spine out of him." He tries to forget her with other women, but to no avail. Although he tries one last time to get her back, she remains as "distant from him as he from his ancestral fishes." Three months later, in a flash of unmotivated insight, he says, "Boys I'm a fool." This is one of Abbott's purest lyrical love stories, creating a roughneck Romeo full of poor-boy poetry.

"THE FINAL PROOF OF FATE AND CIRCUMSTANCE"

This prize-winning story is a lyrical account of a man's masculine identification with his father as he listens to the older man tell stories about his past. As the father tells of driving through the desert when he was in his twenties and accidentally hitting and killing a man, the son imagines the father in such detail that he identifies with him completely. When the father finds the body in the darkness, he feels the kind of tranquility that one feels at the end of a drama when, after the ruin is dealt out fairly, one goes off to drink.

The sense of catharsis felt at the end of a tragedy is continued by the narrator as he listens to more of his father's stories "in which the hero, using luck and ignorance, manages to avoid the base and its slick companion, the wanton." He senses he is in a warm place that few get to experience, where a father admits to being a lot like his son, a place "made habitable by age and self-absorption and fatigue that says much about those heretofore pantywaist emotions like pity and fear."

The father's final story is about the death of his first wife, which occurred so unexpectedly that it was like a death in a fairy tale that left him numb, "no more sentient than a clock." The "sad part" of the story, the father says, occurs during the funeral procession, when he orders the car to stop, gets out, and walks to an ice cream parlor. After eating three cones of the best ice cream he has ever had, he is struck with an insight of such force that he feels light-headed, thinking that if he faints, his last thought, like that of the man he killed in the desert, would be long and complex, featuring "a scene of hope followed by misfortune and doom."

The story ends with the narrator telling his father's stories to his wife, trying to make her see what he only vaguely understands himself. He plans to tell her a story of his own, of wandering through his father's house once and standing over his bed while he slept; this is the part that has the truth in it, he says, about how "a fellow such as me invites a fellow such as him out to do a thing—I'm not sure what—that involves effort and sacrifice and leads, in an hour or a day, to that throb and swell fellows such as you call triumph."

"THE TALK TALKED BETWEEN WORMS"

In this story from Abbott's most recent collection, *Wet Places at Noon*, he focuses once again on the relationship between a father and a son. This time the basis of the relationship is the historical/cultural fact of the report of a flying saucer having landed in the small New Mexico town of Roswell in 1947. Although the official account is that a cowhand named Mac Brazeall found the pieces of metal that were reported to be remnants of a crashed flying saucer, Abbott's story is based on the fictional observation of the spacecraft and aliens by Tot Hamsey, father of the narrator of the story.

Although accounts from the father's journals and recorded tapes of his sighting of the aliens that occurred in 1947 appear throughout the story, the primary events occur in the early 1980's, when the narrator goes to visit his father, who has been institutionalized. The father has extensive records of his knowledge of the aliens: where they live, what they do in space, their beliefs and conquests. Insisting that he is not mad, the father says he is simply a man who has died and come back. The son perceives him as a figure out of a fairy tale, reading his records so often and so thoroughly that he memorizes whole sections.

As he does in other stories, Abbott projects himself into the mind of his father, imagining he is inside his head, feeling the present overwhelmed by the past. The father says, "There's no power, son, no glory. There's nothing—just them and us and the things we walk on. I have proof. . . . My files." Abbott's cultural reference here is to the popular television show *The X-Files*, which is based on the premise of secret government cover-ups and the obsessive belief in the reality of aliens having invaded earth.

When the father dies, the narrator goes to his house looking for evidence of the truth of his father's hallucinations, feeling like a juvenile on a scavenger hunt. Finding a box of papers hidden under the floorboards, he realizes that just as thousands of days ago "a terrible thing had crashed in my father's life . . . something equally impossible had landed in mine." Although he tells his new wife that what he found is trash, just a lot of talk, he recalls his father's admonition about "the talk talked between worms"—the confrontation of human beings with ultimate mystery.

The story is an interesting exploration of basic human choices among logic, common sense, and everyday reality and obsessive commitment to the unknown mysteries of life. Abbott uses the cultural clichés of alien spacecrafts to embody a basic sense that human beings are surrounded by mysteries that they can never fully know, mysteries that they can either ignore or become so captured by that their lives are dominated by them.

OTHER MAJOR WORK

LONG FICTION: *The Putt at the End of the World*, 2000 (with Richard Bausch, Tim O'Brien, and others).

BIBLIOGRAPHY

Abbott, Lee K. "An Interview with Lee K. Abbott." Interview by George Myers. *High Plains Literary Review* 7 (Winter, 1992): 95-108. Abbott rejects being classified as a regional writer, a distinction he says was created for the convenience of reviewers; discusses how the story "How Love Is Lived in Paradise" came into being. Abbott says he is a realist of the "modernist stripe," that character is the center of his fiction. Criticizes such popular writers as Danielle Steel and Sidney Sheldon for trivializing literature by putting formula before fact.

_____. "A Short Note on Minimalism." *Mississippi Review*, no. 40/41 (Winter, 1985): 23. In this special issue on minimalism, Abbott argues that minimalists are basically journalists. Claims he is a "sort of mossback prose-writer who prefers stories with all the parts hanging out and whirling." Says he rides with "Wild Bunch" writers, which include John Updike, John Cheever, Peter Taylor, Walker Percy, and Eudora Welty.

_____. "A Stubborn Sense of Place." *Harper's* 273 (August, 1986): 35-45. Abbott argues that a writer's voice—which he says has to do with character, spirit, custom, practice, habit, and morality—is a function of place, because its authority comes from the crossroads at which the writer learned what he or she knows. Says that literary matters such as voice are really cultural matters; insists that language is culture and that in literature ethos is lingo.

Drury, Tom. "All the Wrong Places." Review of *Wet Places at Noon*, by Lee K. Abbott. *The New York Times*, November 16, 1997, p. 78. Drury says that Abbott draws on American cultural standards to create his own mythology; says Abbott's characters ramble, skip ahead, backtrack, string the reader along, and go on and on as if there is no tomorrow. Notes that recklessness and comic futility are persistent themes in his fiction; says the theme of how stories hold people together as well as hold them back is at work in a number of stories, particularly his best, "The Talk Talked Between Worms."

Pope, Dan. "The Post-Minimalist American Story or What Comes After Carver?" *Gettysburg Review* 1 (Spring, 1988): 331-342. Discusses Abbott's *Strangers in Paradise* and *Love Is the Crooked Thing* to show that the minimalist trap can be avoided and that the American short story is diverse and rich. Argues that Abbott is more influenced by John Cheever than Raymond Carver and that in contrast to the minimalists he is a wordsmith whose love of the rhythm of language is akin to that of Stanley Elkin and Barry Hannah.

Charles E. May

CHINUA ACHEBE

Born: Ogidi, Nigeria; November 16, 1930

PRINCIPAL SHORT FICTION

The Sacrificial Egg and Other Short Stories, 1962
Girls at War, 1972

OTHER LITERARY FORMS

In addition to his short-story collections, Chinua Achebe is known for essays, poetry collections, and children's literature. He is best known, however, for his novel *No Longer at Ease* (1960), which became a modern African classic. The book is the second in a trilogy about change, conflict, and personal struggle to find the "New Africa." The first is *Things Fall Apart* (1958) and the third is *Arrow of God* (1964). Achebe's fourth novel, *A Man of the People* (1966), was followed twenty-one years later by *Anthills of the Savannah* (1987), his fifth novel. In 1984 he became the founder and publisher of *Uwa Ndi Igbo: A Bilingual Journal of Igbo Life and Arts*. Achebe edited volumes of African short fiction, including *African Short Stories* (1985) and *The Heinemann Book of Contemporary African Short Fiction* (1992), both with C. L. Innes.

ACHIEVEMENTS

Chinua Achebe received awards or award nominations for each of his novelistic works, from the Margaret Wrong Memorial Prize for *Things Fall Apart* to a Booker McConnell Prize nomination for *Anthills of the Savannah*. He was also awarded a Rockefeller travel fellowship in 1960 and the United Nations Educational, Scientific, and Cultural Organization (UNESCO) Fellowship for creative artists in 1963. In 1979 he received the Nigerian National Merit Award and was named to the Order of the Federal Republic of Nigeria. Achebe received honorary doctorates from universities around the world, including Dartmouth College in 1972 and Harvard University in 1996.

BIOGRAPHY

Chinua Achebe, christened at birth Albert Chinualumogu Achebe, was born in Ogidi in Eastern Nigeria on November 16, 1930, near the Niger River. His family was Christian in a village divided between Christians and the "others." Achebe's great-grandfather served as the model for Okonkwo, the protagonist of *Things Fall Apart*. Because he was an Ibo and a Christian, Achebe grew up conscious of how he differed not only from other Africans but also from other Nigerians. Achebe was one of the first graduates of University College at Ibadan in 1953. In 1954, he was made producer of the Nigerian Broadcasting Service and in 1958 became the founding editor of Heinemann's African Writers series; this position and the publication, in that series, of *Things Fall Apart*, account for his vast influence among writers of his and the following generation.

Achebe married Christie Chinwe Okoli in 1961 and became the father of four children. When a civil war began in Nigeria in 1966 with the massacre of Achebe's fellow tribesmen in the northern part of the country, Achebe returned to the east, hoping to establish in the new country of Biafra a publishing house with other young Ibo writers. One of this band was the poet Christopher Okigbo, killed later that year in action against federal forces. After Biafra's defeat in the civil war, a defeat which meant for many of his compatriots imprisonment in camps and "reeducation," Achebe has worked as an educator as well as a writer. He traveled to the United States on several occasions to serve as a guest lecturer or visiting professor, and he visited many countries throughout the world. In addition, his interest in politics led to his serving as the deputy national president of the People's Redemption Party in 1983 and then as the president of the town union in Ogidi, Nigeria, in 1986.

Achebe served as visiting professor on an international scale. Universities at which he taught include Cambridge University, the University of Connecticut, and the University of California, Los Angeles. A 1990 car accident injured Achebe's spine, confining him to a wheelchair. He spent six months recovering, then accepted an endowed professorship at New York's Bard College. He continued to teach and write throughout the 1990's.

ANALYSIS

Chinua Achebe is an African English-language writer. As an author, Achebe uses the power of English words to expose, unite, and reveal various aspects of Nigerian culture. His subjects are both literary and political. In general, Achebe's writings reflect cultural diversity in twentieth century African society. He focuses on the difficulty faced by Africans who were once under the rule of British colonials but later had to struggle with issues of democracy, the evils of military rule, civil war, tribal rivalries, and dictatorship.

Achebe seeks to preserve the proverbs and truths of his Ibo tribal heritage by incorporating them into his stories, whether they be in his contemporary novels or his children's tales. His works do more, however, than entertain; they reveal truths about human nature and show the destruction of power corrupted. Achebe's writing does not cast blame but delivers a message to his readers, concerning unity and the necessity for political stability in Nigerian culture.

Chinua Achebe (Rocon/Enugu, Nigeria)

"VENGEFUL CREDITOR"

Achebe's "Vengeful Creditor" is a story that seems to be about what a misconceived government decree guaranteeing free education to all can lead to, including some rather comic developments. It appears to be a story about class struggle, and then, as the reader sees layer after layer of meaning stripped away and one theme leading directly to another, it seems to be—and is—about something really quite different from either education or the class system.

Mr. and Mrs. Emenike are part of the Nigerian upper class: He is a parliamentary secretary, and he and his wife own a Mercedes and a Fiat and employ servants from the still-uneducated masses, most of them from the village of their birth, to which the Emenikes return periodically to shower largesse upon the populace. At the beginning of the story, a free-education bill has caused a mass desertion of servants, even those of college age, all of whom wish to go back to their villages and qualify for an education. Apparently many others have the same idea, for the turnout for free schooling is double what the government statisticians had predicted. The reader sees Emenike and his running buddies at the cabinet meeting at which it is decided to make everyone pay, after all, because the army might have to be called out if new taxes are announced to pay for the unexpected costs of the program.

The Emenikes, finding themselves with this "servant problem," return to their native village and ask Martha, a village woman known to them, if her daughter Vero will be their baby nurse for the princely sum of five pounds per year. Martha has led a rather sad life: She was educated at a Christian school whose reason for being was the education of African girls up to the standards expected of the wives of native pastors. The woman in charge of her school, however, by way of furthering her own romantic aspirations, persuaded Martha to marry a carpenter being trained at an industrial school managed by a white man. Carpentry never came into its own, however, at least not as much as preaching and teaching, and Martha had a "bad-luck marriage," which eventually left her a widow with no money and several children to support, although she was a Standard Three (beginning of high school) reader and her classmates were all married to prosperous teachers and bishops.

The withdrawal of the free-education decree has cast Martha's daughter, Vero, back onto the streets. When Mr. Emenike says that one does not need education to be great, Martha knows he is patronizing her; she knows exactly what the fate of an uneducated person usually is, but she needs the money from this job. Mr. Emenike rounds out his recruiting pitch by saying he thinks there is plenty of time for the ten-year-old girl to go to school. Martha says, "I read Standard Three in those days and I said they will all go to college. Now they will not even have the little I had thirty years ago." Vero turns out to be quick, industrious, and creative, but there also begins to be a connection between her charge's maturing and her own chance of an education. Finally, as she comes to realize the child will need care until hope of an education has past her, she tries to poison him by making him drink a bottle of red ink.

Mrs. Emenike, one of the least sympathetic Africans in any short story ever written by an African, beats Vero unmercifully. They drive back to the village where they were all born and pull her out of the car. Martha hears from Vero that she has been fired, sees the blood on her daughter, and drags her to the Emenikes. Called one who taught her daughter murder, she retorts to Mrs. Emenike that she is not a murderer. Mr. Emenike, trying to break up this confrontation, says, "It's the work of the devil. . . . I have always known that the craze for education in this country will one day ruin all of us. Now even children will commit murder in order to go to school."

"UNCLE BEN'S CHOICE"

"Uncle Ben's Choice" is a ghost or magical story which involves the element of human choice. A succubus-goddess known as the Mami-Wota, capable of many disguises, is both a seducer and a betrayer. She makes it possible for a young girl who offers herself to a man to guarantee not only sexual relations but also success, riches, and whatever material things the man desires. The only condition is that the Mami-Wota prevents the man from marrying her.

"Uncle Ben's Choice" is a monologue told by Uncle Ben in a tone that is skeptical yet simultaneously sincere and ingenuous. Uncle Ben is a clerk determined not to marry, whose passions are scotch, a brand-new phonograph, and his bicycle. His affluence brings him to the attention of the Mami-Wota because he not only lives better than the average African but also is much more concerned with the material rewards of life than even his fellow clerks.

A "light" girl who is Roman Catholic falls for him, and he tries to stay out of her way. However, he comes home one night after some heavy drinking and falls into bed, only to find a naked woman there. He thinks at first that it is the girl who has been making a play for him, then he feels her hair—it feels European. He jumps out of bed, and the woman calls to him in the voice of the girl who has a crush on him. He is suspicious now and strikes a match, making the most fateful decision of his life: to abjure wealth gotten from being the exclusive property of the Mami-Wota, her lover and her slave. "Uncle Ben's Choice" is about the innate morality of men in society. Uncle Ben honors his society by suppressing his own urges and fantasies in favor of remaining a part of his family, clan, and tribe, whose rewards he values more than riches.

"GIRLS AT WAR"

"Girls at War" is a story about the war between the seceding state of Biafra and Nigeria, and both the theme and the plot are foreshadowed in the spare sentence introducing the principal characters: "The first time their paths crossed nothing happened." The second time they meet, however, is at a checkpoint at Akwa, when the girl, Gladys, stops Reginald Nwankwo's car to inspect it. He falls back on the dignity of his office and person, but this fails to impress her, which secretly delights and excites him. He sees her as "a beautiful girl in a breasty blue jersey, khaki jeans and canvas shoes with the new-style hair plait which gave a girl a defiant look." Before, in the earlier stages of the war, he had sneered at the militia girls, particularly after seeing a group recruited from a high school marching under the banner "WE ARE IMPREGNABLE." Now he begins to respect them because of the mature attitude and bearing of Gladys, who seems both patriotic and savvy, knowing and yet naïve.

The third time they meet, "things had got very bad. Death and starvation [had] long chased out the headiness of the early days." Reginald is coming back to Owerri after using his influence as an official to obtain some food, unfortunately under the eyes of a starving crowd who mock and taunt him. He is something of an idealist, and this embarrasses him, but he has decided that in "such a situation one could do nothing at all for crowds; at best one could try to be of some use to one's immediate neighbors." Gladys is walking along in a crowd, and he picks her up, but not because he recognizes her. She has changed: She is wearing makeup, a wig, and new clothes and is now a bureaucrat and no doubt corrupt. She reminds him that she was the one who searched for him so long ago; he had admired her then, but now he just wants her, and as soon as they get into town he takes her into an air-raid bunker after Nigerian planes fly over, strafing.

Later, they go to a party, where in the midst of Biafran starvation there is scotch, Courvoisier, and real bread, but a white Red Cross man who has lost a friend in an air crash tells them all that they stink and that any girl there will roll into bed for a fish or a dol-

lar. He is slapped by an African officer who, all the girls think, is a hero, including Gladys, who begins to appear to the protagonist—and to the reader—as the banal, improvident child she really is. Finally, Gladys goes home and to bed with Reginald, who is shocked by the coarseness of her language. He has his pleasure and writes her off. Then he begins to think she is nothing but a mirror reflecting a "rotten, maggoty society" and that she, like a dirty mirror, needs only some cleaning. He begins to believe she is under some terrible influence. He decides to try to help her; he gives her food and money, and they drive off together to her house. He is determined to see who is there and who her friends are, to get to the bottom of her life of waste and callousness.

On the way he picks up a soldier who has lost part of one leg. Before, he would not have picked up a mere private, not only sweaty but also an inconvenience with his crutches and his talk of war. Then there is another air raid. He pushes past Gladys, who stops to go back to help the crippled soldier, and, terrified, goes into the timberline, where a near-miss knocks him senseless. When he awakes, he finds the driver sobbing and bloody and his car a wreck. "He saw the remains of his car smoking and the entangled remains of the girl and the soldier. And he let out a piercing cry and fell down again." With Gladys's horrible death, the protagonist understands the potential for nobility within the heart and soul of even the most banal and superficial of human beings. "Girls at War" confirms Achebe's faith in humanity and in Africa.

"CIVIL PEACE"

Because of the remarkable portrayal of Nigerian culture, Achebe's works, like the three stories analyzed above, are frequently anthologized. Achebe himself edited and published the collection *African Short Stories* (1985). It is subdivided by regions of the African continent. In the West African section, Achebe included his own work "Civil Peace," originally published in *Girls at War.*

This story takes place in the time period just after the Biafran War. It points out with the ironic title that there may not be much difference between civil war and civil peace. Jonathan Iwegbu feels fortunate that he, his wife, and three of their four children have survived the war. As an added bonus, so has his bicycle, which Jonathan had cleverly buried in his yard to keep it from the marauding troops. After the war, Jonathan's entrepreneurial instincts can flourish because he has the bicycle.

His business ventures do well and, in addition, he receives a cash payment of Nigerian money (called the *ex-gratia* award or egg-rasher by the Nigerians struggling with the foreign term) for turning in rebel money coined during the conflict. Unfortunately, a band of thieves, many of them former soldiers, armed with machine guns and other weapons, learn of his windfall and terrorize Jonathan and his family in a way reminiscent of wartime, until Jonathan gives them the money. Fatalistically, yet realistically, Jonathan realizes he is back to square one, and, at the end of the story, he and his family are once again preparing to go out and start all over again. In Jonathan's own words, "I say, let egg-rasher perish in the flames! Let it go where everything else has gone."

This story illustrates one of Achebe's major themes, a portrayal of both the problems or weaknesses and the strengths of the Nigerian people. The society has been vicious and cruel to itself, yet the strength and spirit of individuals will carry it onward.

OTHER MAJOR WORKS

LONG FICTION: *Things Fall Apart*, 1958; *No Longer at Ease*, 1960; *Arrow of God*, 1964; *A Man of the People*, 1966; *Anthills of the Savannah*, 1987.

POETRY: *Beware: Soul Brother and Other Poems*, 1971, 1972; *Christmas in Biafra and Other Poems*, 1973.

NONFICTION: *Morning Yet on Creation Day*, 1975; *The Trouble with Nigeria*, 1983; *Hopes and Impediments*, 1988; *Home and Exile*, 2000.

CHILDREN'S LITERATURE: *Chike and the River*, 1966; *How the Leopard Got His Claws*, 1972 (with John Iroaganachi); *The Flute*, 1977; *The Drum*, 1977.

EDITED TEXTS: *Don't Let Him Die: An Anthology of Memorial Poems for Christopher Okigbo, 1932-1967*, 1978 (with Dubem Okafor); *Aka Weta: An Anthology of Ibo Poetry*, 1978; *African Short Stories*, 1985 (with C. L. Innes); *Beyond Hunger in Africa*, 1990 (with others); *The Heinemann Book of Contemporary African Short Stories*, 1992 (with Innes).

BIBLIOGRAPHY

Achebe, Chinua. "The Art of Fiction CXXXIX: Chinua Achebe." Interview by Jerome Brooks. *The Paris Review* 36 (Winter, 1994): 142-166. In this interview, Achebe discusses his schooling, work as a broadcaster, and views on other writers, as well as the nature of his writing process and the political situation in Nigeria.

Bolland, John. *Language and the Quest for Political and Social Identity in the African Novel*. Accra, Ghana: Woeli, 1996. This volume examines Achebe's novel *Anthills of the Savannah*, among others, but it is valuable for its examination of African fiction and history, touching on themes found in Achebe's short stories.

Carroll, David. *Chinua Achebe*. New York: Twayne, 1970. Explores Achebe's first four novels. The introductory chapter includes historical details concerning Africa, colonialism, and twentieth century Nigerian political history. Contains a sizable bibliography and an index.

Ezenwa-Ohaeto. *Chinua Achebe: A Biography*. Bloomington: Indiana University Press, 1997. This work reveals information about Achebe's later years. Includes bibliographical references and an index.

Innes, Catherine Lynette. *Chinua Achebe*. Cambridge, England: Cambridge University Press, 1990. Innes's work concentrates on the entire body of Achebe's work. Background information concerning African culture is also included.

Joseph, Michael Scott. "A Pre-modernist Reading of 'The Drum': Chinua Achebe and the Theme of the Eternal Return." *Ariel* 28 (January, 1997): 149-166. In this special issue on colonialism, postcolonialism, and children's literature, Achebe's "The Drum" is discussed as a satirical attack on European colonial values and a text dominated by nostalgia for a lost Golden Age.

Lindfors, Bernth, ed. *Conversations with Chinua Achebe*. Jackson: University Press of Mississippi, 1997. Twenty interviews with Achebe in which he discusses African oral tradition, the need for political commitment, the relationship between his novels and his short stories, his use of myth and fable, and other issues concerning being a writer.

John Carr, updated by Paula M. Miller
and Judith L. Steininger

ALICE ADAMS

Born: Fredericksburg, Virginia; August 14, 1926
Died: San Francisco, California; May 27, 1999

PRINCIPAL SHORT FICTION
Beautiful Girl, 1979
To See You Again, 1982
Molly's Dog, 1983
Return Trips, 1985
After You've Gone, 1989
The Last Lovely City: Stories, 1999

OTHER LITERARY FORMS

Though Alice Adams was first successful in short fiction, she also published several novels, including *Careless Love* (1966), *Families and Survivors* (1974), *Listening to Billie* (1978), *Rich Rewards* (1980), *Superior Women* (1984), *Second Chances* (1988), *Caroline's Daughters* (1991), *Almost Perfect* (1993), *A Southern Exposure* (1995), and *Medicine Men* (1997). In addition, her story "Roses, Rhododendrons" has appeared as an illustrated gift book.

ACHIEVEMENTS

Alice Adams did not publish her first collection of stories until she was in her fifties, but she quickly assumed a place among the leading practitioners of the genre. Twenty-two of her stories have appeared in *Prize Stories: The O. Henry Awards*. In 1976, Adams received a grant from the National Endowment for the Arts and, in 1978, she received a John Simon Guggenheim Memorial Foundation Fellowship. In 1982, Adams received the O. Henry Special Award for Continuing Achievement, given for only the third time; her predecessors were Joyce Carol Oates (in 1970) and John Updike (in 1976). She also received the American Academy of Arts and Letters Award in literature in 1992.

BIOGRAPHY

Alice Boyd Adams was born in Fredericksburg, Virginia, on August 14, 1926, the daughter of Nicholson Adams, a professor, and Agatha (née Boyd) Adams, a writer. Shortly after her birth, the family moved to Chapel Hill, North Carolina, where Adams spent her first sixteen years. After receiving her B.A.

Alice Adams in 1991 (AP/Wide World Photos)

degree from Radcliffe College in 1946, she married Mark Linenthal, Jr. Two years later, they moved to California, and in 1951, their only child, Peter, was born. Their marriage ended in divorce in 1958, following which Adams held a number of part-time clerical, secretarial, and bookkeeping jobs while rearing her son and writing short stories.

It was not until 1969 that she broke into the magazine market when *The New Yorker* bought her story "Gift of Grass." Since then, her stories have continued to appear in *The New Yorker* as well as *Redbook*, *McCall's*, and *The Paris Review*. In addition, Adams has taught at the University of California at Davis, the University of California at Berkeley, and Stanford University. She died on May 27, 1999, in San Francisco after being treated for heart problems.

ANALYSIS

Most of Alice Adams's stories revolve around common themes, and her characters, mostly educated, upper-middle-class women, are defined by a set of common traits and situations which reappear in somewhat different combinations. They find their lives flawed, often by unhappy relationships with lovers, husbands, parents, friends, sometimes with combinations of these, usually with a living antagonist, occasionally with one already dead. Often, they resolve these problems, but sometimes they do not.

Frequently, the tensions of Adams's plots are resolved when her central female characters learn something new or find a new source of strength, which enables them to part with unsatisfactory husbands, lovers, or friends. Claire, in "Home Is Where" (in *Beautiful Girl*), leaves both an unsatisfactory marriage and a miserable love affair in San Francisco, where she feels "ugly—drained, discolored, old," to spend the summer with her parents in her North Carolina hometown, where she had been young and "if not beautiful, sought after." Refreshed and stimulated by the sensual landscape and a summertime affair, Claire returns to San Francisco to divorce her husband, take leave of her unpleasant lover, and, eventually, to remarry, this time happily. Cynthia, in "The Break-in" (*To See You Again*), finds herself so different from her fiancé Roger, when he automati-

cally blames the burglary of his home on "Mexicans," that she leaves him without a word. The narrator of "True Colors" (*To See You Again*) discovers, in Las Vegas, David's ugly side as an obsessive gambler and leaves him: "From then on I was going to be all right, I thought." Clover Baskerville in "The Party-Givers" (*To See You Again*) leaves behind her malicious friends when she realizes that she need not call them if she does not want to see them. All these characters have learned that "home is where the heart" not only "is" but also chooses to be.

Adams's heroines sometimes reach out from their lonely and isolated lives to find sympathetic bonds with poor or troubled people from other cultures. In "Greyhound People" (*To See You Again*), a divorced, middle-aged woman's discovery of kinship with her (mostly black and poor) fellow commuters, along with her discovery that her commuter ticket will take her anywhere in California, is so liberating that she can finally break free of her repressive, domineering roommate and friend Hortense. In "Verlie I Say unto You" (*Beautiful Girl*), Jessica Todd's sensitivity to her black maid Verlie's humanity underscores a fundamental difference between herself and her insensitive husband (see also "The Break-in" in this regard). In "Mexican Dust" (*To See You Again*), Marian comes to prefer the company of the Mexican peasants to that of her husband, friends, and other Americans as they bus through Mexico on vacation; she abandons her party and returns to Seattle, where she plans to study Spanish, presumably to prepare for a return to Mexico alone. In fact, one sign of a strong character in Adams's stories is a marked sensitivity to other cultures. Elizabeth, in the story by that name, purchases her Mexican beach house in the name of her Mexican servant Aurelia and leaves Aurelia in full possession of the house at her death. The central focus in "La Señora" (*Return Trips*) is the friendship between a wealthy, elderly American woman, who vacations annually at a Mexican resort, and Teodola, the Mexican maid in charge of her hotel room. Adams's own concern for the human plight of those of other cultures can be seen in "Teresa," in *Return Trips*, a story about the privation, terror, and grief of a Mexican peasant woman.

"MOLLY'S DOG" AND "A PUBLIC POOL"

In two of Adams's most effective stories, female protagonists learn to live confidently with themselves: "Molly's Dog" and "A Public Pool" (both from *Return Trips*). In the former, Molly returns with her homosexual friend Sandy to a small cabin by the ocean, where she experienced a love affair so intense she cannot think of it without weeping. A friendly dog attaches itself to them on the beach and follows them as they leave; Molly pleads with Sandy to go back for the dog, but he drives faster, and the dog, though running, falls back and shrinks in the distance. Molly and Sandy quarrel over the dog, and Molly, realizing that she is much too dependent on men, comes to see less of Sandy back in San Francisco. She finally learns to think of the dog without pain but cannot forget it, and the place by the ocean becomes in her memory "a place where she had lost, or left something of infinite value. A place to which she would not go back."

In "A Public Pool," the protagonist, though working class, neither part of the literary or artistic world nor so well educated as many of Adams's female characters, shares with many of them a dissatisfaction with her body and a sense of being cut off and alone. She cannot bear to meet people or even look for a job ("We wouldn't even have room for you," she imagines an employer saying), so that life at age thirty is a grim existence in a cold apartment with a penurious mother. Though swimming offers an escape from home and a chance for meeting new people, it also has its fears: of exposing her body in the locker room and enduring the rebukes of strangers, of the faster swimmers whose lane she blocks, of the blond-bearded man who goes by so swiftly that he splashes her, and of a large black woman who tells her that she should stay by the side of the pool.

After a few months of lap swimming, her body changes and her fear of others lessens. An early remark of the blond-bearded man made her babble nervously, but now she responds to his conventional questions with brief assent. On the day the black lady compliments her on her stroke and they leave the pool together, she is finally able to find a job and thinks of moving out of her mother's apartment. She

walks happily about the neighborhood, thinking that she and the black woman might become friends. At that moment, she meets in the street the blond-bearded man, who smells of chewing gum and is wearing "sharp" clothes from Sears. He invites her for coffee, but, "overwhelmed" by the smell of gum and realizing that "I hate sharp clothes," she makes her excuses. Like other Adams women, she has felt loneliness, but, also like many other women in these stories, she finds new strength that will mitigate her isolation by giving her independence. Yet it is primarily achieved by herself, and Adams's always masterful use of language here is especially striking. As Adams's character goes off independently from the blond-bearded man, she says confidently, "I leave him standing there. I swim away."

"YOU ARE WHAT YOU OWN" AND "TO SEE YOU AGAIN"

Not all these stories, however, end so conclusively; in others, it is unclear whether the heroines' chosen resolutions to the problems confronting them will be satisfactory. The young housewife of "You Are What You Own: A Notebook" (*Return Trips*) lives in a house crammed with her domineering mother's furniture, which the girl seems doomed to polish for all eternity. Her boring graduate-student husband complains that she does not polish the furniture enough and even starts to do it himself. She escapes in fantasy, fictionalizing the artists who live in a house down the street from her, assigning them her own names (not knowing their real ones), and indulging in imagined conversations with them. At the end of the story—recorded in her notebook—she tells her husband in a letter that she is leaving him the furniture and going to look for a job in San Francisco. Does she go? Is she capable? Similarly, the lonely young wife in "To See You Again" uses the image of a beautiful adolescent boy in her class to re-create the image of her husband as he was when they fell in love—slim and energetic, not as he is now, overweight and frequently paralyzed by chronic, severe depression. The story ends with her fantasizing that somehow she has escaped her grim life with him, that things are as they once were, her husband somehow reclaimed in the body of the young student.

"BEAUTIFUL GIRL"

The story plots summarized here raise a possible objection to Adams's fiction—that many of her female characters are too obsessed with the attention of men, even to the point where the women's own highly successful careers seem to matter little. This issue, however, must be placed in historical perspective. Most of the women in her stories, like Adams herself, grew up and entered adulthood during the period after World War II, when women's roles in American society were constricted, when women were sent home from their wartime jobs to take on what then seemed an almost patriotic duty: submitting themselves to the roles of wife and mother. From this point of view, Adams's female characters are victims of that culture, dependent on men and falling desperately in love with them because they were expected to do just that. Given these crushing expectations, it is no wonder that Adams's heroines feel lost when bereft, by divorce or widowhood, of the men in their lives. The young people in these stories often reach out to surrogate parents, usually mothers, when the incredible strain on the postwar nuclear family cracks and splinters it (a character in "Roses, Rhododendrons," in *Beautiful Girl*, says "we all need more than one set of parents—our relations with the original set are too intense, and need dissipating").

Emblematic of the plight of this generation is Ardis Bascombe in "Beautiful Girl," an ironic title because Ardis, though in her youth beautiful and popular, is now fleshy, drinking herself to death in her San Francisco apartment. She has failed as a wife and, as her filthy kitchen attests, failed as a homemaker. She had been independent enough to leave her unhappy marriage, but, like other women of her generation, despite her intelligence, idealism, courage, and sophistication, she was unable to make a new life. The life of this beautiful girl demonstrates graphically the destructive pressures on postwar women.

THE LAST LOVELY CITY

In this, her final collection of stories, Alice Adams also focuses on sophisticated contemporary women dealing with wandering husbands, belligerent children, and the tribulations of being divorced or widowed; however, because Adams was in her late six-

ties when she wrote most of these stories, her protagonists are older, albeit not always wiser, veterans of the domestic wars of the 1960's and 1970's.

Adams has always been a favorite of the judges of *Prize Stories: The O. Henry Awards*, and three of these stories were chosen for that prestigious collection: "The Islands" in 1993, "The Haunted Beach" in 1995, and "His Women" in 1996. Two of these are among the best stories in the collection, for they economically and without self-indulgence focus on futile efforts to repeat the past. What "haunts" the beach in "The Haunted Beach" is one woman's previous marriage. Penelope Jaspers, a San Francisco art dealer, takes her new lover, a middle-aged superior court judge to a West Coast Mexican resort that she and her dead husband used to visit. Although she remembers it as charming, she now sees it as "unspeakable shabby" and returns to San Francisco, having decided not to marry the judge.

The persistence of the past also haunts "His Women," as a university professor cannot reconcile with his lover because of memories of the previous women in his life. In the title story, Benito Zamora, a Mexican cardiologist and "sadhearted widow," is forced to dredge up unpleasant moments from his past by an attractive young reporter whom he mistakenly thinks is interested in him sexually. In "Old Love Affairs," a woman's living room is filled with keepsakes that remind her only that she is growing old and can no longer hope for love in her life.

The last four stories in the book—"The Drinking Club," "Patients," "The Wrong Mexico," and "Earthquake Damage"—are linked stories, somewhat like chapters of a novella, in which two Bay Area psychiatrists, who are sometimes lovers, move in and out of various affairs. Both are passive professionals, as are many Adams characters—watchers rather than active participants, caught in a recurrent round of unhappy marriages and unfulfilling affairs.

The weakest stories in the collection—"The Islands," "Raccoons," and "A Very Nice Dog"—are simple paeans to pets. The most interesting, "The Islands," begins with the sentence: "What does it mean to love an animal, a pet, in my case a cat, in the fierce, entire and unambivalent way that some of us do?" Although readers who share such a pet passion might find the question intriguing, many others will view this story about the death of a beloved cat as sentimental rather than sensitive. Although the fact that Adams died at age seventy-two, a few months after this book appeared, gives it some poignancy, on a purely critical level, these stories represent a falling off from the crisp and sophisticated stories of the writer in her prime.

OTHER MAJOR WORKS

LONG FICTION: *Careless Love*, 1966; *Families and Survivors*, 1974; *Listening to Billie*, 1978; *Rich Rewards*, 1980; *Superior Women*, 1984; *Second Chances*, 1988; *Caroline's Daughters*, 1991; *Almost Perfect*, 1993; *A Southern Exposure*, 1995; *Medicine Men*, 1997.

BIBLIOGRAPHY

Adams, Alice. Interview by Patricia Holt. *Publishers Weekly* 213 (January 16, 1978): 8-9. In talking about her life with interior designer Robert McNee, Adams emphasizes the importance of her work as the foundation for the self-respect necessary in a long-term relationship.

Blades, L. T. "Order and Chaos in Alice Adams' *Rich Rewards*." *Critique: Studies in Modern Fiction* 27 (Summer, 1986): 187-195. In an issue devoted to four women writers—Adams, Ann Beattie, Mary Gordon, and Marge Piercy—Blades explores the artificially imposed order created by Adams's female characters and the world of chaos that threatens it. Like Jane Austen's characters, Adams's women enter into unstable relationships but eventually realize that they must concentrate on work and friendships, not romance, to have a healthy self-respect.

Bolotin, Susan. "Semidetached Couples." Review of *The Last Lovely City: Stories. The New York Times*, February 14, 1999. A detailed review of Adams's collection, commenting on several of the stories, particularly the characters and the social world in which they live.

Chell, Cara. "Succeeding in Their Times: Alice Adams on Women and Work." *Soundings* 68 (Spring, 1985): 62-71. Work is the catalyst that enables Adams's characters to realize their self-worth. Chell provides an interesting treatment of this theme throughout Adams's career.

Flower, Dean. "Picking Up the Pieces." *The Hudson Review* 32 (Summer, 1979): 293-307. Flower sets Adams among other American storytellers who look to the past for explanations and intensification of feelings. He explores how this orientation leads to a preoccupation with growing old.

Herman, Barbara A. "Alice Adams." In *Contemporary Fiction Writers of the South*, edited by Joseph M. Flora and Robert Bain. Westport, Conn.: Greenwood, 1993. A brief biography and discussion of Adams's novels and short stories; suggests her two major themes are the maturation of middle-class women seeking self-respect, identity, and independence and women's relationships with husbands, lovers, and friends. Includes a survey of Adams's criticism and a bibliography of works by and about her.

Pritchard, William H. "Fictive Voices." *The Hudson Review* 38 (Spring, 1985): 120-132. Pritchard examines Adams's narrative voice in the context of other contemporary writers. Though the section on Adams is not long, it provides a useful approach to analyzing her stories.

Upton, Lee. "Changing the Past: Alice Adams' Re visionary Nostalgia." *Studies in Short Fiction* 26 (Winter, 1989): 33-41. In the collection of stories, *Return Trips*, Adams's female characters turn to memories of the past as their most valued possessions. Upton isolates three different relationships with the past and shows how each enables Adams's characters to interpret nostalgic images so that they produce more satisfying relationships with the present.

Woo, Elaine. "Alice Adams." *Los Angeles Times*, May 29, 1999, p. B8. Biographical and critical sketch and tribute; notes Adams's specialization in contemporary relationships among white, urban, middle- and upper-class females; charts her career and her critical reception.

Timothy C. Frazer, updated by
Louise M. Stone and Charles E. May

JOSEPH ADDISON

Born: Milston, Wiltshire, England; May 1, 1672
Died: London, England; June 17, 1719

PRINCIPAL SHORT FICTION

The Tatler, 1709-1711 (with Richard Steele)
The Spectator, 1711-1712, 1714 (with Richard Steele)
The Guardian, 1713 (with Richard Steele)
The Freeholder: Or, Political Essays, 1715-1716
The Spectator, 1965 (Donald Bond, editor)

OTHER LITERARY FORMS

Joseph Addison first gained a literary reputation as a poet, writing at Oxford imitation classical poems in Latin and, later, heroic verse in praise of the English war against Louis XIV. His patriotic verse brought him to the attention of the Whig politicians and writers of the Kit-Cat Club. The politicians helped Addison's career in government, and the writers, especially Richard Steele, helped Addison's literary career by introducing him to the theater, political pamphleteering, and periodical journalism. His modern reputation rests mainly on essays he contributed to *The Tatler*, *The Spectator*, and other periodical papers.

ACHIEVEMENTS

Although he was a powerful man of letters and of politics in his own era, Joseph Addison is known more as a journalist and popularizer of neoclassical moral and philosophical trends. His conversational prose style, mild wit, and humor influenced the development of the informal essay. His poetry has been overshadowed by his collaboration with Richard Steele in the establishment of periodical literature for the new middle-class reading public, and these ventures also served in developing his reputation as a literary critic. His vivid portrayals of London life and his focus on middle-class mores were deliberate attempts to inculcate moral values in his audience, and they led in the direction of social commentary. Some judgments of his interest in the imagination and the

natural world have designated him a pre-Romantic, while others have found in his promotion of upper-middle-class values a foreshadowing of the Victorians. A seat in Parliament, patronage, and political appointments secured him enough public presence to gain attention even for his less successful literary works, such as an opera that failed and a neoclassical tragedy that was popular in his lifetime but remains primarily a literary curiosity.

BIOGRAPHY

As the son of an Anglican clergyman, Joseph Addison received a good education, beginning in Lichfield and continuing at the Charterhouse School, where he first met his longtime friend and collaborator, Richard Steele.

After attending Magdalen College, Oxford, Addison determined on a career in public service. Thanks to influential politicians, he received a pension which enabled him to tour Europe (1699-1703) and learn at first hand about the countries with which he might one day have to deal as a diplomat. After the success of his poem "The Campaign," celebrating the victory at Blenheim over the French, Addison was appointed a Commissioner of Appeals. He held a series of increasingly important secretaryships until 1710, when a change of administration cost him his position. An ardent Whig partisan, he was able to combine service in Parliament, political appointments and patronage, and a literary career throughout his adult life. For years, Addison lived solely as a man of letters, writing hundreds of essays for several different papers and bringing a tragedy, *Cato* (1713), to the stage. The accession of George I in 1714 brought Addison back into government service, but he retired in 1718 after a brief tenure as secretary of state. He had married the dowager Countess of Warwick in 1716, only three years before his death.

ANALYSIS

Joseph Addison's essays should not be read as profound pieces; they are meant as vehicles of instruction with two particular intentions. First, he wished to introduce his readers to the great minds of both classical and contemporary cultures: Homer, Marcus Tullius Cicero, John Milton, and Blaise Pascal, to name a few. In *Spectator* 10 he wrote, "It was said of *Socrates*, that he brought Philosophy down from Heaven, to inhabit among Men; and I shall be ambitious to have it said of me, that I have brought Philosophy out of Closets and Libraries, Schools and Colleges, to dwell in Clubs and Assemblies, at Tea-Tables, and in Coffee-Houses."

Second, Addison wished to recommend to his readers a golden mean in politics, manners, morality, and religion. Between 1688 and 1714, England experienced great social change, and Addison championed a middle way between the extreme positions that revolutionary change readily engendered. In politics he advocated constitutional monarchy as a median between Stuart absolutism and Puritan commonwealth; in manners he recommended an educated urbanity between aristocratic hauteur and middle-class utilitarianism; in morality he stressed a gentlemanly Christianity as the mean between libertinism and asceticism; and in religion he argued for a rational faith between superstition and atheism. In sum, Addison offered to his contemporaries the model of the cultured, self-disciplined and pious Roman citizen of antiquity.

If Addison's essays offered in their own time to cultivate the readers' sensibilities and ideas, they interest modern readers mainly for their mode of expression. When Addison moves from straightforward exposition into imaginative presentation, his modest and moral thinking takes on life. Through the accumulation of vivid detail or through humor and dramatization, Addison at his best dresses (to use the favorite metaphor of the age) his thought in attractive garb. Serious presentations of moral or religious truth wear the gossamer veils of allegory (a traditional device for presenting a religious truth) or the exotic trappings of the Asian tale (a genre then recently made popular by translations of the Arabian Nights stories). Comic or satiric exposure of ridiculous fashions and social opinions wears the bright dress of the character sketch and dramatic scene.

Joseph Addison (Library of Congress)

Most often Addison employs an allegory or an Asian tale of paragraph length to illustrate the moral of the expository essay. On several occasions, however, the vision or the tale becomes the whole piece; Addison pays as much attention to the artistic presentation of the setting and events as he does to a clear expression of the lesson. *Tatler* 119, on the world revealed by the microscope, *Tatler* 161, on the blessings of Liberty, and *Spectators* 584-585, about Shalum and Hilpa, are four of Addison's better full-essay efforts in these genres. His best effort, *Spectator* 159, combines allegory and the Asian tale: "The Vision of Mizrah" tells of the dream granted to a young prince as he sits fasting and meditating on a hill outside Baghdad.

"THE VISION OF MIZRAH"

"The Vision of Mizrah" is a completely realized story in which the moral lesson emerges from the events and scenes of the tale. Addison accounts for the tale realistically: Supposedly it comes from a manuscript that was purchased in Cairo. The manuscript is Mizrah's first-person account of the marvelous happenings which occurred when he went to spend a holy day in meditation on the "Vanity of humane life" and on the notion that "Man is but a Shadow and Life a Dream." Enraptured by the melodies of a shepherd playing a pipe, Mizrah soon discovers that the shepherd is actually a "genius" (or genie) known to haunt this hillside.

The genius offers Mizrah a scene representing the plight of human existence, a vision that Addison sublimely describes with vivid and complete detail. Mizrah sees a valley of which the hills on either side are hidden in fog; through the valley flows a sea and across the sea stands a bridge. The genius explains that the fog-shrouded hills are the beginning and the end of time hidden from human sight. The valley is the Vale of Misery in which humans must live, the bridge is the span of human life, and the sea is the eternity into which all men will be swept. Mizrah is most fascinated by the bridge, which the genius tells him was originally built of a thousand sturdy arches but which has now only seventy ruined sections. Mizrah watches the multitude of humanity as it attempts to cross the bridge but plunges into the water below.

When Mizrah despairs at this inevitable destruction of human beings, the genius comforts him with a vision of the land to which the sea of eternity carries them: It "appeared to me a vast Ocean planted with innumerable islands, that were covered with Fruits and Flowers, and interwoven with a thousand little shining Seas that ran among them." These islands are the "Mansions of good Men after Death" filled with all the delightful sights and harmonious sounds that men call by the name of paradise. Having comforted Mizrah, the genius withdraws. Skillfully, Addison works the transition from the marvelous to the mundane: "I turned again to the vision which I had been so long contemplating, but instead of the rolling Tide, and Arched Bridge, and the happy Islands, I saw nothing but the long Hollow Valley of *Bagdat*, with Oxen, Sheep, and Camels, grazing upon the sides of it."

When Addison turns his attention from religious or moral truth to the condition of society, his favorite device is the character sketch. The traditional Theophrastian character described a social type by heaping generalized qualities of appearance and thought upon him in a somewhat helter-skelter manner. Addison, while depicting a type, describes by giving localizing and particularizing characteristics, and by presenting them in dramatic situation.

Some of Addison's best *Tatlers* are elaborated sketches. *Tatler* 155 on the Political Upholsterer, *Tatler* 158 on Tom Folio the Scholar, and *Tatler* 165 on Sir Timothy Tittle, the critic, all achieve success by creating dramatic situations in which a particularized individual exposes his own ridiculousness and that of those who think like him. *Tatler* 163's account of Ned Softly, the modish poet, shows how deftly Addison could let character and action suggest rather than state the thesis of the essay.

TATLER 163
In *Tatler* 163, the narrator Isaac Bickerstaff tells how the young poet-about-town Ned Softly cornered him in a coffeehouse and demanded Bickerstaff's opinion of his latest work, "To Mira on Her Incomparable Poem." More in love with his own verse than with the young lady to whom it is written, Ned Softly insists on reading the poem line by line, commenting on his literary skill, and demanding Bickerstaff's reaction. Not wishing to offend, Bickerstaff replies neutrally or ambiguously; Softly interprets all remarks to his own advantage. With exquisite skill Addison lets the would-be poet reveal the superficiality of his art and the pretentiousness of his claims:

> But now we come to the last, which sums up the whole matter. "For ah! it wounds me like his dart."
>
> Pray, how do you like that *ah!* doth it make not a pretty figure in the place? Ah!—it looks as if I felt the dart, and cried out at being pricked with it.
>
> "For ah! it wounds me like his dart."
>
> My friend Dick Easy (continued he) assured me, he would rather have written that *ah!* than to have been the author of the *Aeneid*.

Bickerstaff hardly gets a word in edgewise, but that is part of Addison's point and method. *Tatler* 163 is the stuff of which the comedy of manners is made: revelation of social character by dialogue and dramatization. *Tatlers* like these indicate how, in the eighteenth century, fiction was gradually adopting one of the stage's most delightful methods of representation.

The possibility of dramatized presentation of particularized social types seems to underlie Addison and Steele's conception of the Spectator Club, from which *Spectator* essays supposedly come. Addison described Mr. Spectator in the first issue of the new series as an eccentric character who observes the whole London world from the Haymarket to the Exchange, but who is so shy that he never speaks in public. Richard Steele described the other members of the club in the second *Spectator*: the country squire Roger de Coverley, the merchant Sir Andrew Freeport, the witty rake Will Honeycomb, and others. Such varied and particularized types, arranged in the dramatic situation of the club, certainly gave Addison and Steele the same material with which later authors would build the novel. Addison and Steele, however, left undeveloped most of the literary possibilities of their material with the one exception of Roger de Coverley, whom they made one of the most memorable characters of English literature.

SIR ROGER DE COVERLEY

Like most other things in *The Spectator*, the character of Sir Roger de Coverley had a didactic purpose. He was intended to represent the class of country squires who constituted a powerful economic and political force in England, a force which Addison and Steele judged reactionary and unchanging. In a long series of essays (*Spectators* 106-130), Mr. Spectator visited Sir Roger's country seat and had an opportunity to comment on various aspects of the squire's life: his relationship with servants and tenants, his ability to manage an estate, and his administration of justice in the country. From all these episodes, Mr. Spectator was to have drawn some useful lessons for other men of property and responsibility.

The Sir Roger whom they intended to tease and use as a vehicle for giving advice, however, took on a life of his own and became lovable. The reader learned through Mr. Spectator how Sir Roger behaved at church, how a "perverse widow" threw him over, and how the values and principles of his ancestors shaped him. The reader also learned little things about Sir Roger: what he liked to eat, the jokes he liked to make concerning Mr. Spectator's familiarity with chickens and ducks, instances of his generosity to tenants. The new attitude is especially evident in the later *Spectators* when Sir Roger comes back to the city. Mr. Spectator describes him less to teach a lesson and more for the sheer fun of showing off a friend whom he loves.

Two things testify to the reality Sir Roger assumed in the imaginations of author and readers alike. Before Addison and Steele ended *The Spectator*, Addison wrote a moving account of the club's learning that Sir Roger had died; he could not let the series end without rounding off Sir Roger's life. Since the eighteenth century, the essays in which Sir Roger appears have often been removed from the numbered sequence of essays that masks their continuity and printed together as "The de Coverley papers."

OTHER MAJOR WORKS

PLAYS: *Rosamond*, pr., pb. 1707 (libretto; music by Thomas Clayton); *Cato*, pr., pb. 1713; *The Drummer: Or, The Haunted House*, pr., pb. 1716.

POETRY: "To Mr. Dryden," 1693; *A Poem to His Majesty*, 1695; *Praelum Inter Pygmaeos et Grues Commisum*, 1699; "A Letter from Italy," 1703; *The Campaign*, 1705; *"The Spectator* Hymns," 1712; "To Her Royal Highness," 1716; "To Sir Godfrey Kneller on His Portrait of the King," 1716.

NONFICTION: *Remarks upon Italy*, 1705; *Dialogues upon the Usefulness of Ancient Medals*, 1721; *The Letters of Joseph Addison*, 1941 (Walter Graham, editor).

TRANSLATION: *Fourth Georgic*, 1694 (of Vergil's *Georgics*).

MISCELLANEOUS: *The Miscellaneous Works*, 1914 (A. C. Guthkelch, editor).

BIBLIOGRAPHY

Addison, Joseph, et al. *The Spectator.* Edited by Donald F. Bond. 5 vols. New York: Oxford University Press, 1965. This standard edition includes ample introductory material and notes that will not intrude on the reading process.

Bloom, Edward A., and Lillian D. Bloom. *Joseph Addison's Sociable Animal: In the Market-Place, On the Hustings, In the Pulpit.* Providence, R.I.:

Brown University Press, 1971. The authors examine Addison's point of view following his own emphasis on the "sociable" dimension of human existence. Without discounting neoclassical belief in the ideal of reason, Addison shows his own fascination with human types in various social settings. His moral emphasis is positioned against the backdrops of trade, politics, and religion.

Elioseff, Lee Andrew. *The Cultural Milieu of Addison's Literary Criticism*. Austin: University of Texas Press, 1963. Addison's development of a critical posture and his critical interests are revealed in their historical setting. His interest in theory as well as in individual judgments of writers and of works is discussed, with an emphasis on his attempts at innovative approaches to genres, such as recognizing the ballad's appeal, psychological problems, as well as political and even cosmological issues.

Gay, Peter. "The Spectator as Actor: Addison in Perspective." In *The Augustan Age: Approaches to Literature, Life, and Thought*, edited by Ian Watt. Greenwich, Conn.: Fawcett, 1968. Gay reviews Donald F. Bond's edition of *The Spectator* and includes a survey of critical views of Addison's thought as well as style. In seeing Addison as a journalist with the public audience in mind, Gay does not denigrate Addison's didactic purpose but points out the writer's dramatic sense of himself and his mission.

Knight, Charles A. *Joseph Addison and Richard Steele: A Reference Guide, 1730-1991*. New York: G. K. Hall, 1994. Contains history, criticism, and bibliographies to the two writers.

_____. "*The Spectator*'s Moral Economy." *Modern Philology* 91 (November, 1993): 161-179. Examines principles of moral economy presented by Addison and Sir Richard Steele in *The Spectator* to control dreams of endless financial gains. Argues that Addison and Steele found in the economic order a secular basis for moral behavior that emphasized the common good over individual gain. Suggests that they connected commercial values to values of politeness and restraint.

Nablow, Ralph Arthur. *The Addisonian Tradition in France: Passion and Objectivity in Social Observation*.Rutherford, N.J.: Fairleigh Dickinson University Press, 1990. Examines Addison's influence on French writers. Includes bibliographical references and an index.

Smithers, Peter. *The Life of Joseph Addison*. Oxford, England: Clarendon Press, 1968. Smithers offers a thorough examination of both the private life—as far as it can be known—and the public life of Addison, the political figure as well as the man of letters. Addison immersed himself in his roles of statesman and administrator without neglecting his craft. He modeled his life after the ancient Augustan ideal of service to the state, combining his public service with learning and a literary career. This biography is the only modern one and it is especially enlightening to compare it with Samuel Johnson's *The Lives of the Poets* (1779-1781).

Varney, Andrew. "The Lascivious Nightingale: Mild Impropriety in *The Spectator*." *Notes and Queries* 41 (June, 1994): 189-191. Discusses a passage in the sequence of papers on the "Pleasures of the Imagination" in *The Spectator*, in which Addison argues that physical beauty arouses the sexual passion in order to assure reproduction and survival.

Robert M. Otten, updated by Emma Coburn Norris

JAMES AGEE

Born: Knoxville, Tennessee; November 27, 1909
Died: New York, New York; May 16, 1955

PRINCIPAL SHORT FICTION

Four Early Stories by James Agee, 1964
The Collected Short Prose of James Agee, 1968
    (Robert Fitzgerald, editor)

OTHER LITERARY FORMS

James Agee is best known for his posthumous novel *A Death in the Family* (1957) and his collection of essays *Let Us Now Praise Famous Men* (1941). He wrote the screenplays for *The Red Badge of Courage* (1951), *The African Queen* (1952), *The Bride Comes to Yellow Sky* (1952), and several other films.

ACHIEVEMENTS

James Agee's greatest literary achievement is his posthumous novel *A Death in the Family*, of which 194 handwritten pages, along with 114 pages of working notes, were completed before his death in 1955. The novel was awarded the Pulitzer Prize in 1958. His collection of essays, *Let Us Now Praise Famous Men*, which included photographs by Walker Evans and has since come to be regarded as a highly perceptive work about tenant farmers, received little notice immediately after its publication because Americans were preoccupied with World War II. In 1949, Agee won an American Academy of Arts and Letters Award, and, in 1952, his screenplay for *The African Queen* was nominated for an Academy Award.

BIOGRAPHY

A defining moment in the life of James Rufus Agee occurred in May, 1916, when his father, Hugh James Agee, was killed in an automobile accident. Hugh's widow, Laura Tyler Agee, recited the details of the accident so often that her children, James and Emma, could repeat them verbatim. These are the details that Agee employed successfully in his most celebrated work, the novel entitled *A Death in the Family*.

In 1919, Laura moved her family to Sewanee, Tennessee, where James attended St. Andrew's Episcopal School, there developing a lifelong friendship with Father James Harold Flye. Agee cycled through Europe with Flye and his wife in 1925 before entering Phillips Exeter Academy, where, as editor of the *Phillips Exeter Monthly*, he gained editorial experience that proved invaluable to him during his seven years as a reporter for *Fortune*. Agee also published some of his earliest writing in the *Phillips Exeter Monthly*.

Continuing his education at Harvard University, from which he was graduated in 1932, Agee worked during the Great Depression as a journalist. Between 1942 and 1948, Agee, starstruck since childhood, wrote the film column for *The Nation*. In 1949 and 1950, he contributed several long film essays (on Charlie Chaplin, D. W. Griffith, and John Huston) to *Life* magazine. This experience was the catapult he needed to embark on a career of writing screenplays. A consistently productive writer, Agee succeeded best when he wrote autobiographically oriented fiction. His novella *The Morning Watch* (1951) recounts a young boy's religious experience in the chapel of a boys' school much like St. Andrew's. His early sketch "Knoxville: Summer of 1915" (1936) recounts the innocent days in the year before his father's death and serves as a prelude to *A Death in the Family*. Suffering for several years from heart trouble, Agee died at age forty-five in a New York City taxicab on his way to his doctor's office. His greatest popular recognition followed his death.

ANALYSIS

Despite his prolonged absence from the South after 1925, James Agee had internalized the details of the area and its people well enough to write about them with exceptional conviction and authenticity. In some of his earliest short prose pieces, such as "Minerva Farmer" (1925), he uses Knoxville, in this case the University of Tennessee, as a backdrop. "A Sentimental Journey" (1928) recounts details about the life of a young widow not unlike his mother, whose marriage had been frowned on by her socially prominent family. "Bound for the Promised Land" (1928) recounts an African American funeral in Tennessee.

In his later work, Agee sometimes writes outside his southern milieu, but he is most convincing in the loosely autobiographical mode that often characterizes his work. His best writing is based on facts that he modifies and embellishes to suit his artistic objectives. The resulting stories, such as the posthumously published "Dream Sequence" (1968), focus on characters who have figured in Agee's life, but he imbues them with a universality, creating archetypes that represent concepts stretching far beyond the narrow geographical range in which his stories take place.

In his novella *The Morning Watch*, Richard, the protagonist, at times is reminiscent of one of James Joyce's protagonists. Agee reveals Richard's subconscious in such a way as to make the reader question whether the twelve-year-old's peak of religious fervor and spiritual insight will last. A master of subtle suggestion, Agee hints that it will not.

Agee brought to his prose poetic qualities that elevated it above the ordinary events about which he wrote. Almost magically, he transformed the commonplace into the extraordinary. His comments about modern society and the inroads it makes on individuality, reflected especially in *Let Us Now Praise Famous Men* and *The Morning Watch*, combine with his preoccupation with innocence and death, as seen so clearly in "Knoxville: Summer of 1915," to produce a body of work unique in modern American literature.

THE COLLECTED SHORT PROSE OF JAMES AGEE

This collection, edited by Robert Fitzgerald, who starts the volume with an extensive memoir, presents four finished pieces of short fiction in the sections "Early Stories" and "Satiric Pieces," along with four fragments and other miscellaneous items. Among the last group, "A Mother's Tale" (1952), a fable, is most interesting. "Death in the Desert" (1930) is reprinted from *The Harvard Advocate*, in which it first appeared during Agee's junior year at Harvard. In the following year, *The Harvard Advocate* published "They That Sow in Sorrow Shall Reap" (1931). The satiric pieces include "Formletter 7G3" (1934), previously

unpublished, and "Dedication Day" (1946). The fragments, undated but likely written in the early 1930's, include "Run Over," "Give Him Air," "Now as Awareness . . . ," and "A Birthday." Each of these pieces is incomplete and brief, seldom occupying more than two pages.

The stories as a whole reveal an author bent on creating believable characters that suggest archetypes. This is particularly true in the allegorical "A Mother's Tale." Agee is very much concerned with the functioning of the subconscious mind, as demonstrated notably in "Death in the Desert." The seeds of his novel *A Death in the Family* and his novella *The Night Watch* are also found in these early stories.

James Agee (Library of Congress)

"KNOXVILLE"

This story, found in the opening pages of *A Death in the Family*, as a prelude to the novel, overflows with innocence and nostalgia. Its protagonist reflects on the last summer of his father's life, soon cut short by an automobile accident. The boy Rufus, through whose eyes the story is told, looks back to a time when his life was secure and comfortable, a time when his father, as is shown in the beginning of *A Death in the Family*, would take his family to an evening's picture show. The tone reminds one of the poet Robert Browning's lines, "God's in his heaven—/ All's right with the world."

Such complacency, however, is not to last. Although this story in itself does not allude to the impending accident that will kill Rufus's father, readers are soon aware that the equilibrium marking the lives of Rufus and his family is about to be disturbed. Included in the original version of the story, which was written in 1936, long before Agee began work on *A Death in the Family*, is a segment that was eventually removed and became a separate entity entitled "Dream Sequence," first published in 1968, thirteen years after Agee's death.

"DREAM SEQUENCE"

"Dream Sequence" begins with a nightmare about a writer who is compelled to write an autobiographical novel in order to sort out his feelings and end the torment of the nightmare, which is based upon a horrible, terrifying event. Whereas in "Knoxville: Summer of 1915" the author returns to his childhood memories and gains a degree of peace by that return, the protagonist in "Dream Sequence" has yet to come to grips with what troubles him and preoccupies his subconscious mind.

When Rufus and his father are brought together in Rufus's dream, the atmosphere of the story changes drastically, and peace descends on the troubled boy. Agee is writing about the inevitability of death while celebrating, simultaneously, the joys of living. He finally brings the two opposites, life and death, into harmony, suggesting that one is the natural outcome of the other.

This story seems in some ways a more valid introduction to *A Death in the Family* than was "Knoxville: Summer of 1915." Rufus's isolation and loneliness pervade much of "Dream Sequence," although the story is resolved quietly and peacefully when the nightmare is finally exorcized.

"DEATH IN THE DESERT"

Written while he was a student at Harvard and first published in *The Harvard Advocate* in 1930, this story might have come directly from the experience of Agee or someone like him: a young man who hits the road for the summer, hitchhiking across a daunting expanse of desert. The young man, on his way to Maine, is picked up by an Oklahoma couple in a five- or six-year-old Buick. He gets into the back seat beside their sleeping son.

As the trip progresses and the characters begin to exhaust their store of things to talk about, the protagonist lapses into a stream-of-consciousness mode. He mentally undresses his hosts, imagining them as skeletons propelling the Buick across the lonely desert. Midway into their journey, they see a desperate African American man stranded in the middle of the desert, facing possible death if he does not get a ride. They pass him by, all of them in their own ways justifying the decision not to pick him up. The social complexities of this situation intrigue Agee and provide his story with the kind of dilemma that forces his readers to wrestle with the ideas he puts before them.

OTHER MAJOR WORKS

LONG FICTION: *The Morning Watch*, 1951; *A Death in the Family*, 1957.

SCREENPLAYS: *The Red Badge of Courage*, 1951 (based on Stephen Crane's novel); *The African Queen*, 1952 (based on C. S. Forester's novel); *The Bride Comes to Yellow Sky*, 1952 (based on Crane's short story); *Noa Noa*, 1953; *White Mane*, 1953; *Green Magic*, 1955; *The Night of the Hunter*, 1955; *Agee on Film: Five Film Scripts*, 1960.

POETRY: *Permit Me Voyage*, 1934; *The Collected Poems of James Agee*, 1968 (Robert Fitzgerald, editor).

NONFICTION: *Let Us Now Praise Famous Men*, 1941 (photographs by Walker Evans); *Agee on Film: Reviews and Comments*, 1958; *Letters of James Agee to Father Flye*, 1962.

BIBLIOGRAPHY

Bergreen, Laurence. *James Agee: A Life*. New York: E. P. Dutton, 1984. This is one of the best biographies of Agee, thorough and well researched. Its critical analyses are cogent and thoughtful. Bergreen's writing style is appealing.

Kramer, Victor A. *Agee and Actuality: Artistic Vision in His Work*. Troy, N.Y.: Whitston, 1991. Kramer delves into the aesthetics of Agee's writing. This study is valuable for identifying controlling themes that pervade the author's writing.

_____. *James Agee*. Boston: Twayne, 1975. Although this well-written book is now dated, it remains one of the more valuable sources available to the nonspecialist, useful for its analyses, its bibliography, and its chronology of the author's life.

Lofaro, Michael A., ed. *James Agee: Reconsiderations*. Knoxville: University of Tennessee Press, 1992. The nine essays in this slim volume are carefully considered. Mary Moss's bibliography of secondary sources is especially well crafted and eminently useful, as are penetrating essays by Linda Wagner-Martin and Victor A. Kramer.

Madden, David, and Jeffrey J. Folks, eds. *Remembering James Agee*, 2d ed. Athens: University of Georgia Press, 1979. The twenty-two essays in this book touch on every important aspect of Agee's life and work. They range from the reminiscences of Father Flye to those of his third wife, Mia Agee. The interpretive essays on his fiction and films are particularly illuminating, as are the essays on his life as a reporter and writer for *Fortune* and *Time*.

Spiegel, Alan. *James Agee and the Legend of Himself*. Columbia: University of Missouri Press, 1998. In this critical study of Agee's writing, Spiegel offers especially sound insights into the role that childhood reminiscence plays in the author's fiction and into the uses that Agee makes of nostalgia. The hundred pages on *Let Us Now Praise Famous Men* represent one of the best interpretations of this important early work. Teachers will appreciate the section entitled "Agee in the Classroom."

R. Baird Shuman

SHMUEL YOSEF AGNON
Shmuel Yosef Czaczkes

Born: Buczacz, Galicia (now Buchach, Ukraine);
July 17, 1888
Died: Rehovoth, Israel; February 17, 1970

PRINCIPAL SHORT FICTION
Agunot, 1909 (English translation, 1970)
"Vehaya he'akov lemishor," 1912
Me'az ume'ata, 1931
Sipure ahavim, 1931
Sefer hama'asim, 1932, 1941, 1951
Beshuva vanachat, 1935
Elu ve'elu, 1941
Shevu'at emunim, 1943 (*Betrothed*, 1966)
Ido ve'Enam, 1950 (*Edo and Enam*, 1966)
Samukh venir'e, 1951
Ad hena, 1952
Al kapot hamanul, 1953

Ha'esh veha'etsim, 1962
Two Tales, 1966 (includes *Betrothed* and *Edo and Enam*)
Twenty-one Stories, 1970
Selected Stories of S. Y. Agnon, 1970
Ir umelo'a, 1973
Lifnim min hachomah, 1975
Pitche dvarim, 1977
A Dwelling Place of My People: Sixteen Stories of the Chassidim, 1983
A Book That Was Lost and Other Stories, 1995

OTHER LITERARY FORMS
    Although it is for his more than two hundred short stories that he has gained worldwide renown, Shmuel Yosef Agnon is also a talented novelist. Three of his novels—*Hakhnasat kala* (1931; *The Bridal Canopy*,

1937), *Bi-levav yamin: Sipur agadah* (1935; *In the Heart of the Seas: A Story of a Journey to the Land of Israel*, 1947), and *Oreach nata lalun* (1939, 1950; *A Guest for the Night*, 1968)—have been published in a twelve-volume set. English translations of his other novels include *T'mol shilshom* (1945), *Sipur pashut* (1935; *A Simple Story*, 1985), and *Shirah* (1971; *Shira*, 1989). In collaboration with Martin Buber, he collected Hasidic tales; among his nonfiction works are *Yamim nora'im* (1938; *Days of Awe*, 1948), a compilation of learned commentaries on the holidays, and *Atem re'item* (1959; *Present at Sinai: The Giving of the Law*, 1994). In 1916, he copublished a book of Polish legends, and later he founded and coedited a journal in Berlin.

Schmuel Yosef Agnon, winner of the Nobel Prize for Literature in 1966
(©The Nobel Foundation)

ACHIEVEMENTS

Shmuel Yosef Agnon's influence on the development of modern Hebrew literature is unparalleled. His contributions to literature earned the Bialik Prize for Literature in 1934 and in 1950, the Ussishkin Prize in 1950, the Israel Prize for Literature in both 1954 and 1958, and the Nobel Prize in Literature in 1966, shared with German-Swedish poet Nelly Sachs.

BIOGRAPHY

Shmuel Yosef Agnon derived his pen name from the novella *Agunot*, which he published in 1909. He was born Shmuel Yosef Czaczkes, the eldest of the five children of Shalom Mordecai and Esther Czaczkes. From his father, an ordained rabbi and merchant with whom he studied Talmudic commentaries, he learned Hebrew scholarship; from his mother, he gained an appreciation of German literature. He had no formal education beyond six years in private hadarim and a short period at the Baron Hirsch School, although he was given honorary doctorates by the Jewish Theological Seminary (1936) and the Hebrew University of Jerusalem (1959). In 1903, when only fifteen, he had his first poems published. At eighteen he moved to Lvov to work on a newspaper. In 1908, he became the first secretary of the Jewish court in Jaffa, Palestine, and Secretary of the National Jewish Council. After two years in Jerusalem, he moved to Berlin, where he taught, wrote,

and met his future publisher. Salman Schocken tried from 1916 to 1928 to have his friend's stories printed and gave him an annual stipend so he could continue writing. Finally, Schocken founded his own publishing firm, which he moved to Tel Aviv in 1938 because of the outbreak of World War II. He opened a New York branch in 1945. Agnon married Esther Marx on May 6, 1919. When his home in Germany burned down in 1924, he lost not only his library of some four thousand volumes but also his seven-hundred-page manuscript of an autobiographical novel called "Eternal Life." Agnon returned to Jerusalem in 1924. From 1950 to 1970, he was president of the society for the publication of ancient manuscripts; he was also fellow of the Bar-Ilan University. Agnon died after suffering a heart attack on February 17, 1970. Some eighty-five of Agnon's works have been published in translation in eighteen languages.

ANALYSIS

To read Shmuel Yosef Agnon's stories is to become immersed in the emerging Jewish state, Eastern

Europe at the beginning of the twentieth century, the Jews in Germany during the Holocaust and throughout history, and individual people struggling to find their niche in these different places and situations. Agnon's sentences are often formed around allusions to Jewish texts and traditions, and the reader benefits from exploring the layers of meaning implied by these references. Agnon frames his stories in a way that begs the reader to struggle with the fine line between fact and fiction.

Much of Agnon's work relies on historical elements for its realism. Its combination of fact and fantasy reveals the breadth of his imagination. His connection to Israel, he said, made him feel as if he had been born in Jerusalem. Agnon, considered the greatest Hebrew writer of the twentieth century, also was inspired by past writers. Although his first book collection was destroyed, before he died he had amassed an even greater collection at his home in Jerusalem. His work, as critic Harold Fisch has said, "reflects the ongoing processes of Jewish life in his time." As a catalog of modern Jewish history and experience, Agnon's work is definitive of, as well as being defined by, its context. His influence on the development of modern Hebrew literature is unparalleled.

"FABLE OF THE GOAT"

In his earliest stories, Agnon established his genre, the medieval ethical tale, through his titles, his rhetorical devices, his use of anonymous, stereotyped figures, and his narrative stance. In 1925 he published a cycle of fourteen legends, the most frequently anthologized of which is the "Fable of the Goat." The figures are flat and unindividuated, a nameless father and his son. The mode of narration is traditional. The pose of transmitting, orally, a story that has been handed down from previous tellers is established by the passive voice of the opening sentence: "The tale is told of an old man who groaned from his heart." The diction is folkloric in its simplicity. Clauses are linked by coordinating rather than subordinating conjunctions; the sentences are compound rather than complex. Events are strung together in a similar fashion, one simply following the other, naïvely oblivious to cause and effect. Magical happenings are taken for granted.

Having set up the folkloric frame through these devices, Agnon persuades his reader to accept the enchantment on the same terms. The old man is cured of his unspecified ailment by the milk of a goat that periodically disappears. When the son offers to follow her by means of a cord tied to her tail, she leads him through a cave to the land of Israel. Desiring his father to follow him there, the son inserts a note in her ear. He assumes that his father will stroke the goat on its return and that, when it flicks its ears, the message will fall out. The father, however, assumes that his son has been killed, and the goat that led him to his death is slaughtered; not until the goat is being flayed does he discover the note. Not only has he deprived himself of joining his son in the Holy Land, because, from that time on, the cave which had afforded his son access has been sealed, but also he has slain the source of the milk "which had the taste of paradise."

The meaning is conveyed stylistically, and the characters indicate their spiritual states by biblical allusions. The son shows that he has attained salvation through a simple leap of faith, by speaking in the language of the Song of Solomon. He sees "pleasant fruits," "a well of living waters," and "a fountain of gardens." He says that he will sit beneath a tree "until the day break, and the shadows flee." This love song between God and Israel is traditionally recited just before the Sabbath evening prayers. When he asks the passersby where he is, he says, "I charge you . . ."; they tell him he is close to Safed, a town which from the sixteenth century has been famous as the center of Jewish mysticism. He sees "men like angels, wrapped in white shawls" going to pray. They are carrying myrtle branches, a Midrashic symbol for a student of the Torah. When he writes his note, it is with ink made from gallnuts, with which the Torah scrolls are inscribed.

The son urges his father to the same simple faith. He writes him not to ask questions but just to hold onto the cord, "then shalt thou walk in thy way safely." The father cannot read this message, however, because it is concealed from him by his own spiritual condition. His speeches echo the dirges of fathers over sons in the Bible; like David mourning

Absalom, he laments, "Would God I had died for thee." Like Jacob grieving for Joseph, he cries "an evil beast hath devoured him; Joseph is without doubt rent in pieces." His lack of faith leads him to slay his one hope of redemption. When he finds the note telling him how to attain salvation "with one bound," it is too late. With the father's realization that he has condemned himself to live out his life in exile, the tale closes, intensified by the ironic contrast with the believing son from whom the father has by his own actions forever separated himself. The closing words quote the Psalm of the Sabbath, the son "shall bear fruit in his old age; full of sap and richness"; that he will live "tranquil and secure" refers to Jeremiah's prophecy of the end of exile.

The goat, whose milk is as sweet as honey, personifies the traditional epithet of Israel as "the land of milk and honey." By drinking the hope of returning to Zion, the old man heals the bitterness of his life. The concealed message sent out from the Holy Land, inscribed like a Torah scroll and promising redemption, reinforces the personification and turns it into a symbol; the words of the Torah are said to be "like milk and honey." The skeptic who deprives himself of this sustenance kills his only link with salvation. The theme, succinctly rendered in three and a half pages through subtle adjustments of biblical overtones, requires an extended explication of those allusions to readers who no longer study the Bible, and that irony is also part of the point of this brief fable.

"THE KERCHIEF"

"The Kerchief," which is also included in *A Book That Was Lost and Other Stories* (1995), shows the changed narrative stance in Agnon's next period, when he turned from the impersonal rendering of folkloric material to the lyrical rendition of subjective experience. The story uses the dual perspective of memoir: The child's initiation is framed by the adult's remembrance. The narrator recalls how he had given his mother's kerchief to a beggar on the day of his Bar Mitzvah; this induction into the adult congregation occurs on his thirteenth birthday. (The story is divided into thirteen episodes, and the first edition was privately issued in thirteen copies.) "The Kerchief" was composed as a Bar Mitzvah present for Gideon

Schocken, the son of Agnon's patron. The tale of how a boy becomes a man opens and closes with the same tableau of the mother waiting at the window. The two scenes are informed by this difference: At the beginning she is waiting for her husband's return and at the end she is waiting for her son's.

The time scheme relates the events to the liturgical calendar and mythicizes them. The narrator says that the week of his father's absence was like Tisha B'ab, a midsummer period of mourning for the destruction of both the first and the second Temples on the ninth of Ab. At this lowest ebb of the year, legend says, the Messiah will be born; he will be found as a ragged pauper, binding his wounds outside the city gates. This event is introduced in a dream of the narrator, who falls asleep thinking of the Messiah's advent and then dreams that a bird has carried him to Rome. There, among a group of poor men, sits a man binding his wounds. The boy averts his eyes from so much suffering. A few days after this dream, his father returns from his trip with presents for the family. His mother opens her gift, a kerchief, and strokes it lovingly, gazing silently at her husband. Because she wears it only on holidays, it becomes associated with family harmony. After she lights the Sabbath candles, the narrator imagines that angels' wings cause it to flutter. He feels a blessing flow into him as she silently strokes his head.

All these elements subtly converge in the climax of the story. On the day of his Bar Mitzvah, his mother has bound her kerchief around his neck. On his way home from the service he encounters a ragged beggar sitting on a pile of stones, tending his open sores; he seems to be the same figure the narrator saw in his dream. Now, having just been initiated into manhood, he does not avert his gaze, and his exchanged glance with the beggar is described with the same phrase used earlier for his parents' looks when the kerchief was first given. With a rush of feeling, the narrator hands him the kerchief, and the beggar bandages his feet and vanishes. The narrator stands for a moment before the now-empty pile of stones, which seem to dazzle, and feels the sun stroke his neck in blessing. Wondering how he can explain the loss of her kerchief, he turns homeward to find his mother waiting at the window with such affectionate acceptance that his apologies are unnecessary.

"A WHOLE LOAF"

The twenty stories in the collection *Sefer hama'asim* (book of deeds) are ironically entitled. The first-person protagonists share an inability to act effectively. Their failed missions, most of them lapses in ritual observance, induce a pervasive anxiety. They are menaced by uncanny figures who seem to be externalizations of their own psyches. "A Whole Loaf," also included in *A Book That Was Lost and Other Stories*, has been the most frequently reprinted of these ambiguous tales. Set in present-day Jerusalem on the weekend before Purim, the story, like its indecisive narrator, circles back on itself, concluding with the same passage with which it began. The speaker, having made no preparations for the Sabbath, must go out to eat, because his family is abroad. It is required to bless a braided white bread in honor of the Sabbath. He is intercepted by Dr. Yekutiel Ne'eman (both of whose names are epithets for Moses, who, according to legend, died on that day, the seventh of Adar). The narrator is asked to mail some registered letters for him. The Hebrew word for "registered" is *ahrayut*, which means "obligation." Thus, he has been allegorically charged with the responsibility of carrying out the Mosaic commandments. The narrator is prevented from entering the post office by Mr. Gressler. An arsonist whose name is derived from the German word for "hateful" (grässlich), Gressler sets fire to a textile shop to get the insurance, and the narrator's entire library goes up in flames. The narrator is both attracted to and repelled by Gressler. Shortly after he enters Gressler's carriage, it overturns; both men fall into the street and grapple in the dust. Bruised and dirtied, the narrator cleans himself off, makes sure that he has not lost the letters, and decides that he had better appease his hunger before mailing them. Entering a restaurant, he orders "a whole loaf," which most likely symbolizes the protagonist's greedy nature. Many times the waiter seems to be approaching him with trays of food, but these are always for some other customer. He begins to reproach himself for having ordered a whole loaf, when he would have been satisfied with just a single

slice. He sees a child eating the saffron-flavored bread his mother used to bake for Purim and longs for a mouthful. The clock strikes, reminding him that the post office will soon close, so he jumps up, knocking down the waiter who is finally bringing his order. He is asked to wait; everyone leaves, and he is locked in for the night. A mouse begins gnawing on the bones, and he fears that it will soon start gnawing him.

In the morning the cleaners ask who this fellow is lying on the littered floor, and the waiter identifies him as the one who had asked for a whole loaf. The narrator heads home in a hunger sweat, in dirty clothes, with a parched throat and heavy legs. Again he cleans himself and sets out once more on his quest for spiritual sustenance. The story closes in *t'shuvah*, which means "return," as it returns to its initial paragraph. The narrator, although he has twice fallen, arises again to seek his tradition (symbolized by the whole hallah and the whole family). Although he is besmirched by life, he cleanses his sins (which is the second meaning of *t'shuvah*, "repentance"). As he is locked in the empty restaurant, his soul is locked in this world for a time. Soon his body and bones will be gnawed away in death, so he must make preparations for the world that is to come. There is a rabbinic saying that the Sabbath is a foretaste of Paradise, so humans must prepare themselves. Although it is Sunday when the story ends, and the post office is closed, he plans to fulfill his commitment. Alienated though he is, he still hungers for the whole loaf of life, even though he has not yet been granted even a crumb.

A BOOK THAT WAS LOST AND OTHER STORIES

A Book That Was Lost and Other Stories is a very readable collection of Agnon's short fiction. Named after one of the included stories, "A Book That Was Lost," the collection follows Agnon's life chronologically and geographically, providing a broad sampling of his many moods, voices, and themes, from pietistic folktales to stark modernism. The literary scope in this collection ranges from coming-of-age tales in "The Kerchief," to magical fables in "Pisces," to accounts of modern alienation in "A Whole Loaf" and "At the Outset of the Day."

The central theme of three stories, "A Book That Was Lost," "The Tale of the Menorah," and "Buczacz," focuses on the significance of Judaism in relation to political turmoil and exile endured throughout history. Other themes in this collection of short fiction include the relationship between the individual and the community, the inability to realize one's ambitions, the alienation of the individual from the community, destruction and redemption, the struggle of the individual in Israel, the intersection of religious and secular life, and human determination versus divine intervention. Throughout the collection, Agnon probes the Jewish condition, his narrators always seeking a balance and understanding between estrangement and community, antiquity and modernity, and destruction and rebirth. "A Book That Was Lost" centers on a book that is actually lost twice. At the beginning of the story, the narrator finds it in an obscure place in the Eastern European village of Buczacz. At the end of the story, the narrator is at the National Library in Israel awaiting the arrival of this same lost book. Jewish history and unity are reiterated throughout the story, bridging the gap from two thousand years ago to present Jewish identity.

"The Tale of the Menorah" and "Buczacz" can be profitably read together. In "The Tale of the Menorah," the symbol of the Menorah is used to relate the history and adaptation of the Jews of Buczacz, the eastern European village where Agnon was born. Throughout the story, the Jews of Buczacz struggle to cope with the challenges faced in understanding life in their Eastern European land of residence. In "Buczacz," Agnon expresses his abiding affection for his hometown village, a community that was swept away during the Holocaust. During the story, Agnon relates his deep feelings for such a great tragedy. By portraying the epic life of this town, Agnon reveals his hope that a single coherent community may become a model for all humans to someday live together in peace.

OTHER MAJOR WORKS

LONG FICTION: *Hakhnasat kala*, 1931 (*The Bridal Canopy*, 1937); *Bi-levav yamin: Sipur agadah*, 1935 (*In the Heart of the Seas: A Story of a Journey to the Land of Israel*, 1947); *Sipur pashut*, 1935 (*A Simple Story*, 1985); *Oreach nata lalun*, 1939, 1950 (*A Guest for the Night*, 1968); *T'mol shilsom*, 1945; *Shirah*, 1971 (*Shira*, 1989); *Bachanuto shel Mar Lublin*, 1974.

NONFICTION: *Sefer, sofer, vesipur*, 1938, 1978; *Yamim nora'im*, 1938 (*Days of Awe*, 1948); *Atem re'item*, 1959 (*Present at Sinai: The Giving of the Law*, 1994); *Sifrehem shel tsadikim*, 1961; *Meatsmi el atsmi*, 1976; *Korot batenu*, 1979.

MISCELLANEOUS: *Kol sippurav shel Shmuel Yosef Agnon*, 1931-1952 (11 volumes); *Kol sippurav shel Shmuel Yosef Agnon*, 1953-1962 (8 volumes).

BIBLIOGRAPHY

Aberbach, David. *At the Handles of the Lock: Themes in the Fiction of S. J. Agnon*. New York: Oxford University Press, 1984. Aberbach sets out the major patterns in Agnon's writing on a work-by-work basis. Much discussion of Agnon's short fiction is included, and the notes and references are detailed. Includes an index.

Band, Arnold J. *Nostalgia and Nightmare: A Study in the Fiction of S. Y. Agnon*. Berkeley: University of California Press, 1968. This comprehensive text covers Agnon's literary development text by text. It is also very useful for the historical background to, and context of, Agnon's work. Band discusses Agnon's life and his career as a writer. The book includes both primary and secondary bibliographies, appendices, and a general index.

Ben-Dov, Nitza. *Agnon's Art of Indirection: Uncovering Latent Content in the Fiction of S. Y. Agnon*. New York: E. J. Brill, 1993. Discusses a number of themes in Agnon's work and includes a chapter entitled "The Web of Biblical Allusion." Also includes a bibliography and index.

Fisch, Harold. *S. Y. Agnon*. New York: Frederick Ungar, 1975. Part of a series on literary greats, this work includes a useful chronology and a brief biography of Agnon's life. An in-depth discussion of individual writings follows the biographical section. Supplemented by notes, primary and secondary bibliographies, and an index.

Fleck, Jeffrey. *Character and Context: Studies in the Fiction of Abramovitsh, Brenner, and Agnon*. Chico, Calif.: Scholars Press, 1984. In this text,

Fleck places Agnon's work alongside that of his contemporaries, especially in the first chapter, "Modern Hebrew Literature in Context." Individual stories such as "The Banished One," "And the Crooked Shall Become Straight," and "Legends" are discussed in detail. Fleck has included notes at the end of each chapter as well as a list of reference works consulted for each author at the end of the book. Includes an index.

Hochman, Baruch. "An Afternoon with Agnon." *The American Scholar* 57 (Winter, 1988): 91-99. A biographical sketch and an account of a meeting with Agnon in Jerusalem; notes how his work elegizes the traditional East European Jewish world, which he saw disappearing through cultural erosion and then through the Holocaust; claims that loss in Agnon's works is counterbalanced by miraculous transformations and restorations. A pervasive self-mockery similarly undercuts whatever the author idealizes.

_____. *The Fiction of S. Y. Agnon.* Ithaca, N.Y.: Cornell University Press, 1970. Hochman presents a detailed interpretation of Agnon's major works, placing them in the context of the time and place in which they were written. A primary bibliographical note is included for locating translations of the original works. Notes on all the chapters are supplied at the end of the book, as is an index.

Ozick, Cynthia. "Agnon's Antagonisms." *Commen-*tary 86 (December, 1988): 43-48. Ozick analyzes Agnon's story "Edo and Enam," discussing the relationship between translation and redemption and the oppositions of safety and obliteration, redemption and illusion, and exile and return.

Patterson, David, and Glenda Abramson, eds. *Tradition and Trauma: Studies in the Fiction of S. J. Agnon.* Boulder, Colo.: Westview Press, 1994. A collection of papers presented at a conference on the centenary of the birth of Agnon. A number of essays focus on such stories as "Forever," "Pat Shlemah," "Friendship," and "The Doctor's Divorce."

Shaked, Gershon. *Shmuel Yosef Agnon: A Revolutionary Traditionalist.* New York: New York University Press, 1989. Shaked details Agnon's progression as a writer, including biographical events that influenced his development. Chapter 5 addresses Agnon's short stories in particular. Contains notes on the chapters and an index.

Yudkin, Leon, ed. *Agnon: Texts and Contexts in English Translation: A Multi-Disciplinary Curriculum, Bibliographies, and Selected Syllabi.* New York: M. Wiener, 1988. A critical study of Agnon's works and their English translations. Includes a bibliography.

Ruth Rosenberg, updated by
Jo-Ellen Lipman Boon and Alvin K. Benson

ILSE AICHINGER

Born: Vienna, Austria; November 1, 1921

PRINCIPAL SHORT FICTION

Rede unter dem Galgen, 1952; pb. as *Der Gefesselte,* 1953 (*The Bound Man and Other Stories,* 1955)

Wo ich wohne: Erzählungen, Gedichte, Dialoge, 1963

Eliza, Eliza, 1965

Selected Short Stories and Dialogue, 1966

Ilse Aichinger, 1969

Nachricht vom Tag: Erzählungen, 1970

Meine Sprache und ich: Erzählungen, 1978

Spiegelgeschichte: Erzählungen und Dialoge, 1979 (stories and dialogue)

Selected Poetry and Prose, 1983

OTHER LITERARY FORMS

Although most critics agree that the stories in *The Bound Man and Other Stories* are Ilse Aichinger's most important work, she is also the author of the novel *Der grössere Hoffnung*, 1948 (*Herod's Children*, 1963); a number of radio plays; a volume of poetry, *Verschenkter Rat* (1978); several dialogues collected in *Besuch im Pfarrhaus: Ein Hörspiel, Drei Dialoge* (1961); *Dialoge, Erzählungen, Gedichte* (1971); and several critical essays.

ACHIEVEMENTS

Ilse Aichinger received the Austrian State Prize for the Encouragement of Literature in 1952, the Prize of Group Forty-Seven in 1952 for the short fiction *Spiegelgeschichte* ("Story in a Mirror"), the Literary Prize of the City of Bremen in 1955, the Immermann Prize of the City of Düsseldorf in 1955, the Bavarian Literature Prize in 1961, and the Nelly Sachs Prize of Dortmund in 1971.

BIOGRAPHY

Ilse Aichinger was born in Vienna, Austria, on November 1, 1921. She spent her childhood in Lenz. In 1942, after her grandmother was sent to a concentration camp, from which she did not return, Aichinger's twin sister Helga was sent to England, but Ilse remained in Vienna with her mother, a physician who was made to work in a factory. After the war, Aichinger studied medicine at the University of Vienna, but decided to become a writer instead.

After her first novel *Herod's Children* was published in 1948, she took a job as a reader for S. Fischer Publishers in Frankfurt, East Germany and Vienna. She became a member of Group Forty-seven, a group of writers that included Günther Grass and Heinrich Böll but refrained from political involvement. Aichinger married the German poet and playwright Günter Eich in 1953, with whom she had two children. After her husband died in 1972, she settled down in a village on the Austrian-Bavarian border and lived in relative seclusion.

ANALYSIS

The most common critical reaction to Aichinger's fiction is to call attention to her similarity to Franz Kafka, for her stories seem dreamlike, hallucinatory, and subtly allegorical. As a number of critics have

pointed out, Aichinger, like Kafka, creates a fictional world that is both real and visionary at once—what one critic has called a sort of "waking dream." Fellow author Wolfgang Hildsheimer has noted that Aichinger and Kafka are both absurdists but that they differ in that, whereas Kafka's narrators question the world of the absurd, Aichinger's narrators adapt to the reality of it.

Although Aichinger has also been compared to Samuel Beckett and James Joyce, with the exception of her two most famous stories, "Spiegelgeschichte" ("Story in a Mirror") and "Der Gefesselte" ("The Bound Man"), her work is not well known in America. Part of the reason for this neglect has been attributed to the European orientation of the absurdist vision and to the demands that Aichinger places on her readers. Described as a skeptic of well-defined terms in particular and language in general, Aichinger is said to be against "easy consumption" and to expect her readers to engage fully with her texts.

"STORY IN A MIRROR"

One of Aichinger's most admired short fictions, this story, also translated as "Life Story in Retrospect," has been frequently commented on, with one critic calling it "one of the most powerful masterpieces of our time." Basically, the story is a narrative trick in which time is reversed much like a film being run backward. The story focuses on the life of a young woman, told by her in second person from the moment of her death back to her birth, at which point she dies in actuality.

The retracing of the girl's life provides no significant cause of her death. Her experience—meeting a young man, falling in love, getting pregnant, having an abortion, contracting a fever, and dying—is too summarized and generalized to provide insight into her character. However, as a narrative experiment, the technique of the story often creates interesting effects, for the girl who tells the story seems quite aware of the reversal taking place. Thus, when she tells of hearing a voice saying "the death struggle is beginning," she can react by saying, "Don't listen to them! What do they know about it?"

The reversal makes possible several ironic implications; for example, when the girl screams to the old woman who has performed the abortion to bring the fetus back to life, her desire is fulfilled by enabling her to walk back away from the abortion appointment in reverse time. When she recounts her relationship with the young man, he mentions the old abortionist before he knows she is pregnant, even before telling her he loves her. As she goes back even further to the death of her mother, she describes her father bringing her mother home from the cemetery where she lies for three days, as the narrator says she once did. The story ends with the day of the woman's birth, at which point she opens her eyes and abruptly a voice says, "She's dead!"

In spite of the story's clever manipulation of narrative time which has fascinated many critics, others suspect that it is merely a trick, similar to the narrative sleight-of-hand Ambrose Bierce perpetuates on the reader in his famous story "Occurrence at Owl Creek Bridge." However, the story has found favor particularly with feminist critics who suggest that the girl's archetypal life experience reflects universal gender issues.

"THE BOUND MAN"

This is Aichinger's most frequently anthologized story, the story that has made many critics compare her to Kafka, particularly because of its similarity in situation and technique to Kafka's *Ein Hungerkünstler: Vier Geschichten*, 1924 (*A Hunger Artist*, 1948) and *Die Verwandlung* (1915; novella; *The Metamorphosis*, 1936). However, Aichinger, who critics nicknamed "Miss Kafka," insists that she had never read Kafka when she wrote the story. The most obvious similarity to Kafka's famous stories is that the transformation or limitation imposed on the central character simply occurs for no ostensible reason; the fact that when he awakes in the first line of the story he is bound hand-and-foot is simply a given fact.

The second important similarity to Kafka's stories is the fact that the limitation is, while a loss of freedom, at the same time the source of a new kind of freedom. Finally, the story reminds the reader of Kafka's techniques in that events shift suddenly without warning or discernible cause. For example, when the circus owner sees the bound man coming down the path, he is enchanted by his "extraordinary gracefulness," and abruptly the story shifts to a later time with the circus owner announcing the bound man as an act in his circus.

The irony of the bound man's situation is that, by staying within the limits of the "free play" of the rope, he is not confined but given wings. Although the circus owner says there is no reason the bound man should remain tied up after the evening performance, the bound man's fame depends on the fact that he is always bound. When other performers, jealous of the bound man's fame, try various ways to release him from his ropes, they are dismissed by the circus owner. The owner's wife, who befriends the bound man, is ironically his greatest threat, for she wishes to release him out of pity.

The story comes to a head when a young wolf escapes and attacks the bound man. However, he has become so skilled in his limitations that he is able to defend himself. Feeling that, if one were tied up in a certain way, one would be able to fly, he is elated that he does not have the "fatal advantage of free limbs which causes men to be worsted." The encounter with the wolf, however, does bring about the bound man's downfall, for people so disbelieve his amazing feat of fending off the wolf that they demand he repeat the act in public. However, when he does so, the owner's wife cuts his rope and frees him. Knowing that fighting the wolf now would prove nothing, he grabs a pistol and shoots the wolf between the eyes, after which he runs away.

Some critics have suggested that the basic thesis of the story is that, by recognizing and accepting the limitations of being human, people can overcome the restrictions and develop spiritual resources. Others suggest the story is an allegory of the artist whose artistic gift masks a basic limitation or handicap.

OTHER MAJOR WORKS

LONG FICTION: *Die grössere Hoffnung*, 1948 (*Herod's Children*, 1963).

PLAYS: *Zu keiner Stunde*, pb. 1957; *Besuch im Pfarrhaus: Ein Hörspiel, Drei Dialoge*, pb. 1961; *Auckland: Vier Hörspiele*, pb. 1969 (radio plays); *Schlechte Wörter*, pb. 1976 (radio plays); *Knöpfe*, pb.

1978 (radio play); *Weisse Chrysanthemum*, pb. 1979.
POETRY: *Verschenkter Rat*, 1978.

MISCELLANEOUS: *Wo ich wohne: Erzählungen, Gedichte, Dialoge*, 1963; *Dialoge, Erzählungen, Gedichte*, 1971; *Selected Poetry and Prose*, 1983; *Werke*, 1991 (9 volumes).

BIBLIOGRAPHY

Alldridge, J. C. *Ilse Aichinger*. London: Oswald Wolff, 1969. In his introduction to this collection of translations of Aichinger's stories, dialogues, and poems, Alldridge provides a summary survey of Aichinger's work. He argues that fairy tale and folklore condition her language and that elements of the collective unconscious are the source of many of her themes and much of her imagery.

Bedwell, Carol B. "Who Is the Bound Man? Towards an Interpretation of Ilse Aichinger's 'Der Gefesselte'." *German Quarterly* 38 (1965): 30-37. A detailed interpretation of "The Bound Man" as an allegory of birth, life, and death. Argues that, although Aichinger shares with Kafka an undercurrent of allegory, she is more lyrical and more optimistic than he is.

Gerlach, U. Henry. "The Reception of the Works of Ilse Aichinger in the United States." *Modern Austrian Literature* 20 (1987): 95-106. A survey of Aichinger's works published in English and a summary of reviews and criticism. Concludes that Aichinger's works have been well received in the United States; claims that although her most popular work is "The Bound Man," "The Mirror Story" has great potential for success, particularly because of its appeal to women readers.

Nicolai, Ral R. "Ilse Aichinger's Response to Kafka: 'The Bound Man'." In *The Legacy of Kafka in Contemporary Austrian Literature*, edited by Frank Pilipp. Riverside, Calif.: Ariadne Press, 1997. Argues that "The Bound Man" formulates a view reminiscent of Kafka—that humans may be inferior to animals and other life forms because of their "fall from grace" and their ability to reason; in other words, although human beings' ability to think is their most distinguishing feature, it is also that which marks their inferior state.

Ratych, Joana M. "Ilse Aichinger." In *Major Figures of Contemporary Austrian Literature*, edited by Donald G. Daviau. New York: Peter Lang, 1987. An introductory survey of Aichinger's work; includes comments on her novel and its relationship to her life, her stories, her radio plays, her dialogues, and her poetry.

Reitner, Andrea. "Ilse Aichinger: The Poetics of Silence." In *Contemporary German Writers, Their Aesthetics and Their Language*, edited by Arthur Williams, Stuart Parkes, and Julian Preece. New York: Peter Lang, 1996. Discusses Aichinger's mistrust of language as an expression of unrest about a chaotic world. Notes that Aichinger's technique of reduction makes her later prose difficult to understand; she demands that her readers become coauthors of her texts.

Stanley, Patricia Haas. "Ilse Aichinger's Absurd 'I'." *German Studies Review* 2 (1979): 331-350. Discusses Aichinger's stories with female narrators in order to examine her treatment of the effects of World War II Nazi atrocities on women after the war and to evaluate her contribution to the literature of the absurd. Provides an extensive discussion of "Spiegelgeschichte," translated as "Life Story in Retrospect" and as "Story in a Mirror."

Wolfschütz, Hans. "Ilse Aichinger: The Skeptical Narrator." In Modern Austrian Writing: Literature and Society After 1945. London: Oswald Wolff, 1980. Survey of Aichinger's fiction, with discussions of "The Bound Man," "The Mirror Story," and several later short fictions. Comments on her skepticism of language and her exploration of a world that suffers from too much interpretation.

Charles E. May

CONRAD AIKEN

Born: Savannah, Georgia; August 5, 1889
Died: Savannah, Georgia; August 17, 1973

PRINCIPAL SHORT FICTION

Bring! Bring! and Other Stories, 1925
Costumes by Eros, 1928
Among the Lost People, 1934
Short Stories, 1950
Collected Short Stories, 1960
Collected Short Stories of Conrad Aiken, 1966

OTHER LITERARY FORMS

Best-known as a poet, Conrad Aiken published dozens of volumes of poetry from 1914 until his death in 1973. He also published novels, essays, criticism, and a play. In addition, he edited a considerable number of anthologies of poetry.

ACHIEVEMENTS

Conrad Aiken's reputation as a writer of short fiction rests on two frequently anthologized short stories: "Silent Snow, Secret Snow," which has twice been adapted to film, and "Mr. Arcularis," which was adapted to a play. Although he published several collections of short stories—they were collected in one volume in 1950—he did not contribute significantly to the development of the short story. Instead, the fictional "voice" so closely approximates Aiken's poetic "voice" that the stories are often seen as extensions of his more famous poems. Both are "poetic" expressions of characters' psychological states. "Silent Snow, Secret Snow," in fact, is often read as the story of a creative artist, a "poet" in a hostile environment. His Freudian themes, his depiction of a protagonist's inner struggle and journey, and his portrait of the consciousness—these are perhaps better expressed in lengthy poetic works than in prose or in individual poems, which are rarely anthologized because they are best read in the context of his other poems.

BIOGRAPHY

When Conrad Aiken was eleven, his father killed his mother and then committed suicide. This incident could very well have influenced the subject matter of a great number of his stories, where one step more may take a character to an immense abyss of madness or death. Graduating from Harvard University in 1911, Aiken became a member of the famous Harvard group which included T. S. Eliot, Robert Benchley, and Van Wyck Brooks. He published his first volume of poems in 1914. A contributing editor of *The Dial* from 1917 to 1919, Aiken later worked as London correspondent for *The New Yorker*. Through the course of his career he was the recipient of many awards, including the Pulitzer Prize in 1930 for *Selected Poems* (1929), the National Book Award in 1954 for *Collected Poems* (1953), and the Bollingen Prize in Poetry in 1956. He died in 1973 at the age of eighty-four.

"SILENT SNOW, SECRET SNOW,"

In "Silent Snow, Secret Snow," a story once included in almost every anthology of short fiction, Conrad Aiken describes a young boy's alienation and withdrawal from his world. The story begins one morning in December when Paul Hasleman, aged twelve, thinks of the postman, whom the boy hears every morning. The progress of the postman as he turns the corner at the top of the hill and makes his way down the street with a double knock at each door is familiar to the boy, and, as he slowly awakens, he begins to listen for the sounds on the cobblestones of the street of heavy boots as they come around the corner. When the sounds come on this morning, however, they are closer than the corner and muffled and faint. Paul understands at once: "Nothing could have been simpler—there had been snow during the night, such as all winter he had been longing for." With his eyes still closed, Paul imagines the snow—how it sounds and how it will obliterate the familiar sights of the street—but when he opens his eyes and turns toward the window, he sees only the bright morning sun. The miracle of snow has not transformed anything.

The moment and his feelings about the snow,

however, remain with him, and later in the classroom as his geography teacher, Miss Buell, twirls the globe with her finger and talks about the tropics, Paul finds himself looking at the arctic areas, which are colored white on the globe. He recalls the morning and the moment when he had a sense of falling snow, and immediately he undergoes the same experience of seeing and hearing the snow fall.

Conrad Aiken (Library of Congress)

As the days go by, Paul finds himself between two worlds—the real one and a secret one of peace and remoteness. His parents become increasingly concerned by his "daydreaming," inattentive manner, but more and more he is drawn into the incomprehensible beauty of the world of silent snow. His secret sense of possession and of being protected insulates him both from the world of the classroom where Deidre, with the freckles on the back of her neck in a constellation exactly like the Big Dipper, waves her brown flickering hand and from the world at home where his parents' concern and questions have become an increasingly difficult matter with which to cope.

Aiken's presentation of the escalation of Paul's withdrawal is skillfully detailed through the use of symbols. The outside world becomes for Paul fragmented: scraps of dirty newspapers in a drain, with the word Eczema as the addressee and an address in Fort Worth, Texas; lost twigs from parent trees; bits of broken egg shells; the footprints of a dog who long ago "had made a mistake" and walked on the river of wet cement which in time had frozen into rock; the wound in an elm tree. In the company of his parents Paul neither sees them nor feels their presence. His mother is a voice asking questions, his father a pair of brown slippers. These images cluster together in such a way as to foreshadow the inevitable and relentless progress of Dr. Howells down the street to Paul's house, a visit which replicates the progress of the postman.

The doctor, called by the parents because their concern has now grown into alarm over Paul's behavior, examines the boy, and, as the examination and questioning by the adults accelerate, Paul finds the situation unbearable. He retreats further into his secret world where he sees snow now slowly filling the spaces in the room—highest in the corners, under the sofa—the snow's voice a whisper, a promise of peace, cold and restful. Reassured by the presence of the snow and seduced by its whisperings and promises, Paul begins to laugh and to taunt the adults with little hints. He believes they are trying to corner him, and there is something malicious in his behavior:

> He laughed a third time—but this time, happening to glance upward toward his mother's face, he was appalled at the effect his laughter seemed to have upon her. Her mouth had opened in an expression of horror. This was too bad! Unfortunate! He had known it would cause pain, of course—but he hadn't expected it to be quite as bad as this. . . .

The hints, however, explain nothing to the adults, and, continuing to feel cornered, Paul pleads a headache and tries to escape to bed. His mother follows him, but it is too late. "The darkness was coming in long white waves," and "the snow was laughing; it spoke from all sides at once." His mother's presence in the room is alien, hostile, and brutal. He is filled with loathing, and he exorcizes her: "Mother! Mother! Go away! I hate you!" With this effort, everything is solved, "everything became all right." His withdrawal is now complete. All contact with the real world is lost, and he gives himself over to a "vast moving screen of snow—but even now it said peace, it said remoteness, it said cold, it said sleep." Paul's withdrawal is, as the snow tells him, a going inward rather than an opening outward: "It is a flower becoming a seed," it is a movement toward complete solipsism and a closure of his life.

"STRANGE MOONLIGHT"

"Strange Moonlight," another story of a young boy's difficulty in dealing with the realities of life and death, could be a prelude to "Silent Snow, Secret Snow." In "Strange Moonlight" a young boy filches a copy of Poe's tales from his mother's bookshelf and in consequence spends a "delirious night in inferno." The next day the boy wins a gold medal at school, which he later carries in his pocket, keeping it a secret from his mother and father. The desire to keep a secret recalls Paul's need to keep from his parents his first hallucination of snow. The gold medal is "above all a secret," something to be kept concealed; it is like a particularly beautiful trinket to be carried unmentioned in his trouser pocket.

The week's events include a visit to a friend's house where the boy meets Caroline Lee, an extraordinarily strange and beautiful child with large pale eyes. Both Caroline Lee and the house in which she lives with its long, dark, and winding stairways excite and fascinate him. Within a few days, however, the boy learns that Caroline Lee is dead of scarlet fever. He is stunned: "How did it happen that he, who was so profoundly concerned, had not been consulted, had not been invited to come and talk with her, and now found himself so utterly and hopelessly and forever excluded—from the house as from her?" This becomes a thing he cannot understand.

The same night he is confronted with another disturbing mystery. He overhears an intimate conversation between his father and mother. Filled with horror, the boy begins at once to imagine a conversation with Caroline Lee in which she comes back from the grave to talk with him. The next day his father unex-

pectedly takes the family to the beach, and the boy wanders away and finds a snug, secret hiding place on a lonely hot sand dune. He lies there surrounded by tall whispering grass, and Caroline's imagined visit of the night before becomes real for him. Rather than ending in unreality as one would expect, however, Aiken inexplicably brings the boy back to reality without resolving any of the problems set up in the story. He thus leaves a gap between the protagonist's conflicts with sexuality, reality, and unreality, and their final resolution.

"YOUR OBITUARY, WELL WRITTEN"

In another story, however, "Your Obituary, Well Written," Aiken presents a young man identified only as Mr. Grant who confronts a similar circumstance. Told in the first person by the protagonist, Mr. Grant, the story repeats what is basically the same pattern of events. Although supposedly a portrait of Katherine Mansfield to whom Aiken is strongly indebted for the forms his stories take, the character of Reiner Wilson is also strongly reminiscent of Caroline Lee, the little girl in "Strange Moonlight." The narrator says of Reiner Wilson: "I was struck by the astonishing frailty of her appearance, an otherworld fragility, almost a transparent spiritual quality—as if she were already a disembodied soul." Knowing from the first that she is not only married but also fatally ill, he manages to see her one time and fall in love with her, and then he almost simultaneously withdraws. "At bottom, however, it was a kind of terror that kept me away. . . . The complications and the miseries, if we did allow the meetings to go further might well be fatal to both of us."

The same conflicts which Paul, the child in "Silent Snow, Secret Snow," experienced are again faced by the man who is not able to resolve the riddles of sex and love, life and death. The narrator never sees Reiner again, and at her death he is left on a park bench under a Judas tree wanting to weep, but unable to: "But Reiner Wilson, the dark-haired little girl with whom I had fallen in love was dead, and it seemed to me that I too was dead." Another similarity between "Silent Snow, Secret Snow" and "Your Obituary, Well Written" is Aiken's use of a natural element as major metaphor. In "Your Obituary, Well Written," rain functions in the same manner that snow does in "Silent Snow, Secret Snow." During Grant's one meeting alone with Reiner Wilson, the room had suddenly darkened, and rain fell, sounding to him as though it were inside the room. The sensations the man feels in response to the rain are similar to those Paul feels in response to the snow. Grant tells Reiner about a time when as a boy he went swimming and it began to rain:

> The water was smooth—there was no sound of waves—and all about me arose a delicious *seething* . . . [T]here was something sinister in it, and also something divinely soothing. I don't believe I was ever happier in my life. It was as if I had gone into another world.

Reiner calls Grant "the man who loves rain," and her estimate of him is correct. Unable to open up himself, unable to make himself vulnerable and live in the real world, he is at the end of the story as withdrawn from reality as is Paul, who chooses the silent and secret snow.

"THISTLEDOWN"

Besides dealing with various subconscious desires projected by means of hallucinating visions, many of Aiken's stories reflect preoccupations of the times in which the stories were written. Chief among these themes is the changing roles of women and sexual mores of the 1920's. In most of Aiken's stories, these conflicts are presented through the male point of view.

"Thistledown," a first-person narrative told by a man who is married and living with his wife, opens with private musings of the narrator, wherein he associates a young woman named Coralyn with thistledown, which is being swept in every direction by the wind but which is ultimately doomed for extinction. Coralyn had been his wife's secretary, and, attracted to her, Phillip, the narrator, became bent on seduction. Far from being "frighteningly unworldly," Coralyn is a "new woman" who has had numerous lovers. He finds her cynical and detached, she finds him an old-fashioned and sentimental fool. The affair is brief. Coralyn leaves, and as the years pass she is in and out of his life, until she disappears altogether,

leaving him bitter, disappointed, and angry. The irony that marks "Thistledown" is characteristic of the stories in which Aiken examines the conventional sexual mores, holding a double-faced mirror to reflect the double standard by which men and women are judged.

"A CONVERSATION"

In "A Conversation," this theme of double standards is examined within the framework of a conversation between two men, probably professors, taking place on a train in a sleeping car. The conversation is overheard by a visiting lecturer at the University who occupies the adjacent sleeping car. The lecturer is tired of "being polite to fools" and wants desperately to go to sleep; but the conversation he overhears keeps him awake, as do clock bells that ring marking every quarter hour. The conversation concerns the fiancée of one of the men, and the other is trying to convince his friend that the woman is not as innocent as she looks; indeed, she has been "manhandled." The engaged man keeps trying to protect his own views of the woman: her central idealism, her essential holiness—views that attach themselves to women who are not prostitutes. By the end of the story, however, the point is made; the engagement will not last, and the woman will be put aside like a used razor or a cork that has been tampered with, images used earlier in the story. The clock bells do not ask a question; they simply continue to toll. In the end, the men cannot accept a female sexuality which is not exclusively directed toward a husband although there is never a question about their own sexual behavior.

OTHER MAJOR WORKS

LONG FICTION: *Blue Voyage*, 1927; *Great Circle*, 1933; *King Coffin*, 1935; *A Heart for the Gods of Mexico*, 1939; *Conversation: Or, Pilgrim's Progress*, 1940; *The Collected Novels of Conrad Aiken*, 1964.

PLAY: *Fear No More*, pr. 1946 (pb. as *Mr. Arcularis: A Play*, 1957).

POETRY: *Earth Triumphant and Other Tales in Verse*, 1914; *Turns and Movies and Other Tales in Verse*, 1916; *The Jig of Forslin*, 1916; *Nocturne of Remembered Spring and Other Poems*, 1917; *The Charnel Rose*, 1918; *Senlin: A Biography and Other*

Poems, 1918; *The House of Dust*, 1920; *Punch: The Immortal Liar*, 1921; *Priapus and the Pool*, 1922; *The Pilgrimage of Festus*, 1923; *Changing Mind*, 1925; *Priapus and the Pool and Other Poems*, 1925; *Prelude*, 1929; *Selected Poems*, 1929; *John Deth: A Metaphysical Legend, and Other Poems*, 1930; *Gehenna*, 1930; *The Coming Forth by Day of Osiris Jones*, 1931; *Preludes for Memnon*, 1931; *And in the Hanging Gardens*, 1933; *Landscape West of Eden*, 1934; *Time in the Rock: Preludes to Definition*, 1936; *And in the Human Heart*, 1940; *Brownstone Eclogues and Other Poems*, 1942; *The Soldier: A Poem by Conrad Aiken*, 1944; *The Kid*, 1947; *Skylight One: Fifteen Poems*, 1949; *The Divine Pilgrim*, 1949; *Wake II*, 1952; *Collected Poems*, 1953, 1970; *A Letter from Li Po and Other Poems*, 1955; *The Fluteplayer*, 1956; *Sheepfold Hill: Fifteen Poems*, 1958; *Selected Poems*, 1961; *The Morning Song of Lord Zero*, 1963; *A Seizure of Limericks*, 1964; *Cats and Bats and Things with Wings: Poems*, 1965; *The Clerk's Journal*, 1971; *A Little Who's Zoo of Mild Animals*, 1977.

NONFICTION: *Skepticisms: Notes on Contemporary Poetry*, 1919; *Ushant: An Essay*, 1952; *A Reviewer's ABC: Collected Criticism of Conrad Aiken from 1916 to the Present*, 1958; *Selected Letters of Conrad Aiken*, 1978.

EDITED TEXTS: *A Comprehensive Anthology of American Poetry*, 1929, 1944; *Twentieth Century American Poetry*, 1944.

BIBLIOGRAPHY

Aiken, Conrad. *Selected Letters of Conrad Aiken.* Edited by Joseph Killorin. New Haven, Conn.: Yale University Press, 1978. Killorin includes a representative sample of 245 letters (from some three thousand) written by Aiken. A cast of correspondents, among them T. S. Eliot and Malcolm Lowry, indexes to Aiken's works and important personages, and a wealth of illustrations, mostly photographs, add considerably to the value of the volume.

Butscher, Edward. *Conrad Aiken: Poet of White Horse Vale.* Athens: University of Georgia Press, 1988. This critical biography emphasizes Aiken's literary work, particularly the poetry. Butscher's book nevertheless contains analyses of about fifteen Aiken short stories, including his most famous ones, "Silent Snow, Secret Snow" and "Mr. Arcularis." Includes many illustrations, copious notes, and an extensive bibliography that is especially helpful in psychoanalytic theory.

Dirda, Michael. "Selected Letters of Conrad Aiken." *The Washington Post*, June 25, 1978, p. G5. A review of Aiken's *Selected Letters*, with a brief biographical sketch; suggests that the letters will help redress the neglect Aiken has suffered.

Hoffman, Frederick J. *Conrad Aiken.* New York: Twayne, 1962. The best overview of Aiken's short fiction. Hoffman's volume contains careful analyses of several individual stories, including "Mr. Arcularis," which receives extensive discussion. Hoffman, who believes Aiken's short stories are more successful than his novels, stresses "Aiken's attitude toward New England, his obsession with "aloneness," and his concern about human relationships. Contains a chronology, a biographical chapter, and an annotated bibliography.

Lorenz, Clarissa M. *Lorelei Two: My Life with Conrad Aiken.* Athens: University of Georgia Press, 1983. Lorenz, Aiken's second wife, discusses the 1926-1938 years, the period when he wrote his best work, including the short stories "Mr. Arcularis" and "Silent Snow, Secret Snow." She covers his literary acquaintances, his work habits, and the literary context in which he worked. The book is well indexed and contains several relevant photographs.

Seigal, Catharine. *The Fictive World of Conrad Aiken: A Celebration of Consciousness.* De Kalb: Northern Illinois University Press, 1993. Chapters on the Freudian foundation of Aiken's fiction, on his New England roots, and on many of his novels. Concluding chapters on Aiken's autobiography, *Ushant*, and an overview of his fiction. Includes notes, selected bibliography, and index.

Spivey, Ted R. *Time's Stop in Savannah: Conrad Aiken's Inner Journey.* Macon, Ga.: Mercer University Press, 1997. Explores Aiken's thought processes and how they translate to his fiction.

Spivey, Ted R., and Arthur Waterman, eds. *Conrad Aiken: A Priest of Consciousness*. New York: AMS Press, 1989. Though their focus is on Aiken's poetry, Spivey and Waterman include essays on the short stories and a review of criticism of the short stories. Contains an extensive chronology of Aiken's life and a lengthy description of the Aiken materials in the Huntington Library.

Womack, Kenneth. "Unmasking Another Villain in Conrad Aiken's Autobiographical Dream." *Biography* 19 (Spring, 1996): 137. Examines the role of British poet and novelist Martin Armstrong as a fictionalized character in Aiken's *Ushant*; argues that Aiken's attack on Armstrong is motivated by revenge for Armstrong's marriage to Aiken's first wife.

Mary Rohrberger, updated by Thomas L. Erskine

RYŪNOSUKE AKUTAGAWA
Ryūnosuke Niihara

Born: Tokyo, Japan; March 1, 1892
Died: Tokyo, Japan; July 27, 1927

PRINCIPAL SHORT FICTION
Kappa, 1927 (English translation, 1970)
Aru ahō no isshō, 1927 (*A Fool's Life*, 1971)
Rashomon and Other Stories, 1930, 1952, 1964
Tales Grotesque and Curious, 1930
Hell Screen and Other Stories, 1952
Japanese Short Stories, 1961
Exotic Japanese Stories: The Beautiful and the Grotesque, 1964

OTHER LITERARY FORMS

Ryūnosuke Akutagawa is known mainly for his short stories, most of which were based on Japanese tales from the twelfth and thirteenth centuries, but he also wrote poetry and essays on literature.

ACHIEVEMENTS

Ryūnosuke Akutagawa gained attention even as a student in English literature at Tokyo University, publishing a short story about a priest with an enormous nose in 1916. Natsumi Sōseki, the foremost novelist of the day, wrote Akutagawa praising his concise style and predicting that if he could write twenty or thirty more such stories he would become famous. He was well recognized as a literary figure by 1918, an unusual accomplishment for such a young writer. Such was his fame that in 1935 the Akutagawa Prize was established in his name. It recognizes promising new writers and is one of the most prestigious literary awards in Japan. Akutagawa is generally considered to be one of the outstanding literary figures in the prewar era, along with Sōseki and Mori Ōgai, and he achieved this in spite of a brief career. His stories are considered classics in modern Japanese literature.

BIOGRAPHY

Ryūnosuke Akutagawa was the son of a dairyman named Niihara Toshizo. Akutagawa's mother went insane seven months after his birth, and she remained so until her death in 1902. At a time when insanity was assumed to be hereditary, Akutagawa feared it most of his life. In fact, he referred to his mother in his suicide note in 1927. Akutagawa was adopted by his mother's brother and reared by his foster mother and a maiden aunt. He was a good student, well read in both Japanese and European literature, including Guy de Maupassant, Anatole France, August Strindberg, and Fyodor Dostoevski.

In 1913, Akutagawa entered the English Literature Department at Tokyo Imperial University, where he published his writing in a university literary magazine. His first important short story, "Rashōmon," appeared in November of 1915, and other modern versions of ancient Japanese tales followed. Akutagawa was graduated in 1916 and briefly held a teaching job, but he soon quit to devote his full time to writing the short stories which already had given him fame.

Akutagawa married Tsukamoto Fumiko in 1918, and in the next few years, well established as a writer, he wrote some of his best stories. These stories were based on old tales from Chinese, Japanese, and Western literature. In 1922, however, he left this genre behind him. It may be that his literary transition and the psychological problems he had were related to his seeming loss of imagination in the early 1920's.

By 1923, Akutagawa's health was deteriorating, and he complained of nervous exhaustion, cramps, and other ailments. Despite his earlier criticisms of the self-confessional I-novel, after 1924 his writing underwent a profound change as he stopped writing imaginative period pieces and turned to contemporary subjects and his own life, especially his childhood. Possibly, he was too ill to muster the creative energy to continue his storytelling. Critics and even some friends had long urged him to reveal himself in his writing, but perhaps he feared facing the insanity that had separated him from his mother when he was a young boy.

From 1923 until his suicide in 1927, Akutagawa turned to contemporary themes that reflected his deteriorating health and increasing depression. In February, 1927, he began a famous literary dispute with Jun'ichirō Tanizaki that lasted until his death in July that year. This "plot controversy" started in a literary magazine where Akutagawa questioned the artistic value of a plot in novels. Tanizaki had denounced unstructured confessional writing in which the author describes his state of mind, ironically a position with which Akutagawa would have agreed in his early career. Month by month in the spring of 1927, they debated structure versus a quality Akutagawa called "purity," but in truth there was little lucidity in the debate, although it aroused great interest in literary circles. The debate ended with Akutagawa's death, which helped make it a turning point in Japanese fiction as writers sought new forms of expression.

With his own artistic shift in 1924, Akutagawa sensed more keenly than most writers the end of his era. He left the brilliant storytelling and plot structure behind in the last three years as he turned to gloomy autobiography that traced his descent into despair and self-destruction. He had become the tormented artist in "Jigokuhen" ("Hell Screen"), one of his most poignant works. Physically and mentally broken, he committed suicide by poisoning in 1927, leaving behind a long, depressing suicide note that has become a classic in itself.

ANALYSIS

Ryūnosuke Akutagawa has come to typify the Taishō era (1912-1926) in Japanese literature, because of his challenge to the confessional and revealing I-novels that prevailed before World War I and the fact that his suicide seemed to end the era, paving the way for prewar proletarian literature. Akutagawa, perhaps influenced by his wide reading of Western authors such as Edgar Allan Poe, used the short-story genre from the start. I-novelists also wrote short stories, and in fact the Japanese term *shōsetsu* is used for both the novel and the short story, but Akutagawa rejected self-disclosure and stressed the narrative element. He saw the writer as a storyteller, and his own stories are twice removed from reality, for they are eclectic, based on other stories in classical Japanese and Chinese literature and stories by Western authors. Frequently, many elements from other works are carefully brought together in new combinations to create a self-contained structure, as Akutagawa let the story define reality in his work. Using old tales allowed him to define reality in symbolic terms and to apply the insights of modern psychology without dealing with the issue of the self.

Mining older literature was a tradition in Japanese literature, a tradition that had disappeared in the confessional novels that dominated early twentieth century Japanese literature. Akutagawa's concise polished style emerged precociously in the stories he published while a student of English literature at Tokyo Imperial University.

"RASHŌMON"

One of them, "Rashōmon," appeared in November, 1915, in a university literary magazine, *Teikoku Bungaku* (imperial literature). Akutagawa borrowed from a twelfth century tale and other sources, setting the story in Kyoto during a period of social and economic chaos. The story begins at a dilapidated gate (the Rashōmon of the title) during a rainstorm. A man seeking shelter from the storm encounters an old woman who is plucking the hair from corpses to use as wigs which she will sell. He, too, descends into depravity as he steals her clothes to sell. Akutagawa mined literature for details which evoke the decadent spirit of the age, adding psychological elements to give the story a modern relevance. In this syncretism, he did not seek to re-create the past but to use it to symbolize a modern theme of social breakdown and the disappearance of universal values.

"THE NOSE"

Although many of his early stories contain sickening details, not all are morbid. His first popular success, "Hana" ("The Nose"), is a story about a Buddhist priest who has an enormous drooping nose which people pity. Embarrassed, he discovers a difficult treatment that shortens it, only to find that those who had previously taken pity on his plight now openly ridicule him for his vanity.

When the nose swells again to its former size one night, the priest is pleased that no one will laugh at him again. This grotesque but humorous story caught the attention of Sōseki, who praised it for its unusual subject and clear style. "The Nose" was reprinted in *Shinshōsetsu* (new fiction), a major literary review, and Akutagawa became a recognized new writer.

"THE SPIDER'S THREAD"

Akutagawa enhanced his reputation with nearly one hundred stories between 1916 and 1924. One of his most famous, "Kumo no ito" ("The Spider's Thread"), explores the theme of self-interest. A robber, Kandata, has been sent to hell for his crimes. Yet the all-compassionate Buddha can save even criminals. Because Kandata had once spared a spider, it spins a thread that drops into hell. Kandata begins to climb up on it, but looking below, he sees other sinners following him. Selfishly, he yells at them to let go lest the thread break. This self-centered thought indeed does break the thread, and he falls back into hell with the others, a victim of selfishness. In this story, as in many others, Akutagawa used a variety of sources, causing some critics to doubt his creativity.

"HELL SCREEN"

Such criticism is unfair, because Akutagawa, while eclectic in his sources of inspiration, recasts tales into a new, more evocative form. An excellent example of his inspired adaptations is "Hell Screen." This powerful story is about an artist, Yoshihide, who puts his art before his family, striving for an inhuman perfection. In the story, Yoshihide is commissioned by his lord to paint a series of screens depicting hell. A slave to accuracy, Yoshihide has his models tortured in varied ways to depict their agony. The last scene requires the burning of a court lady inside a carriage. The lord agrees to stage the hideous scene, but he places Yoshihide's only daughter inside because she has spurned his advances. Horrified, Yoshihide nevertheless finishes the screen. He hangs himself, however, in remorse. The screen is recognized as a masterpiece, as was Akutagawa's moral tale.

"IN A GROVE"

Another well-known story from this period is "Yabu no naka" ("In a Grove"), which was made into a famous film by Akira Kurosawa in 1950, using the title "Rashōmon" from the earlier story and blending the two tales. Again using an old story, he gives conflicting versions of a rape-murder, leaving the reader to guess which is true. The story illustrates the difficulty of finding absolute truth, as each individual describes the incident from a different self-serving perspective. A samurai and his wife encounter a bandit in the forest who, according to the dead samurai speaking through a medium, ties him up and forces him to witness the rape of his wife, who appears to be a willing victim, urging the bandit to kill her weak husband. According to the samurai, the bandit is shocked at the woman's intensity, and he runs off. Humiliated, the samurai uses his wife's dagger to kill himself. Both the bandit and the wife then give their testimony, which glorifies their own actions and contradicts the original version. All the versions of the incident are left unresolved.

In 1924, Akutagawa made a major shift in his writing that signaled a new literary viewpoint. It also coincided with a personal crisis as he fell in love with a poet and began to experience long episodes of depression, trying to reconcile his family commitment with artistic creativity. In 1926, he published a volume of poetry that, for the first time, dealt directly with his own feelings. It marked his turn from stories to the realistic and biographical fiction that characterizes the last years of his life. His literary conversion and death were interpreted as the end of an era and a reflection of the modern debate about plot and expression and the relationship of the narrator to the novel.

Akutagawa's most important fictional work in his last year was *Kappa*, a satire about elves who appear in Japanese folklore, although the long story is similar to Anatole France's novel *L'Île des pingouins*. The grotesque kappa—part human, bird, and reptile—seem to reverse the human order of things, but they also have human problems, such as war and unemployment. Some of these problems have bizarre solutions; for example, the unemployed are eaten. Akutagawa's other stories describe mental breakdown and physical decline, reflecting his deepening gloom.

One of the best of Akutagawa's autobiographical works, "Haguruma," was published posthumously. He wrote of his mental tension and schizophrenic fears of imaginary cogwheels that blocked his vision. In his story, it is difficult to tell reality from hallucination, a reflection of his mental state. It ends with the demented plea, "Will no one have the goodness to strangle me in my sleep?" Another posthumous story written in his final days describes corpses, ennui, and death.

Akutagawa's suicide note itself is well known in Japan. Entitled "Aru kyuyu e okuru shuki" ("Memories Sent to an Old Friend"), it was addressed to Kume Masao. Akutagawa described his reasons for suicide, revealing that for two years he had constantly thought of killing himself, debating the way to carry it out with least trouble to his family. He ruled out a gun since it would leave an untidy mess, and he did not have the courage for the sword. In the end, he took an overdose of sleeping medicine and ended his tormented life on July 27, 1927. His death shocked

the literary world but was no surprise to those knew him well, for he had often talked of suicide.

Akutagawa was the first modern Japanese writer to attract wide attention abroad, and his personal literary conversion and dispute with Tanizaki reflect the modern debate over the direction of the novel. Akutagawa, the consummate storyteller, sensed the weakness of his own writing in his last years, and his dramatic death drew attention to the literary controversy he had begun with Tanizaki. His death signified the end of a period of Japanese literature when writers thought they could balance and reconcile life and art through aesthetic control. Because he was so famous and talented, most of his fellow writers were stunned by his death, and many were forced to reexamine their assumptions about literature. His last works are tragic, and the brutal honesty of his charting of his own demise has gained for him fame in modern Japanese literature. This fame is institutionalized in the Akutagawa Prize, the most sought-after source of recognition for young writers in Japan.

OTHER MAJOR WORK

MISCELLANEOUS: *Akutagawa Ryūnosuke zenshū*, 1967-1969 (11 volumes).

BIBLIOGRAPHY

Gerow, A. A. "The Self Seen as Other: Akutagawa and Film." *Literature/Film Quarterly* 23 (1995): 197-203. Discusses the influence of film on Akutagawa's fiction. Argues that cinema affects the central conflict between East and West and traditional and modern in his work and that Akutagawa's use of film suggests the loss of traditional Japanese culture and an effort to create a new national identity.

Hibbett, Howard. "Akutagawa Ryūnosuke and the Negative Ideal." In *Personality in Japanese History*, edited by Albert M. Craig and Donald H. Shively. Berkeley: University of California Press, 1970. In his essay, Hibbett notes the general conclusion that Akutagawa's suicide is generally interpreted as that of a martyr to the times, and thus symbolic. As the writer's development and various works are discussed, their relationship to his mental condition at various periods is well analyzed. Includes a table of contents and an index.

Hiraoka, Toshio. *Remarks on Akutagawa's Works: With American Students' Opinions*. Tokyo: Seirosha, 1990. Analyses of Akutagawa's works. Includes English translations of some of the fiction.

Keene, Donald. "Akutagawa Ryūnosuke." In *Dawn to the West: Japanese Literature of the Modern Era*. Vol. 1. New York: Holt, Rinehart and Winston, 1984. Keene's comprehensive volume devotes a chapter to Akutagawa and mentions him in other relevant chapters. He provides an overview of many major stories as well as historical, cultural, and literary context. Table of contents, preface, introduction, appendix, glossary, and index.

Lippit, Seiji M. "The Disintegrating Machinery of the Modern: Akutagawa Ryūnosuke's Late Writings." *The Journal of Asian Studies* 58 (February, 1999): 27-50. Discusses Akutagawa's relationship to Japanese modernist concepts. Challenges the critical assumption that he represents aestheticized literary practices and clarifies his advocacy of "pure" literature. Focuses on issues of representation and cultural identity of his late writings.

Ueda, Makoto. "Akutagawa Ryūnosuke." In *Modern Japanese Writers and the Nature of Literature*. Stanford, Calif.: Stanford University Press, 1976. Chapter 5 treats Akutagawa's development as a writer, relates his philosophy of literature to several of his works, and comments on the relationship of Akutagawa's work to his suicide. Notes, a select bibliography, and an index are included.

Yamanouchi, Hisaaki. "The Rivals: Shiga Naoya and Akutagawa Ryūnosuke." In *The Search for Authenticity in Modern Japanese Literature*. New York: Cambridge University Press, 1978. A study of twelve Japanese writers. Includes a chapter on Shiga Naoya and Akutagawa Ryūnosuke, who the author feels can be logically and beneficially compared. Contains a table of contents, a preface, an introduction, notes, and a select bibliography.

Yu, Beongcheon. *Akutagawa: An Introduction*. Detroit: Wayne State University Press, 1972. This fairly slim volume follows the life and the literary development of Akutagawa. In addition to a preface, notes, a list of the works translated into English, and an index, Yu provides a helpful chronology.

Richard Rice, updated by Victoria Price

PEDRO ANTONIO DE ALARCÓN

Born: Guadix, Spain; March 10, 1833
Died: Madrid, Spain; July 20, 1891

PRINCIPAL SHORT FICTION
Historietas nacionales, Cuentos amatorios, and
  Narraciones inverosímiles, 1881-1882 (a three
  volume collection)
Moors, Christians, and Other Tales, 1891
Tales from the Spanish, 1948

OTHER LITERARY FORMS

Having served his apprenticeship in journalism, Pedro Antonio de Alarcón did all the kinds of writing that were normal in that *métier*: sketches of daily life (*cuadros de costumbres*), book reviews, theater criticism, political reporting, and even editorial writing, for he served as editor of several journals in his younger years. His ambition, however, was to be a literary man, and the short stories he published in various journals were the part of his youthful journalistic activity that he took most seriously. They are also the work which first earned him a reputation as a writer. Trading on that reputation, he published his first novel at the age of twenty-two and attracted still more attention with a controversial play when he was only twenty-four. He served as a war correspondent during the fighting in North Africa between Morocco and Spain in 1859-1860, and he published his war articles as a book in 1861. In the edition he prepared of his complete works, Alarcón included a volume of literary criticism, a volume of travel pieces, a volume of *cuadros de costumbres*, and a volume of occasional short poems, all culled from his years as a journalist. His true claim to literary importance, however, resided in his six novels and his more than three dozen short stories.

Pedro Antonio de Alarcón (Library of Congress)

ACHIEVEMENTS

Although Pedro Antonio de Alarcón was not one of the outstanding writers of nineteenth century Spain, he made important contributions to the development of Spain's short story. In Alarcón's time, short fiction was limited to *cuadros de costumbres*, short sketches of popular customs, and the legend or fantastic tale. Alarcón introduced to Spain the techniques of the French short-story writers he admired, such as those of Honoré de Balzac and Théophile Gautier.

Although most of Alarcón's stories are not the products of his imagination, he excelled as a story-

teller. He is known principally as the author of *El sombrero de tres picos* (1874; *The Three-Cornered Hat*, 1886), based on a popular Spanish folktale. His *Historietas nacionales*, which narrate episodes of Spanish history, brought historical fiction into vogue, thus preparing for the *Episodios nacionales* (1873-1912; national episodes) of Benito Pérez Galdós. Alarcón's achievement lies in having captured the spirit of Spain's traditions and its people in his stories.

BIOGRAPHY

Pedro Antonio de Alarcón was the fourth of ten children born to a once-prosperous family come upon hard times. Neither his family's circumstances nor the impoverished environment of Guadix, in southern Spain, served his educational needs well. He had to get his high school diploma in Granada, and once he settled, in his late teens, on a vocation as a man of letters, he knew he would have to leave Guadix in order to establish a career. By the age of twenty-two, he had managed to place himself in Madrid, the active center of Spain's literary life, having previously had some experience as editor of provincial periodicals, having published a first novel, and having contributed stories and sketches to several of the best-known literary journals in the capital. Thus, success came very quickly for this precocious youngster, and between 1855 and 1860 (when he left Madrid to report on the war in North Africa), he made his name prominent by a flood of articles, poems, stories, and sketches, out of which he culled enough material to provide a three-volume book publication called *Cuentos, artículos y novelas* (1859; tales, articles, and novels), a remarkably productive record for a youth of twenty-six.

His work as a war correspondent marked a change of direction for Alarcón which lasted through the decade of the 1860's. He became deeply involved in politics, was elected to the legislature, and gradually shifted his posture from the revolutionary anti-clericalism of his youth to a more moderate outlook, evolving finally to a quite conservative and traditionalist attitude. Meanwhile, he wrote very little and published but one volume, a collection of short stories, throughout the decade of the 1860's. His successful marriage and political defeat combined to reawaken his literary ambitions in the 1870's, during which decade he published three novels, more short stories, and a variety of travel and occasional pieces; won election to the Royal Academy; and attained his greatest eminence as a man of letters. The decade of the 1880's was a period of decline for Alarcón, who preferred to live quietly and privately with his family, publishing little except a collected edition of his works, one more novel, and an account of the origin of his various publications which amounted to an informal literary autobiography. He took no interest whatsoever in politics during that decade and was reported by occasional visitors to his home to be tired, overweight, and ill—in essence, a spent force. Toward the end of the decade, he suffered a series of strokes and died in 1891, at fifty-eight, a prematurely old man, disappointed and depressed.

ANALYSIS

Pedro Antonio de Alarcón developed an impressive variety of narrative techniques over the course of his career by which he could entice his readers into an intriguing story and still reserve for them the kind of surprise he found to be essential to the short-story genre. The most famous story of his younger years, "El Clavo" ("The Nail"), first published in 1853 when he was only twenty, illustrates how early he learned the skills of the artful storyteller. To entice the reader into this rather wildly romantic tale of ungovernable passions, Alarcón used two separate narrative voices, recounting three apparently separate incidents, each involving a different woman of mystery.

The curiosity of readers is promptly piqued. They begin to wonder where lies the connection that unites the three separate incidents. The first incident is the narrator's account of the woman who rejected his love; the second is the account by Zarco, the narrator's friend, of the woman with whom he fell in love and whom he made pregnant, but who failed to appear for their planned wedding; and the third incident is the discovery by the narrator and his friend Zarco, in the town graveyard, of a skull with a nail driven through it, which strongly suggests the murder of a husband by his wife. Since Zarco is a judge, he sets

out to bring the murderess to justice, with the help of his friend Felipe, who is the narrator of the story. Eventually, a tense trial scene reveals that all three women of mystery are one and the same person. Zarco holds true to his judicial calling, suppresses his personal passion, and sees his beloved condemned to death for murder. The final twist to the story comes, however, as she mounts the scaffold to be executed: Zarco, unable to resist his passion for her, has obtained a pardon and comes bearing it to save her at the last moment, where-upon she falls in a faint at his feet and is discovered moments later to be dead. There are several improbabilities and unbelievable coincidences in this intricate plot, but Alarcón manages by his narrative skill to make it an exciting, unpredictable, and spellbinding tale, illustrating the cruel ironies of fate which prevent the consummation of true love.

"THE EMBRACE AT VERGARA"

Similar techniques, which control the narrative point of view and permit the surprise effect at the end, can be seen in other tales of the early period in Alarcón's career. In contrast to the somber drama of "The Nail," for example, one finds a lighthearted comic tale of thwarted love in "El Abrazo de Vergara" ("The Embrace at Vergara"), in which the victim tells his own story in the first person. Thus, the reader can know only what is known by the narrator, who attempts the seduction of a pretty young traveling companion in a stagecoach, thinking she is a foreigner because she says nothing. Just when he thinks he has succeeded, however, the stagecoach stops, the young lady gets out, is greeted by her husband, and says a cheery farewell to her victim in perfect Spanish. As a final ironic twist, the author intervenes at the very end to tease the reader, who must doubtless be disappointed because the title suggests the story is about a political alliance, known popularly as "the embrace at Vergara."

"THE PROPHECY"

In a completely different vein, the story "La Buenaventura" ("The Prophecy") tells of a gypsy who persuades a dangerous outlaw to let him go free by offering to tell his fortune. Although it is a third-person narrative, the perspective through which the reader receives the narrative is constantly that of the gypsy, so that the unexpected fulfillment of the gypsy's prophecy at the end is a surprise not only to the gypsy but also to the reader as well. Among Alarcón's stories, this work has been almost as popular an anthology piece as "The Nail."

"THE NUN"

If the earliest stories bear the imprint of Alarcón's Romantic origins as a writer, his later stories of the 1860's and 1870's clearly demonstrate an altered sensibility. Improbable plots and extravagant diction have vanished, and the focus of interest is more psychological than sentimental, more realistic than fantastic, just as the prose is more concise and restrained. "La Comendadora" ("The Nun"), published in 1868 and probably Alarcón's most admired short story, exemplifies fully Alarcón's manner as a storyteller. The title character is a member of a religious order called *Comendadoras de Santiago* and an attractive woman of thirty whose fate is suggested by the story's subtitle, "The Story of a Woman Who Had No Love Affairs." She had been forced into a religious order by her iron-willed mother while still a young girl so that the family fortune could be passed on intact to her brother. The brother died young, however, and the *Comendadora* is now on leave from her convent to help her aged mother care for the brother's spoiled son, who represents the future of the family name and fortune.

Into this emotionally charged atmosphere intrudes the single event which makes up this story: The little boy, having overhead two artists working in the family palace speak of his aunt's admirably statuesque beauty, suddenly demands to see his aunt naked so that he can understand what the artists meant. To enforce his demand he throws a tantrum, screaming and frothing at the mouth until his fearful grandmother, anxious above all for the future of the family name, orders her daughter to comply because, as she explains, it is God's will. Soon thereafter, the grandmother wishes to comfort her daughter but finds that the *Comendadora* has left the palace. A note explains that, for the first and only time in her life, she has acted without her mother's advice and has returned to her convent with the intention of never leaving it

again. A short time later the *Comendadora* dies. Her mother dies soon thereafter, and the young Count dies in battle some years later without having had time to leave an heir.

The most striking feature of this impressive story is that Alarcón tells it in the sparest possible prose, offering no insight into, or comment on, the state of the *Comendadora*'s feeling or thoughts. The reader is left to imagine and interpret her comportment without any help from the author—a restraint of which the youthful Alarcón would have been incapable. The story nevertheless has the standard pattern of the unexpected event and the ironic vision of life to be found in all Alarcón's short fiction. In this instance, a profound psychological illumination is what is accomplished by the familiar pattern, which is perhaps why this story is thought to be Alarcón's most modern composition as well as his most finished short story, artistically.

"THE LAST ESCAPADE"

In his mature storytelling, Alarcón continued to cultivate his delightful sense of the comic side by side with his sensitivity for the tragic aspects of human destiny such as he portrayed in "The Nun." Two well-known stories of the 1870's illustrate this approach at its best. "La última calaverada" ("The Last Escapade"), published in 1874, is a *tour de force* of the first-person technique, in which the narrator first states, as a general principle, that every rake who reforms does so as a result of a fiasco or failure, then proceeds to entertain his audience of friends with the story of his own last escapade—the incident which persuaded him to give up his pursuit of other women and remain faithful to his wife. The surprise in the story, carefully prepared, is that the narrator, on his way to his amorous rendezvous, loses his way in the darkness, is thrown from his horse, then allows the horse to have his way, with the result that he ends up unknowingly back at his own villa. His wife's passionate greeting convinces him that it is foolish to imagine one will find a superior pleasure with other women. Thus, his little accident ends his career as a dedicated *calavera*, justifying the ironic subtitle of the story: *novela alegre, pero moral*—"a risqué yet moral narrative."

"THE STUB-BOOK"

Three years later, in 1877, Alarcón published one of his few tales with a rural setting, "El libro talonario" ("The Stub-Book"), which has proved to be one of his most popular and most frequently anthologized compositions. The story concerns an instance of the pride and ingenuity with which the gardeners of the Andalusian village of Rota, near Cádiz, take care of their celebrated tomato and pumpkin crop. The hero of the story plans to take forty of his best pumpkins to market in Cádiz and cuts them from their stalks the night before in preparation but finds in the morning that they have been stolen. He goes to the market in Cádiz and is able to identify his own produce to the satisfaction of the police because he has saved the stem cut from the top of each *calabaza* and can show that each stem fits exactly on the top of one of them. Just as the authenticity of a receipt from the tax collector can be verified because it will fit the one stub in the tax collector's book from which it was torn, so the story's hero has ingeniously devised a "stub-book" of his own for authenticating his produce. The thief is thus caught and the hero congratulated.

Alarcón's short-story output was not prolific, but it has the distinction of inaugurating the genre for Spanish literature. Alarcón seemed to have an instinctive understanding of the genre as soon as he discovered it among the French writers he admired, and he demonstrated his devotion to the form by writing short stories throughout his career rather than merely during his apprentice years as a learning device. It was also by instinct, and not by conscious technique, that his stories all turned out to have the common pattern of a surprise ending and a final ironic perspective. For Alarcón, that pattern constituted the essence of the short story as a genre. The common pattern is hardly obtrusive, even for the reader who has recognized it, for the stories possess a rich variety in every other respect: theme, setting, tone, technique, structure, character types, and plot. Some of the stories are weak or contrived, a few are trivial, but there are at least a dozen of high enough quality to earn Pedro Antonio de Alarcón a significant place in the history of the European short story.

OTHER MAJOR WORKS

LONG FICTION: *El final de Norma*, 1855 (*Brunhilde: Or, The Last Act of Norma*, 1891); *El sombrero de tres picos*, 1874 (*The Three-Cornered Hat*, 1886); *El escándalo*, 1875 (*The Scandal*, 1945); *El niño de la bola*, 1880 (*The Child of the Ball*, 1892; also as *The Infant with the Globe*, 1959); *El Capitán Veneno*, 1882 (*Captain Spitfire*, 1886); *La pródiga*, 1882 (*True to Her Oath*, 1899).

PLAY: *El hijo pródigo*, pb. 1857.

NONFICTION: *Diario de un testigo de la Guerra de Africa*, 1859; *De Madrid a Nápoles pasando por París, Ginebra, etc.*, 1861; *Cosas que fueron*, 1871; *Juicios literarios y artisticos*, 1883; *Historia de mis libros*, 1884.

MISCELLANEOUS: *Cuentos, artículos y novelas*, 1859.

BIBLIOGRAPHY

Atkinson, William C. "Pedro Antonio de Alarcón." *Bulletin of Spanish Studies* 10 (July, 1933): 136-141. Written to commemorate the one hundredth anniversary of Alarcón's birth, Atkinson reviews several novels and concludes that Alarcón's characters are types and that he never ceased to be a Romantic.

Combs, Colleen J. *Women in the Short Stories of Pedro Antonio de Alarcón*. Lewiston, N.Y.: Edwin Mellen Press, 1997. Examines Alarcón's treatment of female characters.

DeCoster, Cyrus. *Pedro Antonio de Alarcón*. Boston: Twayne, 1979. The most complete source of material on Alarcón available in English. It provides a complete survey of Alarcón's short fiction and also covers his novels, poetry, drama, sketches, and essays. Supplemented by an annotated bibliography.

Fernandez, James D. "Fashioning the *Ancien Regime*: Alarcón's *Sombrero de tres picos*." *Hispanic Review* 62 (Spring, 1994): 235-247. Discusses the story's use of folktale, its emphasis on historical time and place, and its use of popular sources. Comments on the ambivalence in the story between Alarcon's nostalgia and his modernity.

Hespelt, E. Herman. "Alarcón as Editor of *El látigo*."

Hispania 20 (1936): 319-336. Focuses on Alarcón's brief career as a radical journalist and quotes extensively from the political and social satire he wrote for this short-lived periodical.

Quinn, David. "An Ironic Reading of Pedro de Alarcón's 'La última calaverada.'" *Symposium* 31 (1977): 346-356. Through a structural analysis of the text, David Quinn refutes the notion that the ending of "The Last Escapade" shows the bene-

volent intervention of divine Providence.

Winslow, Richard W. "The Distinction of Structure in Alarcón's *El sombrero de tres picos* and *El Capitán Veneno*." *Hispania* 46 (1963): 715-721. Argues that *El sombrero de tres picos* should be considered a short story, whereas *El Capitán Veneno* is in every sense a novel.

Murray Sachs,
updated by Evelyn Toft

THOMAS BAILEY ALDRICH

Born: Portsmouth, New Hampshire; November 11, 1836

Died: Boston, Massachusetts; March 19, 1907

PRINCIPAL SHORT FICTION

Out of His Head: A Romance, 1862
Marjorie Daw and Other People, 1873
Two Bites at a Cherry, with Other Tales, 1893
A Sea Turn and Other Matters, 1902

OTHER LITERARY FORMS

In addition to short stories, Thomas Bailey Aldrich wrote poems, essays, and novels. His best-known novel is *The Story of a Bad Boy* (1869). He was one of the most prominent men of letters in America in the 1880's, serving as editor of the prestigious *Atlantic Monthly* from 1881 to 1890.

ACHIEVEMENTS

A great popular success during his lifetime, with his collected poems being published in a highly respected series while he was still in his late twenties, Thomas Bailey Aldrich was one of the most influential editors and men of letters of late nineteenth century America. His short story "Marjorie Daw" was one of the most famous stories of his era, earning him an international reputation.

BIOGRAPHY

Born in Portsmouth, New Hampshire, on November 11, 1836, Thomas Bailey Aldrich spent his early years in New York City and New Orleans. Although he returned to Portsmouth in 1849 to prepare for Harvard University, the death of his father made it necessary for him to go to work as a clerk for his uncle in New York instead. During this period, he wrote poetry, became a member of a group of writers that included Walt Whitman, and took a job as a reporter for the *Home Journal*. The popularity of his sentimental verse, "The Ballad of Babie Bell" (1854), encouraged him to quit his clerkship and to devote himself to writing full time.

Aldrich got a job as a literary critic for *The Evening Mirror* in 1855, after which he was soon made an editor. For the next ten years he lived in New York as part of a Bohemian literary circle that centered on the aestheticism of Fitz-James O'Brien. He was invited to Boston after the publication of his popular collection *Marjorie Daw and Other People* in 1873 to assume the editorship of *Every Saturday*, which reprinted European fiction and poetry for American audiences.

Aldrich published a number of stories and poems in *The Atlantic Monthly*, including his widely popular story "Marjorie Daw," and eventually succeeded William Dean Howells as its editor in 1881, a position he held until 1890. In the last years of his life, he traveled and wrote travel literature, sketches, poems, and short prose. He died in Boston on March 19, 1907.

ANALYSIS

Thomas Bailey Aldrich is primarily remembered in literary histories because of the effect of one story; however, that one story, "Marjorie Daw," like those of

Thomas Bailey Aldrich (Library of Congress)

other "one-story" writers—such as Frank Stockton, who wrote "The Lady or the Tiger," and Shirley Jackson, who wrote "The Lottery"—brilliantly manages to exploit a basic human fascination with the blurring of fiction and reality. Often called a masterpiece of its type, "Marjorie Daw" clearly epitomizes the kind of story that O. Henry popularized more than half a century later—a story that seduces the reader into believing that a purely fictional creation is actually reality, only to reveal the ruse in a striking surprise reversal at the end.

Aldrich's remaining stories, like much of his *vers de société*, are lightweight and romantic. Generally,

they are witty and amusing sketches and tales that do not pretend to have any submerged meaning or symbolic significance. They are so unremarkable, in fact, that Aldrich's restrained and self-consciously literary creation of "Marjorie Daw" seems like a fortunate inspirational accident. It is so well crafted, so controlled, and so aware of itself as a self-reflexive play with the basic nature of fiction that it will always remain a favorite anthology piece to represent the surprise-ending story so widely popular during the last half of the nineteenth century.

"MARJORIE DAW"

This story achieved its initial popularity and has remained a representative of the well-made, surprise-ending story because Aldrich so masterfully manipulates reader fascination with imaginative creation taken as reality. Aldrich achieves this deception, which lies at the heart of all fictional creation, by setting up a situation in which the fictional "reader," Flemming, cannot test the reality of the story his friend Delaney sends him via letters because of a broken leg.

Throughout the story, Aldrich makes use of various conventions of fiction-making beginning with Delaney's first letter apologizing that there is nothing to write about since he is living out in the country with no one around. Claiming he wishes he were a novelist so he could write Flemming a "summer romance," Delaney then begins composing by asking Flemming to "imagine" the reality he recounts. After beginning a description of the house across the road from him, Delaney shifts to present tense, as if describing something he sees in reality: "A young woman appears on the piazza with some mysterious Penelope web of embroidery in her hand, or a book." Although the description begins generally, it is enough to catch Flemming, who writes back wanting to know more about the girl, telling Delaney he has "a graphic descriptive touch."

Delaney begins then to create a family for the girl and a name—Marjorie Daw. Although he provides various clues that what he is describing does not exist in the real world, such as noting that it was like "seeing a picture" to see Marjorie hovering around her invented father, Flemming is already convinced. Echoing the experience of many readers who encounter the objectification of a fantasy, Flemming writes back to Delaney, "You seem to be describing a woman I have known in some previous state of existence, or dreamed of in this," claiming that if he saw a photo of her he would recognize her at once. When Delaney writes that, if he himself were on a desert island with Marjorie, he would be like a brother to her, he once again provides a clue to the imaginative nature of the story by saying, "Let me suggest a tropical island, for it costs no more to be picturesque."

Throughout the story Delaney is baffled and fascinated by the strange obsessive effect his account is having on his friend, asking, "Do you mean to say that you are seriously half in love with a woman whom you have never seen—with a shadow, a chimera? for what else can Miss Daw be to you? I do not understand it at all." Later Delaney makes another oblique reference to fiction-making by noting that he accepts things "as people do in dreams." When Flemming insists on writing to Marjorie, Delaney reverses the fictional process by reminding him that because she knows Flemming only through him he is an abstraction to her, a figure in a dream—a dream from which the faintest shock would awaken her. When Flemming threatens to come to see Marjorie, Delaney's letters become increasingly urgent, urging Flemming to stay where he is, for his presence would only "complicate matters."

In the only bit of straight narrative in the story, Flemming arrives to find Delaney gone to Boston and no Marjorie Daw to be found. In the final letter, Delaney, filled with horror at what he has done, says he just wanted to make a little romance to interest Flemming and is regretful that he did it all too well. The story ends with these famous lines: "There isn't any colonial mansion on the other side of the road, there isn't any piazza, there isn't any hammock—there isn't any Marjorie Daw!"

The story is a classic one about the power of fiction to create a convincing sense of reality. Emulating the method of composition described by Edgar Allan Poe, Aldrich once said that he wrote the last paragraph of the story first and then worked up to it, avoiding digressions and side issues. Indeed, "Marjorie Daw" is solely dependent on its final, single effect: surprising and delighting the reader who has been taken in as completely as Flemming has.

"A STRUGGLE FOR LIFE"

This is the only other Aldrich story that has received continued reading and commentary. It depends on a surprise ending, the manipulation of time, and gothic conventions more successfully exploited later by Ambrose Bierce; it also capitalizes on the power of fiction-making, although not in as complex a way as "Marjorie Daw." The frame of this story-within-a-story focuses on an external narrator who, passing a man on the street whose body looks thirty while his face looks sixty, says, half-aloud, "That man has a story, and I should like to know it." When a voice at his side says he knows the man's story, the inner story begins.

The story-within-the-story is about an American in Paris, Philip Wentworth, in love with a young French woman, who is found dead in her bed chamber. During her burial in the family vault, Wentworth faints and is locked in the tomb. The remainder of the story focuses on his efforts to remain alive by dividing his single candle into bite-sized pieces which he portions out to himself to eat until he can be rescued. The minutes pass like hours in the total darkness of the tomb, until two days later when Wentworth is down to his last piece of candle. The door of the tomb is flung open and he is led out, his hair gray and his eyes dimmed like an old man's. The storyteller concludes by revealing that Wentworth had been in the tomb for only an hour and twenty minutes.

However, this is not Aldrich's final surprise. The story so haunts the listener that a few days later, he approaches the old-faced man he thinks is Philip Wentworth. When the man says his name is Jones, the narrator realizes he has been duped by the teller, a gentleman of "literary proclivities" who is trying to write the Great American Novel.

OTHER MAJOR WORKS

LONG FICTION: *The Story of a Bad Boy*, 1869; *Prudence Palfrey*, 1874; *The Queen of Sheba*, 1877; *The Stillwater Tragedy*, 1880.

POETRY: *The Bells: A Collection of Chimes*, 1855; *The Ballad of Babie Bell, and Other Poems*, 1859;

Cloth of Gold and Other Poems, 1874; *Flower and Thorn: Later Poems*, 1877; *Mercedes, and Later Lyrics*, 1884; *Wyndham Towers*, 1890; *Unguarded Gates, and Other Poems*, 1895; *Judith and Holofernes*, 1896; *The Poems of Thomas Bailey Aldrich*, 1897.

NONFICTION: *From Ponkapog to Pesth*, 1883; *An Old Town by the Sea*, 1893; *Pondapog Papers*, 1903.

BIBLIOGRAPHY

Bellman, Samuel I. "Riding on Wishes: Ritual Make-Believe Patterns in Three Nineteenth-Century American Authors: Aldrich, Hale, Bunner." In *Ritual in the United States: Acts and Representations*. Tampa, Fla.: American Studies Press, 1985. Discusses Aldrich's creation of an imaginary individual in three stories, "A Struggle for Life," "Marjorie Daw," and "Miss Mehetabel's Son." Argues that "things are not what they seem" is the principle of these three stories, which are presented ritualistically in the form of a hoax or tall tale intended to trap the unwary.

Canby, Henry Seidel. *The Short Story in English*. New York: Henry Holt and Company, 1909. Canby discusses Aldrich, Frank R. Stockton, and H. C. Brunner as the masters of the type of short story of the "absurd situation" and incongruity. Calls Aldrich a stylist who infused his personality into tales of trivia and made them delightful. Says that in "Marjorie Daw" he was the first American to duplicate the French *conte* of Guy de Maupassant.

Cowie, Alexander. *The Rise of the American Novel*. New York: American Book Company, 1951. Although Cowie discusses Aldrich's novels, his comments on narrative style apply equally well to his short stories. Calls Aldrich a vital writer whose contribution to American literature can be measured in terms of authenticity.

Greenslet, Ferris. *Thomas Bailey Aldrich*. Boston: Houghton Mifflin, 1908. This is the official Aldrich biography; it contains numerous letters not available anywhere else. Describes his friendship with William Dean Howells, his influence on American literary life in the last half of the nineteenth century, and his editorship of *The Atlantic Monthly*; makes passing remarks about his short stories throughout, noting how "Marjorie Daw" was the basis of Aldrich's international reputation as a humorist.

O'Brien, Edward J. *The Advance of the American Short Story*. New York: Dodd, Mead, 1931. The originator of *The Best American Short Stories* series discusses Aldrich's responsibility for the vogue of the surprise ending story in the early twentieth century. Says that although "Marjorie Daw" is flawless, many of Aldrich's stories are "pure sleight of hand." Discusses his relationship to Frank Stockton and Henry Cuyler Bunner and how all three learned their tricks from Maupassant, Alphonse Daudet, and Prosper Mérimée.

Pattee, Fred Lewis. *The Development of the American Short Story: An Historical Survey*. New York: Harper and Brothers, 1923. In this important early history of the American short story, Pattee summarizes Aldrich's career and discusses the importance of "Marjorie Daw" in establishing an influential short-story type. Says that the story stood for art that is artless, that it has a Daudet-like grace and brilliance with the air of careless improvisation.

Samuels, Charles E. *Thomas Bailey Aldrich*. New York: Twayne, 1965. A general introduction to Aldrich's life and art; includes a chapter on his short stories and sketches; describes "Marjorie Daw" as a masterpiece of compression that won an instant international reputation for Aldrich; discusses Aldrich's stories of the fanciful gothic and his taste for the macabre.

Charles E. May

SHOLOM ALEICHEM

Sholom Rabinowitz

Born: Pereyaslav, Russia; March 2, 1859
Died: New York, New York; May 13, 1916

PRINCIPAL SHORT FICTION

Tevye der Milkhiger, 1894-1914 (*Tevye's Daughters*, 1949; also translated as *Tevye the Dairy Man*, 1987)

Menakhem-Mendl, 1895 (*The Adventures of Menachem-Mendl*, 1969)

Mottel, Peyse dem Khazns, 1907-1916 (*The Adventures of Mottel, the Cantor's Son*, 1953)

Jewish Children, 1920

The Old Country, 1946

Inside Kasrilevke, 1948

Selected Stories of Sholom Aleichem, 1956

Stories and Satires, 1959

Old Country Tales, 1966

Some Laughter, Some Tears, 1968

The Best of Sholom Aleichem, 1979

Holiday Tales of Sholom Aleichem, 1979

Tevye the Dairyman and the Railroad Stories, 1987

OTHER LITERARY FORMS

Sholom Aleichem was a prolific writer throughout a career that spanned thirty-six years. His total output comprises more than forty volumes, but much is unavailable in English and would be of little pertinence to most modern readers. Early writings from his rabbinical period, including Hebrew essays on Jewish education, are curiosities but lack originality. His social criticism, never cruel and always mitigated by humor, remains valuable to understanding the now-vanished milieu in which he lived and worked. Journalistic essays, satires, autobiographical sketches, and rhapsodic meditations on biblical and folk themes are often indistinguishable from his short stories and therefore difficult to classify. Though he was less impressive in long narratives and dramas, he did produce several novels still interesting to read. His plays were never total popular and critical successes, but several remain significant for their exploration of themes especially important to Jewish life.

ACHIEVEMENTS

Sadly, Sholom Aleichem's chief legacy is his richly detailed delineation of the world destroyed by Nazi genocide and the Soviet repression of all religious cultures. Read by thousands of Jews dispersed throughout the world, Aleichem evokes nostalgically the society that Jewish ancestors knew; the thick tapestry of Jewish life in czarist Russia—messianic claimants, holy fools, idealistic youth, merchants, scholars, revolutionaries—is resurrected in his sketches. His major achievement may have been his decisive establishment of Yiddish, however briefly, as a worthy vehicle for literary expression. He has been credited with the virtual creation of modern Yiddish literature. Before him and his writing contemporaries, Yiddish was "the tongue without tradition." Only sentimental romances were written in "the jargon," along with simplistic books of scriptural explication and devotional verses for women, who, unlike men, did not read Hebrew.

Aleichem became a godfather to subsequent Yiddish writers. Isaac Bashevis Singer was perhaps the last of international significance. Yet an entire generation of Jewish fiction writers, whose language is English, must also trace its lineage to Aleichem. In the early 1990's in the Ukrainian Republic, the Society of Jewish Culture began moving ahead with plans to establish a museum in the house where Aleichem lived. A special library of mementos and writings, all in Hebrew translation, is maintained in Tel Aviv, Israel. The American stage and screen have far extended the gentile audience of this most characteristic of Yiddish masters. *The World of Sholom Aleichem*, an off-Broadway production written by Arnold Perl and inspired by the writings of Aleichem and Issac Leib Peretz, debuted in 1953, while *Fiddler on the Roof*, a musical based on his stories, had a long run on Broadway and in motion picture theaters throughout Europe and the United States. Music for the Broadway production, which debuted in 1964, was written by Jerry Bock with lyrics by Sheldon Harnick; the film, produced in 1971, was directed by Norman Jewison.

BIOGRAPHY

Much of Sholom Aleichem's life is detailed in his writings, only thinly fictionalized. Born Sholom Rabinowitz, in the Ukrainian town of Pereyaslav, he was the son of a merchant of some education and means. He lost his mother the year of his Bar Mitzvah, only to have her quickly replaced by an unfavored stepmother whose sole contribution to his well-being was a vivid vocabulary of Yiddishisms he would use profitably in his writing. Reversals in family fortune sent the young man in search of employment, as a "crown rabbi" (half religious functionary and half Russian bureaucrat) and as a tutor. By marrying Olga Loyev, his pupil, he acquired a loving life companion, a substantial dowry, and inspiration for lyrical narratives. Moving to Kiev, Aleichem wrote novels and short stories and, through the annuals that he published and the banquets that he hosted, became a patron of Yiddish writers. Financial problems again dislocated him, however, this time to Odessa, another flourishing center of Jewish life. It was finally the social turmoil following the assassination of Czar Alexander II that drove him abroad, to Geneva and New York.

Despite the fame that preceded him to the New World, Aleichem had difficulty supporting his increasingly large family from the proceeds of his writings and theatrical ventures. Through public readings in Western Europe and even Russia, he was still able to earn a living. Remaining a part of the intellectual life of his homeland, he made friends with leading Zionists, corresponded with Leo Tolstoy and Anton Chekhov, and met Maxim Gorky. During his last years, though beset by bereavement and tuberculosis, Aleichem was a revered international man of letters. His funeral in New York, attended by thousands of mourners, became the occasion for an affirmation of the Yiddish culture he had done so much to dignify.

Sholem Aleichem (Library of Congress)

ANALYSIS

It is nearly impossible to summarize the plot of a Sholom Aleichem story. There is no linear, causally enchained sequence in his fiction. The type of plot to which readers have become accustomed in Western fiction—that which moves through clearly defined stages to a predetermined end—is not readily found in Aleichem's work. The reason for this lies in the milieu which is embodied there. Logic and the laws of cause and effect require a stable, orderly world to function. The world of the Russian pale at the close of the nineteenth century was a turbulent chaos of pogroms, revolution, wars, cholera epidemics, starvation, overcrowding, and perpetual hunger.

Except for the few years when he was able to be a patron of letters and to pay his fellow Yiddish writers well for their contributions to his annual, in which he attempted to establish a canon, Aleichem himself was continually in debt. His prodigious output was due to his need to provide for his many dependents. These pressures, the outward instability, and the haste in which he was forced to compose contributed to the absurdist, surrealistic situations he depicted. His plots, rather than moving from explication to complication to resolution, begin in complication and accumulate further complications with ever-increasing momentum to the pitch of madness and then abruptly stop without having been resolved; the story is simply interrupted. One can say that a typical Aleichem plot is a succession of calamities and misfortune, followed by disaster, followed by tragedy.

Aleichem's reputation is nevertheless that of one of the world's greatest humorists. In England, he was compared to Charles Dickens; in America, to Mark Twain. How could he fashion comedy from such dark materials? The answer lies in the authorial stratagems he evolved. He invented a persona, Sholom Aleichem, who is present not as a speaker but only as a listener, to whom others tell their stories. Thus, the act of speech itself is foregrounded, not the events that are related. The linguistic surface predominates. Its exuberance and charm, its wit, its pleasure in homely proverbs and folk wisdom, and its eccentric digressions shield the pain and provide a compensatory pleasure.

TEVYE STORIES

This quality is exemplified in the nine Tevye stories. The first published in 1894 and the last in 1914, they appeared separately over the period of twenty years. They have, however, enough structural similarity to be read as a family chronicle. What gives them their coherence is the voice of Tevye. Each episode begins with Tevye meeting Sholom Aleichem somewhere. After greeting him, he recapitulates what has happened to him since their last encounter and then relates his most recent catastrophe. Each story closes with farewells and the promise of more stories to come at future meetings.

The events related are a series of disasters: loss, early death, revolution, apostasy, suicide, pogroms, and exile. These are so successfully distanced by the mode of narration that they are perceived as comedy. It is Tevye's humane, sardonic voice we hear, quarreling with God about how He runs the universe, using His Own Word against Him with such vigorous audacity and such mangling of the texts that one cannot

help laughing. The monologue form focuses our attention on Tevye's moral resiliency and on his defiant debate with an invisible antagonist. It subordinates the tragic fates of the seven dowryless daughters by keeping these at the periphery. In the foreground is the poor milkman who is their father, with his rickety wagon drawn by a starving horse, punctuating his speech with lines from the prayer book. For example, when he wishes to indicate that no more need be said on any subject, he announces: "Here ends the service for the first Sabbath before Passover." It is his way of saying, "period." He tells how Tzeitl has refused a match with the rich butcher, not because he is widowed and has several children her own age, but because she is already engaged, secretly, to a poor tailor. So she marries Motel and is left with orphans when he dies of tuberculosis. The next daughter, Hodel, marries a revolutionary who is arrested soon after the wedding; Hodel follows him into exile. The third daughter, Chava, is converted by a priest in order to marry a Gentile. According to religious law, Tevye must declare her dead, so he tells his wife Golde that they must "sit shiva" for her (observe the customary period of mourning for the deceased).

The next time they meet, Tevye tells Sholom Aleichem that the reason his hair has turned white is because of what has happened to Schprintze. He says, "God wanted to favor his chosen people, so a fresh calamity descended upon us." The irony of having been especially elected to endure the privilege of suffering permeates these stories.

One of Tevye's customers, a widow summering in Boiberik, asks his advice about her spendthrift son. Having inherited a million rubles he has lived in idleness. Tevye complies: "I sat down with him, told him stories, cited examples, plied him with quotations and drummed proverbs into his ears." Here in this self-description is the essence of Tevye's mode of speech.

Aarontchick, the son, is invited for blintzes on Shavuos. When Tevye wants Golde to bring in another platter-full, he says it, as he does everything, in liturgical metaphors. "What are you standing there for, Golde? Repeat the same verse over again. Today is Shavuos and we have to say the same prayer twice."

Schprintze and the handsome idler fall in love. Tevye, always ready with a quotation, sums it up from the Psalms. "Don't we say in the Psalms: 'Put your trust in God?'—Have faith in Him and He will see to it that you stagger under a load of trouble and keep on reciting: 'This too is for the best.'"

Tevye is summoned to the widow's. He thinks that it is to arrange the details of the wedding. He is asked "How much will this affair cost us?" He answers that it depends on what sort of a ceremony they have in mind. It turns out that they want to buy him off and end the engagement.

Mother and son leave without saying good-bye and still owing for their milk and cheese. Schprintze wastes away from sorrow. One night as Tevye is driving home, "sunk in meditation, asking questions of the Almighty and answering them myself," he sees a crowd gathered at the pond. Schprintze has drowned herself.

Beilke marries a war-profiteer so that she can provide for her father's old age, but he loses his fortune and they are forced to flee to America. Tevye's wife dies and he is driven into exile by Russian peasants, but he remains good-humored and spiritually indestructible. That dignity and self-respect can be sustained under such extreme conditions is the secret of the immense popularity of these stories. It is the narrative strategy that permits this revelation. The monologue form allows an impoverished milkman to reveal the humaneness of his character and the grandeur of his soul without any authorial intervention.

MENACHEM-MENDL LETTERS

Another way of presenting a speaking voice without meditation is the epistolary form. In 1892, Aleichem began the Menachem-Mendl letters, which he continued to publish until 1913. This correspondence constitutes another famous short-story cycle. The hero's name has become synonymous with a *Luftmensch*, someone who builds castles in the air. He is the archetype of Bernard Malamud's luckless businessmen, like Salzman, whose office is "in his socks," and Sussman, whose enterprises are negotiated "in the air." He is the prototype of Saul Bellow's Tommy Wilhelm who loses his last cent on the stock exchange under the influence of a confidence man. He is also the projection of the author's own financial disaster at the Odessa stock exchange and his subsequent bankruptcy.

Each comic episode follows the same repetitive pattern. The husband writes from the city, feverishly detailing his latest scheme for getting rich. His skeptical wife responds from the village, urging him, with innumerable quotations from her mother's inexhaustible store of proverbs, to come home. His next letter always confirms his mother-in-law's forecasts with its news of his most recent disaster. His inevitable failures, however, have taught him nothing about economic realities because he has already flung himself enthusiastically into yet another doomed enterprise. The comedy derives from the repetition of this formula. He is flat, neither aging nor changing; rigid, driven by a single obsessive notion; he is the eternal loser whose hopes are never dimmed.

Menachem-Mendl fails as an investor. He fails as a currency speculator. He fails as a broker in houses, and forests, and oil. He fails as a writer, as a matchmaker, and as an insurance agent; but his irrepressible flow of rhetoric never fails. He says, "The most important thing is language, the gift of speech." He can "talk against time; talk at random; talk glibly; talk himself out of breath; talk you into things; talk in circles." In the pleasure of verbalizing his experiences, relishing his own eloquence, he compensates for them. The comic effect derives precisely from his overvaluation of language. The limited protagonist deludes himself that he has masked the facts in highflown words; the reader penetrates this verbal screen.

To be successful, comedy must sustain a rapid pace. If the events move slowly enough for us to think about them, their essential sadness is exposed. Thus, Menachem-Mendl is kept rushing. He is presented as always in a hurry. His gestures indicate frenzy, accelerated to a dizzying pace. The irony that his busyness is stasis, that his frantic activity is inert because he is speeding only to another dead end, contributes to the comic effect.

Both in these early works and in his later short-story cycles, such as The Railway Tales, the Children's Stories, the Festival Stories, and the Kasril-evke cycles, Aleichem shows his unparalleled mastery of the extended monologue, which he employs with such virtuosity.

OTHER MAJOR WORKS

LONG FICTION: *Natasha*, 1884; *Sender Blank und zayn Gezindl*, 1888; *Yosele Solovey*, 1890 (*The Nightingale*, 1985); *Stempenyu*, 1899 (English translation, 1913); *Blondzne Shtern*, 1912 (*Wandering Star*, 1952); *Marienbad*, 1917 (English translation, 1982); *In Shturm*, 1918 (*In the Storm*, 1984); *Blutiger Shpas*, 1923 (*The Bloody Hoax*, 1991).

PLAYS: *Yakenhoz*, pr. 1894; *Tsuzeyt un Tsushpreyt*, pr. 1905; *Stempenyu*, pr. 1907; *Die Goldgreber*, pr. 1907; *Shver Tsu Zein a Yid*, pb. 1914; *Dos Groyse Gevins*, pb. 1915 (*The Jackpot*, 1989).

NONFICTION: *Fun'm yarid*, 1916 (*The Great Fair: Scenes from My Childhood*, 1955); *Briefe von Scholem Aleichem und Menachem Mendl*, 1921.

BIBLIOGRAPHY

Aarons, Victoria. *Author as Character in the Works of Sholom Aleichem*. Lewiston, N.Y.: Edwin Mellen Press, 1985. An exploration of Aleichem's interesting literary technique and the use of himself as "naive auditor." Religious insights of the fiction also receive suitable attention.

Butwin, Frances, and Joseph Butwin. *Sholom Aleichem*. Boston: Twayne, 1977. The best single introduction in English to the life and writings of Aleichem. Sound, scholarly, and concise.

Frieden, Ken. *Classic Yiddish Fiction: Abramovitsh, Sholom Aleichem, and Peretz*. Albany, N.Y.: State University of New York Press, 1995. Examines the works of Shalom Jacob Abramovich, Aleichem, and Isaac Leib Peretz.

Howe, Irving. *The World of Our Fathers: The Journey of the Eastern European Jews to America and the Life They Found and Made*. New York: Harcourt Brace Jovanovich, 1976. A superbly readable account of the Yiddish culture reflected in Aleichem's writing. This classic study of Jewish immigrant life in the United States gives ample attention to newspapers, journals, and theater, the usual forums for Yiddish literary expression.

Howe, Irving, and Aliezer Greenberg, eds. *A Treasury of Yiddish Stories*. New York: Viking Press, 1954. This volume is not only an enjoyable collection of stories that illustrate Aleichem's proper place within the stream of Yiddish fiction but also a fine survey of the genre. The editor's introduction is the best brief discussion of Yiddish writing that exists in English.

Roskies, David G. *A Bridge of Longing: The Lost Art of Yiddish Storytelling*. Cambridge, Mass.: Harvard University Press, 1995. Places Aleichem in the context of Eastern European Yiddish storytelling as the best loved of all Yiddish folklorists; examines his creation of Tevye, the Milkman as a way to explore life's ironies; discusses Tevye as a Jewish everyman who embodies the invented tradition of storytelling that came to be more authentic than the orthodox rabbinic tradition it replaced.

Sherman, Joseph. "Holding Fast to Integrity: Shalom Rabinovich, Sholom Aleichem, and Tevye the Dairyman." *Judaism* 43 (Winter, 1994): 6-18. Discusses narrative strategy in stories of Tevye, arguing that Aleichem tests the validity of traditional Jewish teaching in the stories through the monologues of the Jewish characters. Suggests that the narratives compel readers to ask questions, which Tevye answers with incomplete, inappropriate, or irrelevant traditional theology.

Waife-Goldbert, Marie. *My Father, Sholom Aleichem*. New York: Simon & Schuster, 1968. This volume is valuable because it is the first complete biography in English and because of its use of Aleichem's own unfinished autobiography. Yet this is a family memoir, lovingly idealized, rather than an objective evaluation of accomplishments.

Ruth Rosenberg, updated by Allene Phy-Olsen

SHERMAN ALEXIE

Born: Spokane Indian Reservation, Wellpinit, Washington; October 7, 1966

PRINCIPAL SHORT FICTION

The Lone Ranger and Tonto Fistfight in Heaven, 1993

The Toughest Indian in the World: Stories, 2000

OTHER LITERARY FORMS

A prolific writer, Sherman Alexie has published well over three hundred stories and poems. His poetry and poetry/short fiction works include *The Business of Fancydancing* (1992), *I Would Steal Horses* (1992), *First Indian on the Moon* (1993), *Old Shirts and New Skins* (1993), *Seven Mourning Songs for the Cedar Flute I Have Yet to Learn to Play* (1994), *Water Flowing Home* (1994), and *The Summer of Black Widows* (1996). He has also written the novels *Reservation Blues* (1995) and *Indian Killer* (1996).

ACHIEVEMENTS

Sherman Alexie began accruing his numerous accolades and awards while in college, including a Washington State Arts Commission poetry fellowship (1991) and a National Endowment for the Arts poetry fellowship (1992). He also won Slipstream's fifth annual Chapbook Contest (1992), an Ernest Hemingway Foundation Award Citation, a Lila Wallace-*Reader's Digest* Writer's Award (1994), an American Book Award (1996), and The Ernest Hemingway Foundation/PEN Award for First Fiction. His first novel, *Reservation Blues* (1995) won the Before Columbus Foundation's American Book Award, the Murray Morgan Prize, and prompted Alexie to be named one of *Granta*'s Best of Young American Novelists. *Indian Killer* (1996), his second novel, was listed as a *New York Times* notable book.

BIOGRAPHY

A self-described Spokane/Coeur d'Alene Indian who believes "Native American" is a "guilty white liberal term," Sherman Joseph Alexie, Jr., grew up in Wellpinit, Washington, on the Spokane Indian Reservation. His father, an alcoholic, spent little time at home, and his mother supported the family by selling hand-sewn quilts at the local trading post. Born hydrocephalic, Alexie spent most of his childhood at home voraciously reading books from the local library. He later attended high school outside the reservation. His academic achievements there secured him a place at Spokane's Jesuit Gonzaga University in 1985. While there, he turned to alcohol as a means of coping with the pressure he felt to succeed. His goal to become a medical doctor was derailed by fainting spells in human anatomy class, and Alexie later transferred to Washington State University in 1987, where he began writing and then publishing his poetry and short stories. During a 1992 National Endowment for the Arts fellowship, he wrote his award-winning *The Business of Fancydancing* and *The Lone Ranger and Tonto Fistfight in Heaven*. With this success came sobriety.

Based on his collection of short stories in *The Lone Ranger and Tonto Fistfight in Heaven*, Alexie wrote and directed the award-winning *Smoke Signals* (1998), the first feature film ever made with an all-Native American cast and crew. Alexie, his child, and wife Diane, a member of the Hidatsa nation and college counselor, settled in Seattle, Washington.

ANALYSIS

According to Sherman Alexie in an interview with *CINEASTE*, the five major influences on his writing are "my father, for his nontraditional Indian stories, my grandmother for her traditional Indian stories, Stephen King, John Steinbeck, and *The Brady Bunch*." It is no wonder then that Alexie's work, in particular the short stories in *The Lone Ranger and Tonto Fistfight in Heaven*, has been described by *American Indian Quarterly* as resembling a "casebook of postmodernist theory" that revels in such things as irony, parody of traditions, and the mingling of popular and native cultures. The result is a body of work that allows Alexie to challenge and subvert the stereotypes of Native Americans seen in the mass media (the warrior, the shaman, the drunk) and explore what it means to be a contemporary Native American.

In commenting on Native American poets and writers, writers such as Leslie Marmon Silko describe how Native American artists often create their strongest work when they write from a position of social responsibility. In Alexie's case, his work is often designed to effect change by exposing other Indians and whites to the harsh realities of reservation life. In Alexie's early work—work influenced by his own alcoholism and father's abandonment (as seen in *The Lone Ranger and Tonto Fistfight in Heaven*)—he uses the Spokane Indian community as a backdrop for his characters, who often suffer from poverty, despair, and substance abuse. Yet it is his use of dark humor and irony that enables these characters to survive both their own depressions and self-loathing and the attitude and activities of the often ignorant and apathetic white society. Alexie writes in his short story "Because My Father Always Said He Was the Only Indian Who Saw Jimi Hendrix Play 'The Star-Spangled Banner' at Woodstock":

> On a reservation, Indian men who abandon their children are treated worse than white fathers who do the same thing. It's because white men have been doing that forever and Indian men have just learned how. That's how assimilation works.

With sobriety, Alexie claims that from *The Business of Fancydancing* in 1992 to *Smoke Signals* in 1998, his vision of Indian society has brightened and his writing has moved from focusing on the effects to the causes of substance abuse and other self-destructive behaviors. In *CINEASTE*, Alexie describes his growth as a writer in this way:

> As I've been in recovery over the years and stayed sober, you'll see the work gradually freeing itself of alcoholism and going much deeper, exploring the emotional, sociological, and psychological reasons for any kind of addictions or dysfunctions within the [Indian]

community. . . . It's more of a whole journey, you get there and you get back.

THE LONE RANGER AND TONTO FISTFIGHT IN HEAVEN

Alexie's first collection of (only) short stories, *The Lone Ranger and Tonto Fistfight in Heaven*, received much critical acclaim. Many of the Native American characters that he introduced in his earlier poetry—like the storyteller Thomas Builds-The-Fire and his friend Victor Joseph—appear here as vehicles through which Alexie illustrates how Indians survive both the hardships they face on reservations and the gulfs between similar and dissimilar cultures, time periods, and men and women.

In a number of the twenty-two often autobiographical stories in this collection, Alexie infuses irony into tales that illustrate the destructive effects of alcohol on both children and adults on reservations. For example, in "The Only Traffic Signal on the Reservation Doesn't Flash Red Any More" he weaves the tradition of storytelling with the contemporary issue of how cultures create their own heroes. In this story, the narrator and his friend Adrian, both recovering alcoholics, are sitting on a porch playing Russian roulette with a BB gun. They stop and watch a local high school basketball player walk by with his friends. As the narrator talks, the reader learns that contemporary heroes on the reservation are often basketball players, and stories about their abilities are retold year after year. Yet, these heroes, including the narrator himself, often succumb to alcoholism and drop off the team. From the narrator's reminisces, it becomes clear that, while all people need heroes in their lives, creating heroes on a reservation can be problematic.

In "A Drug Called Tradition," the narrator tells the story of Thomas Builds-The-Fire and the "second-largest party in reservation history" for which he pays with money he receives from a large utility company land lease. While the narrator claims that "we can all hear our ancestors laughing in the trees" when Indians actually profit in this way, who the ancestors are truly laughing at is unclear. Are they laughing at the white people for spending a lot of money to put ten telephone poles across some land or the Indians for spending that money on large quantities of alcohol? Later in the story, Victor, Junior, and Thomas go off and experience a night of drug-induced hallucinations about the faraway past, the present, and future. In the present, the boys return to a time before they ever had their first drink of alcohol. From this story, the reader learns that it is best for people to stay in the present and keep persevering and not become stuck in the past or an imagined future.

Several of the stories in *The Lone Ranger and Tonto Fistfight in Heaven* that were eventually adapted for the film *Smoke Signals* explore both the connections and fissures between people of different genders and similar or dissimilar cultures. In "Every Little Hurricane," the reader is introduced to nine-year-old Victor, who is awakened from his frequent nightmares by one of the many family fights, this one occurring between his uncles during a New Year's Eve party. Memories of other seasonal alcohol and poverty-induced "hurricanes" ensue, such as that of the Christmas his father could not afford any gifts. At the end of the story, as all the relatives and neighbors pick themselves up and go home, Victor lies down between his father and mother, hoping that the alcohol in their bodies will seep into his and help him sleep. This story is about how Indians continue to be "eternal survivors" of many types of storms.

In "Because My Father Always Said He Was the Only Indian Who Saw Jimi Hendrix Play 'The Star-Spangled Banner' at Woodstock," the narrator details the love-hate relationship between his mother and his father (who would later leave the family), while using a popular music icon to illustrate how Native Americans and whites share at least one common culture. The narrator of this story, the abandoned Victor, later teams up with former childhood friend and storyteller Thomas in "This Is What It Means to Say Phoenix,

Sherman Alexie (Marion Ettlinger)

Arizona," to collect Victor's father's ashes in Phoenix. In their ensuing journey, the characters grow spiritually and emotionally, while exploring what it means today to be a Native American.

OTHER MAJOR WORKS

LONG FICTION: *Reservation Blues*, 1995; *Indian Killer*, 1996.

POETRY: *I Would Steal Horses*, 1992; *Old Shirts and New Skins*, 1993; *The Summer of the Black Widow*, 1996 (poems and short prose).

MISCELLANEOUS: *The Business of Fancydancing*, 1992; *First Indian on the Moon*, 1993.

BIBLIOGRAPHY

Baxter, Andrea-Bess. "Review of *Old Shirts and New Skins*, *First Indian on the Moon*, and *The Lone Ranger and Tonto Fistfight in Heaven*." *Western American Literature* 29, no. 3 (November, 1994): 277-280. A review of the three works with commentary on the appeals of Alexie's writing and its strengths.

Low, Denise. *The American Indian Quarterly* 20, no. 1 (Winter, 1996): 123-125. In examining Alexie's work through a postmodern lens, Low discusses his characters and rhetorical strategies in *The Lone Ranger and Tonto Fistfight in Heaven* and *The Business of Fancydancing*.

McFarland, Ron. "'Another Kind of Violence': Sherman Alexie's Poems." *American Indian Quarterly* 21, no. 2 (Spring, 1997): 251-264. Reviews various anthologies and types of Native American writing and writers with a focus on Sherman Alexie and his work.

Niatum, Duane, ed. *Harper's Anthology of Twentieth-Century Native American Poetry.* San Francisco: Harper & Row, 1988. Features thirty-six contributors and attempts to address what makes Native American poetry unique.

Silko, Leslie Marmon. "Bingo Man—Reservation Blues by Sherman Alexie." *Nation* 260, no. 23 (June 12, 1995): 856-860. A review by a celebrated Native American writer of Alexie's short stories and poems with special focus on his first novel, *Reservation Blues*.

West, Dennis. "Sending Cinematic Smoke Signals: An Interview with Sherman Alexie." *CINEASTE* 23, no. 4 (1998): 28-32. Discusses both the film *Smoke Signals* and short stories in *The Lone Ranger and Tonto Fistfight in Heaven*, followed by an in-depth interview with Alexie about his early influences and work.

Lisa-Anne Culp

NELSON ALGREN
Nelson Algren Abraham

Born: Detroit, Michigan; March 28, 1909
Died: Sag Harbor, New York; May 9, 1981

PRINCIPAL SHORT FICTION

The Neon Wilderness, 1947
The Last Carousel, 1973 (also includes sketches and poems)

OTHER LITERARY FORMS

Nelson Algren is probably best known for films made from his novels *The Man with the Golden Arm* (1949) and *A Walk on the Wild Side* (1956), but his work ranges through those violent novels and short stories to Hemingwayesque essays, verse, work on the avant-garde "little magazine" *Anvil*, sketches on life in major cities, travel sketches, journalistic re-porting, and other factual and fictional pieces about places and people who have "a weakness."

ACHIEVEMENTS

Best known for his novels (*The Man with the Golden Arm* won the first National Book Award in 1950), Nelson Algren was both a popular and critical success with his short stories, which closely resemble his novels in character, setting, and theme. His stories have appeared regularly in both the *O. Henry Memorial Prize Stories* and *The Best American short Stories*, but his popularity waned as the American reading public lost interest in naturalistic fiction. For the most part, his stories are slices of life, packed with details and dialects, grotesques and losers, yet marked with a glimmer of idealism. Influenced by

Ernest Hemingway and Stephen Crane, he has served as an influence on later naturalists as John Rechy and Hubert Selby, Jr., who resemble him in their lower-class characters, urban settings, violent themes, and nightmarish vision.

BIOGRAPHY

Born in Detroit, the descendant of Nels Ahlgren, a Swedish Jew who changed his name to Isaac ben Abraham, Nelson Algren was brought up under the "El" on Chicago's poor West Side and was the "bard of the stumblebum" of the Polish community there in the Depression. He took a degree in journalism at the University of Illinois but found it difficult to get a job after graduating. He drifted to the South and to Texas, where he wrote his first short story, "So Help Me," in an abandoned filling station outside Rio Hondo. This story led to his first novel, *Somebody in Boots* (1935). Algren's novel *The Man with the Golden Arm* reached the top of the best-seller list. He also received praise for his 1956 novel, *A Walk on the Wild Side*. Aside from some interviews, two travel books, and his collected stories, Algren wrote little after 1955. He traveled extensively, taught at various universities, and moved to New Jersey in 1975, finally settling in Sag Harbor, New York, where he died in 1981, shortly after having been elected to the American Academy Institute of Arts and Letters. This belated recognition, for Algren's popularity had declined since the 1950's, was appreciated by Algren, who was having trouble publishing *The Devil's Stocking*, a fictionalized account of Rubin "Hurricane" Carter's life. The book was published posthumously in 1983.

ANALYSIS

Included in the collection *The Neon Wilderness*, the story "Design for Departure" contains the title phrase and sets the tone of the collection. The story contains some heavy-handed Christian symbolism, which can be seen in the names of the main charac-

Nelson Algren (Library of Congress)

ters, Mary and Christy. Mary closely resembles the protagonist of Stephen Crane's novel *Maggie: A Girl of the Streets* (1893); however, her world of "Kleenex, fifty-cent horse (betting) tickets and cigarette snipes" is more a collage than a slice of gutter life. Mary is a shell of a person in her job wrapping bacon and a passive victim of a rape by a deaf man named Christiano, which seems to affect her no more than the moral problems of engaging in a badger game with Ryan, the proprietor of The Jungle (a club) or the subsequent arrest and jail term of her boyfriend Christy. When Christy is released from jail, he finds Mary on the game and on drugs, and she warns him off: She is diseased. At her request, he gives her a fatal overdose. The character of Mary is so void of emotion or response to her life that it is difficult for the reader to feel anything for her. Although there are some bright passages of real-life dialogue in the story, they tend to contribute to the self-conscious tone of the story rather than elevate its quality.

"THE FACE ON THE BARROOM FLOOR"

A less self-conscious and more successful story is "The Face on the Barroom Floor," a sketch that introduces one of the prototypes of *A Walk on the Wild Side*. Algren renders the bloody, senseless fight in the story marvelously. Although he does not seem to understand the psychology of the prizefighter, he effectively describes the brutal poundings of the fight. He creates a similar appeal through vivid description in "He Swung and He Missed." The little guy beaten to a pulp in the ring stands for the victim of "The System"; however, Algren occasionally succeeds in making him more than a symbol.

"HOW THE DEVIL CAME DOWN DIVISION STREET"

Algren's material is most successful when he records in journalistic manner—rather than manipulates as a writer of fiction—the real-life language and insights of his characters. Where "Design for Departure" is ambitious and basically fails, "How the Devil Came Down Division Street" succeeds because Algren has taken the gothic and grotesque elements of an experience and set it down quickly and skillfully. Roman Orlov, trying to "drown the worm" that gnaws at his vitals, sits in the Polonia bar and stumblingly relates his bizarre and drunken tale of how his family's apartment was haunted. By the end of his story his character is clearly revealed—what the lack of hope and even the lack of a bed have made of him; how the consolations of religion are to the very poor only impediments to survival; and how that survival involves the acceptance of extraordinary circumstances which would be farcical if they were not so painful. The reader is moved to understand that for some people "there is no place to go but the taverns." With astonishment, one finds the answer to the question on which the whole story is built: "Does the devil live in a double-shot? Or is he the one who gnaws, all night, within?" In this story we feel Algren has realized his ideal, to identify himself with his subjects.

"A BOTTLE OF MILK FOR MOTHER"

There is even more power of sympathy and understanding in "A Bottle of Milk for Mother," the tale of the "final difficulty" of Bruno "lefty" Bicek. When a street-smart but doomed Polish boxer is charged with the robbery and murder of an old man in a shabby tenement hallway, fierce and unrelenting police interrogation leaves him in despair: "I knew I'd never get to be twenty-one." Kojaz, the wily cop, is also sensitively handled—the story should be read in connection with "The Captain Has Bad Dreams" and "The Captain Is Impaled"—as he inexorably pries from Lefty's grip what still another story calls "Poor Man's Pennies," the transparent alibis and compulsive lies of the downtrodden.

Among the "essential innocents" in Algren's work are the "born incompetents" (such as Gladys and Rudy in "Poor Man's Pennies"), the cops and robbers, the stumblebums, and the prostitutes. In "Please Don't Talk About Me When I'm Gone," the crowd draws back to let Rose be pushed into a paddy wagon, and she reflects: "My whole life it's the first time anyone made room for me." In "Is Your Name Joe?"—all her johns are Joe—another prostitute delivers a raving monologue which has a certain garish and surreal quality, reflecting the details in the world of the former con and former hookers described in the remarkable story entitled "Decline & Fall in Dingdong-Daddyland." It is this surreal quality which salvages the stereotypes of *The Man with the Golden Arm*, the stories in *The Neon Wilderness*, and the best of the later stories ("The Face on the Barroom Floor," "The Captain Is Impaled," "Home to Shawneetown," and "Decline & Fall in Dingdong-Daddyland").

There is in Algren a strain of the surreal and grotesque that links him with William Burroughs and writers who moved from depictions of the weird world of drug addicts to a harsh and often horrifying view of the "real" world from which they are desperately trying to escape. That, not his social realism (in which he is surpassed by Frank Norris, Theodore Dreiser, and many others) or his "poetic" prose (in which Thomas Wolfe, William Faulkner, and others leave him far behind), makes Algren's work more than a mere document of American social protest or a clear precursor of other writers and gives it its own value.

OTHER MAJOR WORKS

LONG FICTION: *Somebody in Boots*, 1935; *Never Come Morning*, 1942; *The Man with the Golden Arm*, 1949; *A Walk on the Wild Side*, 1956; *The Devil's Stocking*, 1983.

NONFICTION: *Chicago: City on the Make*, 1951; *Who Lost an American?*, 1963; *Conversations with Nelson Algren*, 1964 (with H. E. F. Donohue); *Notes from a Sea Diary: Hemingway All the Way*, 1965.

EDITED TEXT: *Nelson Algren's Own Book of Lonesome Monsters*, 1962.

BIBLIOGRAPHY

Cappetti, Carla. *Writing Chicago: Modernism, Ethnography, and the Novel*. New York: Columbia University Press, 1993. Although Cappetti's chapter on Algren focuses primarily on his novel *Never Come Morning*, it is helpful in understanding his short stories, for it deals with Algren's combination of both the realistic/naturalist and the Symbolist/Surrealist traditions. Discusses how Algren's fiction interrupts historicity and factuality with poetic devices that prevent the reader from lapsing into simple referentiality.

Cox, Martha Heasley, and Wayne Chatterton. *Nelson Algren*. Boston: Twayne, 1975. The best overall assessment of Algren's life and work. Contains an early chapter on the short stories, which are analyzed in some detail. The authors provide a chronology, a biographical chapter, an annotated bibliography, and a helpful index that groups the short stories by theme.

Donohue, H. E. F. *Conversations with Nelson Algren*. New York: Hill & Wang, 1964. Donohue's book consists of conversations, arranged chronologically, about Algren's life and work and therefore serves a biographical function. The conversation "The Army and the Writing" concerns, in part, Algren's short-story collection *The Neon Wilderness*, but the book is more valuable for Algren's comments on writing, writers, and politics.

Drew, Bettina. *Nelson Algren: A Life on the Wild Side*. New York: G. P. Putnam's Sons, 1989. The only Algren biography, this volume, which is well researched and readable, mixes biographical material with publication details about Algren's work. One chapter is devoted to *The Neon Wilderness*, a collection of related short stories by Algren. Supplemented by a bibliography of Algren's work.

Giles, James R. *Confronting the Horror: The Novels of Nelson Algren*. Kent, Ohio: Kent State University Press, 1989. Giles provides brief commentary on some of Algren's short stories, but his book is most helpful in relating Algren's naturalism to a literary tradition that extends to later writers such as Hubert Selby, Jr., and John Rechy. For Giles, Algren's fiction reflects his despair over the absurd state of humankind and the obscenity of death.

Ray, David. "Housesitting the Wild Side." *Chicago Review* 41 (1995): 107-116. Anecdotal discussion of acquaintance with Algren in the 1950's and 1960's. Discusses Algren's connection with Chicago, his relationship with Simon de Beauvoir, and efforts to structure and organize Algren's manuscripts.

Leonard R. N. Ashley, updated by Thomas L. Erskine

WOODY ALLEN
Allen Stewart Konigsberg

Born: Brooklyn, New York; December 1, 1935

PRINCIPAL SHORT FICTION
Getting Even, 1971
Without Feathers, 1975
Side Effects, 1980

OTHER LITERARY FORMS

Woody Allen is best known as a filmmaker, for which he provides his own screenplays. He has written extensively for the theater and television, has supplied standup comedians (including himself) with original jokes, and has published numerous comic essays.

ACHIEVEMENTS

Woody Allen is widely accepted as one of the most talented American humorists and filmmakers of his time. This assessment is reinforced by a considerable number of prestigious awards garnered by Allen over the years. These include a Sylvania Award in 1957 for a television script he wrote for the *Sid Caesar Show*, Academy Awards for best director and best original screenplay in 1977 for *Annie Hall* (1977), British Academy and New York Film Critics Awards in 1979 for *Mahattan* (1979), and New York and Los Angeles Film Critics Awards in 1987 for *Hannah and Her Sisters* (1986).

Similar recognition for Allen's dramatic film efforts has been slow in coming. *Interiors* (1978) and *September* (1987) both were greeted unenthusiastically by critics. *Crimes and Misdemeanors* (1989), a more difficult film to categorize, may have been an important breakthrough in this regard.

Though overshadowed by his film career, Allen's short fiction has been well appreciated by critics. His story "The Kugelmass Episode" won an O. Henry Award in 1977. His collections of short fiction have generally been reviewed favorably. In addition to its own considerable merit, Allen's short fiction has served as a breeding ground for themes, ideas, and

images more fully developed later in his films. Thus, while Allen's short stories certainly lack the polish and perfectionism of his motion pictures, they have played an important role in helping Allen to excel as a screenwriter and director. Given Allen's marvelous productivity during his career, they also have contributed to his reputation as an artist whose creative juices never seem to ebb.

BIOGRAPHY

Woody Allen was born Allen Stewart Konigsberg in Brooklyn, New York, on December 1, 1935. He was graduated from Brooklyn's Midwood High School in 1953 and briefly attended New York University and City College of New York. While in the process of abandoning his formal education, Allen took on his soon-to-be-famous pseudonym and became a full-time comedy writer for the David O. Alber public relations firm. At age nineteen, he went to Hollywood as part of the National Broadcasting Company's (NBC) Writers Development Program, soon becoming a highly successful writer for nightclub acts, Broadway revues, and television shows. In 1960, Allen himself began to perform as a stand-up comedian. This led to acting opportunities as well. At the same time, Allen continued to write, turning out comic prose for sophisticated periodicals such as *The New Yorker*, plays good enough to be produced on Broadway, and screenplays that would be made into feature films. Ultimately, Allen's dual career as performer and author came together as Allen wrote, directed, and starred in a number of distinguished motion pictures. Allen has been a longtime resident of New York City and has continued to base much of his work there.

ANALYSIS

The overall emphasis of Woody Allen's short fiction is summarized by the title of his second book-length collection, *Without Feathers*. The title alludes to an Emily Dickinson line: "Hope is the thing without feathers. . . ." The particular hopelessness with which Allen deals, in his mirthful way, is that described, defined, and passed down by such philosophers and literary figures as Friedrich Nietzsche, Søren Kierkegaard, Albert Camus, and Franz Kafka. It is one in which the death of God, existential meaninglessness, and surreal distortions of time and space are the norm. In this world, anxiety abounds, human reason is essentially flawed, and truth disappears into the twin vacuum of moral relativism and perceptual uncertainty.

While Allen demonstrates an instinctive grasp of the issues raised by such a worldview, his treatment is, as one might expect in a humorist, always tongue in cheek. Allen is no scholar, nor is he trying to be one. He accepts the more or less existentialist premises that inform his work and seems to believe in them. He does not take them seriously enough to ponder systematically. In fact, he makes fun of people who do so, particularly those who do it for a

living. Nor does Allen sink into despair. Instead, he uses the philosophical and literary atmosphere of his time as a convenient springboard for laughter. In essence, his work transforms the uncertainty of a Godless universe into fertile ground for his free-flowing style of comedy.

One technique that enables Allen to accomplish this goal is parody, or comic imitation. Most of Allen's fiction contains parody—ranging from imitation of Plato's *Apologia Sōkratous* (399-390 B.C.E.; *Apology*, 1675) to variations on Kafka and Count Dracula—and some stories are multiple parodies. Any mode of thought, scholarship, literary expression, or lifestyle that people celebrate or venerate is fair game to Allen. Indeed, the more seriously a philosophy is taken, the more fun he seems to have tipping it over onto its humorous side. This is not to say that Allen's humor is limited to parody, nor that it is always subtle. Allen is too much the stand-up comedian to let any opportunity for a laugh—no matter how vulgar or easy—pass by unexploited. Nor does he tolerate lulls in his comedic fiction. On the contrary, he shoots for a pace of humor so rapid that the reader will never be left time to wonder when the next joke is coming. Finally, Allen's work often harks back to his roots. While his stories are less autobiographical than some of his films, they often involve—at least in passing—Jewish characters and issues of importance to Jews.

"MR. BIG"

The characteristics listed above are amply illustrated by Allen's story "Mr. Big." In the story, Kaiser Lupowitz, a New York private investigator, is between cases when a beautiful blonde calling herself Heather Butkiss (as suggested above, no joke is too small for Allen) comes to his office and asks him to search for a missing person. The missing person she wants him to find is Mr. Big, that is to say, God. Lupowitz demands to have all the facts before he takes the case. The blonde admits that Butkiss is an alias, claiming that her real name is Claire Rosensweig and that she is a Vassar College student working on an assign-

Woody Allen (AP/Wide World Photos)

ment for her philosophy class. Lupowitz takes the case for his usual daily fee of one hundred dollars plus expenses.

The investigation begins with a visit to a local rabbi for whom Lupowitz had worked previously. After some revealing pokes at the notion of what it means to be God's "chosen people" (Allen likens it to a "protection" racket), Lupowitz visits an informer, Chicago Phil the atheist, in a pool hall to find out more about his client. There, he is told that she is really a Radcliffe student and that she had been dating an empiricist philosopher who dabbled with logical positivism and pragmatism (somehow, Arthur Schopenhauer also is mentioned). That evening, Lupowitz dines with his client. After a bout of lovemaking, the two discuss Kierkegaard. A telephone call from the police interrupts them; it seems someone answering God's description has just showed up in the morgue, a homicide victim. The police suspect an existentialist, possibly even Lupowitz himself.

Lupowitz's next stop is an Italian restaurant in Newark, where he questions His Holiness the Pope, who claims to have an exclusive pipeline to God. Lupowitz learns that his lovely client is actually in the science department at Bryn Mawr College. He makes further inquiries and returns to confront her with what he has learned. Her real name, he tells her, is Dr. Ellen Shepherd, and she teaches physics at Bryn Mawr. In traditional private-eye fashion, Lupowitz reveals a highly tangled plot involving Socrates, Immanuel Kant, and Martin Buber, among others. With a melodramatic flair, he names Ellen Shepherd (and therefore, perhaps, science) as God's killer. The story concludes with an equal mixture of flying bullets and philosophic allusions as the intrepid private eye sees justice through to the end.

Here one can see all Allen's basic ingredients. Philosophy, religion, and the hard-boiled detective genre are all lampooned, the last through the medium of parody. The question of God's existence is explored with a completely earnest lack of earnestness. Truth is treated as something elusive and perhaps irredeemably ephemeral. The wisecracks come one on top of the other and at varying levels of intellectual sophistication.

"THE KUGELMASS EPISODE"

Allen builds on this formula in what some critics believe to be one of his best stories, "The Kugelmass Episode." Here themes are raised that foreshadow his later films. Kugelmass is a professor of humanities at City College of New York. Feeling smothered in his marriage, he seeks approval from his analyst for the adulterous affair he feels to be approaching. When his analyst refuses to condone such behavior, Kugelmass breaks off his therapy. Shortly afterward, he is telephoned by a magician named Persky, who believes he has something that will interest Kugelmass. This turns out to be a cabinet that allows one admittance into the book of one's choice. Though he is skeptical, Kugelmass decides to enter the contraption with a copy of Gustave Flaubert's *Madame Bovary* (1857; English translation, 1886). Quite astonishingly, he is transported to just the right part of the novel so that he can be alone with Emma Bovary, returning to the twentieth century in time to keep his wife from becoming suspicious. (However, literature teachers did begin to wonder when a balding, middle-aged Jew first appeared in the original novel.) After another visit, Emma asks to make the return trip to New York City with Kugelmass. This is arranged by Persky, and the two lovers have a delicious weekend in the city. Emma is particularly taken with the great shopping. (Literature professors now have to ponder why Emma does not appear in the novel at all.)

It is at this point that things begin to go wrong. Persky's cabinet breaks down, and Emma is stuck in New York. Soon she and Kugelmass become permanently soured on each other. Persky finally fixes the cabinet and returns Emma to her fictional time and place. Kugelmass proclaims that he has learned his lesson but three weeks later decides to try Persky's cabinet again. This time he plans to go for more sex and less romance with the "monkey" in Philip Roth's *Portnoy's Complaint* (1969). Something goes wrong, and he is stranded, presumably forever, in a book on remedial Spanish.

Here the emptiness of the universe is merely the backdrop for a story that is about infatuation, magic, and the relation between different kinds of reality. Many of Allen's films involve the finer nuances of infidelity between lovers (or "hanky-panky" as it were), apparently one of the more common ways people deal with the universe's meaninglessness. Magic— perhaps as an alternative manifestation of the miraculous or supernatural—has played a pivotal role in at least two of Allen's films, *Alice* (1990) and *Oedipus Wrecks* (1989). Interestingly enough, the magic goes wrong, just as God might have done somewhere along the line. Most strikingly, the interaction between "real" and fictional characters serves as the central theme of his film *The Purple Rose of Cairo* (1985). In all these instances, Allen has moved from mirthful commentary on the dead end to which humanity has arrived to a more serious look at how people try to cope. Thus "Mr. Big" and "The Kugelmass Episode" illustrate different transitional points in Allen's development as an artist. Taken together, they indicate the general philosophy of life underlying Allen's work and point out the ways in which his stories have provided a foundation for his more elaborate efforts on film.

"THE CONDEMNED"

As is evident in "The Kugelmass Episode," Allen has an abiding interest in the foibles of moral conduct, particularly as it relates to love, sex, infatuation, and fidelity. He also writes quite often about some of the more grave moral-political questions of modern time. In "The Condemned," Allen parodies works by the French existentialists Albert Camus, Jean-Paul Sartre, and André Malraux in order to examine the propriety of political violence. The story begins with a ruthless informer named Brisseau, asleep in his bedroom. Cloquet, who has been assigned to assassinate Brisseau, stands over the bed, wrestling with his conscience. Cloquet has never before killed a human being. He did kill a mad dog once, but only after it had been certified insane by a board of qualified psychiatrists. Gathering his resolve, Cloquet puts his gun to Brisseau's head and is about to pull the trigger. Just then, Madame Brisseau enters the room, failing to notice the gun sticking out of her husband's ear as Cloquet takes cover behind a dresser. After Madame Brisseau exits the room, Cloquet regains consciousness (he had fainted) and resumes his internal dialogue. He wonders whether he is Cloquet the mur-

derer or Cloquet who teaches the Psychology of Fowl at the Sorbonne. He reminisces about his first meeting with Brisseau and finally comes to the conclusion that he cannot possibly shoot anyone, even this man who clearly deserves it.

Dropping his gun, Cloquet flees, stopping off for a brandy before going to Juliet's house. Juliet asks Cloquet if he has killed Brisseau. Yes, he says. Juliet applauds. The two make love. The following morning, Cloquet is arrested for Brisseau's murder. He is subsequently tried and convicted. Awaiting execution, he tries to convert but finds that all the usual faiths are filled. On the eve of his death, Cloquet longs for freedom, relishing the opportunities he has missed to become a ventriloquist or to show up at the Louvre in bikini underwear and a false nose. Just before his execution, as he is about to faint from fear, Cloquet is released. The real murderer has confessed. Overjoyed, Cloquet rushes out to enjoy the life and freedom he had come so close to losing. Three days later he is arrested again, this time for showing up at the Louvre in bikini underwear and a false nose.

Not surprising in the light of what was said above, the issue of whether it is morally acceptable to commit murder for society's greater good is also central to at least two of Allen's films, *Love and Death* (1975) and *Crimes and Misdemeanors*. While the former is an unmitigated comedy, the latter film treats the issue with almost grim seriousness. This is not to say that Allen offers a sermon. He simply lays the issue out in all its complexity for the audience to ponder. Allen's comic treatment of moral and epistemological questions is not meant to disparage the importance of distinguishing right from wrong, truth from falsehood. Rather, Allen offers an alternative to simplistic solutions and, at the other extreme, pretentious intellectualizing as antidotes for modern despair. That alternative is laughter at oneself and at one's predicament. Perhaps, ultimately, this sort of self-recognition will lead to the answers all people seek.

OTHER MAJOR WORKS

PLAYS: *Don't Drink the Water*, pb. 1966; *Play It Again Sam*, pb. 1969; *The Floating Lightbulb*, pb. 1981.

SCREENPLAYS: *What's New Pussycat?*, 1965; *Take the Money and Run*, 1969 (with Mickey Rose); *Bananas*, 1971; *Everything You Wanted to Know About Sex but Were Afraid to Ask*, 1972 (partly based on David Ruben's book); *Play It Again Sam*, 1972 (screen version of his play); *Sleeper*, 1973 (with Marshall Brickman); *Love and Death*, 1975; *Annie Hall*, 1977; *Interiors*, 1978; *Manhattan*, 1979; *Stardust Memories*, 1980; *A Midsummer Night's Sex Comedy*, 1982; *Zelig*, 1983; *Broadway Danny Rose*, 1984; *The Purple Rose of Cairo*, 1985; *Hannah and Her Sisters*, 1986; *Radio Days*, 1987; *September*, 1987; *Oedipus Wrecks*, 1989 (released as part of a *New York Stories* trilogy along with efforts by two other directors); *Crimes and Misdemeanors*, 1989; *Alice*, 1990; *Shadows and Fog*, 1992; *Husbands and Wives*, 1992; *Manhattan Murder Mystery*, 1993; *Bullets over Broadway*, 1994; *Mighty Aphrodite*, 1995; *Everyone Says I Love You*, 1996; *Deconstructing Harry*, 1997; *Celebrity*, 1998; *Sweet and Lowdown*, 1999.

BIBLIOGRAPHY

Baxter, John. *Woody Allen: A Biography*. London: HarperCollins, 1998. Offers insight into the life of the author-filmmaker.

Davis, Robert Murray. "A Stand-Up Guy Sits Down: Woody Allen's Prose." *Short Story*, n.s. 2 (Fall, 1994): 61-68. Compares Allen's stories with those of Donald Barthelme; provides a reading of Allen's best-known story, "The Kugelmass Episode," in terms of its comic techniques.

De Navacelle, Thierry, *Woody Allen on Location*. New York: William Morrow, 1987; Presents an interesting portrait of Allen at work on the film *Radio Days*. Amply demonstrates both Allen's seriousness as an artist and the lengthy process by which his written work is transferred to the medium of film. Indicates the importance of revision as Allen brings his films to fruition (in contrast to the apparent spontaneity of his short fiction).

Hirsch, Foster. *Love, Sex, Death, and the Meaning of Life*. New York: McGraw-Hill, 1984. Explores the philosophical themes that appear consistently throughout Allen's work. Helps to establish a continuous thread in Allen's prolific career and shows how some of the disturbing questions raised in his short fiction are dealt with in his more fully developed film efforts.

Kakutani, Michiko. "The Art of Humor I: Woody Allen." *The Paris Review* 37 (Fall, 1995): 200-222. In this special issue on humor, Allen is interviewed and discusses how humorists perceive reality, which writers most influenced his writing, which filmmakers most influenced his directing, and how he sees his development since his stand-up comedy days.

Lax, Eric. *On Being Funny: Woody Allen and Comedy*. New York: Charterhouse, 1975. Based on firsthand observations, this book presents a detailed account of Allen's very active professional career as well as some of his more interesting recreational endeavors (such as participation in jazz sessions).

_____. *Woody Allen: A Biography*. New York: Alfred A. Knopf, 1991. In this book, Lax covers Allen's formative years more fully than in his previous book and provides detailed discussion of Allen's career through 1990. Offers insight into Allen's many influences, ranging from Ingmar Bergman to the Marx Brothers.

Pinsker, Sanford. "Comedy and Cultural Timing: The Lessons of Robert Benchly and Woody Allen." *The Georgia Review* 42 (Winter, 1988): 822-837. Illuminating comparison of Allen with an earlier master of the one-liner. (Like Allen, Benchly doubled as a performer and writer.)

_____. "Woody Allen's Lovable Anxious Schlemiels." *Studies in American Humor* 5 (Summer/Fall, 1986): 177-189. Examines Allen's most common character type, particularly in his early films. Provides an interesting contrast with Allen's stories, where the characters very often are not nearly so lovable.

Reisch, Marc S. "Woody Allen: American Prose Humorist." *Journal of Popular Culture* 17 (Winter, 1983): 68-74. Focuses on Allen's talent as a comic writer, sorting out his place in a long line of American humorists.

Ira Smolensky

ISABEL ALLENDE

Born: Lima, Peru; August 2, 1942

PRINCIPAL SHORT FICTION

Cuentos de Eva Luna, 1990 (*The Stories of Eva Luna*, 1991)

OTHER LITERARY FORMS

Isabel Allende has published a number of novels, including *La casa de los espíritus* (1982; *The House of Spirits*, 1985), which established her reputation, *De amor y de sombra* (1984), *Eva Luna* (1987), *El plan infinito* (1991), and *Hija de la fortuna* (1999). She has also published an account of her daughter's death in *Paula* (1994), as well as a collection of children's stories entitled *La gorda de Porcelana* (1984), and a collection of humorous pieces poking fun at machismo, originally published in the magazine *Paula*, entitled *Civilice a su troglodita* (1974).

ACHIEVEMENTS

Isabel Allende has been the recipient of numerous prestigious literary prizes, including the Panorama Literario Novel of the Year (1983), Author of the Year in Germany (1984 and 1986), and the Grand Prix d'Évasion in France (1984), as well as the Colima prize for best novel in Mexico (1985). A 1993 film version of *La casa de los espíritus*, directed by Bille August, was a box-office success.

BIOGRAPHY

Though Chilean by nationality, Isabel Angelica Allende was born in Lima, Peru, on August 2, 1942. The niece of the former Chilean president Salvador Allende, who died in September 1973, during the military coup d'état engineered by Augusto Pinochet, Allende attended a private high school in Santiago, Chile, from which she graduated in 1959. She worked as a secretary at the United Nations Food and Agricultural Organization until 1965. She married Miguel Frías in 1962, had a daughter, Paula, and a son, Miguel. In Santiago, she worked as a journalist, editor, and advice columnist for *Paula* magazine from

1967 to 1974 and as an interviewer for a television station from 1970 to 1975. She was also an administrator for Colegio Marroco, in Caracas, from 1979 to 1982. Isabel divorced her husband in 1987 and married William Gordon in 1988. Her daughter died in 1993, and this event formed the basis of the novel named after her.

ANALYSIS

Isabel Allende's literary career is notable in that it stands outside the shifting fashions of the Latin American literary scene. Since the 1960's in Latin America the literary fashion has tended to favor intricate, self-conscious novels that test the reader's interpretative powers. Flying in the face of this trend, however, Allende's novels favor content over form, reality over novelistic devices. Though her fiction has been dismissed by some critics as simply an imitation of Gabriel García Márquez's work, especially his so-called Magical Realist style, it is clear that Allende enjoys unparalleled popularity. Her novels and short stories have attracted an enormous readership in Spanish as well as languages such as English, French, and German. Allende tends to write plot-centered, reader-friendly fiction. Her stories often focus on love and sex as seen from a feminine perspective.

THE STORIES OF EVA LUNA

The short-story collection *The Stories of Eva Luna* is essentially a sequel to her novel *Eva Luna* (1987), published three years earlier; thus the narrator of *The Stories of Eva Luna* is the Eva Luna who appeared in the earlier novel, that is, a resourceful, bright young woman who, though born to poverty, rises to riches as a result of becoming a famous soap-opera writer. Two of the stories provide a direct link to *Eva Luna* the novel. "El huésped de la maestra," for example, finishes a story that was left unresolved in the novel. The novel describes how Inés, the schoolmistress of Santa Agua, saw her son brutally murdered at the hands of a local man, who caught him stealing mangoes in the garden. Riad Halabí, by an ingenious

Isabel Allende (©Miriam Berkley)

There are twenty-three short stories in *The Stories of Eva Luna* and only two of them, as described above, use the same characters that the novels do. In other words, above all, they are new stories that Eva Luna has invented for the enjoyment of her lover, Rolf Carlé. The overriding structure is provided by the theme of *Alf layla wa-layla* (fifteenth century; *The Arabian Nights' Entertainments*, 1706-1708) in which the female narrator, Scherezade, must tell a story each night in order to avoid being executed by the king. The collection of short stories opens, indeed, with Rolf Carlé asking the narrator, who, though unnamed, is obviously Eva Luna, to tell him a story that has never been told to anyone else. The first story, "Dos palabras," explores the same theme. Here the protagonist, Belisa Crepusculario, wrote a speech for a man who wanted to become president; and she also gave him two secret words. The speech was an enormous success, but the Colonel soon discovers that he is fatally attracted to Belisa as a result of the linguistic spell she has cast over him.

There are a number of themes that run through the stories. The most obvious one is that of sexuality and love, which forms the focus for nineteen out of the twenty-three stories in the collection. Love is often presented as occurring purely through chance. In "Tosca," for example, a love relationship begins in this short story as a result of the apparently insignificant fact that Leonardo is seen by Laurizia reading the score of the work *Tosca* by the famous Italian composer Giacomo Puccini. From this chance encounter a passionate affair develops. Of the nineteen stories that focus on love and sexuality, ten focus on illicit sex. A good example is "Si me tocaras el corazón," which tells the story of Amadeo Peralta, who, while on a visit to Santa Agua, seduces a fifteen-year-old girl called Hortensia; when he tires of her, he decides to lock her up permanently in the basement of a sugar refinery. Years later, some chil-

plan, managed to force the murderer to leave town. In the short story, the reader learns that the murderer returns many years later to Santa Agua and is then killed by Inés in an act of revenge; much of the short story is taken up by a description of the ingenious way in which Halabí disposes of the body. Also related to the novel is the short story "De barro estamos hechos." The novel introduces the reader to Rolf Carlé, a cameraman, who eventually becomes Eva's companion. Here the reader sees firsthand his experience of the floods that ravaged the country and that caused a young girl called Azucena to die slowly and painfully, even while he was filming her. The short story focuses on how this experience has changed Rolf's life. These two short stories can be seen as sequels to Allende's long fiction and show continuity of theme and character.

dren hear monstrous noises coming from the basement, and Hortensia is discovered, diseased and at the brink of death, which leads to Amadeo's discomfiture. The moral of this short story seems to be that unbridled sexual passion can have disastrous consequences. Some of the stories, such as "Boca de sapo," "María, la boba," and "Walimai," explicitly allude to prostitution.

Other themes covered in the stories include vengeance, as in "Una venganza," in which revenge for rape is enacted on the rapist; the clash between cultures, as in "Walamai," which describes the struggles between the tribe of the Sons of the Moon and the white man, told from an Indian perspective; the miracle, as in "Un discreto milagro," which tells how Miguel, a priest, has his sight restored by a local saint, Juana de los Lirios; as well as predestination, as in "La mujer del juez," a well-written, suspense story which focuses on the protagonists, Nicolás Vidal and Casilda Hidalgo, who conduct an illicit affair even though they know beforehand that it will lead to their deaths. One particularly powerful story, "Un camino hacia el norte," contains a strong social critique. It describes how Claveles Picero, and her grandfather, Jesús Dionisio Picero, are tricked into giving up Claveles's illegitimate son Juan to a United States adoption agency, which is later discovered to be a front for a contraband agency which sells human organs. The story ends with a description of their journey to the capital in an attempt to discover Juan's fate; they, like the reader, fear the worst. The message is that poverty leads to exploitation and death.

A common technique in the stories involves the story opening with a scene (whose import is not understood) and then cutting to the past, at which point the narrative of the lives of the main protagonists is told. This occurs in a number of stories, including "El camino hacia el norte" and "El huésped de la maestra." Most of the stories are told in the third person, although some, such as "Walimai," are told in the first person.

OTHER MAJOR WORKS

LONG FICTION: *La casa de los espíritus*, 1982 (*The House of the Spirits*, 1985); *De amor y de sombra*,

1984 (*Of Love and Shadows*, 1987); *Eva Luna*, 1987 (English translation, 1988); *El plan infinito*, 1991 (*The Infinite Plan*, 1993); *Afrodita: Cuentos, Recetas y Otros Afrodisiacos*, 1997 (*Aphrodite: A Memoir of the Senses*, 1999); *Hija de la fortuna*, 1999 (*Daughter of Fortune*, 1999).

NONFICTION: *Civilice a su troglodita*, 1974; *Paula*, 1994 (English translation, 1995).

CHILDREN'S LITERATURE: *La gorda de Porcelana*, 1984.

BIBLIOGRAPHY

De Carvalho, Susan. "The Male Narrative Perspective in the Fiction of Isabel Allende." *Journal of Hispanic Research* 2, no. 2 (Spring, 1994): 269-278. Shows that "Walimai" is different from the other short stories in *Los cuentos de Eva Luna* in that it is written in the first person and from a male perspective. Argues that the first-person, male perspective in this story represents the ideal narrative voice.

García Pinto, Magdalena, ed. *Women Writers of Latin America: Intimate Histories*. Austin: University of Texas Press, 1991. Contains an excellent interview with Allende with a great deal of insight into the way she views her writing. It is here that Allende mentions that she sees herself as a troubadour going from village to village, person to person, talking about her country.

Hart, Patricia. *Narrative Magic in the Fiction of Isabel Allende*. Toronto: Associated University Presses, 1989. A good overview of Allende's fiction up to 1987; it has a chapter on Magical Realism and a clearly-written, helpful section on the novel *Eva Luna*, which is useful background for the analysis of the short stories. Argues that Allende parodies rather than imitates García Márquez.

Hart, Stephen M. *White Ink: Essays on Twentieth-Century Feminine Fiction in Spain and Latin America*. London: Tamesis, 1993. Sets Allende's work within the context of women's writing in the twentieth century in Latin America. Examines the ways in which Allende fuses the space of the personal with that of the political in her fiction and shows that, in her work, falling in love with another human being is often aligned with falling in love with a political cause.

Swanson, Philip. *The New Novel in Latin America: Politics and Popular Culture after the Boom.* Manchester: Manchester University Press, 1995. Chapter 9 contains a discussion of the use of popular culture in Allende's fiction, showing that the people and popular culture are seen to challenge official culture and patriarchy in her work. Also has a good introduction which sets Allende's work in the context of other postboom novelists of Latin America.

Williams, Raymond L. *The Postmodern Novel in Latin America: Poltics, Culture, and the Crisis of Truth.* New York: St Martin's Press, 1996. One of Allende's most vigorous critics, who argues that Allende's fiction simply imitates García Márquez's and that it is not postmodern in any real sense.

Stephen M. Hart

HANS CHRISTIAN ANDERSEN

Born: Odense, Denmark; April 2, 1805
Died: Rolighed, near Copenhagen, Denmark; August 4, 1875

PRINCIPAL SHORT FICTION

Eventyr, 1835-1872 (*The Complete Andersen,* 1949; also *Fairy Tales,* 1950-1958; also *The Complete Fairy Tales and Stories,* 1974)
It's Perfectly True and Other Stories, 1937
Andersen's Fairy Tales, 1946
Hans Andersen's Fairy Tales, 1953

OTHER LITERARY FORMS

Hans Christian Andersen's first publication was a poem in 1828, and his first prose work, a fantasy of a nightly journey titled *Fodreise fra Holmens Canal til Østpynten af Amager* (1829; a journey on foot from Holman's canal to the east point of Amager), was an immediate success. He wrote six novels, of which *Improvisatoren* (1835; *The Improvisatore,* 1845) securely established his fame. His nine travel books began with *En digters bazar* (1842; *A Poet's Bazaar,* 1846) and mainly concern his European travels. Other works are *Billebog uden billeder* (1840; *Tales the Moon Can Tell,* 1855) and *I Sverrig* (1851; *In Sweden,* 1852). His autobiographies are *Levnedsbogen, 1805-1831* (1926; *Diaries of Hans Christian Andersen,* 1990), discovered fifty years after his death; *Mit Livs Eventyr* (1847; *The Story of My Life,* 1852); and the revised *The Fairy Tale of My Life* (1855). Other publications include his correspondence, diaries, notebooks and draft material, drawings, sketches, paper cuttings, and plays.

ACHIEVEMENTS

Although hailed as the greatest of all fairy-tale writers in any language, throughout most of his life, Hans Christian Andersen considered his fairy tales to be of far less importance than his other writings. He considered himself much more of a novelist, playwright, and writer of travel books. It was his fairy tales, however, that spread his fame across Europe and, immediately upon publication, were translated into every European language. Andersen was much more famous, courted, and honored abroad than in his native Denmark. In his later years, however, his compatriots did at last recognize Andersen's greatness. He became a friend and guest to royalty, was made a state councillor, and had a touching tribute paid to him in the form of the statue of the Little Mermaid, which sits in the Copenhagen harbor.

BIOGRAPHY

The son of a shoemaker, who died when he was eleven, and an illiterate servant mother, Hans Christian Andersen from his early childhood loved to invent tales, poems, and plays and to make intricate paper cuttings; he loved to recite his creations to any possible listener. Later he yearned to be a creative writer of divine inspiration and an actor. In 1819 he journeyed to Copenhagen where he lived through hard times but developed a talent for attracting benefactors. Among them was Jonas Collin, whose home became Andersen's "Home of Homes," as he called it, who acted as a foster father, and whose son Edvard became a close friend. Through Jonas's influence and a grant from the king, Andersen attended grammar school (1822-1827) and struggled with a difficult headmaster as well as with Latin and Greek. Andersen never married, although he was attracted to several women, among them the singer Jenny Lind. Although he was very tall and ungainly in appearance, with large feet, a large nose, and small eyes, and although he was sentimental and exceptionally concerned with himself, his fears and doubts, Andersen enjoyed the company of Europe's leading professionals

Hans Christian Anderson (Library of Congress)

and nobility, including kings and queens; in later life many honors were bestowed on him. His last nine years he lived at the home of the Moritz Melchiors, just outside Copenhagen, and he died there on August 4, 1875.

ANALYSIS

Following publication of his 1844 collection of tales, Hans Christian Andersen explained in a letter that he wanted his tales to be read on two levels, offering something for the minds of adults as well as appealing to children. Three examples of such adult tales, "The Snow Queen," "The Shadow," and "The Nightingale," demonstrate how, as Andersen said, in writing from his own breast instead of retelling old tales he had found out how to write fairy tales.

"THE SNOW QUEEN"

Comprising seven stories, "The Snow Queen" begins with a mirror into which people can look and see the good become small and mean and the bad appear at its very worst. Andersen could remember, in later years, that his father had maintained that "There is no other devil than the one we have in our hearts"; and this provides a clue to the plot and theme of "The Snow Queen." Only when the demon's followers confront heaven with the mirror does it shatter into fragments, but unfortunately those fragments enter the hearts of many people.

The second story introduces Little Kay and Gerda, who love each other and the summer's flowers until a fragment of the evil mirror lodges in Little Kay's eye and another pierces his heart. Having formerly declared that if the Snow Queen visited he would melt her on the stove, Kay now views snowflakes through a magnifying glass and pronounces them more beautiful than flowers. He protests against the grandmother's tales with a *but* for the logic of each one, and, apparently arrived at adolescence, transfers loyalty from the innocent Gerda to the knowing Snow Queen. He follows the visiting Queen out of town and into the snowy expanses of the distant sky.

The journey from adolescence to maturity becomes for Gerda her quest for the missing Kay, her true love and future mate. Fearing the river has taken Kay, she offers it her new red shoes; but a boat she steps into drifts away from shore, and, riding the river's current, she travels far before being pulled ashore and detained by a woman "learned in magic." Gerda here forgets her search for Kay until the sight of a rose reminds her. In one of the story's most abstract passages, she then asks the tiger lilies, convolvulus, snowdrop, hyacinth, buttercup, and narcissus where he might be; but each tells a highly fanciful tale concerned with its own identity. The narcissus, for example, alludes to the Echo and Narcissus myth in saying "I can see myself" and fails to aid Gerda. Barefoot, Gerda runs out of the garden and finds that autumn has arrived.

A crow believes he has seen Kay and contrives a visit with the Prince and Princess, who forgive the invasion of their palatial privacy and then outfit Gerda to continue her search. All her newly acquired equipage attracts a "little robber girl," a perplexing mixture of amorality and good intentions, who threatens Gerda with her knife but provides a reindeer to carry Gerda to Spitsbergen, where the wood pigeons have reported having seen Kay. At one stop, the reindeer begs a Finnish wise woman to give Gerda the strength to conquer all, but the woman points out the great power that Gerda has already evidenced and adds, "We must not tell her what power she has. It is

in her heart, because she is such a sweet innocent child." She sends Gerda and the reindeer on their way, with Gerda riding without boots or mittens. Eventually the reindeer deposits her by a red-berry bush in freezing icebound Denmark, from which she walks to the Snow Queen's Palace.

Here she finds a second mirror, a frozen lake broken into fragments that is actually the throne of the Snow Queen; the Queen calls it "The Mirror of Reason." Little Kay works diligently to form the fragments into the word "Eternity," for which accomplishment the Snow Queen has said he can be his own master and have the whole world and a new pair of skates. Gerda's love, when she sheds tears of joy at finding Kay, melts the ice in his heart and the mirror within his breast; and Kay, himself bursting into tears at recovering Gerda and her love, finds that the fragments magically form themselves into the word "Eternity." The two young people find many changes on their return journey but much the same at home, where they now realize they are grown up. The grandmother's Bible verse tells them about the kingdom of heaven for those with hearts of children, and they now understand the meaning of the hymn, "Where roses deck the flowery vale,/ There Infant Jesus, thee we hail!" The flowers of love, not the mirror of reason, make Kay and Gerda inheritors of the kingdom of heaven, the Snow Queen's elusive eternity.

Only the style makes such stories children's stories, for "The Snow Queen," with devices such as the snowflakes seen under a microscope, obviously attacks empiricism; at the same time, the story offers the symbol of the foot, important to folklore, and the journey of Gerda through obstacles and a final illumination constitutes a "journey of the hero" as delineated by the mythologist Joseph Campbell. So also Andersen's "The Shadow" presents an alter-ego with psychic dimensions well beyond the ken of children.

"THE SHADOW"

The setting with which "The Shadow" begins reflects Andersen's diary entries from his trip to Naples in June, 1846, when he found the sun too hot for venturing out of doors and began writing the story. With the hot sun directly overhead, the shadow disappears except in morning and evening and begins to assume a life of its own. Its activities, closely observed by its owner, the "learned man from a cold country," leads him to joke about its going into the house opposite to learn the identity of a lovely maiden. The shadow fails to return, but the learned man soon grows a new shadow. Many years later, once more at home, the original shadow visits him but has now become so corporeal that it has acquired flesh and clothes. Further, it divulges, it has become wealthy and plans to marry. Its three-week visit in the house opposite, it now reveals, placed it close to the lovely maiden Poetry, in whose anteroom the shadow read all the poetry and prose ever written. If the learned man had been there, he would not have remained a human being, but it was there that the shadow became one. Emerging thence he went about under the cover of a pastry cook's gown for some time before growing into his present affluence.

Later, the learned man's writing of the good, the true, and the beautiful fail to provide him an income; only after he has suffered long and become so thin that people tell him he looks like a shadow does he accede to the shadow's request that he become a traveling companion. Shadow and master have now exchanged places, but the king's daughter notices that the new master cannot cast a shadow. To this accusation he replies that the person who is always at his side is his shadow. When the new master cannot answer her scientific inquiries, he defers to the shadow, whose knowledge impresses the princess. Clearly, she reasons, to have such a learned servant the master must be the most learned man on earth.

Against the upcoming marriage of princess and shadow, the learned man protests and threatens to reveal the truth. "Not a soul would believe you," says the shadow, and with his new status as fiancé he has the learned man cast into prison. The princess agrees that it would be a charity to deliver the learned man from his delusions and has him promptly executed.

That Poetry would make a human being divine or "more than human" gives Poetry the identity of Psyche, whose statue by Thorvaldsen Andersen had ad-

mired in 1833 in the Danish sculptor's studio. (Also, Andersen in 1861 wrote a story called "The Psyche.") In "The Shadow," the human qualities with which Poetry's presence infuses the shadow function for him as a soul. Thereafter, his incubation under the pastry cook's gown provides him a proper maturation from which, still as shadow, he looks into people's lives, spies on their evils and their intimacies, and acquires power over them. This phase of his existence explains the acquisition of wealth, but as the shadow grows human and powerful the learned man declines.

The shadow, the other self of the learned man, reflects the psychic stress Andersen suffered in his relationship with Edvard Collin. What Andersen desired between himself and Collin has been recognized by scholars as the *Blütbruderschaft* that D. H. Lawrence wrote about—a close relationship with another male. Collin persisted, however, in fending off all Andersen's attempts at informality, even in regard to the use of language. In the story the shadow is obviously Collin, whose separate identity thrives at the expense of the learned man's—Andersen's—psyche. Writing in his diary of the distress and illness brought on by a letter from Edvard Collin, Andersen contemplated suicide and pleaded "he must use the language of a friend" (1834); so also the story's shadow rejects such language and commits the learned man to prison and to death. The problem of language appears twice in the story, although various translations diminish its effect. On the shadow's first visit to his former master, his newly acquired affluence provides him with the daring to suggest that the learned man speak "less familiarly" and to say "sir" or—in other translations—to replace "you" with "thee" and "thou." Frequently argued between Andersen and Collin as the question of *Du* versus *De,* the problem reappears in the story when the learned man asks the shadow, because of their childhood together, to pledge themselves to address each other as *Du.* (In some translations, this reads merely "to drink to our good fellowship" and "call each other by our names.") In the shadow's reply, Andersen improved on Collin's objection by having the shadow cite the feel of gray paper or the scraping of a nail on a pane of glass as similar to the sound of *Du* spoken by the learned man.

"THE EMPEROR'S NEW CLOTHES"

Such touches of individuality made Andersen's writing succeed, as evidenced by a tale he borrowed from a Spanish source, the tale of "The Emperor's New Clothes," which he said he read in a German translation from Prince don Juan Manuel. Andersen's version improved on the original in several respects, including his theme of pretense of understanding as well as ridicule of snobbery and his ending with the objection of the child—an ending which Andersen added after the original manuscript had been sent to the publisher.

Andersen's talent for universalizing the appeal of a story and for capitalizing on personal experiences appears time and again throughout his many tales. Because of his grotesque appearance, which interfered with his longed-for stage career, Andersen knew personally the anguish of "The Ugly Duckling," but his success as a writer made him a beautiful swan. His extreme sensitivity he wrote into "The Princess and the Pea," detailing the adventures of a princess who could feel a pea through twenty mattresses. Andersen in this story borrowed from a folktale in which the little girl understands the test she is being put to because a dog or cat aids her by relaying the information; however, Andersen contrived that her sensitivity alone would suffice. Nevertheless, some translators could not accept the idea of her feeling a single pea and changed the text to read three peas and the title to read "The Real Princess."

Andersen's stories thus objectify psychic conditions, and among these his frequent association with nobility enabled him to depict with humor the qualities of egotism, arrogance, and subservience found at court. In "The Snow Queen" the crow describes court ladies and attendants standing around; the nearer the door they stand the greater is their haughtiness. The footman's boy is too proud to be looked at. The princess is so clever she has read all the newspapers in the world and forgotten them again.

"THE NIGHTINGALE"

One of Andersen's best depictions of court life and, at the same time, one of his best satires is "The Nightingale," which he wrote in honor of Jenny Lind, the singer known as the Swedish Nightingale. The story's theme contrasts the artificial manners and preferences of the court with the natural song of the nightingale and the ways of simple folk. Far from the palace of the Emperor of China where bells on the flowers in the garden tinkle to attract attention to the flowers, the nightingale sings in the woods by the deep sea, so that a poor fisherman listens to it each day and travelers returning home write about it. The Emperor discovers this nightingale from reading about it in a book, but his gentleman-in-waiting knows nothing about it because it has never been presented at court. Inquiring throughout the court, he finds only a little girl in the kitchen who has heard it and who helps him find it. Brought to the court, it must sing on a golden perch, and, when acclaimed successful, it has its own cage and can walk out twice a day and once in the night with twelve footmen, each one holding a ribbon tied around its leg.

When the Emperor of Japan sends as a gift an artificial nightingale studded with diamonds, rubies, and sapphires, the two birds cannot sing together, and the real nightingale flies away in chagrin. The court throng honors the mechanical bird with jewels and gold as gifts, and the Master of Music writes twenty-five volumes about it. The mechanical bird earns the title of Chief Imperial Singer-of-the-Bed-Chamber, and in rank it stands number one on the left side, for even an Emperor's heart is on the left side.

Eventually the mechanical bird breaks down, and the watchmaker cannot assure repair with the same admirable tune. Five years later the Emperor becomes ill, and his successor is proclaimed. Then, with Death sitting on his chest and wearing his golden crown, he calls on the mechanical bird to sing. While it sits mute, the nightingale appears at the window and sings Death away and brings new life to the Emperor. With the generosity of a true heroine, it advises the king not to destroy the mechanical bird, which did all the good it could; however, it reminds the Emperor, a little singing bird sings to the fisherman and the peasant and must continue to go and to return. Although it loves the Emperor's heart more than his crown, the crown has an odor of sanctity also. The nightingale will return, but the Emperor must keep its secret that a little bird tells him everything.

Andersen's comment comparing the heart and the crown of the emperor may be his finest on the attraction of the great, an attraction which he felt all his life. Early in 1874, after visiting a count in South Zealand, he wrote to Mrs. Melchior that no fairy tales occurred to him any more. If he walks in the garden, he said, Thumbelina has ended her journey on the water lily; the wind and the Old Oak Tree have already told him their tales and have nothing more to tell him. It is, he wrote, as if he had filled out the entire circle with fairy-tale radii close to one another. On his seventieth birthday, April 2, 1875, the royal carriage was sent to fetch him to the castle, and the king bestowed another decoration. It was his last birthday celebration, for in a few months Andersen had filled out the circle of his life.

OTHER MAJOR WORKS

LONG FICTION: *Improvisatoren*, 1835 (2 volumes; *The Improvisatore*, 1845); *O. T.*, 1836 (English translation, 1845); *Kun en Spillemand*, 1837 (*Only a Fiddler*, 1845); *De To Baronesser*, 1848 (*The Two Baronesses*, 1848); *At være eller ikke være*, 1857 (*To Be or Not to Be*, 1857); *Lykke-Peer*, 1870 (*Lucky Peer*, 1871).

PLAYS: *Kjærlighed paa Nicolai Taarn: Elle, Hvad siger Parterret*, pr. 1829; *Agnete og havmanden*, pr. 1833; *Mulatten*, pr. 1840.

POETRY: *Digte*, 1830.

NONFICTION: *Fodreise fra Holmens Canal til Østpynten af Amager*, 1829; *Skyggebilleder af en reise til Harzen, det sachiske Schweitz*, 1831 (*Rambles in the Romantic Regions of the Hartz Mountains, Saxon Switzerland etc.*, 1848); *Billebog unden billeder*, 1840 (*Tales the Moon Can Tell*, 1855); *En digters bazar*, 1842 (*A Poet's Bazaar*, 1846); *Mit Livs Eventyr*, 1847 (*The Story of My Life*, 1852); *I Sverrig*, 1851 (*In Sweden*, 1852); *The Fairy Tale of My Life*, 1855; *I Spanien*, 1863 (*In Spain*, 1864); *Et besøg i Portugal*, 1866 (*A Visit to Portugal*, 1870); *Levnedsbogen, 1805-1831*, 1926 (*Diaries of Hans Christian Andersen*, 1990).

MISCELLANEOUS: *The Collected Works of Hans Christian Andersen*, 1870-1884 (10 volumes).

BIBLIOGRAPHY

Book, Frederik. *Hans Christian Andersen*. Norman: University of Oklahoma Press, 1962. This biography studies Andersen's personal and literary history. It considers how psychiatry, folklore, and the history of religion affected Andersen's life. Andersen's autobiographies are examined in the light of what was real and what was the fairy tale he was creating about his life. Contains illustrations of his fairy tales and photographs.

Bresdorff, Elias. *Hans Christian Andersen: The Story of His Life and Work, 1805-1875*. New York: Noonday Press, 1994. This book is divided in two sections: The first part is a biographical study of Andersen's complex personality; the second is a critical study of his most famous fairy tales and stories.

Conroy, Patricia L., ed. *The Diaries of Hans Christian Andersen*. Seattle: University of Washington Press, 1990. A wide selection of excerpts from Andersen's diaries written from as early as when he was a schoolboy and throughout the artist's life. Complete diaries from two trips to England are translated in entirety. Includes illustrations of his drawings and paper cuttings, plus a useful bibliography.

Dollerup, Cay. "Translation as a Creative Force in Literature: The Birth of the European Bourgeois Fairy-Tale." *The Modern Language Review* 90 (January, 1995): 94-102. Discusses the European bourgeois fairy tale's development as the result of translation of the stories of the brothers Grimm into Danish and the stories of Hans Christian Andersen into German because children would not be familiar with foreign languages. Argues that the Grimms and Andersen were adapted to European middle-class values.

Johansen, Jorgen Dines. "The Merciless Tragedy of Desire: An Interpretation of H. C. Andersen's *Den lille Havfrue*." *Scandinavian Studies* 68 (Spring, 1996): 203-241. Provides a psychoanalytic interpretation of "The Little Mermaid," focusing on the tension between earthly love and religious reparation in the story. Discusses the themes of love and salvation in an extensive analysis of love and sexuality in the tale.

Nassaar, Christopher S. "Andersen's 'The Shadow' and Wilde's 'The Fisherman and His Soul': A Case of Influence." *Nineteenth-Century Literature* 50 (September, 1995): 217-224. Argues that Oscar Wilde's tale is a Christian response to Andersen's nihilistic tale. Claims that, while Andersen's tale is about the triumph of evil, Wilde's story is about the triumph of Christian love.

_____. "Andersen's 'The Ugly Ducking' and Wilde's 'The Birthday of the Infanta.'" *The Explicator* 55 (Winter, 1997): 83-85. Discusses the influence of Andersen's "The Ugly Duckling" on Wilde's story. Argues that, in spite of the surface differences, Wilde's story is a direct reversal of Andersen's.

Spink, Reginald. *Hans Christian Andersen and His World*. New York: G. P. Putnam's Sons, 1972. An excellent overview of Andersen's life. Emphasizes how his background and childhood affected his art. Extensively illustrated with photographs, drawings, and reprints of the illustrated fairy tales in several foreign-language editions.

Toksvig, Signe. *The Life of Hans Christian Andersen*. New York: Harcourt, Brace, 1934. An in-depth biography that provides valuable information in spite of its early publication date. Illustrated.

Grace Eckley, updated by Leslie A. Pearl

SHERWOOD ANDERSON

Born: Camden, Ohio; September 13, 1876
Died: Colón, Panama Canal Zone; March 8, 1941

PRINCIPAL SHORT FICTION
Winesburg, Ohio, 1919
The Triumph of the Egg, 1921
Horses and Men, 1923
Death in the Woods and Other Stories, 1933
The Sherwood Anderson Reader, 1947

OTHER LITERARY FORMS

Sherwood Anderson published seven novels, collections of essays, memoirs, poetry, and dramatizations of *Winesburg, Ohio*, as well as other stories. He was a prolific article writer and for a time owned and edited both the Republican and Democratic newspapers in Marion, Virginia. In 1921, he received a two-thousand-dollar literary prize from *The Dial* magazine. While employed as a copywriter, Anderson wrote many successful advertisements.

ACHIEVEMENTS

Sherwood Anderson, a protomodernist, is generally accepted as an innovator in the field of the short story despite having produced only one masterpiece, *Winesburg, Ohio*. In his work, he not only revolutionized the structure of short fiction by resisting the literary slickness of the contrived plot but also encouraged a simple and direct prose style, one which reflects the spare poetry of ordinary American speech. Anderson's thematic concerns were also innovative. He was one of the first writers to dramatize the artistic repudiation of the business world and to give the craft of the short story a decided push toward presenting a slice of life as a significant moment. His concern with the "grotesques" in society—the neurotics and eccentrics—is also innovative as is the straightforward attention he pays to his characters' sexuality. Anderson's contemporaries Ernest Hemingway, William Faulkner, and John Steinbeck were influenced by his work, as were several later writers: Carson McCullers, Flannery O'Connor, Saul Bellow, Bobbie Ann Mason, and Raymond Carver.

BIOGRAPHY

Sherwood Anderson was the third of seven children of a father who was an itinerant harness maker, house painter and a mother of either German or Italian descent. His father was a Civil War veteran (a Southerner who fought with the Union), locally famed as a storyteller. His elder brother, Karl, became a prominent painter who later introduced Sherwood to Chicago's Bohemia, which gained him access to the literary world. Declining fortunes caused the family to move repeatedly until they settled in Clyde, Ohio (the model for Winesburg), a village just south of Lake Erie. The young Anderson experienced a desultory schooling and worked at several jobs: as a newsboy, a housepainter, a stableboy, a farmhand, and a laborer in a bicycle factory.

After serving in Cuba during the Spanish-American War (he saw no combat), he acquired a further year of schooling at Wittenberg Academy in Springfield, Ohio, but remained undereducated throughout his life. Jobs as advertising copywriter gave him a first taste of writing, and he went on to a successful business career. In 1912, the central psychological event of his life occurred. He suffered a nervous breakdown, which led him to walk out of his paint factory in Elyria, Ohio. He moved

Sherwood Anderson (Library of Congress)

to Chicago, where he began to meet writers such as Floyd Dell, Carl Sandburg, and Ben Hecht, a group collectively known as the Chicago Renaissance. A significant nonliterary contact was Dr. Trigant Burrow of Baltimore, who operated a Freudian therapeutic camp in Lake Chateaugay, New York, during the summers of 1915 and 1916. It should be noted, however, that Anderson ultimately rejected scientific probing of the psyche, for he typically believed that the human mind is static and incapable of meaningful change for the better. Publication of *Winesburg, Ohio* catapulted him into prominence, and he traveled to Europe in 1921, where he became acquainted with Gertrude Stein, Ernest Hemingway, and James Joyce. In 1923, while living in New Orleans, he shared an apartment with William Faulkner.

Anderson married and divorced four times. He and his first wife had three children. His second wife, Tennessee Mitchell, had been a lover to Edgar Lee Masters, author of the *Spoon River Anthology* (1915). His last wife, Eleanor Copenhaver, had an interest in the southern labor movement, which drew Anderson somewhat out of his social primitivism, and, for a time in the 1930's, he became a favorite of communists and socialists. His death, in Colón, Panama Canal Zone, while on a voyage to South America, was notable for its unique circumstances: He died of peritonitis caused by a toothpick accidentally swallowed while eating hors d'œuvres.

ANALYSIS

Sherwood Anderson's best-known and most important work is the American classic, *Winesburg, Ohio*. It is a collection of associated short stories set in the mythical town of Winesburg in the latter part of the nineteenth century. The stories catalog Anderson's negative reaction to the transformation of Ohio from a largely agricultural to an industrial society, which culminated about the time he was growing up in the village of Clyde in the 1880's. Its twenty-five stories are vignettes of the town doctor; the voluble baseball coach; the still attractive but aging-with-loneliness high school teacher; the prosperous and harsh farmer-turned-religious fanatic; the dirt laborer; the hotel keeper, the banker's daughter, and her adolescent suitors; the Presbyterian minister struggling with temptation; the town drunk; the town rough; the town homosexual; and the town "half-wit." The comparison to Masters's *Spoon River Anthology* is obvious: Both works purport to reveal the secret lives of small-town Americans living in the Middle West, and ironically both owe their popular success to the elegiac recording of this era, which most Americans insist on viewing idyllically. Anderson's work, however, differs by more directly relating sexuality to the bizarre behavior of many of his characters and by employing a coherent theme.

That theme is an exploration of psychological "grotesques"—the casualties of economic progress—and how these grotesques participate in the maturing of George Willard, the teenage reporter for the *Winesburg Eagle*, who at the end of the book departs for a bigger city to become a journalist. By then his sometimes callous ambition to get ahead has been tempered by a sense of what Anderson chooses to call "sophistication," the title of the penultimate story. The achievement of George's sophistication gives *Winesburg, Ohio* its artistic movement but makes it problematic for many critics and thoughtful Americans.

"The Book of the Grotesque"

The prefacing story defines grotesques. A dying old writer hires a carpenter to build up his bed so that he can observe the trees outside without getting out of it. (While living in Chicago in 1915 Anderson had his own bed similarly raised so that he could observe the Loop.) After the carpenter leaves, the writer returns to his project—the writing of "The Book of the Grotesque," which grieves over the notion that in the beginning of the world there were a great many

thoughts but no such thing as a "truth." People turned these thoughts into many beautiful truths such as the truth of passion, wealth, poverty, profligacy, carelessness, and others; a person could then appropriate a single one of these truths and try to live by it. It was thus that he or she would become a grotesque—a personality dominated by an overriding concern which in time squeezed out other facets of life.

This epistemological fable, which involves a triple-reduction, raises at least two invalidating questions: First, Can there be "thoughts" without the truth to establish the self-differentiating process which generates thought?, and second, If universals are denied and all truths have equal value (they are *all* beautiful), then why should a person be condemned for choosing only one of these pluralistic "truths"?

"Hands"

The stories in *Winesburg, Ohio* nevertheless do grapple with Anderson's intended theme, and a story such as "Hands" clearly illustrates what he means by a grotesque. The hands belong to Wing Biddlebaum, formerly Adolph Myers, a teacher in a Pennsylvania village who was beaten and run out of town for caressing boys. Anderson is delicately oblique about Wing's homosexuality, for the story focuses on how a single traumatic event can forever after rule a person's life—Wing is now a fretful recluse whose only human contact occurs when George Willard visits him occasionally. George puzzles over Wing's expressive hands but never fathoms the reason for his suffering diffidence. "Hands," besides giving first flesh to the word grotesque, makes the reader understand that a character's volition is not necessarily the factor that traps him into such an ideological straightjacket; sympathy can therefore be more readily extended.

"The Philosopher"

"The Philosopher" provides a more subtle illustration of a grotesque and introduces the idea that a grotesque need not be pitiable or tragic; in fact, he can be wildly humorous, as demonstrated at the beginning of the story with the philosopher's description:

Doctor Parcival, the philosopher, was a large man with a drooping mouth covered by a yellow moustache . . .

he wore a dirty white waistcoat out of whose pocket protruded a number of black cigars . . . there was something strange about his eyes: the lid of his left eye twitched; it fell down and it snapped up; it was exactly as though the lid of the eye were a window shade and someone stood inside playing with the cord.

It is George Willard's misfortune that Dr. Parcival likes him and uses him as a sounding board for his wacky pomposity. He wishes to convince the boy of the advisability of adopting a line of conduct that he himself is unable to define but amply illustrates with many "parables" which add up to the belief (as George begins to suspect) that all men are despicable. He tells George that his father died in an insane asylum, and then he continues on about a Dr. Cronin from Chicago who may have been murdered by several men, one of whom could have been yours truly, Dr. Parcival. He announces that he actually arrived in Winesburg to write a book. About to launch on the subject of the book, he is sidetracked into the story of his brother who worked for the railroad as part of a roving paint crew (which painted everything orange); on payday the brother would place his money on the kitchen table—daring any member of the family to touch it. The brother, while drunk, is run over by the rail car housing the other members of his crew.

One day George drops into Dr. Parcival's office for his customary morning visit and discovers him quaking with fear. Earlier a little girl had been thrown from her buggy, and the doctor had inexplicably refused to heed a passerby's call (perhaps because he is not a medical doctor). Other doctors, however, arrived on the scene, and no one noticed Dr. Parcival's absence. Not realizing this, the doctor shouts to George that he knows human nature and that soon a hanging party will be formed to hang him from a lamppost as punishment for his callous refusal to attend to the dying child. When his certainty dissipates, he whimpers to George, "If not now, sometime." He begs George to take him seriously and asks him to finish his book if something should happen to him; to this end he informs George of the subject of the book, which is: Everyone in the

world is Christ, and they are all crucified.

Many critics have singled out one or another story as the best in *Winesburg, Ohio*; frequently mentioned are "The Untold Lie," "Hands," and "Sophistication." However, aside from the fact that this may be an unfair exercise—because the stories in *Winesburg, Ohio* were written to stand together—these choices bring out the accusation that much of Anderson's work has a "setup" quality—a facile solemnity which makes his fictions manifest. "The Philosopher" may be the best story because Dr. Parcival's grotesqueness eludes overt labeling; its finely timed humor reveals Anderson's ability to spoof his literary weaknesses, and the story captures one of those character types who, like Joe Welling of "A Man of Ideas," is readily observable and remembered but proves irritatingly elusive when set down.

"GODLINESS"

Anderson exhibits a particular interest in the distorting effect that religious mania has on the personality, and several stories in *Winesburg, Ohio* attack or ridicule examples of conspicuous religiosity. "Godliness," a tetralogy with a gothic flavor, follows the life of Jesse Bentley, a wealthy, progressive farmer who poisons the life of several generations of his relatives with his relentless harshness until he becomes inflamed by Old Testament stories and conceives the idea of replicating an act of animal sacrifice. Because of this behavior, he succeeds in terrifying his fifteen-year-old grandson, the only person he loves, who flees from him never to be heard from again, thus breaking the grandfather's spirit.

"THE STRENGTH OF GOD" AND "THE TEACHER"

Two stories, "The Strength of God" and "The Teacher," are juxtaposed to mock cleverly a less extravagant example of piety. The Reverend Curtis Hartman espies Kate Swift, the worldly high school teacher, reading in bed and smoking a cigarette. The sight affronts and preoccupies him and plunges him into a prolonged moral struggle which is resolved when one night he observes her kneeling naked by her bed praying. He smashes the window through which he has been watching her and runs into George Willard's office shouting that Kate Swift is an instrument of God bearing a message of truth. Kate remains entirely oblivious of the Reverend, for she is preoccupied with George, in whom she has detected a spark of literary genius worthy of her cultivation. Her praying episode—an act of desperation which the Reverend mistook for a return to faith—was the result of her realization, while in George's arms, that her altruism had turned physical.

"SOPHISTICATION" AND "PAPER PILLS"

It is exposure to these disparate egoisms, the death of his mother and a poignant evening with Helen White, the banker's daughter, which are gathered into the components of George's "sophistication," the achievement of which causes him to leave town. George's departure, however, has a decidedly ambivalent meaning. Anderson as well as other writers before and after him have shown that American small-town life can be less than idyllic, but *Winesburg, Ohio* is problematic because it is not simply another example of "the revolt from the village." In the story "Paper Pills," the narrator states that apples picked from Winesburg orchards will be eaten in city apartments that are filled with books, magazines, furniture, and people. A few rejected apples, however, which have gathered all their sweetness in one corner and are delicious to eat, remain on the trees and are eaten by those who are not discouraged by their lack of cosmetic appeal. Thus the neuroses of Anderson's grotesques are sentimentalized and become part of his increasingly strident polemic against rationality, the idea of progress, mechanization, scientific innovation, urban culture, and other expressions of social potency. Anderson never wonders why pastorals are not written by pastors but rather by metropolitans whose consciousnesses are heightened by the advantages of urban life; his own version of a pastoral, *Winesburg, Ohio*, was itself written in Chicago.

Anderson published three other collections of short stories in his lifetime, and other stories which had appeared in various magazines were posthumously gathered by Paul Rosenfeld in *The Sherwood Anderson Reader*. These are anthologies with no common theme or recurring characters, although some, such as *Horses and Men*, portray a particular milieu such as the racing world or rustic life. Many of the stories, and nearly all those singled out by the critics for their high quality, are first-person narratives. They are told in a rambling, reminiscent vein and are often preferred to those in *Winesburg, Ohio* because they lack a staged gravity. The grotesques are there, but less as syndromes than as atmospheric effects.

"DEATH IN THE WOODS"

The gothic nature of the later stories becomes more pronounced, and violence, desolation, and decay gain ascendancy in his best story, "Death in the Woods," from the collection of the same name. This work also has another dimension: It is considered "to be among that wide and interesting mass of creative literature written about literature," for, as the narrator tells the story of the elderly drudge who freezes to death while taking a shortcut through the snowy woods, he explains that as a young man he worked on the farm of a German who kept a bound servant like the young Mrs. Grimes. He recalls the circular track that her dogs made about her body while growing bold enough to get at her bag of meat when he himself has an encounter with dogs on a moonlit winter night. When the woman's body is found and identified, the townspeople turn against her ruffian husband and son and force them out of town, and their dwelling is visited by the narrator after it becomes an abandoned and vandalized hulk.

Because Mrs. Grimes is such an unobtrusive and inarticulate character, the narrator is forced to tell her story, as well as how he gained each aspect of the story, until the reader's interest is awakened by the uncovering of the narrator's mental operations. This process leads the narrator to ponder further how literature itself is written and guides him to the final expansion: consciousness of his own creative processes. The transfer of interest from the uncanny circumstances of Mrs. Grimes's death to this awareness of human creativity lends some credibility to Sherwood Anderson's epitaph, "Life, Not Death, Is the Great Adventure."

"THE MAN WHO BECAME A WOMAN"

"The Man Who Became a Woman," from *Horses and Men*, is another critic's choice. A young horse groom is sneaking a drink at a bar and imagines that his image on the counter mirror is that of a young girl. He becomes involved in an appalling barroom brawl (its horror contradicts the popular image of brawls in Westerns), and later, while sleeping nude on top of a pile of horse blankets, he is nearly raped by two drunken black grooms who mistake him for a slim young woman. The several strong foci in this long story tend to cancel one another out, and the built-in narrative devices for explaining the reason for the telling of the story succeed only in giving it a disconnected feel, although it is the equal of "Death in the Woods" in gothic details.

"I Am a Fool" and "The Egg"

"I Am a Fool," also from *Horses and Men*, is Anderson's most popular story. Here a young horse groom describes a humiliation caused less by his own gaucheness with the opposite sex than by the gulf of social class and education which separates him from the girl. The story re-creates the universe of adolescent romance so well presented in *Winesburg, Ohio* and brings a knowing smile from all manner of readers. In "The Egg" (from *The Triumph of the Egg*), a husband-and-wife team of entrepreneurs try their hand at chicken-raising and running a restaurant. They fail at both, and the cause in both instances is an egg. This is a mildly humorous spoof on the American penchant for quick-success schemes, which nevertheless does not explain the praise the story has been given.

"The Corn Planting"

"The Corn Planting" (from *The Sherwood Anderson Reader*) is Anderson without histrionics. An elderly farm couple are told that their city-dwelling son has been killed in an automobile accident. In response, the pair rig a planting machine and set about planting corn in the middle of the night while still in their nightgowns. At this concluding point, a generous reader would marvel at this poignant and internally opportune description of a rite of rejuvenation. An obdurate one would mutter Karl Marx's dictum on the idiocy of rural life (not quite apropos since Marx was referring to European peasants, not technologically advanced American farmers); but this reader shall remark that the story itself functions within its confines and breezily add that Anderson's

favorite appellation (and the title of one of his short stories) was An Ohio Pagan.

Other major works

LONG FICTION: *Windy McPherson's Son*, 1916; *Marching Men*, 1917; *Poor White*, 1920; *Many Marriages*, 1923; *Dark Laughter*, 1925; *Beyond Desire*, 1932; *Kit Brandon*, 1936.

PLAY: *Plays: Winesburg and Others*, pb. 1937.

POETRY: *Mid-American Chants*, 1918; *A New Testament*, 1927.

NONFICTION: *A Story Teller's Story*, 1924; *The Modern Writer*, 1925; *Tar: A Midwest Childhood*, 1926; *Sherwood Anderson's Notebook*, 1926; *Hello Towns!*, 1929; *Perhaps Women*, 1931; *No Swank*, 1934; *Puzzled America*, 1935; *Home Town*, 1940; *Sherwood Anderson's Memoirs*, 1942; *The Letters of Sherwood Anderson*, 1953; *Sherwood Anderson: Selected Letters*, 1984; *Letters to Bab: Sherwood Anderson to Marietta D. Finley, 1916-1933*, 1985.

Bibliography

Anderson, David D. *Sherwood Anderson: An Introduction and Interpretation*. New York: Holt, Rinehart and Winston, 1967. This critical biography argues that all Anderson's work, not just *Winesburg, Ohio*, must be considered when attempting to understand Anderson's career and his place in the literary canon.

Appel, Paul P. *Homage to Sherwood Anderson: 1876-1941*. Mamaroneck, N.Y.: Paul P. Appel, 1970. A collection of essays originally published in homage to Anderson after his death in 1941. Among the contributors are Theodore Dreiser, Gertrude Stein, Thomas Wolfe, Henry Miller, and William Saroyan. Also includes Anderson's previously unpublished letters and his essay "The Modern Writer," which had been issued as a limited edition in 1925.

Campbell, Hilbert H. "The 'Shadow People': Feodor Sologub and Sherwood Anderson's *Winesburg, Ohio*." *Studies in Short Fiction* 33 (Winter, 1996): 51-58. Discusses parallels between some of Sologub's stories in *The Old House and Other*

Tales and the stories in *Winesburg, Ohio*. Suggests that the Sologub stories influenced Anderson. Cites parallels to Sologub's tales in such Anderson stories as "Tandy," "Loneliness," and "The Book of the Grotesque."

Campbell, Hilbert H., and Charles E. Modlin, eds. *Sherwood Anderson: Centennial Studies*. Troy, N. Y.: Whitston, 1976. Written for Anderson's centenary, these eleven previously unpublished essays were solicited by the editors. Some of the essays explore Anderson's relationship with other artists, including Edgar Lee Masters, Henry Adams, Alfred Stieglitz, and J. J. Lankes.

Ellis, James. "Sherwood Anderson's Fear of Sexuality: Horses, Men, and Homosexuality." *Studies in Short Fiction* 30 (Fall, 1993): 595-601. On the basis of biographer Kim Townsend's suggestion that Anderson sought out male spiritual friendships because he felt that sexuality would debase the beauty of woman, Ellis examines Anderson's treatment of sexuality as a threat in male relationships in "I Want to Know Why" and "The Man Who Became a Woman."

Hansen, Tom. "Who's a Fool? A Rereading of Sherwood Anderson's 'I'm a Fool.'" *The Midwest Quarterly* 38 (Summer, 1997): 372-379. Argues that the narrator is the victim of his own self-importance and is thus played for a fool. Discusses class consciousness and conflict in the story.

Howe, Irving. *Sherwood Anderson*. Toronto: William Sloane Associates, 1951. This highly biographical work explores why Anderson, a writer with only one crucial book, remains an outstanding artist in American literature. The chapters on *Winesburg, Ohio* and the short stories are noteworthy; both were later published in collections of essays on Anderson. Includes a useful bibliography.

Papinchak, Robert Allen. *Sherwood Anderson: A Study of the Short Fiction*. New York: Twayne, 1992. An introduction to Anderson's short stories that examines his search for an appropriate form and his experimentations with form in the stories in *Winesburg, Ohio*, as well as those that appeared before and after that highly influential book. Deals with Anderson's belief that the most authentic history of life is a history of moments when we truly live, as well as his creation of the grotesque as an American type that also reflects a new social reality. Includes comments from Anderson's essays, letters, and notebooks, as well as brief commentaries by five other critics.

Townsend, Kim. *Sherwood Anderson*. Boston: Houghton Mifflin, 1987. In this biography of Sherwood Anderson, Townsend focuses, in part, on how Anderson's life appears in his writing. Supplemented by twenty-six photographs and a useful bibliography of Anderson's work.

Julian Grajewski, updated by Cassandra Kircher

MAYA ANGELOU

Born: St. Louis, Missouri; April 4, 1928

PRINCIPAL SHORT FICTION

Ten Times Black, 1972

Confirmation: An Anthology of African American Women, 1983

Mrs. Flowers: A Moment of Friendship, 1986 (illustrated by Etienne Delessert)

OTHER LITERARY FORMS

Maya Angelou is known primarily as a poet and autobiographer. She has produced half a dozen volumes of poetry, and *The Complete Collected Poems of Maya Angelou* was published in 1994. She has also written five volumes of autobiography, starting with *I Know Why the Caged Bird Sings* in 1970. In addition, she has written plays, screenplays, and children's stories.

ACHIEVEMENTS

I Know Why the Caged Bird Sings was nominated for the National Book Award in 1970, and Maya Angelou's first volume of poetry (*Just Give Me a Cool Drink of Water 'fore I Diiie*) was nominated for the Pulitzer Prize in 1972. Angelou was also nominated for Tony Awards for her performances in *Look Away* in 1973 and *Roots* in 1977, and she won a Grammy Award for best spoken word or nontraditional album for "On the Pulse of the Morning," the poem she read at the first inauguration of President Bill Clinton in 1993. She holds more than two dozen honorary doctorates, among numerous other awards.

BIOGRAPHY

Maya Angelou was born (as Marguerite Johnson) in St. Louis, Missouri, and spent time as a young girl in Arkansas (in Stamps, near Hope, where Clinton grew up) and California. She was raped at the age of eight by her mother's boyfriend (a story that is retold in *I Know Why the Caged Bird Sings*), had a son by the time she was sixteen, and worked at a number of jobs before she became an artist. In her early career,

she was a singer and actress, appearing in plays and musicals around the world through the 1950's and 1960's. She has since directed plays and films, recorded music and spoken word, and appeared on television as both a narrator and a series host. She has also taught at various American universities since the 1960's and at Wake Forest University since 1981. She has been an outspoken advocate of civil and human rights most of her adult life, and she has lectured and written widely about these issues for decades.

ANALYSIS

Maya Angelou has produced only a few short stories, but those stories, like her multiple volumes of autobiography, deal directly and poignantly with issues of African American life in America. Since her early years, Angelou has been a political activist and educator, and she is knowledgeable and articulate about civil rights and related issues. Her fiction, like her poetry and her nonfiction, reflects social issues and conditions in the second half of the twentieth century, when racial barriers were falling, but the problems behind them continued. In this sense, Angelou must be considered a social realist, for her stories demonstrate the difficulties of growing up an African American woman in an America still riven by racism and sexism. Dozens of anthologies and other collections of contemporary literature have excerpted pieces from one or another of Angelou's autobiographies because they raise so many important issues about modern America—about identity, education, gender, and race. Her short stories are only marginally more fictional and raise many of the same issues.

"STEADY GOING UP"

"Steady Going Up" was first published in the collection *Ten Times Black* in 1972 and has since been reprinted several times, including in Gloria Naylor's *Children of the Night: The Best Short Stories by Black Writers, 1967 to the Present* (1995). The story seems more dated than "The Reunion" but raises several important questions nonetheless. As the story opens, a young black man, Robert, is traveling by bus from his

Maya Angelou recites one of her poems during a performance at St. Bonaventure University in 1996 (AP/Wide World Photos)

home in Memphis to Cincinnati. He has never before been out of Tennessee, but this is hardly a pleasure trip, for he is rushing to pick up his younger sister at the nursing school where she has suddenly become ill (possibly from kidney trouble). Robert has raised Baby Sister since their parents died within six months of each other: "He was three years older than she when, at fifteen, he took over as head of the family." Getting a job as a mechanic at a local garage, he has been able to support Baby Sister, see her through high school, and send her to nursing school. He has had to put his own life on hold (he plans to marry Barbara Kendrick when Baby Sister is finished with school), and now her illness may further complicate his life. The bus ride is full of understandable anxiety for Robert.

When the bus makes its last stop before Cincinnati, Robert gets off to relieve himself but is cornered in the "colored" bathroom by two white men, who have also been traveling on the bus. An older black woman, who was sitting across the aisle from Robert during the trip, has already warned him about the two men, who have been drinking and staring at him.

Now they confront him, accusing him of going north to find white women. Robert cannot "stand the intention of meanness" in the two men, and he decides to act so that he will not miss the bus: "He wasn't going to get left with these two crazy men." When one tries to force him to drink the bourbon that has made them both drunk, Robert kicks him in the groin and then hits the other man over the head with the bottle. Robert manages to get back on the bus, hiding the blood on his hands and shirt, and the bus pulls away with the two men still sprawled in the bathroom. There is no resolution to the story except this escape. Robert has left "those crazy men"—at least for now—but the reader wonders what will happen to him. He may be free of them for the moment, but the hatred and violence they represent will continue to follow him. The story ends with a neutral description of the continuing bus trip: "Then he felt the big motor turn and the lights darkened and that old big baby pulled away from the sidewalk and on its way to Cincinnati." Robert's problems—as for so many African Americans at this time—still lie before him.

"THE REUNION"

"The Reunion" has been collected several times, first in the Amiri and Amina Baraka collection *Confirmation: An Anthology of African American Women*. The story is short (only five pages) but is a much more positive short fiction than the earlier "Steady Going Up," with its lack of resolution. The story is set in 1958 and is narrated by a jazz pianist named Philomena Jenkins, who is playing the Sunday matinee at the Blue Palm Café on the South Side of Chicago with the Cal Callen band. It is a club filled with other African Americans, but suddenly on this day Philomena spots Miss Beth Ann Baker, a white woman sitting with Willard, a large black man. The sight sends Philomena back in memory to her painful childhood growing up in Baker, Georgia, where her parents worked for the Bakers, and she lived in the servants' quarters behind the Baker main house.

The memories are painful because these were "years of loneliness," when Philomena was called "the Baker Nigger" by other children, and she has moved a long way from "the hurt Georgia put on me" to her present success in jazz music. She fantasizes about what she will say to Beth Ann when she meets her, but when they finally face each other at the bar a little later in the story, it is Beth Ann who does all the talking. She is going to marry Willard, who is a south side school teacher, she tells Philomena, and she claims she is very happy. However, her parents have disowned her and even forbidden her to return to Baker. It is clear that she is with Willard to spite her parents, for she sounds to Philomena like "a ten-year-old just before a tantrum," "white and rich and spoiled." When Beth Ann invites "Mena" to their wedding, the narrator replies simply, "'Good-bye Beth. Tell your parents I said go to hell and take you with them, just for company.'" When she returns to her piano after this break, she realizes that Beth Ann

> had the money, but I had the music. She and her parents had had the power to hurt me when I was young, but look, the stuff in me lifted me up above them. No matter how bad times became, I would always be the song struggling to be heard.

Through her tears, Philomena has had an epiphany and experienced a form of reconciliation with her true self, in the recognition that art can transcend social inequity. In the story's last lines, "The piano keys were slippery with tears. I know, I sure as hell wasn't crying for myself." Like a number of other artists (James Baldwin and Amiri Baraka, among them), Maya Angelou posits art—and thus literature—as one way of getting above and beyond the social injustices that her society has created. Philomena cannot erase the painful childhood memories, but her music can lift her and others above them to another, healthier human plane. The hurt may remain, but the "song struggling to be heard" is stronger.

OTHER MAJOR WORKS

PLAYS: *The Least of These*, pr. 1966; *Encounters*, pr. 1973; *And Still I Rise*, pr. 1976.

SCREENPLAYS: *Georgia, Georgia*, 1972; *All Day Long*, 1974.

TELEPLAYS: *Sister, Sister*, 1982; *Brewster Place*, 1990.

POETRY: *Just Give Me a Cool Drink of Water 'fore I Diiie*, 1971; *Oh Pray My Wings Are Gonna Fit Me Well*, 1975; *And Still I Rise*, 1978; *Shaker, Why Don't You Sing?*, 1983; *I Shall Not Be Moved: Poems*, 1990; *On the Pulse of the Morning*, 1993; *The Complete Collected Poems of Maya Angelou*, 1994; *A Brave and Startling Truth*, 1995.

NONFICTION: *I Know Why the Caged Bird Sings*, 1970 (autobiography); *Gather Together in My Name*, 1974 (autobiography); *Singin' and Swingin' and Gettin' Merry Like Christmas*, 1976 (autobiography); *The Heart of a Woman*, 1981 (autobiography); *All God's Children Need Traveling Shoes*, 1986 (autobiography); *Wouldn't Take Nothing for My Journey Now*, 1993 (autobiographical essays).

CHILDREN'S LITERATURE: *Life Doesn't Frighten Me*, 1993 (poetry, with illustrations by Jean–Michel Basquiat); *My Painted House, My Friendly Chicken, and Me*, 1994.

BIBLIOGRAPHY

Bloom, Harold. *Maya Angelou*. Philadelphia, Pa.: Chelsea House Publishers, 1998. The essays in this volume focus mainly on the autobiographies and the poetry, but there are several pieces on larger issues, such as Angelou's audience and the southern literary tradition.

Hagen, Lynn B. *Heart of a Woman, Mind of a Writer, and Soul of a Poet: A Critical Analysis of the Writings of Maya Angelou*. Lanham, Md.: University Press of America, 1996. While there have been a number of scholarly works addressing the different literary forms Angelou has undertaken (most devoted to autobiography), few critical volumes have appeared that survey her entire opus, sand Hagen's is one of the best. Chapters include "Wit and Wisdom/Mirth and Mischief," "Abstracts in Ethics," and "Overview."

King, Sarah E. *Maya Angelou: Greeting the Morning*. Brookfield, Conn.: Millbrook Press, 1994. Includes biographical references and an index. Examines Angelou's life, from her childhood in the segregated South to her rise to prominence as a writer.

Lupton, Mary Jane. *Maya Angelou: A Critical Companion*. Westport, Conn.: Greenwood Press, 1998. While focusing mainly on the autobiographies, Lupton's study is still useful as a balanced assessment of Angelou's writings. The volume also contains an excellent bibliography, particularly of Angelou's autobiographical works.

Pettit, Jayne. *Maya Angelou: Journey of the Heart.* New York: Lodestar Books, 1996. Includes biblio-graphical references and an index. Traces Angelou's journey from childhood through her life as entertainer, activist, writer, and university professor.

David Peck

MAX APPLE

Born: Grand Rapids, Michigan; October 22, 1941

PRINCIPAL SHORT FICTION

The Oranging of America, and Other Stories, 1976
Three Stories, 1983
Free Agents, 1984

OTHER LITERARY FORMS

In addition to writing some critical articles and to editing a book on the fiction of the Southwest, Max Apple has written two novels, *Zip: A Novel of the Left and the Right* (1978) and *The Propheteers: A Novel* (1987), and two memoirs, *Roommates: My Grandfather's Story* (1994) and *I Love Gootie: My Grandmother's Story* (1998). He was a contributor to *Liquid City: Houston Writers on Houston* (1987), a nonfiction work celebrating the Houston International Festival.

ACHIEVEMENTS

In 1971, Max Apple received the National Endowment for the Humanities younger humanists fellowship. *The Oranging of America, and Other Stories* earned him the Jesse H. Jones Award from the Texas Institute of Letters in 1976, as did *Free Agents* in 1985. He won *Hadassah* magazine's Ribalous Award for the best Jewish fiction of 1985. Apple has also contributed stories to a number of periodicals.

BIOGRAPHY

Max Isaac Apple was born October 22, 1941, in Grand Rapids, Michigan, to Samuel and Betty Goodstein Apple. He married Talya Fishman, and together they reared four children (two from a previous mar-riage): Jessica, Sam, Elisheva, and Leah. Apple received a B.A. degree in 1963 and a Ph.D. degree in 1970 from the University of Michigan. He did postgraduate study at Stanford University.

Following his graduation, Apple worked as an assistant professor of literature and humanities at Reed College in Portland, Oregon. In 1972, he accepted an appointment at Rice University in Houston, Texas, where he was assistant professor from 1972 to 1976, associate professor from 1976 to 1980, and professor of English beginning in 1980. Growing up in a three-generation Jewish household in which a respect for language and an appreciation of humor and style in language were the norm, Apple naturally gravitated toward the idea of telling stories. During the early 1970's, Apple contributed to a study of Nathanael West edited by David Madden, *Nathanael West: The Cheaters and the Cheated* (1972), and to the journal *Studies in English*. In 1976, Apple gained recognition as a writer with *The Oranging of America, and Other Stories*.

ANALYSIS

Max Apple's early background no doubt helped to shape his literary career. Acquiring English as a second language after growing up in a Yiddish-speaking home contributed to his viewing mainstream American life as an outsider before becoming a part of that current; thus, he could recast his American life experience in terms that are simultaneously realistic and fantastic. By taking the perspective of the perpetual outsider, Apple remains amazed at daily life in a way that he feels most people cannot.

Throughout his work, Apple develops at least four major themes or issues. He explores the intensity with which Americans expend their energy on pursuing the new, the hitherto unheard of; his writing traces how this restless yearning for the untried is connected to a basic need for safety and for immortality. He also searches for some middle ground between the ideal of the American Dream and the reality of it, aware all along of the impossibility of fulfilling that dream. Likewise, Apple addresses the ambiguity inherent in American enterprise. He perceives it partly as the pitch of a con artist to a gullible client and partly as a dreamer's response to genuine human need and desire. It is the mythic impulse of Americans to enlarge, improve, and keep moving, as opposed to the results of this impulse, that Apple sees as the focus for most Americans.

Whether developed consciously or not, a number of techniques characterize his work. His stories are peopled with well-known public figures, such as Howard Johnson and J. Edgar Hoover. This technique serves as a shortcut by calling up an image of the person in the reader's mind, making long, detailed descriptions unnecessary and leaving Apple free to make the figure into something that is all his own. He deals with what he believes is more real about them than their physical reality: their status in the readers' collective imagination. Another shortcut employed is compression. Apple has cited a line from the story "Inside Norman Mailer" as an example: Following a description of prizefighting, he simply says, "You've all seen it—imagine it yourself!" He is thus spared the task of writing pages of description, when it is only the metaphor in which he is interested.

Again, Apple sometimes recalls an earlier, minor event or thing from his childhood—for example, a gasoline station—and merges that memory with other, more fantastic material. Rhythm is a basic stylistic feature of his work. Whether a sentence is accurate is not nearly as important as whether the sentence sounds right, and, unlike many other writers, he is not concerned with a formal unity in his stories.

There is no thread of anger running through Apple's stories; his wit is tender and soft-edged. In his voice is almost an affection, as if he were admonish-ing a beloved family member with a gentle patience or even amusement. He welcomes diversity and tension for their own sake. Cultural clichés are transformed into shining gems. By polishing the cultural rubble of American life, he rejuvenates our spirits. His stories are basically optimistic.

"THE ORANGING OF AMERICA"

This title story of his 1976 collection demonstrates Apple's overtly fictive strategy. The oranging is that of the rooftops of Howard Johnson motels; he credits the poet Robert Frost as the source of inspiration for making them orange. Howard Johnson, his secretary Millie, and Otis, a former busboy, feel a tingling when they come to a spot where people need to stop and rest; this is how Johnson chooses building sites for new motels. Combining his startling imagination with originality, wit, and economy, Johnson does most of his business in a Cadillac limousine equipped with an ice cream freezer that produces twenty-eight flavors, though Johnson eats only vanilla. Years later, when Millie becomes ill, she investigates having her body frozen after death, and in order to make it possible for Millie to continue traveling with him, Johnson has the steel capsule from the Cryonic Society installed in a U-Haul trailer attached to the Cadillac.

"SELLING OUT"

Although the fantastic element is present, this story is basically plausible. The narrator inherits some money, and when his stockbroker cousin is unsuccessful in turning a satisfactory profit from it, he studies the market himself, sells what he has, and successfully reinvests the money based on his own studies. Like all the stories in *The Oranging of America, and Other Stories*, "Selling Out" is concerned with big-money action in the capitalist system. Here, Apple lives up to his reputation for comic intelligence as he mimics American economics with a tender, insidious wit.

"WALT AND WILL"

Taking the two well-known Disney brothers of cartoon and amusement park fame, Apple uses them for his own purposes. Walt is fixated on motion, which later becomes the principle behind his genius for animation. He is as intensely absorbed in studying the way ants move as any scientist would be in history-making research, for he wants to duplicate the mechanics of animation that he sees in the natural world. His imagination opens to the possibilities of animating great works of art. After the animated Mickey Mouse is born, it is Will, the practical but visionary brother, who goads Walt into developing Disneyworld in Florida; with the California Disneyland, their enterprise would be "like a belt around the country," and America would have her own national monuments, as Europe has. Walt, however, is entranced not with buildings and huge business deals but with movement, with movies. Fantasy, reality, absurdity, and seriousness often merge in Apple's version of the making of the Mickey Mouse Empire.

"FREE AGENTS"

This hilarious fantasy features Apple's internal organs striking for autonomy, insisting that they should have the right to decide where, if ever, they are to be transplanted. His stomach is the narrator of the story. The organs go before a judge, the pituitary gland, who rules that, after a May 11 deadline, all organs, muscles, and tissues, whether Apple's original organs or some added after his birth, will become free agents. As such, they will be able to negotiate with any available bodies. In mock seriousness, the sentence is declared a fair one, made in the spirit of democratic fairness that has characterized the history of collective bargaining. Again, in typical fashion, Apple targets economic, social, and moral issues behind the mask of fantasy and malice-free humor.

OTHER MAJOR WORKS

LONG FICTION: *Zip: A Novel of the Left and the Right*, 1978; *The Propheteers: A Novel*, 1987.

NONFICTION: *Roommates: My Grandfather's Story*, 1994; *I Love Gootie: My Grandmother's Story*, 1998.

BIBLIOGRAPHY

Bellamy, Joe David. *Literary Luxuries: American Writing at the End of the Millennium*. Columbia: University of Missouri Press, 1995. A record of Bellamy's search for a literary life, this book examines various facets of the literary scene in the late twentieth century. A section called "Contemporaries" provides brief overviews of sixteen younger writers, including Max Apple, whom he admires for the way he shows that "the spirit that made America what it is today is still operative" in such fictionalized figures as Howard Johnson in "The Oranging of America" and for his mellowness, which is described as an unusual quality of affection and a certain nostalgia that he generates while at the same time making his characters the butts of his ridicule. While Apple creates fabulous fantasies, few laws of nature are suspended, making his stories strangely plausible. The book lauds Apple's formal economy, balance, and purposefulness of action and plot, and concludes that his whimsicality and imaginative bravado are rarely forced.

Bennett, Patrick. *Talking with Texas Writers: Twelve Interviews*. College Station: Texas A&M University Press, 1980. Interview with Max Apple is included along with those of eleven other Texas writers. Apple shares how he became a writer and what some of his writing habits are: writing in longhand, not preparing an outline, not devoting a set number of hours or words per day to writing. Explains that his use of real names of fictionalized characters helps to bring his voice into the real world. Describes himself as a comic writer who looks for irony but who does not strive for a "punch line."

Chénetier, Marc. *Beyond Suspicion: New American Fiction Since 1960*. Philadelphia: University of Pennsylvania Press, 1996. While relevant references to Max Apple are made throughout the book, Chénetier focuses more extensively on Apple in two chapters. "Cultural Tradition and the Present" finds that Apple devotes the core of his work to using glaring symbols, such as the orange roofs of Howard Johnson motels, to draw a line between the powers of myth and its "puny incarnations." Points out that Apple is able to recycle materials which some might deem unusable in literary writing and to approach them in a fresh way. Another chapter deals with voice in writing. The author uses one of Apple's own analogies, the ventriloquist who has a dummy: For Apple, the dummy is the fiction, the part of himself that gets the best lines, while he is the straight man who provides the tension that he desires in his sentences.

McCaffrey, Larry, and Linda Gregory. *Alive and Writing: Interviews with American Authors of the 1990's*. Urbana: University of Illinois Press, 1987. Max Apple is one of thirteen contemporary writers whom McCaffrey and Gregory interview. Apple explains his sense of realism as being "the way the world is," and cites Gabriel García Márquez's writing as an example of realistic fiction. He prefers fantasy, parody, and myth to more conventional forms. Choosing the short story over the novel as a means of expression was a matter of not having time for the longer genre. Other character-

istics of his work that are discussed include his interest in what his characters' names represent, not in the persons themselves; in fact, he does not research these characters—Howard Johnson or Walt Disney, for example. He admits a decided preference for story writing to writing academic papers.

Shatzky, Joel, and Michael Taub. *Contemporary Jewish-American Novelists: A Bio-Critical Sourcebook*. Westport, Conn.: Greenwood Press, 1997. Max Apple is one of sixty-three Jewish American writers discussed. After biographical data, major works and themes developed by each of the writers are provided. A final section traces each writer's development and emerging critical reception. Primary and secondary bibliographies are provided for each writer discussed.

Victoria Price

JUAN JOSÉ ARREOLA

Born: Zapotlán (now Ciudad Guzmán), Jalisco, Mexico; September 21, 1918

PRINCIPAL SHORT FICTION

Varia invención, 1949 (*Various Inventions*, 1964)
Confabulario, 1952 (*Confabulary*, 1964)
Punto de Planta, 1958 (*Silverpoint*, 1964)
Bestiario, 1958 (*Bestiary*, 1964)
Confabulario total, 1941-1961, 1962 (*Confabulary and Other Inventions*, 1964)
Palindroma, 1971
Confabulario personal, 1980

OTHER LITERARY FORMS

Primarily known for his short stories, fables, and experimental literary sketches, Juan José Arreola also wrote the novel *La feria* (1963; *The Fair*, 1977), some one-act plays, and several essays. Known for his prodigious memory and a legendary ability to talk eloquently and entertainingly about a variety of topics, the best of Arreola's "oral prose" from lectures, round-

table discussions, interviews, and radio and television talks shows over the years has been carefully edited by Jorge Arturo Ojeda and published as *La palabra educación* (1973; the word education) and *Y ahora, la mujer . . .* (1975; and now, woman . . .).

ACHIEVEMENTS

Juan José Arreola has a special place in Latin American literature for successfully experimenting with fictional modes and techniques. A cosmopolitan man of letters, he pushed the genre of the short story in new directions. At the core of his creative representations is the interaction between rational, objective reality and idiosyncratic, subjective perceptions of it. His work includes more than one hundred short prose pieces: stories, fables, parables, biographical portraits, diary entries, advertisements, articles, science-fiction reports, and many sketches best classified as microtexts.

Acclaimed for steering Mexican literature beyond traditional realism with its emphasis on political and socioeconomic problems, Arreola deals imaginatively with the nature of human values in the face of twentieth century materialism. He probes the perverse ways in which alienated people behave when confronted with matters of love, life, and death. Like Jorge Luis Borges, he delights in making philosophical speculations and devising scenarios, although in a more playful manner, in which the line between the real and the unreal is blurred.

Arreola's irreverent humor, clever use of language, prodigious vocabulary, and vast repertoire of images are hallmarks of a unique and stimulating style. Writers from several generations have acknowledged his influence on their work, among them such prominent figures at Rosario Castellanos, Salvador Elizondo, Carlos Fuentes, Luisa Josefina Hernández, José Agustín, Vicente Leñero, Carlos Monsiváis, and Gustavo Sainz.

BIOGRAPHY

Born in 1918 in Zapotlán, Jalisco, Juan José Arreola saw the destruction wrought by warring factions during the Mexican Revolution, which had begun eight years earlier. The fourth of fourteen children, Arreola was neglected by his parents, who could barely provide for the family. He was a mischievous schoolboy, but it was also clear that he was very bright. Blessed with an amazing memory, he could recite huge amounts of literary material to astounded audiences. Strongly influenced by José Ernesto Aceves, an inspiring teacher, Arreola read a number of literary anthologies with samples of the works of authors from around the world. The short story being of particular appeal, he read thousands of these during his early years. His formal schooling ended at the age of twelve, when the local school closed. For several years, he worked at various jobs, including bookbinding and printing, always gravitating toward the cultural life that Guadalajara offered.

At the age of eighteen, he moved to Mexico City, where he held odd jobs and studied acting. His first serious literary attempts resulted in three short theatrical pieces that never circulated. He continued to educate himself by reading constantly in various disciplines. When his theater group failed and a love affair

Juan José Arreola (©Miriam Berkley)

fell apart, Arreola suffered a nervous breakdown, leading him to return to Jalisco. There, in the early 1940's, he tried to settle down by teaching school and getting married to a local woman, but the relationship soon ended in divorce. He spent a considerable amount of his time writing, and he succeeded in having several stories published in local newspapers and literary reviews such as *Pan* and *Eos*, the latter of which he founded with friends. An early piece called "Hizo bien minetras vivió" ("He Did Good While He Lived") drew national attention as an excellent story, bringing the emerging writer a host of contacts. Among them was a prominent French actor who helped Arreola win a scholarship in 1945 to study theater in Paris. Arreola has said that his life can be divided into "before and after" that stimulating sojourn, which he had to abandon after a year as a result of another physical collapse.

Arreola moved back to Mexico City permanently to work at the Fondo de Cultura Económica, a reputable publishing company. There, he met Alfonso Reyes, the world-renowned Mexican scholar and writer who in 1948 gave Arreola a scholarship to the prestigious Colegio de México, a center for humanistic studies, which Reyes headed. Arreola, who was by this time writing in earnest with his new mentor's encouragement, published his first collection of short stories, *Various Inventions*, the following year. Since it largely dealt, although imaginatively, with existential concerns, some critics expressed their disapproval for its lack of "Mexicanness," a reaction that fostered much debate in literary circles. Undaunted, Arreola responded in 1952 with a second collection of stories, *Confabulary*, considered by some critics to be his best for its surprising existential vignettes reminiscent of Jean-Paul Sartre and Franz Kafka.

By now a recognized presence on the literary scene, Arreola joined the Center for Mexican Writers, where he continued writing and where he began tutoring students who would follow him in incorporating imagination and fantasy into Mexican fiction. Another book of stories, *Silverpoint*, appeared in 1958, dazzling readers with whimsical portraits of animals with human traits. Then, in 1962, Arreola issued a new edition of some of his earlier texts, calling it *Confabulario total, 1941-1961*, but added significant new selections that clearly established him as one of Mexico's major writers. During this productive period, he also wrote *The Fair*, his first novel, which appeared in 1963, bringing mixed reviews with a modicum of praise for its multilayered, kaleidoscopic representation of life in a Mexican village. *Palindroma* (palindrome), Arreola's fourth collection of brand-new stories, appeared in 1971. Included in this collection was a theatrical piece, which suggested to some critics that the author's strength was not as a playwright.

In his later years, Arreola continued encouraging young writers, teaching at the University of Mexico, appearing on radio and television talk shows, and writing critical essays, some of which have been occasionally published, such as those in the collection *Inventario* (1976; inventory). His active career consistently reflects his commitment to find new ways through the art of fiction to express the universal conflicts, concerns, and ironies of life, never losing sight of his mission as a writer to challenge and entertain in an aesthetic fashion.

ANALYSIS

The complex fiction of Juan José Arreola, Mexico's acknowledged master of the fantastic, is so unique and varied in its content, forms, tones, and strategies that it practically defies classification. Critics have an easier time defining what his texts are *not* rather than what they actually are. Arreola's work is definitely not within the current of social realism, which is so characteristic of the bulk of the writing associated with Mexico over the centuries. He eschews the conventional mode that depicts socioeconomic and moral injustices in objectified fashion with its focus on verifiable events and the delineation of typically realistic characters. Like Reyes and Julio Torri, predecessors who also marched to a different drummer, Arreola is an innovator. He looks at reality through a different prism in order to represent its multidimensionality, its irrational side, its unexpectedness, its ambiguity.

It is clear from his short prose fiction that, like a growing number of Mexican and Latin American writers in the years since he began experimenting with writing, Arreola's interest lies in representing the personal experience of reality. In his variegated texts, he seeks ways to present what has not yet necessarily been sensed, creating mental images of things unseen, yet to be done, unreal. He chooses to experiment with the short story to show the power of imagination and fantasy as well as the flexibility of the genre itself. Texts as he imagines them include previously established possibilities as well as transformations of those possibilities. In his hands, texts stretch limits and change the rules of the literary game.

Short stories, fables, parables, miniportraits, microtexts, literary miniatures, reveries, diary entries, announcements, essays, advertisements, pseudoreports, prose poems, science-fiction pieces, sketches—Arreola writes all of these and more. Their commonality is their creator's brilliant use of language, penchant for parody, eye for the absurd, outrageous imagery, and relentless sense of humor. Readers are introduced to such figures as a consummate businessman who turns into a bull, a poet who marries a blue whale, a manic-depressive who buys a huge poisonous spider and deliberately loses it in the house, and a man who argues with an angel standing beside him at a urinal, to mention a few of the more memorable. All Arreola's literary inventions serve as scenarios for calling attention to the nature of value, to perverse and hypocritical behavior, to a world whose very survival is threatened by rampaging materialism. His pessimism, however, is not absolute. Arreola does believe that within every human being lies the potential of becoming a better person, even if the odds are against it. His idea of progress lies in the self-realization of human beings as opposed to scientific breakthroughs or technological achievements. This, in fact, is the underlying message of practically all he has written.

"THE SWITCHMAN"

One of the most widely read stories by Arreola is "El guardagujas" ("The Switchman"). In it, he develops one of the main themes and preoccupations that he plays out in a number of other stories: the condemnation of a dehumanized world where human dignity is at the mercy of organized technology. An anonymous traveler meets a gnomelike switchman in an empty train station and inquires about a train to T—, discovering through a lengthy and entertaining dialogue the peculiarities of the railway system: There is no guarantee that the train will ever go to a particular destination; passengers are often left in remote areas to fend for themselves; some immobile trains have moving pictures in the windows to convince the passengers that they are going somewhere; sometimes the tracks end at a river's edge with no bridge, requiring that the train be dismantled and carried to the other side; in some stretches, there is only one rail, and it is on the side of the first-class ticket holders; some passengers end up living in special cars and are taken to a prison car if they misbehave or to a funeral car if they die; spies who work for the company roam throughout the train in disguise; and so on. The lone traveler's train finally arrives, and the miniature switchman goes hopping down the tracks with his little red lantern, laughing as the man's answer to his question about his destination rings in his ears. "I'm heading for X—!" Critics have praised this curious story because it lends itself to interpretation on at least three levels: as a criticism of the railway system, as a satire of social institutions in general, and as an exploration of the nature of reality per se. The irony is that the traveler does not know before boarding the train if what he has heard is all imagined, made up by the little man, or real. In this dreamlike story, Arreola, like Franz Kafka, suggests that everything—family, friends, work—is part of the imagination and nothing more.

"THE PRODIGIOUS MILLIGRAM"

In "El prodigioso miligramo" ("The Prodigious Milligram"), Arreola continues to work with metaphors in the form of a modern allegorical fable involving an ant colony. Like the previous story, it is one of the author's best-known and cleverest pieces. Arreola's main concern is with human social behavior and the nature of human values. A nonconformist ant known for wandering out of line at work time discovers "a prodigious milligram" (it is never defined otherwise) and joyfully carries it back to the colony. There, she is greeted with derision, suspicion, and disapproval for disrupting the routine and introducing something unusual of her own free will, an act that would have led to her execution but for the intervention of a psychiatrist who promptly declares her mentally incompetent and suggests that she be locked up in a cell. The ant dies in her cell while admiring the splendid, glowing milligram. Legends begin to spread about her, and hundreds, then thousands of ants give up their assigned tasks to go out and find prodigious milligrams as she had, carrying them back to a central room in the colony. Conflicts arise between different groups of ants over the quality of the milligrams and their safeguarding. Wealthy ants form private collections. Thievery becomes rampant. War erupts and many ants are killed. Famine follows, for no one has been storing food for the winter. At the end of the story, the entire species is on the verge of extinction.

As in a good fable, ambiguity abounds in this one. Arreola plays with the notion of how arbitrary value can be, starting from an absurd premise and carrying it logically to its extreme conclusion in a convincing fashion. Readers can think about this story in terms of politics, religion, and economics, exploring with the author the tragic consequences to society when people behave in ways that stifle originality, creativity, independence, and human dignity. In many ways, the story is open-ended, for it easily lends itself to myriad interpretations. Whichever conclusions readers may draw, there is a clear sense that definite truths about human nature are represented here.

"BABY H.P."

On an entirely different note, Arreola carries on the theme of the way that human beings allow themselves to be degraded in their embrace of the progress presumably brought by technology in a bizarre short piece written in the form of an advertisement that bears the title in English of "Baby H.P." This is meant as a dig at the capitalist model par excellence of the United States, with its emphasis on utilitarianism and a more comfortable life made possible by the ingenious uses of practical contraptions. Arreola has come up with a "Made in U.S.A." device that is strapped to babies and small children in order to harness their natural energy when they kick, thrash, and run about, funneling their "horse power" into a special transformer that can then be used for operating small appliances such as blenders and radios. An accompanying warning label downplays the possibility that the baby can electrocute itself; as long as the parents carefully follow the directions for proper use, there is no risk. This is Arreola's way of criticizing the excessive interest that people have in functionalism, especially when their self-worth is subordinated to its pursuit.

"SMALL TOWN AFFAIR" AND "EVE"

A more controversial theme that at times seems to consume Arreola is presented in several of his stories, which dramatize the difficulty that men and women have in maintaining harmonious relationships, whether married or not, because of the human tendency toward infidelity and what the author sees as a basic fear that men have of women. In "Pueblerina" ("Small Town Affair"), a husband who discovers that his wife has a lover decides to encourage the affair rather than try to block it. The upshot is that the passion and excitement quickly fade for the lovers when they are no longer stimulated by the risk of getting caught by the husband. In "Eva" ("Eve"),

Arreola represents the notion that originally the platonic human being was complete and bisexual until a primordial split occurred that left male and female feeling incomplete ever since. The flesh component was distributed to the woman, while the man received the spirit. The male, being most vulnerable, seeks to reunite with the woman, an impossible and tragic dream that can end only when a new species is formed through the female reincorporation of the male spiritual component.

"THE BIRD SPIDER"

A kind of existentialist horror story, "La migala" ("The Bird Spider") shows Arreola's skill at creating and maintaining a suspenseful mood in a condensed text. Rejected by the woman he loves, a lonely and insecure man copes with his despair by purchasing a huge spider with a poisonous bite. Deliberately letting it loose in the house, he distracts himself from his despair over his lost love by substituting for it the threat of immediate death, wandering about the house in his bare feet, never knowing when the spider will strike. Arreola's depiction of the strange coping mechanisms that human beings devise for themselves is a grim commentary on the lives of quiet desperation that people are both driven to lead and to which they allow themselves to succumb.

Finally, in another type of text that allows the author to deal more whimsically with his existential concerns, animals are cleverly used to display human traits and weaknesses. Modeled after traditional beast books from medieval times, Arreola's psycho-zoological portraits allow him to unleash his imagination once again as he pokes fun by focusing on what he sees as human in such diverse animals as the hyena, the toad, the monkey, the boa, the seal, the rhinoceros, and a bevy of other creatures. Most of these pieces are a tour de force for their penetrating symbolism, startling use of language, and acerbic wit.

Clearly, a reading of only a sampling of Arreola's texts reveals creative instincts that are unique and multifaceted. A true artisan, he makes skillful use of structure, point of view, brevity, and the power of suggestion in a minimalist fashion, providing readers with just enough detail to trigger their own imaginations so that they will follow his in several possible directions and beyond. His obsession with the threat to the human spirit that excessive materialism and technological progress represent has driven Arreola to display this main theme in kaleidoscopic fashion in a variety of experimental, and for the most part highly effective, literary texts. His success is owed largely to his imaginative approach to reality, his highly creative use of the Spanish language, his colorful imagery, and his bizarre, daring, and even scandalous sense of humor. In the long run, Arreola seems to suggest, the line between the real and the unreal may be just as tenuous as the line between laughing and crying when one contemplates the psychodrama of the human condition.

OTHER MAJOR WORKS

LONG FICTION: *La feria*, 1963 (*The Fair*, 1977).

PLAYS: *La hora de todos*, pb. 1954; *Tercera llamada ¡Tercera! O empezamos sin usted*, pb. 1971.

NONFICTION: *Lectura en voz alta*, 1971; *La palabra educación*, 1973; *Y ahora la mujer . . .* , 1975; *Inventario*, 1976.

EDITED TEXT: *Lectura en voz alto*, 1968 (anthology).

MISCELLANEOUS: *Estas páginas mías*, 1985.

BIBLIOGRAPHY

Gilgen, Read G. "Absurdist Techniques in the Short Stories of Juan José Arreola." *Journal of Spanish Studies: Twentieth Century* 8, no. 1/2 (1980): 67-77. This concise treatment of the notion of the absurd focuses on techniques that help explain Arreola's artistic philosophy. The notes provide references to a few other studies on the absurd as well as on Arreola's work.

Larson, Ross. *Fantasy and Imagination in the Mexican Narrative*. Tempe: Arizona State University Center for Latin American Studies, 1977. A systematic survey of the substantial, although somewhat neglected, body of literature of fantasy and imagination written in Mexico over the years. Arreola is viewed as a major contributor to the movement away from literature with an explicit social purpose. Several of his stories are dealt with, although in somewhat cursory fashion. Contains an extensive bibliography and a useful index.

McMurray, George R. "The Spanish American Short Story from Borges to the Present." In *The Latin American Short Story: A Critical History*, edited by Margaret Sayers Peden. Boston: Twayne, 1983. Argues that "The Switchman" is an excellent example of Albert Camus's philosophy of the absurd. Suggests that the railway journey is a metaphor for life and that the act of boarding the train means accepting life's challenges and uncertainties.

Menton, Seymour. "Juan José Arreola and the Twentieth Century Short Story." *Hispania* 42, no. 3 (September, 1959): 295-308. This study of Arreola by a critic who became his close friend remains the classic introduction to the man and his early work. Arreola is credited with developing the fantastic as a viable way to represent the conflicts and concerns of people trapped under the pressures of modern society. Attention is given to his place within the surrealist movement, his major themes, techniques, and worldview.

_____, comp. *The Spanish American Short Story: A Critical Anthology*. Berkeley: University of California Press, 1980. This collection of Spanish American stories translated into English includes information on the literary movements and tendencies that have shaped the genre in Latin American countries from the 1830's to the "Boom" period of the 1960's and 1970's. Thumbnail sketches introduce Menton's choices as the best and most representative stories available at the time. Brief critical commentaries assist with interpretation of the texts. Arreola's "The Switchman" is included.

Schade, George. Introduction to *Confabulario and Other Inventions*. Austin: University of Texas Press, 1964. This excellent English translation largely follows the text and arrangement of the 1962 edition of *Confabulario total*. Excluded is the one-act play *La hora de todos*, which Schade deems ineffectual and out of place in this collection. Provides a brief but incisive introduction to the stories.

Washburn, Yulan. *Juan José Arreola*. Boston: Twayne, 1983. The most thorough study of Arreola and his work available in English. Drawing on a variety of critical studies in both Spanish and English, as well as on a series of personal interviews with the writer himself, this critic carefully analyzes most of Arreola's major stories, his novel, *The Fair*, and the overall preoccupations reflected in his work as a whole. Detailed plot summaries are followed by

scrupulous textual analyses. Included is an extensive discussion of Arreola's life and times and a substantial select bibliography of primary and secondary sources, most of which are available only in Spanish.

Harry L. Rosser

ISAAC ASIMOV

Born: Petrovichi, Russia; January 2, 1920
Died: New York, New York; April 6, 1992

PRINCIPAL SHORT FICTION
I, Robot, 1950
The Martian Way, 1955
Earth Is Room Enough, 1957
Nine Tomorrows, 1959
The Rest of the Robots, 1964
Asimov's Mysteries, 1968
Nightfall and Other Stories, 1969
The Early Asimov, 1972
Tales of the Black Widowers, 1974
Buy Jupiter and Other Stories, 1975
More Tales of the Black Widowers, 1976
The Bicentennial Man and Other Stories, 1976
Good Taste, 1977
The Key Word and Other Mysteries, 1977
Casebook of the Black Widowers, 1980
The Winds of Change and Other Stories, 1983
The Union Club Mysteries, 1983
Computer Crimes and Capers, 1983
Banquets of the Black Widowers, 1984
The Disappearing Man and Other Mysteries, 1985
Alternative Asimovs, 1986
Isaac Asimov: The Complete Stories, 1990

OTHER LITERARY FORMS
Isaac Asimov was well known as a polymath and

workaholic. His principal works are in the fields of science popularization and science fiction, where both his short stories and novels have been influential, but he also wrote extensively in history and literature, composed books for children and adolescents as well as mystery and detective books for adults, and published books in such areas as mythology, humor, and biblical studies.

ACHIEVEMENTS
Capitalizing on what he called his "lucky break in the genetic sweepstakes," Isaac Asimov used his exceptionally lucid mind and vivid imagination to explain the past and possible future developments of science and technology through his fiction and nonfiction to a large audience of nonscientists. He was a successful communicator of ideas not only in science but also in a wide variety of literary, historical, even theological topics, but it is as a science-fiction writer that he will be best remembered. His ability to generate and extrapolate ideas on the development of science and technology and his creative visions of the human consequences of these developments helped found "social science fiction," which made this formerly pulp genre acceptable to many literary critics.

Asimov was honored for his work in both science fiction and science popularization. The Science-Fiction Writers of America voted his "Nightfall" the best science-fiction story of all time, and his Founda-

Isaac Asimov in 1976 (Library of Congress)

tion Trilogy won a Hugo Award in 1966 as "The Best All-Time Series." His novel *The Gods Themselves*, published in 1972, won both the Hugo and Nebula awards, and his *Foundation's Edge* won a Hugo Award as the best novel in 1982. As a science popularizer, he received the James T. Grady Award of the American Chemical Society in 1965 and the American Association for the Advancement of Science-Westinghouse Science Writing Award in 1967.

BIOGRAPHY

Brought to the United States when he was three, Isaac Asimov was reared in New York by his Jewish parents and was taught to take education seriously, especially science. A child prodigy, he was graduated from high school at fifteen and went on to earn his B.S., M.A., and Ph.D. in chemistry at Columbia University, with a brief interruption for noncombatant military service at the end of World War II. Although he failed to achieve his dream, and that of his parents, to become a doctor, he did join the faculty of the medical school at Boston University, where he be-

came an Associate Professor of Biochemistry before turning to full-time writing. A science-fiction fan since his early teens, he published his first story at eighteen. After nineteen books of fiction in the 1950's, however, he concentrated much more heavily on nonfiction. He was married twice, to Gertrude Blugerman from 1942 to 1973, with whom he had two children, and to psychiatrist Janet Jeppson in 1973. In the early 1980's, Asimov endured a thyroid cancer operation, a heart attack, triple bypass surgery, and his second wife's mastectomy. He treated all these sufferings as temporary setbacks in the "game of immortality" that he played—writing as much as he could with the hope that at least some of his works would live beyond his death. Asimov died of kidney failure on April 6, 1992, in a New York hospital. He was seventy-two.

ANALYSIS

A naïve, untutored writer by his own admission, Isaac Asimov learned the art of commercial fiction by observing the ways of other science-fiction writers before him, with considerable assistance from John W. Campbell, Jr., editor of *Astounding Science Fiction*. Although the diction of pulp writers, for whom every action, however mundane, must have a powerful thrust, colored much of his earlier work, he soon developed a lucid style of his own, spare by comparison with the verbosity of others, which was spawned by the meager word rates for which they worked. Melodramatic action is not absent from his fiction, but confrontations are more commonly conversational than physical. Characters are seldom memorable, and there are few purple passages of description for their own sake; everything is subordinated to the story, itself often an excuse for problem solving to show scientific thinking in action.

Although his first popularity came in the 1930's and 1940's, Asimov's best work was published in the 1950's. In addition to most of his novels, many of his best stories were written then, including "The Ugly Little Boy" (1958), which concerns a Neanderthal child snatched into the present and the consequences of his nonscientific governess's forming an attachment to him. This is one of several stories in which the results of science and technology and devotion to them are cast in a negative or at least ambivalent light, contrary to the view Asimov usually maintains.

Other stories from this period include "Franchise," in which a single voter decides those few issues computers cannot handle; "What If?," in which a newly married couple catches a glimpse of how their lives might have been; and "Profession," in which trends in accelerated education are taken to an extreme. Three stories concern societies so technologically sophisticated that what the reader takes for granted must be rediscovered: writing in "Someday," mathematics in "The Feeling of Power," and walking outdoors in "It's Such a Beautiful Day." "The Last Question" extrapolates computer capabilities in the far future to a new Creation in the face of the heat death of the universe, while "Dreaming Is a Private Thing" concerns a new entertainment form which bears a certain resemblance to traditional storytelling.

Spanning his career, Asimov's robot stories generally involve an apparent violation of one or more of the "Three Laws of Robotics," which Campbell derived from Asimov's earliest variations on the theme. Their classical formulation is as follows:

1. A robot may not injure a human being or, through inaction, allow a human being to come to harm.

2. A robot must obey orders given it by human beings except where such orders would conflict with the First Law.

3. A robot must protect its own existence as long as such protection does not conflict with the First or Second Laws.

"LIAR!"

While this formulation was an attempt to dispel what Asimov called the "Frankenstein complex," it was also a set of orders to be tested by dozens of stories. The best of the robot stories may well be "Liar!," in which a confrontation between robot and human produces an unusually emotional tale, in which the fear of machines is not trivialized away. "Liar!" introduces one of Asimov's few memorable characters, Susan Calvin, chief robopsychologist for U.S. Robots, whose presence between "chapters" of *I, Robot* (1950) unifies to some extent that first collection of

Asimov's short fiction. Usually placid, preferring robots to men, Calvin is shown here in an uncharacteristic early lapse from the type of the dispassionate spinster into that of "the woman scorned."

The story begins with a puzzle, an attempt to discover why an experimental robot, RB-34 (Herbie), is equipped with telepathy. Trying to solve this puzzle, however, Calvin and her colleagues are sidetracked into the age-old problem of human vanity, which ultimately relegates the original puzzle and the robot to the scrap heap. Aware of the threat of harming them psychologically if he tells the truth, Herbie feeds the pride of the administrator, Alfred Lanning, in his mathematics, along with the ambition of Peter Bogert to replace his superior, and the desire of Calvin to believe that another colleague, Milton Ashe, returns her affection, when he is in fact engaged to another.

As the conflict between Bogert and Lanning escalates, each trying to solve the original puzzle, Herbie is asked to choose between them. Present at the confrontation, Calvin vindictively convinces the robot that whatever it answers will be injurious to a human being, forcing it to break down. Since Herbie is a conscious being, more interested in romantic novels than in technical treatises, Calvin's act is not simply the shutting down of a machine but also an act of some malevolence, particularly satisfying to her, and the whole story underlines the human fear of being harmed, or at least superseded, by machines.

"NIGHTFALL"

Asimov's next published story, "Nightfall," is still his best in the opinion of many readers, who have frequently voted it the best science-fiction story of all time, although it shows its age and the author's, since he was barely twenty-one when he wrote it. Written to order for Campbell, it begins with a quote from Ralph Waldo Emerson's *Nature* (1836) which Campbell and Asimov in turn have reinterpreted: "If the stars should appear one night in a thousand years, how would men believe and adore, and preserve for many generations the remembrance of the city of God." Asimov fulfilled Campbell's demand that the event, taken as an astronomical possibility, would drive men mad, but this conclusion is partly counterbalanced by the author's faith in the power of science to explain, without completely succumbing to, awe and superstition.

With the Emerson quote as an epigraph, "Nightfall" was committed to an inevitable, rather than a surprise, ending. From the start, the catastrophe is imminent, predicted by astronomers who have no idea of what is really in store. Aton 77, director of the university observatory where the action takes place, reluctantly permits a newspaper columnist, Theremon 762, to stay and observe, thus setting the stage for a story which is almost all exposition. Sheerin 501, a psychologist, becomes Theremon's major interlocutor, explaining both the physical and behavioral theory behind the predictions which the media and the populace have ridiculed.

Astronomical observation, gravitational theory, and archaeological findings have confirmed the garbled scriptural account of the Cultists' *Book of Revelations* that civilization on the planet Lagash must fall and rise every two millennia. Lit by six suns, Lagash is never in darkness, never aware of a larger universe, except when another world, a normally invisible "moon," eclipses the only sun then in the sky, an event which happens every 2049 years. In hopes of overcoming the anticipated mass insanity, the scientists have prepared a Hideout in which some three hundred people may be able to ride out the half-day of darkness and preserve some vestige of scientific civilization.

While Sheerin is explaining all this and glibly countering commonsense objections, a Cultist breaks in to threaten the "solarscopes," a mob sets out from the city to attack the observatory, and the eclipse indeed begins. Amid flickering torches, the scientists withstand the vandals' charge that they have desecrated the scriptures by "proving" them only natural phenomena. They then speculate ironically about a larger universe, even an Earthlike situation presumed inimical to life, but neither they nor the Cultists are prepared for the truth of "thirty thousand mighty suns" or the gibbering madness which demands light, even if everything must be burned down in order to obtain it.

Other than the astronomical configuration—a highly unlikely and inherently unstable situation—

and its consequences, there is nothing "alien" in the story, which is about potential human reactions. The diction is heavily influenced by 1930's pulp style, some pieces of the puzzle are not rationally convincing, and the story leaves loose ends untied, but it is dramatically convincing, like H. G. Wells's inversion of a similar dictum in "The Country of the Blind." Although Asimov's moral survives, that people can, through scientific observations and reasoning, do something to improve their state, it is largely overshadowed by the effectiveness of the ending. However well-prepared for and rationalized away, the concluding vision of "Nightfall" evokes exactly that quasimystical awe and wonder Asimov is usually constrained to avoid.

"THE MARTIAN WAY"

Relying more on single "impossibilities," correlated extrapolation and reasoning from present-day knowledge, Asimov's best fiction generally stems from the 1950's. The best example of his positive attitude toward future expansion by human beings and their knowledge, "The Martian Way" illustrates the conviction expressed by most of his novels and much of science fiction that the future lies "out there" in space beyond the "cradle" for human beings provided by Earth, its history and prehistory. A "space story" to be sure, "The Martian Way" also concerns political conflict, which is resolved not by drawn blasters at fifty paces but rather by reason and ingenuity, based on a setting and assumptions alien to Earthmen both at the time of writing and at the time period in which the novella is set.

There are a puzzle and a solution, but they are an excuse on which to hang the story. The rise of a demagogic Earth politician, Hilder (modeled on Senator Joseph McCarthy, but echoing Hitler by name), threatens the human colony on Mars which depends on Earth for water, not only for drinking, washing, and industry but also as reaction mass for its spaceships. Among those who will be affected, Marlo Esteban Rioz and Ted Long are Scavengers, who snag empty shells of ships blasting off from Earth and guide them to Martian smelters. Although Rioz is the experienced "Spacer," the "Grounder" Long has a better grasp of "the Martian way," which means not tying one's future to Earth, rather facing outward to the rest of the Solar System and beyond.

Campaigning against "Wasters," Hilder parallels past profligacy toward oil and other resources with the present Martian use of water from Earth's oceans. The Martian colonists recognize the spuriousness of that charge, but they also recognize its emotional impact on Earth. The solution is a marriage of scientific elegance and technological brute force, breathtaking in context even to the Spacers themselves, who set off on a year's journey to bring back an asteroid-sized fragment of ice from Saturn's rings. How they do it is chronicled by the story, along with the euphoria of floating in space, the political wrangling with Earth, and the challenges of colonizing the new frontier.

Throughout the narrative resonates the claim by Long that Martians, not Earthmen, will colonize the Universe. The fundamental difference lies less with the planet of one's birth than with the direction in which one looks to the future. Scientifically more astute and less burdened by racial prejudices, Martians work in teams rather than as individual heroes. Although there are distinct echoes of the legendary American West, the situation on Mars is more radically discontinuous with its predecessors on Earth. The arrival of an independent water supply is just the excuse they need to cut at last the umbilical cord to Earth and the past.

"THE DEAD PAST"

If "The Martian Way" points toward Asimov's novels, most of which take place off Earth, even beyond the Solar System, "The Dead Past" is more typical of the extrapolation Asimov defends in his critical writings as "social science fiction." The novella begins harmlessly enough with a professor of Ancient History being denied access to government-controlled chronoscopy, which would let him see at firsthand the ancient city of Carthage. Although time-viewing is the central science fiction, the focus of the story switches to "the closed society," as Professor Potterly seeks to subvert governmental controls. Scientists in this near-future society have bartered their freedom of inquiry for recognition, security, and financial support. This position is defended by a young physics professor named Foster, whose future de-

pends on his staying within the bounds of his discipline and of the controls which have evolved from governmental support of research.

The point is exaggerated, as is the conspiracy of silence surrounding chronoscopy, but the satirical edge is honed by the subsequent activity of the two academics and Foster's cooperative Uncle Ralph, a degreeless, prestigeless, but well-paid science writer. With his help and the shortcut supplied by his specialty, "neutrinics," Foster reinvents the chronoscope at a fraction of its earlier cost and difficulty, and the conspirators give out the secret to the world. In contrast to Foster's newly gained fanaticism, Potterly has begun to have doubts, in part because of his own wife's nostalgic obsessions. In a melodramatic confrontation with the FBI, they discover that the chronoscope's operating limits are between one hundred and twenty-five years and one second ago, making privacy in the present a thing of the past. Either a whole new utopian society will have to evolve, a doubtful supposition, or the government's suppression of information will turn out, in retrospect, to have been for the good. Although the story has flaws and its fantasy is almost certainly unrealizable, the satire is engaging, and the ending is a thoughtful variation on the theme that there may indeed be some knowledge not worth pursuing.

Asimov's fiction usually has a makeshift quality about it, his characterizations are often featureless, and his propensity for surprise endings and melodramatic diction and situations may irritate some readers. Nevertheless, his exploitation of scientific thought and rationality, his emphasis on the puzzle solving which makes up much of science, and his generally good-humored lucidity have made him, along with Robert A. Heinlein and Arthur C. Clarke, one of the cornerstones of modern science fiction.

OTHER MAJOR WORKS

LONG FICTION: *Pebble in the Sky*, 1950; *Foundation*, 1951; *The Stars Like Dust*, 1951; *The Currents of Space*, 1952; *Foundation and Empire*, 1952; *Second Foundation*, 1953; *The Caves of Steel*, 1954; *The End of Eternity*, 1955; *The Naked Sun*, 1957; *The Death-Dealers*, 1958 (also known as *A Whiff of*

Death); *Fantastic Voyage*, 1966; *The Gods Themselves*, 1972; *Murder at the ABA: A Puzzle in Four Days and Sixty Scenes*, 1976; *Foundation's Edge*, 1982; *The Robots of Dawn*, 1983; *Robots and Empire*, 1985; *Foundation and Earth*, 1985; *Fantastic Voyage II: Destination Brain*, 1987; *Prelude to Foundation*, 1988; *Azazel*, 1988; *Robot Dreams*, 1989; *Nemesis*, 1989; *Robot Visions*, 1990; *Nightfall*, 1991 (with Robert Silverberg); *The Ugly Little Boy* (with Silverberg), 1992; *Forward the Foundation*, 1993; *The Positronic Man*, 1993 (with Silverberg).

NONFICTION: *The Chemicals of Life: Enzymes, Vitamins, Hormones*, 1954; *Inside the Atom*, 1956; *The World of Carbon*, 1958; *The World of Nitrogen*, 1958; *Words of Science and the History Behind Them*, 1959; *Realm of Numbers*, 1959; *The Intelligent Man's Guide to Science*, 1960; *The Wellsprings of Life*, 1960; *Life and Energy*, 1962; *The Search for the Elements*, 1962; *The Genetic Code*, 1963; *The Human Body: Its Structures and Operation*, 1964; *The Human Brain: Its Capacities and Functions*, 1964; *A Short History of Biology*, 1964; *Asimov's Biographical Encyclopedia of Science and Technology*, 1964; *Planets for Man*, 1964 (with Stephen H. Dole); *The Greeks: A Great Adventure*, 1965; *A Short History of Chemistry*, 1965; *The New Intelligent Man's Guide to Science*, 1965; *The Neutrino: Ghost Particle of the Atom*, 1966; *The Roman Republic*, 1966; *Understanding Physics*, 1966; *The Genetic Effects of Radiation*, 1966; *The Universe: From Flat Earth to Quasar*, 1966; *The Roman Empire*, 1967; *The Egyptians*, 1967; *Asimov's Guide to the Bible*, 1968-1969 (2 volumes); *The Dark Ages*, 1968; *Science, Numbers, and I*, 1968; *The Shaping of England*, 1969; *Asimov's Guide to Shakespeare*, 1970 (2 volumes); *Constantinople: The Forgotten Empire*, 1970; *Electricity and Man*, 1972; *The Shaping of France*, 1972; *Worlds Within Worlds: The Story of Nuclear Energy*, 1972; *The Shaping of North America from Earliest Times to 1763*, 1973; *Today, Tomorrow, and . . .*, 1973; *Before the Golden Age*, 1974 (autobiography); *Earth: Our Crowded Spaceship*, 1974; *Our World in Space*, 1974; *The Birth of the United States, 1763-1816*, 1974; *Our Federal Union: The United States from 1816 to 1865*, 1975; *Science Past—Science Future*, 1975; *The Collapsing Universe*, 1977; *The Golden Door: The United States from 1865 to 1918*, 1977; *A Choice of Catastrophes: The Disasters That Threaten Our World*, 1979; *Extraterrestrial Civilizations*, 1979; *In Memory Yet Green: The Autobiography of Isaac Asimov, 1920-1954*, 1979; *The Annotated "Gulliver's Travels,"* 1980; *Asimov on Science Fiction*, 1980; *In Joy Still Felt: The Autobiography of Isaac Asimov, 1954-1978*, 1980; *Visions of the Universe*, 1981; *Exploring the Earth and the Cosmos: The Growth and Future of Human Knowledge*, 1982; *The Roving Mind*, 1983; *The History of Physics*, 1984; *The Edge of Tomorrow*, 1985; *Robots: Machines in Man's Image*, 1985 (with Karen A. Frenkel); *Asimov's Guide to Halley's Comet*, 1985; *Exploding Suns*, 1985; *The Dangers of Intelligence and Other Science Essays*, 1986; *Beginnings: The Story of Origins—of Mankind, Life, the Earth, the Universe*, 1987; *Past, Present, and Future*, 1987; *Asimov's Annotated Gilbert and Sullivan*, 1988; *The Relativity of Wrong*, 1988; *Asimov on Science*, 1989; *Asimov's Chronology of Science and Discovery*, 1989; *Asimov's Galaxy*, 1989; *Frontiers*, 1990; *Asimov's Chronology of the World: The History of the World from the Big Bang to Modern Times*, 1991; *Atom: Journey Across the Subatomic Cosmos*, 1991; *Yours, Isaac Asimov: A Lifetime of Letters*, 1995 (Stanley Asimov, editor).

CHILDREN'S LITERATURE: *David Starr: Space Ranger*, 1952; *Lucky Starr and the Pirates of the Asteroids*, 1953; *Lucky Starr and the Oceans of Venus*, 1954; *Lucky Starr and the Big Sun of Mercury*, 1956; *Lucky Starr and the Moons of Jupiter*, 1957; *Lucky Starr and the Rings of Saturn*, 1958.

BIBLIOGRAPHY

Asimov, Isaac. *Asimov's Galaxy: Reflections on Science Fiction*. Garden City, N. Y.: Doubleday, 1989. This compilation of sixty-six essays presents readers with Asimov's unique perspective on a genre to which he made many important contributions for fifty years. The topics deal with religion and science fiction, women and science fiction, time travel, science-fiction editors, and magazine covers. Particularly interesting are the items in the final section, "Science Fiction and I," in which Asimov writes frankly about his life and work. No index.

"A Celebration of Isaac Asimov: A Man for the Universe." *Skeptical Inquirer* 17 (Fall, 1992): 30-47. Asimov is praised as a master science educator, perhaps of all time; he was responsible for teaching science to millions of people. Tributes are made by Arthur C. Clarke, Frederik Pohl, Harlan Ellison, L. Sprague de Camp, Carl Sagan, Stephen Jay Gould, Martin Gardner, Paul Kurtz, Donald Goldsmith, James Randi, and E. C. Krupp.

Chambers, Bette. "Isaac Asimov: A One-Man Renaissance." *The Humanist* 53 (March/April, 1993): 6-8. Discusses Asimov's stature as a humanist, his presidency of the American Humanist Association; addresses Asimov's support of the Committee for the Scientific Investigation of Claims of the Paranormal and his thoughts on censorship and creationism, pseudoscience, and scientific orthodoxy.

Fiedler, Jean, and Jim Mele. *Isaac Asimov.* New York: Frederick Ungar, 1982. This brief book, part of the Recognitions series, is a primer on Asimov's work as a science-fiction writer. The authors give descriptions of most of Asimov's writings in the genre, including the Foundation trilogy, the robot stories, and the juvenile books. Some critics found the book too long on plot summaries and too short on analyses, but others thought the authors provided a clear and nonacademic treatment of Asimov's major works besides giving some of his less well known works long-overdue recognition. Contains notes, a bibliography, and an index.

Goble, Neil. *Asimov Analyzed.* Baltimore: Mirage, 1972. This unusual study of Asimov's work concentrates on his style in his science fiction and nonfiction. The critical analyses are detailed, with the author going so far as to perform word-frequency counts to make some of his points.

Gunn, James. *Isaac Asimov: The Foundations of Science Fiction.* New York: Oxford University Press, 1982. Rev. ed. Lanham, Md.: Scarecrow Press, 1996. Gunn, a professor of English at the University of Kansas in Lawrence, is a science-fiction writer and a historian and critic of the genre. He has used his long personal friendship with Asimov to show how science fiction shaped Asimov's life and how he in turn shaped the field. The bulk of Gunn's book, a volume in the Science-Fiction Writers series, is devoted to painstaking analyses of Asimov's entire science-fiction corpus. The book concludes with a chronology, a checklist of works by Asimov, a select list of works about him, and an index.

Hutcheon, Pat Duffy. "The Legacy of Isaac Asimov." *The Humanist* 53 (March/April, 1993): 3-5. A biographical account, noting Asimov's efforts to bring scientific understanding to people and to make people realize that to study humanity is to study the universe, and vice versa; claims that Asimov saw the possibility of an eventual organization of a world government, warned against the abandonment of technology in our search for solutions, and predicted the end of sexism, racism, and war.

Olander, Joseph D., and Martin H. Greenberg, eds. *Isaac Asimov.* New York: Taplinger, 1977. This collection of essays is part of a series, Writers of the Twenty-first Century. The essays, which reviewers found useful and illuminating, include analyses of Asimov's social science fiction, his science-fiction mysteries, and his Foundation trilogy. In an afterword, Asimov himself comments, amusingly and enlighteningly, on the essays, asserting that "no purposeful patterns or smooth subtleties can possibly be below the clear surface" of what he has written in his science-fiction stories. The book includes a select bibliography of Asimov's major science-fiction writings through 1976.

Patrouch, Joseph F., Jr. *The Science Fiction of Isaac Asimov.* Garden City, N. Y.: Doubleday, 1974. Patrouch, a teacher of English literature at the University of Dayton, published science-fiction stories, and many reviewers found his critical survey of Asimov's writings in science fiction the best book-length study yet to appear. Patrouch discusses Asimov's style, his narrative skills, and his themes; he also provides detailed analyses of the principal short stories and novels.

Touponce, William F. *Isaac Asimov*. Boston: Twayne, 1991. Part of Twayne's United States Authors series, this volume is a good introduction to the life

and works of the author. Includes bibliographical references and an index.

David N. Samuelson, updated by Robert J. Paradowski

MIGUEL ÁNGEL ASTURIAS

Born: Guatemala City, Guatemala; October 19, 1899
Died: Madrid, Spain; June 9, 1974

PRINCIPAL SHORT FICTION

Leyendas de Guatemala, 1930
Week-end en Guatemala, 1956
El espejo de Lida Sal, 1967
Novelas y cuentos de juventud, 1971
Viernes de dolores, 1972

OTHER LITERARY FORMS

Miguel Ángel Asturias's first published works were translations of Mayan Indian lore whose influence is strongly present in his own writings. His first and most famous novel, *El señor presidente* (1946; *The President*, 1963) is a subjective account of the Estrada Cabrera dictatorship in Guatemala. His "Banana Trilogy" of novels deals with the imperialistic excesses of the United Fruit Company. Because of their use of intense visual images to appeal to the audience's subconscious, his dramas have been regarded as highly experimental. Asturias also wrote poetry, essays, children's stories, and newspaper articles.

ACHIEVEMENTS

Miguel Ángel Asturias sought to give a universal consciousness to the problems of Latin America in his writings. He is best known for fusing native legends, folklore, and myths with harsh reality and even surrealism in his novels.

In 1923, the University of San Carlos in Guatemala awarded Asturias the Premio Galvez for his law

degree dissertation on the sociocultural problems of the Indian; he won the Chavez Prize that same year. The Prix Sylla Monsegur was bestowed upon him in 1931 for his collection of Indian tales entitled *Leyendas de Guatemala*. The Prix du Meilleur Roman Étranger was awarded to him in 1952 for his first novel, *El señor presidente*. The International Lenin Peace Prize from the Soviet Union was awarded to him in 1966 for the three works in the "Banana Trilogy." Asturias's most prestigious award was the Nobel Prize in Literature from the Swedish Academy in 1967.

BIOGRAPHY

Miguel Ángel Asturias was born in 1899 in Guatemala City, Guatemala, only one year after the country succumbed to the dictatorship of Manuel Estrada Cabrera. Asturias's father, a supreme court magistrate, lost his position in 1903, when he refused to convict students who protested against Estrada Cabrera's totalitarian regime. Consequently, Asturias's family was forced to leave the city for a rural area in Guatemala, where the young Asturias's interest in his country's Indian and peasant customs began to develop.

After attending secondary school, Asturias entered the University of San Carlos to study law. There he was politically active, participating in demonstrations that helped to depose Estrada Cabrera. Asturias also helped to found both a student association of Guatemala's Unionist party and the Universidad Popular de Guatemala, an institution providing free evening instruction for the country's poor. In 1923,

Asturias earned his law degree and shortly thereafter founded the weekly newspaper *Tiempos Nuevos*. Later that year Asturias fled the country; his political writings began to endanger his life. After living in London for the next five months, Asturias moved to Paris, where he worked as European correspondent for Mexican and Central American newspapers. He also studied ancient Central American Indian civilizations at the Sorbonne. There he completed a dissertation on Mayan religion and translated sacred Indian texts.

It was in Paris that Asturias began his literary career. There he was introduced to the techniques and themes of the Surrealist literary movement; this movement was to have a significant effect on his writing style. In 1925 Asturias privately published a book of poetry and a prize-winning collection of Indian stories. Asturias returned to Guatemala in 1933 and spent the next ten years working as a journalist and a poet while Guatemala was governed by the military dictatorship of Jorge Ubico Castañeda. Between 1935 and 1940, Asturias published several more volumes of poetry. He entered politics in 1942 with his election as deputy to the Guatemalan national congress. Three years later, after the fall of the Castañeda regime, he joined the Guatemalan diplomatic service. He served in several ambassadorial posts in Mexico and Argentina for the next ten years. During this time, he published several novels and worked on the three novels in his "Banana trilogy"—a portrait of the real-life United Fruit Company.

Stripped of his Guatemalan citizenship in 1954 for supporting president Jacobo Arbenz Guzmán, he lived in exile for the next twelve years in Argentina, Venezuela, and Italy. During this period he continued to write. Regaining his Guatemalan citizenship in 1966, he accepted a position as ambassador to France, which he held until 1970. He died in Madrid, Spain, in 1974.

ANALYSIS

It is likely that, in general terms, Miguel Ángel Asturias is most known for his literature of social denunciation. Indeed, there are those who would claim that his receipt of the Nobel Prize was primarily due to fiction attacking political oppression in Latin America and particularly the deleterious influence of American capitalism. Nevertheless, Asturias is notably prominent in Latin American literature for what one may loosely call a highly "poeticized" fiction; that is, a fictional texture that proposes the dissolution of conventional distinctions between poetic and prosaic registers. Nowhere is this aspect of his writing more apparent than in his first book of short fiction, *Leyendas de Guatemala* (1930; legends of Guatemala).

Like many Latin American writers, Asturias spent his culturally formative years in France. This French experience was doubly significant. Not only was it the opportunity to enter into contact with the most important writers, artists, and intellects of the ebullient *entreguerre* period in Paris, but also it was the transition from a feudal Latin American society of his youth to the free-wheeling, liberal if not libertine society of postwar Europe. The result for many writers like Asturias is the fascinating conjunction of traditional, autochthonous, and folkloric—and even mythic—Latin American material and themes and a mode of literary discourse shaped by surrealism and the other vanguard modernist tendencies of the 1920's and 1930's in the "sophisticated" centers of the West. Surrealism maintained a prominent interest in the primitive and the antirational and had as one of its primary goals the demythification of the primacy of so-called high culture in Western society. Thus it is only natural to find a continuity among the intellectuals of the 1920's and 1930's of the interest in Latin American materials that dates back to early anthropological and archaeological studies of the nineteenth century.

In the case of Asturias, what is particularly significant was his opportunity to work in Paris with Georges Raynaud, who was engaged at that time in preparing a scholarly translation of the *Popol Vuh*, the sacred texts of the Quiché Indians of Guatemala. That is, Asturias, in moving from Guatemala to Paris, exchanged a context of the oppression of indigenous culture for one of scholarly and intellectual interest in the cultural accomplishments of the native population of his own country. In the *Leyendas de Guatemala*,

Miguel Ángel Asturias, Nobel Prize winner for Literature in 1967 (©The Nobel Foundation)

Asturias attempts to stand as a mediator between the Western and Quiché cultures. It is a mediation consisting of both linguistic and cultural "translations" of indigenous materials into cultural idioms or codes of twentieth century literary discourse. This does not mean ethnographic or folkloristic transcription of indigenous legends, nor does it mean the re-creation of indigenous narratives and their rearticulation in terms of homologous modern myths. Rather, it means the semantic reformulation of indigenous materials in terms of the linguistic and cultural symbologies of the modern writer. The representation in Spanish, either directly or indirectly, of indigenous myths can never be only a translation. The rhetorics, styles, and modes of writing of a modern Western language such as Spanish, although they may be influenced by the poetic attempts to incorporate the modalities of an indigenous language such as Quiché, can never be the anthropologically faithful or scientific re-creation of the original materials because of the enormous distance that separates the two linguistic and cultural systems.

The so-called poetic language of Asturias in the *Leyendas de Guatemala*, or in the novel *Hombres de maíz* (1949; *Men of Maize*, 1975) is not, therefore, a translation into Spanish of Quiché materials. Nor is it the attempt to write in Spanish as though one were in reality writing in Quiché. Rather, it is the attempt to attain an independent discourse that, on the one hand, will suggest the melding of the two cultures into an idealized sociohistoric reality and, on the other hand, will attest to the role of the artist and writer as the mediating bridge between two cultures which deplorable but all-too-present circumstances keep separate by a virtually unbreachable abyss.

The influence of surrealism in Latin American literature has meant not merely the recovery of the subconscious and the unconscious as it has in European culture. More significantly, it has meant the recovery of indigenous cultures and the aspects of those cultures that may be seen as prerational or authentically mythic. The discovery by the Latin American of his subconscious reality is, therefore, not simply a psychological discovery; it is the discovery of those mediating cultural elements—usually indigenous but often creole—which were repressed by nineteenth century liberal and Europeanizing ideologies.

"Leyenda del sombrerón"

"Leyenda del sombrerón" (legend of the big hat) is an excellent example of the elaboration in a fictional text of the aforementioned principles. Superficially, it reminds one of those nineteenth century narratives by such writers as Peru's Ricardo Palma or Colombia's Tomás Carrasquilla—narratives that represent an ironic, urbane retelling of traditional or legendary material of a quasi-documentary nature, lightly fictionalized by a somewhat patronizing narrator who claims to have either discovered his material in an out-of-the-way corner of a dusty library or heard it on the lips of gossipy washerwomen and garrulous mule drivers. These narratives were part of the Romantic and prerealist fiction of Latin America and represented that area's version of local color and the discovery of an idealized past and an idealized *Volkspoesie*.

Asturias's story is like these antecedents in that it deals with quasi- or pseudolegendary material: the origin of the devil's big hat. The legend as Asturias tells it concerns a monastery built by the Spanish conquerors of Central America, a monastery inhabited by devout monks, specifically by one monk who spends his time in appropriately devotional readings and meditation. One day, the monk's exemplary otherworldliness is broken by a ball that comes flying through the window, the lost toy of an Indian boy playing outside the walls of the monastery. At first, the monk is entranced by this unknown object which he takes in his hands, imagining that so must have been the earth in the hands of the Creator. Thus distracted from his saintly preoccupations, the monk begins to play with the ball with almost childish joy. A few days later, however, the child's mother comes to the door of the monastery to ask that her son be given religious instruction; it seems that he has been heartbroken since the loss of his ball in the area of the monastery, a ball claimed popularly to be the very image of the devil. Suddenly possessed by a violent rage, the monk runs to his cell, picks up the ball, and hurls it beyond the walls of the monastery. Flying through the air, the ball assumes the form of the black hat of the devil. The story ends with: "And thus is born to the world the big hat."

The superficial resemblance of Asturias's text with its nineteenth century ironic predecessors is borne out by an overt narrator who obliquely addresses himself to the reader. This narrator assumes the function of telling the reader what happened and sharing with him the unusual, surprising, and notable event. Thus, the text is characterized by a number of rhetorical ploys to be seen as markers of this conventional form of ironic storytelling: the explicit allusions to the recovery of the story from antiquarian sources; the fact that the event narrated concerns a remote time and place that because of its strangeness for the reader makes the story all the more notable; the heavy-handed condescension toward the simplicity of manner and ingenuous behavior of the participants—the monk, the Indian child, and his humble mother; and, finally, the explicit allusions to the fact that someone is telling a story. These allusions take the form of phatic formulas such as "Let us continue," "Let us go on," "And thus it happened," "And

thus it was," as well as frequent references to the noteworthiness of the event being related, toward confirming the value of the narrative as narrative and as a form of privileged discourse.

It must be stressed that all these features are only superficial characteristics of nineteenth century ironic, local-color literature. Indeed, the fact that they are superficial echoes in Asturias's text becomes a wholly different sort of irony, an irony at the expense of a reader willing to take them as indicative of peasant superstitions recounted in a straightforward fashion by a narrator slightly amused at folk superstitions. To understand the way in which Asturias's story is much more than such a retelling of a local superstition, it is necessary to keep in mind the presence of two systems of cultural reference in the text. In the first place, it is necessary to recall the enormous sociocultural impact of the activities of religious orders in Latin America during the Colonial period. The conquest was accompanied by religious orders charged with the establishment in the New World of Christianity and the conversion of the indigenous population. In the case of the area known today as Guatemala, this imperative meant the wholesale destruction of the artifacts of indigenous culture, so that today less than a half dozen of the Quiché codices are the survivors of the Christian priests' destructive zeal. It would be no exaggeration to say that, as a consequence, the sort of monastery described with much detail in Asturias's text dominated the daily lives of the conquered indigenous peoples.

Second, ballplaying enjoyed a ritual and religious status in Quiché culture. Indeed, one of the cultural contributions of the Quichés to their conquerors was the ball, an artifact of leisure. Thus, in Asturias's text, the encounter between the priest and the ball—and through the ball, between the former and indigenous culture—may be a circumstantial occurrence. In terms, however, of the cultural system represented on the one hand by the pious monk and the fortress-like monastery he occupies and on the other hand by the system represented by the Indian boy's ball are posited by the story as antagonistic forces. The ball becomes a token in a pattern of cultural invasion and expulsion. In the event narrated, the cultural space of the monk is "penetrated" or "invaded" by the alien object, just as the cultural space of the Quichés had been invaded by the Spanish conquerors and their representatives of an alien religion. The indigenous culture, however, cannot displace the invading culture. The priest's almost hysterical realization of the "diabolical" meaning of the ball with which he has played with such childish abandon is the acknowledgment that the ball is much more than a child's toy. In casting the ball away from the monastery, he is expelling indigenous culture from the fortress of Christianity and reaffirming the primacy and the dominion of the latter. The miraculous transformation of the ball into the devil's hat is not really a fantastic but a phenomenological circumstance. At issue is not a superstitious belief in such occurrences (although an antirational ideology may well affirm them) but rather the perception of the symbolic importance of the object the priest flings away from him with words that recall the "Vade retro, Satanas" commonplace.

It is significant that the narrator of Asturias's story does not end his description of the monk's expulsion from his sanctuary of the artifact of indigenous culture with an explanation of the meaning of that gesture, particularly since, in the opening segments of the text, he takes great pains to describe the setting of the religious community concerned and the monk's initial distraction with the child's stray toy; yet, it is the abrupt end of the text that most confirms the significance of the symbolic interplay between the cultures here described. By not appending an explanatory conclusion, the narrator runs the risk of his reader's taking the event at face value—that is, as a miraculous or fantastic event, the authenticity of which is maintained by conventional and ingenuous superstition. Nevertheless, to the extent that the conventions of serious twentieth century literature preclude the telling of superstitious material for shock effect, the reader is obliged, when confronted with such material, to attribute to it some profound, if only vaguely perceived, semiological value. Such is the case with the encounter between the monk and the ball.

The reader need not endorse the overwhelming significance here implied of the religious community on the one hand and the ritual value of the child's ball on the other to appreciate how the story concerns conflicting antagonistic forces. In terms of the most elemental cultural values in the story one sees the ball interpreted in a conflicting manner by the monk: He sees it first as a symbol of God's creation, and it is only with the appearance of the peasant woman and her casual reference to the ball as the image of the devil that he suddenly becomes enraged with its offending presence. It crosses the monk's mind initially that the ball may be bewitched; nevertheless, he sees in it something less worldly that his books cannot explain. In giving himself over to its humble simplicity, he is, to a certain extent, escaping the treacheries of a bookish culture. Thus there is a subsystem of oppositions whereby on the larger level of the narrative there is a contrast between the monk and the ball, between Christian and indigenous sociocultural values, and there is in the monk's own world a contrast between signs of the devil and signs of God's grace. Before he realizes that the ball is the symbol of the devil, to the extent that it is an artifact of the culture which Christianity is dedicated to eradicating, he considers the errant toy a sign of God's simple grace against the potential treachery of the books with which he surrounds himself. The opposition between grace and evil which the monk perceives in his cell with the appearance of the ball is projected onto the larger plane of the opposition between two alien cultures.

In the world evoked by Asturias's story, there is an impenetrable barrier between two cultures given objective representation by the walls of the monastery. Asturias's text is nevertheless a mediator between these two cultures in the sense that they are brought together as opposing and interdependent elements in a narrative system. Without either one, there would be no story. It is because both are necessary for this narrative to exist that the text then becomes a form of mediation between the two of them, confirming the unique status of the text as a form of unifying cultural discourse. Asturias's text is unquestionably ideological, but not in the sense of sociopolitical denunciation. Rather, it is ideological by virtue of the implied conception of the praxis of narrative art as a form of mediation between two cultures often condemned to an oppressor/oppressed relationship. Writing such as that of Asturias provides the attempt at mediation with a coherence and purpose that is singularly distinctive.

OTHER MAJOR WORKS

LONG FICTION: *El señor presidente*, 1946 (*The President*, 1963); *Hombres de maíz*, 1949 (*Men of Maize*, 1975); *Viento fuerte*, 1950 (*The Cyclone*, 1967; better known as *Strong Wind*, 1968); *El papa verde*, 1954 (*The Green Pope*, 1971); *Los ojos de los enterrados*, 1960 (*The Eyes of the Interred*, 1973); *El alhajadito*, 1961 (*The Bejeweled Boy*, 1971); *Mulata de tal*, 1963 (*Mulata*, 1967); *Maladrón*, 1969.

PLAYS: *Soluna*, pb. 1955; *La audiencia de los confines*, pb. 1957; *Teatro*, pb. 1964.

POETRY: *Sien de alondra*, 1949; *Clarivigilia primaveral*, 1965.

NONFICTION: *Sociología guatemalteca: El problema social del indio*, 1923 (*Guatemalan Sociology*, 1977); *La arquitectura de la vida nueva*, 1928; *Rumania: Su nueva imagen*, 1964; *Latinoamérica y otros ensayos*, 1968; *Tres de cuatro soles*, 1977.

MISCELLANEOUS: *Obras completas*, 1967 (3 volumes).

BIBLIOGRAPHY

Brotherston, Gordon. *The Emergence of the Latin American Novel*. Cambridge, England: Cambridge University Press, 1977. This scholarly work is intended as an introduction to the Latin American novel, particularly from the 1950's to the 1970's. The chapter on Asturias discusses the author's work in the light of his politics, culture, and literary influences. Contains a general bibliography of secondary works on Latin American literature as well as a list of works by and on the major authors mentioned in the text. Accessible to the general reader.

Brushwood, John S. "The Spanish American Short Story from Quiroga to Borges." In *The Latin American Short Story: A Critical History*, edited by Margaret Sayers Peden. Boston: Twayne, 1983. A brief discussion of Asturias's appropriation of legends to use as story material; includes a brief discussion of "The Legend of the Tattooed Woman."

Callan, Richard J. *Miguel Ángel Asturias*. New York: Twayne, 1970. The purpose of Callan's book is both to acquaint English-speaking readers with the author's works and ideas and to outline the substructure of Asturias's work: the depth psychology of Carl G. Jung. Beyond sketching the historical and cultural context of Asturias's work, Callan plunges into its essential depths. Supplemented by an annotated bibliography, a chronology, and notes.

_____. "Miguel Ángel Asturias: Spokesman of His People." *Studies in Short Fiction*, no. 1 (1971): 92-102. This article focuses on both the formal and thematic concerns of Asturias's fiction. Particularly emphasized are the means by which the author represents the Indian culture of Guatemala through myths, legends, and supernatural events.

Gonzalez Echevarria, Roberto. *Myth and Archive: A Theory of Latin American Narrative*. Cambridge, England: Cambridge University Press, 1990. A very helpful volume in coming to terms with Asturias's unusual narratives.

Harss, Luis, and Barbara Dohmann. "Miguel Ángel Asturias: Or, The Land Where the Flowers Bloom." In *Into the Mainstream: Conversations with Latin-American Writers*. New York: Harper & Row, 1967. Based on interviews, the section devoted to Asturias offers useful information on the author's thought. The commentary on the novels and plays, however, reveals an extremely cursory reading of the works.

Henighan, Stephen. "Bearded Self/Heroic Love: M. A. Asturias' *La barba provisional* and Robert Desnos' *La Liberté ou l'amour.*" *Comparative Literature Studies* 33 (1996): 280-296. Claims that Asturias's story is an imaginative transformation of Desnos's novel. Argues that the story also suggests Asturias's unconscious concern that his connection with French writers would affect his successful use of Spanish-American materials. Shows how Asturias reworks themes in Desnos's novel.

Peden, Margaret Sayers, ed. *The Latin American Short Story*. Boston: Twayne, 1983. The essays in this insightful collection chart the main currents and principal figures of the historical mainstream of the Latin American short story, suggesting the outlines of the great depth and breadth of the genre in these lands. The section devoted to Asturias focuses on *Leyendas de Guatemala*. Contains a selected list of authors, collections in English, and critical studies in English.

Prieto, Rene. *Miguel Ángel Asturias's Archaeology of Return*. Cambridge, England: Cambridge University Press, 1993. The best available study in English of the novelist's body of work. Prieto discusses both the stories and the novels, taking up issues of their unifying principles, idiom, and eroticism. See Prieto's measured introduction, in which he carefully analyzes Asturias's reputation and identifies his most important work. Includes very detailed notes and bibliography.

David W. Foster, updated by Genevieve Slomski

MARGARET ATWOOD

Born: Ottawa, Ontario, Canada; November 18, 1939

PRINCIPAL SHORT FICTION
Dancing Girls, 1977
True Stories, 1981
Bluebeard's Egg, 1983
Murder in the Dark, 1983
Wilderness Tips, 1991
Good Bones, 1992 (pb. in U.S. as *Good Bones and Simple Murders*, 1994)

OTHER LITERARY FORMS

Margaret Atwood's publishing history is a testimonial to her remarkable productivity and versatility as an author. She is the author of numerous books, including poetry, novels, children's literature, and nonfiction. In Canada, she is most admired for her poetry; elsewhere, she is better known as a novelist, particularly for *Surfacing* (1972) and *The Handmaid's Tale* (1985). Her other novels include *The Edible Woman* (1969), *Lady Oracle* (1976), *Bodily Harm* (1981), and *Alias Grace* (1996). Among her volumes of poetry are *The Circle Game* (1964), *The Animals in That Country* (1968), *The Journals of Susanna Moodie* (1970), *Interlunar* (1984), and *Morning in the Burned House* (1995). In 1972 she published *Survival: A Thematic Guide to Canadian Literature*, a controversial critical work on Canadian literature, and in 1982, *Second Words: Selected Critical Prose*, which is in the vanguard of feminist criticism in Canada. Atwood has also written for television and theater, one of her successful ventures being "The Festival of Missed Crass," a short story made into a musical for Toronto's Young People's Theater. Atwood's conscious scrutiny, undertaken largely in her nonfiction writing, turned from external political and cultural repression to the internalized effects of various kinds of repression on the individual psyche. The same theme is evident in her fiction; her novel *Cat's Eye* (1988) explores the subordination of character Elaine Risley's personality to that of her domineering "friend" Cordelia.

ACHIEVEMENTS

Margaret Atwood is a prolific and controversial writer of international prominence whose works have been translated into many languages. She has received several honorary doctorates and is the recipient of numerous honors, prizes, and awards, including the Governor-General's Award for Poetry in 1967 for *The Circle Game*, the Governor-General's Award for Fiction in 1986 and the Arthur C. Clarke Award for Best Science Fiction in 1987 for *The Handmaid's Tale*, the Ida Nudel Humanitarian Award in 1986 from the Canadian Jewish Congress, the American Humanist of the Year Award in 1987, and the Trillium Award for Excellence in Ontario Writing for *Wilderness Tips* in 1992 and for her 1993 novel *The Robber Bride* in 1994. The French government honored her with the prestigious Chevalier dans l'Ordre des Arts et des Lettres in 1994.

BIOGRAPHY

Margaret Eleanor Atwood was born in Ottawa, Ontario, Canada, on November 18, 1939. She grew up in northern Ontario, Quebec, and Toronto. Following graduation from Victoria College, University of Toronto, she attended Radcliffe College at Harvard University on a Woodrow Wilson Fellowship, receiving a master's degree in English in 1962. She taught at a number of Canadian universities and traveled extensively. In the early 1990's Atwood was a lecturer of English at the University of British Columbia at Vancouver. She later settled in Toronto with writer Graeme Gibson and their daughter, Jess.

Atwood's output was steady in fiction and particularly in nonfiction. She made successful forays into the fields of script writing for film and musical theater, and she also produced notable novels. It is her prolific, passionate essay and article writing on a variety of national and international social issues, however, of which human rights is her central concern, that made her a bellwether of Canadian opinion. Her involvement with world political and social issues became evident in her vice leadership of the Writers' Union of Canada and her presidency of the International Association of Poets, Playwrights, Editors, and Novelists (PEN), where she waged a vigorous battle against literary censorship. Her association with Amnesty International prompted an increasingly strong expression of her moral vision.

ANALYSIS

One of Margaret Atwood's central themes is storytelling itself, and most of her fiction relates to that theme in some way. The short-story collections each focus on key issues. *Dancing Girls* is primarily con-

Margaret Atwood (©Washington Post; reprinted by permission of the D.C. Public Library)

cerned with otherness, alienation, and the ways in which people estrange themselves from one another. *Bluebeard's Egg* revolves around a favorite theme of Atwood, the Bluebeard tale of a dangerous suitor or husband. The title story explores Sally's excessive concern with her husband and lack of awareness of herself. *Wilderness Tips* centers on the explanatory fiction people tell themselves and one another, on the need to order experience through such fiction, and on the ways in which humans are posing threats to the wilderness, the forests, and open space.

"THE MAN FROM MARS"

In *Dancing Girls*, a gift for comic and satiric invention is evident from the first story, "The Man from Mars." Christine, an unattractive undergraduate at a Canadian university, is literally pursued by an odd-looking, desperately poor exchange student. The daily chases of a bizarre, small, Asian man in hot pursuit of a rather large Christine (a mouse chasing an elephant, as Atwood describes it) attract the attention of other students and make Christine interesting to her male acquaintances for the first time. They begin to ask her out, curious as to the mysterious sources of her charm. She begins to feel and actually to be more attractive. As months pass, however, Christine begins to fantasize about this strange man about whom she knows nothing. Is he perhaps a sex maniac, a murderer? Eventually, through the overreactions and interventions of others, complaints are made to the police, and the inscrutable foreigner is deported, leaving Christine with mingled feelings of relief and regret. She graduates and settles into a drab government job and a sterile existence. Years pass. A war breaks out somewhere in the Far East and vividly revives thoughts of the foreigner. His country is the scene of fighting, but Christine cannot remember the name of his city. She becomes obsessed with worry, studying maps, poring over photographs of soldiers and photographs of the wounded and the dead in newspapers and magazines, compulsively searching the television screen for even a brief glimpse of his face. Finally, it is too much. Christine stops looking at pictures, gives away her television set, and does nothing except read nineteenth century novels.

The story is rich in comedy and in social satire, much of it directed against attitudes that make "a person from another culture" as alien as a "man from Mars." Christine's affluent parents think of themselves as liberal and progressive. They have traveled, bringing back a sundial from England and a domestic servant from the West Indies. Christine's mother believes herself to be both tolerant and generous for employing foreigners as domestic servants in her home; she observes that it is difficult to tell whether people from other cultures are insane. Christine also typifies supposedly enlightened, liberal attitudes, having been president of the United Nations Club in high school, and in college a member of the forensics team, debating such topics as the obsolescence of war. While the story is on the whole a comic and satiric look at the limits of shallow liberalism, there is, however, also some pathos in the end. It seems that the encounter with the alien is the most interesting or significant thing that has ever happened to Christine and that her only feeling of human relationship is for a person with whom she had no real relationship. At the story's conclusion, she seems lost, now past either hope or love, retreating into the unreal but safe world of John Galsworthy and Anthony Trollope.

"DANCING GIRLS"

Another encounter with the alien occurs in the collection's title story, "Dancing Girls," which is set in the United States during the 1960's. Ann, a graduate student from Toronto, has a room in a seedy boardinghouse. Mrs. Nolan, its American proprietor, befriends Ann because a Canadian does not look "foreign." Mrs. Nolan's other tenants are mathematicians from Hong Kong and an Arab who is becoming crazed with loneliness and isolation. Ann's only other acquaintances are Lelah, a Turkish woman studying Russian literature, and Jetske, a Dutch woman studying urban design. Ann also is studying urban design because she has fantasies of rearranging Toronto. She frequently envisions the open, green spaces she will create, but she seems to have the same limitation as "The City Planners" in Atwood's poem of that name. People are a problem: They ruin her aesthetically perfect designs, cluttering and littering the landscape. Finally, she decides that people such as Mrs. Nolan, Mrs. Nolan's unruly children, and the entire collection of exotics who live in the boardinghouse will have to be excluded from urban utopia by a high wire fence.

Yet an event in the story causes Ann to change her mind. The Arab whose room is next to hers throws a rowdy party one night for two other Arab students and three "dancing girls." Ann sits in her room in the dark, fascinated, listening to the music, drinking sherry, but with her door securely bolted. As the noise level of the party escalates, Mrs. Nolan calls the police but cannot wait for them to arrive. Overcome by xenophobic and puritanical zeal, she drives the room's occupants out of her house and down the street with a broom.

Ann finally sees Mrs. Nolan for what she evidently is, a "fat crazy woman" intent on destroying some "harmless hospitality." Ann regrets that she lacked courage to open the door and so missed seeing what Mrs. Nolan referred to as the "dancing girls" (either Mrs. Nolan's euphemism for prostitutes or a reflection of her confused ideas about Middle Eastern culture). The story concludes with Ann again envisioning her ideal city, but this time there are many people and no fence. At the center of Ann's fantasy now are the foreigners she has met, with Lelah and Jetske as the "dancing girls." The implication is clear: Ann has resolved her ambivalent feelings about foreigners, has broken out of the need for exclusion and enclosure, and has rejected the racism, tribalism, and paranoia of Mrs. Nolan, who sees the world in terms of "us" versus "them."

"POLARITIES"

The question of human warmth and life and where they are to be found is more acutely raised in "Polarities," a strange, somewhat abstract story which also comments on the theme of alienation. Louise, a graduate student of literature, and Morrison, a faculty member, are both at the same western provincial university (probably in Alberta). Both are "aliens": Morrison is American and therefore regarded as an outsider and a usurper of a job which should have been given to a Canadian; Louise is a fragile person searching for a place of refuge against human coldness. Louise, a student of the poetry of William Blake, has developed her own private mythology of circles, magnetic grids, and north-south polarities. Her friends, who believe that private mythologies belong in poetry, judge her to be insane and commit her to a mental institution. At first Morrison is not sure what to believe. Finally, he discovers that he loves Louise, but only because she is by now truly crazy, defenseless, "drugged into manageability."

Examining his feelings for Louise and reflecting on her uncanny notebook entries about him, Morrison is forced to confront some unpleasant realities. He realizes that his own true nature is to be a user and a taker rather than a lover and a giver and that all his "efforts to remain human" have led only to "futile work and sterile love." He gets in his car and drives. At the story's end, he is staring into the chill, uninhabitable interior of Canada's far north, a perfect metaphor for the coldness of the human heart that the story has revealed and an ironic reversal of the story's epigraph, with its hopeful reference to humans who somehow "have won from space/ This unchill, habitable interior." The polarities between Louise's initial

vision of a warmly enclosing circle of friends and Morrison's final bleak vision of what poet William Butler Yeats called "the desolation of reality" seem irreconcilable in this story.

"GIVING BIRTH"

The final story in *Dancing Girls* is the most ambitious and complex in this collection. "Giving Birth" is about a physical process, but it is also about language and the relationship between fiction and reality. The narrator (possibly Atwood herself, who gave birth to a daughter in 1976) tells a story of a happily pregnant woman named Jeanie. Jeanie diligently attends natural-childbirth classes and cheerfully anticipates the experience of birth and motherhood. A thoroughly modern woman, she does "not intend to go through hell. Hell comes from the wrong attitude." Yet Jeanie is shadowed by a phantom pregnant woman, clearly a projection of the vague apprehensions and deep fears that Jeanie has repressed. When the day arrives, Jeanie calmly rides to the hospital with her husband and her carefully packed suitcase; the other woman is picked up on a street corner carrying a brown paper bag. As Jeanie waits cheerfully for a room, the other woman is screaming with pain. While Jeanie is taken to the labor room in a wheelchair, the other woman is rolled by on a table with her eyes closed and a tube in her arm: "Something is wrong."

In this story, Atwood suggests that such mysterious human ordeals as giving birth or dying can never be adequately prepared for or fully communicated through language: "When there is no pain she feels nothing, when there is pain, she feels nothing because there is no *she*. This, finally, is the disappearance of language." For what happens to the shadowy woman, the narrator says, "there is no word in the language." The story is concerned with the archaic ineptness of language. Why the expression, "giving birth"? Who gives it? And to whom is it given? Why speak this way at all when birth is an event, not a thing? Why is there no corollary expression, "giving death"? The narrator believes some things need to be renamed, but she is not the one for the task: "These are the only words I have, I'm stuck with them, stuck in them." Her task is to descend into the ancient tar pits of language (to use Atwood's metaphor) and to retrieve an experience before it becomes layered over by time and ultimately changed or lost. Jeanie is thus revealed to be an earlier version of the narrator herself; the telling of the story thus gives birth to Jeanie, just as Jeanie gave birth to the narrator: "It was to me, after all, that birth was given, Jeanie gave it, I am the rez senses: the biological birth of an infant, the birth of successive selves wrought by experience and time, and the birth of a work of literature which attempts to rescue and fix experience from the chaos and flux of being.

"BLUEBEARD'S EGG"

A frequent theme in Atwood's fiction and poetry is the power struggle between men and women. At times, the conflict seems to verge on insanity, as in "Under Glass," "Lives of the Poets," "Loulou: Or, The Domestic Life of the Language," and "Ugly Puss." The title story in *Bluebeard's Egg*, however, seems less bleak. In a reversal of sexual stereotypes, Sally loves her husband, Ed, because he is beautiful and dumb. She is a dominating, manipulating woman (of the type seen also in "The Resplendent Quetzal"), and her relationship to her husband seems to be that of doting mother to overprotected child, despite the fact that he is a successful and respected cardiologist, and she has no meaningful identity outside her marriage. Bored, Sally takes a writing class in which she is admonished to explore her inner world. Yet she is "fed up with her inner world; she doesn't need to explore it. In her inner world is Ed, like a doll within a Russian wooden doll and in Ed is Ed's inner world, which she can't get at." The more she speculates about Ed's inner world, the more perplexed she becomes. Required to write a version of the Bluebeard fable, Sally decides to retell the story from the point of view of the egg, because it reminds her of Ed's head, both "so closed and unaware." Sally is shocked into a new assessment of Ed, however, when she witnesses a scene of sexual intimacy between her husband and her best friend. Ed is after all not an inert object, a given; instead, he has a mysterious, frightening potential. Sally is no longer complacent, no longer certain she wants to know what lies beneath the surface.

"SIGNIFICANT MOMENTS IN THE LIFE OF MY MOTHER"

The first and last stories in *Bluebeard's Egg* reveal Atwood in an atypically mellow mood. "Significant Moments in the Life of My Mother" is a loving celebration of the narrator's (presumably Atwood's) mother and father and of an earlier, simpler time. Yet it is never sentimental because Atwood never loses her steely grip on reality. Looking at an old photograph of her mother and friends, the narrator is interested in

> the background . . . a world already hurtling towards ruin, unknown to them: the theory of relativity has been discovered, acid is accumulating at the roots of trees, the bull-frogs are doomed. But they smile with something that from this distance you could almost call gallantry, their right legs thrust forward in parody of a chorus line.

The "significant moments" of the title inevitably include some significant moments in the life of the narrator as well. Amusing discrepancies between mother's and daughter's versions of reality emerge, but not all are funny. For example, the narrator sees that her compulsive need to be solicitous toward men may be the result of early, "lethal" conditioning; her mother sees "merely cute" childhood behavior. The narrator recalls the shock she felt when her mother expressed a wish to be in some future incarnation an archaeologist—inconceivable that she could wish to be anything other than the narrator's mother. Yet when the narrator becomes a mother herself, she gains a new perspective and "this moment altered for me." What finally emerges between mother and narrator-daughter is not communication but growing estrangement. Recalling herself as a university student, she feels as though she has become as unfathomable to her mother as "a visitor from outer space, a time-traveler come back from the future, bearing news of a great disaster." There are distances too great for maternal love to cross. Atwood is too much of a realist to omit this fact.

"UNEARTHING SUITE"

The final story, "Unearthing Suite," another seemingly autobiographical reminiscence, begins with the parents' pleased announcement that they have purchased their funeral urns. Their daughter is stunned—they are far more alive than she. Mother at seventy-three figure skates, swims daily in glacial lakes, and sweeps leaves off steeply pitched roofs. Father pursues dozens of interests at once: botany, zoology, history, politics, carpentry, gardening. From her torpor, the narrator wonders at their vitality and, above all, at their enviable poise in the face of life's grim realities, those past as well as those yet to come. Perhaps the answer is that they have always remained close to the earth, making earthworks in the wild, moving granite, digging in gardens, and always responding joyously to earth's little unexpected gifts such as the visit of a rare fisher bird at the story's end, for them the equivalent of a visit "by an unknown but by no means minor god." The narrator appreciates her parents' wise tranquillity. She cannot, however, share it.

WILDERNESS TIPS

Atwood's stories are frequently explorations of human limitation, presentations of people as victims of history, biology, or cultural conditioning. The theme of isolation and alienation recurs: There are borders and fences; generational gaps, which make parents and children strangers to each other; failed communication between women and men; gaps between language and felt experience. It is easy to overstate the pessimism which is present in her writings, to see only the wreckage of lives and relationships with which her work is strewn. It is therefore important not to lose sight of the human strength and tenacity (a favorite Atwood word) which also informs her work.

Eight years later, the stories in Atwood's short-fiction collection *Wilderness Tips* ultimately celebrated (still grudgingly) the same human strength and tenacity. This and related themes that shaped Atwood's vision over her writing life are embodied in the sometimes humorous and self-deprecating, often grim and urgent, seekings of the (mostly) female protagonists both to liberate and to preserve themselves in an increasingly ugly world. The conflicts that oppress these characters are rendered more nastily brutish by the realities of middle-class Canadian society in the late twentieth century. The predominant setting

is Toronto, no longer "the Good" but now the polluted, the unsafe, the dingy, the dangerous, and, worst, the indifferent.

The battle between the sexes is again the focus of most of the ten stories, the combatants ranging from youth through middle age. For the most part, the battles are lost or at best fought to a draw; the victories are Pyrrhic. In "True Trash," the consequences of adolescent sexual and social betrayals at a wilderness summer camp are dealt with only by escape into the banal anonymity of adulthood in the city. In "Hairball," Kat, who is in her thirties, is betrayed by both a previously acquiescent lover and her own body. Stripped of the brittle security she had carefully built for herself, she hits back with a spectacularly gross act of revenge. In "Isis in Darkness," conventional, secretly romantic Richard invests the poet Selena with a spiritual transcendence totally at odds with her real-life alienation and pathetic descent to early death over the years of their tenuous relationship. In "Weight," the narrator, a woman of substance, lives by compromise, paying defiant homage to the memory of her scrappy, optimistic friend Molly, who was battered to death by her mad husband. For many of these protagonists (as in Atwood's other works), language is a weapon of choice: In "Uncles," Susanna, though emotionally unfulfilled, is a successful, ambitious journalist; in "Hack Wednesday," Marcia is a freelance columnist; in "Weight," the narrator and Molly, aggressive lawyers, play elaborate word games to ward off threatening realities; in "The Bog Man," middle-aged Julie mythologizes her disastrous youthful affair with Connor. Nevertheless, as it does so often in Atwood's works, the gulf between language and understanding yawns, exacerbating the difficulties of human connections.

In two of the collection's most successful stories, however, that gulf is bridged by messages spoken, ironically, by the dead. In "The Age of Lead," a television documentary chronicles the exhumation from the Arctic permafrost of the body of young John Torrington, a member of the British Franklin Expedition, killed like his fellows by lead poisoning contracted through their consumption of tinned food. The documentary, which protagonist Jane is sporadically watching, weaves in and out of her recollections of Vincent, a friend from her childhood, recently dead. All their lives, his identity was ephemeral and undefined, but as Jane recalls his slow decline and death of an unnamed disease and ponders his enigmatic nature, the television offers the 150-years-dead Torrington, emerging virtually intact from his icy grave to "speak" eloquently to the living. Similarly, in "Death by Landscape," Lois's childhood acquaintance Lucy, who vanished on a camp canoe trip, slyly returns to haunt the adult Lois in Lois's collection of wilderness landscape paintings, assuming a solidity she never had as a live child.

Still, despite the pessimism, inadequacies, and guilt of many of the stories' characters, the reader's lasting impression is a positive one. "Hack Wednesday," the last story, speaks the same grumpy optimism that informs much of Atwood's poetry and prose. Marcia knows she will cry on Christmas Day, because life, however horrific at times, rushes by, and she is helpless to stop it: "It's all this hope. She gets distracted by it, and has trouble paying attention to the real news."

GOOD BONES AND SIMPLE MURDERS

Good Bones and Simple Murders incorporates some material from *Murder in the Dark*. The short pieces in this collection have been termed *jeux d'esprit* and speeded-up short stories. They showcase Atwood's wit, control, and wordplay as she speculates about hypothetical situations, such as "What would happen if men did all the cooking?", and revises traditional tales, such as "The Little Red Hen." In Atwood's version, the hen remains "henlike" and shares the loaf with all the animals that refused to help her produce it. In these pieces, characters who were silent in the original tales get to tell their side of the story. In "Gertrude Talks Back," Hamlet's mother explains matter-of-factly to her son that his father was a prig and that she murdered him. In "Simmering," the women have been cast out of the kitchens and surreptitiously reminisce about the good old days when they were allowed to cook.

Many of the short pieces here are explicitly about storytelling. The first story, "Murder in the Dark," describes a detective game and presents the writer as a trickster, a spinner of lies. "Unpopular Gals" tells of the mysterious women of traditional stories, the witches and evil stepmothers who tell their own side of the story here. "Let Us Now Praise Stupid Women" explains that it is not the careful, prudent, rational women who inspire fiction but rather the careless "airheads," the open, ingenuous, innocent women who set the plots in motion and make stories happen. "Happy Endings" plays with variations on a simple plot, answering in different ways what happens after a man and a woman meet. "The Page" explores the blank whiteness of an empty page and the myriad stories that lurk beneath it.

Atwood does not imply that human experience is beyond understanding, that evil is necessarily beyond redemption, or that human beings are beyond transformation. Her wit, humor, irony, imagination, and sharp intelligence save her and her readers from despair, if anything can. To write at all in this negative age seems in itself an act of courage and affirmation, an act Margaret Atwood gives no sign of renouncing. Though her readers already know Atwood's message, it bears repeating.

OTHER MAJOR WORKS

LONG FICTION: *The Edible Woman*, 1969; *Surfacing*, 1972; *Lady Oracle*, 1976; *Life Before Man*, 1979; *Bodily Harm*, 1981; *The Handmaid's Tale*, 1985; *Cat's Eye*, 1988; *The Robber Bride*, 1993; *Alias Grace*, 1996; *The Blind Assassin*, 2000.

POETRY: *Double Persephone*, 1961; *The Circle Game*, 1964; *Talismans for Children*, 1965; *Kaleidoscopes Baroque: A Poem*, 1965; *Speeches for Dr. Frankenstein*, 1966; *Expeditions*, 1966; *The Animals in That Country*, 1968; *What Was in the Garden*, 1969; *The Journals of Susanna Moodie*, 1970; *Procedures for Underground*, 1970; *Power Politics*, 1971; *You Are Happy*, 1974; *Selected Poems*, 1976; *Two-Headed Poems*, 1978; *True Stories*, 1981; *Snake Poems*, 1983; *Interlunar*, 1984; *Selected Poems II*, 1987; *Poems 1965-1975*, 1991; *Poems 1976-1989*, 1992; *Morning in the Burned House*, 1995.

NONFICTION: *Survival: A Thematic Guide to Canadian Literature*, 1972; *Second Words: Selected Critical Prose*, 1982; *Margaret Atwood: Conversations*,

1990; *Strange Things: The Malevolent North in Canadian Literature*, 1995; *Two Solicitudes: Conversations*, 1998 (with Victor-Lévy Beaulieu; Phyllis Aronoff and Howard Scott, translators).

CHILDREN'S LITERATURE: *Up in the Tree*, 1978; *Anna's Pet*, 1980 (with Joyce Barkhouse); *Princess Prunella and the Purple Peanut*, 1995 (with Maryann Kowalski).

EDITED TEXT: *The New Oxford Book of Canadian Verse in English*, 1982.

BIBLIOGRAPHY

Brown, Jane W. "Constructing the Narrative of Women's Friendship: Margaret Atwood's Reflexive Fiction." *Literature, Interpretation, Theory* 6 (1995): 197-212. In this special issue on Atwood, Brown argues that Atwood's narrative reflects the struggle of women to attain friendship. Maintains Atwood achieves this with such reflexive devices as embedded discourse, narrative fragmentation, and doubling. Discusses the difficulty women have in creating friendships because few women think such friendships are important.

Deery, June. "Science for Feminists: Margaret Atwood's Body of Knowledge." *Twentieth Century Literature* 43 (Winter, 1997): 470-486. Shows how the themes of feminine identity, personal and cultural history, body image, and colonization in Atwood's fiction are described in terms of basic laws of physics. Comments on Atwood's application of scientific concepts of time, space, energy, and matter to the experience of women under patriarchy in an adaptation of male discourse.

Grace, Sherrill E., and Lorraine Weir, eds. *Margaret Atwood: Language, Text, and System*. Vancouver: University of British Columbia Press, 1983. These nine essays by nine different critics treat Atwood's poetry and prose, examining the "Atwood system," her themes and her style from a variety of perspectives, including the feminist and the syntactical.

McCombs, Judith, ed. *Critical Essays on Margaret Atwood*. Boston: G. K. Hall, 1988. This indispensable volume contains thirty-two articles and essays, including assessments of patterns and themes in her poetry and prose. The entries are arranged in the chronological order of Atwood's primary works, beginning with *The Circle Game* and ending with *The Handmaid's Tale*. It includes a primary bibliography to 1986 and a thorough index. McCombs's introduction provides an illuminating overview of Atwood's writing career and is a satisfying rationale for her choices of the critical pieces included in the book.

Meindl, Dieter. "Gender and Narrative Perspective in Atwood's Stories." In *Margaret Atwood: Writing and Subjectivity*, edited by Colin Nelson. New York: St. Martin's Press, 1994. Discusses female narrative perspective in Atwood's stories. Shows how stories such as "The Man from Mars" and "The Sin Eater" focus on women's failure to communicate with men, thus trapping themselves inside their own inner worlds.

Rosenberg, Jerome H. *Margaret Atwood*. Boston: Twayne, 1984. This satisfying book consists of six chapters, examining Atwood's works, poetry, and prose, up to the early 1980's. Chapters 2 and 3 deal exclusively with her poetry. The chapters are preceded by a useful chronology and succeeded by thorough notes and references, a select bibliography, and an index. Rosenberg's writing is lucid and readable; his rationale for this study is presented in his preface, providing insight into the focus of his examination of Atwood's writing. An indispensable study.

Suarez, Isabel Carrera. "'Yet I Speak, Yet I Exist': Affirmation of the Subject in Atwood's Short Stories." In *Margaret Atwood: Writing and Subjectivity*, edited by Colin Nelson. New York: St. Martin's Press, 1994. Discusses Atwood's treatment of the self and its representation in language in her short stories. Demonstrates how in Atwood's early stories characters are represented or misrepresented by language and how struggle with language is a way to make themselves understood; explains how this struggle is amplified in later stories.

Wall, Kathleen. "Representing the Other Body: Frame Narratives in Margaret Atwood's 'Giving Birth' and Alice Munro's 'Meneseteung.'" *Cana-*

dian *Literature*, no. 154 (Autumn, 1997): 74-90. Argues that the nineteenth century nude pictures in these stories are not the traditional object of male observation but rather serve to remove the image of the female body from the reification of Romanticism. Contends that in both stories the images subversively call attention to the margin and the marginal.

Karen A. Kildahl, updated by Jill Rollins
and Karen F. Stein

LOUIS AUCHINCLOSS

Born: Lawrence, New York; September 27, 1917

PRINCIPAL SHORT FICTION

The Injustice Collectors, 1950
The Romantic Egoists, 1954
Powers of Attorney, 1963
Tales of Manhattan, 1967
Second Chance: Tales of Two Generations, 1970
The Partners, 1974
The Winthrop Covenant, 1976
Narcissa and Other Fables, 1983
The Book Class, 1984
Skinny Island: More Tales of Manhattan, 1987
Fellow Passengers: A Novel in Portraits, 1989
False Gods, 1992 (fables)
Tales of Yesteryear, 1994
The Collected Stories of Louis Auchincloss, 1994
The Atonement and Other Stories, 1997
The Anniversary and Other Stories, 1999

OTHER LITERARY FORMS

A practicing attorney on New York's Wall Street for more than forty years, Louis Auchincloss first drew critical attention as a novelist, reaching his peak with such memorable social chronicles as *The House of Five Talents* (1960), *Portrait in Brownstone* (1962), *The Rector of Justin* (1964), and *The Embezzler* (1966); some of his strongest short fiction dates from around the same time. The novel *The Education of Oscar Fairfax* (1995) was well received. Auchincloss also published several volumes of essays and criticism, most notably *Reflections of a Jacobite* (1961), *Reading Henry James* (1975), *False Dawn:* *Women in the Age of the Sun King* (1984), and *The Man Behind the Book: Literary Profiles* (1996). *A Writer's Capital*, a selective autobiographical essay dealing with Auchincloss's inspirations and early evolution as a novelist, appeared in 1974.

ACHIEVEMENTS

Although Louis Auchincloss never won any literary awards, his greatest single achievement as a writer of prose fiction may well be his continued questioning of the distinction between short and long narrative forms. Many of his collections may, in fact, be read with satisfaction either piecemeal or from start to finish, affording the reader an enviable glimpse behind the scenes of power.

BIOGRAPHY

A second-generation Wall Street lawyer, Louis Stanton Auchincloss was born September 27, 1917, at Lawrence, Long Island, the summer home of his parents, J. Howland Auchincloss and the former Priscilla Stanton. Educated at Groton School and at Yale University, Auchincloss began writing as a teenager and submitted his first finished novel as an undergraduate. Although the publisher Charles Scribner's Sons expressed interest in his planned second novel even as the firm rejected his first, young Auchincloss saw fit to take the rejection as an omen of sorts and embark on a law career with all deliberate speed. Actively seeking the best law school that would accept him without a bachelor's degree, he left Yale University after three years and enrolled in1938 at the University of Virginia Law School, having presumably renounced literature for life.

In retrospect, Auchincloss's impulsive decision to leave Yale University prior to graduation turned out to have been a timely one; after receiving his law degree in 1941, he was hired by the well-known Wall Street firm of Sullivan and Cromwell and was actually able to practice his profession for several months before the United States went to war, with a job awaiting him upon his return from inevitable military service.

Louis Auchincloss (Jerry Bauer)

Commissioned in the Navy, Auchincloss served in both the Atlantic and Pacific war theaters after an initial posting to the Canal Zone, an area little touched by the war, where he began to reconsider the option of creative writing. The young officer kept his eyes and ears open throughout the war, also reading voraciously to pass the long, idle hours at sea. At Groton School and at Yale University he had read mainly for academic success, but during the war he began to read for pleasure, incidentally steeping himself in the British, American, and Continental narrative traditions. By the time he was mustered out in 1945, Au-

chincloss had begun plotting a novel, *The Indifferent Children* (1947), combining his wartime observations with characters recalled from his earlier attempts at long fiction. Back in New York, he took an extended furlough to finish the novel before returning to legal practice at Sullivan and Cromwell in 1946.

Published the next year under the pseudonym Andrew Lee and over the objections of Auchincloss's parents (with whom he still lived), *The Indifferent Children* received enough good reviews to encourage the young lawyer to pursue his writing, particularly the short fiction later assembled in *The Injustice Collectors*. Following the publication of the novel *Sybil* in 1951, Auchincloss began to question his "double life" as attorney and author; with the moral and financial support of his parents, he resigned from Sullivan and Cromwell to work full time at his writing, only to conclude that the result—the novel *A Law for the Lion* (1953) and the stories collected in *The Romantic Egoists*—differed little in quality or quantity from what he had done before. By 1954, he was back on Wall Street in search of a job, resigned to juggling dual careers but barred by company policy from returning to his old firm once he had resigned. Hired by the firm of Hawkins, Delafield and Wood, Auchincloss rose to full partnership by 1958, the year following his marriage to Adèle Lawrence, a Vanderbilt descendant some thirteen years his junior with whom he would have three sons. His literary career, meanwhile, continued to flourish along with—and to survive—his legal practice, from which he retired at the end of 1986, in his seventieth year.

Along with his legal and literary work, Auchincloss was active in cultural and civic affairs. A life fellow of the Pierpont Morgan Library, he served as president of the Museum of the City of New York and as a member of the advisory board of *Dictionary of Literary Biography*.

ANALYSIS

A keen and informed observer of American manners and morals, Louis Auchincloss established himself rather early in his career as the peer, if not the superior, of such older social chroniclers as John P. Marquand and John O'Hara, with a particular insider's gift for exposing the well-concealed inner workings of society and politics. Writing in a clear, spare, even classical prose style, Auchincloss credibly "demystifies" for his readers the behavior of those in positions of privilege and power, persons whose actions and decisions help to make the rules by which all Americans should live.

A willing and grateful heir to the "novel of manners" tradition exemplified in the United States by Henry James and perpetuated by Edith Wharton, Louis Auchincloss is first and foremost a writer of "chronicles," long or short, recording observations either topical or historical; well versed in the rules and patterns of Western civilization, Auchincloss tends to perceive historical value even in the topical, giving to his observations a stamp of scholarly authority often lacking in the work of other would-be social satirists. During the 1940's, at the start of his career, Auchincloss tended to deal with the historical present, in the aftermath of World War II; later, in fiction both long and short, Auchincloss focused primarily on the 1930's, the period of his adolescence and young manhood, much as O'Hara in middle age returned to his own adolescent years, the 1920's, in search of clues to what has happened since that time in American society and politics.

Almost from the start, Auchincloss's narratives tended to blur the traditional boundaries separating long fiction from short fiction. In most of his collections, the stories are linked by theme and/or recurrent characters, and in certain volumes the tales are told by a single unifying narrator.

THE INJUSTICE COLLECTORS

Auchincloss's earliest short fiction, assembled in *The Injustice Collectors* in 1950 after being published separately in periodicals such as *Harper's* and *The New Yorker*, is unified by a theme suggested in the title, a nagging suspicion that most people, even—and in the present case, especially—those born to privilege are frequently the authors of their own misfortunes. In his preface to the volume, Auchincloss relates that he has borrowed the title from a popular book by the psychiatrist Edmund Bergler, modifying its meaning to suit his own aspirations as a writer of short stories. A psychiatrist or

even a novelist, he explains, may well probe the causes of the behavior described, while writers of *short* fiction must content themselves with recording the symptoms. Indeed, the evolution of Auchincloss's approach to narrative over the next four decades would frequently test and even cross the boundaries between long and short fiction, with assembled symptoms leading to a rather conclusive diagnosis. In his first volume of stories, however, Auchincloss had yet to unravel the tangled threads implicit in his chosen subject matter, let alone to follow them.

On balance, *The Injustice Collectors* is a rather traditional collection of stories in the manner of James or Wharton, with occasional flashes of originality and even brilliance. One of the tales, "Maud," clearly adumbrates the type of restless, thoughtful heroine that would populate Auchincloss's early novels, a woman whose expectations of life differ sharply from those of her parents. Feeling herself "imprisoned" in her attorney father's household, Maud Spreddon refuses to accept even her own potential capacity for love; engaged to marry her father's junior partner, Halsted Nicholas, who admires her rebellious streak and who has, in fact, waited for her to grow to marriageable age, Maud breaks the engagement abruptly, presumably doubting her fitness for marriage. Several years later, the two meet during World War II in London, where Maud is serving with the Red Cross and Halsted with the Army Air Corps. After a rather stormy reconciliation, Maud accepts Halsted's second proposal; when Halsted's plane is shot down over France two days later, a week before the Normandy invasion, Maud, unwilling to be pitied, resolves to keep the reconciliation a secret for life.

In "Fall of a Sparrow," Auchincloss points the way toward a theme that will loom large in his second collection: the social dynamics between reserve officers and careerists during wartime. Narrated by an officer known only as Ted, "Fall of a Sparrow" shows the shortcomings and eventual disgrace of Victor Harden, Ted's prep-school classmate whose outward success in school and service hides a deep-seated insecurity that proves in time to be his undoing. In *The Romantic Egoists*, Auchincloss will go even further in his delineation of military rivalries and factions, often raising serious questions in the reader's mind as to how the United States and its allies managed to win the war.

THE ROMANTIC EGOISTS

Unified by the narration of Peter Westcott, whose legal and naval experiences run roughly parallel to those of the author, *The Romantic Egoists* shows Auchincloss hitting his stride as a master of prose fiction, as do the novels published around the same time. "Loyalty Up and Loyalty Down," the fictional account of an incident later recalled in *A Writer's Capital*, pits Westcott and his fellow reservists against Harry Ellis, a career officer risen from the ranks, who happens to serve as their skipper. Although perhaps traditional as well as predictable, the tension between the college graduates and their commanding officer is here presented from a somewhat different perspective. What the reservists resent most deeply about their skipper is his apparent willingness to let the rest of the Navy sink, if need be, in order to save his own ship; repeatedly, he will turn down authorized requests from other vessels for food and supplies, and when obliged to rescue surviving marines from a battle station he treats them with contempt, calling them names as he parades before them in a Chinese dressing grown. Westcott, willing but finally unable to serve as peacemaker, eventually allows Ellis to hang himself, observing the skipper's orders to the letter while preserving his own integrity; Westcott watches with combined amusement and consternation as the vessel, lead ship in a convoy, runs over a buoy, followed by all the ships in its wake. Only later will Westcott reflect on the possible danger to the other ships and on the depths to which the running feud with Ellis has finally reduced him.

Written in a similar vein, "Wally" contrasts the ambitions of the title character, one Ensign Wallingford, with those of Lieutenant Sherwood Lane, an Ivy Leaguer and "aristocrat" who, after more than a year of shuffling papers in the Canal Zone, feels that his background and training more than qualify him for a desk job in Washington, D.C. Of all the officers stationed in the Canal Zone and seeking a transfer, only Wallingford and Lane actively seek further shore duty; the others, motivated either by patriotism or by the spirit of adventure, expect to see action at sea. Wallingford, a native of Omaha and a graduate of the hotel school at Cornell University, wants nothing more or less than to serve as he has been trained, managing a hotel for the Navy somewhere in the United States. Whenever possible, Sherwood Lane will block Wally's repeated requests for a transfer, uneasily seeing in the midwesterner's "ridiculous" ambitions a discomfiting and disquieting reflection of his own. In the end, with Westcott's covert assistance, Wally will finish out the war in Florida, helping to run a hotel for the navy with one of his former Cornell professors as his commanding officer; Sherwood Lane, surpassing either his or Westcott's wildest speculations, will have ended the war as a surviving hero, having soon tired of the Washington job and served with high distinction as a line officer. "None of us, least of all Sherwood," concludes Westcott ruefully, "could really stand to live for any length of time with that part of ourselves we recognized in Wally."

"The Great World and Timothy Colt," the longest and arguably the strongest of the tales collected in *The Romantic Egoists*, began the author's detailed exploration of his own working environment as a lawyer on Wall Street and is as painstaking as his examination of social and professional dynamics in the navy. A prototypical "workaholic" married to a former law-school classmate at Columbia University, Timothy Colt personifies the rising postwar "meritocracy," in whom ambition and hard work might well compensate for perceived disadvantages of "background." Seen from the perspective of his slightly younger associate Peter Westcott, "Timmy" Colt is hard-driving and meticulous, yet not without his personable side—at least at first. If Timmy works best under pressure, however, the pressure soon begins to exact its toll, leaving him particularly vulnerable to the gibes and taunts of Sam Liendecker, a rich, influential client to whose case Timmy and Westcott have been assigned by the managing partner. As Flora Colt will explain to Westcott, Liendecker instinctively senses Timmy's fundamental weakness—a nearly total lack of self-esteem that keeps him striving even harder to please those in need of his services. In time,

Timmy, pushed beyond his limits, will insult the aging Liendecker in public, a breach of etiquette for which both his wife and his superiors expect him to apologize. Thus goaded, Timmy in fact will apologize—with Westcott as witness—and it is at that point that Timothy Colt "sells out," in his own mind, to forces that he feels have conspired against him. Thereafter, he quite deliberately and consciously behaves as the antithesis of his former self, incidentally blaming his uncomprehending wife, as well as himself, for the direction that his career has taken. Timmy thus emerges as the ultimate "Romantic Egoist"—not an "egotist" but a self-absorbed dreamer for whom even the best of life will prove a disappointment.

As Auchincloss noted in his preface to the earlier collection, writers of short stories must content themselves with "symptoms." In time, however, the author of "The Great World and Timothy Colt" saw fit to broaden and deepen his analysis of Timmy with a full-fledged novel published under the same title in 1956. In the novel, several of the names are changed and some of the characters are changed or others added, but the central argument of the narrative remains quite the same as the quixotic Timmy Colt, who, risking disbarment, willingly testifies in court to an offense that he did not, in fact, commit—except in his own mind.

Before long, Auchincloss would all but abandon short fiction for the better part of a decade, devoting his increasingly prodigious energies to "Wall Street" novels in the vein of *The Great World and Timothy Colt*. By the time his next collection appeared in 1963, Auchincloss would in turn have deserted the Wall Street novels in favor of the historically dimensional social chronicles, beginning with *The House of Five Talents*.

POWERS OF ATTORNEY

Arguably, Auchincloss by the early 1960's had "relegated" his Wall Street material to the shorter fictional form; the stories collected in *Powers of Attorney* indeed hark back to the themes and settings of novels written before 1960. The narrator Peter Westcott is gone for good, not to reappear—and then as Dan Ruggles—until *Fellow Passengers: A Novel in Portraits*, published as late as 1989. In place of a uni-

fying narrator, however, Auchincloss presents a cast of recurrent characters who move throughout the stories, perhaps serving as focal point in one tale and as part of the background in others. Perhaps predictably, the main "character" of *Powers of Attorney* is a Wall Street law firm whose members often grapple with problems and decisions similar to those that beset Timothy Colt in the short story and later novel bearing his name. "The Deductible Yacht" tells the tale of a hereditary New York "aristocrat," born to high moral principles, for whom the elevation to partnership at Tower, Tilney and Webb is inextricably linked to his professional relationship with the Armenian-born Inka Dahduh, a self-made tycoon who makes no secret of having the law "shaved" in his favor; in the end, Bayard Kip will accept both partnership and client as the price for maintaining his wife and family in the style toward which his background has pointed him.

"The Single Reader," among the more Jamesian of the stories in the collection, portrays the "secret life" of Morris Madison, the firm's senior tax specialist. Deserted early in life by an unfaithful spouse, Madison has devoted decades of his free time to a diary that he imagines as the modern-day equivalent of writer Saint-Simon's *Mémoires du duc de Saint-Simon: Ou, L'Observateur véridique sur le règne de Louis XIV* (1788; *The Memoirs of the Duke of Saint Simon on the Reign of Louis XIV*, 1857); when at last he contemplates remarriage to an eligible widow, Madison makes the mistake of asking the lady to read his multivolume journal, in which she no doubt correctly recognizes an indomitable rival for the aging lawyer's love.

TALES OF MANHATTAN

Tales of Manhattan, published in 1967 with a sequel, *Skinny Island: More Tales of Manhattan*, to follow twenty years later, is somewhat less unified—or novelistic—in its construction than *Powers of Attorney*; notwithstanding, groups of stories are internally linked, more or less demanding that they be read in sequence within each section. The opening sequence, "Memories of an Auctioneer," is narrated by Roger Jordan, an art dealer with the instincts of a sleuth, a keen eye for beauty, and a sharp nose for sniffing out fraud in life as in art. Persuaded that possessions, especially collections, offer psychological clues about their owners, Jordan manages to unearth more than a few juicy secrets; his observations, however, are not limited to artifacts. In "The Question of the Existence of Waring Stohl," Jordan at first suspects the title character, an obnoxious dilettante and would-be novelist, of "sponging off" his and Jordan's former professor, the eminent literary critic Nathaniel Streebe. Unknown to Jordan, however, Stohl is mortally ill; not long after Stohl's early death, Streebe will reveal himself as the true parasite of the pair, having encouraged the young man's literary ambitions in order to write his posthumous biography, published to good reviews under the same title as the Auchincloss story.

SECOND CHANCE

Second Chance, published as a collection in 1970, contains some of Auchincloss's strongest short fiction, particularly "The Prince and the Pauper," ironically sharing its title with a tale by Mark Twain. "The Prince and the Pauper" in many respects summarizes the entire Auchincloss canon, showing the mobility and true pragmatism that lie beneath the apparent structure of "society." Balancing the fortunes of the "aristocratic" attorney Brooks Clarkson against those of Benny Galenti, a former office boy and law-school dropout (owing to the pregnancy of Teresa, now his wife) whom Brooks singled out for special treatment and in time elevated to office manager with appropriate raises in pay, Auchincloss portrays with enviable skill the social dynamics at work in American society. Benny, the son of immigrants, feels that he can never shake off his debt to Brooks, who provided him not only with a decent salary but also with investment advice and, on occasion, a loan with which that advice might be followed. At the time of the story, Brooks Clarkson has lost his position with the law firm, continuing a long slide into alcoholism and general disrepair that he seems to have wished upon himself, together with his wife Fanny; the implication is that Brooks has felt somehow undeserving of, and threatened by, his elevated status both professional and social, finding in the Galentis a vitality and drive somehow lacking in himself and Fanny. The story

ends with Benny somewhat reluctantly accepting for the sake of his family a membership in the Glenville Club, from which the Clarksons have long since been expelled for drunken misbehavior and nonpayment of dues. Society, implies Auchincloss, will continue to make and to break its own rules.

THE PARTNERS

The Partners, published in 1974, differs little in form or concept from the earlier *Powers of Attorney*. Once again, the "life" described is that of a Wall Street law firm in transition. Perhaps the strongest story in the collection is "The Novelist of Manners," in which a best-selling, scandal-mongering novelist is successfully defended against a libel charge by Leslie Carter, a junior partner in the firm, who is stationed in Paris to handle European business. As the case proceeds, Carter, who harbors some literary aspirations of his own, persuades the middle-aged Dana Clyde to try his hand at a "serious" novel, taking a respite from the "good life" of parties and sports cars in order to do so. Clyde does as he is told, but when the novel finally appears it is little different from what he has produced before. Carter, meanwhile, is stunned to find himself portrayed in the novel as a character who commits suicide at the end, having discovered his own importance on his honeymoon with the novel's heroine. As Clyde's wife Xenia explains to Carter, Clyde can never forgive Carter for pushing him beyond his limits and has taken his revenge. Reminiscent of the author's own conclusions after leaving from the law in favor of his writing, the destiny of Clyde and Carter also allows Auchincloss to make his own wry comments on the fate of the "novel of manners," of which he may well be the last traditional, nonsensational practitioner.

FELLOW PASSENGERS

Fellow Passengers, subtitled *A Novel in Portraits*, represents one of Auchincloss's more intriguing experiments in blending long and short fiction. Unlike the vignettes in *The Book Class*, the "portraits" presented here can be read profitably as individual stories, each evoking memorable characters. For the first time since *The Romantic Egoists*, all the tales are told by a semiautobiographical narrator, in the present case a gracefully aging lawyer known as Dan

Ruggles. Like Peter Westcott in the earlier collections, Ruggles tends to stand aside from the action that he recalls, revealing relatively little of himself save for his reactions. If anything, the details of Ruggles's life are drawn even closer to Auchincloss's own than those of Westcott; a case in point, "Leonard Armster" recounts in barely fictionalized form the short, troubled, but somehow exuberant life of the author's friend Jack Woods, recalled in *A Writer's Capital* as a major influence on Auchincloss's aspirations and development as a writer. One cannot help but suspect that the other portraits are drawn equally true to life now that their models are dead, yet in each case Auchincloss moves away from illustration or photography toward archetype and art, portraying the characters against the background of their time, usually but not invariably the 1930's.

THE ATONEMENT AND OTHER STORIES

Auchincloss's attention to short fiction did not stop with publication of *The Collected Stories of Louis Auchincloss* in 1994. *The Atonement and Other Stories*, issued on Auchincloss's eightieth birthday, presents twelve new selections. It portrays characters and situations very similar to those in earlier works. These later stories display no major innovations in theme or technique, but they reveal no diminishing of Auchincloss's narrative powers. As the title suggests, a persistent theme in this collection is the attempt to make amends for past misconduct.

The title story, described by one reviewer as a miniature *Bonfire of the Vanities* (alluding to the 1987 novel by Tom Wolfe), portrays Sandy Tremain, a wealthy Wall Street investment banker whose partner is arrested for illegal insider trading. Equally guilty but able to elude prosecution, Sandy consults his father, a retired teacher who has devoted his entire life to the prep school where he was first a student and then a beloved master. Sandy considers confession, divorce, and solitary exile to a foreign country as a possible response to his dilemma. His father, however, describes such a course as a "bath of self-pity" and affirms that Sandy's real and more difficult obligation is to stand with his wife and family.

In "The Hidden Muse" Auchincloss develops a character much like himself and dramatizes once

more the tug of war between law and literature. The protagonist, David Hallowell, is a young World War II veteran and promising associate at a Wall Street law firm. In this case the misdeed that demands atonement is a sin against himself. David's lawyer father died prematurely, and his mother desperately wants her only son to achieve glory in the same profession. Throughout his school years David indulges his talent for writing fiction, but, in acceding to his mother's demands, he later abandons his secret muse. When his friend and mentor at the law firm rises to a full partnership, David has an epiphany. He realizes that his major concern is not what the firm can do for him, but what he can do with it. He resolves to resign his position and ends the story with plans for transforming his coworkers into characters in a novel.

In "The Last Great Divorce" Clarinda Eberling presents a first-person apology for her life. On the occasion of her daughter's divorce in 1961, Clarinda looks back at the very public breakup of her own marriage in 1938. Joe Eliot and Howard Eberling were best friends and partners in a law firm. Clarinda married Joe but loved the more assertive Howard. After sixteen years with Joe, she engineers an affair with Howard that ultimately terminates two marriages, a long friendship, and a business partnership. To Clarinda's dismay, however, Howard attempts "a kind of atonement" by retiring from public life and becoming an academic. Clarinda accepts her exile but can never completely atone for the pain she has inflicted on her two lovers and her drug-abusing son.

OTHER MAJOR WORKS

LONG FICTION: *The Indifferent Children*, 1947 (as Andrew Lee); *Sybil, 1951; A Law for the Lion*, 1953; *The Great World and Timothy Colt*, 1956; *Venus in Sparta*, 1958; *Pursuit of the Prodigal*, 1959; *The House of Five Talents*, 1960; *Portrait in Brownstone*, 1962; *The Rector of Justin*, 1964; *The Embezzler*, 1966; *A World of Profit*, 1968; *I Come as a Thief*, 1972; *The Dark Lady*, 1977; *The Country Cousin*, 1978; *The House of the Prophet*, 1980; *The Cat and the King*, 1981; *Watchfires*, 1982; *Exit Lady Masham*, 1983; *The Book Class*, 1984; *Honorable Men*, 1985; *Diary of a Yuppie*, 1986; *The Golden Calves*, 1988;

Fellow Passengers, 1989; *The Lady of Situations*, 1990; *Three Lives*, 1993 (novellas); *The Education of Oscar Fairfax*, 1995; *Her Infinite Variety*, 2000.

NONFICTION: *Reflections of a Jacobite*, 1961; *Pioneers and Caretakers: A Study of Nine American Women Novelists*, 1965; *Motiveless Malignity*, 1969; *Edith Wharton: A Woman in Her Time*, 1971; *Richelieu*, 1972; *A Writer's Capital*, 1974 (autobiography); *Reading Henry James*, 1975; *Life, Law, and Letters: Essays and Sketches*, 1979; *Persons of Consequence: Queen Victoria and Her Circle*, 1979; *False Dawn: Women in the Age of the Sun King*, 1984; *The Vanderbilt Era: Profiles of a Gilded Age*, 1989; *J. P. Morgan: The Financier as Collector*, 1990; *Love Without Wings: Some Friendships in Literature and Politics*, 1991; *The Style's the Man: Reflections on Proust, Fitzgerald, Wharton, Vidal, and Others*, 1994; *The Man Behind the Book: Literary Profiles*, 1996; *La Gloire: The Roman Empire of Corneille and Racine*, 1996; *Woodrow Wilson*, 2000.

BIBLIOGRAPHY

Gelderman, Carol W. *Louis Auchincloss: A Writer's Life*. New York: Crown, 1993. A good, updated biography of the writer. Includes bibliographical references and an index.

Parsell, David B. *Louis Auchincloss*. Boston: Twayne, 1988. Parsell's sixth chapter, entitled "The Novel as Omnibus: Auchincloss's Collected Short Fiction," is recommended for those seeking to explore Auchincloss's singular approach to short and long fiction.

Piket, Vincent. *Louis Auchincloss: The Growth of a Novelist*. Basingstoke, England: Macmillan, 1991. Part of the New Directions in American Studies series, this critical look at Auchincloss's career includes bibliographical references and an index.

Plimpton, George. "The Art of Fiction CXXXVIII: Louis Auchincloss." *The Paris Review* 36 (Fall, 1994): 72-94. In this interview, Auchincloss discusses his fiction and nonfiction, commenting on his relationship with editors, how important plot and character are in his fiction, and his notion of literary style as a reflection of the personality of the writer.

Tintner, Adeline R. "Louis Auchincloss Reinvents Edith Wharton's 'After Holbein.'" *Studies in Short Fiction* 33 (Spring, 1996): 275-277. Argues that Auchincloss uses a section of Edith Wharton's "After Holbein" in the episode "The Dinner Out," in his novelistic collection *The Partners*. Suggests that in these two stories the fear of death lingers over royal feasts.

David B. Parsell, updated by Albert Wilhelm

JANE AUSTEN

Born: Steventon, England; December 16, 1775
Died: Winchester, England; July 18, 1817

PRINCIPAL SHORT FICTION

Minor Works, 1954 (Volume 6 of the *Oxford Illustrated Jane Austen*, R. W. Chapman, editor)

OTHER LITERARY FORMS

Jane Austen is best known for her six novels about middle-class life in the nineteenth century. Four were published during her lifetime: *Sense and Sensibility* (1811), *Pride and Prejudice* (1813), *Mansfield Park* (1814), and *Emma* (1815). *Northanger Abbey* (1818) and *Persuasion* (1818) were published posthumously.

ACHIEVEMENTS

Although she was not widely recognized in her own day, Jane Austen did enjoy the appreciation of discriminating readers whose contemporary esteem has since become the critical consensus. The scrupulous accuracy, complex irony, and serious moral speculation of Austen's novels of middle-class life provided the groundwork for the "great tradition" of the nineteenth century novel. Austen's short fiction,

Jane Austen (Library of Congress)

written before she turned seventeen, is experimental work in which the beginning writer mocks the absurdities and limitation of the sentimental novel popular at the end of the eighteenth century and tentatively explores the possibilities of themes and literary techniques that she will later develop in her mature work. By slightly exaggerating the sensibility of a heroine, the refinement of a hero, the effusiveness of their conversations, and the unlikelihood of their adventures, Austen makes plain the absurdity of the worldview purveyed by sentimental novels.

Biography

Jane Austen was the seventh of eight children born to a Steventon, Hampshire clergyman. A large family of gentle lineage and no fortune, the Austens were a lively, literary household whose quiet country life left time for novel reading and charades. In 1801, Austen's father moved with his wife and daughters to Bath, an expensive and populous watering place, possibly because his daughters were still unmarried. Jane is reported to have fallen in love in that year, but the

gentleman died before a formal engagement had occurred. She never married. Jane's elder sister by three years, Cassandra, was closest to her, and they lived together continually until Jane died in Winchester in 1817.

Analysis

With unsurpassed charm and subtlety, Jane Austen's novels of country life present and appraise the manners, morals, and relationships of Regency England's prosperous middle class. In choosing to depict what she called her "bits of ivory," the segment of the world she knew best, Jane Austen steered the course of the English novel away from the melodramatic implausibilities that dominated popular fiction at the turn of the nineteenth century. Sir Walter Scott, who recognized the importance of Austen's choice, also praised her for the literary finesse that made such a choice workable, "the exquisite touch which renders commonplace things and characters interesting from the truth of the description and the sentiment."

Although the subject of Jane Austen's novels was contemporary life, it was contemporary literature with its various excesses and deficiencies which inspired her earliest attempts at fiction. In the short pieces collected as her juvenilia—tales, miniature novels, and epistolary narratives—Austen applies the conventions of sentimental fiction, which she and her family read avidly but critically, with rigorous consistency and pushes them to their logical extremes to demonstrate that such standards produce slipshod literature and convey a false view of the world.

Austen's juvenile fiction differs from the novels in its audience as well as in its subject matter. The young author wrote these short pieces for the private amusement of her family, and as an experienced novelist never contemplated revising and publishing them. Consequently the reader familiar with the decorous elegance of the public prose sees a new side of Jane Austen in the short fiction which, like her letters, voices a tough candor and a blunt humor that the novels mute: Remarks such as "Damme Elfrida *you* may be married but *I* wont" seldom make their way from the nursery of Austen's short fiction to the drawing rooms of her adult novels.

Many of the apprentice pieces are literary parodies and burlesques poking fun at the distinctive features of the novel of sensibility: the high-flown language, incredible coincidences, instant friendships, immoderate loves, unaccountable lapses of memory, and sudden recognitions. For example, "Evelyn" amusingly points out the dangers of the cult of sensibility's much-vaunted "sympathetic imagination" unallied with judgment by portraying a village full of utterly and undiscriminatingly benevolent people. "The Beautifull Cassandra" achieves its comic effect by yoking two shortcomings of the popular novel: absurd, unmotivated action included to engage readers and trivial details supplied to convince them. A typical effusion from "Frederic and Elfrida" demonstrates the emptiness of the sentimental novel's stock praises and the egocentricity of its refined protagonists:

Lovely & too charming Fair one, notwithstanding your forbidding Squint, your greasy tresses & your swelling Back, which are more frightfull than imagination can paint or pen describe, I cannot refrain from expressing my raptures, at the engaging Qualities of your Mind, which so amply atone for the Horror, with which your first appearance must ever inspire the unwary visitor.

Your sentiments so nobly expressed on the different excellencies of Indian & English Muslins, & the judicious preference you give the former, have excited in me an admiration of which I alone can give an adequate idea, by assuring you it is nearly equal to what I feel for myself.

LOVE AND FRIENDSHIP

Perhaps the most wide-ranging and successful of the literary burlesques is *Love and Friendship* (1922), in which Laura, a paragon of sensibility, relates her adventures through a series of letters. Here, Jane Austen lampoons most of the conventions of the sentimental novel and its popular successor, the gothic romance: the convoluted plots, star-crossed loves, cruel families, and in particular the transports of emotion that, in the world of sensibility, are the index of personal excellence. At the climax of this story containing enough harrowing incident for a triple-decker novel, Laura and her bosom friend Sophia discover "two Gentlemen most elegantly attired but

weltering in their blood" who turn out to be their husbands. The heroines react in the prescribed manner:

Sophia shreiked & fainted on the Ground—I screamed and instantly ran mad—. We remained thus mutually deprived of our Senses some minutes, & on regaining them were deprived of them again—. For an Hour & a Quarter did we continue in this unfortunate situation—Sophia fainting every moment & I running Mad as often. At length a Groan from the hapless Edward (who alone retained any share of Life) restored us to ourselves—. Had we before imagined that either of them lived, we should have been more sparing of our Grief—.

Sophia, in fact, literally dies of the sensibility that has engendered her "shreiks and faints," though not before warning Laura of the medical risks that she now, too late, knows attend on swoons: "Run mad as often as you chuse," Sophia concludes, "but do not faint." These last words undercut many a sentimental deathbed.

In *Love and Friendship*, Jane Austen's satire points out the weaknesses of the literary fashion of sensibility but extends its criticism to include the code of behavior as well. Sensibility as embodied by Laura and Sophia, who meddle, lie, and even steal with perfect complacency, is ethically bankrupt as well as absurdly unrealistic. In several of the juvenile pieces, among them *The Three Sisters* (1933), *Lesley Castle* (1922), and *Catherine* (1818), literary parody gives way to concern with the social and moral themes that pervade the mature novels; but the most sophisticated example of Austen's "serious" short fiction is *Lady Susan* (1871, 1925), an epistolary narrative written after the juvenilia but before the versions we now possess of the six novels.

LADY SUSAN

Lady Susan is unique among Jane Austen's works for several reasons. Lady Susan Vernon, the beautiful and brilliant main character, is Austen's only aristocratic protagonist, and her only *femme fatale*. Unlike the heroines of the novels, whose characters are being formed by experience and who will place themselves in society by the ultimate act of self-definition, marriage, Lady Susan possesses a character matured, even hardened, by years of social skirmishing in the Great World. Furthermore, as a titled widow she already has an established place in society, a most respectable public position she has every intention of retaining without sacrificing her private taste for amorous adventures. Whereas the heroines of the novels gradually learn what they need to know, Lady Susan knows from the start of the story exactly what she wants: "Those women are inexcusable," she observes, "who forget what is due to themselves and to the opinion of the World."

The substance of *Lady Susan* is social and romantic intrigue. Lady Susan balances the attentions of her kindly brother-in-law, her married lover, the rich and well-born fool she has marked out for her insignificant daughter, and the self-assured young man of fashion whose heart she wins for amusement and thinks of retaining as an investment, while two virtuous but worldly women, the brother-in-law's wife, Mrs. Vernon, and her mother, Lady De Courcy, do their best to frustrate her efforts. Although *Lady Susan*'s action, deftly manipulated by the protagonist until luck finally thwarts her, is interesting as pure narrative, its chief fascination is psychological revelation. Lady Susan is as honest with herself as she is false to others; and the epistolary format, often a clumsy way of presenting a story, is ideally suited to pointing up this contrast between her social roles and her true character. The letters Lady Susan's dupes and foes exchange with one another and with her show how easily she can identify and play on the follies of "virtuous" people; Lady Susan's candid letters to her confidante Mrs. Johnson let us see how far the scheming adventuress surpasses the other characters in the quality that is the first step to true virtue: self-knowledge.

Thus, this important piece of short fiction is more than a chronological transition from Jane Austen's juvenilia to her novels; it is a moral bridge as well. In *Lady Susan*, Austen moves from the realm of literary burlesque into sustained, serious treatment of moral problems, but the conclusion she leaves us to draw is more completely ironic and hence more "literary" than any found in the later works. Never again in Jane Austen is vice so attractive and successful and virtue so unappealing.

OTHER MAJOR WORKS

LONG FICTION: *Sense and Sensibility*, 1811; *Pride and Prejudice*, 1813; *Mansfield Park*, 1814; *Emma*, 1815; *Northanger Abbey*, 1818; *Persuasion*, 1818; *Lady Susan and the Watsons*, 1882; *Love and Friendship*, 1922; *Fragment of a Novel*, 1925; *Plan of a Novel*, 1926; *Sanditon*, 1975.

NONFICTION: *Jane Austen's Letters to Her Sister Cassandra and Others*, 1932 (edited by R. W. Chapman).

CHILDREN'S LITERATURE: *Catherine*, 1818; *Lesley Castle*, 1922; *Three Sisters*, 1933.

BIBLIOGRAPHY

Austen, Jane. *Jane Austen's Letters to Her Sister Cassandra and Others*. Edited by R. W. Chapman. 2 vols. Oxford, England: Clarendon Press, 1932. The first collection of surviving Austen letters arranged chronologically in two volumes with appendices that give summary identifications of anyone who is ambiguously mentioned in the text of the letters. With corrected spelling and punctuation. Includes a map of eighteenth century Berkshire and Surrey, England.

Brown, Julie Prewit. *Jane Austen's Novels*. Cambridge, Mass.: Harvard University Press, 1979. A somewhat feminist perspective of Jane Austen as a conscious artist who masterfully employed ironic comedy and satiric realism. Five chapters explore the purpose and subtleties of each novel. Includes an eye-opening chapter on the artist as a woman writer.

Bush, Douglas. *Jane Austen*. New York: Macmillan, 1975. This work, addressed to general readers, shows how Austen re-created themes from many minor eighteenth century writers. Each of Austen's major works is summarized and briefly analyzed in an individual chapter.

Grey, J. David, ed. *The Jane Austen Companion*. New York: Macmillan, 1986. A collection of sixty-four essays from a wide range of academic and nonacademic lovers of Austen's art. Individual essays cover a great variety of subjects and have diverse approaches. Includes "A Dictionary of Jane Austen's Life and Works," written by H. Abigail

Bok. This volume is a comprehensive guide to both real and imagined places, people, and literary allusion in Austen's work.

Halperin, John. *The Life of Jane Austen*. Baltimore: The Johns Hopkins University Press, 1984. A biographical study of Jane Austen's life with a focus on the association between the life of the artist and the works she produced. Valuable for a realistic look at the life of a legendary figure. Includes illustrations.

Le Faye, Deidre. *Jane Austen: A Family Record*. London: The British Library, 1989. A revision of the 1913 edition of *Life and Letters of Jane Austen*, written by a descendant of Austen's nephew, James Edward. In addition, Le Faye has done extensive contemporary research. This book provides a thorough look at Austen's life and the close-knit family on which she was financially dependent. Includes a thorough chronology of Jane Austen's life and an extensive family pedigree. With illustrations.

Selwyn, David. *Jane Austen and Leisure*. London: Hambledon Press, 1999. Examines the manners and customs of Austen's class in her era and how Austen portrays them in her works.

Waldron, Mary. *Jane Austen and the Fiction of Her Time*. Cambridge, England: Cambridge University Press, 1999. Puts Austen's writings in the context of other literary output of her era. Includes bibliographical references and an index.

Peter W. Graham, updated by Leslie A. Pearl

B

ISAAC BABEL

Born: Odessa, Ukraine, Russia; July 13, 1894
Died: Siberia, U.S.S.R.; March 17, 1941

PRINCIPAL SHORT FICTION

Rasskazy, 1925
Istoriia moei golubiatni, 1926
Konarmiia, 1926 (*Red Cavalry*, 1929)
Odesskie rasskazy, 1931 (*Tales of Odessa*, 1955)
Benya Krik, the Gangster and Other Stories, 1948
The Collected Stories, 1955
Izbrannoe, 1957, 1966
Lyubka the Cossack and Other Stories, 1963
The Lonely Years, 1925-1939: Unpublished Stories and Private Correspondence, 1964
You Must Know Everything: Stories, 1915-1937, 1969

OTHER LITERARY FORMS

Although Isaac Babel spent most of his career writing short stories, he tried his hand at other genres without making significant contributions to them. He wrote two plays: *Zakat* (1928; *Sunset*, 1960) and *Mariia* (1935; *Maria*, 1966). He also wrote several screenplays, most of which remain unpublished. Babel was known to have worked on several novels, but only a few fragments have been published. If he ever completed them, either he destroyed them or they were confiscated by police when he was arrested in 1939, never to be seen in public again. Because of their fragmentary nature, the tendency among critics is to treat them as short fiction. He also wrote a brief autobiography, a diary, reminiscences, and newspaper articles.

ACHIEVEMENTS

Isaac Babel's greatest achievement lies in short fiction. From the outset, he established himself as a premier short-story writer not only in Russian but also in world literature as well. He achieved this reputation not only through his innovative approach to the subject matter—the civil war in Russia, for example, or the Jewish world of his ancestry—but also through his stylistic excellence. His mastery of style earned for him, early in his career, a reputation of an avant-garde writer—a model to be emulated, but at the same time difficult to emulate. He elevated the Russian short story to a new level and attracted the attention of foreign writers such as Ernest Hemingway, who read him in Paris. At the same time, it would be unjust to attribute his greatness only to the uniqueness of his subject matter or to his avant-garde style. Rather, it is the combination of these and other qualities that contributed to his indisputably high reputation among both critics and readers, a respect that seems to grow with time.

BIOGRAPHY

Isaac Emmanuilovich Babel was born in Odessa on July 13, 1894, into a Jewish family that had lived in southern Russia for generations. Soon after his birth, the family moved from this thriving port on the Black Sea to the nearby small town of Nikolayev, where Babel spent the first ten years of his life. His childhood was typical of a child growing up in a colorful Jewish environment and, at the same time, in a Russian society replete with prejudices against Jews. In his stories, Babel describes the difficult lessons of survival that he had to learn from childhood on, which enabled him not only to survive but also to keep striving for excellence against all odds. He was a studious child who read under all conditions, even on his way home, and his imagination was always on fire, as he said in one of his stories. Among many other subjects, he studied Hebrew and French vigorously, becoming more proficient in them than in Russian.

After finishing high school in Odessa—which was difficult for a Jewish child to enter and complete— Babel could not attend the university, again because of the Jewish quota. He enrolled in a business school in Kiev instead. It was at this time that he began to write stories, in French, imitating his favorite writers, François Rabelais, Gustave Flaubert, and Guy de Maupassant. In 1915, he went to St. Petersburg, already thinking seriously of a writing career. He had no success with editors, however, until he met Maxim Gorky, a leading Russian writer of the older generation, who published two of his stories and took him under his wing. This great friendship lasted until Gorky's death in 1936. Gorky had encouraged Babel to write and had protected him but had published no more of his stories, and one day Gorky told Babel to go out into the world and learn about real life. Babel heeded his advice in 1917, setting off on a journey lasting several years, during which he volunteered for the army, took part in the revolution and civil war, married, worked for the secret police, was a war correspondent, and finally served in the famous cavalry division of Semyon Mikhaylovich Budenny in the war against the Poles. Out of these dramatic experiences, Babel was able to publish two books of short stories, which immediately thrust him into the forefront of the young Soviet literature. The period from 1921 to 1925 was the most productive and successful of his entire career.

By the end of the 1920's, however, the political climate in the Soviet Union had begun to change, forcing Babel to conform to the new demands on writers to serve the state, which he could not do, no matter how he tried. His attempts at writing a novel about collectivization never materialized. His inability (or, more likely, unwillingness) to change marks the beginning of a decade-long silent struggle between him and the state. Refusing to follow his family into emigration, he tried to survive by writing film scenarios, unable to publish anything else. In May, 1939, he was arrested and sent to a concentration camp. In 1954, it was revealed that he had died on March 17, 1941, but neither the location nor the exact circumstances of his death were specified. His confis-

cated manuscripts—a large crate of them—were never found.

ANALYSIS

Isaac Babel's short stories fall into three basic groups: autobiographical stories, tales about Jews in Odessa, and stories about the Russian Revolution and Civil War. Even though the stories were written and published at different times, in retrospect they can be conveniently, if arbitrarily, classified into these three categories. A small number of stories do not fall into any of these groups, but they are exceptions and do not figure significantly in Babel's opus.

While it is true that many of Babel's stories are autobiographical, even if indirectly, a number of them are openly so. Several refer to his childhood spent in Nikolayev and Odessa. In one of his earliest stories, "Detstvo: U babushki" ("Childhood: At Grandmother's"), Babel pays his emotional due to his kind grandmother, who kept quiet vigil over his studying for hours on end, giving him her bits of wisdom every now and then: "You must know everything. The whole world will fall at your feet and grovel before you. . . . Do not trust people. Do not have friends. Do not lend them money. Do not give them your heart!" Babel loved his childhood because, he said, "I grew up in it, was happy, sad, and dreamed my dreams— fervent dreams that will never return." This early wistful realization of the inevitable transience of all things echoes through much of his writings. The mixture of happiness and sadness is reflected in one of his best stories, "Istoriia moei golubiatni" ("The Story of My Dovecote"), where a child's dream of owning a dovecote is realized during a pogrom, but the dove, which his father had promised him if he was accepted to high school, is squashed against his face. The trickling of the dove's entrails down his face symbolizes the boy's loss of innocence and a premature farewell to childhood.

Babel's discovery of love as the most potent feeling of humankind came to him rather early. As he describes in "Pervaia liubov" ("First Love"), he was ten years old when he fell in love with the wife of an officer, perhaps out of gratitude for her protection of Babel's family during the pogrom in Nikolayev. The puppy love, however, soon gave way to fear and prolonged hiccuping—an early indication of the author's rather sensitive nervous system that accompanied him all his life. This innocent, if incongruous, setting points to a sophisticated sense of humor and to irony, the two devices used by Babel in most of his works. It also foreshadows his unabashed approach to erotica in his later stories, for which they are well known.

As mentioned already, Babel lived as a child in a world of books, dreams, and rampant imagination. In addition, like many Jewish children, he had to take music lessons, for which he had no inclination at all. He had little time for play and fun and, as a consequence, did not develop fully physically. He was aware of this anomaly and tried to break out of it. During one such attempt, as he describes it in "Probuzhdenie" ("Awakening"), he ran away from a music lesson to the beach, only to discover that "the waves refused to support" him. Nevertheless, this experience made him realize that he had to develop "a feel for nature" if he wanted to become a writer. Another experience of "breaking out" concerns Babel's awareness of his social status, as depicted in the story "V podvale" ("In the Basement"). In the story, he visits the luxurious home of the top student in his class and has to use his power of imagination to convince the rich boy that socially he is on equal footing with him. When the boy visits the apartment of Babel's family, "in the basement," however, the truth becomes obvious, and the little Isaac tries to drown himself in a barrel of water. This realization of the discrepancy between reality and the world of dreams and the need and desire to break out of various imposed confines were constant sources of aggravation in Babel's life. Other autobiographical stories, as well as many other stories seemingly detached from the author's personal life, attest this perennial struggle.

TALES OF ODESSA

The stories about the life of Jews, in the collection *Tales of Odessa*, demonstrate Babel's attachment to his ethnic background as well as his efforts to be objective about it. In addition to being an economic and cultural center, Odessa had a strong underground world of criminals made mostly of Jews, which fueled the imagination of the growing Isaac; later, he

used his reminiscences about the Jewish mafia in some of his best stories. He immortalized one of the leaders, Benya Krik, alias the King, in "Korol" ("The King"). Benya's daring and resourcefulness are shown during the wedding of his elderly sister, whose husband he had purchased. When the police plan to arrest Benya's gang during the wedding celebration, he simply arranges for the police station to be set on fire. He himself married the daughter of a man he had blackmailed in one of his operations.

An old man who saw in Babel a boy with "the spectacles on the nose and the autumn in the heart" told him the story of Benya's rise to fame in "Kak eto delalos v Odesse" ("How It Was Done in Odessa"). Here, Benya orders the liquidation of a man who did not give in to blackmail, but Benya's executioner kills the wrong man, a poor clerk who had very little joy in life. Benya orders a magnificent funeral for the unfortunate clerk and a lifelong financial support for his mother, thus showing his true nature and revealing that it is not crime that attracted him to the underground life but rather a subconscious desire to right the wrongs and help the downtrodden. Through such characters and their motives, Babel is able to lend his stories a redeeming grace, neutralizing the mayhem saturating them.

Loyalty is another quality that binds these lawbreakers, as illustrated in the story "Otec" ("The Father"), where Benya helps an old gangster, who had given him his start, to marry off his daughter to the son of a man who had rejected the marriage. They are assisted by another legendary figure, Lyubka, known also from the story "Liubka Kazak" ("Lyubka the Cossack"). Lyubka, a middle-aged shop and whorehouse keeper, reigns supreme in her dealings with customers, who, in turn, help her wean her baby from breast-feeding. This interdependency in a life fraught with danger and risks gives Babel's characters a human face and his stories a patina of real drama.

Not all stories about Jews in Odessa deal with the underground world, as "Di Grasso," a colorful tale about theater life in Odessa, shows. Di Grasso, a Sicilian tragedian, and his troupe flop the first night of the show. After a favorable newspaper review praising Di Grasso as "the most remarkable actor of the century," the second night the theater is full and the spectators are so enthralled that the wife of the theater "mogul," to whom the fourteen-year-old Isaac had pawned his father's watch, makes the husband return the watch, sparing Isaac much trouble. Babel's uncanny ability to intertwine high aspirations and small concerns, pathos with bathos, turns seemingly insignificant events into genuine human dramas. This is even more evident in the story "Konets bogadel'ni" ("The End of the Old Folks' Home"), where the inmates of a poorhouse near the Jewish cemetery make a living by using the same coffins again and again, until one day the authorities refuse to allow a used coffin for the burial of a revolutionary hero. The ensuing rebellion by the inmates leads to their dispersal and to the end of their life-sustaining scheme. Thus, what began as a clever business proposition turns into tragedy, making Babel's story a timeless statement of the human condition.

RED CAVALRY

Babel uses a similar technique in the collection *Red Cavalry*. Although the stories here are based on Babel's real-life experiences in the war between the Russian revolutionaries and the Poles, their real significance lies beyond the factual presentation of a historical event, as the author endows every gesture, almost every word, with a potential deeper meaning. It is not coincidental that the entire campaign is seen through the eyes of, and told by, a baggage-train officer named Liutov (a persona standing for Babel), not by a frontline participant. Readers learn about the general nature of the conflict, recognize the place names, and even follow the course of the battles, but they cannot piece together the exact history of the conflict simply because that was not the author's intention. Babel gives readers single episodes in miniature form instead, like individual pieces of a mosaic; only after finishing the book are readers able to take in the complete picture.

The first story, "Perekhod cherez Zbruch" ("Crossing into Poland"), sets the tone for the entire collection. The opening lines reveal that a military objective has been taken, but Liutov's baggage train that follows sinks into a hazy, dreamy, impressionistic atmosphere, as if having nothing to do with the campaign:

Fields flowered around us, crimson with poppies; a noontide breeze played in the yellowing rye; on the horizon virginal buckwheat rose like the wall of a distant monastery. The Volyn's peaceful stream moved away from us in sinuous curves and was lost in the pearly haze of the birch groves; crawling between flowery slopes, it wound weary arms through a wilderness of hops. . . .

This passage shows a poetic proclivity of Babel, but it is also his deliberate attempt to take his readers away from the factual course of events and move them to what he considers to be more important—the human perception of the events. Many of the stories in the collection bear the same trademark.

Although many stories deserve detailed comment, several stand out for their "message" or meaning that can be culled from the story. Nowhere is the brutal nature of the civil war depicted more poignantly than in "Pis'mo" ("A Letter"). A young, illiterate cossack, Vasily, dictates to Liutov a letter to his mother. He inquires about his beloved foal back home, and only after giving detailed advice about handling him does he tell how his father, who is on the other side, killed one of his sons and was then killed in return by another. This most tragic piece of news is relayed matter-of-factly, as if to underscore the degree of desensitization to which all the participants have fallen prey through endless killing.

The cruelty of the civil war is brought into sharp focus by an old Jewish shopkeeper in "Gedali." Gedali reasons like a legitimate humanitarian and libertarian: "The Revolution—we will say 'yes' to it, but are we to say 'no' to the Sabbath? . . . I cry yes to [the Revolution], but it hides its face from Gedali and sends out on front naught but shooting." He understands when the Poles commit atrocities, but he is perplexed when the Reds do the same in the name of the revolution. "You shoot because you are the Revolution. But surely the Revolution means joy. . . . The Revolution is the good deed of good men. But good men do not kill." Gedali says that all he wants is an International of good people. Liutov's answer that the International "is eaten with gunpowder," though realistic, falls short of satisfying the old man's yearning for justice, which, after all, was the primary driving force of the revolution. It is interesting that, by presenting the case in such uncompromising terms, Babel himself is questioning the rationale behind the revolution and the justification of all the sacrifices and suffering.

A similar moral issue is brought to a climactic head in perhaps the best story in *Red Cavalry*, "Smert' Dolgushova" ("The Death of Dolgushov"). Dolgushov is wounded beyond repair and is left behind the fighting line to die. He is begging Liutov to finish him off because he is afraid that the Poles, if they caught him alive, would mutilate his body. Liutov refuses. The commander gallops by, evaluates the situation, and shoots Dolgushov in the mouth. Before galloping away, the commander threatens to kill Liutov, too, screaming, "You guys in specks have about as much pity for chaps like us as a cat has for a mouse." Aside from the revolutionaries' mistrust of Liutov (alias Babel) and the age-old question of euthanasia, the story poses a weighty moral question: Has a human being the right to kill another human being? Even though Babel seems to allow for this possibility, he himself cannot make that step, making it appear that he is shirking his responsibility (after all, he is fighting alongside the revolutionaries). More likely, he is hoping that there should be at least someone to say no to the incessant killing, thus saving the face of the revolution (as if answering Gedali's mournful plea). More important, this hope hints at Babel's real attitude toward the revolution. For such "misunderstanding" of the revolution he was criticized severely, and it is most likely that through such attitudes he sowed the seeds of his own destruction two decades later.

Not all stories in *Red Cavalry* are weighed down with ultimate moral questions. There are stories of pure human interest, colorful slices of the war, and even some genuinely humorous ones. In "Moi pervyi gus' " ("My First Goose"), Liutov is faced with the problem of gaining the respect of the illiterate cossacks in his unit. As a bespectacled intellectual ("a four-eyed devil," as they called him), and a Jew at that, he knows that the only way to win them over is by committing an act of bravery. He thinks of raping a woman, but he sees only an old woman around. He finally kills a goose with his saber, thereby gaining

the respect of his "peers." Only then are they willing to let him read to them Vladimir Ilich Lenin's latest pronouncements. With this mixture of mocking seriousness and irony, Babel attempts to put the revolution in a proper perspective. His difficulties at adjusting to military life are evident also in the story "Argamak," where he ruins a good horse by not knowing how to handle it.

The Jews are frequently mentioned in these stories because the war was taking place in an area heavily populated by them. Babel uses these opportunities to stress their perennial role as sufferers and martyrs, but also to gauge his own Jewish identification. In "Rabbi" ("The Rabbi"), he visits, with Gedali, an old rabbi, who asks him where he came from, what he has been studying, and what he was seeking—typical identification questions. Later, they and the rabbi's son, "the cursed son, the last son, the unruly son," sit amid the wilderness of war, in silence and prayers, as if to underscore the isolation of people threatened by an alien war. In "Berestechko," a cossack is shown cutting the throat of an old Jewish "spy," being careful not to stain himself with blood. This one detail completes the picture of a Jew as an ultimate victim.

Many characters are etched out in these miniature stories. There is Sandy the Christ in the story by the same title ("Sashka Khristov"), a meek herdsman who at the age of fourteen caught "an evil disease" while carousing with his stepfather and who later joined the Reds and became a good fighter. There is Pan Apolek ("Pan Apolek"), an itinerant artist who painted church icons in the images not of the saints but of local people. There is Afonka Bida ("Afonka Bida"), the commander who almost shot Liutov because of Dolgushov, who loses his horse Stepan and disappears hunting for another. After several weeks, he reappears with a gray stallion, but the loss of Stepan still makes him want to destroy the whole world. In "So" ("Salt"), a woman carrying a bundled baby uses him to gain sympathy and hitch a train ride. It turns out that the bundle is nothing but a two-pound sack of salt; she is thrown out of the moving train and then shot from the distance. The man who killed her pronounces solemnly, "We will deal mercilessly with all the traitors that are dragging us to the dogs and want to turn everything upside down and cover Russia with nothing but corpses and dead grass," which is exactly what he has just done. Finally, in one of the best stories in the book, "Vdova" ("The Widow"), a lover of the dying commander is bequeathed all of his belongings, with the request that she send some of them to his mother. When the widow shows signs of not following the will of the deceased, she is beaten, and, if she forgets the second time, she will be reminded again in the same fashion. These stories are perfect illustrations of Babel's ability to create unforgettable but credible characters, to set up dramatic scenes, and to conjure a proper atmosphere, while endowing his creations with a truly human pathos—qualities that characterize most of his stories but especially those in *Red Cavalry*.

Among the stories outside the three groups, several are worth mentioning. An early story, "Mama, Rimma, i Alla" ("Mama, Rimma, and Alla"), resembles a Chekhov story in that the domestic problems in a family (a mother finds it difficult to cope with her daughters in absence of her husband) are not solved and the story dissolves in hopelessness. "Iisusov grekh" ("The Sin of Jesus") is a colorful tale of a woman whose husband is away at war and who goes to Jesus for advice about loneliness. When Jesus sends her an angel, she accidentally smothers him to death in sleep. She goes again to Jesus, but now he damns her as a slut, which she resents, for it is not her fault that she lusts, that people drink vodka, and that he has created "a woman's soul, stupid and lonely." When finally Jesus admits his error and asks for forgiveness, she refuses to accept it, saying, "There is no forgiveness for you and never will be." The story displays Babel's exquisite sense of humor along with a keen understanding of human nature and the complexities of life. A variant, "Skazka pro babu" ("The Tale of a Woman"), another Chekhovian story, again depicts the plight of a widow who, in her loneliness, asks a friend to find her a husband. When she does, he mistreats her and walks out on her, which causes her to lose her job. Finally, "Ulitsa Dante" ("Dante Street") is a Paris story in the tradition of Guy de Maupassant, showing Babel's versatility and imagination.

Babel's stylistic excellence has been often praised by critics. His style features a Spartan economy of words, and he is known to have spent years reworking and revising his stories. Babel's attention to detail, especially to line and color, often result in fine etchings. There is a pronounced poetic bent in his stories, whether they are located in a city milieu or in the countryside. This is reinforced by a prolific use of images and metaphors in the style of the following passages, quoted at random:

> A dead man's fingers were picking at the frozen entrails of Petersburg. . . . The gentleman had drooping jowls, like the sacks of an old-clothes man, and wounded cats prowled in his reddish eyes.

One finds in Babel also a surprising amount of humor, as if to offset the cruelty and gruesome injustice of his world.

Babel's artfulness is especially noticeable in his treatment of irony as his strongest device. He refuses to accept reality as one perceives it. He also plays games with the reader's perceptions, as he says openly, "I set myself a reader who is intelligent, well educated, with sensible and severe standards of taste. . . . Then I try to think how I can deceive and stun the reader." This cool intellectual approach, coupled with the strong emotional charge of his stories, gives his stories an aura of not only skillfully executed works of art but also pristine innocence of divine creation.

OTHER MAJOR WORKS

PLAYS: *Zakat*, pb. 1928 (*Sunset*, 1960); *Mariia*, pb. 1935 (*Maria*, 1966).

SCREENPLAYS: *Benia Krik: Kinopovest'*, 1926 (*Benia Krik: A Film Novel*, 1935); *Bluzhdaiushchie zvezdy: Kinostsenarii*, 1926.

BIBLIOGRAPHY

Avins, Carol J. "Kinship and Concealment in *Red Cavalry* and Babel's 1920 Diary." *Slavic Review* 53 (Fall, 1994): 694-710. Shows how a diary Babel kept during his service in the 1920 Polish campaign was a source of ideas for his collection of stories *Red Cavalry*. Claims that Babel's efforts to conceal his Jewishness, recounted in the diaries, is also reflected in the stories.

Carden, Patricia. *The Art of Isaac Babel*. Ithaca, N.Y.: Cornell University Press, 1972. In this discerning study of Babel's art, Carden combines biography and analysis of his main works and themes, especially his search for style and form, and philosophical, religious, and aesthetic connotations. The meticulous scholarship is accompanied by keen insight and empathy, making the book anything but cut-and-dried. Includes a select bibliography.

Ehre, Milton. "Babel's *Red Cavalry:* Epic and Pathos, History and Culture." *Slavic Review* 40 (1981): 228-240. A stimulating study of Babel's chief work, incorporating its literary, historical, and cultural aspects. No attention to detail, but rather a sweeping overview.

Falen, James E. *Isaac Babel, Russian Master of the Short Story*. Knoxville: University of Tennessee Press, 1974. Falen's appraisal of Babel is the best overall. Following the main stages of Babel's life, Falen analyzes in minute detail his works, emphasizing the short stories. Lucidly written and provided with the complete scholarly apparatus, the study offers an exhaustive bibliography as well.

Hyman, Stanley Edgar. "Identities of Isaac Babel." *The Hudson Review* 8 (1956): 620-627. Hyman sees as one of the major themes in Babel's stories changes of identity through ritual of rebirth. Their true dichotomy is that of culture and nature, of art and the life of action, of necessity and freedom. For Hyman, the Jews are the heirs of all world cultures. A thought-provoking essay.

Luplow, Carol. *Isaac Babel's Red Cavalry*. Ann Arbor, Mich.: Ardis, 1982. This detailed, full-length study of Babel's most famous collection focuses on the narrative perspective of the stories, the basic dialectic between the spiritual and the physical which they embody, their style and romantic vision, and the types of story structure and epiphanic vision they reflect.

Mendelson, Danuta. *Metaphor in Babel's Short Stories*. Ann Arbor, Mich.: Ardis, 1982. A schol-arly discussion, drawing from linguistic and psychological studies as well as structuralist studies of narrative. Analysis of *Red Cavalry* as an episodic novel in the modernist tradition, rather than as a strictly linear realist work, makes clear how the action of the book takes place on several poetic planes at once.

Poggioli, Renato. "Isaac Babel in Retrospect." In *The Phoenix and the Spider*. Cambridge, Mass.: Harvard University Press, 1957. Poggioli discusses the three curses of Babel's life: race, poverty, and the calling of an artist. He also comments on Babel's attitude toward war and his inferiority complex, resulting in his admiration for the cossacks as men of action.

Shcheglov, Yuri K. "Some Themes and Archetypes in Babel's *Red Cavalry*." *Slavic Review* 53 (Fall, 1994): 653-670. Discusses initiatory and otherworldly thematic patterns in "My First Goose," showing how Babel used archetypes subtly and selectively. Concludes that "My First Goose," with its density reinforced by archetypal connotations, is an emblematic prototype of later works of Soviet fiction that focus on similar themes.

Sicher, Efraim. *Style and Structure in the Prose of Isaak Babel*. Columbus, Ohio: Slavica, 1986. Primarily a formalist study of the style of Babel's stories. In addition to discussing Babel's lyrical prose, the book analyzes setting, characterization, narrative structure, and point of view in Babel's stories.

Terras, Victor. "Line and Color: The Structure of I. Babel's Short Stories in *Red Cavalry*." *Studies in Short Fiction* 3, no. 2 (Winter, 1966): 141-156. In one of the best treatments of a particular aspect of Babel's stories, Terras discusses his style in terms of line and color and of his poetic inclination.

Trilling, Lionel. Introduction to *The Collected Stories*. Cleveland: World Publishing, 1955. Trilling stresses the difference between the cossacks and the Jews as one of the backbones of *Red Cavalry* and Babel's relationship to them in terms of test and initiation. A good general introduction to Babel's works.

Zholkovskii, A. K. "How a Russian Maupassant Was Made in Odessa and Yasnaya Polyana: Isaak Babel and the Tolstoy Legacy." *Slavic Review* 53 (Fall, 1994): 671-693. Examines the influence of Tolstoy on Babel, arguing that although both sought to liberate the individual from impersonal routine, Babel's approach is the opposite of Tol-stoy's; whereas for Tolstoy finding the self meant relinquishing falsehood and society and returning to truth and childlike innocence, for Babel, one finds the self through erotic contact, culture, art, and invention.

Vasa D. Mihailovich

JAMES BALDWIN

Born: New York, New York; August 2, 1924
Died: St. Paul de Vence, France; November 30, 1987

PRINCIPAL SHORT FICTION
Going to Meet the Man, 1965

OTHER LITERARY FORMS

In addition to one edition of short stories, James Baldwin published more than twenty other works, including novels, essays, two plays, a screenplay on Malcolm X, one play adaptation, a children's book, two series of dialogues, and a collection of poetry, as well as numerous shorter pieces embracing interviews, articles, and recordings.

ACHIEVEMENTS

James Baldwin received numerous awards and fellowships during his life, including the Rosenwald, John Simon Guggenheim Memorial Foundation, and Partisan Review fellowships, a Ford Foundation Grant, and the George Polk Memorial Award. In 1986, shortly before his death, the French government made him a Commander of the Legion of Honor.

BIOGRAPHY

James Arthur Baldwin grew up in Harlem. While he was still attending DeWitt Clinton High School in the Bronx he was a Holy Roller preacher. After high school, he did odd jobs and wrote for *The Nation* and *The New Leader*. A turning point for him was meet-ing Richard Wright, who encouraged him to write and helped him obtain a fellowship that provided income while he was finishing an early novel. After moving to Paris in 1948 he became acquainted with Norman Mailer and other writers. His first major work, *Go Tell It on the Mountain*, appeared in 1953 and was followed by a long list of books. He moved back to New York in 1957, and during the 1960's his writing and speeches made him an important force in the Civil Rights movement. Following the assassination of Martin Luther King, Jr., Baldwin returned to Europe several times and again settled in France in 1974, where he lived until his death. He continued his productivity in the 1980's. In 1985, for example, Baldwin wrote three works, including his first book of poetry. He died in 1987 of stomach cancer and is buried near Paul Robeson's grave at Ferncliff Cemetery, Ardsley, New York.

ANALYSIS

James Baldwin is widely regarded as one of the United States' most important writers in the latter part of the twentieth century. Baldwin's writing career spanned more than four decades and is remarkable for its wide diversity of literary expression, encompassing fiction, nonfiction, poetry, and plays. He was considered the most important American writer during the 1950's, 1960's, and 1970's on the issue of racial inequality. The repeated thrust of his message, centered on being black in a white America, touched a responsive chord. Disgusted with American bigotry, social discrimination, and inequality, he exiled himself in France, where he poured out his eloquent and passionate criticism. Baldwin also wrote with compelling candor about the Church, Harlem, and homosexuality. He often fused the themes of sex and race in his work. Today, Baldwin's essays are considered his most important contribution to literature.

"THE MAN CHILD"

Baldwin's "The Man Child," the only story in *Going to Meet the Man* that has no black characters, scathingly describes whites, especially their violent propensities. The central character is Eric, an eight-year-old. The story opens as he, his mother, and his father are giving a birthday party for Jamie, his father's best friend. In the next scene Eric and his father walk together and then return to the party. After a brief summary of intervening events, the story moves forward in time to a day when Jamie meets Eric, entices him into a barn, and breaks his neck. The story described thus, its ending seems to be a surprise, and it certainly is a surprise to Eric. In fact, his sudden realization that he is in grave danger is an epiphany. "The Man Child" is thus a coming-of-age story, an account of a young person's realization of the dark side of adult existence. Eric, however, has little time to think about his realization or even to generalize very much on the basis of his intimation of danger before he is badly, perhaps mortally, injured.

The story, however, contains many hints that violent action will be forthcoming. A reader can see them even though Eric cannot because Eric is the center of consciousness, a device perfected, if not invented, by Henry James. That is, Eric does not narrate the story so the story does not present his viewpoint, but he is always the focus of the action, and the story is in essence an account of his responses to that action. The difference between his perception of the events he witnesses (which is sometimes described and sometimes can be inferred from his actions) and the perception that can be had by attending carefully to the story encourages a reader to make a moral analysis and finally to make a moral judgment, just as the difference between Huck Finn's perception and the perception that one can have while reading *The*

Adventures of Huckleberry Finn (1884) at first stimulates laughter and then moral evaluation. Eric's lack of perception is a function of his innocence, a quality that he has to an even larger extent than has Huck Finn, and thus he is less able to cope in a threatening world and his injury is even more execrable. If the measure of a society is its solicitude for the powerless, the miniature society formed by the three adults in this story, and perhaps by implication the larger society of which they are a part, is sorely wanting.

To be more specific about the flaws in this society and in these persons, they enslave themselves and others, as is suggested very early in the story: "Eric lived with his father . . . and his mother, who had been captured by his father on some faroff unblessed, unbelievable night, who had never since burst her chains." Her husband intimidates and frightens her, and his conversation about relations between men and women indicates that he believes she exists at his sufferance only for sex and procreation. Her role becomes questionable because in the summary of events that happen between the first and last parts of

James Baldwin in 1982 (AP/Wide World Photos)

the story one learns that she has lost the child she had been carrying and cannot conceive anymore. The two men enslave themselves with their notions about women, their drunkenness (which they misinterpret as male companionship), their mutual hostility, their overbearing expansiveness, in short, with their machismo. Eric's father is convinced that he is more successful in these terms. He has fathered a son, an accomplishment the significance of which to him is indicated by his "some day all this will be yours" talk with Eric between the two party scenes. Jamie's wife, showing more sense than Eric's mother, left him before he could sire a son. Jamie's violent act with Eric is his psychotic imitation of the relation of Eric's father to Eric, just as his whistling at the very end of the story is his imitation of the music he hears coming from a tavern. Eric is thus considered by the two men to be alive merely for their self-expression. His father's kind of self-expression is potentially debilitating, although somewhat benign; Jamie's version is nearly fatal.

"GOING TO MEET THE MAN"

"Going to Meet the Man" is a companion to "The Man Child," both stories having been published for the first time in *Going to Meet the Man*. Whereas the latter story isolates whites from blacks in order to analyze their psychology, the former story is about whites in relation to blacks, even though blacks make only brief appearances in it. The whites in these stories have many of the same characteristics, but in "Going to Meet the Man" those characteristics are more obviously dangerous. These stories were written during the height of the Civil Rights movement, and Baldwin, by means of his rhetorical power and his exclusion of more human white types, helped polarize that movement.

The main characters in "Going to Meet the Man" are a family composed of a southern deputy sheriff, his wife, and his son, Jesse. At the beginning of the story they are skittish because of racial unrest. Demonstrations by blacks have alternated with police brutality by whites, each response escalating the conflict, which began when a black man knocked down an elderly white woman. The family is awakened late at night by a crowd of whites who have learned that the

black has been caught. They all set off in a festive, although somewhat tense, mood to the place where the black is being held. After they arrive the black is burned, castrated, and mutilated—atrocities that Baldwin describes very vividly. This story, however, is not merely sensationalism or social and political rhetoric. It rises above those kinds of writing because of its psychological insights into the causes of racism and particularly of racial violence.

Baldwin's focus at first is on the deputy sheriff. As the story opens he is trying and failing to have sexual relations with his wife. He thinks that he would have an easier time with a black, and "the image of a black girl caused a distant excitement in him." Thus, his conception of blacks is immediately mixed with sexuality, especially with his fear of impotence. In contrast, he thinks of his wife as a "frail sanctuary." At the approach of a car he reaches for the gun beside his bed, thereby adding a propensity for violence to his complex of psychological motives. Most of his behavior results from this amalgam of racial attitudes, sexual drives, fear of impotence, and attraction to violence. For example, he recalls torturing a black prisoner by applying a cattle prod to his testicles, and on the way to see the black captive he takes pride in his wife's attractiveness. He also frequently associates blacks with sexual vigor and fecundity. The castration scene is the most powerful rendition of this psychological syndrome.

The deputy sheriff, however, is more than a mere brute. For example, he tries to think of his relation to blacks in moral terms. Their singing of spirituals disconcerts him because he has difficulty understanding how they can be Christians like himself. He tries to reconcile this problem by believing that blacks have decided "to fight against God and go against the rules laid down in the Bible for everyone to read!" To allay the guilt that threatens to complicate his life he also believes that there are a lot of good blacks who need his protection from bad blacks. These strategies for achieving inner peace do not work, and Baldwin brilliantly describes the moral confusion of such whites:

They had never dreamed that their privacy could contain any element of terror, could threaten, that is, to reveal itself, to the scrutiny of a judgment day, while remaining unreadable and inaccessible to themselves; nor had they dreamed that the past, while certainly refusing to be forgotten, could yet so stubbornly refuse to be remembered. They felt themselves mysteriously set at naught.

In the absence of a satisfying moral vision, violence seems the only way to achieve inner peace, and the sheriff's participation in violence allows him to have sex with his wife as the story ends. Even then, however, he has to think that he is having it as blacks would. He is their psychic prisoner, just as the black who was murdered was the white mob's physical prisoner.

Late in this story one can see that Jesse, the sheriff's eight-year-old son, is also an important character. At first he is confused by the turmoil and thinks of blacks in human terms. For example, he wonders why he has not seen his black friend Otis for several days. The mob violence, however, changes him; he undergoes a coming of age, the perversity of which is disturbing. He is the center of consciousness in the mob scene. His first reaction is the normal one for a boy: "Jesse clung to his father's neck in terror as the cry rolled over the crowd." Then he loses his innocence and it becomes clear that he will be a victim of the same psychological syndrome that afflicts his father: "He watched his mother's face . . . she was more beautiful than he had ever seen her. . . . He began to feel a joy he had never felt before." He wishes that he were the man with the knife who is about to castrate the black, whom Jesse considers "the most beautiful and terrible object he had ever seen." Then he identifies totally with his father: "At that moment Jesse loved his father more than he had ever loved him. He felt that his father had carried him through a mighty test, had revealed to him a great secret which would be the key to his life forever." For Jesse this brutality is thus a kind of initiation into adulthood, and its effect is to ensure that there will be at least one more generation capable of the kind of violence that he has just seen.

"SONNY'S BLUES"

Whereas "The Man Child" has only white charac-

ters and "Going to Meet the Man" is about a conflict between whites and blacks, "Sonny's Blues" has only black characters. Although the chronology of "Sonny's Blues" is scrambled, its plot is simple. It tells the story of two brothers, one, the narrator, a respectable teacher and the other, Sonny, a former user of heroin who is jailed for that reason and then becomes a jazz musician. The story ends in a jazz nightclub, where the older brother hears Sonny play and finally understands the meaning of jazz for him. The real heart of this story is the contrast between the values of the two brothers, a contrast that becomes much less dramatic at the end.

The two brothers have similar social backgrounds, especially their status as blacks and, more specifically, as Harlem blacks. Of Harlem as a place in which to mature the narrator says, "boys exactly like the boys we once had been found themselves encircled by disaster. Some escaped the trap, most didn't. Those who got out always left something of themselves behind, as some animals amputate a leg and leave it in a trap." Even when he was very young the narrator had a sense of the danger and despair surrounding him:

> When lights fill the room, the child is filled with darkness. He knows that every time this happens he's moved just a little closer to that darkness outside. The darkness outside is what the old folks have been talking about. It's what they've come from. It's what they endure.

For example, he learns after his father's death that his father, though seemingly a hardened and stoical man, had hidden the grief caused by the killing of his brother.

At first the narrator believes that Sonny's two means for coping with the darkness, heroin and music, are inextricably connected to that darkness and thus are not survival mechanisms at all. He believes that heroin "filled everything, the people, the houses, the music, the dark, quicksilver barmaid, with menace; and this menace was their reality." Later, however, he realizes that jazz is a way to escape: He senses that "Sonny was at that time piano playing for his life." The narrator also has a few premonitions of the epiphany he experiences in the jazz nightclub. One occurs when he observes a group of street singers and understands that their "music seemed to soothe a poison out of them." Even with these premonitions, he does not realize that he uses the same strategy. After an argument with Sonny, during which their differences seem to be irreconcilable, his first reaction is to begin "whistling to keep from crying," and the tune is a blues. Finally the epiphany occurs, tying together all the major strands of this story. As he listens to Sonny playing jazz the narrator thinks that

> freedom lurked around us and I understood, at last, that he could help us be free if we would listen, that he would never be free until we did. Yet, there was no battle in his face now. I heard what he had gone through, and would continue to go through.

The idea in that passage is essentially what Baldwin is about. Like Sonny, he has forged an instrument of freedom by means of the fire of his troubles, and he has made that instrument available to all, white and black. His is the old story of suffering and art; his fiction is an account of trouble, but by producing it he has shown others the way to rise above suffering.

OTHER MAJOR WORKS

LONG FICTION: *Go Tell It on the Mountain*, 1953; *Giovanni's Room*, 1956; *Another Country*, 1962; *Tell Me How Long the Train's Been Gone*, 1968; *If Beale Street Could Talk*, 1974; *Just Above My Head*, 1979.

PLAYS: *The Amen Corner*, pr. 1955; *Blues for Mister Charlie*, pr., pb. 1964; *One Day When I Was Lost: A Scenario Based on "The Autobiography of Malcolm X,"* pb. 1972; *A Deed from the King of Spain*, pr. 1974.

POETRY: *Jimmy's Blues: Selected Poems*, 1983.

NONFICTION: *Notes of a Native Son*, 1955; *Nobody Knows My Name: More Notes of a Native Son*, 1961; *The Fire Next Time*, 1963; *Nothing Personal*, 1964 (with Richard Avedon); *No Name in the Street*, 1971; *A Rap on Race*, 1971 (with Margaret Mead); *A Dialogue*, 1975 (with Nikki Giovanni); *The Devil Finds Work*, 1976; *The Evidence of Things Not Seen*, 1985; *The Price of the Ticket*, 1985; *Conversations with James Baldwin*, 1989.

CHILDREN'S LITERATURE: *Little Man, Little Man*, 1976.

BIBLIOGRAPHY

Kinnamon, Kenneth, ed. *James Baldwin: A Collection of Critical Essays*. Englewood Cliffs, N.J.: Prentice-Hall, 1974. A good introduction to Baldwin's early work featuring a collection of diverse essays by such well-known figures as Irving Howe, Langston Hughes, and Eldridge Cleaver. Includes a chronology of important dates, notes on the contributors, and a select bibliography.

Leming, David. *James Baldwin: A Biography*. New York: Alfred A. Knopf, 1994. A biography of Baldwin written by one who knew him and worked with him for the last quarter century of his life. Provides extensive literary analysis of Baldwin's work and relates his work to his life.

O'Daniel, Therman B., ed. *James Baldwin: A Critical Evaluation*. Washington, D.C.: Howard University Press, 1981. This useful introduction to Baldwin groups essays in six categories such as "Baldwin as Novelist," "Baldwin as Essayist," and "Baldwin as Playwright." Supplemented by a detailed bibliography, notes on contributors, and an index.

Porter, Horace A. *Stealing the Fire: The Art and Protest of James Baldwin*. Middletown, Conn.: Wesleyan University Press, 1989. Originally a doctoral dissertation; the author expanded his original material and published it following Baldwin's death. Porter attempts to relate Baldwin to the larger African American tradition of social protest.

Pratt, Louis H. *James Baldwin*. Boston: Twayne, 1978. This well-balanced evaluation of Baldwin emphasizes the artist and his literary art. Pratt firmly believes that Baldwin's major contribution to American letters is in the essay form. Complemented by a chronology, a select bibliography, and an index.

Romanet, Jerome de. "Revisiting Madeleine and 'The Outing': James Baldwin's Revision of Gide's Sexual Politics." *MELUS* 22 (Spring, 1997): 3-14. A discussion of Baldwin's story "The Outing" in terms of its contrast with Gide's Calvinist guilt.

Discusses sexual identity in this story and other Baldwin fictions. Argues that Baldwin's exile in France was as concerned with racial identity as with sexual emancipation.

Sanderson, Jim. "Grace in 'Sonny's Blues.'" *Short Story*, n.s. 6 (Fall, 1998): 85-95. Argues that Baldwin's most famous story illustrates his integration of the personal with the social in terms of his residual evangelical Christianity. Argues that at the end of the story when the narrator offers Sonny a drink, he puts himself in the role of Lord, and Sonny accepts the cup of wrath; the two brothers thus regain grace by means of the power of love.

Sherard, Tracey. "Sonny's Bebop: Baldwin's 'Blues Text' as Intracultural Critique." *African American Review* 32 (Winter, 1998): 691-705. A discussion of Houston Baker's notion of the "blues matrix" in Baldwin's story; examines the story's treatment of black culture in America as reflected by jazz and the blues. Discusses how the "blues text" of the story represents how intracultural narratives have influenced the destinies of African Americans.

Standley, Fred L., and Nancy V. Burt, eds. *Critical Essays on James Baldwin*. Boston: G. K. Hall, 1988. An attempt to anthologize the important criticism on Baldwin in one definitive volume. More than thirty-five articles focus on Baldwin's essays, fiction, nonfiction, and drama.

Sylvander, Carolyn Wedin. *James Baldwin*. New York: Frederick Ungar, 1980. This good overview of Baldwin's work provides an aesthetic perspective, a bibliographical summary, and an analysis of individual works, with greater emphasis given to Baldwin's plays, novels, and short stories.

Tomlinson, Robert. " 'Payin' One's Dues': Expatriation as Personal Experience and Paradigm in the Works of James Baldwin." *African American Review* 33 (Spring, 1999): 135-148. A discussion of the effect of life as an exile in Paris had on Baldwin. Argues that the experience internalized the conflicts he experienced in America. Suggests that Baldwin used his homosexuality and exile as a metaphor for the experience of the African American.

Tsomondo, Thorell. "No Other Tale to Tell: 'Sonny's Blues' and 'Waiting for the Rain.'" *Critique* 36 (Spring, 1995): 195-209. Examines how art and history are related in "Sonny's Blues." Discusses the story as one in which a young musician replays tribal history in music. Argues that the story represents how African American writers try to reconstruct an invalidated tradition.

Weatherby, W. J. *James Baldwin: Artist on Fire*. New York: Donald I. Fine, 1989. A lengthy personal reminiscence of Baldwin by a close friend who calls his biography a portrait. Rich in intimate detail and based on conversations with more than one hundred people who knew Baldwin. Reveals the man behind the words.

John Stark, updated by Terry Theodore

J. G. BALLARD

Born: Shanghai, China; November 15, 1930

PRINCIPAL SHORT FICTION
The Voices of Time, 1962
Billenium, 1962
The Four-Dimensional Nightmare, 1963
Passport to Eternity, 1963
The Terminal Beach, 1964
The Impossible Man, 1966
The Disaster Area, 1967
The Overloaded Man, 1967
The Atrocity Exhibition, 1969 (also known as *Love and Napalm: Export U.S.A.*)
Vermilion Sands, 1971
Chronopolis and Other Stories, 1971
The Best Short Stories of J. G. Ballard, 1978
Myths of the Near Future, 1982
Memories of the Space Age, 1988
War Fever, 1990

OTHER LITERARY FORMS

J. G. Ballard has written an impressive array of novels, all of which deal with the fantastic, and among which *Crash* (1973), *Concrete Island* (1974), *High Rise* (1975), and *The Day of Creation* (1987) are considered the best. Both *Rushing to Paradise* (1994) and *Cocaine Nights* (1996) are ostensibly set in the present, but they still contain Ballard's trademark fascination with the surreal. His autobiographical novel *Empire of the Sun* (1984), which tackles the subject of his childhood in war-torn China, was made into a 1987 motion picture directed by Steven Spielberg. Ballard has also written some literary and cultural criticism.

ACHIEVEMENTS

Within the genre of science fiction, J. G. Ballard's texts have been instrumental in the success of the New Wave movement, which brought literary respectability and serious attention to a literature formerly dismissed. *Empire of the Sun* won for Ballard the *Guardian* Fiction Prize in 1984, nearly won Great

Britain's prestigious Booker McConnell Prize in 1984, and earned the James Tait Black Memorial Prize in 1985.

BIOGRAPHY

James Graham Ballard was born on November 15, 1930, in Shanghai, where his father, businessman James Ballard, and his mother, Edna (née Johnstone), were members of the international European and American community of the ancient Chinese trading city. The outbreak of World War II in the Pacific in 1941 changed the boy's life dramatically: When the Japanese began interning Westerners, the Ballard family, too, came to spend the war years in a camp.

Liberated by the Japanese surrender, but with civil war looming in China, the boy accompanied his mother and sister to Great Britain in 1946 (while his father remained in China, for the last year as a captive, until 1951). After he was graduated from Leys School, Cambridge, Ballard studied medicine at King's College; anatomy became his favorite subject before he dropped out and enlisted in the Royal Air Force. After receiving some flight training in Canada, Ballard returned to England, where, in 1955, he married Helen Mary Matthews. Before her death in 1964, they had a son and two daughters.

In 1956, Ballard sold his first story, "Prima Belladonna," to *Science Fantasy* magazine; despite working full time as assistant editor of a chemical journal in London he soon turned into a productive writer with a distinct literary voice, something of a rarity in his chosen field at the time. After publishing his first novel, *The Wind from Nowhere,* in 1962, Ballard successfully continued to write both short and long fiction and became a full-time author.

Bringing up his three small children in London's tranquil suburb of Shepperton, Ballard became an increasingly unlikely author of a series of progressively dark texts, which during the 1960's turned for their topics from natural disasters to the perturbing icons of American culture. From Cadillacs to film stars—images first encountered in the *Life* magazines that found their way into the boy's prison camp—this new material experienced a radical stylistic transformation at the hands of the artist who created such masterpieces as the 1969 collection of "condensed novels," *The Atrocity Exhibition*.

Throughout the 1970's and 1980's, Ballard startled the world with texts that defy any easy categorization. Whether he writes about a desertified America (*Hello, America*, 1981), a troubled African continent (*The Day of Creation*, 1987), or the mischievous offspring of the upper-class residents of a gated community (*Running Wild*, 1988), Ballard, in his own words, feels strangely liberated in a world which, in the words of one critic, has called his work the product of a man totally beyond psychiatric help.

During the 1990's, Ballard continued to invent characters whose bizarre actions turn contemporary events made familiar by the mass media into surreal spectacles with their own diabolical logic. The civil war in Lebanon becomes a psychosocial laboratory in "War Fever"; the environmentalists in *Rushing to Paradise* have their own sinister agenda; and *Cocaine Nights* mischievously challenges the conventions of the detective story. Ballard's novel *Crash* was made into a film in 1997. After his three children grew up and left home, Ballard remained in his house in Shepperton, from where, in addition to his steady output of original novels and short stories, he continued to be an active writer of essays and book reviews. His voice is familiar in British literary circles.

J. G. Ballard (©Miriam Berkley)

ANALYSIS

Writing against the grain of conventional realism has become the trademark of an author whose fiction is after bigger game: the fantastic truth hidden behind the scintillating facade of contemporary Western culture. A writer of extraordinarily imaginative and intellectually challenging science fiction, J. G. Ballard centers his short and long fiction on questions of humanity's mental and physiological relationship with a drastically altered environment, in which change is brought about either by advanced technology or by a global natural disaster.

From the beginning, J. G. Ballard's short stories demonstrated his preoccupation with the internal

landscapes of the mind and humanity's mental reaction to profound changes in everyday environment. Ballard, however, typically refuses to deal with his subject matter in a realist fashion. Instead of presenting "true" psychological conflicts and offering obvious and well-accepted solutions, he often imagines his own mental diseases and has his characters embark on apparently irrational but certainly innovative courses of action. This defiance of the "normal" in the widest sense and this fictional probing of the radically new are crucial aspects of Ballard's fiction. In turn, his authorial insistence on total imaginative freedom has also led Ballard to write fiction that successfully experiments with style and language. Imbued with the postmodern consciousness, Ballard has been compared with such key American authors as Thomas Pynchon, Donald Barthelme, and William S. Burroughs. His work, with its uncomfortable dissection of Western cultural icons, has also been hailed as a fictional equivalent of the literary and cultural criticism of scholars such as Roland Barthes.

Overall, Ballard's continuous revisiting of his favorite themes, which has become a mark of his fiction, is artistically successful because it always leads to a reshaping and sharpening of the highly original myths of his imagination. Furthermore, Ballard is at his best when he gracefully embraces the surreal and does not even try to establish an overt link to the natural world. Stories such as "The Subliminal Man" or "The Largest Theme Park in the World," which deal with subliminal advertising and the emergence of a European beach culture that leaves the interior of the continent deserted for foreign visitors, are less successful than the more outrageously imaginative stories that present an inner truth unconnected to any naturalistic scenario. The beautiful resurrection story of Ballard's "Myths of the Near Future," in which Elaine Sheppard, the victim of space sickness, is in essence brought back to life through the power of her former husband Roger's loving imagination, hints at exactly such a truth as the imagination Ballard presents to his readers.

In imagining his protagonists, who are often thrust into strange new worlds and alien landscapes that they accept with little questioning, Ballard typically creates well-educated, articulate, and emotionally controlled men and women with an apparently solid upper-middle-class background. Yet, underneath this tranquil facade of reason, control, and often literally clinical detachment, Ballard installs a second, deeper layer of strange obsessions and aberrant needs that the new world, in which the characters find themselves, causes to spring to the surface. This evolution of the everyday postmodern person into a driven, irrational, yet also strangely liberated character who, through a subjective reading of his or her unfolding situation, finds a sense of meaning previously missing from the "real" world is clearly the trademark of Ballard's short fiction.

"CONCENTRATION CITY"

In one of his first stories, "Concentration City," Ballard skillfully maps out the complex relationship between obsession, liberation, and a surreal landscape. Franz Mattheson's (re)invention of an airplane spurs him to search ingeniously for the limits of a jam-packed futuristic city that has built up even the sky, thus depriving the young inventor of the medium in

which to fly his plane. Not only is the motif of flying introduced here—Ballard's central metaphor for humanity's yearning for freedom—but also, in a surprising turn at the end, Ballard's fascination with time serves, for the first time in his fiction, as the ultimate medium for the fantastic. Thus, upon his return to his exact geographical point of departure after an uninterrupted railway journey across the globe-spanning city, Franz finds out that even the fourth dimension, time, is a prison: Incomprehensibly, the clock turns back to the day of his departure weeks earlier, confirming the impossibility of flight from the metropolis.

"MANHOLE SIXTY-NINE"

Turning from a four-dimensional prison to the incarceration of the mind, "Manhole Sixty-nine" is the first of Ballard's stories in which a hospital setting serves as the nexus of modern technology, the scientific method of reasoning, and the new tortures for the human soul. His story chronicles the result of a neurosurgical experiment that has enabled three men to live without sleep. Unable to cope with ever-present consciousness, however, each of the patients mentally forces his universe to collapse into a space just large enough to contain a single body. Drawing on his familiarity with the knowledge, jargon, methodology, and mind frame of medical research, Ballard presents a haunting picture that derives its uncanny effect from a masterful mix of the real and the fantastic. Here, as elsewhere in his fiction, scientific language itself becomes part of the new world that confronts an old humanity.

"THE CAGE OF SAND"

The fact that many of his early stories introduce themes and visions that will persistently return in Ballard's work has led to the existence of strings of Ballard stories treating an overriding theme that is developed over the course of decades. Ballard's series of stories dealing with the return to Earth of its dead astronauts constitutes such a cycle. Written in 1962, "The Cage of Sand" is the first. It opens in the vicinity of a deserted Cape Canaveral, an area poisoned by the Martian sand that spaceships have brought back as interplanetary ballast. There, two men and a woman have gathered to watch the nightly appearance of one or more of the seven dead astronauts who, still flying in the capsules in which they died, have become a ghastly group of satellites.

Typically the landscape, the living, and the dead form a complex system held together by mutual attraction, for the wounds they have suffered can be traced back to the crisis brought on by humanity's quest for the stars. Consequently, in "The Cage of Sand," among the living, Bridgman's plans for a Martian city are rejected, Travis's nerves fail during the countdown to his first launch, and Louisa Woodward's husband is one of the dead.

Yet, characteristically, Ballard's story transcends failure and disaster and offers instead the quintessential Ballardian sense of a final surreal fulfillment. When the capsule of Merrill, the oldest of the dead space pioneers, finally falls out of its orbit and crashes into the dunes of Martian sand around the Cape, the narrator remarks dryly that the astronaut has finally accomplished his mission, for Merrill "had reached Mars after all." The reader should take these words seriously, since their positive, if clearly unconventional, interpretation is perhaps all for which postmodern humanity can hope.

"THE DEAD ASTRONAUT"

Always viewed from a new angle, the theme of this ghostly reentry of dead astronauts at the exact spot of their launch returns and replays. In the 1968 story laconically entitled "The Dead Astronaut," Philip and Judith Groves return to Cape Kennedy days before the anticipated fall out of orbit of Judith's former husband Robert Hamilton. Eventually, Philip and Judith indeed receive the charred remains of Hamilton but are poisoned by their radioactivity, which stems from the fact that his capsule carried a nuclear bomb. At the moment of their realization that their bodies have been terminally corrupted by radiation disease, Philip also confides that he has used the memory of Hamilton to make Judith love him, a former National Aeronautics and Space Administration (NASA) flight programmer, and that their marriage was based not only on a dead man but also on false pretenses.

"MEMORIES OF THE SPACE AGE"

Fourteen years later, in "Memories of the Space Age," Ballard adds a new twist as he returns to the deserted Cape, which like all Florida has been quarantined after the outbreak of a strange space sickness brought back with the starships. Now it is Gale Shepley, the daughter of the first astronaut murdered in space by a colleague, who awaits the imminent return of her father's body. His murderer, Hinton, has come back as well and tries to heal the "psychic fissure" that the space program has rent in the human collective unconscious. He does so by flying replica after replica of the first planes across the deserted spaceport, thus searching in the roots of aviation for a clue to the "evolutionary crime" of space travel. Against the backdrop of Hinton's struggles with Gale Shepley and a space-sick former NASA doctor and his wife, who have come back to the source of their disease, the imminent reentry of Alan Shepley again serves to highlight the experience of a private vision of grace: the space-sick end by "freezing" in time, living forever in the moment of their death.

"THE TERMINAL BEACH"

Given Ballard's fascination with such imaginative material and his admiration for surrealist painters such as Salvador Dalí and Max Ernst, his stylistic experimentation with the form of the short story is hardly surprising. Beginning in the mid-1960's, Ballard published such innovative texts as his 1964 story "The Terminal Beach," one of the best of his "condensed novels." In this story, he strips conventional storytelling of such accumulated "ballast" as the naturalistic description of character, dialogue, and conflict and focuses instead—exclusively—on the evocation of the particular mind frame that has guided Traven, the protagonist, to maroon himself on the Pacific island of Eniwetok, the historical site of American nuclear tests in the 1950's.

Presenting one scene after another of Traven's stay, and with deliberate disregard for transitional paragraphs or the convention of helpful objective narration, "The Terminal Beach" instead seeks to create a series of still pictures that derive their artistic force from the selected images of the atomic age that they conjure up—empty camera bunkers and abandoned military staff cars are juxtaposed with half-drained target basins full of partially molten test dummies.

All of this is presented through the eyes and via the apparently mad consciousness of Traven, who seeks truth by immersing himself in the landscape and trying to become part of the scene in order to understand its meaning; characteristically, he hides from a navy patrol by mingling with the abandoned dummies, thus indirectly stating their true relationship to himself.

"THE ATROCITY EXHIBITION"

Ballard's formal experimentalism led him to the creation of his 1966 masterpiece "The Atrocity Exhibition," a powerful text that lent its title to a famous 1969 collection presenting an unreality shaped out of the blown-up fragments of the everyday world. Taking its cue from the genuine psychiatric practice of occupational therapy, "The Atrocity Exhibition" is a series of violent pictures painted by imaginary inmates of an insane asylum and chronicles the reaction to them by the medical staff and the protagonist, Travis, who becomes obsessed with his self-imposed task of creating a fitting piece to portray a future World War III.

At the core of the story's narrative lies the unsettling idea that the products of human culture that the text presents, mainly taken from the fields of warfare, technology, art, and popular entertainment, not only are intrinsically violent but also correspond to the biological makeup of humanity. The head of the asylum, Dr. Nathan, is thus convinced that

World War III . . . will be fought out on the spinal battlefields, in terms of the postures we assume, of our traumas mimetized in the angle of a wall or balcony.

In this world, to understand the true meaning of human architectural design requires discovering the underlying mental pain and physical anguish of architect and client, which quite literally has been written into the walls of modern housing complexes.

This narrative adventure seeks to find a stylistic counterpart to the apparent chaos of modern culture by presenting no continuous, traditional text but brief scenes containing action, dreams, dialogue, lists of disasters, and putative explanations proffered by characters who possess a highly private view of their world. From here, Ballard moved on to write both more experimental short fiction and texts that offer

their imaginative content in more conventional form. His pair of short stories written in the mid-1980's, minimalistically titled "Answers to a Questionnaire" and "The Index," for example, both tell their stories through the form that their title pronounces. In Ballard's hands, a book index—the ultimate "condensation"—can successfully stand in for the whole text of the book.

"THE OVERLOADED MAN"

Occasionally, Ballard has been attacked by critics who have failed to grasp the premises of his fiction and its deliberately paradoxical view of reality; like the reviewer-turned-psychiatrist who perceived a psychopathic mind behind Ballard's work, they have mistakenly read his stories as "straight" advocacy of criminal insanity. Ballard's exploration of a possible drive toward psychic self-annihilation through a deliberately alternative, or "psychotic," perception of reality is particularly vulnerable here. As early as 1961, "The Overloaded Man" probed this theme within the context of Harry Faulkner's developing facility to blot out physical reality and perceive his suburban neighborhood as "a cubist landscape, a collection of random white forms below a blue backdrop" instead of a carefully tended condominum project. Consequently, to test fully his new gift of disassociating himself from reality, Faulkner ends up drowning himself in his shallow ornamental pool; again a strange sense of absurd achievement breaks through the tragedy as the protagonist "waited for the world to dissolve and set him free."

"THE ENORMOUS SPACE"

In 1989, Ballard ingeniously returned to a man who dreams a similar dream of dropping out of reality. Geoffrey Ballantyne, in "The Enormous Space," however, is caught somewhat unawares by his discovery that just as he has retreated from the world outside, so his family house and space itself have retreated from him, leaving him stranded and unable to move. Yet Ballantyne, too, considers his fate a positive one. Nearly immobilized and ready to take up cramped final residence next to his secretary in the freezer, he congratulates himself on "finding at last the still centre of the world."

"WAR FEVER"

"War Fever" is indicative of Ballard's trademark trend to provide apparently paradoxical explanations for the inner workings of current events that hold the media-fed attention of the public. Taking the civil war in Lebanon as its cue, which still raged unresolved at the time of the short story's publication in 1990 and provided the world with haunting footage of real atrocities, the text focuses on Ryan, a seventeen-year-old orphan of Canadian descent. With his sister and aunt, he is stranded in the city of Beirut, which has seen nothing but warfare for nearly three decades.

A fighter for the Christian militias in the city, Ryan becomes disillusioned and appalled by the horror of war, with its ever-shifting alliances which led to his killing of his friend Angel. Ballard's depiction of the devastation wrought by war is uncannily realistic as he turns to hotels-turned-battlegrounds, offering their shattered lobbies as background for pictures of war atrocities. Ryan devises an ingenious but improbable plan for peace. Donning the blue helmet of the United Nations (U.N.) peacekeeping forces, which still operate on an apparently humanitarian mission throughout the city, he challenges friends and rivals alike to follow his example.

Just as peace is about to settle, sudden explosions rock the city, and fighting quickly flares up again. Taken into U.N. custody by Dr. Edwards, who follows an apparently deranged inner calling, Ryan learns that the peacekeepers have secretly fueled the war. In a surreal twist typical of Ballard's dark imagination, Dr. Edwards explains that just as the World Health Organization has singled out an impoverished nation to study the mutations of the smallpox virus, the virus of warfare has been kept alive in Beirut while the rest of the world has seen its eradication. The fighters are young men and women taken from all over the world and given false family associations; thus, while they feel like blood relatives to him, Ryan's sister and aunt are not really related to him.

Yet when Ryan discovers their murdered bodies, he directs his rage toward Dr. Edwards and the rest of the world, which has turned the city into a bio-psychological test tube. In a turn familiar in Ballard's

fiction, Ryan fiercely embraces his identity as a virus. He kills Dr. Edwards and prepares to unite the fighters, to spread out to contaminate the world with the virus it has nurtured in them. "War Fever" reveals Ballard's continued interest in imaginative diseases, similar to his concern with space viruses in other texts. Ultimately, Ballard's characters are left alone in a universe devoid of common moral guidance systems. Yet within the idiosyncratic worlds they inhabit, the characters consider their decisions the most reasonable courses of action.

OTHER MAJOR WORKS

LONG FICTION: *The Wind from Nowhere*, 1962; *The Drowned World*, 1962; *The Drought*, 1964 (also known as *The Burning World*); *The Crystal World*, 1966; *Crash*, 1973; *Concrete Island*, 1974; *High Rise*, 1975; *The Unlimited Dream Company*, 1979; *Hello, America*, 1981; *Empire of the Sun*, 1984; *The Day of Creation*, 1987; *Running Wild*, 1988 (novella); *The Kindness of Women*, 1991; *Rushing to Paradise*, 1994; *Cocaine Nights*, 1996; *Super-Cannes*, 2000.

NONFICTION: *A User's Guide to the Millennium: Essays and Reviews*, 1996.

BIBLIOGRAPHY

Brigg, Peter. *J. G. Ballard*. San Bernardino, Calif.: Borgo Press, 1985. The most exhaustive book-length discussion of the author and his work. Brigg treats his subject with great competency and offers a well-grounded analysis. The book is especially valuable for its fine bibliography.

_____. "J. G. Ballard: Time Out of Mind." *Extrapolation* 35 (Spring, 1994): 43-59. Discusses Ballard's characters as figures who act according to the internal absolutes of their own reasonably processed observations. Asserts the key to his characters' perceptions of their needs and actions is how they respond to time as they know and define it.

Lathan, Rob. "The Modern World Is an Enormous Fiction: J. G. Ballard and the Millennium." *The New York Review of Science Fiction* 9 (March, 1997): 1, 8-12. Discusses Ballard's nonfiction in *A*

User's Guide to the Millennium as a useful supplement to his fiction. Notes Ballard's common theme in fiction and nonfiction: that the modern world is an enormous fiction created by media.

Luckhurst, Roger. *The Angle Between Two Walls: The Fiction of J. G. Ballard.* New York: St. Martin's Press, 1997. A study of Ballard's work that attempts to account for both the fascination and repulsion often felt by his readers. Argues not that the cause of this unease is the difficulty of finding the right framework for approaching Ballard's fiction, but that his work is a prolonged meditation on the question of frames.

Pringle, David. *Earth Is the Alien Planet: J. G. Ballard's Four-Dimensional Nightmare.* San Bernardino, Calif.: Borgo Press, 1979. Pringle offers an overview of Ballard's work and discusses literary context, symbolism, and key returning themes and motifs of his texts. Sympathetic, readable, and informed, this book is a good, if somewhat dated, introduction to Ballard.

Re/Search 8-9 (1984). A flashy but informative special celebration of the author's work. Includes valuable interviews, an illustrated autobiography, and a selection of the fiction and critical writing. Full of photographic and literary material on and by Ballard and about his subjects. The useful bibliography includes a complete chronological list of Ballard's short stories.

Stephenson, Gregory. *Out of the Night and into the Dream: A Thematic Study of the Fiction of J. G. Ballard.* New York: Greenwood Press, 1991. Focuses on Ballard's science-fiction motifs. Includes bibliographical references and index.

R. C. Lutz

HONORÉ DE BALZAC

Born: Tours, France; May 20, 1799
Died: Paris, France; August 18, 1850

PRINCIPAL SHORT FICTION

Les Contes drolatiques, 1832-1837 (*Droll Stories*, 1874, 1891)

OTHER LITERARY FORMS

Although he was an accomplished short-story writer, Honoré de Balzac is famous above all as a novelist. Between 1829 and 1850, he created a series of more than ninety interconnected novels with recurring characters. In 1841, he gave this collection of novels the general title of *La Comédie humaine* (1829-1848; *The Human Comedy*, 1895-1896, 1911). He was also a prolific essayist, and he wrote five plays, which enjoyed some popular success during his lifetime, but have long since fallen into oblivion.

ACHIEVEMENTS

Balzac was the most influential and creative French novelist in the first half of the nineteenth century. The French poet and literary critic Charles Baudelaire expressed a profound insight into Balzac's genius when he stated that Balzac was not a realist but rather a visionary who taught readers to see and understand the exploitation and alienation of modern men and women. His novels described the radical transformation of French society after the French Revolution and the Napoleonic era. Balzac did not depict the broad sweep of history but rather the intense and very personal suffering of key characters whose vulnerability and innocence allowed them to be destroyed by others. Balzac created the narrative technique of recurring characters whom readers find at different moments in their lives in various novels. His *The Human Comedy* revealed his ability to describe with sensitivity and psychological depth characters from the full spectrum of French society. His masterpieces included works such as *Les Chouans* (1829; *The Chouans*, 1885), which denounced the violation of basic human rights during the French Revolution, his lyrical and autobiographical novel *Le Lys dans la vallée* (1836; *The Lily in the Valley*), and *La Peau de chagrin* (1831; *The Wild Ass's Skin*), which is a variation on the Faust legend.

BIOGRAPHY

Honoré de Balzac grew up in a bourgeois family in Tours, then moved with them to Paris, where he completed his undistinguished education—he was apparently too much of a dreamer to perform well in classes. Working as a clerk in law and financial practices and attending the Sorbonne lectures of Victor Cousin and François Guizot in the evenings led him to develop an abhorrence for the mundane existence of the salaried working class. In 1819, he suddenly announced that he intended to become a writer, and there followed years of misery as he eked out his living in rented attics, existing like a hermit by extraordinary economy and by producing a flood of anonymous cheap tracts and novels. Although his family hoped that these conditions would bring Balzac back to his senses, unyielding patterns were formed instead, traits that would continue for the rest of his life. His prodigious energy, combined with a strong will, established his daily regimen of writing—often twenty hours, nonstop—which he sustained by his own blends of coffee. His penniless existence helped whet his appetite for financial success to the degree that he was often tempted to embark on the most elaborate schemes to make his fortune. It was not that his ideas, such as forming a publishing company that would produce inexpensive copies of the classics, were unsound; in fact, his notions were far ahead of his time. His sense of management, however, as well as his choice of partners and financial backers were inevitably naïve, and few, if any, of his financial ventures were to succeed.

As a result, Balzac turned to the newspapers, where he sold essays and short stories and where his real apprenticeship took place. Publishing deadlines and payment by the word encouraged him to prolific

writing as a means of paying off his debts. In 1829 came his first success under his own name; this was a historical novel influenced by Sir Walter Scott, *The Chouans*, which dealt with the royalist uprising in Brittany during the French Revolution. After this, his output became truly prodigious, for in addition to the normal demands of journalism, he produced ninety-three novels between 1829 and 1850. Like both Scott and Fyodor Dostoevski, he was constantly writing to satisfy his creditors; that he managed under these circumstances to produce enduring works of art is testimony to his genius.

The year 1829 was also the date that Balzac's anonymous *La Physiologie du marriage (The Physiology of Marriage)* appeared; although seemingly satirical, it demonstrated the same profound empathy and understanding for women that would lead him toward numerous enduring relationships. Many were begun by correspondence, the most famous being that with the Polish Countess Éveline Hanska, whom he pursued for eighteen years. Their correspondence, published posthumously as *Letters to Madame Hanska* (1900), forms a fascinating account of Balzac's life

Honoré de Balzac (Library of Congress)

and works. Although they married in March, 1850, by then he was in very poor health, and it was too late for her fortune to be of assistance to him in his constant financial entanglements. Balzac died, exhausted, in August of 1850.

ANALYSIS

Honoré de Balzac's immense production and his celebrated writing schedule of some two thousand pages per year suggest an artist who gave no thought to theory or form, and a glance at some of his journalistic endeavors will readily confirm these clichés. Quite early in his career, however, examples of Balzac's genius were expressed in his short fiction.

"THE UNKNOWN MASTERPIECE"

"Le Chef-d'œuvre inconnu" ("The Unknown Masterpiece") was first published in newspaper form in 1831, and was later included in *The Human Comedy* under the classification of *Études philosophiques* (1831-1835; *Philosophical Studies*). The story deals with the lifelong obsession of master-painter Frenhofer to discover ideal beauty and its representation. Two admiring disciples, Franz Purbus and Nicolas Poussin, real-life artists used by Balzac to add verisimilitude to his story, come to seek advice; in exchange, they propose that the mistress of Poussin be the model for the work that Frenhofer has been trying to complete after all these years. No sooner does the master see the young woman than his inspiration permits him to complete without further delay the elusive painting. When he unveils the work for his friends, however, they are dumbfounded to see on the canvas a mass of colors and lines, but no figure. Embarrassed and wondering if Frenhofer may not be playing a joke on them, they hem and haw, examine the painting with great attention, and finally discern a foot, a beautiful, living foot, lost in the haze of colors and details. When the master, lost in ecstasy, understands the reality of his disciples' incomprehension and realizes that even his fellow artists are unable to grasp the significance of his creation, he sends them away, burns his paintings, and dies.

Balzac's story fits into the tradition of the *ars poetica*, works about the act of artistic creation. It reveals to what extent the young and busy author himself meditated on this critical topic, on the distinction between artistic theory and artistic practice, and, in this case at least, anticipated the aesthetic revolution to be launched by the Impressionists.

DROLL STORIES

Completely different in tone, *Droll Stories* recalls the gross farce of François Rabelais and the bawdy dimensions of the *esprit gaulois*. Like the *fabliaux* of the late Middle Ages, the stories poke good-humored fun at indecency. Like Giovanni Boccaccio's *Decameron: O, Prencipe Galeotto* (1349-1351; *The Decameron*, 1620) there is a semblance of morality, but it is spread so thin that the reader has to laugh, along with the author, at the adulterous couples, lascivious men of the Church, deceived husbands, and others who constitute the universal menagerie of the farce. Whereas the form is inspired by Geoffrey Chaucer and Boccaccio, the style Balzac adopts is very similar to that of Rabelais, and it shows tendencies that later become Balzac's trademark: long lists of synonyms and abundant technical details that in fact have little to do with the story line but which permit the author to indulge his passion for words and his delight at demonstrating his verbal dexterity. The collection is signed by the author as "de Balzac," the first use of the snobbish *particule* that Balzac used consistently thereafter, along with a family coat of arms that he either "discovered" or invented himself. The vivid and racy spirit of Rabelais, which is so close to that of Balzac himself, permeates his other works, as does the Renaissance spirit of enthusiasm and lust for life. His sheer exuberance sustained him throughout his complex career.

"THE GRANDE BRETÈCHE"

A typical story is "La Grande Bretèche" ("The Grande Bretèche"), which continues the tradition of a story within a story. In this case, Dr. Bianchon, a character who recurs throughout *The Human Comedy* and for whom Balzac called as he lay dying, tells of a strange property he visited in the Vendôme and of the provocative tale that lay behind it. A suspicious husband returns home earlier than expected and confronts his wife, asking her to open her closet door so that he can see her lover. On her affirmation that there is no one there, and that, further, if her husband should doubt her word and actually open the door to verify it, their relationship will be forever dissolved, the husband agrees; he then promptly has a worker build up a wall over the doorway, smiling with assurance at his distressed wife. Balzac here presents a fascinating study of conjugal jealousy with medieval overtones, and he anticipates scenes later exploited by Alexandre Dumas, *père*, and Edgar Allan Poe.

"Facino Cane"

These same melodramatic touches distinguish "Facino Cane," a story evoking the sensuality and political corruption of eighteenth century Venice (another idea borrowed by Dumas for *The Count of Monte-Cristo*, 1844), which gives Balzac full rein for his use of local color, obsessive emotions, and money as a prime motivating force in modern society. It is difficult for the modern reader to realize to what extent Balzac's treatment of money in literature was truly new. While greed has always been represented in literature, Balzac was among the first to dwell on what he termed "la nécessité de calculer."

It is important to note that Balzac made no clear distinctions between the novel and the short story, and that many of his best early works are in fact works of short fiction now scattered throughout the framework of *The Human Comedy*. The magnum opus, including its recurring characters, was first conceived of in 1834, and carried a preface by Felix Davin, a friend of Balzac. Three years later, however, Balzac had written so much more than anticipated that the project was expanded, and by 1840, the unifying title, recalling Dante's work, was established. The finishing touches were applied in 1842, when Balzac replaced Davin's earlier preface with his own preface—a critical document and the cornerstone of his aesthetics. His extraordinary range of knowledge and precise powers of observation, combined with a vigorous personality which could not resist sharing its personal views with others, make Balzac one of the great chroniclers of nineteenth century life.

Other major works

LONG FICTION: *La Comédie humaine*, 1829-1848 (17 volumes; *The Comedy of Human Life*, 1885-1893, 1896 [40 volumes]; also as *The Human Com-* edy, 1895-1896, 1911 [53 volumes]; includes all titles listed below); *Les Chouans*, 1829 (*The Chouans*, 1885); *Physiologie du marriage*, 1829 (*The Physiology of Marriage*); *Gobseck*, 1830 (English translation); *La Maison du chat-qui-pelote*, 1830, 1869 (*At the Sign of the Cat and Racket*); *Le Chef-d'oeuvre inconnu*, 1831 (*The Unknown Masterpiece*); *La Peau de chagrin*, 1831 (*The Wild Ass's Skin*; also as *The Fatal Skin*); *Sarrasine*, 1831 (English translation); *Le Curé de Tours*, 1832 (*The Vicar of Tours*); *Louis Lambert*, 1832 (English translation, 1889); *Maître Cornélius*, 1832 (English translation); *La Femme de trente ans*, 1832-1842 (includes *Premiéres fautes*, 1832, 1842; *Souffrances inconnues*, 1834-1835; *À trente ans*, 1832, 1842; *Le Doigt de Dieu*, 1832, 1834-1835, 1842; *Les Deux Rencontres*, 1832, 1834-1835, 1842; *La Vieillesse d'une mère coupable*, 1832, 1842); *Eugénie Grandet*, 1833 (English translation, 1859); *La Recherche de l'absolu*, 1834 (*Balthazar: Or, Science and Love*, 1859; also as *The Quest of the Absolute*); *Histoire des treize*, 1834-1835 (*History of the Thirteen*; also as *The Thirteen*; includes *Ferragus, chef des dévorants*, 1834 [*Ferragus, Chief of the Devorants*; also as *The Mystery of the Rue Solymane*]; *La Duchesse de Langeais*, 1834 [*The Duchesse de Langeais*]; *La Fille aux yeux d'or*, 1834-1835 [*The Girl with the Golden Eyes*]); *Melmoth réconcilié*, 1835 (*Melmoth Converted*, 1900); *Le Père Goriot*, 1835 (*Daddy Goriot*, 1860; also as *Père Goriot*); *Le Lys dans la vallée*, 1836 (*The Lily in the Valley*); *Histoire de la grandeur et de la décadence de César Birotteau*, 1837 (*History of the Grandeur and Downfall of César Birotteau*, 1860; also as *The Rise and Fall of César Birotteau*); *Illusions perdues*, 1837-1843 (*Lost Illusions*); *Splendeurs et misères des courtisanes*, 1838-1847, 1869 (*The Splendors and Miseries of Courtesans*, 1895; includes *Comment aiment les filles*, 1838, 1844 [*The Way that Girls Love*, 1895]; *À combien l'amour revient aux viellards*, 1844 [*How Much Love Costs Old Men*, 1895]; *Où mènent les mauvais chemins*, 1846 [*The End of Bad Roads*, 1895]; *La Dernière incarnation de Vautrin*, 1847 [*The Last Incarnation of Vautrin*, 1895]); *Pierrette*, 1840 (English translation); *Le Curé de village*, 1841 (*The Country Parson*);

Mémoires de deux jeunes mariées, 1842 (*The Two Young Brides*); *Une Ténébreuse Affaire*, 1842 (*The Gondreville Mystery*); *Ursule Mirouët*, 1842 (English translation); *La Cousine Bette*, 1846 (*Cousin Bette*, 1888); *Le Cousin Pons*, 1847 (*Cousin Pons*, 1880).

PLAYS: *Vautrin*, pr., pb. 1840 (English translation, 1901); *La Marâtre*, pr., pb. 1848 (*The Stepmother*, 1901, 1958); *Le Faiseur*, pr. 1849 (also as *Mercadet*; English translation, 1901); *The Dramatic Works*, pb. 1901 (2 volumes, includes *Vautrin*, *The Stepmother*, *Mercadet*, *Quinola's Resources*, and *Pamela Giraud*); *Cromwell*, pb. 1925 (wr. 1819-1820).

NONFICTION: *Correspondance*, 1819-1850, 1876 (*The Correspondence*, 1878); *Lettres à l'étrangére*, 1899-1950; *Letters to Madame Hanska*, 1900 (translation of volume 1 of *Lettres à l'étrangére*).

BIBLIOGRAPHY

Charlton, D. G., et al., eds. *Balzac and the Nineteenth Century*. Leicester, England: Leicester University Press, 1972. This volume of essays describes very well the profound influence of Balzac on important nineteenth century French writers such as Charles Baudelaire, Émile Zola, and Victor Hugo. This book also contains thoughtful interpretations of Balzac's short stories by Anthony Pugh and Peter W. Lock.

Festa-McCormick, Diana. *Honoré de Balzac*. Boston: Twayne, 1979. An excellent introduction to the works of Balzac. Festa-McCormick describes with much subtlety Balzac's evolution as a novelist, and she makes insightful comments on his representation of women. This book contains a very well annotated bibliography.

Guenther, Beatrice Martina. *The Poetics of Death: The Short Prose of Kleist and Balzac*. Albany: State University of New York Press, 1996. Examines the short fiction of Balzac and Heinrich von Kleist, especially the theme of death in their works.

Maurois, André. *Prometheus: The Life of Balzac*. Translated by Norman Denny. New York: Harper & Row, 1965. The standard biography of Balzac. Maurois analyzes Balzac's formative years, his place in the Parisian literary circles of the 1830's and 1840's, and his long relationship with Éveline Hanska. Maurois made judicious use of Balzac's extant letters in order to give readers a sense of Balzac's personality.

Mileham, James. "Labyrinths in Balzac's Ferragus." *Nineteenth-Century French Studies* 23 (Spring/Summer, 1995): 356-364. Discusses two sorts of images of the labyrinth in Balzac's novella: the Cretan, which is deceptive, and the oneiric, which is dreamlike. Argues that in the novella the streets of Paris are basically a Cretan labyrinth, but that some of them are oneiric.

Pritchett, V. S. *Balzac*. New York: Alfred A. Knopf, 1973. A beautifully illustrated book by an eminent writer and literary critic. Pritchett enables readers to understand the milieu in which Balzac wrote. Pritchett's interpretations of Balzac's short stories and his novel *The Wild Ass's Skin* are especially thought-provoking. Includes a good bibliography of recent critical studies on Balzac.

Robb, Graham. *Balzac: A Life*. New York: W. W. Norton, 1994. A detailed biographical account of the life and work of Balzac. Focuses on his philosophic perspectives and well as his fiction; speculates on the psychological motivation underlying his work.

Rogers, Samuel. *Balzac and the Novel*. Madison: University of Wisconsin Press, 1953. A thoughtful study of Balzac's narrative techniques and his use of recurring characters in *The Human Comedy*. Rogers also describes Balzac's portrayal of different social classes in his novels. This book contains a very useful bibliography, but readers should consult the books of Diana Festa-McCormick and V. S. Pritchett (above) for information on later critical studies on Balzac.

Schlossman, Beryl. "Balzac's Art of Excess." *MLN* 109 (December, 1994): 872-896. Discusses Charles Baudelaire's analysis of Balzac's "aesthetic of excess" as a translation of the pictorial into language. Discusses Balzac's use of language as visible form and paintings as linguistic discourse.

Thomas, Gwen. "The Case of the Missing Detective: Balzac's *Une Ténébreuse Affaire*." *French Studies*

48 (July, 1994): 285-298. Discusses how Balzac anticipates a number of detective story conventions. Argues that Balzac retains gaps and indeterminacies in his work and that his final revelation is a literary device rather than a logical conclusion.

Robert W. Artinian, updated by Edmund J. Campion

TONI CADE BAMBARA
Miltona Mirkin Cade

Born: New York, New York; March 25, 1939
Died: Philadelphia, Pennsylvania; December 9, 1995

PRINCIPAL SHORT FICTION
Gorilla, My Love, 1972
The Sea Birds Are Still Alive: Collected Stories, 1977
Deep Sightings and Rescue Missions: Fiction, Essays, and Conversations, 1996

OTHER LITERARY FORMS

Before Toni Cade Bambara published her first collection of stories, *Gorilla My Love* (1972), she edited two anthologies, *The Black Woman* (1970) and *Tales and Stories for Black Folks* (1971), under the name Toni Cade. Her 1980 novel, *The Salt Eaters*, was well received and won many awards. She was also an active screenwriter whose credits included Louis Massiah's *The Bombing of Osage Avenue* (1986), about the bombing of the Movement (MOVE) Organization's headquarters in Philadelphia, and Massiah's *W. E. B. Du Bois: A Biography in Four Voices* (1995). Her friend and editor, Toni Morrison, edited a collection of her previously uncollected stories and essays in 1996 called *Deep Sightings and Rescue Missions: Fiction, Essays, and Conversations*, and her final novel, *Those Bones Are Not My Child*, was published in 1999.

ACHIEVEMENTS

The Salt Eaters won numerous awards, including the American Book Award, the Langston Hughes Society Award, and an award from the Zora Neale Hurston Society. Toni Cade Bambara's work on *The Bombing of Osage Avenue* led to an Academy Award for Best Documentary and awards from the Pennsylvania Association of Broadcasters and the Black Hall of Fame. Her other honors include the Peter Pauper Press Award (1958), the John Golden Award for Fiction from Queens College (1959), a Rutgers University research fellowship (1972), a Black Child Development Institute service award (1973), a Black Rose Award from *Encore* (1973), a Black Community Award from Livingston College, Rutgers University (1974), an award from the National Association of Negro Business and Professional Women's Club League, a George Washington Carver Distinguished African American Lecturer Award from Simpson College, *Ebony*'s Achievement in the Arts Award, and a Black Arts Award from the University of Missouri (1981), a Documentary Award from the National Black Programming Consortium (1986), and a nomination for the Black Caucus of the American Library Association Literary Award (1997).

BIOGRAPHY

Toni Cade Bambara was born Miltona Mirkin Cade in New York City in 1939 and grew up in Harlem, Bedford-Stuyvesant, and Queens, New York, and in Jersey City, New Jersey. She attended Queens College in New York and received a B.A. degree in theater arts in 1959, the same year she published her first short story, "Sweet Town." From 1960 to 1965, she worked on an M.A. degree in American literature at City College of New York, while also working as a caseworker at the Department of Welfare, and later as program director of the Colony Settlement House. Starting in 1965, she taught at City College for four years before moving on to Livingston College at Rutgers University in 1969. She also taught at Emory University, Spelman College (where she was a writer-in-residence during the 1970's), and Atlanta University, at various times teaching writing, theater, and social work.

Her publication of *The Black Woman*, an anthology of poetry, fiction, and nonfiction by established writers (such as Nikki Giovanni, Alice Walker, and Paule Marshall) and students demonstrated her com-

Toni Cade Bambara (Joyce Middler)

mitment to both the women's movement and the Civil Rights campaign. By the time she had published her first collection of short stories, *Gorilla, My Love*, in 1972, she had adopted the last name of Bambara from a signature she found on a sketch pad in a trunk of her grandmother's things.

Bambara's belief in the connection between social activism and art was strengthened by a trip to Cuba in 1973, when she met with women's organizations

there. The increased urgency of concern for social activism appears in her second collection of short stories, *The Sea Birds Are Still Alive*. After her first novel, *The Salt Eaters*, was published in 1980 and received numerous awards, she increasingly turned her attention to her work in the arts, becoming an important writer of independent films, though she never stopped working on fiction. She died of cancer on December 9, 1995.

ANALYSIS

Toni Cade Bambara's short fiction is especially notable for its creativity with language and its ability to capture the poetry of black speech. In a conversation that was printed in her posthumous collection *Deep Sightings and Rescue Missions* as "How She Came by Her Name," she claimed that in the stories from *Gorilla, My Love* about childhood, she was trying to capture the voice of childhood, and she was surprised that readers received these efforts to use black dialect as a political act. Nonetheless, her writing (like her work as a teacher, social worker, and filmmaker) was always informed by her sense of social activism and social justice in the broadest sense. In her later work outside the field of short fiction (in films and in her last novel) she focused on the bombing of the black neighborhood in Philadelphia where the MOVE Organization was headquartered, the life of W. E. B. Du Bois, and the Atlanta child murders of the 1980's, all topics that were rife with political meaning.

Nonetheless, what enlivens her writing is her originality with language and a playful sense of form which aims more to share than to tell directly. Another essay from *Deep Sightings and Rescue Missions*, "The Education of a Storyteller" tells of Grandma Dorothy teaching her that she could not really know anything that she could not share with her girlfriends, and her stories seem to grow out of the central wish to share things with this target audience of black women peers. Her stories are usually digressive, seldom following a linear plot. Most of them are structured in an oral form that allows for meaningful side issues with the aim of bringing clear the central point to her audience. Though this technique can be daunting when used in the novel-length *The Salt Eaters*, it allows her to make her short stories into charming, witty, and lively artistic performances whose social messages emerge organically.

GORILLA, MY LOVE

Gorilla, My Love was Toni Cade Bambara's first collection of her original work, and it remains her most popular book. The stories in it were written between 1959 and 1970, and as she explains in her essay, "How She Came by Her Name," she was trying to capture the language system in which people she knew lived and moved. She originally conceived it as a collection of the voices of young, bright, and tough girls of the city, but she did not want it to be packaged as a children's book, so she added some of the adult material to it. "My Man Bovane," for instance, features a matronly black woman seducing a blind man at a neighborhood political rally, while her children look on in disapproval. Similarly, among the fifteen stories (most of which are written in the first person) that make up this book is "Talkin Bout Sonny," in which Betty and Delauney discuss their friend Sonny's recent breakdown and assault on his wife. Delauney claims he understands exactly how such a thing could happen, and it is left unclear how this unstable relationship between Betty and Delauney (who is married) will resolve itself.

Most of the stories, however, focus on young girls determined to make their place in the world and the neighborhood. "The Hammer Man," for instance, tells of a young girl who first hides from a mentally disturbed older boy she has humiliated in public but later futilely attempts to defend against two policemen who try to arrest him. The adult themes and the childhood themes come together best in "The Johnson Girls," in which a young girl listens in as a group of women try to console Inez, whose boyfriend has left with no promise of return. As the young narrator listens in the hope that she will not have to endure "all this torture crap" when she becomes a woman, it becomes clear that the intimate conversation between women is a form of revitalization for Inez.

A delightful preface to *Gorilla, My Love* assures the reader that the material in the book is entirely fictional, not at all autobiographical, but it is hard for a reader not to feel that the voices that populate the work speak for Bambara and the neighborhood of her youth.

"GORILLA, MY LOVE"

The title story of Bambara's first book-length collection of her own work, "Gorilla, My Love" is also her most irresistible work. The narrator is a young girl named Hazel who has just learned that her "Hunca Bubba" is about to be married. She is clearly upset about both this news and the fact that he is now going by his full name, Jefferson Winston Vale. The story proceeds in anything but a linear manner, as Hazel sees a movie house in the background of Hunca Bubba's photos, and starts to tell about going to the movies on Easter with her brothers, Big Brood and Little Jason. When the movie turns out to be a film about Jesus instead of "Gorilla, My Love," as was advertised, Hazel gets angry and demands her money back, and not getting it, starts a fire in the lobby—"Cause if you say Gorilla My Love you supposed to mean it."

What is really on her mind is that when Hunca Bubba was baby-sitting her, he promised he was going to marry her when she grew up, and she believed him. Hazel's attempt to keep her dignity but make her feeling of betrayal known by confronting Hunca Bubba is at once both a surprise and a completely natural outgrowth of her character. Her grandfather's explanation, that it was Hunca Bubba who promised to marry her but it is Jefferson Winston Vale who is marrying someone else, is at once both compassionate and an example of the type of hypocrisy that Hazel associates with the adult world. The example she gives in her story about going to the movie makes it clear that she has always seen her family as better than most, but she sees hypocrisy as a universal adult epidemic.

"RAYMOND'S RUN"

"Raymond's Run," a short story that was also published as a children's book, is about the relationship between the narrator, Hazel (not the same girl from "Gorilla, My Love," but about the same age), her retarded brother, Raymond, and another girl on the block, Gretchen. Hazel's reputation is as the fastest thing on two feet in the neighborhood, but coming up to the annual May Day run, she knows that her new rival, Gretchen, will challenge her and could win. Mr. Pearson, a teacher at the school, suggests it would be a nice gesture to the new girl, Gretchen, to let her win, which Hazel dismisses out of hand. Thinking about a Hansel and Gretel pageant in which she played a strawberry, Hazel thinks, "I am not a strawberry . . . I run. That is what I'm all about." As a runner, she has no intention of letting someone else win.

In fact, when the race is run, she does win, but it is very close, and for all her bravado, she is not sure who won until her name is announced. More important, she sees her brother Raymond running along with her on the other side of the fence, keeping his hands down in an awkward running posture that she accepts as all his own. In her excitement about her brother's accomplishment, she imagines that her rival Gretchen might want to help her train Raymond as a runner, and the two girls share a moment of genuine warmth.

The central point of the story is captured by Hazel when she says of the smile she shared with Gretchen that it was the type of smile girls can share only when they are not too busy being "flowers of fairies or strawberries instead of something honest and worthy of respect . . . you know . . . like being people." The honest competition that brought out their best efforts and enticed Raymond to join them in his way brought them all together as people, not as social competitors trying to outmaneuver one another but as allies.

"THE LESSON"

"The Lesson" is a story about a child's first realization of the true depth of economic inequity in society. The main characters are Miss Moore, an educated black woman who has decided to take the responsibility for the education of neighborhood children upon herself, and Sylvia, the narrator, a young girl. Though it is summer, Miss Moore has organized an educational field trip. This annoys Sylvia and her friend, Sugar, but since their parents have all agreed to the trip, the children have little choice but to cooperate. The trip is actually an excursion to a high-priced department store, F. A. O. Schwartz.

The children look with astonishment at a toy clown that costs $35, a paperweight that sells for $480, and a toy sailboat that is priced at $1,195. The children are discouraged by the clear signs of economic inequality. When Miss Moore asks what they have learned from this trip, only Sugar will reply with what she knows Miss Moore wants them to say: "This is not much of a democracy." Sylvia feels betrayed but mostly because she sees that Sugar is playing up to Miss Moore, while Sylvia has been genuinely shaken by this trip. At the end, Sugar is plotting to split the money she knows Sylvia saved from the cab fare Miss Moore gave her, but Sylvia's response as Sugar runs ahead to their favorite ice cream shop, "ain't nobody gonna beat me at nothin'," indicates she has been shaken and is not planning to play the same old games. However, Sylvia cannot so easily slough it off.

"MEDLEY"

The most popular story from *The Sea Birds Are Still Alive*, "Medley" is the story of Sweet Pea and Larry, a romantic couple who go through a poignant breakup in the course of the story. Though neither of them is a musician, both are music fans, and their showers together are erotic encounters in which they improvise songs together, pretending to be playing musical instruments with each other's body. Sweet Pea is a manicurist with her own shop, and her best customer is a gambler named Moody, who likes to keep his nails impeccable. Because he goes on a winning streak after she starts doing his nails, he offers to take her on a gambling trip as his personal manicurist, for which he pays her two thousand dollars. Sweet Pea takes the offer, though Larry objects, and when she gets back, he seems to have disappeared from her life. Nonetheless, she remembers their last night in the shower together, as they sang different tunes, keeping each other off balance, but harmonizing a medley together until the hot water ran out.

Though Sweet Pea is faced with the choice of losing two thousand dollars or her boyfriend and chooses the money, the story does not attempt to say that she made the wrong choice. Rather, it is a snapshot of the impermanence of shared lives in Sweet Pea's modern, urban environment. This transience is painful, but is also the basis for the enjoyment of life's beauty.

OTHER MAJOR WORKS

LONG FICTION: *Tales and Stories for Black Folks*, 1971; *Gorilla My Love*, 1972; *The Salt Eaters*, 1980; *Those Bones Are Not My Child*, 1999.

SCREENPLAYS: *Zora*, 1971; *The Johnson Girls*, 1972; *The Long Night*, 1981; *The Bombing of Osage Avenue*, 1986; *W. E. B. Du Bois—A Biography in Four Voices*, 1995.

MISCELLANEOUS: *Deep Sightings and Rescue Missions: Fiction, Essays, and Conversations*, 1996.

BIBLIOGRAPHY

Butler-Evans, Elliott. *Race, Gender, and Desire: Narrative Strategies in the Fiction of Toni Cade Bambara, Toni Morrison, Alice Walker*. Philadelphia: Temple University Press, 1989. The first book-length study to treat Bambara's fiction to any extent, this study uses narratology and feminism to explore Bambara's works.

Hargrove, Nancy. "Youth in Toni Cade Bambara's *Gorilla, My Love*." In *Women Writers of the Contemporary South*, edited by Peggy Whitman Prenshaw. Jackson: University Press of Mississippi, 1984. A thorough examination of an important feature of Bambara's most successful collection of short fiction—namely, that most of the best stories center on young girls.

Vertreace, Martha M. *Toni Cade Bambara*. New York: Macmillan Library Reference, 1998. The first full-length work devoted to the entirety of Bambara's career. A part of the successful Twayne series of criticism, this will be quite helpful for students interested in Bambara's career.

Willis, Susan. "Problematizing the Individual: Toni Cade Bambara's Stories for the Revolution." In *Specifying: Black Women Writing the American Experience*. Madison: University of Wisconsin Press, 1987. Though largely centered on an analysis of *The Salt Eaters*, this essay also has clear and informative analysis of Bambara's most important short fiction.

Thomas Cassidy

MELISSA BANK

Born: near Philadelphia, Pennsylvania; 1961

PRINCIPAL SHORT FICTION

The Girls' Guide to Hunting and Fishing, 1999

OTHER LITERARY FORMS

Melissa Bank's story collection is her first book. She has, however, completed a screenplay based on the book's title story.

ACHIEVEMENTS

Melissa Bank won the Nelson Algren award in 1993 for her story "My Old Man." *The Girls' Guide to Hunting and Fishing* was on *The New York Times* best-seller list for more than two months. On her reading tours, she drew standing-room only crowds. Her work has been broadcast on National Public Radio's "Selected Shorts." The bidding war that ended with a $275,000 advance for her first book, a collection of short stories which obviously struck a chord with many young women, created the biggest publishing story of 1999. The book was reviewed by every major newspaper in the English-speaking world, and Bank has been interviewed by numerous papers, magazines, television shows, and Internet sites.

BIOGRAPHY

Melissa Bank was born in 1961 and grew up in a suburb of Philadelphia. Her father was a neurologist, who died of leukemia in his late fifties. She studied art at Hobart College in upstate New York, but did not do well in that subject, changing her major and graduating in 1982 with a degree in American Studies. She moved to New York City, where she worked for two years as an editorial assistant in a publishing house. She then entered graduate school at Cornell

University in 1985 and earned an M.F.A., after which she taught English at Cornell for three years.

Bank moved back to New York City in 1989, where she worked as a copywriter at McCann-Erickson advertising agency. During the nine years she worked in advertising, she took some creative writing classes at Columbia University and spent all her free time after work and on weekends writing stories. However, she had little luck in publishing them except in small-circulation journals; her first story, "Lucky You," appeared in 1989 in *The North American Review.*

Bank's big break came in 1997, when Francis Ford Coppola commissioned her to write a story in reaction to the popular book *The Rules: Time Tested Secrets for Capturing the Heart of Mr. Right* (1996), a how-to guide for getting a man, for his *Zoetrope* magazine. As a result, she sent the story and others to an agent who in turn sent them out to ten publishers, nine of whom wanted to publish them in a book. Viking Press won a bidding war for the manuscript, giving Bank an unusually large advance for a first book of short stories. She has since been commissioned to write a screenplay based on the title story for a film for Coppola's studio. Bank settled in New York City with her Labrador retriever, Maybelline.

ANALYSIS

Although it may be primarily a case of "being at the right place at the right time," few collections of short stories, particularly collections by a new author, receive the kind of media attention that Melissa Bank's *The Girls' Guide to Hunting and Fishing* received during the summer of 1999. Billed by publishers as "fiction" on the book jacket, hoping readers would take it as a novel rather than the less popular short-story form, these seven loosely connected stories became one of the most popular "take-to-the-beach books" of the year.

Much of the ballyhoo resulted from Bank being commissioned by the prestigious filmmaker Francis Ford Coppola to write the title story; however, part of the fuss is also due to the popularity of the British single-girl novel, *Bridget Jones's Diary: A Novel* (1999), and the negative reaction of many feminists

to the retrograde book *The Rules*, which instructed women how to attract men by playing manipulative games.

The central character of most of Bank's stories is Jane Rosenthal, the classic wise-cracking young Jewish working girl, who "comes of age." With the exception of the longest story in the collection, "The Worst Thing a Suburban Girl Could Imagine," which deals with Jane's ways of coping with the death of her father, most depend primarily on clever one-liners typical of stand-up comedy routines. Bank's witticisms puts her in the camp of similar 1990's writers, such as Amy Hempel and Lorrie Moore.

"ADVANCED BEGINNERS"

This is probably the most conventional, creative-writing-class story in the collection, and because it is so well made, it is in some ways the most satisfying. The story focuses on young Jane Rosenthal's reaction to her brother's first serious girlfriend, Julia—a reaction which combines jealousy, because she feels Julia is the "kind, helpful, articulate daughter" her parents really wanted and deserved, and sisterly affection, because she can talk to her about such things as love and sex about which she cannot talk to her parents.

Even this story, however, gets much of its energy from the smart talk of the young protagonist, which has made some reviewers call her a kind of female Holden Caulfield. For example, when she tells her friend that breasts are to sex what pillows are to sleep, she adds, "Guys might think they want a pillow, but they'll sleep just as well without one." The most effective parts of the story are the conversations and camaraderie between Jane and the older Julia, who gives her a copy of *The Great Gatsby.*

Overall, the story has more depth than most stories in the collection because of Jane's gradual coming-ofage understanding of the difficulty of loving and having a relationship. At the end, after her brother breaks up with Julia, Jane goes out on her dock looking for the green light that Gatsby looked for, feeling scared that her brother has failed at loving someone, for, she says, "I had no idea myself how to do it." The story's treatment of this theme is a promising introit to the book that is not always fulfilled by later stories.

"THE WORST THING A SUBURBAN GIRL COULD IMAGINE"

Bank has told interviewers that this is her favorite story in the collection. Either because it deals with a subject so central to the collection—Jane's relationship with her father and her resulting relationship with an older man—or because it is the longest, most serious and most ambitious story in the collection, this is the story that best determines if Bank can write a sustained and serious fiction.

Almost as important to this story as her father, who is dying of leukemia, is Archie Knox, an older man with whom Jane has had an affair in the earlier story "My Old Man," but with whom she has broken up. Here, Archie, an editor, returns to further complicate her life, which is already complicated by her father's illness and a new editor, Mimi, who treats Jane as a menial assistant on whom she foists most of her own work.

"The Worst Thing a Suburban Girl Could Imagine" is the closest thing to a novel that Bank has written, and indeed, it reads much more like an abbreviated novel than the tightly built short story that opens the book. The emphasis in this story is a young professional woman's dilemma of coping with paternalistic older men and exploitative professional women. At the climax of the story, Jane's lover Archie is hospitalized with a disease of the pancreas as a result of his alcoholism, and her father dies. As a result, she is able to see her life "in scale" and understand that it is just her life, not momentous as she had always thought. Putting things in perspective, she stands up to her dominating female superior, who then delivers what is probably the central thematic line of the story, "We are all children until our fathers die." At the end of the story, Jane's realization about her life after her father's death also gives her the courage to say no to Archie's proposal of marriage.

"THE GIRLS' GUIDE TO HUNTING AND FISHING"

The title story of Bank's collection, a title that made some booksellers stock it in the sports section, is the story that began Bank's phenomenal career with its publication by Francis Ford Coppola. It is not a profound story by any means, rather more like a story typical of the old-fashioned sophistication of *Cosmopolitan* magazine. In this story, Jane Rosenthal is the young working woman often depicted in slick magazines, television situation comedies, and films. She is smart, witty, and attractive, but for some reason, in spite of dating often, she faces that age-old "girl problem": men who cannot commit.

The story is based on the premise that Jane meets a man at a friend's weddings and carries on a courtship, against her better judgment, according to a book entitled *How to Meet and Marry Mr. Right*. Throughout the story, she imagines the faces of the two authors of the book, Faith Kurtz-Abromowitz and Bonnie Merrill, giving her advice every time she is tempted to follow her intuition and be herself. In an obvious parody of the popular advice book *The Rules*, Bank peppers the story with one-line advice in boldface type, of which the most important for Jane is to suppress her one-liners; the rule is: "Don't be funny . . . Funny is the opposite of sexy."

As Jane follows such advice as "don't accept a date less than four days in advance," "don't say 'I love you first'," and "don't bring up marriage," the manipulation tactics seem to be working. So she continues to "keep him guessing," to "let him pay," and to "be mysterious," even though she tries to rebel against the advice, for she wants this relationship to "be real." The story advances in predictable sitcom fashion when Robert, tiring of the games Jane plays, stops calling her, and Jane decides in a final bit of fantasy dialogue with Faith and Bonnie, that she will be herself. "No more hunting or fishing," Jane says. At the end of the story, Robert tells her that he was interested in her at first but became less interested when she began the manipulative games. Jane saves all by being her irresistibly clever self. When Robert says he is a "goofball in search of truth," she replies, "I'm a truthball in search of goof," and, naturally, he falls in love with her all over again. The story ends with the feel-good line "There is no stopping us now. Both of us are hunters and prey, fishers and fish."

OTHER MAJOR WORKS
SCREENPLAY: *The Girls' Guide to Hunting and Fishing*, wr. 1999.

BIBLIOGRAPHY

Caldwell, Gail. "Bright Girl, Big City." *The Boston Globe*. May 30, 1999, p. D1. Says *The Girls' Guide to Hunting and Fishing* is the American book industry's answer to *Bridget Jones's Diary*, with the hope that a well-timed trend may constitute "a Zeitgeist, or at least a barrelful of profits." Argues that the experiences in the book are predictable and the over-the-top one-liners "stick out like drugstore jewelry on a little girl."

Carey, Lynn. "Hunting and Fishing Frenzy." *The Buffalo News*, August 21, 1999, p. 7C. In this interview article, Bank says the father in the stories is mostly autobiographical, but she refuses to discuss the origins of the story about breast cancer. Bank argues against the frequent comparison of her book to British author Helen Fielding's *Bridget Jones's Diary*.

Chonin, Neva. "A Guide Women Can Identify With." *The San Francisco Chronicle*, June 22, 1999, p. E1. An interview story that discusses the buzz that developed around Bank's *Zoetrope* story months before it was printed. Bank says she is "flattered but flummoxed" by her sudden popularity; says her goal was just to get published so she could get a decent university teaching job but that she now both loves and hates her new celebrity status.

Iovine, Julie V. "At Home with Melissa Bank." *The New York Times*, July 22, 1999, p. F1. This interview story provides biographical notes, discusses the media attention Bank has received, and quotes Bank on her reaction to being in the literary limelight after years of writing alone.

Lanham, Fritz. "Love, Happiness Are Trophies Melissa Bank's Heroine Seeks." *Houston Chronicle*, August 1, 1999, p. 18. An interview story with biographical background. Bank discusses her relationship to Jane Rosenthal, the heroine of her stories, as well as Rosenthal's development throughout the stories.

Lehmann-Haupt, Christopher. "She Lives to Tell About Growing Up." *The New York Times*, June 17, 1999, p. E9. In this review, Lehmann-Haupt calls *The Girls' Guide to Hunting and Fishing* a charming, funny collection of seven linked fictions. Argues that all the humor of the stories turns on Jane's "wonderfully clear sense of the trickiness of language."

Weaver, Courtney. "Jane's Addiction." *The New York Times*, May 30, 1999, p. 23. Relates the stories to themes and types from women's magazines. Argues there is no real character development in the stories and no unified structure; says it feels like an unfinished novel, divided up into stories.

Charles E. May

RUSSELL BANKS

Born: Newton, Massachusetts; March 28, 1940

PRINCIPAL SHORT FICTION

Searching for Survivors, 1975
The New World, 1978
Trailerpark, 1981
Success Stories, 1986
The Angel on the Roof, 2000 (omnibus collection)

OTHER LITERARY FORMS

Russell Banks has published several collections of poetry and many novels. *Continental Drift* (1985) was a finalist for the Pulitzer Prize and *Affliction* (1989) was nominated for both the PEN/Faulkner Award for Fiction and the Irish International Prize. Other major works include *Family Life* (1975), *Hamilton Stark* (1978), *The Sweet Hereafter* (1991), *Rule of the Bone* (1995), and *Cloudsplitter* (1998). His poems, stories, and essays have appeared in *The Boston Globe Magazine*, *Vanity Fair*, *The New York Times Book Review*, *Esquire*, and *Harper's*.

ACHIEVEMENTS

Russell Banks has been awarded a Woodrow Wilson Foundation Award, a John Simon Guggenheim Memorial Fellowship, a National Endowment for the Arts grant, the Ingram Merril Award, the Fels Award, the John Dos Passos Award, the St. Lawrence Award for Fiction from St. Lawrence University and *Fiction International*, and the American Academy of Arts and Letters Award for work of distinction. His work has been anthologized in *Prize Stories: The O. Henry Awards* and *The Best American Short Stories*.

BIOGRAPHY

Russell Earl Banks was born in Newton, Massachusetts, on March 28, 1940, and raised in New Hampshire. The first in his family to attend college, Banks found the atmosphere at Colgate University incompatible with his working-class background and relinquished his scholarship after eight weeks. He headed for Florida, fully intending to align himself

with rebel Cuban leader Fidel Castro, but, lacking enough incentive and money, worked at odd jobs until his career path became clear. He was at various times a plumber (like his father), a shoe salesman, a department store window dresser, and an editor.

In 1964 he enrolled at the University of North Carolina at Chapel Hill and graduated Phi Beta Kappa in 1967. His sense of political and social injustice became more finely honed in this city, which is touted as the most northern of the southern states, the most dramatic incident being the disruption of an integrated party by gun-wielding members of the local Ku Klux Klan.

A John Simon Guggenheim Memorial Foundation Fellowship in 1976 allowed him to move to Jamaica, where he immersed himself in the culture, trying to live as a native rather than as a tourist. The experience of living in an impoverished nation helped him professionally as well as personally and gave him a broad perspective on issues of race. Married four times and the father of four grown daughters, Banks has taught at major universities, including Columbia University, Sarah Lawrence College, New York University, and Princeton University. Critic Fred Pfeil called Banks

the most important living white male American on the official literary map, a writer we, as readers *and* writers, can actually learn from, whose books help and urge us to change.

ANALYSIS

Russell Banks's work is largely autobiographical, growing out of the chaos of his childhood: the shouting and hitting, physical and emotional abuse inflicted on the family by an alcoholic father, who abandoned them in 1953. Being forced at age twelve to assume the role of the man in the family and always living on the edge of poverty greatly influenced Banks's worldview and consequently his writing. Banks's struggle to understand the tight hold that the past has on the present and the future led him to create a world in which people come face to face with similar dilemmas. Banks's characters struggle to get out from under, to free themselves from the tethers of race, class, and gender. He writes of working people, those who by virtue of social status are always apart, marginalized, often desperate, inarticulate, silenced by circumstances. He aims to be their voice, to give expression to their pain, their aspirations, their angsts. Their emotional makeup can be as complex as those more favored by birth or power. In an interview in *The New York Times Book Review*, Banks noted that

> part of the challenge . . . is uncovering the resiliency of that kind of life, and part is in demonstrating that even the quietest lives can be as complex and rich, as joyous, conflicted and anguished, as other seemingly more dramatic lives.

Banks's main strength, besides his graceful style, keen powers of observation, intelligence, and humanity, is his ability to write feelingly of often unlovable people. He never condescends or belittles. He does not judge. He always attempts to show, rather than tell, why a person is as he or she is, and it is in the telling that Banks is able to understand himself and exorcize the devils of his own past. He did not necessarily set out on self-discovery, but learned, through writing, who he was and what he thought. He grew to understand himself through understanding the elements of his past that shaped him.

Banks is sometimes grouped with Raymond Carver, Richard Ford, and Andre Dubus as writers in a "Trailer-Park Fiction" genre, which, according to critic Denis M. Hennessy,

> examine[s] American working-class people living their lives one step up from the lowest rung on the socioeconomic ladder and doing battle every day with the despair that comes from violence, alcohol, and self-destructive relationships.

Some of Banks's plots and themes are derivative, with heavy borrowings from Mark Twain and E. L. Doctorow, but his unique touch sets them apart. Banks is both a chronicler and a critic of contemporary society.

Russell Banks (©Miriam Berkley)

Influenced by James Baldwin, who said that the true story about race would have to be "written from the point of view of a member of a lynch mob," Banks attempts to elicit an understanding of the perpetrators as well as of the victims of crimes, cruelties, and injustices. He believes that understanding a situation depends on knowing how the players who created it were created themselves. His characters all search for transformation, for something that will redeem them, lift them above their present circumstances. Their searches lead them to greater desolation and very seldom to contentment. The lower echelon is forever pitted against and at the mercy of the middle class. Hennessy has called Banks's short fiction the "testing ground of his most innovative ideas and techniques." The major themes revolve around disharmony, both in the family and in society, and the eternal search for the lost family. Banks admits that much of his fiction centers on "Russell Banks searching for his father. . . . I spent a great deal of my youth running away from him and obsessively returning to him."

SEARCHING FOR SURVIVORS

Banks's first collection combines reality and fantasy, with the fourteen stories divided into three general groups: five moral and political parables, a trilogy of stories that feature Latin American revolutionary Che Guevara, and six substantially autobiographical tales set in New England. Banks's experiments with narrative style, structure, and point of view met with mixed response. He was credited for trying but faulted for lacking a unifying thread. Critic Robert Niemi says of the parables that if the

> theme . . . is the modern divorce between cognition and feeling [they] stylistically enact that schism with a vengeance . . . almost all [being] solemn in tone, and written in a detached, clinically descriptive style that tends toward the cryptic.

Each story ends on a note of either defeat or disillusionment. Survival is highly unlikely. The American Dream has failed.

The opening tale deals with a man driving along the Henry Hudson Parkway, thinking about his childhood friend's car, a Hudson, and about the explorer, who was set adrift in 1611 in the waters that eventually bore his name. The narrator imagines going to the shores of Hudson Bay to look for evidence of the explorer's fate. Therein is an attempt to understand the past. Banks often deals with

> the Old World and the early exploration of North America, and he shows the connections between those who set out from their comfortable but unjust homelands to settle the unknown, and modern Americans who have been shunted out of their safe cocoons of fixed values and family security into the relativistic reality of the latter half of the twentieth century.

In a story confirming Thomas Wolfe's thesis that one "can't go home again," a young man returns from adventures with guerrilla leader Che Guevara, only to find his hometown irrevocably changed and himself so different that no one recognizes him. In another story, "With Che at Kitty Hawk," a newly divorced woman and her two daughters visit the Wright Brothers Memorial. An almost-happy ending has the woman feeling somewhat liberated after being

trapped in marriage, but that optimism is fleeting. In yet another, "Blizzard," Banks shifts the narrator, first having him be omniscient, then having him speak through a man who is losing touch with reality, succumbing to guilt and bleak wintery surroundings.

THE NEW WORLD

Banks's search for a comfortable voice caused him to continue to experiment with narrative voice, switching from first- to second-person, and sometimes third-, at times unsettling readers and critics who deemed his shifts haphazard rather than intentional. Never fully at ease with an omniscient, all-knowing narrator, yet not wanting his storyteller to be a character, an integral player, and hence subject to the vagaries of plot, Banks tries to approach his writing as the telling of a story to a partner, perhaps in a darkened room while lying comfortably in bed. He wants to share his story, yet not to tell it from a position of privilege. This approach gives the reader the immediacy needed for involvement in the story, but, at the same time, enough detachment on the part of the narrator to trust him.

Banks called his second collection, which was far more positively received,

> a carefully structured gathering of ten tales that dramatize and explore the process and progress of self-transcendence, tales that . . . embrace the spiritual limits and possibilities of life in the New World.

The collection is divided into two parts: "Renunciation" and "Transformation." The opening story, "The Custodian," deals with a forty-three-year-old man whose father's death finally frees him "to move to a new village . . . to drink and smoke and sing bawdy songs." As he is now also free to marry, he, "reasoning carefully . . . conclude[s] that he would have good luck in seeking a wife if he started with women who were already married." Fortuitously, he has many married male friends and thus begins his series of conquests. He proposes to a few likely prospects; they succumb; he changes his mind; they return to their husbands, never to know satisfaction again.

In another story, "The Conversion," a young boy is wracked by guilt at not being a good person, at engaging in excessive masturbation, always falling short of what he thought he should be. Alvin wants to change. He wants to be good, decent, and chaste. He fails miserably until one day he sees an angel in a parking lot and decides to become a preacher. His conversion, the reader realizes is not so much religious as it is a hope to start anew. His new religious life starts as a dishwasher in a religious camp. Robert Niemi observes that, "much like Banks in his youth, Alvin is torn between the promise of upward mobility and loyalty to his father's proletarian ethos." Alvin's father suspects him of "selling out his working-class identity by associating himself with a bourgeois profession," reflecting Banks's own social background in which attempts to move upward were considered a criticism of what was left behind.

Historical figures are featured in some of the stories: Simón Bolívar, Jane Hogarth (wife of the eccentric painter William), Edgar Allan Poe, and others. In the Hogarth tale, "Indisposed," the wife is sadly used by the husband, who treats her as a sexual convenience and housekeeper. She is overwhelmed by the nothingness of her existence. She is fat and self-loathing until she experiences a sickbed transformation which allows her to move beyond "pitying [her large, slow] body to understanding it." She is then, according to Niemi, able to "inhabit her body fully and without shame, thus reclaiming herself." Then, when her husband is caught in the upstairs bed with the young domestic helper, Jane is able to exact swift punishment and completely change the tenor of the home. Niemi observes that Banks's history

> shades into fiction and fiction melds into history. [His] central theme, though, is the enduring human need to reinvent the self in order to escape or transcend the constrictions of one's actual circumstances. This means creating a "new world" out of the imagination, just as the "discovery" of the Americas opened up vast horizons for a culturally exhausted Old World Europe.

Banks believes that "the dream of a new life, the dream of starting over" is the quintessential American Dream, the ideological keystone of American civilization from its inception to the present day.

TRAILERPARK

In this collection, perhaps his most structurally satisfying, Russell Banks takes the reader into the very heart of a community of people who, while not having lowered expectations, do have less grandiose or unrealistic ambitions than those in the mainstream. They go through life earning enough to meet basic needs, never going far beyond their environs. Some work full time, some seasonally; some leave for a while and then return. Most seem to find the day-to-day process of getting by nearly enough. Heartaches, anger, depression, and just plain weirdness are often eased with marijuana and alcohol.

This collection's twelve stories are interrelated because they all deal with the residents of the Granite State Trailerpark in Catamount, New Hampshire. They have little in common other than the circumstances of their housing. They are detached physically as well as emotionally, yet they do form a community with at least some common concerns. One of the residents notes that when you are "a long way from where you think you belong, you will attach yourself to people you would otherwise ignore or even dislike." Each story deals with one of the dozen or so denizens, all of whom are "generally alone in the world."

Trailer #1 is the heartbeat of the park, where French Canadian manager Marcelle Chagnon oversees operations. She lost a child when an unscrupulous doctor found her more interesting than her illness. Bank teller Leon LaRoche lives in #2 next to Bruce Severance, in #3, a college student who is an afficionado of homegrown cannabis. Divorcée Doreen Tiede and her five-year-old daughter are in #4 next to the burned remains of #5, where Ginnie and Claudel Bing lived until Ginnie left the stove burner on. Retired army captain Dewey Knox is in #6; Noni Hubner and her mother Nancy are in #7. Merl Ring, in #8, enjoys self-imposed isolation, eagerly awaiting the blasting winters when he can set up his equipment in the middle of frozen Skitters Lake and spend months of solitary ice fishing. The former resident of #9, Tom Smith, killed himself, and the place remains empty. The only black resident, Carol Constant, sometimes shares #10 with her brother Terry. Number 11 houses Flora Pease and more than 115 guinea pigs, which threaten to overtake the trailer and the whole park. The opening story, "The Guinea Pig Lady," introduces all the residents as they share their concerns about the situation. Most notable is the trailer and occupant not mentioned at all—#12, probably the narrator's place. Banks's park people have offbeat but understandable pathologies. Some are just achingly lonely. Critic Johnathan Yardley credits Banks with drawing together a "small but vibrant cast of characters, a human comedy in microcosm" made up of "utterly unconnected people [who] find themselves drawn together by the accident of living in the same place; the trailer park, grim and dreary as it may be, is a neighborhood."

SUCCESS STORIES

This 1986 collection of twelve stories, six autobiographical, six parabolic, has more to do with failed attempts to change the course of lives than it does with acquisition of fame and fortune. The characters in the collection have been called "dreamers, nourished on giddy expectations, but disenfranchised by accidents of class, economy, looks or simple luck." They think that life holds all sorts of possibilities but learn quickly that fate has not cast a favorable eye on them. Banks sets out to show that success is more elusive for the disenfranchised.

Four stories revolve around Earl Painter, a young child in the story "Queen for a Day," who writes to the host of the popular television show of the same name numerous times hoping that his mother's plight will land her a place as a contestant. In subsequent stories, Earl attempts to come to grips with his parents and their lies and imaginings. His search for fulfillment leads him to Florida, where he experiences short-lived success. He toys with the idea of marrying into a new life but instead engages in adultery with a neighbor's wife, learning from her husband that he is just one of her many dalliances.

These stories are interspersed with ones that are either fabular or close to surreal. Three deal with situations possibly slated to show a similarity between Third World exploitation and an American tendency to disenfranchise the working class. All deal with the terrible consequences of false promises of success.

One story, "Sarah Cole: A Type of Love Story," shows the impermeability of the walls separating the classes. The hero, exceptionally handsome, develops an unlikely relationship with his antithesis, an alarmingly ugly barroom pickup named Sarah. His initial curiosity about lovemaking with someone so badly put together turns into a kind of commitment but not one strong enough to be made public. The contrast in their appearances proves too great for him. He is indeed superficial and acts hatefully. Years later, the truth of his love dawns on him, but Sarah is long gone, and he is left with his shame.

Critic Trish Reeves notes in an interview that "the irony of finally becoming a literary success by writing about the failure of the American Dream was not lost on Banks." He said:

> I still view myself in the larger world the way I did when I was an adolescent. . . . [as a member of] a working class family: powerless people who look from below up. I'm unable to escape that—how one views oneself in the larger structure is determined at an extremely early age. The great delusion is that if you only can get success then you will shift your view of yourself . . . you will become a different person. That's the longing, for success is really not material goods, but in fact to become a whole new person.

OTHER MAJOR WORKS

LONG FICTION: *Family Life*, 1975 (revised, 1988); *Hamilton Stark*, 1978; *The Book of Jamaica*, 1980; *The Relation of My Imprisonment*, 1983; *Continental Drift*, 1985; *Affliction*, 1989; *The Sweet Hereafter*, 1991; *Rule of the Bone*, 1995; *Cloudsplitter*, 1998.

POETRY: *Fifteen Poems*, 1967 (with William Matthews and Newton Smith); *Waiting to Freeze*, 1969; *30/6*, 1969; *Snow: Meditations of a Cautious Man in Winter*, 1974.

NONFICTION: *The Autobiographical Eye*, 1982 (Daniel Halpern, editor); *The Invisible Stranger: The Patten, Maine Photographs of Arturo Patten*, 1999.

EDITED TEXT: *Brushes with Greatness: An Anthology of Chance Encounters with Greatness*, 1989 (with Michael Ondaatje and David Young).

BIBLIOGRAPHY

Chapman, Jeff, and Pamela S. Dean. *Contemporary Authors* 52 (1996). A short but information-packed study under the headings "Personal," "Career," "Memberships," "Awards and Honors," "Writings," and "Sidelights" (containing author quotes and discussions, mostly of longer fiction but also touching on *Trailerpark*) followed by an invaluable list of biographical and critical sources.

Contemporary Literary Criticism 37, 1986. Provides a good overview of Banks's life up to 1985 and gives a substantial sampling of literary criticism.

Contemporary Literary Criticism 72, 1992. A strong biographical overview of Banks's life and influences, followed by critical analyses of work published between 1986 and 1991. Included is a valuable interview conducted by writer Trish Reeves that provides a good understanding of the author.

Top literary critics provide illuminating commentary.

Meanor, Patrick, ed. *American Short Story Writers Since World War II*. Vol. 130 in *Dictionary of Literary Biography*. Detroit, Mich.: Gale Research, 1993. Good background material on Banks's life and the general content of his fiction with some discussion of thematic and narrative approaches.

Niemi, Robert. *Russell Banks*. Twayne's United States Authors series. New York: Twayne, 1997. A comprehensive biography that includes critical analyses of all his major literary works. It is rife with charming and telling details that convey the essence of the author, but it maintains the objectivity necessary to present a fair portrait.

Gay Annette Zieger

AMIRI BARAKA
Everett LeRoi Jones

Born: Newark, New Jersey; October 7, 1934

PRINCIPAL SHORT FICTION
Tales, 1967
The Fiction of LeRoi Jones/Amiri Baraka, 2000

OTHER LITERARY FORMS

Amiri Baraka has been a cultural activist and professional writer for more than four decades and in that time has produced a wide range of works, including plays, essays, stories, and poems. Best known for dramas produced in the 1960's (*The Baptism*, pr. 1964; *The Toilet*, pr., pb. 1964), he has also written a novel (*The System of Dante's Hell*, 1965), collections of poetry (*Preface to a Twenty Volume Suicide Note*, 1961), *The Autobiography of LeRoi Jones/Amiri Baraka* (1984), and several books on black music (*Blues People: Negro Music in White America*, 1963; *The Music: Reflections on Jazz and Blues*, 1987).

ACHIEVEMENTS

Amiri Baraka has won a number of awards and fellowships, particularly for his poetry and drama (such as the Playwright's Award at North Carolina's Black Drama Festival in 1997). His play *Dutchman* (pr., pb. 1964) won an Obie Award for Best American Off-Broadway Play, and the following year Jones was granted a John Simon Guggenheim Memorial Foundation Fellowship. In 1984 he received an American Book Award, and in 1989 he won a PEN/Faulkner Award for Fiction. He has also founded or supported numerous journals (such as *Yugen* magazine), theater groups (like the Black Arts Repertory Theatre), and other cultural organizations, especially in the African American community, and he has edited several important books on black culture (such as *Home: Social Essays*, 1966). In 1989, Baraka was given the Langston Hughes Medal for outstanding contribution to literature. His work has been translated and published in a number of other languages and countries.

Biography

Born Everett LeRoi Jones, Imamu Amiri Baraka was born and raised in Newark, New Jersey, and has lived for most of his life in or near New York City, where many of his plays were first staged. He served in the U.S. Air Force from 1954 to 1957, mainly in Puerto Rico. He attended Rutgers and Howard universities and did graduate work at the New School for Social Research and Columbia University. He has been a faculty member at a number of American universities, including the New School (1962 to 1964) and Yale University (1977-1978). In 1980, Baraka accepted a teaching position at the State University of New York at Stony Brook. Baraka was married twice and has several children.

Analysis

Amiri Baraka's literary career has had three distinct periods. In the first period—the late 1950's and early 1960's—he was influenced by, and became a part of, the predominantly white avant garde Beat movement in the arts. By the mid-1960's, Baraka had become a black nationalist (indicated by his rejection of the name LeRoi Jones), and many of his better-known plays, like *Dutchman*, reflect his confrontational racial views from this period. Since the 1970's, Baraka has continued working as a political activist and writer, but his writing has increasingly encompassed a Marxist economic analysis in addition to his strong racial views. Nearly all of Baraka's short stories—although they continued to be reprinted into the 1980's and 1990's—first appeared in his earlier black nationalist period in the 1960's and reflected both the literary experiments of his Beat period and the increasingly political attitudes of his black nationalism. While many of these stories hold mainly historical interest today, the best are still compelling examples of how radical political views and experimental prose styles could be fused in the 1960's, when a number of writers, both white and black, were trying to merge their art and their politics.

Tales

This collection of fiction was published in 1967 and contains sixteen short prose pieces written during the previous decade and published in various small

LeRoi Jones, later Amiri Baraka, in 1964 (AP/Wide World Photos)

literary magazines. Most of these stories are distinguished by an experimental prose style wedded to a strong political analysis. The first nine in the collection have a fairly traditional narrative line. "Uncle Tom's Cabin: Alternate Ending," for example, is a six-page story that centers on the interaction between a fifth-grader and his racist teacher, but the brief story also includes multiple points of view and a surprise ending. The last seven stories in the collection, however, reject traditional storytelling for a poetic prose style closer to the rhythms of jazz. "Words" is prose poetry written in "the alien language of another tribe" and dated "Harlem 1965." "Answers in Progress"—reprinted along with "Words" in Baraka's 1979 *Selected Plays and Prose*—features spaceships and the musical group Art Blakey and the Jazz Messengers. So, while the prose content can often be combative and challenging, Baraka's style is increasingly fragmentary in structure, poetic in style, and cryptic in meaning, particularly in the last stories collected in

Tales. Put another way, readers can see Baraka in this collection moving away from traditional fiction toward poetry and essay.

"A CHASE (ALIGHIERI'S DREAM)"

The story that opens *Tales* is only a few pages in length, but into it Baraka has packed a great deal of meaning. The title is the first clue, leading readers back through his novel (*The System of Dante's Hell*) to the Italian writer Dante Alighieri, whose *La divina commedia* (c. 1320; *The Divine Comedy*, 1802) contains one of the most powerful descriptions of hell in all of literature. Baraka's hell is the modern ghetto, and in particular Newark, New Jersey, where he grew up. As critic Lloyd Brown describes "A Chase," "The story as a whole is a nightmarish series of images through which the writer presents an overview of life in the black ghetto." The story's narration is a surreal and staccato stream of consciousness through which the young protagonist links together a number of disparate images:

Faces broke. Charts of age. Worn thru, to see black years. Bones in iron faces. Steel bones. Cages of decay. Cobblestones are wet near the army stores. Beer smells, Saturday. To now, they have passed so few lovely things.

Like the protagonist in "The Screamers," the narrator here is in a dreamlike, and finally nightmarish, flight through the streets of the inner city. Hell, Baraka shows, is here and now, and there seems to be no escape from it.

"THE SCREAMERS"

Reprinted at least half a dozen times since its appearance in *Tales*, generally in collections of African American fiction, "The Screamers" is by far Baraka's best-known short story. The narrative covers one night in a black jazz nightclub in Newark (probably in the early 1950's) from the perspective of a young man listening to "Harlem Nocturne" and other popular dance tunes. What makes this night unique is the performance of saxophonist Lynn Hope, who in an inspired moment leads the musicians through the crowd and out into the streets. "It would be the form of the sweetest revolution, to hucklebuck into the fallen capital, and let the oppressors lindy hop out."

The police arrive and attack the crowd, a riot ensues, and the marchers "all broke our different ways, to save whatever it was each of us thought we loved." The story has a number of elements common to Baraka's fiction: the positive depiction of African American cultural forms (including a kind of "bop" jazz language), the conflict between this culture and white oppressors, and the metaphor of black art—here music, but it could as easily stand for writing—as an inspirational cultural form which, while it cannot finally overcome white oppression, at least achieves a moment of heightened consciousness for the people (here called "Biggers," in reference to the central character, Bigger Thomas, of Richard Wright's 1940 novel *Native Son*) listening to the music and moved by it.

"THE DEATH OF HORATIO ALGER"

The titles of Baraka's stories—such as "Uncle Tom's Cabin: Alternate Ending" or "A Chase (Alighieri's Dream)"—often carry the larger meaning of the work, even when the story makes no further reference to it. In the case of "The Death of Horatio Alger," the tale seems a fairly simple description of a childhood fight. The narrator of the tale, Mickey, is playing dozens—a black word game of insults aimed at participants' parents—with his best friend, J.D., and in front of three white friends. J.D. misunderstands one of the insults and attacks Mickey, and then they both attack the three white boys (who do not understand the black word game to begin with). The story is thus about communication and its failure, but also about the Horatio Alger myths of equality and freedom and about the alienation Baraka's protagonists often experience. As Lloyd Brown accurately writes of the story, "In stripping himself of insensitive white friends and Horatio Alger images of American society, Mickey is putting an end to his alienation from his black identity."

"THE ALTERNATIVE"

Plot line in "The Alternative" has been replaced by multiple images substituting for short-story narrative. The setting is a black university, and the story reverberates with references from that environment (such as Thomas Hobbes, Albert Camus, Federico García Lorca, and Nat King Cole) and the piece is thus the most allusive in the *Tales* collection. It is clear that this setting is also part of the cause of the alienation of the central character, Ray McGhee, in this surreal depiction of college dormitory life. Like many of Baraka's plays (such as *Dutchman*), "The Alternative" describes the tension between an individual outsider and the group. In Lloyd Brown's interpretation of the story, he says,

> The erudition that is the key to middle-class success and future leadership also sets him apart from other blacks, even from those who, like himself, have chosen the middle-class 'alternative.'

The lack of a linear plot line, and its replacement by lines of dialogue and images, may explain why in later decades Baraka has dropped attempts at fiction to write nonfiction prose, poetry, and drama, to the exclusion of prose fiction.

OTHER MAJOR WORKS

LONG FICTION: *The System of Dante's Hell*, 1965.

PLAYS: *The Baptism*, pr. 1964; *Dutchman*, pr., pb. 1964; *The Slave*, pr., pb. 1964; *The Toilet*, pr., pb. 1964; *Experimental Death Unit #1*, pr. 1965; *Jello*, pr. 1965; *A Black Mass*, pr. 1966; *Arm Yourself, or Harm Yourself*, pr. pb. 1967; *Great Goodness of Life (A Coon Show)*, pr. 1967; *Madheart*, pr. 1967; *Slave Ship: A Historical Pageant*, pr., pb. 1967; *The Death of Malcolm X*, pb. 1969; *Bloodrites*, pr. 1970; *Junkies Are Full of (Shhh . . .)*, pr. 1970; *A Recent Killing*, pr. 1973; *S-1*, pr. 1976; *The Motion of History*, pr. 1977; *The Sidney Poet Heroical*, pb. 1979 (originally as *Sidnee Poet Heroical*, pr. 1975); *What Was the Relationship of the Lone Ranger to the Means of Production?*, pr. pb. 1979; *At the Dim'cracker Convention*, pr. 1980; *Weimar*, pr. 1981; *Money: A Jazz Opera*, pr. 1982; *Primitive World*, pr. 1984; *The Life and Life of Bumpy Johnson*, pr. 1991; *Meeting Lillie*, pr. 1993.

POETRY: *Spring and Soforth*, 1960; *Preface to a Twenty Volume Suicide Note*, 1961; *The Dead Lecturer*, 1964; *Black Art*, 1966; *A Poem for Black Hearts*, 1967; *Black Magic: Sabotage—Target Study—Black Art: Collected Poetry, 1961-1967*, 1969; *It's Nation Time*, 1970; *In Our Terribleness: Some Elements and Meaning in Black Style*, 1970

(with Fundi [Billy Abernathy]); *Spirit Reach*, 1972; *Afrikan Revolution*, 1973; *Hard Facts*, 1975; *Selected Poetry of Amiri Baraka/LeRoi Jones*, 1979; *Reggae or Not!*, 1981; *Wise, Why's, Y's*, 1995; *Transbluesency: The Selected Poems of Amiri Baraka*, 1995; *New Poems (1984-1995)*, 1997.

NONFICTION: *Blues People: Negro Music in White America*, 1963; *Home: Social Essays*, 1966; *Raise Race Rays Raze: Essays Since 1965*, 1971; *The New Nationalism*, 1972; *The Autobiography of LeRoi Jones/Amiri Baraka*, 1984; *Daggers and Javelins: Essays*, 1984; *The Music: Reflections on Jazz and Blues*, 1987 (with Amina Baraka).

EDITED TEXTS: *The Moderns: New Fiction in America*, 1963; *Black Fire: An Anthology of Afro-American Writing*, 1968 (with Larry Neal); *A Black Value System*, 1970; *African Congress: A Documentary of the First Modern Pan-African Congress*, 1972; *Confirmation: An Anthology of African-American Women*, 1983 (with Amina Baraka).

MISCELLANEOUS: *Selected Plays and Prose*, 1979.

BIBLIOGRAPHY

Brown, Lloyd W. *Amiri Baraka*. Boston: Twayne, 1980. Chapter 4 focuses on the short stories and includes the sections "The Writer as Divided Self" and "Toward Black Nationalism." Brown's is clearly the best analysis of individual Baraka short stories, and, like Werner Sollors, he identifies both the formal and thematic elements that tie these different stories together.

Fox, Robert Eliot. *Conscientious Sorcerers: The Black Post-Modernist Fiction of LeRoi Jones/Baraka, Ishmael Reed, and Samuel R. Delaney*. New York: Greenwood Press, 1987. Chapter 2 is a discussion of Baraka's novel and the stories collected in *Tales*, in a comparative study of "three of the most important and gifted American authors to have emerged in the tumultuous period of the 1960's."

Gwynne, James B., ed. *Amiri Baraka: The Kaleidoscopic Torch*. Harlem, N.Y.: Steppingstones Press, 1985. This collection of poems and essays for and about Amiri Baraka includes Richard Oyama's analysis of "The Screamers," titled "A Secret

Communal Expression," as well as essays by Clyde Taylor and E. San Juan, Jr.

Lacey, Henry C. *To Raise, Destroy, and Create: The Poetry, Drama, and Fiction of Imamu Amiri Baraka (LeRoi Jones)*. Troy, N.Y.: Whitston, 1981. In the last chapter, "Recapitulation," Lacey traces the autobiographical origins of many of Baraka's short stories. While he recognizes Baraka's faults—"extreme privacy of reference, frequent experimental failure, and racist dogma, to name only a few"—he also identifies Baraka's main merits: "daring and frequently successful verbal approximations of jazz music, vibrant rec-

reation of black speech, and a consummate portrayal of the black middle-class psyche."

Sollors, Werner. *Amiri Baraka/LeRoi Jones: The Quest for a "Populist Modernism."* New York: Columbia University Press, 1978. In Chapter 7 of this early study, Sollors examines the themes and forms of Baraka's lone novel and his short stories. The stories in *Tales* "may be considered the logbook of a fiction writer who under the social pressures of the 1960's, catapulted himself out of writing fictions while writing a swan-song to telling tales."

David Peck

JULIAN BARNES

Born: Leicester, England; January 19, 1946

PRINCIPAL SHORT FICTION
Cross Channel, 1996

OTHER LITERARY FORMS

Julian Barnes is the author of several novels, including *Metroland* (1980), *Before She Met Me* (1982), *Flaubert's Parrot* (1984), *Staring at the Sun* (1986), *A History of the World in 10½ Chapters* (1989), *Talking It Over* (1991), *The Porcupine* (1992), and *England, England* (1998). He has also published a collection of essays, *Letters from London* (1995).

ACHIEVEMENTS

Julian Barnes's first novel, *Metroland*, won the Somerset Maugham Award, and his third novel, *Flaubert's Parrot*, was nominated for a Booker McConnell Prize and won both the Geoffrey Faber Memorial Prize and the Prix Médicis. Barnes won an American Academy of Arts and Letters award in 1986 and was awarded the Prix Gutembourg in 1987, the Premio Grinzane Carour in 1988, and the Shakespeare Prize in 1993. He has also been named an Officier de l'Ordre des Arts et des Lettres.

BIOGRAPHY

Julian Patrick Barnes was born in Leicester, England, on January 19, 1946, and educated at the City of London School. He graduated with honors from Magdalen College, Oxford, in 1968, and for the next four years was a lexicographer for the *Oxford English Dictionary Supplement*. In 1977, he began reviewing for a number of British periodicals and between 1979 and 1986 was a television critic for *The Observer*. He has been a visiting professor at The Johns Hopkins University in Baltimore, Maryland. He has also written a number of popular thrillers under the pseudonym Dan Kavanagh.

ANALYSIS

Julian Barnes's collection of short stories, *Cross Channel*, contains ten stories appearing previously in *The New Yorker*, *Granta*, and elsewhere. Despite Barnes's small output, *Cross Channel* has received a great deal of positive attention partially because of critical admiration of his novels, particularly *Flaubert's Parrot* and *England, England*, and partially because of his narrative experiments with the short-story form.

The collection is thematically of a piece, all the stories focusing on the British in France, from the seventeenth to the twenty-first century. The stories also share the common characteristic of being grounded as much on historical fact and cultural values as they are on individual characters. As a result, his stories sometimes lean as much toward the essayistic as they do toward the fictional. Although this creates a strong factual context for the stories, giving them a sense of historical reality, it tends to make them focus more on social abstractions than on individual characters.

"DRAGONS"

"Dragons" focuses on the occupation of a Protestant village in southern France in the seventeenth century by mercenaries working for Louis XIV. Three soldiers, or "dragonnades," from the north are placed in the household of Pierre, a French carpenter, ostensibly because he has not paid a tax but actually because he is Protestant and thus considered an enemy of the king's religion. The soldiers burn his furniture and his fine wood and sell his tools for bargain prices.

One by one, the members of Pierre's family are forced to recant their religion and return to the Church. His child Daniel is taken to a Jesuit college; another son abjures when his sister is raped by the dragons, but when they continue to treat her as a whore, he spits out the holy wafer and wine and is condemned to death by burning. To force the girl to abjure, the dragons tell her that she will get pregnant and that they will testify that her father used her as a whore, which will result in her and her father's deaths.

The climax of the story comes when the reader learns that the dragons are Irish Catholics, who have become mercenaries for the French Catholics out of revenge for Oliver Cromwell's Protestant atrocities against them many years earlier. When the heretics are reduced in number from 176 to 8, the dragons move farther south and start work in another area. However, Pierre still goes into the forest to join his secret religious sect.

"Dragons" is an ironic story about persecution and social intolerance, told in the formal language and tones of the folktale. However, as the story progresses, it moves slowly from an anonymous folktale country to a precise historical context. The fact that

Julian Barnes (©Miriam Berkley)

the dragons are from Ireland seems a kind of poetic justice, as they have also been victims of religious persecution. Thus, the story begins to resonate with cultural meaning after the reader learns the historical context.

"INTERFERENCE"

The movement in this story of an aging and egotistical English composer, who lives in a French village in the 1930's with his longtime lover Adeline, is toward his inevitable death; the narrative interest is in which poetically just way that death will occur. The emphasis of the story is on Adeline, who has pampered and tolerated his egotism for years. An important motivating device in the story is the composer's wireless radio, with which he listens to concerts from England. When the villagers use electric motors to pump water and cattle feed on their farms, it interferes with his radio reception, so he asks Adeline to have them turn off their motors when he wishes to listen to a concert.

The story comes to a climax when he tells her to alert the village of a concert that, unknown to her, is of his last and most famous composition. Tired of his imperious posturing, she refuses; thus when the concert begins, and she discovers that it is his own piece that is to be played, she howls and dashes to the village in desperation, wanting to strike the whole countryside into silence. However, everywhere she goes the machines are running, as if the village conspired, as the world has always conspired, against the artist, waiting until he was at his weakest to destroy him. When she returns to the house, she finds him dead, his eyes closed, either by nature or by human "interference." Three weeks after the funeral, when the recordings of the symphony, entitled *Four English Seasons*, arrives, she methodically puts them in the order of the seasons and then breaks them one by one.

"EVERMORE"

"Evermore" is about an elderly English woman who has visited France for years to attend to the grave of her brother, who was killed during World War I. A "connoisseur of grief," hungry for its "voluptuous selfishness" and solitude, she cannot imagine her life without it. The story has no plot but is rather like an elegiac commemoration of grief itself. The title of the story derives from the legend carved on the stones, "Their name liveth for evermore," but she wonders if there is such a thing as a collective memory, something more than the sum of individual memories. The story is about an individual effort to extend a personal memory to the level of cultural history. The question it raises is this: What is the difference between one person's memory and effort to preserve the past and the cultural nature of history itself, which seeks to preserve the past?

"HERMITAGE"

"Hermitage" takes place in the last decade of the nineteenth century as two Englishwomen, perhaps quietly lesbian, leave England to buy a vineyard in the Médoc area of France. A metaphor announced early in the story concerns a rule that grape pickers are not to eat the grapes: Women pickers are made to stick out their tongues for inspection, and if their tongues are purple, the women must kiss the overseer as their punishment. The story is about the English-

women's efforts to impose English ways on the French vineyards and their gradual acceptance of French ways; they do not wish to disturb the lives of their French neighbors but rather wish to achieve tranquillity in their own lives. The story ends on the last evening of the nineteenth century as the two women drink a glass of wine together on the terrace of their château. One teasingly asks the other to let her see her tongue, which she does in mock contrition, and then the two women turn out the light and go to bed.

"TUNNEL"

Of all the essaylike stories in *Cross Channel*, "Tunnel" is perhaps the most essayistic, for it assumes the convention of a personal autobiographical account of an elderly Englishman who travels on the Eurostar from London to Paris in the year 2015 via the tunnel beneath the English Channel, commenting both on his past journeys to France and on his observations on this journey. Like a writer, he observes people on the train and makes up stories about them. He also thinks of the verb "remember" as being inexact, for he knows that the word also means to "retrospectively imagine" or to "reconstruct."

The word "tunnel" in the story suggests not only a conduit between two cultures but also the "tunnel of memory" that connects the past with the present. Several motifs in "Tunnel" refer to the other stories in *Cross Channel*, ending with a reference to "Evermore," as the man thinks of history as being a process of deletion and of World War I cemeteries being deleted. He thinks of himself as a gatherer, sifter, and grafter of memories, passing them on to others. The story ends with a self-reflexive reference to Barnes and his own book: "And the elderly Englishman, when he returned home, began to write the stories you have just read."

OTHER MAJOR WORKS

LONG FICTION: *Metroland*, 1980; *Duffy*, 1980 (as Dan Kavanagh); *Fiddle City*, 1981 (as Dan Kavanagh); *Before She Met Me*, 1982; *Flaubert's Parrot*, 1984; *Putting the Boot In*, 1985 (as Dan Kavanagh); *Staring at the Sun*, 1986; *Going to the Dogs*, 1987 (as Dan Kavanagh); *A History of the World in*

10½ Chapters, 1989; *Talking It Over*, 1991; *The Porcupine*, 1992; *England, England*, 1998; *Love, etc.*, 2000.

NONFICTION: *Letters from London*, 1995.

BIBLIOGRAPHY

Barnes, Julian. "Established Novelist Turns to Short Stories." Interview by James Hollings. *The Evening Post*, March 12, 1998, p. 14. In this interview, Barnes says he had not intended to write short fiction, but in 1990, he started having ideas that presented themselves as short stories rather than as novels; says *Cross Channel* is about why the British are drawn to France; claims that the short story is harder to write than the novel because one needs to know the tone and the theme and how these will be treated before writing can begin.

_____. "Interview with Julian Barnes." Interview by Patrick McGrath. *Bomb* 21 (Fall, 1987): 20-23. Barnes argues that there is no norm to a sex life; claims that a first-rate critic is less important than a second-rate writer; talks about his relationship to the French; and insists that he is not obsessed with obsession.

_____. "Inventing England." Interview by Penelope Dening. *The Irish Times*, September 8, 1998, p. 12. A interview with Barnes just after the publication of *England, England*; says his work is rarely autobiographical and that disparities between the public and the private and between the false and the authentic run through his fiction; Barnes says he does not write to solve problems but that he writes about themes that make him itch.

_____. "Open Channels." Interview by Penny Fox. *The Scotsman*, January 13, 1996, p. 16. In this interview, Barnes says writing is the most enjoyable work he has ever done; he is amused that Sharon Stone was flown to Paris to receive a French award, while he was only invited down to the local embassy to receive the same honor; talks about the origins of *Cross Channel* and speculates about new writers from Scotland.

Higdon, David Leon. " 'Unconfessed Confessions': The Narrators of Graham Swift and Julian Barnes." In *The British and Irish Novel Since 1960*, edited by James Acheson. New York: St. Martin's Press, 1991. Argues that the fiction of Swift and Barnes defines what is meant by British postmodernism; claims they share themes of estrangement, obsession, and the power of the past; examines their creation of "the reluctant narrator," who, although quite perceptive, has experienced something so traumatic he must tell it through indirections, masks, and substitutions.

May, Derwent. "More than Just Sleeve Notes." *The Times*, January 11, 1996, p. 1. A review of *Cross Channel*; notes that there is little emotion or personal drama in the stories but rather that they wittily re-create a passage of social history; discusses several of the stories, especially "Hermitage" and "Evermore," which May says are the best in the collection.

Mosely, Merritt. *Understanding Julian Barnes*. Columbia: University of South Carolina Press, 1997. A general introduction to Barnes's life and work that briefly discusses his novels, stories, and nonfiction. In the chapter on short fiction, Mosely discusses "Dragons," "Interference," and "Experiment" from *Cross Channel*. Includes a bibliography of criticism of Barnes's fiction.

Stout, Mira. "Chameleon Novelist." *The New York Times Magazine*, November 22, 1992, 28-29. A brief biographical sketch discussing Barnes's experiments with various narrative forms and his common themes of obsession, dislocation, death, art, and religion. Discusses his childhood, his circle of friends, and his marriage to agent Patricia Kavanagh.

Charles E. May

ANDREA BARRETT

Born: Cape Cod, Massachusetts; July 17, 1955

PRINCIPAL SHORT FICTION
Ship Fever and Other Stories, 1996

OTHER LITERARY FORMS

Andrea Barrett published four moderately successful novels before *Ship Fever and Other Stories* catapulted her to fame. Since then her ambitious historical novel *The Voyage of the Narwhal* was published to very good reviews in 1998, although it has not received the critical attention her collection of stories did.

ACHIEVEMENTS

In 1992, Andrea Barrett won a National Endowment for the Humanities Fellowship, using the time that award provided to write the stories in *Ship Fever and Other Stories*, which won the 1996 National Book Award. She has received a John Simon Guggenheim Memorial Foundation Fellowship and an honorary degree from Union College.

BIOGRAPHY

Andrea Barrett grew up on Cape Cod; her father was a ski racer and later a ski patrolman. Uncertain about a chosen career, she was in and out of graduate school in the late 1970's and early 1980's, doing advanced study first in zoology and then in medieval and reformation history. She held a number of low-paying jobs—receptionist, billing clerk, customer service representative, greenhouse technician, clerk, secretary, and research assistant—and in the late 1980's, she did freelance medical editing, book reviewing, and teaching. She has said she learned a great deal of biology and medicine from several of these jobs, which she has used in her fiction.

Barrett has said that she shifted from science to writing because she realized while in graduate school that what she had was a passion for the passion of science; she says that it took her many years to realize that what she mistook for her own obsessions with

science were, in fact, other people's obsessions. Although she devotes most of her time to research and writing, she has been a faculty member at the Bread Loaf Writer's Conference and has taught regularly in the M.F.A. program at Warren Wilson College in North Carolina, where she was living in 2000 with her husband, a biologist.

ANALYSIS

Although the stories in Andrea Barrett's National Book Award-winning *Ship Fever and Other Stories* focus on characters caught up in pursuits in the natural sciences, her real emphasis is on the vulnerable human element behind the scientific impulse. Many of the stories are historical fictions in the classic sense: They involve real people from the past, often very famous scientists such as Gregor Mendel and Carl Linnaeus, and they present the past as it impinges upon and informs the present. All of Barrett's stories use scientific fact and historical events to throw light on basic human impulses and conflicts.

Barrett is a consummate stylist, a writer who chooses words carefully and never wastes a single one. In "The Behavior of the Hawkweeds," Mendel's paper on the hybridization of edible peas is held up by his present-day admirer as a "model of clarity. . . . It represented everything that science should be." Indeed, Barrett's stories are similarly models of clarity, representing everything that narrative art should be.

"THE BEHAVIOR OF THE HAWKWEEDS"

"The Behavior of the Hawkweeds," which was selected for *The Best American Short Stories* in 1995, is typical of Barrett's short fiction. Told by the wife of a mediocre twentieth century science professor, who greatly admires the geneticist Gregor Mendel, it includes the historical account of how Mendel allowed himself to be misdirected from his valuable studies of the hybridization of the edible pea to a dead-end study of the hawkweed by the botanist Carl Nageli until he finally gave up in despair.

"The Behavior of the Hawkweeds" also contains the more personal story of how the narrator's grandfather accidentally killed a man who he thought was trying to abuse her as a child. These stories from the past are paralleled by stories in the present in which the narrator finds herself leading a meaningless life at middle age and in which her husband, having achieved nothing of scientific value himself, spends his retirement continually retelling the Mendel stories his wife told him.

"Birds with No Feet"

"Birds with No Feet" is about the difference between the impulse that drives the true scientist and that which compels the mere collector and observer. It is the story of contrasting parallels between Alec Carriere, a young man who gathers specimens in the Amazon in the 1850's, and Alfred Wallace, a more established scientist, who is also a collector of biological specimens. The basic difference between the two men is that whereas Wallace is interested in the method whereby species mutate into new species, Carriere has no concept of "method" and no time to theorize.

Obsessed by the urgency to capture and name everything he sees, "caught like a fly in the richness around him, drowning in detail," Carriere wonders why all he has observed has not crystallized into some "shimmering structure." Even his capture of the great Bird of Paradise, which lacks wings or feet, is superseded by Wallace's return to London with the same bird. The story ends with Carriere's fear he has never been a true scientist.

"The Littoral Zone"

One of the most compact stories in the collection, "The Littoral Zone" centers on Jonathan and Ruby, teachers of zoology and botany who met fifteen years earlier while doing summer research on an island off New Hampshire. The story is about the inexplicable puzzle of what draws two people together and what holds them together. At the time of the story, Jonathan and Ruby are near fifty and their children cannot imagine them young and strong and wrung by passion.

The title of the story refers to the space between high and low watermarks where organisms struggle to adapt to the daily rhythm of immersion and exposure. When the two meet and realize their mutual attraction, Barrett describes it in terms of the littoral zone metaphor: "They swam in that odd, indefinite zone where they were more than friends, not yet lovers, still able to deny to themselves that they were headed where they were headed." The littoral zone, Barrett seems to suggest, is that time in a relationship between the high point of passion and the lowest point of everyday life. Neither of the two could now, if pressed, explain what drew them together.

"Ship Fever"

The longest story in the collection, long enough to be designated a novella rather than a short story, is "Ship Fever," another name for typhus in the nineteenth century, when it was particularly prevalent among poor immigrants and refugees who fled Europe for North America. The story takes place in the 1840's when thousands of poor people fled the great Famine in Ireland. The central focus is on a fictional young doctor, Lauchlin Grant of Quebec, who volunteers for the pubic health service on Grosse Isle, a quarantine station for Irish immigrants.

The plot of the story is driven by the doctor's initial motivation to volunteer for this seemingly hopeless effort because of his love for the young Susannah Rowley, whose husband is a journalist in Ireland sending back stories and letters about the famine. Stung by her accusation that he is doing nothing to help the suffering Irish immigrants, the doctor goes to Grosse Isle and is so affected by the horrors he sees there that he becomes obsessed with doing what he can to care for the sick and dying and to prevent the spread of the disease.

Barrett's fondness for parallel actions is manifested in this story when the doctor rescues Nora Kynd, who looks very much like Susannah Rowley, a young woman who has been given up for dead. Separated from her two brothers, who are sent into the central part of Canada because they have not been infected by the disease, Nora is nursed back to health by the doctor. Because of her own fine nursing skills, she stays on and helps others. When the doctor becomes ill himself, she tries unsuccessfully to bring him back to health.

The story ends when Nora leaves Grosse Isle and goes to the city to tell Susannah about the doctor's death, only to discover that she too is now ill. Finally,

Nora goes to look for her brothers, saying she will travel to the United States if she cannot find them. Thematically, the idea of starting fresh, that which brought the many immigrants to North America in the first place, is thus the story's final emphasis.

OTHER MAJOR WORKS

LONG FICTION: *Lucid Stars*, 1988; *Secret Harmonies*, 1989; *The Middle Kingdom*, 1991; *The Forms of Water*, 1993; *The Voyage of the Narwhal*, 1998.

BIBLIOGRAPHY

Barrett, Andrea. "An Interview with Andrea Barrett." Interview by Marian Ryan. *The Writer's Chronicle* 32 (December, 1999): 4-9. An extensive interview in which Barrett talks more candidly than usual about a wide variety of concerns important to her. Barrett talks about how stories are a way of knowledge, about how the lens of historical fiction allows her to express her deepest feelings, and about the technical experimentation that gave rise to many of the stories in *Ship Fever and Other Stories*.

Basbanes, Nicholas A. "Author's 'Private Passion' Goes Public." *The Memphis Commercial Appeal*, March 16, 1997, p. G4. An interview story about Barrett's publicity tour after winning the National Book Award. Barrett describes the origin of *Ship Fever and Other Stories* and how she taught herself to write short fiction for the book.

Greene, Janice. "Science as a Metaphor for Longing." Review of *Ship Fever and Other Stories*, by Andrea Barrett. *The San Francisco Chronicle*, January 28, 1996, p. 5. This review claims Barrett's stories of the past have more vitality than those of the present. Singles the title story out as one that is rich with contrasts; says it sums up the focus of all her stories—that the pursuit of fulfillment, like the pursuit of science, is a quest for truth.

Lanham, Fritz. "Keeping Success in Perspective." *The Houston Chronicle*, November 1, 1998, p. Z26. An interview-based story about Barrett on the publication of *The Voyage of the Narwhal*. Provides biographical information about Barrett's education and research methods. Barrett describes her decision to shift from history to fiction and her first disappointing efforts to write a novel.

Lippman, Laura. "The Very Humble Andrea Barrett." *St. Louis Post Dispatch*, March 9, 1997, p. 1D. An interview story which includes biographical information and quotes Barrett on the writing life: "If people knew how happy it can make you, we would all be writing all the time. It's the greatest secret of the world."

Mallon, Thomas. "Under the Microscope." Review of *Ship Fever and Other Stories*. *The New York Times*, January 28, 1996, p. 24. Notes that Barrett's scientific bent is sufficiently rare among fiction writers; praises her ability to weave science and fiction together; argues that the charge that Barrett works too hard to make her connections is out of place.

Martelle, Scott. "Lost in the Pursuit of Love and Science." *The Buffalo News*, February 4, 1996, p. 5E. Says that Barrett has found a nexus in the schism in American culture between art and science. Says the title story of *Ship Fever and Other Stories* is the weakest work in the collection, for the real history never gets integrated into the fiction the way it does in her better stories.

Streitfeld, David. "A Literary Write of Passage." *The Washington Post*, November 23, 1996. P. G1. An interview-based story on the occasion of Barrett's winning the National Book Award. Streitfeld describes Barrett's reaction to receiving the award and speculates on its influence on her writing career.

Charles E. May

JOHN BARTH

Born: Cambridge, Maryland; May 27, 1930

PRINCIPAL SHORT FICTION
  Lost in the Funhouse, 1968
  On with the Story, 1996

OTHER LITERARY FORMS

The majority of John Barth's fiction is in the novel form. He has also written critical articles and essays on the nature of fiction and the state of the art. Some of his material has been recorded, since several of his stories require an auditory medium to achieve their original purposes and effects.

ACHIEVEMENTS

Honors accorded to John Barth and to his work include a Brandeis University Creative Arts Award in 1965, a Rockefeller Foundation grant for 1965-1966, a National Institute of Arts and Letters grant in 1966, the National Book Award for *Chimera* in 1973, and the F. Scott Fitzgerald Award for outstanding achievement in American literature in 1997. In 1974, he was elected to both the National Institute of Arts and Letters and the American Academy of Arts and Sciences.

BIOGRAPHY

John Simmons Barth's first artistic interest was in music, and he studied briefly at the Juilliard School of Music before entering The Johns Hopkins University in Baltimore, Maryland, in the fall of 1947. He married Harriette Anne Strickland in January, 1950. In 1951, he received his B.A. in creative writing, and his first child, Christine, was born. Barth completed his M.A. in 1952 and began work on his Ph.D. in the aesthetics of literature. His second child, John, was born in 1952, and with his wife expecting a third child (Daniel, born in 1954), Barth abandoned work on his Ph.D. and took a teaching job at Pennsylvania State University in 1953. In 1965, he left Pennsylvania State to teach at the State University of New York at Buffalo. Divorced from his first wife in 1969, Barth married Shelly Rosenberg on December 27,

1970. Barth was Alumni Centennial Professor of English and Creative Writing at The Johns Hopkins University from 1973 to 1990, when he became professor emeritus.

ANALYSIS

As a leading developer and writer of metafiction, John Barth wrote a body of work that, through the use of the fantastic and the absurd as well as the realistic and the romantic, portrays the human experience in the second half of the twentieth century. He is considered a leading writer in the field of postmodernist fiction.

Barth, who always hoped to bring alive philosophical alternatives in his stories, reviving old themes of literature and life—literature's because they *are* life's—is able to make a progression through these short fictions, retackling the problems, not by repetition but by constantly distilling the possibilities of technique. He has clearly opened the narrative consciousness, the academic ear, and the imagination of readers and writers alike. While he never presumes to answer one of his posed questions, his inventiveness and sincerity make his stories experiences of real substance, as well as of words. Throughout the collection, words and stories help to ease human pain and serve as a source of curious investigation and delight.

LOST IN THE FUNHOUSE

Although John Barth is best known for his novels, his stories "Night-Sea Journey," "Lost in the Funhouse," "Title," and "Life-Story" from his collection of short fiction *Lost in the Funhouse* are frequently anthologized. The book is a sequence of related stories which operate in a cycle beginning with the anonymity of origins and concluding, like the serpent with its tail in its mouth, with the anonymity of a life's conclusion and the narrator's exhaustion of his art. Some of Barth's characters are nameless, having both a personal and a universal dimension. Others, such as those in "Echo" and "Menelaiad," take their names from mythology. Three stories, "Ambrose His

Mark," "Water Message," and "Lost in the Funhouse," reveal three turning points in the life of a developing character, Ambrose: his naming as an infant; his first consciousness of *fact*, in both conflict and alliance with a romanticized truth; and a larger apprehension of life suffused with his first sexual consciousness. Barth's characters, or voices, are all natural storytellers compelled to make sense of what they experience; they become living metaphors for states of love, art, and civilization. As they quest, the author joins them, so that Barth's technique often

John Barth (Teturo Maruyama)

conforms with his subject matter. Only the first two Ambrose stories could be considered conventional in structure; the remaining stories are fictions which investigate each individual's experience through voice shift, idea, and the self-evident play of language.

In these stories Barth questions the meaning of love, love in relation to art, and the artist's and lover's place within civilization—not merely time-bounded culture, but art's progress through history, its aspirations and its failures. Barth's characters face the reve-

lation that the individual facts of their lives are painful, that self-knowledge hurts and is in conflict with their original visions of the world. The characters turn to storytelling, not only to comprehend the complexities of their personal lives but also to preserve their sanity as they encounter knowledge. The creation of artifice literally kills time, and by virtue of narrative organization, even when suffering cannot be explained, life may become bearable. In "Life-Story," which spans only part of a day, the narrator speaks of himself:

> Even as she left he reached for the sleeping pills cached conveniently in his writing desk and was restrained from their administration only by his being in the process of completing a sentence. . . . There was always another sentence to worry about.

In "Autobiography," a story written for monophonic tape, the speaker says, "Being me's no joke," and later, "I'm not what either parent or I had in mind."

The tradition underlying Barth's stories is the language itself, the very process of storytelling, not merely the genre of story. In this sense his work has much in common with experimental films and some contemporary poetry, as his characters transform their personal worlds of fact into worlds of fiction. For Barth, that is one solution of the fact of existence. The question remains: Does one then become nothing more than one's story? If the body does not live, does it matter that the words might, even if they can solve nothing? The very playfulness and intrigue of Barth's language, along with its intellectual complexity, suggests that romantic disillusion may be at least temporarily combated through the vehicle of self-examining narrative. The underlying fear is that the story might exhaust itself, that fiction might become worn out and the words have nowhere to go but back into the narrator's mind.

"Night-Sea Journey," which opens the collection, is the story of the life of a single sperm cell as it travels toward the possibility of linkage and conception upon the shores of a mythic Her. The narrator is the sperm and is quoted throughout by the authorial voice, yet the narrator addresses himself and finally the being he may become, not an audience, so the story reads as a first-person interior monologue. Being "spoken inwardly," "Night-Sea Journey" is similar to later stories in the collection which are first-person accounts by the author. This similarity effects a parallel between the struggles of the sperm cell and later struggles by the author, which, in turn, parallel the struggles everyone faces in the journey through life.

At first, the narrator shares the determination of the other "swimmers" to "reach the shore" and "transmit the Heritage." His enthusiasm, however, wanes as he considers the philosophy of a friend, who has since "drowned." The friend claimed that since their ultimate destiny is to perish, the noble thing to do is to commit suicide. He considered the hero of heroes to be he who reached the shore and refused "Her." Pondering this and such questions as whether the journey is real or illusory, who or what causes the difficult passage, and whether arrival will mean anything at all, the narrator considers various possible explanations of the meaning, if any, of the journey. Here Barth parodies philosophical and religious positions familiar to the sophisticated reader. He also parodies common adolescent ramblings about the meaning of life: "Love is how we call our ignorance of what whips us." The whipping here results from the sperm's tail, causing movement toward an unknown destiny. Barth makes deliberate use of clichés and puns to ease the reader into identification with the narrator's voice, which speaks phrases we have all spoken in our most baffled or despairing moments. The humor is as adolescent as the state of the speaker's anxieties: "I have seen the best swimmers of my generation go under."

Constantly suspicious that the journey is meaningless, the speaker is finally swayed to accept his pessimistic friend's advice; he gives up and ceases to swim; however, his decision has come too late. By continuing to live he has been drawn ever nearer to the "shore" and is pulled by the force of the female element. He reaches "a motionless or hugely gliding sphere" and is about to become a link in another cycle of life and death. Before joining with Her, however, he expresses his "single hope" that he might transmit to the being he is becoming "a private legacy

of awful recollection and negative resolve." The speaker declares: "You to whom, through whom I speak, do what I cannot: terminate this aimless, brutal business! Stop your hearing against her song! Hate Love!" In spite of the speaker's desire to end all night-sea journeys, all life—"Make no more"—he cannot resist biological fate and plunges "into Her who summons, singing . . . 'Love! Love! Love!'" This conclusion and Barth's parody throughout the story of attempts to understand life suggest that the meaning of life may be nothing more than life itself. To borrow a statement from *Chimera*, "the key to the treasure is the treasure."

"Lost in the Funhouse" appears midway in the collection. It opens with young Ambrose, perhaps the being formed through the union of the sperm with Her in "Night-Sea Journey," traveling to Ocean City, Maryland, to celebrate Independence Day. Accompanying him through this eventual initiation are his parents, an uncle, his older brother Peter, and Magda, a thirteen-year-old neighbor who is well developed for her age. Ambrose is "at that awkward age" when his voice and everything else is unpredictable. Magda is the object of his first sexual consciousness, and he experiences the need to do something about it, if only barely to touch her. The story moves from painful innocence and aspects of puppy love to the stunned realization of the pain of self-knowledge. Barth uses printed devices, italics, and dashes to draw attention to the storytelling technique throughout the presentation of conventional material: a sensitive boy's first encounters with the world, the mysterious "funhouse" of sexuality, illusion, and consciously realized pain.

As the story develops, Barth incorporates comments about the art of fiction into the narrative:

He even permitted the single hair, fold, on the second joint of his thumb to brush the fabric of her skirt. Should she have sat back at that instant, his hand would have been caught under her. Plush upholstery prickles uncomfortably through gaberdine slacks in the July sun. The function of the *beginning* of a story is to introduce the principal characters, establish their initial relationship, set the scene for the main action . . . and initiate the first complication or whatever of the "rising action."

Such moments, when the voice seems to shift outside Ambrose's consciousness, actually serve to unite the teller with the tale, Barth with his protagonist, and life with art. Among other things, "Lost in the Funhouse" is a portrait of the artist as an adolescent. The developing artist, "Ambrose . . . seemed unable to forget the least detail of his life" and tries to fit everything together. Most of all, he needs to know himself, to experience his inner being, before he will have something to express.

Ambrose develops this knowledge when he becomes lost in the carnival funhouse, which, on one level, represents the mind. Just before emerging from the funhouse, he strays into an old, forgotten part of it and loses his way. Here, separated from the mainstream—the funhouse representing the world for lovers—he has fantasies of death and suicide, recalling the "negative resolve" of the sperm cell from "Night-Sea Journey." He also finds himself reliving incidents with Magda in the past and imagining alternative futures. He begins to suffer the experience of illusion and disillusion: "Nothing was what it looked like." He finds a coin with his name on it and imagines possible lives for himself as an adult.

These experiences lead to a new fantasy: Ambrose dreams of reciting stories in the dark until he dies, while a young girl behind the plyboard panel he leans against takes down his every word but does not speak, for she knows his genius can only bloom in isolation. This fantasy is the artistic parallel to the sperm's union with "Her" in "Night-Sea Journey." Barth thus suggests that the artist's creative force is a product of a rechanneled sexual drive. Although Ambrose "would rather be among the lovers for whom funhouses are designed," he will construct, maybe operate, his own funhouse in the world of art. His identity as artist derives from the knowledge he has gained of his isolation, the isolation of the artist, who is not "a person," but who must create a self and a world, or, rather, selves and worlds. The difference between lovers and artists, however, may not be as definitive as it seems, for Barth's fiction implies that Ambrose's predicament may be universal.

The final story in *Lost in the Funhouse* is "Anonymiad," the life-story of a minstrel who becomes an artist, perhaps an Ambrose grown up, as well as an alter ego for Barth himself. If translated into realistic terms, the life of the minstrel would parallel Barth's literary career. The minstrel grows up singing in a rural setting with the most lovely goatherd maiden as his mistress. Dreaming of fame, he takes his song to the city, where he meets Queen Clytemnestra and becomes a court minstrel. As he becomes more musically adept, he spends more time in court intrigues than with his maiden, Merope. When King Agamemnon goes off to war, an interloper, Aegisthus, steals the Queen's love, woos Merope, and casts the minstrel on a deserted island with nine casks of wine. To each of these the minstrel gives the name and properties of one of the nine muses. For the remainder of his life the minstrel, now without his lyre, composes something new, literature, which he casts adrift in the empty wine bottles. These bottles parallel the sperm cell of "Night-Sea Journey," transmitting the Heritage.

Isolated on his island, like Ambrose in the funhouse, the minstrel is unhappy. His life has not worked out; his work has been mediocre and unacclaimed; love has failed; and later he says that his "long prose fictions of the realistical, the romantical and fantastical" are not what he meant them to be. He writes these fictions on the island to structure his life; he tans the hides of native goats and sends his manuscripts out to sea in the large urns after drinking up all the wine. Urn by urn, he writes his way through the panorama of fiction's possibilities. Then he loses interest and decides that all he has written is useless. There is one amphora left, and one goat, hard to catch, whom he names Helen. Rousing himself, he decides to write one final, brilliant piece, his "Anonymiad," which he hopes will be filled with the "pain of insight, wise and smiling in the terror of our life." Everything must be deliberated to get all this on a single skin. This is vital, as an earlier work had come floating back to shore in its urn, drenched and unreadable. After painstakingly writing this final piece, the writer sees it only as a "chronicle of minstrel misery." No more living creatures exist on the island; the writer is totally alone. In spite of these facts, however, the minstrel is content. He has sent his "strange love letter" to Merope, now his muse. He knows that "somewhere outside myself, my enciphered spirit drifted, realer than the gods, its significance as objective and undecoded as the stars." He imagines his tale "drifting age after age, while generations fight, sing, love, expire." Sadly, he thinks: "Now it passes a hairsbreadth from the unknown man or woman to whose heart, of all hearts in the world, it could speak fluentest, most balmly—but they're too preoccupied to reach out to it, and it can't reach out to them." Like the minstrel, his tale will drift and perish, but as the story ends, "No matter." A noontime sun "beautiful enough to break the heart" shines on the island where "a nameless minstrel wrote it." The collection of stories ends, turning back toward its *tabula rasa* of origin.

ON WITH THE STORY

On with the Story gathers together twelve short pieces that Barth had previously published separately in periodicals. He insisted that *Lost in the Funhouse*, many pieces of which had similarly been published separately, was "neither a collection nor a selection, but a series . . . meant to be received 'all at once' and as here arranged." Reviewers of *On with the Story* were quick to see that it also constituted a work with its own unity and integrity. Ron Loewinsohn, for example, found a clear structural arrangement: "a dozen stories arranged in three groups of four, concerning beginnings, middles, and endings." D. Quentin Miller noted the focus provided by Barth's device of "concluding the book with continuations of the eleven stories that precede the conclusion, in reverse order," as well as the coherence provided by "the series of interchapters depicting a vacationing husband and wife who exchange stories in bed"—a recycling of the dramatic situation of Shahriar and Scheherazade in *Alf layla wa-layla* (fifteenth century; *The Arabian Nights' Entertainments*, 1706-1708)—which he links to Barth's frequent reliance on the device of the frame-tale in his novels. A number of the stories suggest parallels with this framing story of the couple, who appear to be at the end of or at least at a turning point in their relationship, though these connections are left open for the reader's speculation rather than filled out in detail.

A thematic principle of coherence is suggested by the book's two epigraphs, one from the physicist Werner Heisenberg and one from a standard textbook on narrative (coauthored by Barth's early critical champion Robert Scholes), and several of the stories explicitly parallel the laws of physics with those of narrative. In "Ad Infinitum: A Short Story" and "On with the Story," for example, Barth takes two of ancient philosopher Zeno of Citium's paradoxes—Achilles' inability to catch the tortoise, and the arrow that can never hit its target—as the core of stories designed to demonstrate the range of narrative techniques available for the depiction of temporal and spatial relations in fiction.

Barth also forges links between *On with the Story* and his first book of short stories, *Lost in the Funhouse*. The narrator of the final story in *On with the Story*, "Countdown: Once Upon a Time," was himself "once briefly lost in a funhouse, and a quarter-century later found a story in that loss," suggesting his identity with Ambrose, the author-figure from the earlier work. Even the title connects the two works, as the phrase "on with the story" appeared at the end of the author's note to *Lost in the Funhouse*. As Loewinsohn stipulates, however, the connection is to be thought of not as a return, the closing of a circle, but as the typical Barthian spiral, a near-repetition with a difference: "There it signified a beginning, meaning 'Let's get the story started.' Here it is a plea for continuity: 'Let's not allow the story to end.'"

OTHER MAJOR WORKS

LONG FICTION: *The Floating Opera*, 1956; *The End of the Road*, 1958; *The Sot-Weed Factor*, 1960; *Giles Goat-Boy: Or, The Revised New Syllabus*, 1966; *Letters*, 1979; *Sabbatical: A Romance*, 1982; *The Tidewater Tales: A Novel*, 1987; *The Last Voyage of Somebody the Sailor*, 1991; *Once upon a Time: A Floating Opera*, 1994.

NONFICTION: *The Friday Book: Essays and Other Nonfiction*, 1984; *Further Fridays: Essays, Lectures, and Other Nonfiction*, 1995.

BIBLIOGRAPHY
Barth, John. "Interview." *Short Story*, n.s. 1 (Spring,

1993): 110-118. Discusses Barth's love for the short story and why he does not write more of them. Talks about minimalism and self-reflexivity; examines the nature of the story in *The Arabian Nights' Entertainments* and Edgar Allan Poe; explains why he tries to stay as non-ideological as possible; surveys the changes in short fiction from the mid-1970's to the early 1990's.

Bowen, Zack. *A Reader's Guide to John Barth.* Westport, Conn.: Greenwood Press, 1994. A concise overview of Barth's first ten books of fiction (through *The Last Voyage of Somebody the Sailor*), with a short but thoughtful chapter on *Lost in the Funhouse.* Contains good bibliographies (including one of articles and book chapters on *Lost in the Funhouse*), a brief biographical sketch, and an interesting appendix: "Selected List of Recurrent Themes, Patterns, and Techniques."

_____. "Barth and Joyce." *Critique* 37 (Summer, 1996): 261-269. Discusses how Barth followed James Joyce in the grandness of his narrative scheme, his ironic focus on a region, and his personal overtones in his fiction. Explores Barth's anxiety about this influence.

Fogel, Stan, and Gordon Slethaug. *Understanding John Barth.* Columbia: University of South Carolina Press, 1990. In this text, the authors present a comprehensive interpretation of Barth's works, from *The Floating Opera* to *The Tidewater Tales.* Chapter 6 is devoted entirely to *Lost in the Funhouse,* with discussion of how Barth's short fiction fits into his oeuvre. Each chapter includes notes at its end. Fogel and Slethaug have included both a primary and a secondary bibliography. The primary bibliography is especially useful for its list of uncollected short stories, and it includes the stories' date and place of publication. An index divided by work and a general index conclude the book.

Harris, Charles B. *Passionate Virtuosity: The Fiction of John Barth.* Urbana: University of Illinois Press, 1983. This work has a chapter entitled " 'A Continuing, Strange Love Letter': Sex and Language in *Lost in the Funhouse*," which concentrates on Barth's stories from the aspect of the reader and writer relationship. Exhaustive notes at the end of the chapter direct the reader to further sources, as does the secondary bibliography at the end of the book. Includes an index.

Kiernan, Robert F. "John Barth's Artist in the Fun House." *Studies in Short Fiction* 10 (Fall, 1973): 373-380. Calls "Autobiography" a tour de force, capturing a fiction in the process of composing its own autobiography. Fiction tends necessarily to a life of its own and to an inordinate degree of self-reflection.

Schulz, Max F. *The Muses of John Barth: Tradition and Metafiction from "Lost in the Funhouse" to "The Tidewater Tales."* Baltimore: The Johns Hopkins University Press, 1990. Schulz concentrates on the themes of "romantic passion and commonsense love" in Barth's work, with an emphasis on "the textual domestication of classical myths." In the chapter entitled "Old Muses and New: Epic Reprises, Self-Reflexive Bedtime Stories, and Intertextual Pillow Talk," Schulz discusses what he calls the "Thalian design" of *Lost in the Funhouse.* Notes to the chapters are included at the end of the text, as is an index.

Waldmeir, Joseph J., ed. *Critical Essays on John Barth.* Boston: G. K. Hall, 1980. Although an early critical work, this text does contain four essays specifically on *Lost in the Funhouse.* Each essay includes notes, and a general index can be found at the end of the book.

Walkiewicz, E. P. *John Barth.* Boston: Twayne, 1986. This book is very useful for biographical details: It includes a chronology of Barth's life and work. Contains also considerable discussion of *Lost in the Funhouse,* which makes this book a good all-around reference. Supplemented by primary and secondary bibliographies as well as notes and an index.

Zhang, Benzi. "Paradox of Origin(ality): John Barth's 'Menelaiad.'" *Studies in Short Fiction* 32 (Spring, 1995): 199-208. Argues that in the story "Menelaiad" Barth transforms a mythological story into a postmodern "trans-tale" about the tension between past and the present and between originality and repetition.

James L. Green, updated by Jo-Ellen Lipman Boon and William Nelles

DONALD BARTHELME

Born: Philadelphia, Pennsylvania; April 7, 1931
Died: Houston, Texas; July 23, 1989

PRINCIPAL SHORT FICTION
  Come Back, Dr. Caligari, 1964
  Unspeakable Practices, Unnatural Acts, 1968
  City Life, 1970
  Sadness, 1972
  Amateurs, 1976
  Great Days, 1979
  Sixty Stories, 1981
  Overnight to Many Distant Cities, 1983
  Forty Stories, 1987

OTHER LITERARY FORMS

In addition to his one hundred and fifty or so short stories, Donald Barthelme published four novels, a children's volume that won a National Book Award, a number of film reviews and unsigned "Comment" pieces for *The New Yorker*, a small but interesting body of art criticism, and a handful of book reviews and literary essays, two of which deserve special notice: "After Joyce" and "Not Knowing."

ACHIEVEMENTS

For nearly three decades, Donald Barthelme served as American literature's most imitated and imitative yet inimitable writer. One of a small but influential group of innovative American fictionists that included maximalists John Barth, Robert Coover, and Thomas Pynchon, Barthelme evidenced an even greater affinity to the international minimalists Samuel Beckett and Jorge Luis Borges. What distinguishes Barthelme's fiction is not only his unique "zero degree" writing style but also, thanks to his long association with the mass-circulation magazine *The New Yorker*, his reaching a larger and more diversified audience than most of the experimentalists, whose readership has chiefly been limited to the ranks of college professors and their students. For all the oddity of a fiction based largely upon "the odd linguistic trip, stutter, and fall" (*Snow White*, 1967),

Barthelme may well come to be seen as the Anthony Trollope of his age. Although antirealistic in form, his fictions are in fact densely packed time capsules—not the "slices of life" of nineteenth century realists such as Émile Zola but "the thin edge of the wedge" of postmodernism's version of Charles Dickens's hard times and Charles Chaplin's modern ones. For all their seeming sameness, his stories cover a remarkable range of styles, subjects, linguistic idioms, and historical periods (often in the same work, sometimes in the same sentence). For all their referential density, Barthelme's stories do not attempt to reproduce mimetically external reality but instead offer a playful meditation on it (or alternately the materials for such a meditation). Such an art makes Barthelme in many respects the most representative American writer of the 1960's and of the two decades that followed: postmodern, postmodernist, post-Freudian, poststructuralist, postindustrial, even (to borrow Jerome Klinkowitz's apt term) postcontemporary.

BIOGRAPHY

Often praised and sometimes disparaged as one of *The New Yorker* writers, a narrative innovator, and a moral relativist whose only advice (John Gardner claimed) is that it is better to be disillusioned than deluded, Donald Barthelme was born in Philadelphia on April 7, 1931, and moved to Houston two years later. He grew up in Texas, attended Catholic diocesan schools, and began his writing career as a journalist in Ernest Hemingway's footsteps. His father, an architect who favored the modernist style of Ludwig Mies Van Der Rohe and Le Corbusier, taught at the University of Houston and designed the family's house, which became as much an object of surprise and wonder on the flat Texas landscape as his son's oddly shaped fictions were to become on the equally flat narrative landscape of postwar American fiction. While majoring in journalism, Barthelme wrote for the university newspaper as well as the *Houston Post*. He was drafted in 1953 and arrived in Korea on the day the truce was signed—the kind of coincidence one comes to expect in Barthelme's stories of strange juxtapositions and incongruous couplings. After his military service, during which he also edited an Army newspaper, he returned to Houston, where he worked in the university's public relations department ("writing poppycock for the President," as he put it in one story), and where he founded *Forum*, a literary and intellectual quarterly that published early works by Walker Percy, William H. Gass, Alain Robbe-Grillet, Leslie Fiedler, and others. He published his first story in 1961, the same year that he became director of the Contemporary Arts Museum of Houston. The following year, Thomas Hess and Harold Rosenberg offered him the position of managing editor of their new arts journal, *Location*. The journal was short-lived (only two issues ever appeared), but Barthelme's move to New York was not. Taking up residence in Greenwich Village, he published his first story in *The New Yorker* in 1963, his first collection of stories, *Come Back, Dr. Caligari*, in 1964, and his first novel, *Snow White* (among other things an updating of the Grimm Brothers' fairy tale and the Walt Disney feature-length animated cartoon), in 1967. Although he left occasionally for brief periods abroad or to teach writing at Buffalo, Houston, and elsewhere, Barthelme spent the rest of his life chiefly in Greenwich Village, with his fourth wife, Marion Knox. He lived as a writer, registering and remaking the "exquisite mysterious muck" of contemporary urban American existence, as witnessed from his corner of the global (Greenwich) village.

Donald Barthelme (Bill Wittliff)

ANALYSIS

Donald Barthelme's fiction exhausts and ultimately defeats conventional approaches (including character, plot, setting, theme—"the enemies of the novel" as fellow writer John Hawkes once called them) and defeats too all attempts at generic classification. His stories are not conventional, nor are they Borgesian *ficciones* or Beckettian "texts for nothing." Thematic studies of his writing have proved utterly inadequate, yet purely formalist critiques have seemed almost as unsatisfying. To approach a Barthelme story, the reader must proceed circuitously via various, indeed at times simultaneous, extraliterary

forms: collage, caricature, Calder mobile, action painting, jazz, atonality, the chance music of John Cage, architecture, information theory, magazine editing and layout, ventriloquism, even Legos (with all their permutational possibilities, in contrast with the High Moderns' love of cubist jigsaw puzzles). In Barthelme's case, comparisons with twentieth century painters and sculptors seem especially apropos: comical like Jean Dubuffet, whimsical and sad like Amedeo Modigliani, chaste like Piet Mondrian, attenuated like Alberto Giacometti, composite like Kurt Schwitters, improvisational like Jackson Pollock, whimsical like Marc Chagall and Paul Klee. Like theirs, his is an art of surfaces, dense rather than deep, textured rather than symbolic, an intersection of forces rather than a rendered meaning. Adjusting to the shift in perspective that reading Barthelme entails—and adjusting as well to Barthelme's (like the poet John Ashbery's) unwillingness to distinguish between foreground and background, message and noise—is difficult, sometimes impossible, and perhaps always fruitless.

However attenuated and elliptical the stories may be, they commit a kind of "sensory assault" on a frequently distracted reader who experiences immediate gratification in dealing with parts but epistemological frustration in considering the stories as wholes, a frustration which mirrors that of the characters. Not surprisingly, one finds Barthelme's characters and the fictions themselves engaged in a process of scaling back even as they and their readers yearn for that "more" to which Beckett's figures despairingly and clownishly give voice. Entering "the complicated city" and singing their "song of great expectations," they nevertheless—or also—discover that theirs is a world not of romantic possibilities (as in F. Scott Fitzgerald's fiction) but of postmodern permutations, a world of words and undecidability, where "our Song of Songs is the Uncertainty Principle" and where "double-mindedness makes for mixtures." These are stories that, like the red snow in Barthelme's favorite and most Borgesian work, "Paraguay," invite "contemplation" of a mystery that there is "no point solving—an ongoing low-grade mystery." Expressed despondently, the answer to the question, "Why do I live this way?"—or why does Barthelme write this way?—is, as the character Bishop says, "Best I can do." This, however, sums up only one side of Barthelme's double-mindedness; the other is the pleasure, however fleeting, to be taken "in the sweet of the here and the now."

"ME AND MISS MANDIBLE"

Originally published as "The Darling Duckling at School" in 1961, "Me and Miss Mandible" is one of Barthelme's earliest stories and one of his best. Written in the form of twenty-six journal entries (dated September 13 to December 9), the story evidences Barthelme's genius for rendering even the most fantastic, dreamlike events in the most matter-of-fact manner possible. The thirty-five-year-old narrator, Joseph, finds himself sitting in a too-small desk in Miss Mandible's classroom, having been declared "officially a child of eleven," either by mistake or, more likely, as punishment for having himself made a mistake in his former life as claims adjuster (a mistake for justice but against his company's interests). Having spent ten years "amid the debris of our civilization," he has come "to see the world as a vast junk-

yard" that includes the failure of his marriage and the absurdity of his military duty. At once a biblical Joseph in a foreign land and a Swiftian Gulliver among the Lilliputians, he will spend his time observing others and especially observing the widening gap between word and world, signifier and signified, the ideals expressed in teachers' manuals and the passions of a class of prepubescents fueled by film magazine stories about the Eddie Fisher/Debbie Reynolds/Elizabeth Taylor love triangle. Unlike his biblical namesake, Joseph will fail at reeducation as he has failed at marriage and other forms of social adjustment, caught by a jealous classmate making love to the freakishly named Miss Mandible.

"A SHOWER OF GOLD"

The coming together of unlike possibilities and the seeming affirmation of failure (maladjustment) takes a slightly different and more varied form in "A Shower of Gold." The former claims adjuster, Joseph, becomes the impoverished artist, Peterson, who specializes in large junk sculptures that no one buys and that even his dealer will not display. Desperate for money, he volunteers to appear on *Who Am I?*, the odd offspring of the game show craze on American television and of existentialism transformed into pop culture commodity. (There is also a barber who doubles as an analyst and triples as the author of four books all titled *The Decision to Be*.) Peterson convinces the show's Miss Arbor that he is both interesting enough and sufficiently de trop to appear on *Who Am I?*, only to feel guilty about selling out for two hundred dollars. Watching the other panelists be subjected to a humiliating barrage of questions designed to expose their bad faith, Peterson, accepting his position as a minor artist, short-circuits the host's existential script by out-absurding the absurd (his mother, he says, was a royal virgin and his father, a shower of gold). Peterson's situation parallels Barthelme's, or indeed any American writing at a time when, as Philip Roth pointed out in 1961, American reality had begun to outstrip the writer's imagination, offering a steady diet of actual people and events far more fantastic than any that the writer could hope to offer. What, Roth wondered, was left for the writer to do? "A Shower of Gold" offers one possibility.

"THE INDIAN UPRISING"

"The Indian Uprising" and "The Balloon" represent another possibility, in which in two quite different ways Barthelme directs the reader away from story and toward the act of interpretation itself (interpretation as story). As Brian McHale and Ron Moshe have demonstrated, "The Indian Uprising" comprises three overlapping yet divergent and even internally inconsistent narratives: an attack by Comanche on an unidentified but clearly modern American city; the narrator's (one of the city's defender's) unsatisfying love life; and the conflict between modern and postmodern sensibilities manifesting itself in a variety of allusions to modernist texts, including T. S. Eliot's *The Waste Land* (1922). Near the end of his poem, Eliot writes, "These fragments I have shored against my ruins." "The Indian Uprising" presents a very different approach, transforming Eliot's shoring up of high culture into a "barricade" that recycles Eliot and Thomas Mann along with ashtrays, doors, bottles of Fad #6 sherry, "and other items." Behind Eliot's poem lies the possibility of psychic, spiritual, and sociocultural wholeness implied by Eliot's use of the "mythic method." Behind Barthelme's story one finds recycling rather than redemption and instead of the mythic method what Ronald Sukenick has called "the Mosaic Law," or "the law of mosaics, a way of dealing with parts in the absence of wholes." Short but beyond summary, filled with non sequiturs, illogic, self-doubts, and anti-explanations, "The Indian Uprising" rises against readers in their efforts to know it by reducing the story to some manageable whole. At once inviting and frustrating the reader's interpretive maneuvers, "The Indian Uprising" follows the "plan" outlined in "Paraguay" insofar as it proves "a way of allowing a very wide range of tendencies to interact."

Attacking and defending are two operant principles at play here, but just who is attacking and what is being defended are never made clear. Sides change, shapes shift in a story in which American Westerns, the Civil Rights movement, and American involvement in Vietnam all seem to have their parts to play, but never to the point where any one can be said to dominate the others. Small but indomitable, the story resists the linearity of an interpretive domino theory in favor of a semiotic quagmire (more evidence of Barthelme's interest in current affairs—Vietnam, in this case—and "mysterious muck"). In "The Indian Uprising," there is no final authority to come like the cavalry to the rescue and so no release from the anxiety evident in this and so many other Barthelme stories. While there may be no permanent release, however, there is some temporary relief to be had in the "aesthetic excitement" of "the hard, brown, nutlike word" and in the fact that "Strings of language extend in every direction to bind the world into a rushing ribald whole."

"THE BALLOON"

"The Balloon" is a more compact exploration and a more relentless exploitation of interpretation as a semiotic process rather than a narrowly coded act. Covering only a few pages (or alternately an area forty-five city blocks long by up to six blocks wide), "The Balloon" is Barthelme's American tall-tale version of the short French film *The Red Balloon* and an *hommage* to Frederick Law Olmsted (who designed New York's Central Park) and environmental artist Cristo (one of his huge sculptural wrappings). Analogies such as these help readers situate themselves in relation to the inexplicable but unavoidable oddity of "The Balloon" in much the same way that the viewers in the story attempt to situate themselves in relation to the sudden appearance of a balloon which, even if it cannot be understood ("We had learned not to insist on meanings"), can at least be used (for graffiti, for example) and appreciated despite, or perhaps because, of its apparent uselessness. Ultimately the narrator will explain the balloon, thus adding his interpretive graffiti to its blank surface. The balloon, he says, was "a spontaneous autobiographical disclosure" occasioned by his lover's departure; when, after twenty-two days, she returns, he deflates the balloon, folds it, and ships it to West Virginia to be stored for future use. His explanation is doubly deflating, for while the balloon's "apparent purposelessness" may be vexing, in a world of "complex machinery," "specialized training," and pseudoscientific theories that make people marginal and passive, it has come to exist as the "prototype" or "rough draft" of the kind of solution to which people will increasingly turn, to what the Balloon Man calls his best balloon, the Balloon of Perhaps. Until the narrator's closing comments, the balloon is not a scripted text but a blank page, not an object but an event, not a ready-made product, a prefab, but a performance that invites response and participation. It is a performance that the narrator's explanation concludes, assigning both an origin (cause) and destination (result, function, use, addressee). Yet even as the explanation brings a measure of relief, it also adds a new level of anxiety insofar as the reader perceives its inadequacy and feels perhaps a twinge of guilty pleasure over having made so much of so little. In a way, however, the balloon was always doomed to extinction, for it exists in a consumer culture in which even the most remarkable objects (including "The Balloon") quickly become all too familiar, and it exists too in a therapeutic society in thrall to the illusion of authoritative explanations.

"ROBERT KENNEDY SAVED FROM DROWNING"

Appearing only two months before the real Robert F. Kennedy's assassination, "Robert Kennedy Saved from Drowning" explores epistemological uncertainty by exploiting the contemporary media's and its audience's claiming to know public figures, whether politicians or celebrities (a distinction that began to blur during the eponymous Kennedy years). The story exists at the intersection of two narrative styles. One is journalistic: twenty-four sections of what appear to be notes, each with its own subject heading and for the most part arranged in random order (the last section being a conspicuous exception) and presumably to be used in the writing of a profile or essay "about" Kennedy. The other is Kafkaesque fantasy and is evoked solely by means of the reporter's use of journalistic shorthand, the initial "K," which "refers" to Kennedy but alludes to the main characters of the enigmatic (and unfinished) novels *Der Prozess* (1925; *The Trial*, 1937) and *Das Schloss* (1926; *The Castle*, 1930) and ultimately to their equally enigmatic author, Franz Kafka himself. The narrator of "See the Moon?" claims that fragments are the only forms he trusts; in "Robert Kennedy Saved from Drowning," fragments are the only forms

the reader gets. The conflicting mass of seemingly raw material—quotes, impressions, even fragments of orders to waiters—saves Kennedy from drowning in a media-produced narcissistic image that turns even the most inane remarks into orphic sayings. Kennedy cannot drown; he can only float on the postmodern surface. Instead of the Kennedy image, Barthelme turns Kennedy into a series of images, the last being the most ludicrous and yet also the most revealing: Kennedy as Zorro, masked and floundering in the sea, his hat, cape, and sword safely on the beach. Saved from drowning (by the narrator), Kennedy is unmasked as a masked image, a free-floating signifier, a chameleon in super-hero's clothing who proves most revealing when most chameleon-like, offering a summary of Georges Poulet's analysis of the eighteenth century writer Pierre Marivaux. Only here, at this third or even fourth remove, will many readers feel that they have gotten close to the "real" Kennedy:

> The Marivaudian being is, according to Poulet, a pastless, futureless man, born anew at every instant. The instants are points which organize themselves into a line, but what is important is the instant, not the line. The Marivaudian being has in a sense no history. Nothing follows from what has gone before. He is constantly surprised. He cannot predict his own reaction to events. He is constantly being *overtaken* by events. A condition of breathlessness and dazzlement surrounds him. In consequence he exists in a certain freshness which seems, if I may say so, very desirable. This freshness Poulet, quoting Marivaux, describes very well.

"VIEWS OF MY FATHER WEEPING"

"Views of My Father Weeping" combines epistemological uncertainty with typically postmodern problematizing of the relationship between past and present (hinted at in the above quotation). Several days after his father has died under the wheels of an aristocrat's carriage, the narrator sets out to investigate whether the death was accidental, as the police reported, or an example of the aristocracy's (and the police's) indifference to the poor. Spurred on less by a desire for truth and justice than a vague sense of filial obligation and even more by the slight possibility of financial gain, but fearful that he may be beaten for making inquiries, perhaps (like his father) even killed, the narrator-son proceeds, more hesitant than Hamlet. Hamlet had his father's ghost appear to remind him of his duty to avenge a murder most foul. Barthelme's story also has a ghost (of sorts), a weeping father who sits on his son's bed acting in decidedly untragic fashion like a spoiled, sulky child whose very identity as father the son quietly questions. Complicating matters still further, this father seems to appear in a second story within "Views of My Father Weeping," which takes place in a more contemporary and clearly, although fantastically, American setting. These important if often blurred differences aside, the two narrators suffer from the same twin diseases that are pandemic in Barthelme's fiction: abulia (loss of the ability to decide or act) and acedia (spiritual torpor). They certainly would benefit from a reading of a slightly later story, "A Manual for Sons," a self-contained part of Barthelme's second novel, *The Dead Father* (1975), which concludes with this advice:

> You must become your father, but a paler, weaker version of him. The enormities go with the job, but close study will allow you to perform the job less well than it previously has been done, thus moving toward a golden age of decency, quiet, and calmed fever. Your contribution will not be a small one, but "small" is one of the concepts that you should shoot for. . . . *Fatherhood can be, if not conquered, at least "turned down" in this generation*—by the combined efforts of all of us together.

The extreme brevity of his densely allusive and highly elliptical stories suggests that Barthelme sides with the smallness of sons in their comic struggle with their various fathers (biological, historical, cultural). Against the authoritative word of the All Father, Barthelme offers a range of ventriloquized voices. "Here I differ from Kierkegaard," says one of the characters in "The Leap." "Purity of heart is not," as Kierkegaard claimed, to will one thing; it is, rather, "to will several things, and not know which is the better, truer thing, and to worry about this forever." Barthelme's own double-mindedness and preference

for mixtures and the guilty pleasures of the son's uncertainty and anxiety of influence become especially apparent in his collages of verbal and visual materials in which he puts the magazine editor's skills—layout in particular—to the fiction writer's use in order to achieve for fiction the kind of "immediate impact" generally available only to those working in the visual arts. "At the Tolstoy Museum," one of the best of these collages, literalizes, chiefly through visual means, the canonization of Leo Tolstoy as a metaphorical giant of literature, a cultural institution, an object of public veneration. Visitors to the "Tolstoy museum" must gaze at the prescribed distances and times and in the proper attitude of awe and submission. Readers of "At the Tolstoy Museum," on the other hand, find all the rules broken, temporal and spatial boundaries transgressed, and distances subject to a new and fantastic geometry. Against the museum as a repository of cult(ural) memorabilia, the story serves a narrative riposte in the form of a study in perspective. Barthelme whittles Tolstoy down to manageable size by exaggerating his proportions (much as he does with another dead father in his second novel): the thirty thousand photographs, the 640,086 pages of the Jubilee edition of Tolstoy's works, the coat that measures at least twenty feet high, the head so large it has a hall of its own (closed Mondays, Barthelme parenthetically adds), even a page-long summary of one of Tolstoy's shortest stories, "The Three Hermits." There are also the two huge Soviet-style portraits on facing pages, identical in all but one feature: the tiny figure of Napoleon I (The Little Emperor), from Tolstoy's *Voyna i mir* (1865-1869; *War and Peace*, 1886), playing the part of viewer/reader. Best of all is Barthelme's rendering of The Anna-Vronsky Pavilion devoted to the adulterous pair from *Anna Karenina* (1875-1877; English translation, 1886), a cut-out of a nineteenth century man and woman superimposed on an early (and now adulterated) study in perspective dating from 1603. "At the Tolstoy Museum" does more than merely mix and match, cut and paste. It makes hilariously clear the artifice of art and of what the passive consumer of culture may naïvely assume is both natural and eternal.

"SENTENCE"

"Sentence" makes a similar point, but it does so by exploring the literal in a quite different way. As its title suggests, the story takes the form of a single sentence of approximately twenty-five hundred words and manages to combine the brevity, open-endedness, and formal innovation that together serve as the hallmarks of Barthelme's idiosyncratic art. The subject of "Sentence" is the sentence itself: its progress and process. Beginning with one of Barthelme's favorite words, "or" ("etc." and "amid" are others), it proceeds by means of accretion and ends (if a work without any terminal punctuation can be said to end) as much an "anxious object" as any of those works of modern art to which Harold Rosenberg applied that phrase. Even as it pursues its own meandering, self-regarding, seemingly nonreferential way down the page, "Sentence" remains mindful of its reader, no less susceptible to distraction than the sentence itself and lured on by whatever promise the sentence holds out yet also feeling threatened by the sentence's failure to play by the rules. As the narrator sums up, "Sentence" is "a man-made object, not the one we wanted of course, but still a construction of man, a structure to be treasured for its weakness, as opposed to the strength of stones."

Earlier in "Sentence," Barthelme alludes to the Rosetta Stone that Champollion used to decipher the ancient Egyptian hieroglyphs. Barthelme's fiction, although written in a familiar language, proves more resistant to decoding. Barthelme uses the past as he uses the present, but neither offers anything approaching an interpretive touchstone, only the raw material, the bits and bytes out of which he constructs his oddly shaped but nevertheless aesthetically crafted "archaeological slices." Built upon the cultural ruins of an ancient Norse tale entitled "The Princess and the Glass Hill," "The Glass Mountain" resembles "Sentence" and "The Balloon" more than it does its nominal source in that it too is largely about one's reading of it. "I was trying to climb the glass mountain," the narrator declares in the first of the story's one hundred numbered sections (most only one sentence long). Like the reader, the narrator is "new to the neighborhood," persistent, comically me-

thodical, and methodologically absurd; the plumber's friends he uses to scale the glass mountain at the corner of Thirteenth Street and Eighth Avenue seem no less inappropriate than his by-the-book how-to approach drawn from medieval romance—or the reader's efforts to climb (surmount, master) Barthelme's see-through metafiction by means of equally outdated reading strategies. Once atop the glass mountain the narrator finds exactly what he hoped to, "a beautiful enchanted symbol" to disenchant. Once kissed (like the frog of fairy tales), the symbol proves disenchanting in a quite different sense of the word, changed "into only a beautiful princess" whom the narrator (now himself disenchanted) hurls down in disappointment. Having staked his life on the eternal symbol of medieval romance, the narrator finds the temporary and the merely human (princess) disappointing.

Making a postmodern something, however small and self-consuming, out of the existential nothing became Barthelme's stock-in-trade, most noticeably in "Nothing: A Preliminary Account." His art of the nearly negligible works itself out comically but almost always against a sympathetic understanding for the permanence for which the climber in "The Glass Mountain" and the characters in so many of his other stories, "The New Music," for example, yearn. A fusion of two stories published earlier the same year, one with the same title, the other entitled "Momma," "The New Music" takes the dialogue form that Barthelme often used to new and dizzying heights of nearly musical abstraction, akin to what Philip Roth would accomplish more than a decade later in his novel, *Deception* (1990). The subject here is slight (even for Barthelme), as the story's two unidentified, no-longer-young speakers go through (or are put through) a number of routines analogous to vaudeville comedy and improvisational jazz. After a few opening bars, one speaker suggests that they go to Pool, "the city of new hope. One of those new towns. Where everyone would be happier." They then segue into an exchange on, or consideration of, the new music done as a version of the familiar song "Momma don' 'low." Among the many things that Momma (now dead) did not allow was the new music. "The new music burns things together, like a welder," or like the sculptor Peterson from "A Shower of Gold" or like Barthelme who along with his two speakers understands that the new music always has been and always will be: ever changing, ever ephemeral, ever new, and forever beyond momma's prohibitions and the reader's explanations.

OTHER MAJOR WORKS

LONG FICTION: *Snow White*, 1967; *The Dead Father*, 1975; *Paradise*, 1986; *The King*, 1990.

CHILDREN'S LITERATURE: *The Slightly Irregular Fire Engine: Or, The Hithering Thithering Djinn*, 1971.

MISCELLANEOUS: *Guilty Pleasures*, 1974 (parodies and satire).

BIBLIOGRAPHY

Couturier, Maurice, and Regis Durand. *Donald Barthelme*. London: Methuen, 1982. This brief study focuses on the performance aspect of Barthelme's stories and considers them in relation to the multiplicity of varied responses that they elicit from readers. Readings are few in number but highly suggestive.

Gordon, Lois. *Donald Barthelme*. Boston: Twayne, 1981. This volume, in Twayne's United States Authors series, makes up in breadth what it lacks in depth. Although the book has no particular point to make about Barthelme and his work, it does provide useful and accurate summaries of most of his work. A comprehensive introduction for undergraduates unfamiliar with the fiction, as is Stanley Trachtenberg's *Understanding Donald Barthelme*.

Klinkowitz, Jerome. *Donald Barthelme: An Exhibition*. Durham, N.C.: Duke University Press, 1991. Klinkowitz is easily the best informed and most judicious scholar and critic of contemporary American fiction in general and Barthelme in particular. Building on his Barthelme chapter in *Literary Disruptions* (see below), he emphasizes the ways in which Barthelme reinvented narrative in the postmodern age and places Barthelme's fiction in the larger aesthetic, cultural, and historical contexts. The single most important study of Barthelme.

_____. *Literary Disruptions: The Making of a Post-Contemporary American Fiction*. 2d ed. Urbana: University of Illinois Press, 1980. Informed, accurate, and intelligent, Klinkowitz's book is the necessary starting point for any serious discussion of Barthelme and his work. The emphasis is on Barthelme's interest in structure, his revitalizing of exhausted forms, his words as objects in space rather than mimetic mirrors, and the imagination as a valid way of knowing the world.

McCaffery, Larry. *The Metafictional Muse: The Works of Robert Coover, Donald Barthelme, and William H. Gass*. Pittsburgh: University of Pittsburgh Press, 1982. After situating the three writers in their historical period, McCaffery provides excellent readings of individual works. Views Barthelme as a critic of language whose "metafictional concerns are intimately related to his other thematic interests."

Molesworth, Charles. *Donald Barthelme's Fiction: The Ironist Saved from Drowning*. Columbia: University of Missouri Press, 1982. Objecting to those who emphasize the experimental nature of Barthelme's fiction, Molesworth views Barthelme as essentially a parodist and satirist whose ironic stance saves him from drowning in mere innovation.

Olsen, Lance, ed. *Review of Contemporary Fiction* 11 (Summer, 1991). In addition to the editor's excellent bio-critical introduction and Steven Weisenburger's bibliography of works by and about Barthelme, this special issue on Barthelme reprints an early story and offers seven new essays (including especially noteworthy ones by Jerome Klinkowitz on the uses to which Barthelme put his unsigned "Comment" pieces from *The New Yorker* and Brian McHale and Ron Moshe on "The Indian Uprising") and shorter appreciations of and critical commentary on Barthelme from twenty critics and fiction writers.

Patteson, Richard, ed. *Critical Essays on Donald Barthelme*. New York: G. K. Hall, 1992. A collection of critical essays on Barthelme from book reviews and academic journals. Provides an over-view of critical reaction to Barthelme in the introduction. Essays deal with Barthelme's use of language, his fragmentation of reality, his montage technique, and his place in the postmodernist tradition.

Roe, Barbara L. *Donald Barthelme: A Study of the Short Fiction.* New York: Twayne, 1992. An introduction to Barthelme's short stories, with discussion of the major stories arranged in chronological order. Also includes several interviews with Barthelme, as well as previously published essays by other critics.

Stengel, Wayne B. *The Shape of Art in the Stories of Donald Barthelme.* Baton Rouge: Louisiana State University Press, 1985. Discusses such themes as play, futility, stasis, affirmation, and education in four types of stories: identity stories, dialogue stories, social fabric stories, and art-object stories. Focuses on Barthelme's emphasis on art in his self-reflexive stories.

Waxman, Robert. "Apollo and Dionysus: Donald Barthelme's Dance of Life." *Studies in Short Fiction* 33 (Spring, 1996): 229-243. Examines how the interplay between the Apollonian search for order and the Dionysian longing for freedom from convention informs much of Barthelme's work and is often embodied in the metaphor of music.

Robert A. Morace

FREDERICK BARTHELME

Born: Houston, Texas; October 10, 1943

PRINCIPAL SHORT FICTION
Rangoon, 1970
Moon Deluxe, 1983
Chroma, 1987
The Law of Averages: New and Selected Stories,
   2000

OTHER LITERARY FORMS
Frederick Barthelme has written several novels; they include *Second Marriage* (1984), *Tracer* (1985), *Natural Selection* (1990), *The Brothers* (1993), *Painted Desert* (1995), and *Bob the Gambler* (1997). An essay, "On Being Wrong: Convicted Minimalist Spills Bean," was published in 1988.

ACHIEVEMENTS
Also a visual artist, Frederick Barthelme has exhibited in the Seattle Art Museum (1969) and the Museum of Modern Art in New York (1970). He won the Eliot Coleman Award for prose from The Johns

Hopkins University for his story "Storyteller" in 1976-1977. He also received grants from the National Endowment for the Arts in 1979 and 1980.

BIOGRAPHY
Frederick Barthelme was born in Houston, Texas, on October 10, 1943. Two of his brothers, Donald and Steven, have also published fiction. Initially desiring to be a painter, he studied at Tulane University (1961-1962), and the University of Houston (1962-1965, 1966-1967). He briefly attended the Museum of Fine Arts in Houston in 1965-1966. After working on his visual arts career for a few years, he started writing fiction. In 1976-1977 Barthelme received the Eliot Coleman Award for Prose from The Johns Hopkins University. He also received grants from the National Endowment for the Arts and the University of Southern Mississippi. Receiving his M.A. from The Johns Hopkins University in 1977, he was then appointed professor at the University of Southern Mississippi, where he still teaches and edits the *Mississippi Review*.

ANALYSIS

Frederick Barthelme's short stories are frequently offered as examples of "minimalism." Focusing on the surface of events, minimalism generally refuses to delve into a character's psychological motivations and avoids overt narratorial commentary. Because this style is often attacked for its supposed moral defeatism and lack of historical sensibility, it is especially useful to consider Barthelme's essay "On Being Wrong: Convicted Minimalist Spills Bean" (1988) when examining his writing. In this playful manifesto, Barthelme maintains that minimalist stories deliberately react against the postmodernist obsession with language, while simultaneously rejecting conventional realism. Human experience, according to Barthelme, "is so enigmatic that only the barest suspicion of it can be got on the page with any assurance."

Barthelme usually sets his stories in malls, restaurants, and apartment complexes, rendering a vision of contemporary America that fastens upon the subdued sublimities of day-to-day existence. Suggesting that most people overlook or repress the weird peculiarity of the objects and situations they face in their daily lives, Barthelme augments the uncanny dimensions of suburban experience through stylistic experimentation. Narrators startle the reader by using the second-person form of address ("you"); everyday objects take on qualities independent from their common uses, creating an atmosphere that is both disturbing and quietly celebratory. Usefully locating this fiction within the literary mode of the "grotesque," Robert H. Brinkmeyer maintains that Barthelme's fiction "knots together the alien with the familiar and challenges the beholder to resolve the ambivalence that this intermingling evokes."

Uncomfortable in their lives and with each other, yet at ease with incongruity, Barthelme's characters find little to distinguish public from private experience. Although they are keen observers of their environments' particularities, popular culture often forms the basis of their relationship with each other and the world. Desiring change while suspecting that attempts at personal transformation will only be cosmetic or, worse, result in self-deception, these char-

acters face the confusions of late twentieth century life with integrity and an appreciable curiosity. Critic Timothy Peters detects a modest heroism in their unwillingness "to look back, to be nostalgic, or even to scheme for a more aesthetically or materially rewarding future."

"SHOPGIRLS"

"Shopgirls," from *Moon Deluxe*, encapsulates one of the central themes of Barthelme's work: how a consumer- and media-based culture influences the men and women who live within it. Initially set in a mall, "Shopgirls" follows a chronic voyeur who scrutinizes the female clerks in a department store. Andrea, who oversees purses, forces an encounter with the narrator, surprisingly inviting him to have lunch with the various women he has been observing. They tease and fawn over him, then bicker among themselves, after which Andrea invites him to spend the night. In her apartment, she relates a bizarre story about her hurricane-obsessed father, who once attempted suicide when a storm failed to arrive, leaving him crippled. The couple does not sleep together; instead, the narrator fantasizes about further voyeuristic meanderings on another floor of the department store. When, during lunch, one of the women confesses that their cultural obligation is to "make the women feel envious and . . . men feel cheated," the reader sees voyeurism's frustrating disconnections extending to social relations as a whole. Barthelme's innovative narrative strategy—the subject of the narration is a second-person "you"—is a practice drawn from film. Skillfully manipulating readers into identifying with situations to which most would be unaccustomed, this technique resembles the way an audience unconsciously adopts a motion picture camera's point of view. Although Barthelme often uses this stylistic maneuver, his particular application of it in "Shopgirls" heightens the story's emphasis on voyeurism, foregrounding the degree to which media technology and the image have influenced contemporary American culture.

"SAFEWAY"

"Safeway," from *Moon Deluxe*, employs one of Barthelme's favorite plot devices: A man and woman negotiate the unpredictable waters of initiating a sexual relationship. "Safeway" also adopts the second-person, but on this occasion, "you" are directed through the viewpoint of a man shopping for waffles. Waiting in the checkout line with Sarah, a woman he has just met, the narrator becomes embroiled in the unexplained anger of two men. These men add a peculiar twist to the story when one of them refers to a photograph of the other's wife. She is standing in front of a Confederate painting with a cast on one leg, supported by cane from World War I, presumably in a pornographic pose. Barthelme passes quickly over this startling image, devoting the remainder of the story to Sarah and the narrator flirting in a restaurant, making plans for a tryst. No affair begins because the narrator gives Sarah a false address to his apartment, the story offering no rationale for his deception. Inundating the story with brand names, Barthelme shows individuals being evaluated on the basis of their consumer choices. When someone glances at the narrator after noticing his waffles, he recognizes that "his opinion of your entire life is instantly communicated." Brand names also provide the only reliability in a life controlled by chance.

Because the narrator is keenly observant of the "random data" his day presents to him, Barthelme implies that one's understanding of the world is thoroughly shaped by the incidental. Although the narrator is acutely sensitive to the nuances of his environment—the grocery store's "parking lot [has] a close, magical look"—he seems oblivious to the workings of his mind, as his playing football with the cream cartons in the restaurant demonstrates. This equivocation of significance affects interpretation. The nuns in their "brilliant blue habits" would ordinarily suggest a religious symbol; here, however, such a moment is a visual tableau rather than a sign of potential redemption. Similarly, the historically ironic photograph contributes to the story's atmosphere without offering a readily understandable meaning. This commitment to unrooted images connects Barthelme to postmodernism.

"DRIVER"

This story from *Chroma* fulfills Brinkmeyer's comment that almost all "of Barthelme's protagonists are haunted by the fear that their lives are . . . ordered

but repetitious, without worry but without wonder." While the narrator's wife, Rita, sleeps, he watches a television program on customized low-riding cars. The next morning he trades in his Toyota for a low-rider airbrushed with a painting showing the Virgin Mary surrounded by salivating wolves. If the narrator is going through a mid-life crisis, it is not the usual kind. Going out for a drive with Rita, he finds her delightful. Discovering kids roller skating in a parking lot, Rita comments on the scene's "amazing" charm. Later, the narrator channel surfs almost until dawn, when he decides to take the car out again. The deserted downtown looks "like one of those end-of-the-world movies." Once again, he stops in a parking lot, convincing two dogs that had been chasing a bird to get into the car. Heading home, he tells the dogs about his dissatisfactory old life. The narrator's admiration of the dogs' single-minded pursuit coincides with his own gratification in having followed a series of impulses. His astonished perception that a larger reality has been going on outside his previously confined, egocentric existence leads to a classic epiphany. Whether Barthelme undercuts this private revelation by having the narrator recount it to the uncomprehending dogs depends on the reader. The diverse references scattered throughout "Driver" complicate its emotional range. Hollywood's generic films are juxtaposed uneasily with the untapped story that the man who painted the discomfiting image on the car died in Vietnam. Should the reader be suspicious when the narrator drives around his secretary's apartment? Why are the dogs identical twins and what of their owner or owners? By hinting at but not resolving these narrative dilemmas, Barthelme dramatizes the claim in "On Being Wrong: Convicted Minimalist Spills Bean" that an empty parking lot "might as well be an ancient temple."

"CHROMA"

The title story from this collection reveals an intricate network of sexual politics. The narrator's wife, Alicia, spends alternate weekends with her young lover, George. Next door live Juliet and Heather, a lesbian couple, although Juliet offers to sleep with the narrator to offset Alicia's infidelity. On a weekend when Alicia is supposed to be with George, she returns home early, the story concluding with the narrator sitting beside the bathtub, overcome by Alicia's loveliness while he watches her bathe. Barthelme does not judge this unusual sexual dynamic, but neither does he gloss over the pain, anger, and confused tenderness shared by these people. The word "chroma" refers to a pure color, suggesting the subtle but distinctly rendered portrayals of the four major characters. Like many of Barthelme's stories, "Chroma" is written in the present tense; in this instance, the effect is to magnify the inherent perplexities of time. Early in the story, Juliet and the narrator have a late breakfast in a section of town that has been subject to urban renewal. After rejecting many of the restaurants, they choose an old restaurant which also has its faults, but it has "been there for thirty years, so all the things wrong with it are deeply wrong." Age confers authenticity over fashion. The narrator worries over saying things to Juliet that will be true in the present moment but will seem false at a later time. The notion that the passing of events reconfigures, even mitigates, their original importance becomes clear when Juliet plays Nat King Cole on a tape—not the original record, Barthelme notes—and the narrator suddenly remembers what it was like to hear the music for the first time decades earlier. To the narrator, people float along the surface of time without truly living within it, a condition that undermines communication and self-knowledge. Alicia's remarks when the narrator queries her on a seemingly meaningful gesture—"If I thought something I only thought it for a second and I don't remember what it was, so leave me alone"—typify the isolation and bewilderment caused by temporal experience. If the couple's relationship is erratic, it provides the narrator with a complex understanding of time.

OTHER MAJOR WORKS

LONG FICTION: *War and War*, 1971; *Second Marriage*, 1984; *Tracer*, 1985; *Two Against One*, 1988; *Natural Selection*, 1990; *The Brothers*, 1993; *Painted Desert*, 1995; *Bob the Gambler*, 1997.

NONFICTION: "On Being Wrong: Convicted Minimalist Spills Bean," 1988; *Double Down: Reflections on Gambling and Loss*, 1999 (with Barthelme Barthelme).

BIBLIOGRAPHY

Brinkmeyer, Robert H., Jr. "Suburban Culture, Imaginative Wonder: The Fiction of Frederick Barthelme." *Studies in the Literary Imagination* 27 (Fall, 1994). Discusses Barthelme's fiction in terms of the southern tradition and its examination of place. Ties Barthelme's evocation of suburban mystery to the grotesque, concluding that Barthelme's fiction celebrates wonder.

Peters, Timothy. "The Eighties Pastoral: Frederick Barthelme's *Moon Deluxe* Ten Years On." *Studies in Short Fiction* 31 (Spring, 1994): 175-195. Begins by comparing Vladimir Nabokov's *Lolita* (1955) to Barthelme's fiction. Engages critics who disparage Barthelme's writing by arguing that it confronts the dreamscape of contemporary suburban America.

Michael Trussler

RICK BASS

Born: Fort Worth, Texas; March 7, 1958

PRINCIPAL SHORT FICTION
The Watch, 1989
Platte River, 1994
In the Loyal Mountains, 1995
The Sky, the Stars, the Wilderness, 1997

OTHER LITERARY FORMS

Rick Bass's first two collections of essays, *The Deer Pasture* (1985) and *Wild to the Heart* (1987), revealed both his active concerns as an environmentalist and his passion for hunting and fishing. Bass's 1989 book, *Oil Notes*, revealed his wealth of specialized knowledge as a petroleum geologist. He is also the author of a novel, *Where the Sea Used to Be* (1998).

ACHIEVEMENTS

Many of Rick Bass's short stories have been selected for the annual *The Best American Short Stories*, the O. Henry Award, and the Pushcart Prize. In 1987 he received the General Electric Younger Writers Award, and in 1988 he was awarded a PEN/ Nelson Algren Award special citation.

BIOGRAPHY

Rick Bass was born in Fort Worth, Texas, on March 7, 1958. While growing up in south Texas, he often went deer hunting with his grandfather. While on these hunting trips his grandfather told him stories about his family. Those stories and Bass's personal experiences on the hunting trips formed the basis of Bass's first book, *The Deer Pasture* (1985), and many of his subsequent works. In 1976 he enrolled at Utah State University and in 1979, following in his father's footsteps, received a degree in geology. After college he took a job as a petroleum geologist in Jackson, Mississippi, and, while prospecting for oil, wrote *Oil Notes*, a journal of his work and meditations.

In 1987 Bass decided to write full time. He gave up his job as a petroleum geologist and moved to a remote ranch in Yaak, Montana, near the Canadian border. Within his first two years in Montana he had stories published in several prestigious magazines, *The Paris Review*, *The Southern Review*, *Cimarron Review*, *Antaeus*, and *The Quarterly*. In 1988, he published his first collection of short stories, *The Watch*. He has written and published several novellas, some illustrated by Elizabeth Hughes Bass (his wife), and he published his first full-length novel, *Where the Sea Used to Be*, in 1998.

ANALYSIS

Rick Bass is a writer preoccupied with the connections between the human animal and wilderness. His characters work with and against the wilderness in which he places them and are defined by this struggle. The physical environment in a Bass story is as alive and intricate as any of the human characters. He is a minimalist whose narrators are usually first-person, rarely named, and seem often to have inherited their fated behaviors from other family members. Many of these first-person narratives have as one of their major themes the maturation of the narrator. The narrator of "In the Loyal Mountains" is greatly influenced by an uncle, a bizarre and strong-willed man, whose devotion to hunting and fishing make him sound like Bass's descriptions of his own grandfather, and by a girl from "the wrong side of the tracks," one of society's more "civilized" wildernesses. Bass's female characters, both major and minor, seem always to function as satellites of male characters, even in "The Myths of Bears," where he gives the woman a role as large as that of her male counterpart. At times this makes the women of Bass's stories seem secondary, sometimes even superfluous. Consequently, the men often seem immature or incomplete.

In his review of *The Watch*, Bass's first collection of short stories, Joseph Coates writes about other critics' use of the term "Magical Realism" in regard to Bass's stories, that quality, if it exists in his work, appears not in the kind of surreal events or atmosphere that we see in García Márquez but in the arbitrary strangeness of Bass' situations, which he somehow makes plausible.

Coates compares Bass's voice to those "particularly American" voices of Twain, Fitzgerald, and Hemingway.

"The Watch"

This title story from the book *The Watch* was reprinted in *New Stories from the South 1988*. The

Rick Bass (©Miriam Berkley)

dominant theme of the story is the power of loneliness and feelings of alienation to warp an individual's senses of reality and morality. Hollingsworth and his seventy-seven-year-old father Buzbee are the only inhabitants of a town most of whose inhabitants were killed long ago. Because Buzbee is only fourteen years older than his son, their relationship has, at times, been more like that of brothers. When Buzbee runs off to the swamps and establishes a commune with women from a local town who have been abused

by husbands and lovers, Jesse, an aging cyclist who can never quite keep up with the pack that daily rides past Hollingsworth's general store, stops to drink his usual half a Coke and offers to help catch Buzbee for the thousand-dollar reward Hollingsworth has posted. When they catch Buzbee, Hollingsworth chains him to the store porch. The great irony here is that Hollingsworth risks life and limb to bring his father back so he will have someone to talk to, but Buzbee grieves like a caged animal and refuses to talk or listen. Jesse, who became fat and out of shape during the hunt, buys a new bike and goes into intensive training to keep up with the pack of cyclists who pass by Hollingsworth without ever stopping or speaking.

"In the Loyal Mountains"

This title story from the book *In the Loyal Mountains* was reprinted in *New Stories from the South 1991*. The first-person narrator, a man born with one leg noticeably shorter than the other, tells the story of how he was raised by his father, a minor professional golfer, and his mother, a housewife who often traveled with her husband. Whenever they traveled the boy stayed with his uncle Zorey and, for one summer, with a girl "from the wrong side of the tracks" named Spanda, who was the boy's companion, lover, and the only one he ever knew who was "attracted" to his shorter leg. Most of the story concentrates on the adventures the boy experienced that one summer in the Loyal Mountains with his uncle Zorey, a very rich and eccentric man who had a passion for eating wild game and fish that he had killed himself, and with Spanda, his first lover but a person he never believed did or could love him. In his adult life he seems to have lost his adoration for Zorey; he refers to him as a crook. When his three-year-old son becomes moody and distant or has temper tantrums, he fears that the boy may be destined to become like Zorey. His greatest fear seems to be that everyone is helplessly fated to become what they become.

"Fires"

"Fires" appears in *In the Loyal Mountains* and was reprinted in *The Best American Short Stories 1996*. As in most of Bass's stories, two of the driving themes of this story are isolation and the fear of being trapped. An unusual element of this story is that the protagonist's fear is not of being trapped; he is afraid of being a trapper, of somehow emotionally holding someone against his or her will: "I haven't lived with a woman for a long time. Whenever one does move in with me, it feels as if I've tricked her, caught her in a trap, as if the gate has been closed behind her. . . ." This fear has become so strong that when Glenda, a competitive runner, comes to the remote area where the protagonist lives for high-altitude training, he fails to recognize her offerings of love. In a final act of seeming madness, she starts a grass fire, and they have to take refuge together in a pond. When the heat of the burning world around them becomes so hot they have to move to the center of the pond and keep ducking under to protect their faces, she tries to make her feelings known: "'Please, love' Glenda was saying, and I did not understand at first that she was speaking to me. 'Please.'" At the end she runs away.

"WEJUMPKA"

"Wejumpka" won a Pushcart Prize in 1996. On a camping trip with boys his age, eight-year-old Montrose drew the name "Wejumpka" while pulling Indian names out of a wooden box. When the camping trip ended, the rest of the boys, who had also taken Indian names, went back to their real names, but Montrose liked his new name so much that he insisted from then on that everyone call him Wejumpka. When he was eleven the unnamed narrator of the story lost a game of liar's poker to Wejumpka's father, Vern, and thus became Wejumpka's godfather. Vern and the narrator decided that before entering junior high school, Wejumpka had to change his name. From a wooden bowl he drew the name Vern, Jr. His behavior is unusual for a boy his age. His first response to people is to grab and hug them, a habit he is forced to break while in junior high school, and in the final scene of the story he demonstrates a remarkable ability to endure physical stress. There is virtually no plot to this story. It is a character study and a gentle reminder that fate can be the quirkiest of characters.

"THE MYTHS OF BEARS"

An O. Henry Award winner in 1998, "The Myths of Bears" is a wild and gruesome story of escape,

pursuit, freedom, and survival. Trapper, a hunter of virtually anything with fur, has been going through some dramatic changes. At night "he imagines that he is a wolf, and that the other wolves in his pack have suddenly turned against him . . . he's roused in bed to snarl and snap at everything in sight." His wife Judith, a six-foot-tall woman with curved feet so large she does not need snowshoes, becomes so afraid of him that she breaks through a window of their cabin and flees into the night during a blizzard. Trapper feels "Betrayed; abandoned. He'd thought she was tame. He'd not understood she was the wildest, most fluttering thing in the woods." It takes him almost a year to track her, trap her, and bring her back. Judith often thinks of allowing him to catch her. She misses his attentions, but her view of their relationship has changed. "It is not that he is a bad man, or that I am a bad woman, she thought. It's just that he is a predator, and I am prey." Both characters evolve as products of the wilderness in which this story is set.

OTHER MAJOR WORKS

LONG FICTION: *Fiber*, 1998; *Where the Sea Used to Be*, 1998.

NONFICTION: *The Deer Pasture*, 1985; *Wild to the Heart*, 1987; *Oil Notes*, 1989; *Winter: Notes from Montana*, 1991; *The Ninemile Wolves: An Essay*, 1992; *The Lost Grizzlies: A Search for Survivors*, 1995; *The Book of Yaak*, 1996; *The New Wolves*, 1998; *Brown Dog of the Yaak*, 1999; *Colter: The True Story of the Best Dog I Ever Had*, 2000.

BIBLIOGRAPHY

Bass, Rick. "Rick Bass: Lessons from the Wilderness." Interview by David Long. *Publishers Weekly* 242 (June 26, 1995): 82-83. Discussion of Bass's daily writing schedule, how he began writing while working as a geologist, and his passion for the environment.

Dixon, Terrell F. *American Nature Writers* 1. New York: Charles Scribner's Sons, 1996. A lengthy discussion of Bass's love of nature and the wilderness essays of *Wild to the Heart*. Emphasizes the importance of natural settings in his writing and includes some biographical information.

Gorra, Michael. "Outside: Rick Bass's Novellas Offer Meticulous Observations of the Natural World." *The New York Times* (December 14, 1997; July 20, 1999). In this review of the three novellas in Bass's *The Sky, the Stars, the Wilderness*, Gorra praises Bass for his ability to bring the wilderness alive, to pin it to the page for all to experience. He explains why he thinks the first two novellas, *The Myths of Bears* and *Where the Sea Used to Be*, are

not as successful as the final novella, *The Sky, the Stars, the Wilderness*.

Johnson, Anne Janette. "Rick Bass." *Contemporary Authors* (July 20, 1999). Contains basic biographical information, a list of books by the author, a list of anthologies in which some of his works have appeared, and a list of articles in periodicals, most of which are book reviews.

Edmund August

H. E. BATES

Born: Rushden, England; May 16, 1905
Died: Canterbury, England; January 29, 1974

PRINCIPAL SHORT FICTION
The Seekers, 1926
Day's End and Other Stories, 1928
Seven Tales and Alexander, 1929
The Black Boxer: Tales, 1932
Thirty Tales, 1934
The Woman Who Had Imagination and Other Stories, 1934
Cut and Come Again: Fourteen Stories, 1935
Something Short and Sweet: Stories, 1937
Country Tales: Collected Short Stories, 1938
The Flying Goat: Stories, 1939
My Uncle Silas: Stories, 1939
The Beauty of the Dead and Other Stories, 1940
The Greatest People in the World and Other Stories, 1942
How Sleep the Brave and Other Stories, 1943
The Bride Comes to Evensford and Other Tales, 1943
Dear Life, 1949
Colonel Julian and Other Stories, 1951
The Daffodil Sky, 1955
The Sleepless Moon, 1956
Death of a Huntsman: Four Short Novels, 1957
   (U.S. edition, *Summer in Salandar*, 1957)
Sugar for the Horse, 1957

The Watercress Girl and Other Stories, 1959
An Aspidistra in Babylon: Four Novellas, 1960
   (U.S. edition, *The Grapes of Paradise*, 1960)
The Golden Oriole: Five Novellas, 1961
Now Sleeps the Crimson Petal and Other Stories, 1961 (U.S. edition, *The Enchantress and Other Stories*, 1961)
Seven by Five: Stories, 1926-1961, 1963 (U.S. edition, *The Best of H. E. Bates*, 1963)
The Fabulous Mrs. V., 1964
The Wedding Party, 1965
The Four Beauties, 1968
The Wild Cherry Tree, 1968
The Good Corn and Other Stories, 1974
The Yellow Meads of Asphodel, 1976

OTHER LITERARY FORMS

H. E. Bates's major literary achievements are, without much question, his short stories. He was also a successful and prolific novelist; among his best and most representative work in this form are *The Two Sisters* (1926), *The Poacher* (1935), *Fair Stood the Wind for France* (1944), *The Purple Plain* (1947), *Love for Lydia* (1952), and *The Darling Buds of May* (1958). Other works include several juveniles; books of verse; *The Modern Short Story: A Critical Survey* (1941); and a three-volume autobiography: *The Vanished World* (1969), *The Blossoming World* (1971), and *The World in Ripeness* (1972).

ACHIEVEMENTS

H. E. Bates's creative output was prodigious—approximately a book a year for almost a half century. In spite of this formidable productivity, Bates from the beginning was a demanding taskmaster who held himself accountable to a high standard. Inevitably, there is a temptation to think that any writer as prolific as Bates cannot match the quality with the quantity of his work. The temptation is misleading, however, and its conclusion is erroneous. There are, indeed, misses and near-misses among his hundreds of collected stories. Yet, in spite of his amazing productivity, Bates was from first to last a dedicated craftsman and a keen observer of the human condition.

BIOGRAPHY

Herbert Ernest Bates was born and reared in what he later described as the "serene pastures" of the Nene Valley in the Northamptonshire village of Rushden, which later furnished subject, setting, and themes for much of his fiction. From a workingclass family, he grew up in a period of transition, often mirrored in his stories, in which one finds the contrast between rural and urban values, the individual up against the dehumanizing influence of the factory, and industrial blight clashing with the natural beauty of the Midlands. He entered school in Rushden when he was four; in a few years, he was "voraciously reading" the works of Arthur Conan Doyle and Edgar Wallace, unconsciously assimilating methods and techniques that, later, emerged as "guiding principle[s] when . . . [he] began to handle the short story." After failing an examination for a fellowship to a private school, Bates entered the grammar school at nearby Kettering, where his "solitary ambition . . . was to become a painter." Subsequently praised by one of his teachers, he "suddenly knew," he wrote years later, that he "was or was going to be, a writer."

After leaving school before his seventeenth birthday, Bates worked briefly for a newspaper (which he hated), became a competent amateur athlete between jobs, labored in a warehouse, and subsequently "discovered" Stephen Crane, the first of a group of "cho-

H. E. Bates (AP/Wide World Photos)

sen idols" which included Ivan Turgenev, Anton Chekhov, Guy de Maupassant, and Joseph Conrad. It was to Crane, Bates said years later, that "I really owe my first conscious hunger to begin writing."

The Two Sisters, his first novel, for the most part written at the warehouse, was published when Bates was twenty; his second collection of short stories, *Day's End and Other Stories*, was published two years later; he married Marjorie Helen Cox in 1931 and subsequently moved to Little Chart, in the green and golden meadowlands of Kent (where he and his wife would live until Bates's final illness and death in Canterbury). The next few years were among the most productive—and significant—of Bates's career. In addition to several novels, he published eight collections of short fiction in the 1930's, rounding out the decade with two radically different collections: *My Uncle Silas*, which includes fourteen brisk tales centering on a robust ninety-three-year-old rascal based on the author's recollections of his great-uncle, and *The Flying Goat*, the least impressive of Bates's early collections.

In the summer of 1941, Bates received a commission as a writer in the Royal Air Force; out of this grew two small collections, as much reportage as fiction, published under the pseudonym of Flying Officer "X." These pieces mark a turning point in Bates's career and were immediately popular in England, a popularity that became international with *Fair Stood the Wind for France*, an American Book-of-the-Month Club selection, and *The Purple Plain*, the first of his novels to be made into a motion picture. For various reasons, Bates then virtually abandoned the short story for several years but returned with *Colonel Julian and Other Stories* in 1951. He vowed that he would "never, never write another novel" (a vow, incidentally, soon forgotten) and returned in 1955 to his "first love, the short story" with *The Daffodil Sky*, an impressive collection and apparently the one which Bates valued the most. *The Watercress Girl and Other Stories*, thirteen stories concerned primarily with children, or with an adult's recollections of childhood experiences, contains half a dozen or more stories that are among his best work. His remaining collections—including *Now Sleeps the Crimson Petal and Other Stories*, *The Wedding Party*, *The Wild Cherry Tree*, and the posthumous *The Yellow Meads of Asphodel*—added relatively little to his by then established reputation as one of the major twentieth century writers of short fiction.

Following the success of the first of the Larkin family series, Bates devoted more and more of his energy to the novel. Though he occasionally returned to stories of rural and village life and would resurrect Uncle Silas from time to time, these later collections are for the most part less important than those of his earlier years. He was made Commander of the British Empire shortly before his death in Canterbury on January 29, 1974.

ANALYSIS

H. E. Bates's relatively few unsuccessful stories (in which Angus Wilson finds "some sense of sentimentality . . . that spoils what would otherwise be perfection") are animated by Bates's unwavering sense of wonderment in life, his feeling for the beauty in nature, and his insatiable appetite for pondering and re-creating the variety and richness of the human experience. Before Bates's second collection, *Day's End and Other Stories*, what E. M. Forster called the battle against the "tyranny of plot" had already been won by pioneers from Chekhov, Maupassant, and Crane to James Joyce, A. E. Coppard, Katherine Mansfield, and Sherwood Anderson. Bates admired Chekhov for freeing the short story from the nineteenth century sin of wordiness, for his simplicity, and for implying rather than commenting; he had learned, too, from what he called Crane's "sharp and dominant" lyricism, his "painterly quality," and his depicting of life not in "wooly, grand, or 'literary' prose, but in pictures." Perhaps the most important influences on Bates's early short fiction, however, were his conversations with Coppard on the relationship between film and the short story: "I want to see it," Coppard had insisted. "I must see it."

This is not to suggest that the works in *Day's End and Other Stories* are essentially derivative or imitative. Bates was already finding his own narrative voice, his own subject matter, and his own methods; his major concerns were with character, mood, and the evocation of a sense of time and place. He was to insist later, "I never had the slightest interest in plots . . . the idea of plot is completely foreign to my conception of the short story."

DAY'S END AND OTHER STORIES

Most of the twenty-five stories in *Day's End and Other Stories* are set in the English Midlands that Bates knew so intimately; all but five or six are concerned with simple country folk, offering highly concentrated glimpses into the lives of his characters—single-episode sketches illuminated by muted revelations not unlike those of Joyce's *Dubliners* (1914). The world of *Day's End and Other Stories* is one in which a Creator—benign or malevolent—has no place; no divinity shapes his people's lives. Spiritual poverty, frustration, and isolation are as much a part of one's destiny as are their opposites, just as cold and rain, drought and decay, are as much a part of Nature as their opposites. The collection's stories are short and simple annals of the poor, the lonely, and the unfulfilled. Yet almost without exception, the pictorial and lyric quality of the collection is remarkable, as a distinguished fiction writer was to comment a quarter of a century later: "In lucid, effortless prose, Bates can write for the fiftieth time of a field in summer as though he had never seen a field before."

Throughout his long and productive career, Bates would explore other fields, utilize more traditional storytelling techniques and methods, and find more melodramatic or exotic settings. At the same time, he would continue to examine, recall, and write about the particular part of England that is the world of most of the collection's stories.

THE BLACK BOXER

The title story of *The Black Boxer*, the first of Bates's collections published after his marriage, is interesting, particularly because of its atypical subject matter. The main character is an American black twenty years older than the local favorite he knocks out at a match at a county fairground. "The Hessian Prisoner," perhaps the best as well as the best known of the collection's stories, is similarly unusual, centering as it does on the death of a young German prisoner of war and the English couple in whose farm the prisoner is interned. More characteristic are "The Mower" and "A Flower Piece," the first depicting a conflict between a farmer and his hired man, a competition reverberating with the farmer's wife's repressed sexual attraction for her husband's worker, the second being a delicious little parody of genteel, middle-class mores. Such contrasts, so characteristic of Bates's early fiction, become more sharply defined in *The Woman Who Had Imagination and Other Stories*. "Sally Go Round the Moon" and "The Story Without an End," for example, are dark depictions of loneliness, lovelessness, and decadence; after such excursions into the depths, the quiet good humor of a brief sketch such as "Time" comes as a welcome relief, as does "The Lily," another sketch introducing Uncle Silas, who would become Bates's most popular character.

SOMETHING SHORT AND SWEET

Something Short and Sweet is the darkest and perhaps the finest of Bates's prewar collections. In "Cloudburst," Bates examines a farm couple's futile efforts to save their barley crop from a devastating storm; the story is powerful and unerring in its specificity. At the other extreme are several stories involving grotesques who would be at home in the worlds of Flannery O'Connor or James Purdy. The most memorable of these include "Purchase's Living Wonders," a fablelike account of a midget; "The Palace," a study of loneliness, frustration, and isolation set in The Palace, a London landmark converted into an internment camp for Austrian and German prisoners during World War I; and "Breeze Anstey," possibly the best story in the collection, a memorable depiction of lesbianism.

MY UNCLE SILAS *and* THE FLYING GOAT

Though published in the same years, *My Uncle Silas* and *The Flying Goat* are completely unrelated. The first contains fourteen brisk tales, narrative sketches, and reminiscences centering on a robust ninety-three-year-old based on Bates's recollections of a relative. The result is a pleasing, unpretentious, happy book, far removed in subject matter and tone from many of Bates's brooding stories of the 1930's. The sketches have about them the flavor and gusto of the oral tradition of folktales ranging from the fabliaux of the Middle Ages to A. B. Longstreet's *Georgia Scenes, Characters, Incidents, Etc. in the First Half Century of the Republic* (1835) and Mark Twain's frontier tales. Uncle Silas, called "reprobate, rapscallion, crafty as a monkey, liar, gardener of much cunning, drinker of infinite capacity," is one of Bates's most memorable characters. *The Flying Goat*, on the other hand, is the least important of Bates's prewar collections; apparently fully aware of its limitations, he included only one of its stories, "The Ox," in *Seven by Five*, the first important anthology of his short fiction. "I have rarely enjoyed writing as I did in . . . [that] decade," he would recall in *The World in Ripeness*, "when I produced half a dozen volumes of short stories."

COLONEL JULIAN AND OTHER STORIES

More varied in setting than its predecessors—four of the fifteen stories take place outside England—and in one way or another concerned with the war and its aftermath, *Colonel Julian and Other Stories* is a memorable and disturbing collection. Soldier or civilian, young or old, male or female, most of the characters in *Colonel Julian and Other Stories* have reached the end of their rope in one way or another, because of the war, fatigue or disappointment, or some congenital inability to confront life on its terms rather than on their own. With the exception of two genuinely humorous Uncle Silas stories, *Colonel Julian and Other Stories* constitutes a kind of postwar anatomy of loneliness and despair. Some characters, such as the masculine protagonist of "A Girl Named Peter," are denied love because of physical or emotional traits over which they can exercise little or no control. Some, such as the lovers of "The Lighthouse," are frustrated by custom, tradition, or contemporary mores, others by fear or the sheer perversity of things as they are. Still others, like the protagonist of "The Frontier,"

> . . . had been travelling up and down there, in the same way, for twenty years. . . . He had learned, very early, that in the East time . . . does not matter; that it is better not to get excited; that what does not happen today will happen tomorrow and that death, it is very probable, will come between. His chief concern was not to shout, not to worry, not to get excited, but to grow and manufacture a tolerably excellent grade of tea.

All of Bates's people are similarly far from heroic. There is a sixtyish major with three different pairs of false teeth and a shrewish wife, a naïve farmer who finds only temporary relief by way of the agony columns, and a sensitive young woman badgered beyond endurance in a world of philistines. They are not ignoble, however, and long after their fate has been settled, they tend to linger disturbingly in the reader's mind.

Less dramatic and a return to more familiar Bates territory and subject matter is "The Little Farm," a Midlands story depicting the dismal aftermath of a naïve countryman's obtaining, through a want ad, a "young lady housekeeper." Quite different in form and content is "A Christmas Story," revolving around a small-town teacher, a bashful young man, and the local Babbitts. Effectively low-key and unassuming, this depiction of one person's life of quiet desperation is unforgettable.

THE DAFFODIL SKY *and* THE WATERCRESS GIRL AND OTHER STORIES

The Daffodil Sky and *The Watercress Girl and Other Stories* are others of Bates's finest collections. The first is impressive in its variety: The protagonist of the title piece is a young Midlands countryman who begins to live only after a chance encounter with a lusty Lawrentian woman "full of the uncanny instinct of the blood"; not an ungentle man, he reacts with his blood, not his reason, and as the violent climax of the story-within-the-story indicates, the blood can save or destroy with equal indifference. In a very different mood, "The Good Corn," depicting the tensions between a Midlands farmer and his wife, has an unmistakable ring of authenticity and does not suffer by comparison with the best of D. H. Lawrence; there is an especially marvelous final scene reminiscent of the ritualistic baptism-by-sunlight episode of *Sons and Lovers* (1913). Best of all, perhaps, is the quiet, poignant creation of mood and characters of "The Maker of Coffins," which depicts a single episode in the life of a no-longer-young man who in his childhood had aspired to be a violinist. Without a single false note, the story ends as quietly and effectively as the young man's music, "like the sounds of pigeons' voices echoing each other far away in summer trees, and in the sound . . . was . . . love."

Unique among Bates's collections, the thirteen stories of *The Watercress Girl and Other Stories* are concerned primarily with children or with an adult's recollection of childhood; it contains several classic Bates stories. "The Cowslip Field," for example, is characteristic, representing a few moments in the lives of a young boy and Pacey, a small, eccentric woman. As in many of Bates's single-scene stories, nothing dramatic occurs externally, child and adult wander through the flowering countryside and pick flowers; the boy makes a small chain of blossoms; Pacey lets down her long hair. The boy places the blossoms on Pacey's forehead, and he suddenly, unthinking, removes her glasses. Before him stands a "strange transformed woman he does not know." There, the story ends, after a moment of grace and happiness before what the reader knows will be a harsh future. The story is a small masterwork, alive and joyous but poignant in the reader's awareness that the magic and beauty of the moment are ephemeral.

As already noted, Bates's remaining collections—*Now Sleeps the Crimson Petal and Other Stories, The Wedding Party, The Wild Cherry Tree,* and *The Yellow Meads of Asphodel*—do relatively little to add to his reputation as one of the major twentieth century writers of short fiction. Following the success of the first of the Larkin family series—*The Darling Buds of May* and *A Breath of French Air* (1959)—Bates tended to devote more and more of his energies to the novel. Though he occasionally returned to the nostalgic re-creation of rural and village life and would resurrect Uncle Silas from time to time, his later collections tend to vary more widely, both in subject matter and in quality, than their predecessors. Yet Bates never lost his enthusiasm for the short story. Relatively early in his career, in the preface to the first important anthology of his short fiction, he had written: "The best I can hope is that [the reader] will read these stories with something of the spirit in which they were written: for pleasure and out of a passionate interest in human lives." That "pleasure" and "passionate interest" animated Bates's short fiction from his first collection to his last.

OTHER MAJOR WORKS

LONG FICTION: *The Two Sisters,* 1926; *Catherine Foster,* 1929; *Charlotte's Row,* 1931; *The Fallow Land,* 1932; *The Poacher,* 1935; *A House of Women,* 1936; *Spella Ho,* 1938; *Fair Stood the Wind for France,* 1944; *The Cruise of the Breadwinner,* 1946; *The Purple Plain,* 1947; *The Jacaranda Tree,* 1949; *The Scarlet Sword,* 1950; *Love for Lydia,* 1952; *The Nature of Love: Three Short Novels,* 1953; *The Feast of July,* 1954; *The Sleepless Moon,* 1956; *Death of a Huntsman: Four Short Novels,* 1957; *The Darling Buds of May,* 1958; *A Breath of French Air,* 1959; *An Aspidistra in Babylon: Four Novellas,* 1960; *When the Green Woods Laugh,* 1960; *The Day of the Tortoise,* 1961; *A Crown of Wild Myrtle,* 1962; *The Golden Oriole: Five Novellas,* 1962; *Oh! To Be in England,* 1963; *A Moment in Time,* 1964; *The Distant Horns of Summer,* 1967; *A Little of What You*

Fancy, 1970; *The Triple Echo,* 1970.

PLAYS: *The Last Bread,* pb. 1926; *The Day of Glory,* pb. 1945.

NONFICTION: *Through the Woods,* 1936; *Down the River,* 1937; *The Modern Short Story: A Critical Survey,* 1941; *In the Heart of the Country,* 1942; *Country Life,* 1943; *O More Than Happy Countryman,* 1943; *Edward Garnett,* 1950; *The Country of White Clover,* 1952; *The Face of England,* 1952; *The Vanished World: An Autobiography,* 1969; *The Blossoming World: An Autobiography,* 1971; *The World in Ripeness: An Autobiography,* 1972.

BIBLIOGRAPHY

Baldwin, Dean R. "Atmosphere in the Stories of H. E. Bates." *Studies in Short Fiction* 21 (Summer, 1984): 215-222. Discusses Bates's naturalistic and romantic stories, focusing on how Bates uses atmosphere; argues that Bates's stories seem simple on the surface, but deserve more attention than they have received for the subtlety of their technique.

_____. *H. E. Bates: A Literary Life.* Selinsgrove, Pa.: Susquehanna University Press, 1987. The only full-length biography of Bates and a more reliable source of information about the author than Bates's own three-volume autobiography. Contains extensive commentary on the stories.

Beachcroft, T. O. *The Modest Art: A Survey of the Short Story in English.* London: Oxford University Press, 1968. Beachcroft discusses Bates numerous times in the context of the modern English short story. Most interesting is his discussion of the author's use of Midland characters and themes.

Eads, Peter. *H. E. Bates: A Bibliographical Study.* Winchester, England: St. Paul's Bibliographies, 1990. A good collection of bibliographical material on Bates.

Frierson, William. *The English Novel in Transition, 1885-1940.* New York: Cooper Square, 1965. Frierson discusses the influence of Anton Chekhov, Thomas Hardy, and D. H. Lawrence on Bates's work and sees pessimism as the most fundamental connective thread in his fiction.

Hughes, Douglas. "The Eclipsing of V. S. Pritchett and H. E. Bates: A Representative Case of Critical Myopia." *Studies in Short Fiction* 19 (Fall, 1982): iii-v. Complains that Pritchett and Bates have been allowed to slip into oblivion by editors and critics; argues that editors and groups of professors should not presume to dictate which story writers can or cannot be written about.

Miller, Henry. Preface to *The Best of H. E. Bates*, by H. E. Bates. Boston: Little, Brown, 1963. Miller discusses Bates's use of nature imagery and themes, plus his humor and "obsession with pain."

Vannatta, Dennis. *H. E. Bates*. Boston: Twayne, 1983. Contains less biographical information than Dean R. Baldwin's book but more critical commentary. A useful bibliography of primary and secondary sources follows the text.

William Peden, updated by Dennis Vannatta

RICHARD BAUSCH

Born: Fort Benning, Georgia; April 18, 1945

PRINCIPAL SHORT FICTION

Spirits and Other Stories, 1987
The Fireman's Wife and Other Stories, 1990
Rare and Endangered Species, 1994
Aren't You Happy for Me? and Other Stories, 1995
The Selected Stories of Richard Bausch, 1996
Someone to Watch over Me: Stories, 1999

OTHER LITERARY FORMS

Richard Bausch has published several novels. *Take Me Back* (1981) was nominated for a PEN/Faulkner Award.

ACHIEVEMENTS

Richard Bausch's collection *Spirits and Other Stories* was nominated for a PEN/Faulkner Award. His stories frequently appear in *New Stories from the South: The Year's Best* and in *The Best American Short Stories* series. Bausch received a National Endowment for the Arts grant in 1982 and a John Simon Guggenheim Memorial Foundation Fellowship in 1984. In 1992, he won the Lila Wallace-*Reader's Digest* Writers Award and in 1993, an American Academy of Arts and Letters Award in Literature.

BIOGRAPHY

Richard Carl Bausch was born April 18, 1945, in Fort Benning, Georgia, and grew up in rural Virginia, outside Washington, D.C. After high school, he worked as a rock singer, songwriter, and comedian. From 1966 to 1969, he was a survival instructor in the United States Air Force. In 1969, he married Karen Miller, a photographer, and started a family. When he was twenty-five, Bausch entered George Mason University; he received his B.A. in 1974. With his wife and a new baby, he moved to Iowa, where he enrolled in the prestigious University of Iowa Writers' Workshop and in 1975 was awarded an M.F.A. When his works did not sell, Bausch began looking for a job. First he took a temporary position at George Mason University, then taught for two years at Northern Virginia Community College. Finally, he returned to George Mason, where he eventually became a full professor of English and the holder of the Heritage Chair of Creative Writing. Bausch has also been a visiting professor at the University of Virginia-Charlottesville and at Wesleyan University.

ANALYSIS

The fact that Richard Ford wrote the introduction to Richard Bausch's first British collection of short stories indicates how closely Bausch is allied to such contemporary realists as Ford, Bobbie Ann Mason, and Raymond Carver. As critic Paul Elie explains in *Commonweal* (November 9, 1990), these writers have been nicknamed the "Dirty Realists" because they write about ordinary people whose lives have taken a turn for the worse and are not likely to get any better. The fiction of the Dirty Realists is all the more poignant because the characters are perceptive enough to see how little the future holds for them.

However, Bausch's Catholicism sets him apart from the other Dirty Realists. Where they see heartbreak and despair as simply a part of life, Bausch often views them as the product of sinful human nature. Over and over again, his characters distance themselves from each other. As a result, marriages end, families disintegrate, and individuals are left alone and desolate. "Wedlock," from *The Fireman's Wife and Other Stories*, is about a relationship that dies after a day and a half. Once the new bride begins to view her husband objectively, rather than with the eyes of love, she first finds him ridiculous and then repulsive.

Some of Bausch's stories may be read as showing the operation of divine grace in human life, whether by prompting someone to plead the case for forgiveness, as Tom does in "The Brace," or by bringing people together in a new relationship, as in "The Billboard" from *Rare and Endangered Species*. Admittedly, in his short fiction Bausch seems much more certain about sin than he is about grace. However, he clearly believes that only by loving others can we make our own lives bearable.

"Aren't You Happy for Me?"

The title work in Bausch's first British collection, which previously appeared in *Rare and Endangered Species*, is one of the author's most admired short stories. "Aren't You Happy for Me?" begins with a telephone call from Melanie Ballinger in Chicago to her parents in Charlottesville, Virginia, informing them that she is pregnant and that she plans to marry the man responsible, William Coombs, who was her college literature professor. Coombs is forty years older than Melanie and, as her father John points out rather nastily, old enough to be his father, rather than

Richard Bausch (©Miriam Berkley)

his son-in-law. While Melanie is talking to her mother Mary, John realizes that if he does not pretend to accept Melanie's decision, he will lose her, and he promises Melanie that he will work on his feelings. He never does tell her his own news: that Mary and he are getting a divorce. When out of habit John turns to Mary for comfort, he discovers that he can no longer reach her. All John and Mary have left is the past; the best they can do is to remember how happy they were when Melanie was a toddler and they were as sure of their love as Melanie and William are of theirs. "Aren't You Happy for Me?" is typical of Bausch's short fiction both in its subject, the erosion of relationships, and in its bleak ending. While John may now have new insights about time, love, and loss, he is still left uncomfortable.

"Not Quite Final"

In "Not Quite Final" from *Someone to Watch over Me*, the Ballingers get another chance. Evidently Melanie has forgiven her parents for not approving of her marriage. She has even persuaded William to move to Charlottesville because, as she puts it, their baby needs to become acquainted with her grandparents. On moving day, while Mary keeps the baby, John is helping Melanie haul furniture into her new apartment. William just watches; he is too arthritic to help. When she discovers that he also forgot to get the water turned on, Melanie becomes irritated. However, she insists that she knew what William was like when she married him, and their affection toward each other is no different from that of any other newlyweds. John is trying very hard to be tactful about his son-in-law. He slips only once, when he rebukes two young telephone installers for staring at Melanie. After they leave, William makes it clear that he did not need John's aid, and John feels impelled to apologize to William. Oddly, that incident seems to bring the two men closer to an understanding. Mary also appears to soften toward John. While taking care of her granddaughter, she admits, she thinks of how much she missed her husband, and the two embrace. Thus Bausch indicates that people who care enough can transcend their differences. If divine grace truly operates in this world, it may be by inspiring them to try.

"THE BRACE"

"The Brace," from *The Fireman's Wife and Other Stories*, is narrated in the first-person by a young wife and mother. She is worried because her father, a famous playwright, is on his way to visit them, and she fears a confrontation between him and her brother James, who is staying with them. James has hated his father ever since he portrayed their mother as a useful but trivial woman in a play called "The Brace." The narrator, too, dislikes their father. Though she has spent her life trying to please him, she could never do so. He does not bother to hide his contempt for her husband Tom, a good but unsophisticated man, and their mundane life together. During this visit, however, it is the narrator who is inflexible. When her father attempts some explanation of his past conduct, she will not listen to him. Left alone, she suddenly imagines a time when her own son will treat her in the same way. She also realizes that when her father, her husband, and her brother spend the evening to-

gether, they will ignore their differences and connect in a way that excludes her. She now knows that there is no one to "brace" her, not even Tom. She is quite alone. In a *Publishers Weekly* interview that coincided with the publication of *The Fireman's Wife and Other Stories*, Bausch identified "The Brace" as his favorite story in the collection, primarily, he says, because the narrator is so brave. It is not easy to face isolation or to anticipate the loss of love.

"VALOR"

Next to compassion for others, Bausch admires courage. The protagonist of "Valor," from *Someone to Watch over Me*, has both. A middle-aged shoe salesman with a domineering wife and a parasitical brother-in-law, Gabriel Aldenburg has come to Sam's bar for a little peace and quiet. Standing by the door, Aldenburg sees a Cadillac ram into a school bus. Immediately he rushes out, gets the driver to safety, then pulls the children out of the burning bus. When he gets home, no one wants to hear his story. His wife has her own announcement to make: She is moving out. When she refuses to watch the news report, Aldenburg becomes so angry that she feels a bit frightened. Realizing that he cannot reach her, he slips back into his usual insignificance. Though Aldenburg cannot impress his family, whether or not he will now have a higher opinion of himself is left an open question. Bausch's habit of ending his stories with some issue still unresolved is evidence of his commitment to realism. Life is rarely as neat as one would like it to be.

OTHER MAJOR WORKS

LONG FICTION: *Real Presence*, 1980; *Take Me Back*, 1981; *The Last Good Time*, 1984; *Mr. Field's Daughter*, 1989; *Violence*, 1992; *Rebel Powers*, 1993; *Good Evening Mr. and Mrs. America, and All the Ships at Sea*, 1996; *In the Night Season*, 1998; *The Putt at the End of the World*, 2000 (with Lee K. Abbott, Dave Barry, Tim O'Brien, and others).

BIBLIOGRAPHY

Bausch, Richard. Interview by Dulcy Brainard. *Publishers Weekly* 237 (August 10, 1990): 425-426. The author explains why he finds the short-story genre so satisfying and expresses hope that he will soon reach a larger audience. Moral issues, he says, are central in his life and in his fiction.

Bell, Madison Smartt. "Everyday Hazards." *The New York Times Book Review* (June 14, 1987): 16. The subject of *Spirits and Other Stories* is the "hazards" of everyday life. Most of the stories end unhappily; "Spirits" is an exception.

Cahill, Thomas. "Fireworks Hidden and Deep." *Commonweal* 114 (October 9, 1987): 568-569. In this review of *Spirits and Other Stories*, it is argued that Bausch's superb style and well-drawn characters will cause him to be remembered when more fashionable writers are forgotten. His preoccupation with fatherhood and "caring" is linked to the Catholic doctrine of the Real Presence.

Desmond, John F. "Catholicism in Contemporary American Fiction." *America* 170 (May 14, 1994): 7-11. Bausch is one of a number of fine Catholic writers who, avoiding "sentimentality and easy dogmatism," show their characters facing very real evils, which they can survive only with the aid of divine grace.

Dorris, Michael. "The Drama of Ordinary Life." *The Washington Post Book World* (June 28, 1987): 6. Bausch's mastery of the short-story genre is evident throughout *Spirits and Other Stories*. The title story is discussed at length, others more briefly.

Elie, Paul. "The Way Things Are: Richard Bausch's Unadorned World." *Commonweal* 177 (November 9, 1990): 642-646. Explains how Bausch differs stylistically from the other Dirty Realists and thematically from other Catholic writers. Because his short stories differ from the novels in their emphasis on separation and loss, Bausch's work should be viewed as a whole.

O'Brien, Sean. "Drifting Westwards." *The Times Literary Supplement* (July 21, 1995): 21. A favorable review of the first British collection of Bausch's short fiction, *Aren't You Happy for Me? and Other Stories*. Analyzes the title story, "What Feels Like the World," "Design," and "To the Lady of the House."

Pesetsky, Bette. "Quarrels over Who Said What and When." *The New York Times Book Review* (August 19, 1990): 9. Insists that though Bausch's characters are often called ordinary, they are unusual in their intelligence and in their yearning for meaning. Seven of the stories in *The Fireman's Wife and Other Stories* are discussed in terms of a common theme, "redemption through understanding."

Shields, Carol. "The Life You Lead May Be Your Own." *The New York Times Book Review* (August 14, 1994): 6. Ignoring the literary fashions of the 1970's and the 1980's, Bausch has continued to write realistic domestic fiction. Again in *Rare and Endangered Species*, various relationships, including marriages, are threatened by change, betrayal, and sheer boredom, and yet his characters try valiantly to remain true to each other and to their own best selves.

Rosemary M. Canfield Reisman

CHARLES BAXTER

Born: Minneapolis, Minnesota; May 13, 1947

PRINCIPAL SHORT FICTION
Harmony of the World, 1984
Through the Safety Net, 1985
A Relative Stranger, 1990
Believers, 1997

OTHER LITERARY FORMS

Charles Baxter has written such novels as *First Light* (1987) and *Shadow Play: A Novel* (1993) and the collection of poetry *Imaginary Paintings and Other Poems* (1989). In addition, Baxter writes fine literary nonfiction, including his essays on imagination and daily life collected in *Burning Down the House: Essays on Fiction* (1997).

ACHIEVEMENTS

Editors consistently select Charles Baxter's stories for the annual *The Best American Short Stories*, *The Pushcart Prize*, and *Prize Stories: The O. Henry Awards*. He won the Associated Writing Programs Award in 1984 for his first collection of fiction and has been awarded National Endowment for the Arts and Lila Wallace-*Reader's Digest* Fund grants, as well as a John Simon Guggenheim Memorial Fellowship. His list of awards also includes a Lawrence Foundation award, Michigan Author of the Year Award, and a *Harvard Review* award.

BIOGRAPHY

Charles Morley Baxter was born in Minneapolis, Minnesota, on May 13, 1947. Baxter attended Macalester College in St. Paul, Minnesota, earning his bachelor's degree in 1969. Baxter published his first book of poetry in 1970. After teaching high school English in the small town of Pinconning, Michigan, during 1969-1970, he began graduate work at the State University of New York at Buffalo, completing a Ph.D. in 1974, the same year he published *The South Dakota Guidebook*. He returned to Michigan to teach at Wayne State University in De-

troit in 1974. In July of 1976, he married Martha Ann Hauser. At Wayne State, Baxter moved through the ranks, achieving full professorship in 1985.

In 1984, Baxter published his first collection of short stories, *Harmony of the World*, for which he received both the Associated Writing Programs Award and the Lawrence Foundation Award. The following year, he published his second collection of short stories, *Through the Safety Net*, followed by his novel *First Light* in 1987. In 1989, Baxter left Wayne State to begin teaching at the University of Michigan at Ann Arbor. He also began teaching in the Warren Wilson writing program in 1986.

During the 1990's, Baxter continued regularly to contribute literary criticism and short stories to a host of literary journals of the highest quality including *Prairie Schooner*, *Michigan Quarterly*, and *Minnesota Review*, a journal he had edited in 1967-1969. During the same decade, he published a volume of poetry, two collections of short stories (*A Relative Stranger* in 1990 and *Believers* in 1997) and a novel, *Shadow Play* (1993).

ANALYSIS

The stories in each of Charles Baxter's three collections are internally linked by theme, image, and motif. The title story in each collection suggests thematic ties to other stories in the collection. As a musician composes a symphony, building variations around an initial theme, Baxter works and reworks connecting ideas in multiple ways. While some stories seem more closely linked than others, taken as a whole, each collection says something different about the human experience.

For example, in *Harmony of the World*, a number of stories concern music, musicians, or artists. Thematically, Baxter plays with notions of harmony and discord and the way these notions play out in human relationships. Likewise, in *A Relative Stranger*, Baxter explores both the relatedness of strangers and the strangeness of relatives. In these stories he seems to tell the reader that no matter how different or far apart people are, they are nonetheless connected. Conversely, he also demonstrates in these stories that no matter how closely related people may be, they still have to live their lives alone in their skins. Finally, in *Believers*, an especially fine collection, Baxter meditates on the relationship between belief and truth. He demonstrates in these stories both how belief can change the perception of truth and how truth can impact belief.

Baxter accomplishes these sophisticated linkages through the invention of characters who are both varied and individual, rich and self-contradictory. Baxter develops these characters by offering snapshots of their lives, brief still shots revealing where each is located in the moment of the story. Like real people, they are not all one way or another; rather, they are a complicated stew of thoroughly human qualities.

HARMONY OF THE WORLD

Baxter's first collection of short stories, published in 1984, met with strong and favorable reviews. The title of the collection is ironic; the ten stories focus not on harmony but on discord and tricks of fate. The characters in the stories (many of them musicians, a further irony) fail to establish harmonious relationships with other people. Moreover, they do not realize that they are out of harmony with themselves and the culture. Although often mediocre in talent and intellect, they demand perfection in others, as if the harmony they seek can be found outside themselves. The title "Harmony of the World," for instance, is taken from an opera by composer Paul Hindemith, an opera that music critics generally consider a failure. Likewise, the main character is a music reviewer, a failed concert pianist who has settled for passing judgment on the music of others rather than on creating music himself. He breaks off a relationship with a singer because she, too, is mediocre. The story, included in *The Best American Short Stories 1982*, reveals Baxter's strong sense of character, dialogue, and detail.

A RELATIVE STRANGER

Critics often cite "Fensted's Mother" as one of Baxter's best stories. It first appeared in the *Atlantic*, and noted writer Margaret Atwood chose it for inclusion in *The Best American Short Stories 1989*. The

Charles Baxter (©Miriam Berkley)

opening story in the collection, it takes as its subject Fensted, a publicist for a computer company, and his aging mother, a socially progressive atheist. Fensted, who attends church regularly, invites his mother to attend the English composition class he teaches at night school. She is a great hit, siding with Fensted's students in a discussion of the logical inconsistency of the sentence "I, like most people, have a unique problem." Fensted wants to talk about logic; the students, egged on by his mother, want to talk about problems. Although closely related, Fensted and his mother seem unable to speak the same language. Further, in spite of their obvious love for each other, they remain relative strangers.

The title story of the collection, "A Relative Stranger," expands the theme explored in "Fensted's Mother." Baxter seems to be asking, what does it mean to be related to someone else? In this story, a middle-aged man, Oliver, suddenly discovers that he has a brother, Kurt. Although Oliver knew that he had been adopted as an infant, he did not realize that he had a sibling. Kurt chooses to contact Oliver at a time when Oliver's wife has left him and his life is a mess. Kurt, on the other hand, is a successful businessman. The meeting between the brothers does not go as planned. Although related, the two are strangers to each other. Baxter carefully reveals the odd sense of familiarity and strangeness Oliver feels. After Oliver punches Kurt in a bar, the two establish a relationship that is, while not close, brotherly. Through this story, Baxter once again demonstrates that fraternity does not guarantee compatibility. Although the two brothers struggle to understand each other, like Fensted and his mother, they speak different languages.

BELIEVERS

Baxter's 1997 collection contains seven stories and a novella and represents some of Baxter's finest work. The characters in *Believers* struggle with issues of truth and belief, and the conflict such issues often produce. The range of characters in this collection seems wider than in his earlier work, and the believers in the stories include a young woman who believes she is in love, a man who believes that his former wife waves to him to cross a flooded river, a group of friends who believe they know each other well, and a former priest who loses his belief on a trip into Nazi Germany. Although the stories in *Believers* are about faith and truth, and although the stories carry with them religious imagery and theological undertones, they do not close with epiphanies. In his book of essays on fiction, *Burning Down the House*, Baxter includes a whole chapter, "Against Epiphanies," in which he argues that too much contemporary fiction depends on the epiphanic ending. Baxter's stories do not provide characters who arrive at some important insight in the closing paragraphs. Rather, the stories end as they have grown, moving toward inevitable yet complicated and ambiguous endings, endings that seem to point to some truth hidden somewhere just under the surface.

Believers is the novella that gives the collection its name and establishes a number of important thematic concerns. Jack Pielke narrates the story, trying to piece together the fragments of his father's life in order to arrive at the truth. Issues of belief are strong in

the story. Jack's father Franz, the son of German immigrants, was a former Catholic priest, a man who believed profoundly in God and God's creation until a trip to Nazi Germany with a jaded American couple irreversibly changed him. Jack is the quintessential researcher, supplying genealogical background, interviewing everyone who knew his father, hounding his mother for details about their union. The one person who could perhaps help him the most is mute: Franz Pielke, a stroke victim, has not spoken for more than two years. Jack's struggle, then, is to give voice to his father's life. He believes a careful reconstruction of that life will reveal some sort of truth. Jack wants to understand his father, his rejection of the priesthood, his marriage to his mother, and his fatherhood. Most of all, he wants to know what happened to his father's faith and what both the gift and the loss of that faith has cost him. What Jack discovers, however, is that like all lives, his father's is more than the sum of its parts, and that all he, Jack, can render is a textual reconstruction of lived experience, not the truth at all.

OTHER MAJOR WORKS

LONG FICTION: *First Light*, 1987; *Shadow Play: A Novel*, 1993; *The Feast of Love*, 2000.

POETRY: *Chameleon*, 1970; *Imaginary Paintings and Other Poems*, 1989.

NONFICTION: *Burning Down the House: Essays on Fiction*, 1997.

BIBLIOGRAPHY

Baxter, Charles. "An Interview with Charles Baxter." Interview by Kevin Breen. *Poets and Writers* 22 (September, 1994): 60. An interview focusing on Baxter's creation of characters. Especially useful for fiction writers trying to refine their craft.

Baxter, Charles. *Burning Down the House: Essays on Fiction*. Saint Paul, Minn.: Graywolf Press, 1997. In nine essays, written with humor, insight, and care, Baxter explores the relationship between imagination and daily life, the way characters develop, and his ideas about fiction. An important collection for anyone who wants to know more about Baxter and his art.

Griffiths, Sarah, and Kevin J. Kehrwald. *Delicious Imaginations: Conversations with Contemporary Writers*. West Lafayette, Ind.: NotaBell Books, 1998. Provides a chapter-length interview with Baxter, who shares his ideas about the writing of fiction. Other chapters include interviews with such important contemporary writers as Larry Brown, Rick Bass, and Robert Olen Butler.

Van Wert, William F. "Charles Baxter and the Rites of Fiction." *Michigan Quarterly Review* 38 (Winter, 1999): 135-143. A review of *Believers* and *Burning Down the House* offering close and convincing analyses of "Flood Show," "Kiss Away," "Reincarnation," and "Saul and Patsy Are in La-bor," as well as examining some of the features of fiction Baxter explores in his book of essays.

Winans, Molly. "Bigger than We Think: The World Revealed in Charles Baxter's Fiction." *Commonweal* 124 (November 7, 1997): 12-16. Argues that Baxter's best work is his short fiction, a genre that allows him to develop interesting characters and small truths in the exploration of the ordinary. Compares Baxter to other short-story writers such as Frank O'Connor and Flannery O'Connor. Suggests that Baxter's stories can be discussed in "theological terms" including forgiveness, sin, and faith.

Diane Andrews Henningfeld

ANN BEATTIE

Born: Washington, D.C.; September 8, 1947

PRINCIPAL SHORT FICTION

Distortions, 1976
Secrets and Surprises, 1978
Jacklighting, 1981
The Burning House, 1982
Where You'll Find Me and Other Stories, 1986
What Was Mine and Other Stories, 1991
Park City: New and Selected Stories, 1998

OTHER LITERARY FORMS

While Ann Beattie's reputation rests primarily on her short stories, particularly those that first appeared in *The New Yorker*, she has also written several novels. The first, *Chilly Scenes of Winter* (1976), appeared simultaneously with *Distortions*, a rare occurrence in the publishing world, especially for a first-time author. Her second novel, *Falling in Place* (1980), is her most ambitious and her best. In *Love Always* (1985), she uses an approach that is closer to that of her short stories than in either of the previous novels. The subject matter is narrower, and the characters are more distanced from the narrative voice.

Her novel *Picturing Will* was published in 1989. In 1986 and 1987, she worked on her first nonfiction project, the text to accompany a monograph containing twenty-six color plates of the paintings of Alex Katz. Her last novel, *My Life, Starring Dara Falcon* (1997), has been scorned as her weakest yet; *The New York Times* called it an "ill-conceived experiment" that "must surely mark a low point" in her career.

ACHIEVEMENTS

Ann Beattie has been called the most imitated short-story writer in the United States, an amazing claim for a woman whose publishing career began in the early 1970's. Along with such writers as Raymond Carver, she is a premier practitioner of minimalism, the school of fiction-writing that John Barth has characterized as the "less is more" school. In 1977, she was named Briggs-Copeland Lecturer in English at Harvard, where she was apparently uncomfortable. She used a John Simon Guggenheim Memorial Foundation grant to leave Harvard and move back to Connecticut, where she had attended graduate school. In 1980, she received an award of excellence from the American Academy of Arts and

Letters and a Distinguished Alumnae award from American University. In 1992, she was elected to the American Academy and Institute of Arts and Letters.

BIOGRAPHY

Born on September 8, 1947, Ann Beattie grew up with television, rock music, and all the other accouterments of the baby boomers. The child of a retired Health, Education, and Welfare Department administrator, Beattie took a B.A. in English at American University in 1969 and completed her M.A. at the

Ann Beattie (Benjamin Ford)

University of Connecticut in 1970. She began, but did not complete, work on her Ph.D. In 1972 she was married to, and was later divorced from, David Gates, a writer for *Newsweek* and a singer. Together they had one son. Before her appointment at Harvard, Beattie taught at the University of Virginia in Charlottesville. After living in the Connecticut suburbs and in New York City, she returned to Charlottesville and the university in 1985. She appeared as a waitress in the film version of *Chilly Scenes of Winter* and, after her di-

vorce, was named one of the most eligible single women in America. In 1985, Beattie met painter Lincoln Perry, whom she later married. The couple lived for a time in Charlottesville. Later, Beattie and Perry settled in a turn-of-the-century farmhouse in York, Maine, one of America's oldest cities. Beattie says she does not go to book-publishing parties, does not know many writers, has an unlisted phone number, and shies away from writers' colonies.

ANALYSIS

Ann Beattie has been called the spokesperson for a new lost generation, a sort of Ernest Hemingway for those who came of age during the 1960's and 1970's. Many of her themes and much about her style support the assertion that she, like Hemingway, voices a pervasive and universal feeling of despair and alienation, a lament for lost values and lost chances for constructive action. Yet to limit one's understanding of Beattie's work to this narrow interpretation is a mistake.

Beattie shares much with writers such as Jane Austen, who ironically portrayed the manners and social customs of her era, and with psychological realists such as Henry James, who delved into the meanings behind the subtle nuances of character and conflict. Her primary themes are loneliness and friendship, family life, love and death, materialism, art, and, for want of a better term, the contemporary scene. Her short fiction tends to be spare and straightforward. Her vocabulary and her sentence structure are quite accessible, or minimalist, to use a more literary label. Even when the stories contain symbols, their use is most often direct and self-reflexive.

Her combination of subject matter and style leads to a rather flat rendering of the world, and Beattie is sometimes criticized for that flatness. Because her narrators usually maintain a significant distance from the stories and their characters, critics and readers sometimes assume that Beattie is advocating such remove and reserve as the most feasible posture in contemporary life. Even her most ironic characters and narrative voices, however, experience a profound longing for a different world. Despite the ennui that dominates the texture of their lives, Beattie's characters hold on to the hope of renewal and redemption, often with great fierceness, even though the fierceness frequently suggests that these people are clutching at hope so hard that they are white-knuckling their way through life. If members of the generation about which she writes are indeed lost, they have not accepted their condition, even though they recognize it. They are still searching for the way out, for a place in which to find themselves or to be found.

"DWARF HOUSE"

"Dwarf House," the first story in *Distortions*, establishes an interest in the grotesque, the bizarre, and the slightly askew that surfaces several times in this first of Beattie's collections. The main characters of the story are James and MacDonald, brothers who struggle to find understanding and respect for each other and to deal with their possessive and intrusive mother. Because James, the older of the two, is a dwarf, Beattie immediately plays upon the collection's title and places the story beyond the plane of realism.

The irony of the story develops as the reader realizes that MacDonald's supposedly normal life is as distorted as the life of his sibling. When MacDonald goes to visit James in the dwarf house where he lives, along with several other dwarfs and one giant, he finds himself repulsed by the foreign environment. Yet, when he gets home, he cannot face his own "normal" world without his martinis. He is as alienated and isolated at home and at work as he would be if he were a dwarf. Beattie uses the ludicrous, the exaggerated scenario of James's life, complete with his wedding to a fellow dwarf, conducted by a hippie minister and culminating in the releasing of a caged parrot as a symbol of hope and the new freedom of married life, to bring into focus the less obvious distortions of regular American life.

MacDonald is typical of many Beattie characters. He is relatively young—in his late twenties—and well educated. He works, but his work provides little challenge or stimulation. He has enough money to live as he wants, but he struggles to define what it is he does want. His wife is his equal—young, well educated, hip—but they have less than nothing to talk about.

MacDonald wants to make his brother's life more normal—that is, get him out of the dwarf house, the one place where James has ever been happy, and back into their mother's home, where James and MacDonald will both be miserable. MacDonald is motivated not by malice toward James but by an overdeveloped sense of guilt and responsibility toward his mother, a trait he shares with many of Beattie's young male characters. By the story's end, the reader cannot say who is better off: James, whose life is distorted but productive and satisfying to him, or MacDonald, who has everything a man could want but still lacks an understanding of what it is he should do with what he has.

"THE LIFEGUARD"

In "The Lifeguard," the final story in *Distortions*, Beattie portrays the offbeat and grotesque elements that permeate the collection in a sharply realistic setting, where their humor and irony disappear. The impact of these elements is, then, all the more forceful for the reader's sense of sudden dislocation. Without warning, the book becomes too real for comfort, and at the same time it continues to use shades of the unreal to make its point.

"The Lifeguard" tells the story of the Warner family and their summer vacation. The mother, Toby, finds herself fantasizing about the young college student who is the lifeguard on the beach. Yet when her children Penelope and Andrew die in a boat deliberately set afire by their playmate Duncan Collins, the inappropriateness and incapacity of the lifeguard and of her infatuation are too vividly brought home to Toby. The monstrousness of Duncan Collins's action is but another kind of distortion; there are no simple lives in a distorted world.

"A VINTAGE THUNDERBIRD"

If *Distortions* emphasizes the outward manifestations of the disordered contemporary world, *Secrets and Surprises*, the second collection, turns inward, as its title suggests. "A Vintage Thunderbird" features a woman who comes to New York to have an abortion against the wishes of her husband. The friends to whom she turns, Karen and Nick, have their own problems in love. By mirroring the sense of loss that follows the abortion with the sense of loss felt by Ka-

ren and Nick when she sells the vintage car of the title, Beattie addresses the connection between spiritual and emotional needs and material needs.

Very few of the people in Beattie's fiction suffer
for want of material goods; almost all suffer from
lack of spiritual and emotional fulfillment. The interesting aspect of this dichotomy is that the characters
do not, as a rule, actively pursue material well-being.
Their money is often inherited, as are their houses
and many of their other possessions. The main character in "Shifting," for example, inherits an old Volvo
from an uncle to whom she was never very close. The
money earned by these characters is almost always
earned halfheartedly, without conspicuous ambition
or enthusiasm. These are not yuppies, who have sub-
stituted acquisition for all human emotion; they are
people who, by accident of birth or circumstance,
have not had to acquire material wealth; for whatever
reason, wealth comes to them.

What does not come is peace, satisfaction, and
contentment. When a material object does provide
emotional pleasure, as the Thunderbird does for Karen and Nick, Beattie's characters tend to confuse the
emotion with the symbol and to conclude, errone-
ously, that ridding themselves of the object will also
rid them of the gnawing doubts that seem to accompany contentment and satisfaction. It is sometimes as
frightening, Beattie seems to suggest, to be attached
to things as to people.

"THE CINDERELLA WALTZ"

In *The Burning House*, Beattie's third collection,
she turns to the darker, more richly textured veins of
her standard subject matter to produce stories that are
less humorous but more humane, less ironic but wiser
than those in the earlier collections. Infidelity, divorce,
love gone bad—all standard Beattie themes—are connected to parenthood and its attendant responsibilities, to homosexuality, to death, and to birth defects.
The affairs and the abortions that were entered into, if
not concluded, with a "me-generation" bravado suddenly collide with more traditional values and goals.

Many of Beattie's characters, both married and
single, have lovers. In fact, having a lover or having
had one at some time during a marriage is almost
standard. In "The Cinderella Waltz," Beattie adds a

further complication to the de rigueur extra-marital
affair by making the husband's lover a male. Yet, in
much the same way that she makes the unusual work
in a story such as "Dwarf House," Beattie manages to
make this story more about the pain and suffering of
the people involved than about the nontraditional
quality of the love relationship.

The wife in "The Cinderella Waltz," left to understand what has happened to her marriage and to help
her young daughter to reach her own understanding,
finds herself drawn into a quiet, resigned acceptance
of her husband's relationship with his lover. She laments the loss of innocence in the world, for her child
and for them all, but she chooses to go forward with
the two men as part of her life and the child's. She rejects—really never even considers—the negative, destructive responses that many women would have.

"The Cinderella Waltz" ends with images of enormous fragility—glass elevators and glass slippers.
Yet they are images that her characters embrace and
cling to, recognizing that fragile hope is better than
none. The cautious nature of such optimism is often
mistaken for pessimism in Beattie's work, but her intention is clearly as affirmative as it is tentative.

"WINTER: 1978"

Another story from *The Burning House*, "Winter:
1978," offers a glimpse of most of Beattie's concerns
and techniques. An unusually long story for Beattie,
"Winter: 1978" features a selfish mother who is host-
ing a wake for her younger son, who has drowned in a
midwinter boating accident. His death is mystifying,
for there were life preservers floating easily within
his reach, a fact that suggests the ultimate despair and
surrender often present in Beattie's characters. An
older son blames the mother for placing too much
guilt and responsibility on the dead son, but he himself has done nothing to assume some of that burden.
The older son's former wife, their child, his current
girlfriend, and his best friend are all present at the
wake. The best friend's girlfriend is alone back in
California, having her uterus cauterized. His former
wife seems inordinately grief-stricken until it is revealed that the dead man was her lover. During the
course of the wake, which lasts several days, she becomes the lover of her former husband's best friend.

This extremely baroque and convoluted situation contains much that is ironically humorous, but it also reflects deep pain on the part of all the characters, not only the pain of having lost a loved one but also the pain of reexamining their own lives and measuring them against the idea of death. That sort of existential questioning, rarely overt but frequently suggested, contributes to the idea of a lost generation brought to life on the pages of Beattie's fiction.

Yet Beattie rarely leaves her characters in perpetual existential angst, as is the case in a Hemingway story such as "A Clean, Well-Lighted Place," an embodiment of the existential despair and the longing for some minute, self-created order and refuge typical of the original literary lost generation. Instead, Beattie often opts for a neo-Romantic, minimalist version of hope and redemption, of continued searching as opposed to acquiescence.

"Winter: 1978" concludes with the absentee father, the surviving son, taking his own child upstairs for a bedtime story. The little boy, like the daughter in "The Cinderella Waltz," is far too wise to take comfort from the imaginary world of the story; he has been exposed to far too much of the confused adult world of his parents. On this occasion, however, he pretends to believe, and he encourages his father's tale about the evolution of deer. According to the story, deer have such sad eyes because they were once dinosaurs and cannot escape the sadness that comes with having once been something else.

This story serves as a metaphor for the melancholy cast of characters in this and Beattie's other collections of short fiction. Almost all of her characters have a Keatsian longing to connect with a better, more sublime existence that seems to be part of their generational collective consciousness. Far too aware and too ironic to follow the feeling and thereby to transcend reality, they linger in their unsatisfactory lesser world and struggle to accommodate their longing to their reality.

"Snow"

More than her other collections, *Where You'll Find Me* displays Beattie's awareness of her own reputation as a writer. In particular, in a story called "Snow," she appears to write a definition of the kind

of story her work has come to define. Less than three pages long, the story takes a single image, that of snow, and uses it not only as a symbol of the lost love the narrator is contemplating but also as a metaphor for storytelling as practiced by the author.

The remembered lover has explained to the narrator at one point that "any life will seem dramatic if you omit mention of most of it." The narrator then tells a story, actually one paragraph within this story, about her return to the place where the lovers had lived in order to be with a dying friend. She offers her story-within-the-story as an example of the way in which her lover said stories should be told.

The narrator goes on to say that such efforts are futile, bare bones without a pattern to establish meaning. For her, the single image, snow in this case, does more to evoke the experience of her life with the man than does the dramatized story with the details omitted. In the story's final paragraph, the narrator concludes that even the single image is too complex for complete comprehension. The mind itself, let alone the narratives it creates, is incapable of fully rendering human experience and emotion. The best a writer, a storyteller, can do is to present the essence of the experience in the concrete terms in which his or her consciousness has recorded it.

What the reader inevitably receives, then, is minimal, to return to John Barth's theory. It is equally important, however, that Barth argues that the minimal can be more than enough. The characters in this fourth collection are generally older and wiser than their predecessors. They have, as a rule, survived an enormous loss and are still hoping for a richer, more rewarding life, or at least one in which they feel less out of place and alone.

"Janus"

Andrea, the real-estate agent who is the main character of "Janus," is typical. Safely married to a husband who is interesting and financially secure, she is also successful in her career. The two of them take great pleasure in the things that they have accumulated. Yet Andrea takes most pleasure in a relatively inexpensive and quite ordinary-looking ceramic bowl, a gift from a former lover who asked her to change her life, to live with him.

Although she has long since turned him down, Andrea finds herself growing increasingly obsessed with the bowl. She begins to believe that all of her career success comes from the bowl's being precisely placed in the homes that she shows to her clients. A mystery to her, the bowl seems to be connected to the most real, the most private parts of herself. She loves the bowl as she loves nothing else.

She fears for its safety. She is terrified at the thought that it might disappear. She has lost the chance that the lover represents, choosing instead stasis and comfort, remaining intransigent about honoring her previous commitments. Sometimes she goes into her living room late at night and sits alone contemplating the bowl. She thinks, "In its way, it was perfect; the world cut in half, deep and smoothly empty."

Such is the world that Beattie observes, but Beattie is, after all, an artist, not a real-estate agent. All that Andrea can do is contemplate. Beattie can fill the bowl, to use a metaphor, with whatever she chooses. She can capture, again and again, the story behind the "one small flash of blue, a vanishing point on the horizon," that Andrea can only watch disappear.

Barth's description of the impulse behind minimalism, the desire "to strip away the superfluous in order to reveal the necessary, the essential," is a fair assessment of Beattie's work. Yet it is equally important to recall what necessary and essential elements remain after the superfluous has been stripped away. They are love, friendship, family, children, music, and creativity. Beattie fills the bowl of her fiction with much the same fruits that other writers have used.

"WINDY DAY AT THE RESERVOIR"

In contrast to her earlier, so-called minimalist stories, Beattie's more recent short fictions seem to be moving more toward length and elaboration, making more use of novelistic techniques of character exploration and realistic detail. "Windy Day at the Reservoir," the longest story in her collection *What Was Mine*, focuses on two people who, while housesitting for another couple, make a number of discoveries both about the homeowners and about themselves—for example, about the vacationing couple's

impending breakup because of the wife's mastectomy and their own inability to have children. The point of view moves from the house-sitting husband, to the wife, to the mentally disabled son of the housekeeper, who walks into the reservoir and drowns. The final section focuses on the housekeeper, who provides a novelistic resolution to the two couples who have both broken up. Ending with a realistic resolution rather than a metaphoric embodiment of conflict, the story reflects Beattie's moving away from short-story techniques to novelistic devices.

"GOING HOME WITH UCCELLO" AND "PARK CITY"

A clear contrast between short-story and novelistic technique can be seen in the difference between two of the eight new stories in Beattie's collection of selected stories, *Park City*—"Going Home with Uccello" and the title story "Park City." In the former, a woman on a trip to Italy with her boyfriend has a realization about why he has taken her there when he flirts with a Frenchwoman about an Uccello painting. She understands that he has taken her to Italy not to persuade her to join him in London forever, but to persuade himself that he loves her so much that no other woman can come between them. The story ends in a typical Beattie ambiguity about whether the man in the story can commit himself to a relationship or whether he is continuing, as so many of Beattie's male characters do, to look for some ineffable dream.

In "Park City" the central character spends a week at a Utah ski resort during the off-season looking after her half-sister's daughter, Nell, who is three, and her half-sister's boyfriend's daughter, Lyric, who is fourteen. The story is filled with dialogue between the three females in which it seems increasingly clear that the woman is more naïve than the precocious fourteen-year-old. In one particular encounter, the girl spins out a long invented tale to a stranger about having had breast implants. The story ends when the central character tries to get on a ski lift with the child Nell and the two almost fall off. They are saved by a man who, significantly, tells her, "the one thing you've got to remember next time is to request a slow start."

In the twenty odd years that Beattie has been publishing short stories, mostly in *The New Yorker*, her milieu and her method have changed little, which has led some to complain that she has nothing new to say about the era she has evoked so sharply. However, Beattie has said, "My test was not did I get it right about the sixties, but is it literature. I am not a sociologist."

OTHER MAJOR WORKS

LONG FICTION: *Chilly Scenes of Winter*, 1976; *Falling in Place*, 1980; *Love Always*, 1985; *Picturing Will*, 1989; *Another You*, 1995; *My Life, Starring Dara Falcon*, 1997.

NONFICTION: *Alex Katz*, 1987.

CHILDREN'S LITERATURE: *Goblin Tales*, 1975; *Spectacle*, 1985.

BIBLIOGRAPHY

Atwood, Margaret. "Stories from the American Front." *The New York Times Book Review*, September 26, 1982, 1, 34. Discusses *The Burning House* as it represents the loss of the American dream for the children of the 1960's. For Beattie, freedom equals the chance to take off, run away, split. Beattie's stories chronicle domesticity gone awry, where there are dangers and threats lurking beneath the surface of even the most mundane events. Observes that most of the stories in this collection concern couples in the process of separating.

Barth, John. "A Few Words About Minimalism." *The New York Times Book Review*, December 28, 1986, 1, 2, 25. Explores Beattie's spare style and considers her fiction as it represents a current stylistic trend in the American short story. Spends a considerable amount of space describing the origins of the contemporary minimalist movement in American short fiction. Sees this form as a nonverbal statement about theme: the spareness of life in America. Places Beattie's work among that of other minimalists, including Raymond Carver, Bobbie Ann Mason, James Robison, Mary Robison, and Tobias Wolff. Discusses Edgar Allan Poe as an early proponent of minimalism. Says that

Beattie's fiction is clearly shaped by the events surrounding the Vietnam War. A helpful essay for gaining an understanding of Beattie as a minimalist.

Beattie, Ann. "An Interview with Ann Beattie." Interview by Steven R. Centola. *Contemporary Literature* 31 (Winter, 1990): 405-422. Contains a photograph of Beattie. This article is useful to the general reader, providing information about Beattie's biography. Beattie discusses herself as a feminist writer and talks about how she goes about creating credible male protagonists. Asserts that most of her fiction centers on exploring human relationships. Discusses *Falling in Place, Love Always, Chilly Scenes of Winter*, and *Picturing Will*. Talks about F. Scott Fitzgerald and his novel, *The Great Gatsby* (1925). Says that she is not interested in capturing American society but in capturing human nature.

Berman, Jaye, ed. *The Critical Response to Ann Beattie*. Westport, Conn.: Greenwood Press, 1993. Includes contemporary reaction to Beattie's novels and collections of short stories, as well as scholarly and academic analyses of her work by various critics.

Gelfant, Blanche H. "Ann Beattie's Magic Slate: Or, The End of the Sixties." *New England Review* 1 (1979): 374-384. Examines Beattie's short stories as reflecting the concerns of adults who came of age during the hippie years. Discusses Beattie's desolate landscapes and the pervading sense of doom found in much of her fiction. Focuses on *Secrets and Surprises* and *Distortions*, saying that they are a requiem for the freedom and wildness of the United States of the 1960's. Beattie concentrates on what amounts to the trivia of the everyday in order to make her points about the minutiae of the average person's life. Also compares Beattie's fiction with that of Joan Didion. Sees Beattie as a writer who explores the violence, inertia, futility, and helplessness of contemporary American culture.

Hansen, Ron. "Just Sitting There Scared to Death." *The New York Times Book Review*, May 26, 1991, 3, 14. Discusses Beattie's collection *What*

Was Mine and Other Stories. Hansen says that Beattie's fiction provides insightful portraits of people in their thirties and forties who experience broken marriages and shattered dreams. Comments on Beattie's ability to portray a realistic male point of view. Says that her females in this book are ill-defined and hard to understand. Hansen is critical of Beattie's style as being too elliptical and relying too much on inference rather than on direct commentary. Despite this shortcoming, he says that the collection is a success, describing it as an almost photojournalistic chronicle of the disjunctions in the contemporary world. Categorizes *What Was Mine and Other Stories* as being more introspective than Beattie's earlier collections of short fiction.

McKinstry, Susan Jaret. "The Speaking Silence of Ann Beattie's Voice." *Studies in Short Fiction* 24 (Spring, 1987): 111-117. Asserts that Beattie's female speakers puzzle readers because they tell two stories at once: an open story of the objective, detailed present juxtaposed against a closed story of the subjective past, which the speaker tries hard not to tell.

Murphy, Christina. *Ann Beattie*. Boston: Twayne, 1986. Good general introduction to Beattie's work. Discusses her major stories, illustrating her central themes and basic techniques. Discusses the relationship of her stories to her novels and her place in the development of the contemporary American short story.

Opperman, Harry, and Christina Murphy. "Ann Beattie (1947-): A Checklist." *Bulletin of Bibliography* 44 (June, 1987): 111-118. A useful guide to Beattie's work. Contains a helpful brief introductory essay that identifies Beattie as an important authorial voice that came of age during the 1960's. Views her as a descendant of Ernest Hemingway. Her characters are refugees from the Woodstock generation, idealistic dreamers caught by ennui, drifters and people who are emotional burnouts. Says that her characters resemble F. Scott Fitzgerald's: Both have outlived their youthful romanticism and are now materialistic rather than idealistic. Also compares her to John Cheever and John Updike. Provides both primary and secondary bibliographies through 1986.

Porter, Carolyn. "The Art of the Missing." In *Contemporary American Women Writers: Narrative Strategies*, edited by Catherine Rainwater and William J. Scheick. Lexington: University Press of Kentucky, 1985. Argues that Beattie economizes not by developing a symbolic context, as James Joyce and Sherwood Anderson did, but rather by using the present tense and thus removing any temptation to lapse into exposition, forcing the background to emerge from dialogue of character consciousness.

Jane Hill, updated by Melissa E. Barth and
Charles E. May

SAMUEL BECKETT

Born: Foxrock, Ireland; April 13, 1906
Died: Paris, France; December 22, 1989

PRINCIPAL SHORT FICTION

More Pricks than Kicks, 1934
Nouvelles et textes pour rien, 1955 (*Stories and Texts for Nothing*, 1967)
No's Knife: Collected Shorter Prose, 1947-1966, 1967
First Love and Other Shorts, 1974
Pour finir encore et autres foirades, 1976 (*Fizzles*, 1976, also as *For to Yet Again*, 1976)
Four Novellas, 1977 (as *The Expelled and Other Novellas*, 1980)
Company, 1980
Collected Short Prose, 1991 (vol. 1)

OTHER LITERARY FORMS

Although Samuel Beckett began to write for publication in the pre-World War II period, he had little success until after the war. His first worldwide acclaim came as a dramatist, with the production of the play *En attendant Godot (Waiting for Godot)* first in Paris in 1952, in French, then in 1954 in London, in English. His ultimate reputation was to rest primarily on his plays, but he was also a novelist, again of major importance. His three novels *Molloy* (1951; English translation, 1955), *Malone meurt* (1951; *Malone Dies*, 1956), and *L'Innommable* (1953; *The Unnamable*, 1958) can be read separately but are, in fact, usually published under the title *Trilogy* and are his best work in that medium. He is also an interesting literary critic and something of a poet, but his greatest contributions have been to drama and the novel.

ACHIEVEMENTS

Samuel Beckett is the unchallenged master of "absurd" literature, not only in English but also in French, which he often used as the original language for his work. He is, for many critics, the great novelist, and, at the same time, the great dramatist of the second half of the twentieth century, despite the fact

that he is not a popular writer; his work is often difficult to read, pays very little attention to pleasing the reader or the audience, and is generally pessimistic and often repetitive.

Despite his late recognition and the lack of much published material in his later years, Beckett was a prolific writer in the 1950's and 1960's, and his occasional works after that time, usually in the form of short fictions (which were sometimes cheekily called "novels"), were always received with great interest. There is a large critical industry providing comment upon his work, not only because of its artistic quality or experimental daring but also because of its themes and attitude, which are recognized as authentically, if disturbingly, accurate in representing the relentlessly despairing sensibility of much of the post-World War II intelligentsia, particularly in Europe. His work in general, even when it seems eccentrically ambiguous, has a ring of credibility that mirrors the angst and helplessness of late twentieth century life in the face of worldwide unrest and violence. He has made art out of human beings' failure to find meaning in a world that has gone so badly off the rails that many have lost confidence in religion, politics, society, or personal relationships. He never makes chiding statements on these problems, but his stories seem to be metaphors for modern humankind's situation. He is, therefore, unusual in being considered by many to be the greatest writer of the last half of the twentieth century, while rarely read by the general public because his work is considered too difficult.

BIOGRAPHY

Samuel Beckett was born on April 13, 1906, in Foxrock, Ireland. His family was financially and socially comfortable, and his parents sent him to a good private school and then to a university, hoping that he would join the family firm of surveyors upon graduation. Beckett belonged to the "Anglo-Irish" wing of Irish society. He was not a Celt or a Roman Catholic; his family had come to Ireland in the seventeenth century, and the original family name was "Becquet," his ancestors being French Huguenots, who fled religious persecution.

The Anglo-Irish contribution to Irish letters is considerable, the works of Jonathan Swift, for example, being a rich addition to Irish literature. Swift's family came from England in the late seventeenth century, and he was educated, as was Beckett, at Trinity College, Dublin, the Protestant university. Beckett was a brilliant scholar, and there was some hope that he would become an academic. He studied in Paris and was given a chance to teach at a university in Dublin, but he proved erratic at best as a lecturer, and ultimately, at worst, incompetent. His parents wanted him to face the facts and come into the mundane world of business; he, however, was determined to live in Paris and to become a writer, but he was so feckless and seemingly untalented that he was obliged to live on handouts of money from his mother, who continually pressed him to give up and come home. He was often unwell, impoverished, and self-destructive in his personal life, and sometimes he seemed headed for disaster. He wrote a bit but could rarely get anything published. He associated with the literary figures in Paris, and for a time was a close friend of James Joyce. At the time of the invasion of France by Germany in 1939, he was still without a literary reputation and with only a few works published. During the war, he worked in the French underground movement and barely missed being arrested by the Gestapo. He had been joined in these activities by Suzanne Deschevaux-Dumesnil, who was living with him and was, eventually, to become his wife; they fled Paris together, spending the rest of the war in a mountain village, Roussillon, in the Vaucluse, living hand to mouth in poverty.

After the war, the couple returned to Paris. Beckett was still determined to be a writer, despite the fact that he had managed to publish only a few poems, a small critical monograph on Marcel Proust in 1931, and one novel, *Murphy* (1938), which had gone unnoticed. Beckett had many faults, but he had one virtue: He was exceedingly stubborn, and he would not cease pursuing his goals. *Murphy* appeared in French in 1947, and a second novel, *Molloy*, came out in 1951, but to little acclaim.

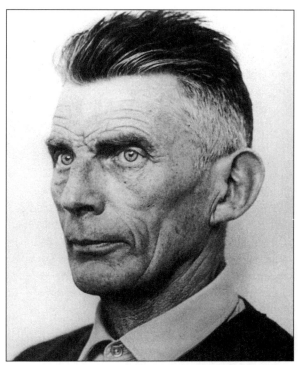

Samuel Beckett, Nobel Prize winner for Literature in 1969
(©The Nobel Foundation)

Although his major literary interest was in the novel, he began writing plays, and in 1952, with the Paris production of *Waiting for Godot*, his reputation began to develop, although slowly. The 1954 production of the play in English started the international enthusiasm for his work, and from that time on, he had little difficulty in getting his prose published. The plays, however, were most responsible for his reputation. During the ten years following the appearance of *Fin de partie* (1957; *Endgame*, 1958), his short list of plays appeared at regular intervals. During that time, he wrote full-length dramas, one-act plays, and a considerable amount of radio drama. In 1965, his one screenplay, called, appropriately, *Film*, was released, with Buster Keaton, the silent-film comic, in the major role.

Beckett continued to live in Paris, and his success, particularly in the theater and as a university author (in the sense that he became a major subject for study not only for scholars but also for undergraduates and graduates), allowed him to purchase a small house just outside Paris, and he spent the remainder of his life in his Paris apartment and in the country house, traveling occasionally, particularly to keep an eye on productions of his plays. He often would collaborate with a director and, on occasion, direct his own productions of his dramas.

His work has not always been unanimously praised, and some critics find little value in his art. Despite the skepticism, he was awarded the Nobel Prize in Literature in 1969. He continued to write, if somewhat sparingly, into old age, and in 1989, he produced *Stirrings Still*, the last work published before his death. His wife died in July, 1989, and Beckett, who had always been reluctant to make any public display of himself (he did not, for example, appear at the Nobel Prize ceremony), had made arrangements to be buried in a private ceremony at Montparnasse cemetery. Although he was shy, reluctant to socialize in the world of letters, and reclusive, he was not unapproachable. Many tales have been told of his kindness to strangers and scholars who approached him or who were able to find him as he slipped about the streets of Paris.

ANALYSIS

Samuel Beckett does not write short fiction in the tradition of the short story as it has developed in Europe and the United States over the last 150 years. He is not interested in telling a story with a beginning, a middle, and an end, and there are no trick revelations; nothing is withheld to the last minute that makes everything suddenly clear. He is not interested in social problems, personal confrontations, or the day-to-day eccentricities of modern life. His characters are usually nameless, barely existing in unidentifiable huts and hovels, at no special time, in no special place. If his art is a comment upon the meaningless nature of the human condition, he does not explore that problem sociologically as many writers do but draws the problem into a barren landscape barely inhabited by characters who often do not know who they are, have little—if any—memory, and simply want to die. To die is not an easy thing in Beckett's world, and to exist is often simply torment. Beckett, in a sense, piles on the agony of late twentieth century unhappiness

and meaninglessness by isolating his characters in a symbolic landscape, often with faint echoes of a post-atomic-bomb desert.

His characters are often physically tattered and psychologically distraught, and they can sometimes be so traumatized that they are speechless, but there is always an overriding intelligence present that attempts to shape the situation with precision but often fails in the act. Indeed, Beckett's short fiction is often about the problem of writing short fiction that involves subjects who are so minimalized, so debased and confined that it is impossible to know what to say about them. On occasion, therefore, his stories are about the act of failing to capture the subjects artistically. This failure can be maddening, particularly for readers with a strong sense of what a short story or novella should be, and it is the first lesson in how to read Beckett. He is not slow to apprehend or unlettered; he knows what is expected of the writer; he has, however, like many contemporary painters, refused to accept the medium as it came to him.

"FIRST LOVE"

"First Love," written in 1946, can be helpful because it still uses some of the elements that are expected in short fiction, but it is also ripe with hints of things to come as Beckett works his way toward his ideal of the short story. Written originally in French and titled "Premier amour," Beckett withheld publication until 1970, and admitted then that he only allowed it to be printed because of the pressure for material caused by the award of the Nobel Prize. Part of his reluctance came, as he admitted, from the fact that it was based in small part on an incident in his own life; as he told the actor Patrick Magee, it no longer mattered in 1970, since the woman had died. This habit of using stray bits of his own life continued to appear throughout his career, but was never very systematically pursued and hard to pin down.

The major character, however, is a much used type that is common in his novels. Nameless, shiftless, unpleasant, and unsanitary in his personal habits with a jaundiced view of humankind and a lively, vulgar way of looking at the world, he is happiest when left alone, able to live on the meagerest of provisions. He looks like a tramp and smells like one; his temperament is depressed, but he is intelligent. He can be very witty, if mordantly so, and he seems, given the arcane allusions that he makes, to be very well read and very well educated.

This story begins with the narrator telling how he was evicted from the family home at the time of his father's death, how he managed to survive as a tramp, and how he met a woman who took him in and allowed him to occupy a room in her apartment, where she worked occasionally as a prostitute. The woman managed to slip into bed with the narrator who, reluctantly, had sexual relations with her once in a while. She eventually becomes pregnant, and a child is born. The narrator gathers up his rags and leaves, followed down the street by the cries of the child.

In his very early work, Beckett was often a humorous writer, and some of that humor is still present in "First Love." The narrator, in fact, resembles Murphy, the major character in his 1938 novel *Murphy*, who also wants to be alone, but he also has the rather unpleasant, nasty streak in him that appears in the leading characters in the *Trilogy*. Perhaps the story can be seen as a kind of preliminary exercise in the line of stories that are going to become increasingly pessimistic and withdrawn in their exploration of solipsistic life among the homeless, who are often quite satisfied to be so, even if they suffer physically and mentally in the process of surviving completely outside society.

What will be noticed, however, is that the story does not make any point, save from the obvious one that the narrator is not fit for human intercourse and sees no reason to apologize for his preference. There is no trick to the ending; he just goes. Being seduced occasionally is one thing, but having a baby is too much. He is not a bad man, and he is not stupid. He simply wants to be left alone.

Later stories, however, are not quite that easy to understand. Even "First Love" has passages of monologue that have to be reread carefully. Much of the later material, however, *must* be reread. The stories are often monologues, rambling, discursive, contradictory, muddled in syntax, often denying previous passages, and usually deliberately short on facts. The stories have no names, no place, no time, often no

reason for being written. The best way to read them is to understand them straight, in the first reading, in a simple paraphrase, perhaps by making a written précis, step by step. Once what is being said is understood and the sometimes excessive punctuation worked out, the story can be read again, and that will be when the aesthetic power of the story will work. It is, in fact, similar to the way in which much late twentieth century poetry must be read. What is said and in what order one idea leads to another must first be understood; then the artistic virtue of the story (or the poem) can be met; the second reading becomes a kind of aesthetic experience.

"THE END"

"The End," originally published in French as "La Fin" in 1955 and in English in 1960, still retains some measure of structure and, like "First Love," makes sense, if oddly so. The point about this work is that it is only "absurd" in the sense that odd things are taking place. They may be improbable but are not impossible, and they have a touch of authenticity, given the debased way in which the characters are living. Beckett, for all his perverseness, often is accurate in his understanding of how humans live on the very lowest level of survival. In "The End," the major character is, as the character in "First Love" was, thrown out of his room. This time, however, there is no family connection; he seems to have been living in a public institution. The rest of the tale is occupied with his modest adventures, finding shelter, losing it, and ultimately achieving a kind of morbid contentment, hiding in an old boat and dreaming of going down with it. The tale has the short-story structure of beginning, middle, and end, but it is slightly farther away from civilization than "First Love." Aside from the character passing his son on the street, there is no family connection, and he rejects the tentative friendship offered by an old friend. He so wants to be alone that he cannot tolerate the roar of the sea. Although he has adequate shelter in a cave, he must move on until he finds the comparative silence of the abandoned boat. The mordant Irish humor is still there, and the old man, however disgustingly unsanitary he may be, is not unintelligent. He is the teller of the tale, and it is important in Beckett's work to remember that his speakers are often quite aware of what is taking place and quite able to comment on it, which is certainly the case in "First Love" and "The End."

"IMAGINATION DEAD IMAGINE"

This kind of genial absurdity, however, is to give way as the years pass to that other line of deep malevolence and imploded melancholy that has an early place in his art. "Imagination Dead Imagine" (originally entitled "Imagination morte imaginez"), seems to be a snippet from a science-fiction story or from a tale about the aftermath of a nuclear holocaust. It is tersely written (a mark of Beckett's work as he became older) by a character who describes the discovery of a small mound-shaped building in the wilderness. He, himself, seems to descend to it from some kind of flying vehicle, which is never described, and he finds inside it a male and a female, side by side in fetal position, alternately assaulted by light and heat, dark and cold. It is written without feeling, as a sort of scientific report, and may be as finely honed a metaphor for the possible aftermath of nuclear disaster as has ever been written, or it may not mean anything at all. Beckett would certainly deny any specific meaning, but his stories often reverberate with ambiguous, multilayered possibilities, which are part of their power.

"ALL STRANGE AWAY"

This story should be read in conjunction with "All Strange Away," a story that appeared in the 1970's. "Imagination Dead Imagine" is the last of the Beckett monologues but not the last time that he would reuse ideas and situations. In "All Strange Away," the immured couple appears again in much the same state as in the previous story, but now the main problem has become how to describe them. The laconic, brisk confidence of the narrator in "Imagination Dead Imagine" has disappeared, and the story is not so much about the couple lying on the floor, but about how to write about them, and it is cluttered with false starts, rejections, and alternatives. It is comparable to seeing all the drafts of a story piled up in frustration to be handed to the reader in place of the finished product. The story, in other words, has become a work in progress, replete with a sense that there is no true way of expressing it.

Over the years, there has been a tendency for Beckett's prose fictions to become shorter and shorter, despite the occasional description of these materials as novels. If they are "novels," they are dehydrated ones. "All Strange Away," however, is going in the opposite direction, opening up the tight bud of "Imagination Dead Imagine," in a sense, adding further imaginative energy and improvisation to the idea and displaying Beckett's gift for making an old idea new.

COMPANY

Company, published first in French as *Compagnie* and then as *Company* in the same year, 1980, is one of the most successful attempts by Beckett to explore the problem of how to make a work of art about the problem of solipsistic isolation while retaining some measure of narrative structure and tonal tenderness. A man lies on his back in the dark; he is old, immobile, and does not speak, but the narrator, who can enter his mind, makes it clear that he can hear a Voice that is speaking to him, retelling the story of the old man's life. That Voice is some company to the man, and it in part explains the title of the story, but there is also a suggestion that the narrator may be, in fact, allowing the story of his own life to be narrated. He, the narrator, may be constructing this tale of a Voice telling a tale to an old man in order to keep himself company.

Behind this triple line of shadowy characters is another commentator, who claims to be responsible for everything: He is involved in a kind of constant criticism of the story as it progresses, keeping a wary eye on how well the tale is being related. As a result, the ordinary shape of third-party narration has been breached in order that someone who claims to be the author may enter the artistic object. The question is whether this is the end of it: Is the real author behind this figure?

Beyond this, however, is the story of the old man's childhood, richly anecdotal and often seen as directly related to Beckett's own history. Eccentric and somewhat morbid, it possesses, nevertheless, a comic and sometimes elegiac tonality, which is not often seen in his later work, and it draws the starkly symbolic setting of the story into conjunction with the real world, which is suprising this late in his career. *Company* rewards careful rereading with the best of Beckett's literary concerns, fusing his concern with composition and structure with the unrelenting symbol of human isolation, relieved ever so slightly by the memory of life before it all goes wrong with age and experience; it is a kind of Wordsworthian absurd.

Beckett never wavered in his commitment to using short fiction as he saw fit rather than complying with its traditions. Fiction in his hands is not simply a comment, in realistic terms, upon life, but an object separate and apart from it, and his fiction is closer to poetry than to the novel. If his fiction is read as an aesthetic experience in which facts are of secondary and sometimes irrelevant concern, then Beckett's contribution may be understood. It need not make sense, just as nonrepresentational painting, sculpture, or music need not make sense. It is much more difficult to draw language into a nonrepresentational mode than to draw the raw materials of the other arts into simply existing artistic objects, but Beckett, in part, is trying to do just that. He is also trying to say something about the "absurd" nature of twentieth century life. The form and content of a Beckett story make little sense because late twentieth century life makes no sense—that is, it is absurd. The question is whether one can make art out of that conclusion. Beckett's fictions are attempts to do just that: to make form and content imitate the absurd.

OTHER MAJOR WORKS

LONG FICTION: *Murphy*, 1938; *Molloy*, 1951 (English translation, 1955); *Malone meurt*, 1951 (*Malone Dies*, 1956); *L'Innommable*, 1953 (*The Unnamable*, 1958); *Watt*, 1953; *Comment c'est*, 1961 (*How It Is*, 1964); *Mercier et Camier*, 1970 (*Mercier and Camier*, 1974); *Le Dépeupleur*, 1971 (*The Lost Ones*, 1972); *Company*, 1980; *Mal vu mal dit*, 1981 (*Ill Seen Ill Said*, 1981); *Worstward Ho*, 1983.

PLAYS: *En attendant Godot*, pb. 1952 (*Waiting for Godot*, 1954); *Fin de partie: Suivi de Acte sans paroles*, pr., pb. 1957 (music by John Beckett; *Endgame: A Play in One Act, Followed by Act Without Words: A Mime for One Player*, 1958); *Krapp's Last Tape*, pr., pb. 1958; *Act Without Words II*, pr., pb.

1960 (one-act mime); *Happy Days*, pr., pb. 1961; *Play*, pr., pb. 1963 (English translation, 1964); *Come and Go: Dramaticule*, pr., pb. 1965 (one scene; English translation, 1967); *That Time*, pr., pb. 1976; *Footfalls*, pr., pb. 1976; *Ends and Odds*, pb. 1976; *A Piece of Monologue*, pr. 1979; *Rockaby*, pr., pb. 1981; *Ohio Impromptu*, pr. 1981; *Catastrophe*, pr. 1982; *Company*, pr. 1983; *Collected Shorter Plays*, pb. 1984.

SCREENPLAY: *Film*, 1965.

TELEPLAYS: *Eh Joe*, 1966 (*Dis Joe*, 1967); *Not I*, 1972; *Tryst*, 1976; *Shades*, 1977; *Quad*, 1981.

RADIO PLAYS: *Embers*, 1959; *Words and Music*, 1962 (music by John Beckett); *Cascando*, 1963 (music by Marcel Mihalovici); *All That Fall*, 1957, revised 1968.

POETRY: *Whoroscope*, 1930; *Echo's Bones and Other Precipitates*, 1935; *Poems in English*, 1961; *Collected Poems in English and French*, 1977.

NONFICTION: *Proust*, 1931.

TRANSLATION: *An Anthology of Mexican Poetry*, 1958 (Octavio Paz, editor).

MISCELLANEOUS: *I Can't Go On, I'll Go On: A Selection from Samuel Beckett's Work*, 1976 (Richard Seaver, editor).

BIBLIOGRAPHY

Alvarez, Alfred. *Beckett*. New York: Viking Press, 1973. A short, lively, and sometimes opinionated discussion of Beckett by a critic who does not altogether trust the author and who knows how to argue not only for his strengths but also against his limitations. Contains a good short discussion of the intellectual climate that precipitated absurd literature.

Bair, Deirdre. *Samuel Beckett: A Biography*. New York: Harcourt Brace Jovanovich, 1978. Although Beckett was often reluctant to talk about himself, he cooperated with Bair, who was then an American Ph.D. student. It is the fullest, most helpful version of his life in print, and to know his life is to understand his art. Contains good illustrations. The criticism of the specific texts is often limited, but Bair is very good in putting the work in conjunction with his very odd life.

Carey, Phyllis, and Ed Jewinski, eds. *Re: Joyce'n Beckett*. New York: Fordham University Press, 1992. This collection of essays on the relationship between Joyce and Beckett includes two essays that discuss their influence on the short story. One compares Joyce's "Ivy Day in the Committee Room" with Beckett's "Fingal," and another compares the hero of Beckett's *More Pricks than Kicks* with Joyce's Stephen Dedalus.

Cronin, Anthony. *Samuel Beckett: The Last Modernist*. New York: HarperCollins, 1997. A fully documented and detailed biography of Beckett, describing his involvement in the Paris literary scene, his response to winning the Nobel Prize, and his overall literary career.

Esslin, Martin, ed. *Samuel Beckett: A Collection of Critical Essays*. Englewood Cliffs, N.J.: Prentice-Hall, 1965. Esslin is the editor of this collection of major essays by some of the best Beckett critics. Includes essays on all phases of his work, not only by English-speaking critics but also by European writers, who see Beckett not as a writer in English but as part of the European tradition.

_____. *The Theatre of the Absurd*. Garden City, N.Y.: Anchor Books, 1961. This volume is specifically about Beckett's work in the theater, but Esslin's discussion of the absurd in general is perhaps the clearest, most succinct and helpful definition of the movement.

Hill, Leslie. *Beckett's Fiction*. Cambridge, England: Cambridge University Press, 1990. In his preface, Hill briefly characterizes previous criticism and finds it reductive. Chapters on the trilogy, on duality, repetition, fables of genealogy, experiment, and failure. Includes notes and bibliography.

Kenner, Hugh. *A Reader's Guide to Samuel Beckett*. London: Thames and Hudson, 1973. Part of the dependable Reader's Guide series, this volume allows Kenner to comment clearly and simply on the individual texts and is an essential companion for anyone determined to get Beckett to make some kind of sense. Beckett's work will never be completely clear, but with Kenner, it sometimes makes sense, if only for the moment, which is all Beckett wanted.

_____. *Samuel Beckett: A Critical Study*. Berkeley: University of California Press, 1968. Kenner is probably the best commentator on Beckett. He has been writing about him since early in his career and has continued to do so. He is lively, imaginative, and extremely good at placing Beckett in the Irish tradition, as well as assessing his part in the movement of experimental literature.

Knowlson, James. *Damned to Fame: The Life of Samuel Beckett*. New York: Simon & Schuster, 1996. A comprehensive biography with much new material, detailed notes, and bibliography.

McCarthy, Patrick A., ed. *Critical Essays on Samuel Beckett*. Boston: G. K. Hall, 1986. Includes essays on how the collection *More Pricks than Kicks* suggests the majority of Beckett's later thematic and aesthetic preoccupations and how the most familiar story from that collection, "Dante and the Lobster," was revised by Beckett to sharpen its comic incongruity.

Pireddu, Nicoletta. "Sublime Supplements: Beckett and the 'Fizzing Out' of Meaning." *Studies in Short Fiction* 29 (Summer, 1992): 303-314. Argues that the constitutive element of the stories in *Fizzles* is the fiasco of narration itself, the idea of an aborted endeavor. Provides a detailed Derridean analysis of the stories, suggesting that they embody the ritual of deterioration and that they replace the paternal figure of the Romantic sublime with a sense of exhaustion and belatedness typical of postmodernism.

Rabinovitz, Rubin. *The Development of Samuel Beckett's Fiction*. Urbana: University of Illinois Press, 1984. An interesting discussion of the radical techniques that Beckett brought into his early work as a fictionist, and how they marked his art throughout his career.

Charles Pullen

MAX BEERBOHM

Born: London, England; August 24, 1872
Died: Rapallo, Italy; May 20, 1956

PRINCIPAL SHORT FICTION

A Christmas Garland, Woven by Max Beerbohm,
1912, 1950 (enlarged)
Seven Men, 1919, 1950 (enlarged as *Seven Men
and Two Others*)

OTHER LITERARY FORMS

Max Beerbohm's eclectic published work includes biography, caricatures and cartoons (with captions), dramatic and literary criticism, essays, letters, plays, radio broadcasts, and verse. Although critics often see Beerbohm as a many-sided figure, dabbling superficially in myriad literary forms, he nevertheless has a consistent comic development and outlook. The reader will find this special style of invention, exaggeration, and parody displayed in all his works, especially in his short fiction.

ACHIEVEMENTS

Labeled by George Bernard Shaw as "the incomparable Max," Max Beerbohm was a major figure in describing and parodying late Victorian and Edwardian society. Artist, critic, and fiction writer, Beerbohm is best known for the sharp wit and biting satire of his caricatures, fiction, and critical essays, which expose the pretentions of the literary and social world. Beerbohm was awarded honorary degrees from Oxford, Cambridge, and Edinburgh universities, was made an honorary fellow of Merton College, and was finally knighted in 1939. Perhaps the greatest testament to his literary legacy is the enduring Maximilian Society, founded in 1942. Beerbohm influenced many artists and writers; the popularity of his work in magazines such as *The Yellow Book, Strand*, and *Saturday Review* contributed to the success of such publications and generated an audience for more of their kind. The influence of his style on *The New Yorker* has often been acknowledged. Only Oscar Wilde is equally responsible for giving modern readers the vivid image of the Victorian dandy. Beerbohm's influence can be detected in the works of Thornton Wilder, W. Somerset Maugham, Evelyn Waugh, Muriel Spark, Kingsley Amis, and many others.

BIOGRAPHY

Sir Henry Maximilian Beerbohm was educated at Charterhouse and at Merton College, Oxford, where he made friends with many luminaries such as painters William Rothenstein and Aubrey Beardsley and writers Oscar Wilde and Bernard Shaw. He contributed often to the famous magazine *The Yellow Book* and frequently sold essays and caricatures to various other magazines. When Shaw resigned as dramatic critic of the *Saturday Review*, Beerbohm succeeded him and for twelve years was one of the English theater's most celebrated critics. In 1910 he married Florence Kahn and moved to Rapallo, Italy, where he remained until 1956. He stayed in England during both world wars and periodically returned there to publish his books and exhibit his caricatures. Beerbohm died in Rapallo, Italy, on May 20, 1956.

ANALYSIS

Max Beerbohm is both a product and a critic of the late nineteenth century aesthetic movement. He emphasizes the quality of beauty in a work of art, rather than its moral implications; this beauty is perceived by the reading audience in the writer's style, his ability to choose the appropriate word. Although Beerbohm's style develops from the stunning effects of exaggeration and fantasy in the 1890's to a more measured, classical style in the 1920's, his temperament and attitude remain the same through all forms of his writing. His delicate, elegant style, balanced by humor, biting satire, and accurate parody, treats the reader to some of the most amusing short fiction of the twentieth century.

Beerbohm understands that his work does not include that which is called "important"; he aims more for "the perfect adjustment of means to ends," yet his writing is not merely surface brilliance. Within this approach of intelligent good sense Beerbohm's criticism of art, artists, and life shows a subtle insight into people's behavior and the ambiguities of human nature. In his fantasy stories he captures the moods and social conventions of the society of his time; in his parodies he dissects not only the style but also the thought of famous authors. His art, then, reveals a good measure of truth.

SEVEN MEN

Seven Men is a collection of stories that blurs the distinction between fact and fiction. In a very modern way Beerbohm self-consciously introduces himself as a character in the story, reminiscing about some of his extraordinary experiences. The stories also follow different periods in Beerbohm's life. The autobiographical and realistic elements are further reinforced by the introduction of actual persons into the narrative. The two central stories, "Enoch Soames" and "'Savonarola' Brown," focus upon this relationship of life to art and the illusions that can dominate both. Beerbohm characteristically parodies himself and his susceptibility to the manners and modes of the time; as an author he also comments obliquely on the nature of art itself.

"Enoch Soames" begins with Max looking eagerly into Mr. Holbrook Jackson's book of the 1890's for the entry SOAMES, ENOCH. Finding it missing as he had suspected, Beerbohm tells us about his meetings with the poet and author Enoch Soames and tells us why his story *must* be written. Sprinkled throughout the sketch are the names of the masters of the 1890's: Wilde, Rothenstein, Walter Richard Sickert, and Beardsley. Soames patronizes the café society of this decade and tries to be as intellectually daring as the other famous artists and poets. We understand very soon, however, that the personality of the "stooping, shambling" Soames is of a different order from that of his colleagues. Max describes him as ridiculous and "dim," and Rothenstein does not remember him. Rothenstein, in fact, will not even draw him, asking, "How can one draw a man who doesn't exist?" Beerbohm reads Soames's book *Negations*, but he cannot understand what it is about. It seems to have form but no substance, like Soames himself.

Max Beerbohm (Archive Photos)

Soames is well aware that people, especially reviewers, do not notice him, and what he wants more than anything else is artistic recognition, especially for posterity. While dining with Max at le Restaurant du Vingtième Siècle, Soames, who earlier confessed to Max that he was a Catholic Diabolist, says he wants to go one hundred years into the future to see the editions, commentaries, and bibliographies of himself in the British Museum. For this, he says, "I'd sell myself body and soul to the devil." The gentleman sitting next to them *is* the Devil and quickly accepts Soames's terms. Soames disappears and then returns to Beerbohm, confirming the author's suspicion that Soames's search would be fruitless. The only reference to Soames, in the phonetic language of 1897, is that he is an imaginary character in a "sumwot labud sattire" by Max Beerbohm. Soames's last words before the Devil fulfills his bargain are, "*Try* to make them know that I did exist." Later, Max sees the Devil "over-dressed as usual" and is deliberately snubbed.

It seems that Soames, and possibly Max himself, is typical of the young authors of the 1890's whose talent was imaginary or at least of little value to later generations. There are many like Soames who are only parodies of the French Symbolists or the Decadent novelists. The satire, however, succeeds at a deeper level. Beerbohm creates reflections and images that mirror the nature and the problems of art and artists. There is a fine distinction between art and life, and the author must create his own reality, which may be ephemeral. Max both acknowledges and fears the Soames side of his own character, the mediocre element, the part rebuffed by the Devil. In fashioning this type of narrative, Beerbohm examines the truth of fiction and our attitudes toward it. Soames is a fiction trying to become real, and the truth of his predicament both within the circumscribed world of the story and without is problematic. Beerbohm, on the other hand, is the working storyteller trying to get inside his fiction to make it more authentic and artistic. As he says about the Café Royal in the story, "This indeed . . . is life." For Beerbohm, art and life coalesce, one imitating the other, each a part of the other's style and reality.

In "'Savonarola' Brown" Beerbohm disrupts our sensibilities by giving us a play within a story. The satire is ostensibly against the conventions of Elizabethan drama and the blank verse imitations of Algernon Charles Swinburne, Alfred, Lord Tennyson, and Robert Browning; but the formal qualities of the work make it a satire on the conventions of short fiction. Beerbohm first meets Brown at school; then later in life, when Max is drama critic for the *Saturday Review*, he sees him frequently at the theater. Brown is writing a play about Savonarola, and he discusses it at length with Beerbohm over a number of years. Max argues against Brown's improvised view of how a play should end. Brown wants Savonarola to work out his own destiny, to come alive as a real character. Max says, "My dear Brown, the end of the hero *must* be logical and rational." Not believing in this kind of causality, Brown says that there is nothing to prevent a motor-omnibus from knocking him down and killing him. By a strange coincidence, one Beerbohm says playwrights ought to avoid, Brown is

knocked down and killed by a bus. Beerbohm is made literary executor and attempts to publish Brown's unfinished play.

The play is disappointing to Beerbohm, but he thinks it a virtue that there is not one line that does not scan, a telling admission for a theater critic on a major magazine. Beerbohm presents us with the play itself, a lively, absurd parody involving such figures as Dante, Lucrezia Borgia, St. Francis of Assisi, Lorenzo and Cosimo de' Medici, Machiavelli, and other incongruous historic characters. The play has Lucrezia plotting her revenge on Savonarola for spurning her. Lorenzo de' Medici attempts to turn a mob, in which "cobblers predominate," against Savonarola. When Lucrezia enters, the mob attends her arguments also and is swayed, in a wildly comic scene, by whoever is speaking. Pope Julius settles the issue by putting both Lucrezia and Savonarola in a dungeon. A Fool helps them to escape and is killed by mistake by Cesare Borgia. Brown's play ends here, and Beerbohm apologizes for forcing us to judge a work that is unfinished.

As in "Enoch Soames," Max suffers the apprehension that the play would, if completed, have merit. The story now illustrates the problem of art on two levels. As a serious play by Brown, it is ludicrous and unintentionally humorous with all the worst elements of Renaissance drama and some poor examples of twentieth century language. Savonarola's hair turns white in only three hours; of this he says, "The scandal, the incredible come down!" Being outside the events of the fiction, however, we find it a fine example of parody. Beerbohm, again, is playing with our attitudes toward art.

Although Max tries to get the play produced, no one will accept it without an ending. He finishes it, having Machiavelli betray Savonarola and the now-mad Lucrezia, who together take deadly nightshade to avoid capture by Pope Julius. The significance of Beerbohm's conclusion is that he acknowledges Brown as a master in that Brown's conception is greater than his own. The characters will not breathe for Max, and he begins to hate them. By finishing the play, he also accepts Brown's view of probability and coincidence. Beerbohm is changing ideas, not only of

Elizabethan blank verse but also of literature itself. Readers are taken into the fiction and brought back out again until they are unsure about the nature of art and its designs upon them.

A CHRISTMAS GARLAND, WOVEN BY MAX BEERBOHM

One of the most unusual collections of modern short stories is *A Christmas Garland, Woven by Max Beerbohm*, in which Beerbohm further comments on technique and fiction through parodies of famous authors. Some of these certainly miss the mark because authors such as A. C. Benson, G. B. Street, and Maurice Hewlett are little known to the general public. Nevertheless, parodies of Henry James, G. K. Chesterton, Rudyard Kipling, and Joseph Conrad are still effective since many readers have a necessary familiarity with these authors. It is ironic that Beerbohm excels in a form that is significantly bound to the vagaries of time. All Beerbohm's best qualities of observation, satire, style, and wit, however, are to be found in these parodies.

The artistic center of *A Christmas Garland, Woven by Max Beerbohm* is the work of Henry James, for Beerbohm the most notable expression of imaginative fiction. In the story "The Mote in the Middle Distance, H*nry J*m*s," Beerbohm parodies the style and thought of James found in *The Wings of the Dove*, with echoes of *The Turn of the Screw* (1898) and other James novels. Simply, we are taken on a journey into the minds of the two children, Keith Tantalus and his sister Eva, as they consider whether or not to peer into their Christmas stockings at the foot of their bed. We encounter a typical Jamesian situation with limited action and heightened perceptual and moral awareness. Each thought is qualified by another, reflected in the syntactically complex, broken sentences which raise James's style almost to the point of absurdity. Although the detail and word choice is obvious, a criticism of James's often pretentious and serious manner, we are compelled to evaluate the dilemma in both comic and artistic terms. We feel the sexual tension underlying the brother-and-sister relationship that is present in much of James's work, and we feel that block of moral perception which complicates human choice. The narrator says

of Keith, "That his fear of what she was going to say was nothing to his fear of what she might be going to leave unsaid." This precocious insight in a small child and the recognition of James's style of creating effect by the use of negatives triggers the reader's humorous reaction. It seems that James goes wrong in excess, and Beerbohm makes clear the value and the flaw in this idiosyncrasy. At the same time, the sentence seems so right, so subtle in its representation, that we almost believe it is the work of James himself. Thus we have an astute criticism of James, a comment upon the act of literary creation, and a new work of art which is Beerbohm's. Beerbohm involves himself in the work of art to a greater extent—and in a different way—than he does in *Seven Men*, more effectively challenging the definition between form and content, between art and artist.

Beerbohm continues, throughout *A Christmas Garland, Woven by Max Beerbohm*, to submerge himself in what John Keats called "negative capability" to parody Chesterton's paradoxes, Kipling's authoritarianism, Conrad's foreign style, and many others. Ultimately, valid questions about art are raised, but there are no resolutions; only ambiguities remain. Beerbohm's achievement, then, is the creation of a style that is as complex as life. He develops a language and an image of himself in his fiction, often through self-parody, which mirrors and distorts both the real world and the imaginative one. With the self-consciousness of the modern author, he parodies with elegance and charm the forms, conventions, and ideas found in late nineteenth and early twentieth century writing. Although his purpose is always to amuse and delight, he makes the reader more aware of the nature of art and its deceptions, what John Felstiner aptly calls "the lies of art."

OTHER MAJOR WORKS

LONG FICTION: *Zuleika Dobson: Or, An Oxford Love Story*, 1911.

PLAY: *The Happy Hypocrite: A Fairy Tale for a Tired Man*, pr. 1890 (one-act dramatization), pr. 1936 (three-act dramatization).

POETRY: *Max in Verse*, 1963.

NONFICTION: *The Works of Max Beerbohm*, 1896;

The Happy Hypocrite: A Fairy Tale for Tired Men, 1897; *More*, 1899; *Yet Again*, 1909; *And Even Now*, 1920; *Around Theatres*, 1924; *A Variety of Things*, 1928; *Lytton Strachey*, 1943; *Mainly on the Air*, 1946, 1957 (enlarged); *Selected Essays*, 1958; *More Theatres, 1898-1903*, 1969; *Last Theatres, 1904-1910*, 1970; *A Peep into the Past, and Other Pieces*, 1972; *Max and Will: Max Beerbohm and William Beerbohmn, Their Friendship and Letters, 1893-1945*, 1975; *Letters of Max Beerbohm, 1892-1956*, 1989.

CARICATURES: *Caricatures of Twenty-five Gentlemen*, 1986; *The Poet's Corner*, 1904; *A Book of Caricatures*, 1907; *Fifty Caricatures*, 1913; *A Survey*, 1921; *Rossetti and His Circle*, 1922; *Things New and Old*, 1923; *Observations*, 1925; *Heroes and Heroines of Bitter Sweet*, 1931.

BIBLIOGRAPHY

Behrman, S. N. *Portrait of Max: An Intimate Memoir of Sir Max Beerbohm*. New York: Random House, 1960. Behrman sentimentally recounts his personal friendship with Beerbohm during the last four years of the author's life.

Bonaparte, Felicia. "Reading the Deadly Text of Modernism: Vico's Philosophy of History and Max Beerbohm's *Zuleika Dobson*." *Clio* 27 (Spring, 1998): 335-361. Discusses the connection between Beerbohm and Italian philosopher Giambattista Vico in an effort to show that Vico's influence on nineteenth century thought has been underestimated. Argues for a reading of Beerbohm from the perspective of Vico's philosophy of history.

Cecil, David. *Max: A Biography*. Boston: Houghton Mifflin, 1965. A more complete, objective biography than S. N. Behrman's (above), drawing heavily on quotations from people who knew Beerbohm and from his personal papers.

Epstein, Joseph. "Portraits by Max." *The New Yorker* 73 (December 8, 1997): 108-110. In this biographical sketch, the relationship between Beerbohm's prose and his drawings is discussed; asserts that his draftsman's line is the perfect visual equivalent of his prose and his prose the perfect verbal match of his line; notes that both his drawings and his writing exhibit painstaking attention to detail, energized by parody and inspired by merry malice.

Felstiner, John. *The Lies of Art: Max Beerbohm's Parody and Caricature*. New York: Alfred A. Knopf, 1972. Rejecting the superficial studies of the dandy image that belie Beerbohm's depth, Felstiner traces the evolution of Beerbohm's comic art which culminates in parody. Illustrations, bibliography.

Grushow, Ira. *The Imaginary Reminiscences of Sir Max Beerbohm*. Athens: Ohio University Press, 1984. Focuses more on Beerbohm's quest for form, his prose and caricatures as reminiscences of imagination. Offers an in-depth look at *Seven Men* and *Rossetti and His Circle*.

Hall, N. John. *Max Beerbohm Caricatures*. New Haven, Conn.: Yale University Press, 1997. Examines Beerbohm's characters. Includes illustrations, bibliographical references, and indexes.

Lynch, Bohun. *Max Beerbohm in Perspective*. New York: Alfred A. Knopf, 1921. One of the earliest serious looks at Beerbohm's writings and caricatures as being part of the same serious artistic statement. Bibliography, illustrations.

McElderry, Bruce R. *Max Beerbohm*. New York: Twayne, 1972. A helpful general look at Beerbohm's work from a traditional approach. Contains primary and secondary bibliographies.

Mortimer, John Clifford. "'The Last Civilized Man on Earth': The Incomparable Max Beerbohm." *The New York Times Book Review* 100 (September 3, 1995): 11-12. Notes that Beerbohm, a dandy of the Victorian era, took great pleasure in the vulgarity of the music hall, leading some critics to say he wasted time there that could have been spent writing; discusses Beerbohm's short story "Enoch Soames," his novel *Zuleika Dobson: Or, An Oxford Love Story*, and his caricatures and parodies.

Riewald, J. G. *Sir Max Beerbohm, Man and Writer: A Critical Analysis with Brief Life and a Bibliography*. The Hague: Martinus Nijhoff, 1953. A comprehensive, critical overview of Beerbohm's life and work. Includes a bibliography.

James MacDonald, updated by Lou Thompson

MADISON SMARTT BELL

Born: Franklin, Tennessee; August 1, 1957

PRINCIPAL SHORT FICTION
Zero db and Other Stories, 1987
Barking Man and Other Stories, 1990

OTHER LITERARY FORMS

Madison Smartt Bell's essays on literary topics have appeared in such publications as *Harper's* and *The Review of Contemporary Fiction*. His historical novel *All Souls' Rising* (1995) was a finalist both for a National Book Award and for a PEN/Faulkner Award. It won a Maryland Library Association Award and an Annisfield-Wolf Award. In 1996, Bell was included in *Granta* magazine's list of "Best American Novelists Under Forty."

ACHIEVEMENTS

Madison Smartt Bell's short stories have been selected for such series as *The Best American Short Stories* and *New Stories from the South: The Year's Best*, as well as for various anthologies, including *That's What I Like (About the South) and Other New Southern Stories for the Nineties*. In 1980, Bell was awarded Hollins College's Andrew James Purdy Fiction Award. Bell received a Lillian Smith Award in 1989, a John Simon Guggenheim Memorial Foundation Fellowship in 1991, and both a Maryland State Arts Council Individual Artist Award and a George A. and Eliza Gardner Howard Foundation Award in 1991-1992. He was awarded a National Endowment for the Arts Fellowship in 1992.

BIOGRAPHY

Madison Smartt Bell was born on August 1, 1957, in Franklin, Tennessee. He was educated at the Montgomery Bell Academy in Nashville and at Princeton University, where he won awards for fiction writing and was elected to Phi Beta Kappa. In 1979, he graduated summa cum laude. He then spent a year in New York working at various jobs and doing research and

writing for the Franklin Library. From 1979 to 1984, Bell was a director of a film production company, the 185 Corporation.

After a year's study at Hollins College, Bell received his master's degree in English and creative writing in 1981. Back in New York, he continued working for the Franklin Library and also for the Berkeley Publishing Corporation. His first novel, *The Washington Square Ensemble*, was published in 1983.

The following year, Bell moved to Baltimore, Maryland, and became an assistant professor of English at Goucher College, a position he held until 1986. In 1985, he married the poet Elizabeth Spires. After a year as a lecturer at the University of Iowa Writers' Workshop, Bell returned to Goucher as writer-in-residence in 1988. He has also taught graduate writing seminars at The Johns Hopkins University.

ANALYSIS

In his essay "Less Is Less: The Dwindling American Short Story," Madison Smartt Bell classifies himself as a traditional writer, one who believes that only by observing the most minute details can one arrive at universal truths. Although Bell's methods are traditional, his characters are the products of contemporary society. Whether they live in the rural South or in the urban Northeast, they are lonely, alienated figures without a clear sense of purpose. Their world is marked by cruelty, violence, and death, all of which Bell describes in harrowing detail. In "Triptych I," from *Zero db and Other Stories*, gruesome descriptions of hog butchering frame the central incident, a human death in which the victim's arm is charred on a hot stove burner. Here and elsewhere, Bell uses structure to remind his readers that they are animals, too, not much different from the hogs, rats, and cockroaches that they kill.

However, human beings can rise above their animal nature. Some of Bell's characters act on principle. The dog trainer in "Black and Tan," from

Barking Man and Other Stories, stops working with boys because he has doubts about his methods; the waitress in "Monkey Park," from *Zero db and Other Stories*, will not leave her husband even though she loves another man. Other characters are compassionate. In "Move on Up," from *Barking Man and Other Stories*, homeless people display a touching generosity toward one another. One also has to admire the semiliterate narrator of one of Bell's funniest stories, "The Naked Lady," from *Zero db and Other Stories*. Although he enjoys shooting rats and watching barroom brawls, this character is essentially a kindly soul, who worries about his roommate's career as a sculptor and even lets their rat-eating snake warm itself in his bed. Even if we have lost our faith in the myths that once sustained us, Bell believes that we can still find meaning in our willingness to connect with one another.

"IRENE"

In "Irene," from *Zero db and Other Stories*, a young girl becomes the central reality in the narrator's life. After experiencing some personal disappointments, the narrator moves into a Puerto Rican neighborhood in Newark, New Jersey, hoping that in isolation he will turn into a creative genius. In fact, however, he sinks into apathy. One night his neighbors invite him to join them on their steps, and he is so struck by the beauty of a twelve-year-old girl named Irene that he cannot get her out of his mind. He even fantasizes about marrying her. On one occasion, when he sees her crying, he takes her into his apartment until she calms down. The narrator finally pulls himself together, gets a job, and moves away, but he can never forget Irene. He only hopes that she has some recollection of him. Though he now knows that his fantasies of instantaneous success and marriage to Irene will never be realized, the narrator has found himself by connecting with another human being.

"TODAY IS A GOOD DAY TO DIE"

"Today Is a Good Day to Die," from *Zero db and Other Stories*, is an initiation story. The protagonist is a young army lieutenant, who in 1875 has been assigned to General George A. Custer's unit at Fort Robinson as an observer. That is also his function in terms of the story. Though he is a West Point graduate, the lieutenant has a great deal to learn about war and even more to learn about this conflict. His initiation begins when a whiskey trader tries to sell him a leather-like object that was once a squaw's breast. The falsity of the trader's justification, that Native Americans are not human beings, becomes clear to the lieutenant when one saves him from death in the snow. While they sit together beside the fire, the Native American draws a sketch to show the lieutenant how Custer's men massacred unarmed Native American women and children. Though he does fight at the Little Bighorn, the lieutenant later deserts and starts walking toward the mountains, discarding his uniform and then destroying his watch. His final words, which urge a buzzard to eat of his body, echo the Eucharist, suggesting that he sees his death as expiation for the sins of his race. The lieutenant is no longer an observer; he has become a participant in the eternal battle between good and evil.

"CUSTOMS OF THE COUNTRY"

One of Bell's major themes is that one can find goodness and heroism at even the lowest levels of society. The first-person narrator of "Customs of the Country," from *Barking Man and Other Stories*, is a reformed drug addict. While she was in the throes of withdrawal, she became irritated with her little boy Davey and threw him across the room, breaking his leg. As a result, he was taken away from her. Ever since, her one goal has been to get Davey back. She is now free of drugs, visits Davey whenever she can, and with her earnings as a waitress has hired a lawyer and fixed up her apartment for a social worker's approval. However, the authorities' supposed "evaluation" is a fraud; they have long since decided to give Davey to foster parents. In the end, the narrator shows herself to be far more compassionate than the bureaucrats. When she hears the man next door beating his wife even more viciously than usual, she incapacitates him with a skillet and then offers to take the wife along with her. The wife does not leave; as the narrator says, she is stuck in her rut. Ironically, in her refusal to take chances, the wife is no different from the bureaucrats. By contrast, in the narrator the reader sees true heroism.

"DRAGON'S SEED"

Unlike most of Bell's short fiction, "Dragon's Seed," from *Barking Man and Other Stories*, ends in poetic justice. Mackie Loudon, an elderly sculptor, lives in a decaying house, alone except for her demons. After she discovers that a boy she has befriended, who stays next door with a man called Gil, is a kidnap victim in the hands of a child pornographer, Mackie informs the police. However, Gil has no difficulty convincing them that Mackie is crazy. Later, he tells her that he has disposed of the boy and then pushes her off an embankment. Mackie ends up in the hospital. After she is released the following spring, Mackie breaks into Gil's place, sets him on fire, and burns down the house. Bell's use of mythology makes the story even more effective. The reader first sees Mackie carving a head of Medusa, the Gorgon who turned men to stone; later she shapes that head into her own likeness, and as Medusa, kills Gil. The dragon's teeth sowed by the Greek hero Jason emerged as fighting men; similarly, when Mackie returns, her memories of the boy, whose name was Jason, give her the strength to effect retribution.

OTHER MAJOR WORKS

LONG FICTION: *The Washington Square Ensemble*, 1983; *Waiting for the End of the World*, 1985; *Straight Cut*, 1986; *The Year of Silence*, 1987; *Soldier's Joy*, 1989; *Doctor Sleep*, 1991; *Save Me, Joe Louis*, 1993; *All Souls' Rising*, 1995; *Ten Indians*, 1996.

NONFICTION: *History of the Owen Graduate School of Management*, 1985; *George Garrett: An Interview*, 1988; *Narrative Design: A Writer's Guide to Structure*, 1997.

BIBLIOGRAPHY

Bell, Madison Smartt. "An Essay Introducing His Work in a Rather Lunatic Fashion." *Chattahoochee Review* 12 (Fall, 1991): 1-13. Bell explains how he came to share the southern Agrarians' distrust of technology. His own spiritual pilgrimage led him to Giordano Bruno and animism, a faith that Bell believes could save the world from environmental disaster.

_____. Interview by Bob Summer. *Publishers Weekly* 232 (December 11, 1987): 45-46. A lengthy biographical essay, supported by extensive quotations. Bell will always consider himself a southerner. He went to New York only because he had to move outside the South in order to find his own voice. Comments on "Triptych II," his first published story.

_____. "An Interview with Madison Smartt Bell." Interview by Mary Louise Weaks. *The Southern Review* 30 (Winter, 1994): 1-12. In this 1992 interview, Bell explains how he came to know Andrew Lytle and Allen Tate and why he still holds Agrarian views. He comments at length on "Today Is a Good Day to Die."

_____. "Less Is Less: The Dwindling American Short Story." *Harpers* 272 (April, 1986): 64-69. Criticizes the minimalists because their fiction merely reflects the sameness and emptiness of contemporary life. Traditional writers, like Ellen Gilchrist, George Garrett, Peter Taylor, and Bell himself, know that one must observe the most minute details before attempting generalizations about people or society.

_____. "Time and Tide in the Southern Short Story." In *That's What I Like (About the South) and Other New Southern Stories for the Nineties*, edited by George Garrett and Paul Ruffin. Columbia: University of South Carolina Press, 1993. Insists that short stories by the newer southern writers lack the historical perspective that has defined southern literature. Fortunately, a few writers, Fred Chappell, Richard Bausch, and Mary Hood, for example, still remain true to their roots. However, southern literature may be less distinctive now because so many writers from other regions are expressing their sense of alienation.

Bernays, Anne. "Heartbreak in the Monkey Park." *The New York Times Book Review* (February 15, 1987): 15. *Zero db and Other Stories* displays an amazing variety of voice and tone. Five of the stories are discussed. Comments that the author combines affection for his characters just as they are with anger because they are not better people.

Chappell, Fred. "The Helplessness of Compassion."

The Washington Post Book World (February 1, 1987): 7. In *Zero db and Other Stories*, Bell shows his characters responding in different ways to the cruelty around them. Some retreat into despair, while others find that by empathizing with those around them, they can make their own lives better.

DeMarinis, Rick. "The Hero Is a Mouse." *The New York Times Book Review* (April 8, 1990): 11. A thoughtful analysis of *Barking Man and Other Stories*. Sums up Bell's world as a perilous place in which ordinary people are often extraordinarily heroic. Though the author is no sentimentalist, he can find good in seemingly worthless characters.

McCarthy, Paul D. "Pounding Out the Dents." *Los Angeles Times Book Review* (September 30, 1990): 12. Points out how the two parts of *Barking Man and Other Stories* differ in tone and theme. Notes also how recurring motifs unify the collection.

Rosemary M. Canfield Reisman

SAUL BELLOW

Born: Lachine, Quebec, Canada; June 10, 1915

PRINCIPAL SHORT FICTION

Mosby's Memoirs and Other Stories, 1968
Him with His Foot in His Mouth and Other Stories, 1984
Something to Remember Me By: Three Tales, 1991
The Actual, 1997 (novella)

OTHER LITERARY FORMS

Saul Bellow is known primarily for his novels, which include *The Adventures of Augie March* (1953), *Herzog* (1964), *Mr. Sammler's Planet* (1970), and *Ravelstein* (2000). He also published plays, a book of nonfiction prose about a trip to Jerusalem, and a number of essays.

ACHIEVEMENTS

Few would deny Saul Bellow's place in contemporary American literature. Any assessment of his contributions would have to account for his realistic yet inventive style, the rich Jewish heritage upon which he draws, the centrality of Chicago in his fictional world, the role of the intellectual, and a fundamental wit, rare in contemporary American fiction. In 1976, Bellow's achievement was internationally recognized when he was awarded the Pulitzer Prize and the Nobel Prize in Literature. He also won the 1988 National Medal of Arts and four National Book Awards—for

The Adventures of Augie March in 1954, for *Herzog* in 1965, for *Mr. Sammler's Planet* (1970) in 1971, and for *The Bellarosa Connection* (1989) in 1990. In 1997, *The Actual* (1997) won the National Jewish Book Award, given by the Jewish Book Council.

BIOGRAPHY

Saul Bellow was born in Canada, spent his first nine years in the Montreal area, then moved to Chicago and graduated from high school there. He spent his first two years of college at the University of Chicago and the last two at Northwestern, graduating in 1937. That same year he began a brief interlude of graduate work in anthropology at the University of Wisconsin. A few years later he started his writing career. He also taught at the University of Chicago from 1962 to 1993, moving to Boston University thereafter. He has been married five times and has three children. In 1996, he became coeditor of a new literary journal, *The Republic of Letters*.

ANALYSIS

Saul Bellow's stature in large measure owes something to the depths to which he plumbs the modern condition. He addresses the disorder of the modern age, with all its horror and darkness as well as its great hope. Though intensely identified with the United States, his heroes are preoccupied with dilemmas arising out of European intellectual and cultural history. Bellow's fictional world is at once cerebral and sensual. His concern is with the interconnections between art, politics, business, personal sexual proclivities and passions, the intellectual, and the making of culture in modern times. He is heady, like German writer Thomas Mann, revealing the limitations and powers of the self. Few contemporary American writers deal with such weighty issues as masterfully as does Bellow.

Bellow's honors and reputation document but do not explain his importance, although it will be more clearly seen in the future when some of the main tendencies of American fiction of his era have been fully developed. He is important because he has both preserved and enhanced qualities that are present in the great fictional works of the eighteenth and nineteenth centuries yet has fully participated in the tumult and uncertainty of the modern era. Though he has often opposed the political left and has espoused "traditional" cultural positions, Bellow is not primarily a polemical writer. His main concern is not with maintaining social or cultural order but is more spiritual and philosophical in nature. In this, he differs from the group of "New York intellectuals" that centered in the 1940's and 1950's on the journal *Partisan Review*. Although Bellow was for a time friendly with members of this group he took pains to distance himself from it and to stress his essential independence of any creed or ideology, as his paramount concern is for the individual. This theme is especially prominent in his short fiction, whose smaller canvas gives heightened emphasis to Bellow's stress on the struggle of the individual for self-definition and development against the background of the sundry obstacles the world has in store.

Bellow's characters have selves and interact with a society and a culture that Bellow has created in detail after careful observation. In some of his works, especially *Mr. Sammler's Planet*, Bellow's attitude toward that society and that culture borders on scorn, but his attitude has been earned, not merely stated in response to limitations on his own sensibility. The interaction between self and society in his work occurs against the backdrop of moral ideas. This is not to say that Bellow is didactic; rather, his work is infused

Saul Bellow, Nobel Laureate for Literature in 1976 (©The Nobel Foundation)

with his sophisticated understanding of moral, social, and intellectual issues. In addition to preserving a rich but increasingly neglected tradition, Bellow enriched that tradition. After the exuberant opening words of *The Adventures of Augie March*, he also added new possibilities to the prose style of American fiction. In short, his work offers some of the benefits that readers in previous centuries sought in fiction—most notably, some ideas about how to be a person in the world—yet it also offers a technical brilliance that Bellow keeps in rein instead of letting it control his work.

MOSBY'S MEMOIRS AND OTHER STORIES

The stories collected in *Mosby's Memoirs and Other Stories* explore characteristic Bellow themes and clearly demonstrate the writer's moral and aesthetic vision. "Looking for Mr. Green" is set in Chicago during the Depression and recounts the efforts of a civil servant, George Grebe, to deliver relief checks to black residents of the south side. This is the stuff of social protest literature, and Bellow's story does dramatize the suffering that was endemic at that time, but it is much more than didactic. Bellow avoids a single-minded attack on economic injustice and the resulting inartistic story by, among other things, using a number of contrasts and ironies. For example, two scenes set on the streets and in the tenements of Chicago are separated by a scene at Grebe's office, and in that scene a philosophical discussion between Grebe and his boss, Raynor, is interrupted by a welfare mother's tirade. The basic situation of the story is ironic, because it seems odd that anyone would have trouble delivering checks to persons who desperately need them. These persons, however, are difficult to ferret out, and their neighbors will not reveal their whereabouts because they fear that Grebe is a bill collector, process-server, or other source of trouble, and because he is white. This irony vividly illustrates the degree to which the Depression has exaggerated the instinct of self-preservation and widened the gulf between blacks and whites.

Grebe's name points out several of the contrasts in "Looking for Mr. Green." Grebes are birds known for their elaborate courtship dances, but George Grebe is a bachelor. More important for the story, grebes live in pairs rather than in flocks and remain in their own territories, but George, because of his job, is forced into society and into territory where he is an alien, not only because he is white but also because he is the son of the last English butler in Chicago and was a professor of classics. This is not to say that he is a stranger to trouble: He "had had more than an average seasoning in hardship." Despite his troubles, Grebe is shocked by suffering, distrust, and decrepit physical settings.

Oddly enough, these conditions are for him not only a moral problem but also an epistemological one. Raynor, his supervisor, brings up this problem by asserting that "nothing looks to be real, and everything stands for something else, and that thing for another thing." In contrast, Grebe later concludes that objects "stood for themselves by agreement, . . . and

when the things collapsed the agreement became visible." The physical setting and the social and economic structure in this story are rapidly deteriorating, if not collapsing. Grebe complicates his analysis by asking "but what about need?" thereby suggesting that because of the Depression the agreement itself is collapsing and perhaps with it reality. Some of the persons he meets want to hasten that collapse. The welfare mother "expressed the war of flesh and blood, perhaps turned a little crazy and certainly ugly, on the place and condition," and another person advocates an alternate agreement, a plan whereby blacks would contribute a dollar apiece every month to produce black millionaires. Grebe's finding Mr. Green indicates that he can do something about this obscure world in which appearance and reality are mixed. Near the end of the story he asserts that it "was important that there was a real Mr. Green whom they could not keep him from reaching because he seemed to come as an emissary from hostile appearances."

"The Gonzaga Manuscripts" is a subtle story that traces changes in a young man, Clarence Feiler, and puts those changes in the context of important issues pertinent to the proper functions of literature and to its relation to everyday reality. Bellow carefully delineates the psychological state of Feiler, to whom literature makes an enormous difference, and shows the impingement upon him of Spanish society, which also was the environment of the writer about whom he cares passionately, Manuel Gonzaga. These themes are developed in the context of Feiler's search in Madrid and Seville for the unpublished manuscripts of poems written by Gonzaga. Feiler learns finally that the poems are lost forever, buried with Gonzaga's patron.

When Feiler arrives in Spain he is a confirmed Gonzagan, and while searching for the manuscripts he immerses himself in Spanish society and even in Gonzaga's former milieu. Bellow meticulously paints in the Spanish background by describing the cities, religious processions, political climate, and a representative group of Spaniards. As a result of his immersion Feiler begins virtually to relive Gonzaga's poems. For example, early in the story Feiler quotes part of a poem:

I used to welcome all
And now I fear all.
If it rained it was comforting

And if it shone, comforting,
But now my very weight is dreadful.

The story ends thus: "as the train left the mountains, the heavens seemed to split. Rain began to fall, heavy and sudden, boiling on the wide plain. He knew what to expect from the redheaded Miss Walsh at dinner." That is, the rain is not comforting, and he fears that Miss Walsh will continue to torment him.

Feiler maintains his allegiance to Gonzaga, but there is considerable evidence in the story indicating that his allegiance is misplaced. For example, Gonzaga's friends are unimpressive. His best friend, del Nido, is a babbling mediocrity who sees little need for more poetry, and Gonzaga's patron has had the poems buried with her, thus denying them to the world. Another acquaintance misunderstands Feiler's search, thinking that he is after mining stock. One of Gonzaga's main beliefs is that one needs to take a dim view of human potential; he advocates being little more than a creature and avoiding the loss of everything by not trying to become everything. Even though Feiler himself has few aspirations besides finding the lost poems, he ends in despair. In fact, Gonzaga resembles the writers whom Bellow castigates in "Some Notes on Recent American Fiction" because of their minimal conception of human potential and their concomitant solicitousness for their own sensibility. Bellow's essay is a defense of a view of literature that Feiler unflatteringly contrasts to Gonzaga's.

"Mosby's Memoirs" was published in 1968, two years before *Mr. Sammler's Planet*, and, like that novel, is a study in world weariness. Mosby is writing his memoirs in Oaxaca, Mexico, where the fecund land and the earthy existence of the people contrast to his own dryness. His mind ranges back through his life, particularly to recall two friends: Ruskin, a poet who has a theoretical bend of mind, and Lustgarden, who alternates between endlessly elaborated Marxism and piratical capitalism. At the end of the story Mosby is in a tomb that, along with his inability to

get enough air to breathe, suggests that he is moribund. Although *Mr. Sammler's Planet* depicts a sympathetic character fending off as best he can the horrors of contemporary life, "Mosby's Memoirs" shows the danger of rejecting one's era.

Mosby's critique is conservative: He had worked for Hearst, had shaken Franco's hand, had agreed with Burnham's emphasis on managing, even to the point of admiring Nazi Germany's skill at it. Partly because Lustgarden's Marxism is not made to appear attractive either, Mosby's politics are not as unattractive as his attitude toward other persons. He is intolerant and is characterized by "acid elegance, logical tightness, factual punctiliousness, and merciless laceration in debate." Even more damaging to him is a scene at a concert in which he is described as "stone-hearted Mosby, making fun of flesh and blood, of those little humanities with their short inventories of bad and good." His attitude is also obvious in his treatment of Lustgarden in his memoirs. Rather than using his friend's disastrous attempts to make money as a political parable or as an occasion to demonstrate pity, Mosby plans to use them for comic relief, in the process eschewing his "factual punctiliousness" in order to make Lustgarden more laughable.

HIM WITH HIS FOOT IN HIS MOUTH AND OTHER STORIES

The stories brought together in *Him with His Foot in His Mouth and Other Stories* can be divided into two types: The title story and *What Kind of Day Did You Have?* (both novella-length pieces) feature powerful, aging Jewish intellectuals trying to come to grips with the course their lives have taken and bridge the world of ideas with the sensate, real world around them; the other three stories in the volume—"Zetland: By a Character Witness," "A Silver Dish," and "Cousins"—are cut from the same fabric as is "Looking for Mr. Green." They vividly, almost nostalgically, evoke a past, between the wars and after, and portray the assimilation of Jews in the United States. What is impressive in all of these stories is the wide historical swath they cut; Bellow's concern here, as elsewhere, is no less than the human condition in the twentieth century.

Herschel Shawmut, the narrator of *Him with His*

Foot in His Mouth, a man in his sixties, is a successful Jewish musicologist. His story, a sort of confession, is addressed to a "Miss Rose" whom he evidently mortally offended with an inadvertent verbal barb years ago. Shawmut confesses to other slips of the tongue as well. As he writes about all the incidents, revealing a certain pattern of personality, he attributes them simply to fate. His confession also reveals that he has been swindled by his own brother Philip, a materialist living a sumptuous bourgeois life in Texas. Philip convinces his naïve brother to hand over all of his hard-earned money (made from his musicological ventures) and form a partnership in a company rife with fraud and other illegal activities. After Philip's untimely death, Shawmut, hounded by creditors, seeks exile. He is, in the end, living a lonely life in Canada. Through his confessions, Shawmut seems to find some kind of order and the satisfaction of having articulated the nature of his fate, for better or worse.

Victor Wulpy, the older Jewish intellectual in *What Kind of Day Did You Have?* is a charismatic figure who sweeps a much younger Katrina Goliger, mother of two, off her feet. On the day in question, Wulpy calls Katrina to ask her to come to Buffalo and fly back to Chicago with him for a speaking engagement. Not daring to question this cultural giant, she takes off immediately, cancelling an appointment with a psychiatrist for an evaluation of her psychiatric condition in a fierce battle with her former husband for custody of her children. In the climactic scene of the story, the small Cessna plane they are in seems, in the thick of a winter storm, to be in a fatal dive toward Lake Michigan. In the face of possible death Katrina wants him to say he loves her, but he refuses. "If we don't love each other," she then wonders aloud, "What are we doing? How did we get here?" In the end, Wulpy makes his speaking engagement and Trina makes it home, to find her children gone. Soon they return, escorted by Krieggstein, a police officer and a suitor waiting for the passing of the Wulpy phase.

Bellow's Jewish wit, evident in all these stories, sparkles in "A Silver Dish" and "Cousins," both cleverly conceived. In "A Silver Dish," a sixty-year old

Woody Selbst mourns his father's death and recalls an incident in his youth. Woody's mother and father had split up, leaving Woody's upbringing in the hands of his mother and a Protestant evangelical minister. Woody's father, "Pop," returns one day to ask his son a favor. Would he introduce his father to a certain wealthy Protestant, Mrs. Skoglund, who had made money in the dairy business? Woody reluctantly agrees and takes his father to the woman's home. While she and her suspicious maid leave the room to pray and decide whether or not to comply with Pop's request for money, Pop steals a silver dish from a locked cabinet. Woody and his father get into a scuffle, and his father promises to put the dish back if Mrs. Skoglund coughs up the money. She does, but Pop, unbeknownst to his son, keeps the dish. When the dish is missed, Woody gets the blame and falls from grace in the eyes of the evangelical crowd—which is exactly the effect his father desired.

In "Cousins," the narrator, Ijah Brodsky, an international banker, tells the story of his contact with three cousins. The first, Tanky Metzger, is connected to mobs and wants Ijah to use his influence with a certain judge and gain a lighter sentence. The second cousin is Mordecai, or "Cousin Motty," whom Ijah goes to visit in the hospital after he has been hurt in an automobile crash. Cousin Motty has letters to deliver to Ijah from another cousin, Scholem Stavis. The intellectual in the family, Stavis has ended up, however, driving a cab. All through the narrative are reminiscences, a calling up of the past, a restitching of old relationships. Ijah's existence seems somehow to be tied to, and defined by, his connection to these cousins.

THE ACTUAL

The Actual, a short, self-contained novella, has many of the traits and characteristics associated with Bellow's earlier work. In fact, for these reasons it is an excellent introduction to Bellow's fictional world. Yet, strikingly for a work published in its author's eighty-second year, it also breaks new ground for Bellow. The hero of *The Actual* is a man named Harry Trellman, who is at the time of the action semi-retired and living in Chicago. Trellman has always been perceived by those he encounters as a bit different from everybody else, standing out from the rest of the crowd. Trellman worked as a businessman in Asia and later served as an adviser to Siggy Adletsky, a tycoon and racketeer who controls a huge financial empire and who is now ninety-two years old. Adletsky finds Trellman valuable because of his wide-ranging knowledge. This is a situation often found in Bellow's work: the alliance between the shady millionaire and the intellectual.

As a teenager, Trellman had been in love with Amy Wustrin, who had eventually chosen as her second husband Trellman's best friend in high school, Jay Wustrin. Throughout the years, Harry Trellman had kept firm to the inner image of Amy in his mind even as he went through his varied career and activities. After Jay Wustrin dies prematurely, he is buried in the cemetery plot originally reserved for Amy's father, who had sold it to him years earlier. Now Amy wants to remove Jay's body to the burial plot of his own family so that her father, who is still alive at an advanced age, can eventually be buried there. In a limousine provided by Adletsky, Amy and Trellman disinter and rebury the body. Moved by this scene of death and renewal, Trellman confesses to Amy that he has always loved her, that he has what he terms an "actual affinity" for her (hence the title of the story). He then asks her to marry him.

This declaration of love is striking as Trellman, for most of his life, has remained uncommitted and rather inscrutable, not exposing his inner secrets to others. Harry's privacy is contrasted with the willful self-exposure of men such as Jay Wustrin, who love making a spectacle of themselves. This dichotomy between the public and private man is mirrored by the tensions in Trellman's relationship with Adletsky, who is concerned only with money and profit-making, yet needs the intellectual-minded, knowledgeable Trellman in order to succeed; equally, Trellman becomes dependent on the financial largesse of Adletsky. Trellman stands slightly outside the world's network of relationships yet cannot do entirely without them.

In most of his fictions, Bellow's male protagonists tend to have troubled relationships with women and are often suffering in the aftermath of divorce. The

serenity of Trellman's love for Amy stands in vivid contrast, especially to earlier short fictions of Bellow's such as *What Kind of Day Did You Have?* and sounds a note of romantic celebration that is basically unprecedented in Bellow's work.

OTHER MAJOR WORKS

LONG FICTION: *Dangling Man*, 1944; *The Victim*, 1947; *The Adventures of Augie March*, 1953; *Seize the Day*, 1956; *Henderson the Rain King*, 1959; *Herzog*, 1964; *Mr. Sammler's Planet*, 1970; *Humboldt's Gift*, 1975; *The Dean's December*, 1982; *More Die of Heartbreak*, 1987; *A Theft*, 1989; *The Bellarosa Connection*, 1989; *Ravelstein*, 2000.

PLAYS: *The Wrecker*, pb. 1954; *The Last Analysis*, pr. 1964; *A Wen*, pb. 1965; *Under the Weather*, pr. 1966 (also known as *The Bellow Plays*; includes *Out from Under*, *A Wen*, and *Orange Soufflé*).

NONFICTION: *To Jerusalem and Back: A Personal Account*, 1976; *It All Adds Up: From the Dim Past to the Uncertain Future*, 1994.

EDITED TEXTS: *Great Jewish Stories*, 1963.

BIBLIOGRAPHY

American Studies International 35 (February, 1997). A special issue on Bellow, in which a number of distinguished contributors discuss the importance of Bellow's work as a symbol of the civilization of the United States. The issue contains tributes, critiques, and analyses of Bellow's thought and art.

Bellow, Saul. "Moving Quickly: An Interview with Saul Bellow." *Salmagundi* (Spring/Summer, 1995): 32-53. In this special section, Bellow discusses the relationship between authors and characters, John Updike, intellectuals, gender differences, Sigmund Freud, and kitsch versus avantgarde art.

Bloom, Harold, ed. *Saul Bellow*. New York: Chelsea House, 1986. This volume, with an introduction by Bloom, is an omnibus of reviews and essays on Bellow. Collected here are comments on Bellow by writers such as Robert Penn Warren, Malcolm Bradbury, Tony Tanner, Richard Chase, and Cynthia Ozick. Gives the reader a good sense of early critical responses to Bellow.

Boyers, Robert. "Captains of Intellect." *Salmagundi* (Spring/Summer, 1995): 100-108. Part of a special section on Bellow. A discussion of characters in stories from the collection *Him with His Foot in His Mouth and Other Stories* as captains of intellect who pronounce authoritatively on issues of the modern. Discusses Bellow as an intellectual leader with a multifaceted perspective.

Cronin, Gloria L., and L. H. Goldman, eds. *Saul Bellow in the 1980's: A Collection of Critical Essays.* East Lansing: Michigan State University Press, 1989. This anthology brings together a sampling of a wave of criticism that focuses variously on Bellow's women, his debts to Judaism, connections to theories of history, and modernism.

Freedman, William. "Hanging for Pleasure and Profit: Truth as Necessary Illusion in Bellow's Fiction." *Papers on Language and Literature* 35 (Winter, 1999): 3-27. Argues that Bellow's realism is a search for truth, not the discovery of it. Discusses how Bellow deals with the question of whether a man is isolated or a member of a human community. Contends that for Bellow the value of literature is the ceaseless search for truth in a world that promises truth but seldom provides it.

The Georgia Review 49 (Spring, 1995). A special issue on Bellow in which a number of contributors discuss his life and art, his contribution to American thought and culture, and the wide range of his works.

Kiernan, Robert. *Saul Bellow.* New York: Continuum, 1989. Provides a useful chronology of Bellow's life and production. Traces the writer's development from *Dangling Man* to *More Die of Heartbreak.* The best book on Bellow for the general reader.

Miller, Ruth. *Saul Bellow: A Biography of the Imagination.* New York: St. Martin's Press, 1991. Traces Bellow's travels, linking the author's life to his work. Contains useful appendices, a bibliography, a listing of interviews, and a table of contents from *The Noble Savage,* a journal edited by Bellow.

Pifer, Ellen. *Saul Bellow Against the Grain.* Philadelphia: University of Pennsylvania Press, 1990. In a study that deals comprehensively with the writer's oeuvre, Pifer's central observation is that Bellow's heroes are divided against themselves and conduct an inner strife that dooms and paralyzes them. Their struggle, like Bellow's, is a search for language to articulate the modern condition.

John Stark, updated by Allen Hibbard and Nicholas Birns

AIMEE BENDER

Born: 1969

PRINCIPAL SHORT FICTION
The Girl in the Flammable Skirt, 1998

OTHER LITERARY FORMS
Aimee Bender's first novel, *An Invisible Sign of My Own,* was published in 2000.

ACHIEVEMENTS
Aimee Bender's early work ("Fugue") was accepted by the *Santa Monica Review* and was published in *Absolute Disaster: Fiction from Los Angeles* in the spring of 1997. *The Girl in the Flammable Skirt* is Aimee Bender's first book.

BIOGRAPHY
Aimee Bender grew up in Santa Monica, California, in the early 1980's. Her father was a psychiatrist and her mother, a dancer. As a child, Bender was a budding writer but let this fall by the wayside after elementary school. At Palisades High School, Bender followed her mother's artistic bent in choir and drama but did no further writing until college. Her instructors at the University of California at San Diego, where she received a bachelor's degree in 1991, en-

couraged her writing. She moved to San Francisco and taught reading in an elementary school dominated by Russian immigrants. In the fall of 1995, the University of California at Irvine (UCI) accepted Bender in their graduate writing workshop program as one of only eleven students. She received a master's of fine arts in 1997 and was awarded a one-year fellowship to teach composition and creative writing as well as edit the campus literary journal, *Faultline*. During her graduate studies, Bender lived on Balboa Island but moved to West Hollywood after attaining her degree.

Bender's works have appeared in numerous literary periodicals. Her first published work was "Dreaming in Polish," which appeared in the *Santa Monica Review* (Spring, 1995). This was followed in short succession by "Skinless" (also entitled "Erasing") in the Spring, 1996, issue of the *Colorado Review*. One year later, "Legacy" was printed in *Cream City Review*. "The Rememberer" was first published in the *Missouri Review* in the fall of 1997, at the same time that "The Ring" appeared in the same journal, "What You Left in the Ditch" in *The Antioch Review*, and "Fell This Girl" in *Faultline*. Spring, 1998, saw the publication of "Call My Name" in the *North American Review* as well as "Quiet Please" in the May issue of *GQ*; later that year, "The Healer" appeared in *Story* and "Loser" in *Granta*.

ANALYSIS

When she was at UCI, Aimee Bender was the only one of her class to concentrate on the short-story form. While she claims to admire both this format and that of the novel, perhaps she chose the former because it lent itself to her type of mythic, didactic style. Bender admits to feeling more comfortable in this form. Her early influences included the tales and fables of Jacob and Wilhelm Grimm, Hans Christian Andersen, and others, and the quality of her work certainly mimics these children's stories but in an adult manner. Although many of her classmates wrote their first novels in the custom of the young—set in seedy, angst-ridden apartments—Bender "did try to write more traditional things, but . . . didn't en-

joy it as much." In fact, she found mythic tales "liberating."

Bender's characters live in a never-never land somewhere between life and the pages of a story by Sir James Barrie, but their problems and conflicts are very real because they are precisely those that real people avoid at all costs. They are the unconscionable burdens of life that make humanity wake up in the middle of the night, sweating and frightened. Her characters feel incredibly isolated and yearn for human contact to the point of sacrificing their moral beliefs. They suffer inhuman loss and deformity yet must cope with the results of these losses and the results (sometimes offspring) of these deformities. Just as Hansel and Gretel were unthinkably abandoned in the forest, so Bender's characters must adapt to their trying tragedies with humor, compassion, and creativity.

However, sometimes they fail. As Hugh Garvey pointed out in *The Village Voice*, "the tales in *Flammable* are also unified by the characters' disturbing inability to resolve the conflicting desires for obliteration and connection." While this conflict may seem to be a paradox, it parallels the very human choice of fight or flight when faced with distasteful dilemmas. Bender's characters cannot decide (as many people cannot) whether to accede to the incomprehensible, and sometimes fatal, vagaries of life or to do battle with the unknown and unloved. Through them, she provides the solution that there is no solution at all. Everyone must simply cope as best as he or she can with the abilities and afflictions of life.

"CALL MY NAME"

The speaker in this first-person narrative is decked out like a bird of prey in a dress the color of dried blood. Like many single women, she seeks a mate for a sex-driven relationship, but he must be someone nonthreatening, someone she can dominate—or can she? Spreading her spoor around the subway, she spots a likely target. At first he ignores her slithery advances, but then she senses "he's getting the sexual vibe which makes me feel . . . alive." The speaker follows him home, trying to make her lust transform him, but he remains steadfast in his refusal of her. He has no wish to make the connection. Finally, he lets her into his apartment, after which she finds herself naked and tied to a chair. Has she won? Has she failed? She hears the sound of winning, but the reader has to wonder if this tale of power and its fatal links is not also an anti-Edenic refutation of the irrefutable attraction of sex.

"WHAT YOU LEFT IN THE DITCH"

A young woman's husband returns home from the war without lips. As with many of Bender's stories focusing on the recurring theme of mutilation and loss, this very bizarre image must be viewed in the larger context of loss of communication and contact that may occur after a debilitating rift in a relationship. The wife cannot cope with the return of only a partial husband, in fact hardly a husband at all, as he must wear a pacifier-like prosthesis until his lips can be restored. He becomes her child, someone who must be fed and nurtured, even if this chore is distasteful. She buries her loyalty to him as she buries in the backyard the "dead sweaters" she has knitted and sets off to seduce the grocery checker. However, he is too perfect to "save" her and restore her loss. In the end, she returns to her husband, covering her ears in an imitation of his disability, equalizing their losses so that they may recover their lost relationship.

"SKINLESS"

Superficially, this story is about the naïve notion that love and trust will overcome racial and ethnic hatred. Beneath it all, there are undertones of frustration, loss, and contempt. Renny, a neo-Nazi inmate of a halfway house, and Jill, the activities director of the facility, are in conflict but not necessarily with each other. In fact, each is looking for a mother. For Renny, this madonna figure takes the form of the mothers of his brother's amours; for Jill, this figure is herself. The found object must also be destroyed, and Renny finds himself scratching out the images of women in photos, while Jill wonders what lies, literally, beneath the skins of her lover and her rabbi. She needs to find "what exactly they were made of." In an odd replication of the death of the philosopher Hypatia, she needs to do more than scratch the surface of their beings. However, this story is not about the connection between Jew and neo-Nazi but rather a look at forced coexistence between enemies. The

ending is ambiguous, as Renny has the opportunity to either make love to Jill or push her off a cliff. The only clue offered is the sexual connection they appear to make, which may or may not salvage a relationship forged in hell.

"DREAMING IN POLISH"

"There was an old man and an old woman and they dreamed the same dreams." In a small town, prophets are easily believed and often revered, and so it is in this tale of two Holocaust victims, who repeat their visions, in fragments, to the villagers. When the dreams begin to come true, the town is thrown into a frenzy of obedience. Whatever is augured must be fulfilled, even to the covering of a vague statue of a Greek figure. The caretaker of the statue is a young woman, who works in a store during the day but must care for her invalid father at night. Her mother, who is inclined to walking excursions and Holocaust museums, decides to abandon them for a short trip to a nearby display. Her absence causes an undue share of their responsibilities to fall on the daughter, which is the theme of the story. She is overwhelmed by her love for her father and by the burden his illness has placed on her. The statue, strong and silent, becomes an icon of hope and recovery, a regeneration of their family unit. The old couple? They begin to speak only in Polish, and even in their glossolalia they are revered and upheld as New-World Isaiahs.

"THE RING"

Two robbers break into kitchens and find precious jewels in counter canisters of dry goods. They steal diamond, ruby, and emerald rings, but only the ruby turns out to be cursed. It starts to turn everything red, and in a frenzy they return it, but the wife of the robber cannot live without it, so her husband resteals it to make her happy. They fly to Tahiti, but the ring turns the sea red for a mile, so they destroy it "in [the] red wet mouth of the ocean." This is the most fablelike of the stories in its simplistic rhetoric; however, the magic lies not in the extraordinary jewels—which are amazingly easy to come by, being guarded only by a large white cat—but in the ordinary items. The sugar in the ruby's canister is the only essence in the world, it seems, not affected by its crimson taint. The robber's wife characterizes her husband as a "baker," and they delight in flour-coated sex. A celebration of the commonplace, this is a venue where thieves are safe.

OTHER MAJOR WORK

LONG FICTION: *An Invisible Sign of My Own*, 2000.

BIBLIOGRAPHY

Garvey, Hugh. "Writers on the Verge: Aimee Bender." *The Village Voice* 43 (June 2, 1998): 79-80. This is a profile of Aimee Bender with some helpful insight into her overall themes and influences.

Lewis, William Henry. "Tales of Sexual Zealots." *The Washington Post*, October 18, 1998, p. X10. Aimee Bender's initial offering defies expectations of the typical first novel/anthology. This collection describes what fables can do when used as social tools. A variety of narrative methods are displayed, and the author concentrates on the conflict between the modern and the old-fashioned, between nonsectarian and Jew. In addition, she concentrates on the trade-off of power and sex between men and women.

Luis, Fiona. "Bender Evokes Laughter Subdued by Absurdity." *Boston Globe*, August 11, 1998, p. E2. Bender's stories would be hilarious except for the way they evoke a certain sympathy in the reader. She carefully dissects the seasick soul in a fashion that leaves the reader with a sense of loss and grief. Each story both repels and compels the reader to finish it and, in the end, find a certain comfort there.

McLellen, Dennis. "Making a Myth in the Space of a Short Story." *The Los Angeles Times*, September 9, 1998, p. 1. Aimee Bender started writing as a young girl in Santa Monica. She expanded her writing expertise in the University of California at Irvine writing program and has returned to her roots in the city to publish her first collection.

Jennifer L. Wyatt

STEPHEN VINCENT BENÉT

Born: Bethlehem, Pennsylvania; July 22, 1898
Died: New York, New York; March 13, 1943

PRINCIPAL SHORT FICTION

Thirteen O'Clock, 1937
Tales Before Midnight, 1939
Twenty-five Short Stories, 1943
The Last Circle, 1946

OTHER LITERARY FORMS

Stephen Vincent Benét's *John Brown's Body* (1928), a long epic poem, created a sensation when it was published and remains, despite his many volumes of poems, including *Western Star* (1943), his best-known and most popular work. He also wrote Hollywood scripts, librettos, and an opera, and he composed radio addresses and scripts, used for patriotic propaganda during World War II. Benét also published five novels.

ACHIEVEMENTS

American history, especially that of the Civil War, is integral to the fiction of Stephen Vincent Benét. Whether folklore, fantasy, or parable, his writing reverberates with history, not only American but also European, since he lived in France for several years. His characters range from European immigrants to expatriates from America, from slaves to frontiersmen, from the World War I lost generation eccentrics to religionists. His fictional modes include irony, satire, sentimentality, and romanticism. Benét imbues his fiction with themes of national pride, freedom with responsibility, the cardinal virtues, and the fair play of living the good life.

His honors and prizes include a John Simon Guggenheim Memorial Foundation Fellowship (1926), which was extended for six months (1927), a Pulitzer Prize (1929) for *John Brown's Body*, election to the National Institute of Arts and Letters (1929), an O. Henry Memorial Prize for the short story (1936), an honorary degree by Yale University (1937), election to the American Academy of Arts and Sciences (1938), and a Pulitzer Prize, awarded posthumously, for *Western Star*.

BIOGRAPHY

Descendant of a grandfather and father, both West Pointers and Army men, Stephen Vincent Benét traveled and lived with his family on military posts throughout the United States. This familiarity with the locales and terrains of the United States provided a rich background to his short stories and poems. Colonel James Walker Benét, an omnivorous reader with a deep love of country and history, inflamed his younger son with these same passions. Like his older brother William Rose Benét, a well-known writer, editor, and magazine founder, Stephen Vincent Benét was graduated from Yale University in 1919. He was given a Yale travel award and a John Simon Guggenheim Memorial Foundation grant, permitting him to spend initially eighteen months in France and to attend the Sorbonne in Paris. He lived in France several years and attributed his particular love for the United States to having gained perspective on his native land from his European travels. On his return to the United States in 1923, he published three volumes: *King David; The Ballad of William Sycamore, 1790-1880*; and *Jean Huguenot*, a novel. In 1926, he returned with a John Simon Guggenheim Memorial Foundation Fellowship to France, where he worked on *John Brown's Body*, a poem about the Civil War, which won the Pulitzer Prize in 1929. He was also elected to the National Institute of Arts and Letters the same year. In 1933 he became editor of the Yale Series of Younger Poets Competition and two years later began reviewing for the New York *Herald Tribune* and *Saturday Review of Literature*. In 1936 his short story "The Devil and Daniel Webster" was awarded the O. Henry Memorial Prize for the best American short

Stephen Vincent Benét (Library of Congress)

story of the year. In 1937 his story "Johnny Pye and the Fool-Killer," and in 1940 "Freedom's a Hard-Bought Thing," won similar honors.

ANALYSIS

Stephen Vincent Benét achieved mastery of the short fiction form only after laborious and persistent efforts. His preference was for poetry and the freedom it offered as opposed to the restrictions of the short story. Perhaps because of this, he never experimented with the short-story form and unflinchingly favored the traditionally-structured stories with a definite beginning, middle, and end. He also skillfully employed the traditional device of the narrator to bring about a sense of immediacy and the interesting possibility of self-revelation and concealment which this perspective offered; he was not, however, an innovator of any new form of the short story.

Early in his career, Benét reconciled his conscience with his economic needs by writing original short stories designed to elicit popular appeal. He achieved this self-appeasement by basing his stories on material from American history and folklore and transfusing it with his vivid imagination. The reconciliation resulted in such stories as "The Devil and Daniel Webster," "Daniel Webster and the Sea Serpent," "Daniel Webster and the Ides of March," "Jacob and the Indians," "A Tooth for Paul Revere," "Freedom's a Hard-Bought Thing," and "Johnny Pye and the Fool-Killer."

"THE DEVIL AND DANIEL WEBSTER"

The first Webster story, "The Devil and Daniel Webster," was published in 1936 in the *Saturday Evening Post*, and its tremendous success gave Benét immediate national recognition and fame. The cause of its success was deeply rooted; it sparked the latent historic and cultural feelings in the American mind. Moreover, in Webster, Benét found an ideal folk hero who had all the myth surrounding his character to provide ample material for productive characterization. The basis for the conflict in the story is extremely interesting. Webster was renowned for his superb oratorical powers, and consequently he was the perfect protagonist to meet the Devil in an oratorical contest and defeat him. This symbolic contest between the representatives of good and evil had wide appeal and was complemented not only by Benét's use of local humor but also by the story's inherent universal significance. These elements of the story, combined with the tones of pathos and human nobility, make it more than a simple humorous fantasy—it is a classic American fable. The New England dialect of the narrator forms a striking blend with the rhythm and visual imagery drawn from several literary sources. In addition, Benét's use of little-known historical characters on the jury—Simon Girty, the renegade, and the Reverend John Smeet, the strangler—adds novelty and helps give the story a sustained interest. The narrator's final comment that the Devil "hasn't been seen in the state of New Hampshire from that day to this" and "I'm not talking about Massachusetts or Vermont" redeems the story from heavy didacticism.

The story, however, has a moral derived from the grass roots of American tradition. It is, from one perspective, an American version of the story of Job and the Faust legend. Although the name Jabez Stone is implicitly suggestive, Stone is initially unlike Job. He is a poor man plagued by bad luck. When his troubles multiply, he sells his soul to the Devil, not for power like Faust, but for the typically American goal of material prosperity. Unlike Faust, the tug-of-war for Jabez's soul is not between God and the Devil but between the epitome of Americanism, Daniel Webster, and Mr. Scratch. Jabez, however, is not damned like Faust, for the American virtues embedded in Webster make him use his capacity to reason, to awaken pity from a biased jury. Webster points out that since the Devil is a foreign prince, he has no authority over an American citizen. The Devil's line of argument is clever and logical. He dates his citizenship back to the day when the first injustice was done to the Indians and when the first slave ship set sail from Africa; and when Webster permits the Devil to choose any judge and jury as long as they are American citizens, the Devil selects Judge Hathorne of the Salem witch trials and a dozen wicked men from hell. Webster uses his powers of elocution to awaken pity from the jury by reviving their sense of manhood. He recalls the simple pleasures of life that can only be enjoyed in freedom. He concedes that although errors and discrimination had taken place in America, something new had been born out of all this—a freer, more vital way of life built by everybody's efforts. Although Jabez is a mean man, he is a man and thus has some good in him. Webster then stresses the fact that being a man is a matter of pride because even in hell a man's mettle can be recognized.

In his concluding statements Webster makes, through his plea for Jabez, a plea for himself and for humankind. Webster observes that the jurors were out to get Jabez, as well as condemn him, if he fought them with their own weapons. He evokes their sympathy by recalling the symbolic journeying of all men, which is filled with failures and deceptions. Only real men, he stresses, can see the inherent greatness of the journey. This triggers the latent chords of manhood in the jury and their spokesman declares: "The jury has considered its verdict. We find for the defendant, Jabez Stone." The verdict is tempered by the spirit rather than the letter of the law, for the spokesman adds: "but even the damned may salute the eloquence of Mr. Webster." Resorting to a similar spirit Webster also lets the Devil go. The Devil will be back, but his evil has been conquered in some of the United States by humanity, justice, and the representative of a country that symbolizes all of humankind's positive hopes. These layers of symbolic connotations give Benét's story a depth which equals the humor.

Benét's other two Webster tales cannot measure up to the quality of "The Devil and Daniel Webster." In "Daniel Webster and the Sea Serpent," for example, Benét weaves another humorous myth, but the story has little, if any, national significance. Nevertheless, he often channeled this penchant for history into realism and achieved aesthetically laudable results.

In stories such as "The Die-Hard," "Jacob and the Indians," and "Freedom's a Hard-Bought Thing," Benét uses the historical base to portray realism. His technique in these stories is to focus on a protagonist who represents a given historical period and to make his experiences reflect the essence of that period. This type of story obviously requires a strong central character who has to be typical and yet distinct and plausible enough to sustain the reader's interest. Probably the best story of this genre is "Freedom's a Hard-Bought Thing," which won the O. Henry Memorial Award for the best short story of 1940. The story, which derives its effect from its realism and its moral, is equally notable for depicting faithfully the colorful dialect and point of view of specific ethnic groups. The story has a strong narrative core with the narrator, a black woman, telling the children the story of Cue, a plantation slave. Benét's faithful depiction of her speech patterns, rhythms, and diction helps to individualize her but does not obstruct the flow of the plot.

"FREEDOM'S A HARD-BOUGHT THING"

Cue, the protagonist of "Freedom's a Hard-Bought Thing," grows up to be a proud, strong, and affable young man. He likes his work at the plantation blacksmith shop and has no complaints about his life until his parents die in an epidemic. Soon after

this, their cabin is given to new slaves, and all that remains is their burial ground. The tragedy changes Cue's complacent outlook on life, and he begins to ask himself questions. This state leads him to Aunt Rachel, a conjure woman, who diagnoses his problem as freedom sickness:

> It's sickness in your blood. . . . It's a sickness in your liver and veins. Your daddy never had it that I know of—he took after his mommy's side. His daddy was a corromante and they is bold and free, and you takes after him. It is the freedom sickness, son Cue.

Aunt Rachel then tells Cue about the underground road and how to find it. Cue then runs away but is caught and whipped. Because of his good record, however, his owners are easy on him. The failure of his attempted escape makes him ponder Aunt Rachel's advice about learning the wisdom of nature by observing her creatures. He even channels his effort toward learning to read so he may acquire some of the wisdom of the white people.

Eventually he meets a white man who tells him of freedom and the underground railroad. Yet Cue again fails to escape because he gives the last place on a boat to his girlfriend Sukey. Cue is branded a runaway and all his bitterness is diverted toward Aunt Rachel because the burden of gaining freedom literally drains him. She then reassures him by reminding him of the ancient freedom of her people and the long tedious road ahead for him. Her words of wisdom solidify Cue's faith, and he feels that he is bound to be a witness to freedom. Soon after this, Cue is sold to new owners and he confronts deliberate cruelty and suffering for the first time. Finally he manages to escape and through the underground railways arrives in Canada—a free man finally. Unable at first to grasp totally the ramifications of his new state, he ultimately gives himself a full name—John H. Cue—to symbolize his nascent freedom.

One of the reasons for the overwhelming impact of the story is its resemblance to biblical parables. Cue's dual strength of body and mind make him a symbol for all slaves who have struggled to attain freedom, and the dialect of his narrator, as well as the direct invocations of God, remind the reader of the

King James Bible. The storyteller's name, "Aunt Rachel," recalls the Old Testament, and her specific memory of her past juxtaposed with the symbolic connotations of Cue's story makes "Freedom's a Hard-Bought Thing" a narrative of a whole people. In addition, Benét's portrayal of Cue is specific and select enough to individualize him and make the overall effect of the story extremely realistic. Details in setting, such as the bubbling pot in Aunt Rachel's cabin and her advice to Cue to study the wisdom embedded in the creatures of nature add both realism and a dash of local color. Finally Benét's sentimentalism in rewarding Cue with another Sukey at the end has a thematic justification; it represents the reevolution and continuity of the race under its newly acquired freedom.

"JOHNNY PYE AND THE FOOL-KILLER"

Benét was not always an optimist and did not always stress fulfillment of hopes in his tales. Through "Johnny Pye and the Fool-Killer" Benét vented a subdued preoccupation to illustrate the dismal aspect of folklore. This story deals with the failure of people who do not follow the rudiments of common sense. Johnny Pye, the protagonist, is the typical naïve youth who is initiated to the ways of the world through hard experience. Johnny, an orphan in a small town, has foster parents, a miller and his wife, who treat him like a fool because they think that is the proper way to bring up a child. When the miller tells him that he is the most foolish boy he has ever seen (Johnny being already fearful of the legendary Fool-Killer), he runs away. Johnny's life after this is a series of apprenticeships with a quack doctor who makes the mistake of returning to a town he had previously visited, and a merchant who is totally obsessed with making money. These follies make Johnny run away again to avoid entrapment in similar situations. He then meets an inventor of a perpetual motion machine, a drunken fiddler, impetuous soldiers and Indians, a Republican Congressman, a Democratic Congressman, and finally a President of the United States; the last three barrage Johnny with the notion of the omniscience of their respective parties.

On the night he wins the hand of the girl he loves, Johnny hears the dogged steps of the Fool-Killer, but

he marries her anyway and accepts the President's appointment to be the postmaster in his hometown. Soon after this, Johnny encounters the Fool-Killer, an old scissors-grinder, putting an edge on a scythe. The Fool-Killer tells Johnny that it is his time. The old man, however, gives Johnny a deferral when he protests. He even agrees to give Johnny the first reprieve in history if he can answer one question: How can a person be a human being and not be a fool?

When Johnny is forty he faces the first major tragedy in his own family—his eldest son drowns. Obsessed with grief, Johnny confronts the Fool-Killer. The Fool-Killer evades him and reminds him that even though his grief cannot be healed, time will pass by, and that his present responsibilities lie in taking care of his wife and the other children. Time passes and Johnny becomes a grandfather, although his wife dies. When Johnny is ninety-two years old, he meets the Fool-Killer for the final time. Since the last meeting, Johnny has gone through a great deal and has an answer to the Fool-Killer's question. All humans are basically fools although the wise and the brave account for the occasional progress. Humanity is a conglomerate of different types and qualities of humans, and only a creature foolish by nature could have been ejected from the Garden of Eden or chosen to come out of the sea onto dry land. Johnny realizes that he has no use for a man who has not been labeled a fool by any of his acquaintances. This answer satisfies the Fool-Killer, who offers Johnny eternal life. Johnny, after pondering the problem, declines on the grounds that his physical decay will continue with the progression of years. In addition, Johnny realizes that with his wife and friends gone, he would have no one to talk to if he decided to accept the Fool-Killer's offer. He questions the Fool-Killer to find out if he would see his friends eventually on the Day of Judgment if he decided to stay around. The Fool-Killer answers: "I can't tell you that . . . I only go so far." Johnny leaves with him, content to go that distance.

In "Johnny Pye and the Fool-Killer," Benét varies his style to suit his material. Although the story begins with a direct address to the reader—"You don't hear much about the Fool-Killer these days"—the narrator has no symbolic identity other than that specific function. He remains anonymous and blends the elements of humor, folklore, and native wisdom to enhance the total impact. He narrates the tale without serious moralizing and integrates a subtle, refined humor directed to underline the pretensions and eccentricities of the American character. The shift in tone implicit in Johnny's discovery that the "Fool-Killer" is a manifestation of time is achieved smoothly and without any abrupt recourse to philosophical discourse. The theme of the story finally comes into focus when Johnny realizes that folly is an essential and humanizing frailty. His recognition is a reflection of the vision of the "New American Adam" as a creature with distinct possibilities and human flaws. Benét's larger focus, however, is on human morality. The pathos in the final scene, tempered with hope, seems to be a fitting epitaph for Johnny and a fitting ending to an American Fable.

Benét's forte was not the short story, yet his tales will always be popular because of their typically American grass roots. Although his stories were written during a period of national and world upheavals, their patriotic blend of American history, wisdom, and folklore has a timeless quality because it captures the essence of the American spirit—freedom, justice, equality, opportunity, and plain common sense.

OTHER MAJOR WORKS

LONG FICTION: *The Beginning of Wisdom*, 1921; *Young People's Pride*, 1922; *Jean Huguenot*, 1923; *Spanish Bayonet*, 1926; *James Shore's Daughter*, 1934.

PLAYS: *Nerves*, pr. 1924 (with John Farrar); *That Awful Mrs. Eaton*, pr. 1924 (with Farrar); *The Headless Horseman*, pr., pb. 1937; *The Devil and Daniel Webster*, pr. 1938; *We Stand United and Other Radio Scripts*, pb. 1945.

POETRY: *Five Men and Pompey*, 1915; *Young Adventure*, 1918; *Heavens and Earth*, 1920; *King David*, 1923; *The Ballad of William Sycamore, 1790-1880*, 1923; *Tiger Joy*, 1925; *John Brown's Body*, 1928; *Ballads and Poems, 1915-1930*, 1931; *A Book of Americans*, 1933 (with Rosemary Carr Benét); *Burning City*, 1936; *The Ballad of the Duke's Mercy*, 1939; *Western Star*, 1943.

NONFICTION: *America*, 1944; *Stephen Vincent Benét on Writing: A Great Writer's Letters of Advice to a Young Beginner*, 1946; *Selected Letters of Stephen Vincent Benét*, 1960.

MISCELLANEOUS: *Selected Works of Stephen Vincent Benét*, 1942 (Basil Davenport, editor); *Stephen Vincent Benét: Selected Poetry and Prose*, 1942 (Basil Davenport, editor).

BIBLIOGRAPHY

Benét, Stephen Vincent. *Selected Letters of Stephen Vincent Benét*. Edited by Charles A. Fenton. New Haven, Conn.: Yale University Press, 1960. A broad selection of letters reflecting Benét's moods and perceptions about places in the United States and Europe, the people and the literary and social scenes, especially during the 1920's, 1930's, and the few years that he lived in the 1940's.

Bleiler, Everett Franklin. *The Guide to Supernatural Fiction*. Kent, Ohio: Kent State University Press, 1983. Includes a list and commentary on several stories by Stephen Vincent Benét that deal with themes of fantasy and extrasensory perceptions and hallucinations.

Fenton, Charles A. *Stephen Vincent Benét: The Life and Times of an American Man of Letters*. New Haven, Conn.: Yale University Press, 1958. A definitive biography that not only presents the well-documented life of Benét but also comments on the works. Fenton had the cooperation of Rosemary Carr (Mrs. Benét) and access to Benét's diaries.

Partenheimer, David. "Benét's 'The Devil and Daniel Webster.'" *The Explicator* 55 (Fall, 1996): 37-39. Discusses how Benét makes a legend out of Webster, the great American politician and orator, and at the same time paradoxically damns him for his willingness to sell his soul for fame.

Roache, Joel. "Stephen Vincent Benét." In *Dictionary of Literary Biography*. Vol. 102. Detroit: Gale Research, 1991. Delineates the writings of Benét and provides a short biography and a commentary on the subject matter and themes of representative short stories. A straightforward and readable article, succinctly written.

Singer, Robert. "One Against All: The New England Past and Present Responsibilities in 'The Devil and Daniel Webster.'" *Literature/Film Quarterly* 22 (1994): 265-271. Discusses the 1941 film version of Benét's story. Argues that the Faust theme in the story and the screenplay that he co-authored uniquely dramatize the conflict between Satan and the American statesman. Argues that the film is a perceptive political treatment of the Depression and the coming of war in the late 1930's.

Snow, Richard F. "Benet's Birthday." *American Heritage* 49 (October, 1998): 6-7. A biographical sketch that comments on Benét's winning of the Pulitzer Prize and his attempts to forge a clear American language that was large enough for poetry but also idiomatic and spare.

Stroud, Parry. *Stephen Vincent Benét.* New York: Twayne, 1962. A critique that focuses on Benét's liberalism, reflected in his writings. Stroud places the writer in a historical and cultural frame in an interpretation of Benét's themes. The analysis is clear in its literary perspective and its biographical framework.

Zia Hasan, updated by Julia B. Boken

GINA BERRIAULT

Born: January 1, 1926; Long Beach, California
Died: July 15, 1999; Greenbrae, California

PRINCIPAL SHORT FICTION

The Mistress, and Other Stories, 1965
The Infinite Passion of Expectation, 1982
Women in Their Beds: New and Selected Stories, 1996
The Great Petrowski: A Fable, 2000

OTHER LITERARY FORMS

Gina Berriault authored five novels, *The Descent* (1960), *Conference of Victims* (1962), *The Son* (1966), *The Lights of Earth* (1984), and *Afterwards: A Novel* (1998). She also wrote a screenplay, adapted from her story of the same title, *The Stone Boy* (pr. 1984). The film version was directed by Christopher Cain.

ACHIEVEMENTS

Gina Berriault received numerous awards, including a fellowship from Centro Mexicano de Escritores, Mexico City, Mexico (1963), the National Book Critics Circle Award (1996), the Commonwealth Club Gold Medal and the Bay Area Book Reviewers Award (1997), and the PEN/Faulkner Award for Fiction and the Rea Award (1997). She also received awards from *The Paris Review*, including the Aga Khan Prize for Fiction, and her work has appeared in *Prize Stories: The O. Henry Awards*.

BIOGRAPHY

Gina Berriault was born in Long Beach, California, to Russian-Jewish immigrants. Her father, who worked as a marble cutter and later as a writer, was not always able to secure employment. Her mother went blind when Berriault was fourteen years old, which, Berriault suggested, influenced her writing. An avid reader, Berriault started to write her own stories in grammar school. Although a drama teacher in high school offered to pay her tuition at a prestigious drama school, the death of Berriault's father prevented her from taking the offer, and she received no further formal education or any formal training as a writer. Instead, Berriault worked various jobs including clerk, waitress, and news reporter in order to support her mother, brother, and sister.

Berriault was married to J. V. Berriault, a musician, whom she later divorced. Supporting herself and her daughter through her writing, her first success came in 1958 when seven of her stories were collected in Scribners's *Short Story I*. In the 1960's, Berriault lived and wrote in Mexico for a time and wrote articles for *Esquire*, eventually gaining recognition as a writer of serious fiction. She taught creative writing at San Francisco University and at Ohio State University, and received an appointment as a scholar at the Radcliffe Institute for Independent Study. She died in 1999 at the age of seventy-three.

ANALYSIS

Although Gina Berriault wrote short stories for three decades, she is still considered an undervalued writer who does not receive the critical or commercial attention she deserves. She is often described as a "writer's writer," that is, somebody with an enthusiastic following within the literary community but who is unknown outside of it. It is as a writer of short stories that she is best known and admired, and many of her stories have appeared in anthologies. These often brief stories deploy a detached economical prose style to empathically but unsentimentally portray a wide variety of characters in crisis situations. Unable to change their lives or to fully identify or express their feelings of loss, despair, and loneliness, Berriault's characters often suffer in silence and isolation. Particularly important is the theme of unrealized expectations, which contrast with the hard realities in which her characters actually live.

Another virtue of Berriault's work was that she could write convincingly from both male and female perspectives and from the vantage point of both youth and age. Her characters also come from a variety of social, ethnic, and economic backgrounds. Using California, especially the Bay Area, as the setting for many of her stories, her picture of modern California is a far cry from its image as a land of milk and honey. Many of her West Coast denizens lead bleak lives in diminished circumstances, having ended up in dead-end marriages or dead-end jobs.

Berriault's brevity and her pessimistic vision of life have much in common with the minimalist writers of the 1980's, such as Raymond Carver. Her unsentimental depiction of hardship has given her a reputation as a writer of gritty realism, but her work also has an intellectual and poetic side, which gives complexity and mystery to her otherwise often very short stories.

"THE BYSTANDER"

Although this is a very short story, Berriault is

Gina Berriault (AP/Wide World Photos)

able to imply a larger social world, depicting the marginal side of American life and featuring people who are down on their luck, living out their years in inexpensive boarding houses and state institutions. Told from the perspective of eighteen-year-old Arty, the "bystander" of the title, the story reveals that Arty's father, Lewis, has become an embittered and disappointed man, who has worked all his life and feels he has nothing to show for it. An irrational assault on his girlfriend has landed him in a mental ward, where Arty, whom he has raised since his wife's death, has come to visit him. Much of the story is taken up by the disjointed conversation between father and son, so that it appears to be more of a vignette in which inconsequential details dominate—the two talk in a desultory way about where to eat, how to treat a cold, tool boxes, and travel directions. The underlying point, however, is that Lewis has become weak and dependent and that Arty has assumed a more parental role. When Arty departs, it dawns on him that the strong man he once saw as a good father and provider no longer exists and that he must stand by helplessly as his father utterly loses his old, heroic identity and becomes simply another inmate warehoused in a bleak asylum.

"DEATH OF A LESSER MAN"

"Death of a Lesser Man" is a stream-of-consciousness story, which mixes memory, fantasy, and reality. When Claudia's husband Gerald suddenly faints at a party, they both fear he has a terminal illness. While they wait for him to undergo a series of tests, Claudia undergoes a psychological crisis in which she guiltily realizes that Gerald's death would constitute a liberation for her, the possibility of another existence filled with new chances for passion, adventure, and intellectual stimulation. Claudia is also haunted by an imagined stalker, a nightmarish figure, who seems be stealing away the dreams that have sustained her in her daily life. These dreams are fueled by memories of a special time in her past, a brief visit to Paris, where she prowled the streets looking for the French writer Albert Camus. Instead of finding Camus, however, the menacing dolt of her previous dreams and fears seems to invade her bed at the end of the story, cropping her hair with large, cold scissors and leaving her in a state of utter desolation.

"THE INFINITE PASSION OF EXPECTATION"

"The Infinite Passion of Expectation" is told from the perspective of a young waitress, who has been paying a small fee for therapy from an elderly English psychiatrist. The old man tells the waitress that he still allows himself great expectations of love and other pleasures and has advised her to do the same. In fact, at age seventy-nine, the ever-youthful psychiatrist is actually considering marriage to or at least a love affair with the young waitress, beginning a tentative if somewhat manipulative courtship of her. Learning from the lessons of the psychiatrist, however, she rejects him, realizing a love affair with the old man would cut off many other possibilities for her, virtually ending her life. Because of her diminished circumstances, the waitress had always thought that to dream was to delude herself, but inspired by the old man's advice and example she gives herself over to "the infinite passion of expectation."

"DIARY OF K. W."

"Diary of K. W." is told through a series of entries in the diary of an old woman known only by her initials, K. W. She is undergoing a psychological crisis, which begins when she is fired from a job as a substitute helper in a grammar school cafeteria. Reasoning that if the children eat their food they will only grow up to suffer as she has, she refuses to serve them their hot lunches. She also begins deliberately to starve herself as well, even while trying to reach out to the neighbors in her apartment building, notably a new tenant, a self-involved Dutch architect. She occasionally leaves in his mailbox samples of her art work, which she signs, semi-anonymously, "K. W." The reader begins to realize that, although her last job was a poorly paid and unglamourous one, K. W. is actually an artist and an intellectual, and that she had once been valedictorian of her class, been married, and had a promising life. It all ended, however, in poverty and isolation. Although she is scrupulous about feeding the architect's neglected cats, she allows herself to starve to death without seeking help, and her neighbors never realize that she is dying. More than the hungry body, however, this is a story about the hungry soul. Her diaries tell us that she wishes to be judged not by her body or by her external circumstances but by her soul, which she describes as a Janus-like entity, which can simultaneously look at who she is and who she might have been.

"THE STONE BOY"

This story, set on a family farm, concerns the tragic accidental shooting of the family's older brother Eugie by his younger brother Arnold. The nine-year-old Arnold seems to show no remorse for accidentally shooting and killing Eugie while they were on their way to do their morning chores. Shunned by his community and family, Arnold begins to live within himself, unable to articulate his grief and denied the comfort he needs from others. Although Arnold tries to reach out to his parents, and they, in spite of their grief and anger, try to reach out to him, there is never a reconciliation. Arnold is left permanently estranged from his family, presenting a unreadable, unreachable "stone face" to the world that does not reveal his inner world of anguish and loneliness.

OTHER MAJOR WORKS

LONG FICTION: *The Descent*, 1960; *Conference of Victims*, 1962; *The Son*, 1966; *The Lights of Earth*, 1984; *Afterwards: A Novel*, 1998.

SCREENPLAY: *The Stone Boy*, 1984.

BIBLIOGRAPHY

Amdahl, Gary. "Women in Their Beds." *The Nation* (1996). Important review of Berriault's work, which suggests she ought to be as familiar to readers as Toni Morrison or John Updike. Laments her lack of recognition, praises her as a writer who has written magnificently and consistently for forty years, and singles out the depth of understanding she brings to the creation of her characters.

Berriault, Gina. "An Interview with Gina Berriault." Interview by Bonnie Lyons and Bill Oliver. *Literary Review* (Summer, 1994): 7, 14-23. Discusses Berriault's childhood, her father, her favorite authors, her opinions of contemporary fiction, and the pressures on contemporary writers to evade or falsify the truth. Describing the purpose of her fiction as compassion and comprehension, Berriault also notes that, like all serious writers of fiction, she is a political writer.

Dubus, Andre. "The Infinite Passion of Expectation." *America* (September 8, 1984). This important review by one of the finest contemporary American short-story writers praises this collection as the best book of short stories by a living American author.

Harshaw, Tobin. "Women in Their Beds." *New York Times Book Review* (May 5, 1990): 22. Praises her gift for language, the complexity of her characterization, and her ability to engage the reader sympathetically in the crises her characters face. Faults Berriault's stories for being too low-key.

Milton, Edith. "Lives that Touch Without Intimacy." *The New York Times Book Review* (January 8, 1983). Positive review of *The Infinite Passion of Expectation*, describes the stories as flawless miniatures presenting paralyzed characters whose shattered expectations have led them to live in dreams or in the past rather than the present world.

Poore, Charles. "Books of the Times: The Moment of Truth Doesn't Need Stretching." *The New York Times* (September, 1965). Praises Berriault for finding originality in what otherwise might be seen as predictable subjects. Draws attention to her economy and her minimalist, open endings, her sympathetic picture of the down-and-out, and her satiric look at intellectual bohemia in the Bay Area.

Shelnutt, Eve, ed. "Almost Impossible." In *The Confidence Woman: Twenty-six Woman Writers at Work*. Atlanta, Ga.: Longstreet Press, 1991. Insightful interview with Berriault in which she discusses the nature of writing, her own creative process, her identity as a woman writer, and her students' reactions to her short stories.

Margaret Boe Birns

DORIS BETTS

Born: Statesville, North Carolina; June 4, 1932

PRINCIPAL SHORT FICTION

The Gentle Insurrection and Other Stories, 1954
The Astronomer and Other Stories, 1965
Beasts of the Southern Wild and Other Stories,
1973

OTHER LITERARY FORMS

Doris Betts is the author of several novels: *Tall Houses in Winter* (1957), *The Scarlet Thread* (1964), *Heading West* (1981), a February, 1982, Book-of-the-Month Club selection, *Souls Raised from the Dead* (1994), and *The Sharp Teeth of Love* (1997).

ACHIEVEMENTS

Doris Betts won the 1954 University of North Carolina G. P. Putnam Award for her first short-story collection, *The Gentle Insurrection and Other Stories*, and her third collection, *Beasts of the Southern Wild and Other Stories*, was a National Book Award finalist. The state of North Carolina presented her with its Medal for Literature in 1975. She won a John Dos Passos Award in 1983 and a Medal of Merit from the Academy of Arts and Letters in 1989.

BIOGRAPHY

Doris June Waugh Betts is the daughter of William Elmore and Mary Ellen Freeze Waugh. She was educated in the public schools of Statesville, North Carolina, and at the University of North Carolina at Greensboro (1950-1953) and later at Chapel Hill (1954). On July 5, 1952, she married Lowry Matthew Betts, a lawyer. They had three children. Betts claimed that her childhood experiences as an Associate Reform Presbyterian have stayed with her. "The Bible is a strong source in my writing because I grew up in a strict religious family, strongly fundamentalist. . . . Bible stories themselves are marvelous, really marvelous, background for a writer—a lot of the rhythms, to begin with, in the Bible are good for writers. And secondly, all these stories are very physical, very spe-

cific and concrete." Betts taught English, including writing, at the University of North Carolina at Chapel Hill. She received a Tanner Award for excellence in undergraduate teaching in 1973, the same year that *Beasts of the Southern Wild and Other Stories* was nominated for a National Book Award. She and her husband bought a farm near Chapel Hill. Betts declined a nomination for chancellorship of the University of North Carolina but continued to teach.

ANALYSIS

Doris Betts's fiction is strongly rooted in the landscape and experiences of North Carolina. Her first collections were solidly realistic stories about her own part of that state, the Piedmont Upper South, and they focus on everyday concerns such as growing up, growing old, racial tensions, family relationships, and death as it is perceived by the dying and the living left behind. Her later work, although still centered on everyday experiences and characters, time, and mortality, also moved into fantasy and passed through a concern with death into a consideration of the afterlife. Her later stories, as always rich in diction and image, operate on several levels simultaneously.

THE GENTLE INSURRECTION AND OTHER STORIES

Betts's earliest collection, *The Gentle Insurrection and Other Stories*, presents twelve tales, each involving a paradox or oxymoron. In all of them, characters who would cause an insurrection by breaking out of their situations or typical lifestyles go no further than contemplating changes or making plans for them. The plots concern race relations in a small southern town in the 1950's, mothers deserting children, children coming of age, love, illness, and death. The characters face the burdens of ordinary life as they struggle against serious odds, especially loneliness. Betts's universal theme is the difficulty of achieving real understanding between people.

In this collection, then, there is at least momentary defiance by individuals toward their situations and their discovery that life is not a matter of finding happiness on some climactic day. While the characters seek self-identity, independence, and, often, love, the issue of morality usually lurks in the background. These threads remained central to Betts's fiction, long and short, throughout her writing career. Her style is suggestive, metaphysical, economical, flexible, and religiously allusive; her sobriety and humor are also in evidence. The setting is characteristically southern, in terms of both geography and mindframes.

Doris Betts (©Miriam Berkley)

An example of someone involved in a "gentle insurrection" by attempting to break out of her mold is Agnes Parker in "Miss Parker Possessed." Here a fortyish public librarian tries to jettison her persona of an unloved old maid who focuses on her library duties completely and efficiently. Her "other self" longing to emerge reveals an inner being that presses her to declare her love for Lewis Harvey, a widower and the head teller at the Merchants' and Industrial Bank in her town.

At a meeting of the Committee of Councilmen Supervising Library Management, Miss Parker evi-

dences her state of mind when she suggests that the library acquire a competent textbook on sex. Previously, her "second personality" had shocked some prudish women at the Ladies Bi-Monthly Book Club, which Agnes Parker has attended regularly. Overhearing Mr. Harvey and another council member discussing the possibility of first hiring a library assistant and then pensioning off the apparently sickly Miss Parker, she enters the meeting room and resumes her former demeanor. She can now meet Mr. Harvey's glance and let out a long breath without the earlier fluttering in her chest. Rather, she sees the longed-for lover of her timid desires as a balding individual with protruding front teeth, an unpleasant-looking scar on his left index finger, and a similarly unattractive mole behind his ear.

The resumption of her former routines, responsibilities, and persona suggest the sorrow of a lost opportunity to love and communicate—elements so crucial in Betts's thinking—and thus the return to her earlier empty life. That is how the author achieves the oxymoron promised in the collection title.

THE ASTRONOMER AND OTHER STORIES

In the first movement of Betts's *The Astronomer and Other Stories*, the eponymous hero (his real name is Horton Beam) retires from the huge, noisy textile mill in North Carolina where he has spent most of his adult life. It is his last day, and they give him a gold watch as he collects his last paycheck. At last, after a lifetime of subservience to the machine, he crosses a patch of grass outside the plant in defiance of a Keep Off the Grass sign and mutters (under his breath), "They can all go to hell." It is important for the tone of the story and for Beam's ultimate position in life that he does not have the courage to yell it out loud or to commit any major infraction of the rules. He tells his coworkers on that last day that he is going to do nothing. At the house where he has lived alone since his wife died years ago, his watch off, he begins looking at the books left in the house and comes across his dead son's copy of Walt Whitman's *Leaves of Grass* (1855) and sees the line ". . . heard the learned astronomer." Beam decides on impulse to become a Learned Astronomer. This is a novel (or novella) of ideas, a short allegory set in prose form, a multileveled symbolic novel in the tradition of Nathaniel Hawthorne, and, as it turns out, a consummate exercise in mythopoetic fiction—for Betts's artistry is such that it can be all these things, and in such a short space.

The next day, a young man, Fred Ridge, appears on Horton Beam's doorstep, wanting to rent a room. The Astronomer ignores him and studies his star charts all day, but the young man is still there at nightfall, so Beam rents him a room. The next morning Ridge presents The Astronomer with his paramour—and the representative of the labyrinth—Eva, who has abandoned her husband and children and run off with Ridge, one of her husband's used-car salesmen. These characters are not merely people but are the allegorical embodiment of ideas or forces or human options and choices. Eva reminds one of Eve by her name, but she is more like Lilith, the first (and evil) wife of Adam. Lilith, according to legend, objected to the recumbent position in sexual intercourse, preferring the superior one; when Adam tried to compel her obedience, she uttered the name of God and left. Lilith became the destroyer of the newborn (just as, later in the short story, Eva aborts the love child she conceived during her affair with Ridge). God is supposed to have sent three angels, Senoy, Sansenoy, and Semangelof, to fetch Lilith back; she would not go but agreed to spare newborn children if the names of the three or their likenesses on an amulet appeared above the infants. This led to the apotropaic rite formerly practiced by devout Jews in which a message in charcoal was written inside a charcoal circle on the wall of the newborn's room: "ADAM AND EVE. OUT, LILITH!" Jewish children who laughed in their sleep were supposed to have been caressed by Lilith.

The other Hebrew legend about Lilith is that she ruled as queen in Zmargad and in Sheba; in another, because she left Adam before the Fall, she was immortal, and she not only strangled sleeping infants but also seduced men in their sleep. In this novella, The Astronomer, at the height of his infatuation for Eva, feels that he has for a moment seen through sheet and mattress and boards and earth right down to hell, which is certainly congruent to Eva's represent-

ing Lilith. If Lilith is a demon, then The Astronomer represents Judeo-Christian spiritual history against the forces of darkness, another reading of the allegorical content of this novella. The Astronomer at another point claims identification with Adam in that he gives names to stars. It might also be noted, however, that this allegory is not merely religious, but also aesthetic; its conflict is between the artists and those involved in the quotidian burdens of life. To give the story a "middle reading," these are real people, too, in a real workaday North Carolina. The car lot where Fred Ridge used to work for Eva's husband was depressing, Eva says. The progress of life annoys her; for her, the momentary pleasures of life, the feeling of slight removal from things rushing to their conclusions, are part and parcel of living. She fears final things, and so, from the beginning, her adventure with Ridge and her abandonment of the children can only be a momentary loop in the straight road to death through alienation and despair. She is not, perhaps, a good example of those who live recklessly by improvisation, dedicated to survival by their wits, but here, as in so many Betts stories, there are no final winners.

Eva is a sensualist. She has, like her little girl, chewed tar from the telephone poles, and she asks The Astronomer if he has ever chewed peach-tree gum or eaten wild locusts (this reference is almost biblical). Eva is pregnant with Fred's child, however, and she goes to an abortionist on the street running between the black and white communities. He makes her prostitute herself as the price of the abortion. Eva's troubles, her new sordid life, and his going down into Nighttown to find her force a conversion upon The Astronomer (and it might be remembered that in Hebrew legend, Lilith goes East, beyond Eden, to live by the Red Sea, home of the lascivious demons). It is not quite a religious experience; Betts's control does not leave her for an instant. The Astronomer begins to think of Ridge, and he begins to feel sexual desire for Eva as she recovers from her abortion; desire is something he has not felt for a long, long time. He comes alive; he thinks he can hear the grass growing. His telescope becomes covered with dust. After Eva recovers, both of them disappear, an ending that shocks the reader but provides a perfect conclusion to the story.

"THE SPIES IN THE HERB HOUSE"

"The Spies in the Herb House," in *The Astronomer and Other Stories*, is a beautiful evocation through unobtrusive prose of a happy childhood; it is based on a wickedly funny conceit: that two innocent young girls growing up in Piedmont, North Carolina, during World War II could believe that a popular graffito could stand for Fight Until Children Killed. There is not much motion in the story, in the great tradition of stories of childhood remembered, and it is rather closely autobiographical (one little girl's name is Doris), but the diction, the timing of the joke (and it is timed as expertly as any stand-up comedian's), and the characterization of the girls all make the story more than worthwhile. The Herb House of the story is a large, ugly wooden building in the Herb Capital of the World (Statesville, North Carolina), where elder flowers, true love, wild cherry bark, blackberry and pokeweed roots, sumac berries, ginseng, sassafras bark, catnip, balm of Gilead buds, and other herbs were stored until a few years before the story opened; the warehouse is no longer in use. It is the sort of place two tomboys like Doris and Betty Sue would break into, and they do.

Once inside, they discover an "X" on a box, which they mistake for a swastika (this story takes place during World War II, and Doris's playmate has boyfriends in the service who write her letters). Later, the girls, who believe that they have discovered a German spy hideout, have "other dreadful discoveries to make." They see "two long glass counters against one wall. They were about as high as the glass counters which held candy at the dime store. By taking turns, by twisting our necks, we could see they were lined with velvet." Doris immediately deduces the German spies are engaged in diamond smuggling. "Why would the Germans do that?" Betty Sue asks. "Submarines cost money!" Doris says. Then they see the graffito written on the wall and deduce its meaning too and feel utterly powerless and alone. "There was so much I understood that day—valor, and patriotism, and the nature of the enemy. Even my fear was specific. The war had come to me and I did not have

to go to it. I was one with all the innocent victims of history." This is not a bad discovery, however frightening, to make at any age.

"BENSON WATTS IS DEAD AND IN VIRGINIA"

Betts said about the story "Benson Watts Is Dead and in Virginia" that it "is a logical extension of the things that interest me most in fiction, which, as I say, are mortality and time. . . ." The premise is intriguing. It is in fact the one question that has tormented every human culture since time began: Where do we go when we die? In this first-person narrative, Benson Watts, a sometime schoolteacher, dies and wakes up in Virginia. He is sixty-five and survived by grandchildren, "none of whom I liked very much." He looks like John L. Lewis and teaches United States and world history in high schools all over Texas.

When he wakes up one day, he is bald, younger, forty again, dressed in Dacron trousers and a pair of shoes he has never owned. Around his neck hangs a medallion which says:

1. Dwell, then travel
2. Join forces
3. Disremember

He finds a house he immediately recognizes as the one Henry David Thoreau built by Walden Pond. Shortly thereafter Olena, a pregnant red-headed woman in a hairdresser's white uniform, appears; she is in her late twenties and has stayed alive eating persimmons. Next, as throughout the story, animals from medieval bestiaries once read by Benson Watts begin to follow them everywhere, coming almost close enough to be seen in detail. Then the two are joined by Melvin Drum, a connoisseur of religions and a streetcorner preacher, who is beaten to death in an alley by men who mistake his identity. This is, at this point, a welter of religious ideas, allusions, references, symbols, and speculations entering the story. Betts is writing here of Everyman Dead, not just a meditation on the Christian heaven or purgatory, limbo or paradise.

The three have been following, at first separately and then together, the first injunction written on Watts's disc: "Travel." All three begin to travel through endless virgin forests, over pure limpid streams, deeper and deeper into a world that none of them recognizes. Now, with the exception perhaps of Benson Watts, they begin to obey the third injunction: "Disremember." Benson Watts begins to make love to Olena. Drum disappears. They continue to drift across an empty planet thick with forests. The baby in Olena's body disappears, the first disconcerting sign: Perhaps their time in this limbo is keyed to the number of years each has lived. Finally Olena dies, leaving Watts alone. The tale ends with Watts closing his journal (the story has been a sort of epistle intended for dispatch to the Void, or perhaps for the next one to come along) and waiting for an end he cannot imagine. The novella is built around a powerful idea, which accounts for most of its thrust, but its execution and the expert blending of philosophy with realistic rendering of the human beings involved make it almost unique in American letters. Betts breaks new ground in her first fantasy short story and dramatizes many beliefs and attitudes toward death. The most important thing about the story, however, is that it reads almost like a biblical tale: It is authentic, human, and cathartic.

OTHER MAJOR WORKS

LONG FICTION: *Tall Houses in Winter*, 1957; *The Scarlet Thread*, 1964; *The River to Pickle Beach*, 1972; *Heading West*, 1981; *Souls Raised from the Dead*, 1994; *The Sharp Teeth of Love*, 1997.

BIBLIOGRAPHY

Brown, W. Dale. "Interview with Doris Betts." *The Southern Quarterly* 34 (Winter, 1996): 91-104. In this detailed interview, Betts discusses her Christian faith and how it relates to her fiction.

Evans, Elizabeth. "Another Mule in the Yard: Doris Betts's Durable Humor." *Notes on Contemporary Literature* 11 (March, 1981): 5-6. Evans's thesis is that "Doris Betts produces durable humor which often turns funny lines and situations into dark melancholy where humor remains, but overrun with pessimism and despair." This creates an incongruity that "frequently emphasizes the bitterness that undergirds the characters' lives." The article focuses on the story "The Dead Mule."

_____. *Doris Betts*. New York: Twayne, 1997. An authoritative critical interpretation of Betts's long and short fiction.

Holman, David Marion. "Faith and the Unanswerable Questions: The Fiction of Doris Betts." *The Southern Literary Journal* 15 (Fall, 1982): 15-22. This article contains analyses of Betts's characterization, treatment of faith, and use of the grotesque in her short fiction. The discussion centers on three short stories: "The Ugliest Pilgrim," "The Astronomer," and "The Mandarin," although the longer fiction is also discussed briefly.

Lang, John. "Mapping the Heart's Home: Doris Betts's 'The Astronomer.'" *The Southern Literary Journal* 31 (Fall, 1998): 70-77. Examines themes of love, forgiveness, and the search for order in "The Astronomer." Shows that as the protagonist moves spatially through the story, he also moves socially from isolation to a sense of family and community and morally from complacency to active questioning.

Ragan, Sam, et al. "A Tribute to Doris Betts." *Pembroke Magazine* 18 (1986): 275-284. Included in the transcript of the 1985 North Carolina Writer's Conference is this tribute to and analysis of Betts's fiction by Sam Ragan, Robert Mason, Lee Smith, and William Friday. Contains both personal and critical appraisal of Betts's career, concerns, and short and long fiction, as well as anecdotes and fond remembrances.

Scura, Dorothy M. "Doris Betts at Mid-Century: Her Voice and Her Art." In *Southern Women Writers: The New Generation*, edited by Tonette Bond Inge. Tuscaloosa: The University of Alabama Press, 1990. A general discussion of Betts's themes and techniques, focusing particularly on the short stories, which Scura contends are her natural forte. Summarizes the critical reception of Betts's stories and her themes of love and death, relationships between the sexes, and growing up.

Walsh, William. "An Interview with Doris Betts." *High Plains Literary Review* 4 (Winter, 1989-1990): 82-102. The most extensive of the interviews Betts has granted, this article allows the reader to hear her views on her work, past and present, and her thoughts on the future. Also contains examples of her wit and humor.

Wolfe, George. "The Unique Voice: Doris Betts." In *Kite-Flying and Other Irrational Acts: Conversations with Twelve Southern Writers*, edited by John Carr. Baton Rouge: Louisiana State University Press, 1972. This article provides an introduction to Betts's philosophy, her critical approach to writing, anecdotes about her early experiences in

writing and publishing, and sources for some of her works. Betts also discusses biblical and other religious influences in her work and talks about the South, where she grew up. The introduction includes a brief biographical summary and a physical description of Betts.

John Carr, updated by Mary LeDonne Cassidy and Peter B. Heller

---

AMBROSE BIERCE

Born: Horse Cave Creek, Ohio; June 24, 1842
Died: Mexico(?); 1914(?)

PRINCIPAL SHORT FICTION

Cobwebs: Being the Fables of Zambri the Parse, 1884

Tales of Soldiers and Civilians, 1891 (republished under the title *In the Midst of Life*, 1898)

Can Such Things Be?, 1893

Fantastic Fables, 1899

The Cynic's Word Book, 1906

My Favourite Murder, 1916

Ghost and Horror Stories of Ambrose Bierce, 1964

OTHER LITERARY FORMS

As a lifelong journalist and commentator, Ambrose Bierce wrote prodigiously. He was fond of vitriolic epigrams and sketches, together with miscellaneous works of literary criticism, epigrams, and both prose and verse aphorisms.

ACHIEVEMENT

For many years, Ambrose Bierce was labeled a misanthrope or pessimist, and his dark short stories of murder and violence were understood as the work of a man who, obsessed with the idea of death, showed himself incapable of compassion. A less moralistic and biographical reevaluation of Bierce's work, however, reveals his intellectual fascination

with the effect of the supernatural on the human imagination. Many of his morally outrageous stories are "tall tales," which certainly cannot be taken at face value. Their black humor, combined with the coolly understated voices of their criminal or psychopathic narrators, reflects a society gone to seed and pokes fun at the murderous dangers of American life in the West during the Gilded Age.

BIOGRAPHY

Ambrose Gwinett Bierce was brought up on the farm in Horse Cave Creek, Ohio, where he was born in 1842. Although information about his early life is sparse, the evidence of his stories and the fact that he quarreled with and repudiated his large family with the exception of one brother indicate an unhappy childhood and an abnormal hatred of parental figures. His only formal education consisted of one year at a military academy. He fought with the Indiana infantry in the American Civil War, was wounded at the battle of Kennesaw Mountain, and ended the conflict as a brevet major. After the war, he settled in California, where, following a brief stint as a watchman at the San Francisco mint, he drifted into literary work. He wrote for the San Francisco *Argonaut* and *News Letter* and published his first story, "The Haunted Valley" (1871), in the *Overland Monthly*. He married and, on money received as a gift from his father-in-law, traveled abroad to England in 1872, returning to

California in 1876 because of bad health. Upon his return he again became associated with the *Argonaut*. From 1879 to 1881 he took part in the Black Hills gold rush, returning in 1881 to San Francisco, having found no success as a miner. There he began, in association with the San Francisco *Wap*, his famous column "The Prattler," transferred to William Randolph Hearst's San Francisco *Examiner* upon the *Wap*'s failure, and continued at the *Examiner* until 1896, when Hearst sent him to Washington as a correspondent for the New York *American*. Much of Bierce's subsequently collected work appeared first in "The Prattler." Divorced in 1904, Bierce resigned from the Hearst organization in 1909 and, in a final quixotic gesture, disappeared into Mexico in the thick of the Mexican Revolution. He was never heard from again.

ANALYSIS

Perhaps the most rewarding way to approach Ambrose Bierce's writing is to note that it was in many respects the product of two intertwined biographical factors, inseparable for purposes of analysis. The first of these reflects Bierce's thorny and irascible personality which made him, on the one hand, quarrel with practically everyone he ever knew, and on the other, follow romantic and often impossible causes, the last of which led to his death. The second reflects his lifelong employment as a journalist, more specifically as a writer of short columns, generally aphoristic in nature, for various newspapers. The interaction of these two often contradictory strands explains, as well as any single factor can, both the strengths and weaknesses of Bierce's writing.

Philosophically, Bierce's work is almost completely uncompromising in its iconoclasm; his view of existence is despairing, revealing only the bitterness of life within a totally fallen world promising neither present happiness nor future redemption. This "bitterness," which almost every critic has remarked in Bierce's work, is not completely fortunate. It can, and in Bierce's case often does, lead to that kind of adolescent cynicism which delights in discovering clouds in every silver lining. Too many of the insights which once seemed sterling are now fairly obviously only tinfoil. The definition of "economy" in *The*

Ambrose Bierce (Library of Congress)

Devil's Dictionary (1906) is a case in point: "Purchasing the barrel of whiskey that you do not need for the price of the cow that you cannot afford"—an arresting idea, certainly, succinctly expressed, but by no means a profound one. In fact, it is precisely the kind of item one would expect to find on the editorial page of the morning newspaper and perhaps remember long enough to repeat at the office. Indeed, this particular aphorism did first appear in a newspaper, with most of the other contents of *The Devil's Dictionary* and, predictably, did not really survive the transformation into book form. *The Devil's Dictionary*, like much of Bierce's work, is now much more generally read about than actually read.

"AN OCCURRENCE AT OWL CREEK BRIDGE"

At its best, however, Bierce's cynicism is transformed into often-passionate statements of the tragedy of existence in a world in which present joys are unreal and future hopes vain, as a glance at one of Bierce's best-known stories, "An Occurrence at Owl Creek Bridge," will show.

This story, for all its apparent simplicity, has attracted uniform critical admiration and has been complimented not only by being extensively anthologized but also by having been made into an award-winning film. Purporting to be an incident from the American Civil War, the story opens with the execution by hanging of a Confederate civilian. His name, Peyton Farquhar, is revealed later, as is his apparent crime: He was apprehended by Union soldiers in an attempt to destroy the railroad bridge at Owl Creek, from which he is about to be hanged. The hangman's rope breaks, however, precipitating Farquhar into the current below. He frees his bound hands and, by swimming, manages to escape both the fire of the Union riflemen who have been assembled to witness the execution and, more miraculously, the fire of their cannon. Reaching shore, Farquhar sets out for home along an unfamiliar road, and after a night-long journey in a semidelirious condition arrives at his plantation some thirty miles away. His wife greets him at the entrance, but as he reaches to clasp her in his arms he suffers what is apparently a stroke and loses his senses. He has not, it develops, suffered a stroke; the last sentence of the story tells us what has really happened. The rope had not broken at all: "Peyton Farquhar was dead; his body, with a broken neck, swung gently from side to side beneath the timbers of the Owl Creek bridge."

"An Occurrence at Owl Creek Bridge" sounds, in summary, contrived. What is it, after all, more than a tired descant on the familiar theme of the dying man whose life passes before his eyes, coupled with the familiar trick of the unexpected happy ending put in negative terms? The answer, from the perspective of one who has read the story rather than its summary, is that it is much more. For one thing, the careful reader is not left totally unprepared for the final revelation; he has been alerted to the fact that something may be amiss by Bierce's remark that Farquhar had, before his apparent death, fixed "his last thoughts upon his wife and children." Moreover, Farquhar's journey

home is described in terms which become constantly less real. The unreality of the details of his homeward journey not only expresses Farquhar's growing estrangement from the world of reality, his "doom," perhaps, or—for those more at home in modern Freudianism—his "death wish," but also subtly indicates that what *seems* to be happening in the story may not in fact actually *be* happening, at least in the real world. In any event, Bierce's point is clear and reinforced within the story by a consistent movement in grammatical usage from the actual, "he was still sinking" (speaking of Farquhar's fall from the bridge into the water), toward the hypothetical, such as "doubtless," the word Bierce uses to describe Farquhar's apparent return to his plantation.

What, then, makes this story more than the predictable reverse of the typical tricky story with the illogical happy ending? The difference is to be found simply in Bierce's uncompromisingly negative view of the world. The reader begins in a world where everyone is symbolically sentenced to death, from which his or her reprieve is only temporary, and the reader wanders with him through a field of illusions which become more attractive as they escape the confines of reality. The reader ends, reaching for a beauty and love which was sought but which was unobtainable, dead under Owl Creek Bridge. The symbolism of Owl Creek is not gratuitous: Wise old owls discover that every road leads only to death.

"CHICKAMAUGA"

The master image of "An Occurrence at Owl Creek Bridge" of a delusory journey leading to an ultimately horrible and horrifying revelation is central to many of Bierce's stories, one more of which is worth brief mention here. "Chickamauga," not as well known as the former story, is equally chilling and equally cunning in its artistry. It tells of a nameless young boy, "aged about six years," who with toy sword in hand wanders away from his home one day into the adjacent woods, where he successfully plays soldier until, unexpectedly frightened by a rabbit, he runs away and becomes lost. He falls asleep, and when he awakens it is nearly dusk. Still lost, his directionless night journey through the forest brings him upon a column of retreating soldiers, all horribly wounded and unable to walk, who are trying to withdraw from a battle (presumably the 1863 Battle of Chickamauga in the American Civil War, although this is never specifically stated) which has been fought in the neighborhood and of which the child, whom we later discover to be both deaf and mute, has been unaware. In a ghastly parody of military splendor, the child takes command of these horribly wounded soldiers and leads them on, waving his wooden sword. As the ghastly cavalcade limps forward, the wood mysteriously begins to brighten. The brightness is not the sun, however, but the light from a burning house, and when the little boy sees the blazing dwelling he deserts his troops and, fascinated by the flames, approaches the conflagration. Suddenly he recognizes the house as his own, and at its doorway he finds the corpse of his mother.

Again, the magic of this story vanishes in paraphrase, in which the masterfully controlled feeling of horror inevitably sounds contrived, the revelation slick rather than profound. The compelling quality of "Chickamauga" is largely a function of Bierce's style, which at once conceals and reveals what is going on. The story of a small boy who wanders off into the woods with a toy sword and who is frightened by a rabbit scarcely seems to be the kind of fictional world in which such uncompromising horrors should logically take place. Yet on a symbolic level, the story has a curiously compelling logic. The first reading of the tale leaves one with a slightly false impression of its meaning. The story does not tell us, as it seems to, and as so many fairy tales do, that it is better not to leave home and venture into the wild wood; the story's meaning is darker than this. In the world of "Chickamauga," safety is to be found neither at home nor abroad. By wandering away into the woods the boy perhaps escaped the fate of those who remained at home, and yet his symbolic journey has only brought him back to a world where death is everywhere supreme. To emphasize this point more strongly, in 1898 Bierce retitled the book of short stories in which both the above tales appeared *In the Midst of Life*. Readers are expected to complete the quotation themselves: " . . . we are in death."

Although most of Bierce's stories which are

widely remembered today deal with military themes, many of his other stories are quite frankly supernatural. By and large these supernatural stories seem less likely to survive than his military ones, if only because Bierce has less sense for the implicit thematic structure of supernatural tales than he does for macabre stories about the military. His ghost stories are avowedly "shockers," without the psychological depth to be found in the works of true masters of the supernatural. They do not have the profundity, for example, of Mary Shelley's *Frankenstein* (1818) or Bram Stoker's *Dracula* (1897). Nevertheless, the best of them do have a certain compelling quality simply because of the bizarre nature of the revelation of what lies at the heart of the supernatural event which Bierce relates.

"THE DAMNED THING"

"The Damned Thing" offers a convenient case in point. This is, quite simply, the story of a man who is hunted down and finally killed by some kind of animal, apparently a wildcat. The reader never knows precisely what kind of animal it is, however, since it has one peculiar quality: It is invisible. The story is told with the last scene first. This last scene, entitled "One Does Not Always Eat What Is on the Table," takes place at the coroner's inquest over the body of one Hugh Morgan, who has met a violent death. His friend, William Harker, explains how Morgan had acted inexplicably on a hunting trip, apparently falling into a fit. The coroner's jury agrees, at least to an extent. Their ungrammatical verdict is "We, the jury, do find that the remains come to their death at the hands of a mountain lion, but some of us thinks, all the same, they had fits." In the closing scene of the story, Morgan's diary is introduced as explanation, and in it we read of his growing awareness that he is being stalked by some kind of invisible animal. A pseudoscientific rationale is given for this invisibility. The animal is "actinic," at least according to Morgan. "Actinic" colors, we are informed, are colors that exist at either end of the spectrum and that cannot be perceived by the human eye. We have, in other words, either an infrared or an ultraviolet mountain lion. Neither choice is particularly satisfactory, and the difficulty with our willing suspension of disbelief in the tale is indicated by precisely this: The science is bad, and yet it pretends not to be. The notion of an ultraviolet mountain lion is basically more silly than chilling, and since the story has no fiber to it other than the revelation of what the mountain lion actually consists of, we cannot take it seriously. In fact, the reader feels vaguely victimized and resentful, as though having been set up as the butt of some kind of pointless joke.

Yet even in this story, relatively unsuccessful as it is, we see at work the underlying preoccupations which make some of Bierce's other stories unforgettable. The attempt in a Bierce story is always to shock someone by removing him from a commonplace world and placing him—like the little boy in "Chickamauga"—in another world whose laws are recognizable, though strange. The logic of a Bierce story is often very like the logic of a nightmare, in which the reader is placed in the position of the dreamer. When trapped in a nightmare, the reader feels the presence of a certain inexorable logic, even though one may not, at the moment, be able to define exactly how that logic operates or of what precisely it consists. It is the feeling for the presence of this hostile and malevolent order which gives the best of Bierce's stories their perennial fascination.

OTHER MAJOR WORKS

POETRY: *Black Beetles in Amber*, 1892; *How Blind Is He?*, 1896; *Vision of Doom*, 1890; *Shapes of Clay*, 1903.

NONFICTION: *The Fiend's Delight*, 1873; *Nuggets and Dust Panned in California*, 1873; *Cobwebs from an Empty Skull*, 1874; *The Dance of Death*, 1877; *The Dance of Life: An Answer to the Dance of Death*, 1877 (with Mrs. J. Milton Bowers); *The Devil's Dictionary*, 1906; *The Shadow on the Dial and Other Essays*, 1909; *Write It Right: A Little Blacklist of Literary Faults*, 1909; *The Letters of Ambrose Bierce*, 1922; *Twenty-one Letters of Ambrose Bierce*, 1922; *Selections from Prattle*, 1936; *Ambrose Bierce on Richard Realf by Wm. McDevitt*, 1948.

TRANSLATION: *The Monk and the Hangman's Daughter*, 1892 (with Gustav Adolph Danziger; of Richard Voss's novel).

MISCELLANEOUS: *The Collected Works of Ambrose Bierce*, 1909-1912.

BIBLIOGRAPHY

Butterfield, Herbie. "'Our Bedfellow Death': The Short Stories of Ambrose Bierce." In *The Nineteenth Century American Short Story*, edited by A. Robert Lee. Totowa, N.J.: Barnes & Noble, 1985. A brief, general introduction to the themes and techniques of some of Bierce's most representative short stories.

Conlogue, William. "A Haunting Memory: Ambrose Bierce and the Ravine of the Dead." *Studies in Short Fiction* 28 (Winter, 1991): 21-29. Discusses Bierce's symbolic use of the topographical feature of the ravine as a major symbol of death in five stories, including "Killed at Resaca," "Coulter's Notch," and "The Coup de Grace." Shows how the ravine symbolizes the grave, the underworld, and lost love for Bierce, all derived from his Civil War memories and the death of his first love.

Davidson, Cathy N. *The Experimental Fictions of Ambrose Bierce: Structuring the Ineffable*. Lincoln: University of Nebraska Press, 1984. Discusses how Bierce intentionally blurs distinctions between such categories as knowledge, emotion, language, and behavior. Examines how Bierce blurs distinctions between external reality and imaginative reality in many of his most important short stories.

Davidson, Cathy N., ed. *Critical Essays on Ambrose Bierce*. Boston: G. K. Hall, 1982. A comprehensive compilation of thirty essays and reviews of Bierce's work, this collection is an essential tool for any serious study of Bierce. Davidson's introduction locates the essays in relation to the ongoing process of reevaluating Bierce's work, and her thoroughly researched bibliography contains more than eighty further critical references.

Fatout, Paul. *Ambrose Bierce, the Devil's Lexicographer*. Norman: University of Oklahoma Press, 1951. Fatout's impressive collation of painstakingly researched biographical data represents an important landmark in the scholarly study of Bierce's life. Supplemented by illustrations and a bibliography.

Grenander, Mary Elizabeth. *Ambrose Bierce*. New York: Twayne, 1971. This volume is well researched, balanced, and readable, and it is perhaps the single most accessible study of Bierce's work and life. Contains a valuable, annotated bibliography and a list of primary sources.

Hoppenstand, Gary. "Ambrose Bierce and the Transformation of the Gothic Tale in the Nineteenth-Century American Periodical." In *Periodical Literature in Nineteenth-Century America*, edited by Kenneth M. Price and Susan Belasco Smith. Charlottesville: University Press of Virginia, 1995. Examines Bierce's relationship to the San Francisco periodicals, focusing on the influence he had in bringing the gothic tale into the twentieth century; discusses themes and conventions in "The Damned Thing" and "Moxon's Master."

McWilliams, Carey. *Ambrose Bierce: A Biography*. Hamden, Conn.: Archon Books, 1967. A reprint of the 1929 edition, with a new introduction that tells of the book's origin in McWilliams's collaboration with Bierce's surviving daughter Helen. Based on oral interviews of people who knew Bierce, this is the first scholarly study of his life.

O'Connor, Richard. *Ambrose Bierce*. Boston: Little, Brown, 1967. A popular biography by a prolific writer on the American West. Very readable, the book interprets Bierce's work as that of a despairing moralist. Complemented by a select bibliography.

Schaefer, Michael W. *Just What War Is: The Civil War Writings of De Forest and Bierce*. Knoxville: University of Tennesse Press, 1997. Examines the pervasive theme of the Civil War in Bierce's stories as well as John William De Forest's.

Woodruff, Stuart C. *The Short Stories of Ambrose Bierce: A Study in Polarity*. Pittsburgh: University of Pittsburgh Press, 1964. Argues that Bierce's fiction derives from a series of violent oscillations between art and life and idealism and cynicism; argues that Bierce's major theme is the inscrutable universe which blocks man's every effort to live his dreams; discusses the polarity between the true and permanent art Bierce hungered for and the popular journalism he took up.

James K. Folsom, updated by R. C. Lutz

ALGERNON BLACKWOOD

Born: Shooters Hill, Kent, England; March 14, 1869
Died: London, England; December 10, 1951

PRINCIPAL SHORT FICTION
The Empty House and Other Ghost Stories, 1906
The Listener and Other Stories, 1907
John Silence: Physician Extraordinary, 1908
The Lost Valley and Other Stories, 1910
Pan's Garden, 1912
Ten Minute Stories, 1914
Incredible Adventures, 1914
Day and Night Stories, 1917
The Wolves of God, and Other Fey Stories, 1921
    (with Wilfred Wilson)
Tongues of Fire and Other Sketches, 1924

The Dance of Death and Other Tales, 1927
Shocks, 1935
The Doll, and One Other, 1946
Tales of the Uncanny and the Supernatural, 1949

OTHER LITERARY FORMS

Algernon Blackwood's early life, especially his adventures in Canada and New York, was summarized in his autobiography *Episodes Before Thirty* (1923). He also wrote plays, several novels on mystical themes, and children's novels.

ACHIEVEMENTS

In 1949 Algernon Blackwood received the British Television Society Medal for Outstanding Artistic

Achievement for his popular storytelling programs. A month earlier he was named a Commander of the British Empire, an honor recognizing his service as writer, storyteller, and entertainer during World War II.

BIOGRAPHY

Algernon Henry Blackwood was born on August 15, 1869, in the small village of Shooters Hill, now a suburb of London, England. His father was an official in the British Post Office, and his mother was the widow of the sixth duke of Manchester. A strict religious upbringing and a year studying at the School of the Moravian Brotherhood in Germany developed in Blackwood a distrust of fundamentalist religions and a lifelong interest in Eastern wisdom, alternative religions, and mystical studies.

From 1890 to 1899 Blackwood lived in Canada and New York, trying a variety of businesses and careers, eventually becoming a reporter for *The New York Times* and a private secretary for a wealthy banker. His experiences camping in the wilderness of Canada as well as a period of ill health and poverty in New York provided settings and events he would use later in his fiction.

Upon his return to England in 1899, Blackwood began writing, traveling widely, and seriously investigating paranormal and mystical subjects. His volumes of ghost stories and mystical, nature adventures began to sell, and his reputation grew. As the Ghost Man, Blackwood became a staple on Saturday night television until his death in 1951 at age eighty-two.

ANALYSIS

Algernon Blackwood is primarily known as a writer of ghost stories, but of his more than two hundred published stories bibliographer Mike Ashley lists only thirty under the subject categories of ghosts and haunted houses. Blackwood's other stories cover themes as diverse as nature worship, psychic experiences, and reincarnation. Almost all of his work, though, concerns the expansion of consciousness and the ability of humans to perceive supernatural forces and even briefly contact other worlds just beyond ordinary reality. His stories are powerful and convinc-

ing because the reader can sense that the author really believes in what he is writing. In the introduction to a 1938 collection of stories, Blackwood listed numerous events in his own life that inspired his stories. In the same introduction, he wrote, "If a ghost is seen, what *is* it interests me less than what sees it." He was concerned with the human faculties that, under the right stimulation, can sense sights, sounds, and feelings normally imperceptible.

Blackwood has also been called a nature mystic, and many of his stories effectively evoke the feelings of terror or awe that individuals experience when they come face-to-face with the universe, usually when alone in a spectacular landscape. Nature then assumes a spiritual consciousness that can be malevolent and dangerous, as in "The Willows," or beautiful and alluring, as in "The Man Whom the Trees Loved" and "The Glamour of the Snow."

Blackwood's power as a writer lies in his ability to minutely describe subtle feelings and emotions, letting the coming event or vision build up over many pages. His writing also has the ability to sustain suspense and an otherworldly atmosphere through long stories, often with several climactic events and scenes. At the same time, he has occasionally been criticized for his wordy style, which often tells the reader what to feel, and his lengthy quasi-scientific explanations of the phenomena portrayed.

"THE EMPTY HOUSE"

This is the title story of Blackwood's first collection and demonstrates his approach to the traditional haunted-house story. Jim Shorthouse is convinced by his aunt, who is interested in psychical research, to spend the night in a reportedly haunted house. Well prepared with blankets and "strong spirits," and acquainted with the story of murder and unrequited love associated with the house, they undertake their vigil. Mysterious events build up gradually, including an early apparition of a ghostly woman, doors that close by themselves, and a grotesque vision of a man's face so close that Shorthouse could have touched it with his lips. Though the reader expects such events, Blackwood's descriptive and narrative skills provide surprise and a real "suspension of disbelief." Predictably at midnight, the two witness a noisy yet ghostly reenactment of the original chase and murder, entirely through sound and feeling, without any visible apparitions. This extended supernatural occurrence is effectively portrayed and demonstrates Blackwood's skill at holding his ghostly spell over the reader for several pages at a time. Also shown in this early story is the author's tendency to use a series of frights or shocks, any one of which could be the climax in a lesser story.

"THE MAN WHOM THE TREES LOVED"

A fine example of Blackwood's nature mysticism, this story invokes feelings of awe and wonder as it animates nature with consciousness and desire. David Bittacy, a retired forester, begins to notice an attraction to trees and forests beyond his professional capacity. This attraction is explained to him by Sanderson, an artist who specializes in paintings of trees, as due to the fact that the trees are aware of him and appreciate his service to their species. Bittacy's sensitivity to nature is also partially explained by his having a Eurasian ancestor, a testament to Blackwood's interest in Eastern philosophies and religions. Gradually, over the one hundred pages of the story, Bittacy's soul is assimilated into the greater spirit of the forest. The only fear or terror in the story belongs to Mrs. Bittacy, who loses not only her husband but also her faith in her traditional religion.

"THE DAMNED"

In this eighty-five-page tale Blackwood seems to have set for himself the task of writing an extended ghost story in which virtually nothing happens (a phrase repeated throughout the story). The narrator and his sister visit the country house of friend whose husband, a man of intolerant religious beliefs, has recently died. The three are haunted by subtle "feelings" and indescribable sensations of unease, but no ghosts appear. The story illustrates one of Blackwood's strongest messages: his distaste for exclusive religions or creeds that consign all unbelievers to eternal damnation. The house, and the land before it, had been occupied (in an unlikely coincidence) by a series of intolerant religious leaders, from druids and Romans to strict Catholics and radical orthodox Jews. Blackwood believed, at least for the purposes of his fiction, that thoughts and emotions, especially of an

intense or violent nature, can remain in a physical place to be detected later by a particularly sensitive individual. In this story, many centuries' worth of negative thoughts, hate, and fear were released at the same time, each conflicting with the others and canceling one another out, so that there was no spiritual manifestation of any one of them but rather an intense psychic struggle. The narrator himself says at the end of the story that there was no climax and nothing happened, yet Blackwood has spun a fascinating tale of suspense and atmospheric power.

"THE WILLOWS"

This is Blackwood's most frequently anthologized story, and arguably one of his best. It is the tale of two men camping on a river island within a vast wilderness of water and willow shrubs. The beauty and solitude of the natural setting gradually give way to feelings of claustrophobic isolation and vulnerability to powerful forces, which seem to attack the campers. Strange and otherworldly phenomena, including shifting shapes in the wind-tossed willows, the force of which damages their canoe, and loud, ringing, sometimes buzzing sounds in the air around them vie with eerie descriptions of an otter that looks like a dead body in the river and a man dimly seen in a boat to create an atmosphere of bewildering mystery. The narrator's supposed "unimaginative" friend explains that they have encountered a space where the ordinary world intersects with another dimension, inhabited by entities beyond our imagination. Using the interplay between these two men, Blackwood here explores the types of personalities that can perceive, and then best withstand, supernatural forces. What exactly these forces are, and which other world has been inadvertently glimpsed, is left a mystery in this powerful, atmospheric tale.

JOHN SILENCE

Blackwood's first major commercial success came with the publication of this collection in 1908. Capitalizing in part on the popular Sherlock Holmes stories, it presented a series of hauntings and other supernatural cases, investigated, solved, and explained by the enigmatic Dr. Silence, sometimes with the help of his Watson-like assistant, Hubbard. The five stories in the original volume (a sixth, originally published in a later collection, was added to the 1997 Dover edition) cover a broad menu of occult subjects, including a haunted house, a werewolf, devil worship, reincarnation, witchcraft, and fire elementals that guard a stolen Egyptian mummy. In each case, Dr. Silence provides a detailed explanation, based on "occult science," of the phenomena involved.

OTHER MAJOR WORKS

LONG FICTION: *Jimbo, A Fantasy*, 1909; *The Human Chord*, 1910; *The Centaur*, 1911; *Julius Le Vallon*, 1916; *The Wave: An Egyptian Aftermath*, 1916; *The Promise of Air*, 1918; *The Garden of Survival*, 1918; *The Bright Messenger*, 1921; *Dudley and Gilderoy: A Nonsense*, 1929; *The Fruit Stoners*, 1934.

PLAYS: *The Starlight Express*, pr. 1915 (adapted from *The Promise of Air*); *Karma: A Re-incarnation Play*, pb. 1918; *Through the Crack*, pb. 1925.

NONFICTION: *Episodes Before Thirty*, 1923 (autobiography).

CHILDREN'S LITERATURE: *The Education of Uncle Paul*, 1909; *A Prisoner in Fairyland*, 1913.

BIBLIOGRAPHY

"Algernon Blackwood: The Ghostly Tale's Great Visionary." *Rod Serling's Twilight Zone Magazine* 5, no. 2 (May/June, 1985): 56-63. Written in the form of a fictitious interview, this article contains much useful information taken from Blackwood's letters and published essays. Details his early life and development as a writer, his beliefs in spiritualism and reincarnation, and the personal experiences that were the sources of many of his stories.

Ashley, Mike. *Algernon Blackwood: A Bio-Bibliography*. New York: The Greenwood Press, 1987. An extensive and detailed bibliography, listing newspaper articles, stories, novels, and other writings. Provides publishing histories and various indexes and cross-references, including an index to themes and settings in the stories. An extensive secondary bibliography lists reviews, articles, and books about Blackwood and his works through 1987. Also includes a complete, thirty-three page biography.

Joshi, S. T. "Algernon Blackwood: The Expansion of Consciousness." In *The Weird Tale*. Austin, Tex.: University of Texas Press, 1990. A thoughtful overview, which divides Blackwood's work into the categories of awe, horror, and stories of and for children. Explores the spiritual and religious underpinnings of the stories.

_____. Introduction to *The Complete John Silence Stories*, by Algernon Blackwood. Mineola, New York: Dover, 1997. A brief but excellent introduction to Blackwood and the Silence stories in particular. Compares John Silence to other psychic detectives and traces the probable influence of Sherlock Holmes. Discusses narrative techniques and Blackwood's attempts to explain supernatural phenomena in terms of occult or psychic science.

Penzoldt, Peter "Algernon Blackwood." In *The Supernatural in Fiction*. New York: Humanities Press, 1965. An enthusiastic overview of Blackwood's work (Penzoldt dedicates the entire book to him), although it is colored by an emphasis on Freudian psychoanalysis. Examines in detail the style and storytelling methods that make Blackwood's stories successful.

Sullivan, Jack. "The Visionary Ghost Story: Algernon Blackwood," In *Elegant Nightmares: The English Ghost Story from Le Fanu to Blackwood*. Athens, Ohio: Ohio University Press, 1978. Examines Blackwood, especially in relation to other ghost story writers, aligning him with visionaries and believers, such as Arthur Machen and Walter de la Mare, and against the objective, skeptical storytellers M. R. James and J. S. Le Fanu. Sullivan points out the inconsistencies in Blackwood's work, the shortcomings in his style, and the occasional heavy-handed occult explanations, but he cannot deny the powerful effect of Blackwood's writing at its best.

Joseph W. Hinton

GIOVANNI BOCCACCIO

Born: Florence or Certaldo, Italy; June or July, 1313
Died: Certaldo, Italy; December 21, 1375

PRINCIPAL SHORT FICTION

Decameron: O, Prencipe Galetto, 1349-1351 (*The Decameron*, 1620)

OTHER LITERARY FORMS

Although Giovanni Boccaccio's greatest work is the masterfully framed collection of one hundred Italian short stories known as *The Decameron*, he also left a large and significant corpus of poetry. His earliest poetry, written in Naples, is in Italian and includes the *Rime* (c. 1330-1340; poems), which comprises more than one hundred lyrics, mostly sonnets and not all of sure attribution. These short poems are largely dedicated to the poet's beloved Fiammetta, who is identified in some of Boccaccio's pseudoautobiographical writings as Maria d'Aquino; supposedly, she was the illegitimate daughter of King Robert of Naples, but more probably she was the invention of the poet. Similarly, the longer poem *La caccia di Diana* (c. 1334; Diana's hunt), *Il filostrato* (c. 1335; *The Filostrato*, 1873), *Il filocolo* (c. 1336; *Labor of Love*, 1566), and *Teseida* (1340-1341; *The Book of Theseus*, 1974) are all poems ostensibly inspired by Boccaccio's ardor for Fiammetta, whose name means "little flame." Other poems that were composed in the 1340's also treat the formidable power of love and include the *Commedia delle ninfe*, entitled *Il ninfale d'Ameto* by fifteenth century copyists (1341-1342; the comedy of the nymphs of Florence), *L'amorosa visione* (1342-1343; English translation, 1986), *Elegia di Madonna Fiammetta* (1343-1344; *Amorous Fiammetta*, 1587), and *Il ninfale fiesolano* (1344-1346; *The Nymph of Fiesole*, 1597).

ACHIEVEMENTS

Giovanni Boccaccio created many literary firsts in Italian letters. He is often credited, for example, with the first Italian hunting poem (*La caccia di Diana*), the first Italian verse romance by a nonminstrel (*The*

Filostrato), the first Italian prose romance (*Labor of Love*), and the first Italian idyll (*The Nymph of Fiesole*). Many scholars also regard Boccaccio as the greatest narrator Europe has produced. Such high esteem for the Tuscan author assuredly arises from his masterpiece, *The Decameron*, which has provided a model or source material for many notable European and English authors, from Marguerite de Navarre and Lope de Vega Carpio to Gotthold Ephraim Lessing and Alfred, Lord Tennyson. Even if Boccaccio had never composed his magnum opus, however, he would still enjoy significant acclaim in European literary history for his presumedly minor writings. For example, many consider his *Amorous Fiammetta* to be the first modern (that is, postclassical) psychological novel. Certainly his *Il ninfale d'Ameto* anticipates Renaissance bucolic literature. Contemporary medieval authors also looked to Boccaccio for inspiration. In *The Filostrato*, Geoffrey Chaucer found ample material for his *Troilus and Criseyde* (1382), and in *The Book of Theseus* Chaucer discovered the source for "The Knight's Tale." Boccaccio's encyclopedic works in Latin resulted in his being regarded as one of the most prominent Trecento humanists. Indeed, it was as a Latin humanist, rather than as a raconteur of vernacular tales, that Boccaccio was primarily remembered during the first century following his demise.

BIOGRAPHY

The exact place and date of the birth of Giovanni Boccaccio are not known. Until the first half of the twentieth century, it was believed that he was born in Paris of a noble Frenchwoman; scholars now regard that story as another one of the author's fictional tales. Most likely, he was born in Florence or Certaldo, Italy, in June or July, 1313, the natural son of Boccaccio di Chellino and an unidentified Tuscan woman. His father, an agent for a powerful Florentine banking family (the Bardi), recognized Giovanni early as his son; the boy, as a result, passed both his infancy and his childhood in his father's house.

Giovanni Boccaccio (Library of Congress)

Boccaccio's teacher in his youth was Giovanni Mazzuoli da Strada, undoubtedly an admirer of Dante Alighieri, whose *La divina commedia* (c. 1320; *The Divine Comedy*, 1802) greatly influenced Boccaccio's own writings.

In his early teens, sometime between 1325 and 1328, Boccaccio was sent to Naples to learn the merchant trade and banking business as an apprentice to the Neapolitan branch of the Bardi Company. The Bardi family, as the financiers of King Robert of Anjou, exerted a powerful influence at the Angevin court in Naples. The experiences Boccaccio enjoyed with the Neapolitan aristocracy and with the breathtaking countryside and beautiful sea are reflected in many of his early poems. During his sojourn in Naples, Boccaccio also studied canon law, between 1330 or 1331 and 1334. While studying business and law, however, he anxiously sought cultural experiences to broaden his awareness of belles lettres. Largely self-taught in literary matters, he soon began to study the writings of his somewhat older contemporary, Francesco Petrarca, known as Petrarch. Later,

the two men became friends and met on a number of occasions (1350 in Florence, 1351 in Padua, 1359 in Milano, 1363 in Venice, and 1368 in Padua again).

Boccaccio left Naples and returned to Florence between 1340 and 1341 because of a financial crisis in the Bardi empire. Although Boccaccio rued having to leave Naples, so often associated in his imagination and writings with love and adventure and poetry, his highly bourgeois Florentine experience added an important and desirable dimension of realism to his work. Unfortunately, very little is documented about Boccaccio's life between 1340 and 1348, although it is known (from one of Petrarch's letters) that he was in Ravenna between 1345 and 1346 and that he sent a letter from Forlì in 1347. He was back in Florence in 1348, where he witnessed at first hand the horrible ravages of the Black Death, or bubonic plague. Between 1349 and 1351, he gave final form to *The Decameron*, which takes as it *mise en scène* Florence and the Tuscan countryside during the plague of 1348.

After his father's death in 1349, Boccaccio assumed many more familial responsibilities and financial burdens. As his fame as an author and scholar burgeoned, his fellow Florentines began to honor him with various ambassadorial duties, starting with his 1350 assignment as ambassador to the lords of Romagna. Such posts, however, did little to alleviate the financial difficulties caused by the collapse of the Bardi Company. Boccaccio longed to return to the pleasant life he had known in Naples, but visits there in 1355 and again in 1362 and 1370 to 1371 were extremely disappointing. Between 1360 and 1362, he studied Greek, the first among the literati of his time to do so seriously; from that time until his death, his home became the center for Italian humanism. Sometime around 1361 or 1362, he left Florence to take up residence in the family home in Certaldo, where he died, on December 21, 1375, the year after the death of his friend and fellow humanist, Petrarch.

ANALYSIS

Giovanni Boccaccio's short fiction, one hundred *novelle*, or tales, is collectively and contemporaneously his longest work of fiction, known as *The*

Decameron. That fact must be kept foremost in mind in any serious analysis of the tales. In other words, Boccaccio's individual short stories are best understood when examined as part of a much larger work of fiction which has an elaborate *cornice*, or frame, striking symmetry, and selective and oft-repeated themes.

The word *decameron*, Greek for "ten days," refers to the number of days Boccaccio's fictional characters (three young men and seven young women) dedicate to swapping tales with one another in the tranquil Tuscan countryside away from the plague-infested city of Florence. The work's subtitle, "Prencipe Galeotto" (Prince Galahalt), refers to the panderer Galahalt, who brought Guinevere and Lancelot together, and emphasizes that Boccaccio's book—dedicated to women—is written, not unlike many of his early poems, in the service of love. As the narration of the first day begins, three men—Panfilo ("all love"), Filostrato ("overcome by love"), and Dioneo ("the lascivious"), alluding to the love goddess Venus, daughter of Dione—come by chance one Tuesday upon seven women, who are between the ages of eighteen and twenty-eight, in the Church of Santa Maria Novella. The year is 1348, and the Black Death is the macabre background for what happens in the course of the telling of the tales. The seven women—Pampinea ("the vigorous"), Fiammetta (whose name echoes that of Boccaccio's beloved), Filomena ("lover of song"), Emilia ("the flatterer"), Lauretta (in homage to Petrarch's beloved Laura), Neifile ("new in love"), and Elissa (another name for Vergil's tragic heroine Dido)—anxiously wish to remove themselves from the diseased and strife-torn city and repair to the healthful and peaceful countryside. The young men agree to accompany the ladies, and the following day (a Wednesday) the group leaves for a villa in nearby and idyllic Fiesole. Better to enjoy what is essentially a fortnight's holiday, Pampinea suggests that they tell stories in the late afternoon when it is too hot to play or go on walks. It is decided that one of them will be chosen as king or queen for each day, and he or she will select a theme for the stories to be told on that day. Only Dioneo, who tells the last tale each day, has the liberty of ignoring the gen-

eral theme if he so desires. They then proceed to tell ten stories per day over a two-week period, refraining from tale-telling on Fridays and Saturdays out of reverence for Christ's crucifixion and in order to prepare properly for the Sabbath. On a Wednesday, the day following the last day of telling tales and exactly two weeks from the day the group left Florence, they return to their respective homes.

The emphasis on order and propriety, the presentation of the countryside as a *locus amoenus*, the repetition of the number ten (considered a symbol of perfection in the Middle Ages), and even the total number of tales (one hundred, equal to the number of cantos in Dante's *The Divine Comedy*) are all aspects of the work which contrast sharply with the disorder, impropriety, and lack of harmony which characterized Florence during the 1348 plague. The author graphically depicts, in the opening pages of the book, examples of the social chaos caused by the plethora of plague-induced deaths. The pleasant pastime of telling tales in the shade of trees and the skillful ordering of the stories serve, in other words, as an obvious antidote or salutary response to the breakdown of society which resulted from the deadly pestilence which swept Italy and much of Europe in the mid-fourteenth century. Further supporting the notion that *The Decameron* presents an ordered universe as an alternative to the chaos and anarchy created by the plague is Boccaccio's insistence that his storytellers, though they may occasionally tell ribald tales, are uniformly chaste and proper in their behavior toward one another.

THEMES

The stories told on each of the ten days which make up *The Decameron* explore a predetermined subject or theme. On the first day, everyone is free to choose a topic—one is the character "Abraam giudeo" ("Abraham the Jew"). On the second day, the stories treat those, such as the subject of "Andreuccio da Perugia" ("Andreuccio of Perugia"), who realize unexpected happiness after serious misfortune. Then, on the third day, the stories discuss people who have accomplished difficult goals or who have repossessed something once lost, among which is the tale "Alibech" ("Alibech and Rustico"). The next day, the narrators tell love stories which end unhappily (see "Tancredi, Prenze di Salerno" and its English translation). On the fifth day, they tell love stories which depict misfortune but end felicitously (see "Nastagio degli Onesti" and the English translation). The stories told on the sixth day deal with the role of intelligence in helping one avoid problems—one of the most famous among these is "Cisti fornaio" ("Cisti the Baker"). On the seventh day, the stories relate tricks which wives play on husbands (see "Petronella mette un so amante in un doglio," or "Petronella and the Barrel"), and on the eighth day, the stories recount tricks men and women play on each other, as in "Calandrino" ("Calandrino and the Heliotrope"). On the ninth day, once again everyone is free to choose a topic (one is described in "Le vasi una badessa in fretta ed al buio per trovare una sua monaca a lei accusata" and its translation, "The Abbess and the Nun"). Finally, on the tenth day, the narrators tell of men and women who have performed magnanimous deeds and acquired renown in so doing (see "Il Marchese di Saluzzo," or "The Marchese di Saluzzo and Griselda").

In addition to the pronounced framing technique created by the introductions to the various days and by the themes themselves, there seems to be a degree of subtle thematic framing within the stories themselves from first to last. The first story of the first day, "Ser Cepparello," tells how a most wicked man—clearly a *figura diaboli*, or type of the devil—deceived a friar with a false confession and came to be reputed a saint. On one hand, the tale ridicules gullible priests and credulous common folk, but on the other hand, it presents the undeniable power of human cunning. The tenth story of the tenth day recounts the story of how the Marquis of Saluzzo marries the peasant Griselda and subjects her to inhuman trials to ascertain her devotion; for example, he pretends to have their two children killed. His cruelty is ostensibly designed to test her love or respect for him; her extraordinary patience in responding to his bestiality assuredly makes of her a *figura Christi*, or type of Christ. From the comedic devil figure of Cepparello to the tragic Christ figure of Griselda there appears to be in *The Decameron* a rev-

elation of the breadth of the human condition and the wide-ranging possibilities of human experience. Nevertheless, Boccaccio explores a variation on at least one of two themes in almost all of his stories: the power of human intelligence (for good or bad) and the effect of love or human passion (for the well-being or detriment of those involved). At times, these themes are intermingled, as in so many of the stories of the seventh day having to do with the ingenious tricks wives play on their (usually cuckolded) spouses.

SETTINGS

Often when treating the advantages of human wit, the author provides a Florentine or Tuscan setting to his story. For example, in the sixth day, "Cisti the Baker" is set in Florence and illustrates the rise and power of the hardworking and hard-thinking merchant class Boccaccio knew so well in his hometown. Similarly, "Guido Cavalcanti," told on the same day, has Florence as its setting and reveals the barbed wit of one of the city's native sons. There are also tales told of Florentines who are dull-witted; examples would include the various eighth and ninth day stories about the simple-minded painter Calandrino, who is constantly being tricked by his supposed friends Bruno and Buffalmacco. Those who outsmart him, however, are fellow Florentines. By contrast, many of the highly adventurous tales are set in cities far away from Florence, often in exotic locations. Not surprisingly, Naples figures prominently in perhaps the most notable of the adventure tales—that is, "Andreuccio of Perugia," the story of a provincial young man who goes to a big city (Naples) to buy horses and ends up suffering a series of misfortunes only to return home with a ruby of great value. In the tale, Naples symbolizes adventure and daring and is undoubtedly meant to recall the city of the author's youth.

THE LOVE TALES

Boccaccio's love tales repeatedly, though not exclusively, present realistic women in place of the idealized and angelic women Dante was wont to exalt. In stories scattered throughout *The Decameron*, but especially in those of the third and fifth day, the physical and pleasurable union of man and woman is portrayed as the healthy and correct goal of human love. While some interpret such unabashed celebration of humankind's sexuality as a sure indication that *The Decameron* is a Renaissance work, it should be remembered that approximately ninety percent of Boccaccio's tales derive from medieval sources. G. H. McWilliam, in the introduction to his excellent English translation of *The Decameron*, reviews with insight the problem of how to classify the book with regard to historical period. He points out that the harsh judgment leveled against friars and monks, whether they are philanderers or simoniacs, has numerous precedents in the literature of the Middle Ages, including Dante's thoroughly medieval *The Divine Comedy*.

This is not to say, however, that *The Decameron* does not look to the future, for it most certainly does. For one thing, when Boccaccio attacks the superstitious religious beliefs and corrupt ecclesiastical practices of his times, he does so with more severity than did his predecessors; for another, he presents the centrality of sexuality to the human condition without recourse to sermons or condemnations of the same. In both ways, he draws closer to the spirit of a new age and distances himself from the Middle Ages. His overriding purpose in the tales, however, is to illuminate the spectrum of humankind's experiences and to point, in a world accustomed to pain and disease, a way to happiness and health. Boccaccio's medium is always the well-worded and exquisitely framed story; his best medicine, more often than not, is laughter or the praise of life.

OTHER MAJOR WORKS

POETRY: *Rime*, c. 1330-1340; *La caccia di Diana*, c. 1334; *Il filostrato*, c. 1335 (*The Filostrato*, 1873); *Il filocolo*, c. 1336 (*Labor of Love*, 1566); *Teseida*, 1340-1341 (*The Book of Theseus*, 1974); *Il ninfale d'Ameto*, 1341-1342 (also known as *Commedia delle ninfe*); *L'amorosa visione*, 1342-1343 (English translation, 1986); *Elegia di Madonna Fiammetta*, 1343-1344 (*Amorous Fiammetta*, 1587); *Il ninfale fiesolano*, 1344-1346 (*The Nymph of Fiesole*, 1597); *Buccolicum carmen*, c. 1351-1366 (*Boccaccio's Olympia*, 1913).

NONFICTION: *Genealogia deorum gentilium*, c. 1350-1375; *Trattatello in laude di Dante*, 1351, 1360, 1373 (*Life of Dante*, 1898); *Corbaccio*, c. 1355 (*The Corbaccio*, 1975); *De casibus virorum illustrium*, 1355-1374 (*The Fall of Princes*, 1431-1438); *De montibus, silvis, fontibus lacubus, fluminubus, stagnis seu paludibus, et de nominbus maris*, c. 1355-1374; *De mulieribus claris*, c. 1361-1375 (*Concerning Famous Women*, 1943); *Esposizioni sopra la Commedia di Dante*, 1373-1374.

BIBLIOGRAPHY

Bergin, Thomas G. *Boccaccio*. New York: Viking Press, 1981. An excellent general introduction to Boccaccio. It begins with a historical background to Florentine life in the fourteenth century and proceeds to delineate the life of the author with emphasis on the major influences on his work. The early works are analyzed individually for their own merit and for their relationship to *The Decameron*. Contains lengthy but lucid discussion of *The Decameron* followed by notes and a useful list of works.

Branca, Vittore. *Boccaccio: The Man and His Works*. Translated by Richard Monges. New York: New York University Press, 1976. The definitive biography of Boccaccio by an eminent scholar in the field of medieval literature. Branca analyzes Boccaccio from a historical perspective, provides an overview of the Middle Ages, discusses Florentine life during the period of the emerging merchant middle class, and focuses on the episode of the horrendous Black Plague. Branca offers many scholarly insights into Boccaccio's prose production within a readable style that is accessible to the general public.

Caporello-Szykman, C. *The Boccaccian Novella: The Creation and Waning of a Genre*. New York: Peter Lang, 1990. Defines the novella as a form that existed only between Boccaccio and Cervantes. Discusses generic characteristics of the *Decameron*, Boccacio's narrative theory, and the novella's place within the oral tradition.

Cottino-Jones, Marga. *An Anatomy of Boccaccio's Style*. Napoli, Italy: Cymba, 1968. While the influence of Boccaccio on prose literature and the novel is of major importance, his linguistic contribution cannot be ignored. Boccaccio's style was to be emulated by the writers of ensuing generations, and in the Renaissance he officially became the model for all Italian prose. Cottino-Jones analyzes the style of Boccaccio, its mixture of Latin and Florentine idioms, and illustrates how a study of its linguistic peculiarities can offer interesting insights into an interpretation of *The Decameron.*

Forni, Pier Massimo. *Adventures in Speech: Rhetoric and Narration in Boccaccio's "Decameron."* Philadelphia: University of Pennsylvania Press, 1996. Examines Boccaccio's style in his seminal work. Includes bibliographical references and an index.

Hollander, Robert. *Boccaccio's Two Venuses.* New York: Columbia University Press, 1977. A thorough analysis of all Boccaccio's works except *The Decameron.* The author contrasts classical and Christian influences in Boccaccio's work and concludes that, although the latter predominates in the later works, even in the earlier prose the classical Venus is tempered by the use of irony. Concludes that Boccaccio is a moral philosopher who, unlike Dante, is not concerned with human appetites that lead to a spiritual death but with their negative effects in this world. More than one hundred pages of notes provide a tool for further research.

Moe, Nelson. "Not a Love Story: Sexual Aggression, Law and Order in *Decameron* X 4." *Romanic Review* 86 (November, 1995): 623-638. Discusses the fourth tale of the tenth day as a reworking of an earlier Boccaccio treatment; examines his reformulation of the social significance of sexual transgression that is at the center of both versions of the tale. Argues that the revision transforms a tale of passion into a tale of property and discusses the use of legal discourse in the revision.

Stierle, Karlheinz. "Three Moments in the Crisis of Exemplarity: Boccaccio-Petrarch, Montaigne, and Cervantes." *Journal of the History of Ideas* 59 (October, 1998): 581-595. Discusses Boccaccio's response to the exemplum as a form of narration that presumes more similarity in human behavior than diversity; analyzes Boccaccio's turn from exemplum to novella as a shift that indicates a crisis of exemplarity.

Wright, Herbert G. *Boccaccio in England, from Chaucer to Tennyson.* London: Athlone Press, 1957. Boccaccio's fame is not limited to Italy, and it is particularly in England that his works had a major impact. This book analyzes the influence of Boccaccio on well-known authors such as Geoffrey Chaucer, William Shakespeare, and Alfred, Lord Tennyson, with an especially lengthy and perspicacious discussion of the presence of Boccaccio in *The Canterbury Tales.* This volume is also a fine introduction to the comparative study of literatures, and it illustrates how masterpieces of literature in any language belong to the world community.

Madison V. Sowell, updated by Victor A. Santi

HEINRICH BÖLL

Born: Cologne, Germany; December 21, 1917
Died: Merten, West Germany; July 16, 1985

PRINCIPAL SHORT FICTION

Wanderer, kommst du nach spa . . . , 1950 (*Travel-
ler, If You Come to Spa*, 1956)
So ward abend und morgen, 1955
Unberechenbare gäste, 1956
*Doktor Murkes gesammeltes schweigen und andere
satiren*, 1958
Der fahnhof von zimpren, 1959
Erzählungen, hörspiele, aufsätze, 1961
Entfernung von der truppe, 1964 (*Absent Without
Leave*, 1965)
Eighteen Stories, 1966
Absent Without Leave and Other Stories, 1967
Children Are Civilians Too, 1970
Die verwundung und andere frühe erzählungen,
1983 (*The Casualty*, 1986)
*Veränderungen in Staech: Erzählungen, 1962-
1980*, 1984
The Stories of Heinrich Böll, 1986

OTHER LITERARY FORMS

A prolific writer, Heinrich Böll is best known for
his novels, many of which might better be called novellas, like his first two, *Der Zug war pünktlich*
(1949; *The Train Was on Time*, 1956) and *Wo warst
du, Adam?* (1951; *Adam, Where Art Thou?*, 1955).
Other novels include *Und sagte kein einziges wort*
(1953; *Acquainted with the Night*, 1954), *Billard um
halbzehn* (1959; *Billiards at Half-Past Nine*, 1961),
and *Die verlorene ehre der Katharina Blum: Oder,
Wie gewalt entstehen und wohin sie führen kann*
(1974; *The Lost Honor of Katharina Blum: Or, How
Violence Develops and Where It Can Lead*, 1975). In
addition, he frequently wrote essays, statements, radio plays, translations, poems, and dramas.

ACHIEVEMENTS

Heinrich Böll arrived on the German literary
scene shortly after the total collapse of Adolf Hitler's

National Socialism. Deeply suspicious of all authority and mistrustful of much that he saw about him in
the fledgling Federal Republic, the young former
Wehrmacht veteran dedicated his writing to the cause
of democratic humanism. Early associated with the
young left-leaning writers and thinkers of Gruppe 47
(for the year 1947), such as Günter Grass, Stefan
Lenz, Uwe Johnson, and Ilse Aichinger, Böll turned
out a stream of fiction that attracted attention and
won numerous prizes, first in his own country and
then in the world. In 1969, he was elected president
of the West German PEN Club (a writers' union) and
in 1971 of the International PEN. In 1972, he became
the first German to win the Nobel Prize in Literature
since Thomas Mann in 1929.

BIOGRAPHY

Although Heinrich Böll belonged to the generation that was most attracted to the Nazis, he was
never deluded by their rhetoric and promises. He
even recognized their success in alleviating the distress of workers ravaged by a worldwide depression
as achieved only by means of a conspiracy with capitalism.

Coming from a large family of Rhineland Catholics, Böll grew up in broad-minded Cologne, happy
and well adjusted. Despite the nation's hard times and
the limited means of his father, who ran a small wood-
working business, Böll's childhood was rich in the
pleasant qualities of German life alluded to in his stories: a loving family, decorated tables for special occasions, Christmas trees and songs, and flowers, gather-
ings, books, music, wines, and stately churches.

In 1937, Heinrich Böll was graduated from the
Gymnasium (the German name for the demanding
preparatory school). After a few months of work as a
clerk in a bookstore in Bonn, he entered the University of Cologne to study literature. Previous labor service and an aversion to Nazi affiliations, however, led
to his precipitate induction into eight weeks of military training, weeks that turned into six endless years
when war broke out in September, 1939. Wounded

Heinrich Böll, Nobel Laureate for Literature in 1972
(©The Nobel Foundation)

four times and serving on both the Eastern and Western fronts, Böll, who despised the cause for which he was fighting, succeeded in surviving only by a combination of luck and desperate ruses. Captured on April 9, 1945, he was released by the Americans the following September to join millions of his dazed compatriots wandering through the ruins, hoping to find food, shelter, and lost family members.

Reunited with his wife Annemarie, whom he had married on leave in 1942, he found work first with his father and later with the City of Cologne. In these awful years of cold, hunger, and death, during which his little son died, Böll started to write stories based on his war and postwar experiences. While he had been interested in writing as early as his teenage years, it was in this period that his career commenced. Böll began publishing stories in newspapers and maga-

zines and soon acquired a German and then an international readership. As a pacifist and a democrat with leftist sympathies, his work was recognized by Europe's socialist countries as acceptable reading for the masses. Thus, Böll, who regarded himself as espousing antiauthoritarian, Christian, and humanistic values, was surprised to find himself claimed by East and West as a spokesperson—a role he disclaimed, largely to deaf ears.

While he has written many works, not always of a consistent quality, it seems safe to predict that he will be remembered less for his satiric depictions of a West Germany on the way to an "economic miracle" than for his moving stories and novellas of decent people, in the cataclysmic decade from 1939 to 1949, who longed for a world of charity, understanding, and tolerance.

Böll died on July 16, 1985, from illnesses aggravated by his early suffering and long years of heavy smoking. In his last years, he often came to be regarded as something of a crank for his sympathy toward the radical Left and his repetitive chidings of an affluent *Bundesrepublik*.

ANALYSIS

Heinrich Böll often appears both stylistically and philosophically to be a fusion of Ernest Hemingway and Franz Kafka, unlikely as that combination might seem. He frequently wrote in a simple prose style, recounting the day-to-day affairs of soldiers or former soldiers who smoke cigarette after cigarette and drink as much as Hemingway's characters. Despite a surface reality, however, his world is often as surrealistic as Kafka's, as stories such as "Unberechenbare gäste" ("Unexpected Guests"), "Wie in schlechten romanen" ("Like a Bad Dream"), "Der wegwerfer" ("The Thrower Away") or "Er kam als bierfahrer" ("He Came as a Beer-Truck Driver") testify. Böll has not decided whether his allegiance is ultimately to those who see humanity triumphing over the myriad disasters that dog it or to those who regard decency and justice hopelessly as overpowered by chaos, force, and intolerance.

Perhaps it is because his most formative and productive years were spent either in the field-gray uniform of the Third Reich or in cast-off civilian clothes observing its successor that his judgment wavers. Though he witnessed or heard of countless horrors, he also experienced incidents of kindness, love, and compassion that seemed to redeem them. From his experience came a hatred of intolerance but also an understanding that accusations of innate German moral inferiority themselves constituted a kind of racism. Thus, despite Hitler, the Holocaust, and those whose greatest joy is to lord it over others, he is always more interested in people like himself (often little people, eccentrics, or women—for Böll is a pronounced feminist), who are filled with awe at the miracles of nature, human life, and creative ability. These—whether Jewish teachers, German infantry men, American soldiers, or Hungarian pub keepers—are the people to whom he belongs. It is they who will inherit the earth—always provided the others can be kept at bay.

Böll associates authority with evil and good with youth, innocence, and women. Although he did not translate J. D. Salinger's *The Catcher in the Rye* (1951) into German until many years after he had established himself as a writer, the attraction that book had for him is easy to grasp. Like Holden Caulfield, Böll distrusts "phonies," and like Salinger, he expresses himself in a language purged of abstractions, avoiding the syntax of authority, the gaseous bureaucratese, and perversions of vocabulary indulged in by the Nazis. His recognition of the damaged state of the German language after the dictatorship might be compared to Winston Smith's similar realization about "Newspeak" in George Orwell's *Nineteen Eighty-Four* (1949). Böll's attempt to rescue German from its kidnappers is not always apparent in translation but endeared him to postwar readers. Moreover, his language often incorporates a kind of childlike quality reflective of his themes, in which "tenderness" relieves "anarchy," to borrow two helpful terms from a perceptive introductory essay by an editor of his works.

"And There Was the Evening and the Morning"

Thus, in "So ward abend und morgen" ("And There Was the Evening and the Morning"), a story that comes perilously close to the sentimental, a husband estranged from his wife describes to her on a postwar Christmas Eve the presents that he has been able to afford for her: "It's an umbrella . . . two books and a little piano made of chocolate; it's as big as an encyclopedia, the keys are made of marzipan and brittle." Then he asks her if she is pleased, "Freust du dich?," the sort of simple question that one might ask a child but in a language that touches the heart in a way almost impossible to convey in English.

"As the War Ended" and "Murke's Collected Silences"

In "Als der krieg zu ende war" ("As the War Ended"), a "story" that, like a few others, seems almost a personal reminiscence, a fellow prisoner of war tries to explain to the first-person narrator that a German nationalist need not be a Nazi, that words such as "honor," "loyalty," "fatherland," and "decency" still have meaning. The narrator offers as refutation merely a list of German "patriots": Wilhelm II, Papen, Hindenburg, Blauberg, Keitel; he adds gratuitously and mischievously to the reader: "It made him furious that I never even mentioned Hitler."

Böll has had good fortune in his authorized English translator Lelia Vennewitz, who renders his sensitive prose into excellent English. If her Britishisms distract or confuse American readers on rare occasions, those readers can be grateful for her many inconspicuous, clarifying additions. Böll's Germany of simple pleasures, of belt-tightening, railroad stations, bicycles, and how it was both before and after the swastika darkened the skies has almost disappeared. In a satirical story chiding a recovering nation rapidly heading again for world prominence, "Dr. Murkes gesammeltes schweigen" ("Murke's Collected Silences"), Böll refers casually to a *Paternosteraufzug*. Vennewitz deftly interrupts the narrative to explain that this is an elevator of "open cages carried on a conveyor belt, like beads on a rosary, moving slowly and continuously from bottom to top, across the top of the elevator shaft, down to the bottom again, so that passengers could step on and off at any floor." While none of these are Böll's words, few would argue that they do anything but increase the clarity of the story.

Undoubtedly, Böll's short fiction about the war and its aftermath will most interest foreign readers. Satires such as "Veränderung in Staech" ("The Staech Affair") or the bittersweet "Rendezvous mit Margaret" ("Rendezvous with Margaret") are fine works in their way but not comparable to "Wanderer, kommst du nach spa . . ." ("Stranger, Bear Word to the Spartans We . . .") or "Die dachrinne" ("The Rain Gutter"). Such a judgment does not mean that all earlier stories are necessarily better than late ones. For example, the labored "Abenteuer eines Brotbeutels" ("Adventures of a Haversack") cannot compare with the previously mentioned "Stranger, Bear Word to the Spartans We . . . ," published the same year. Furthermore, "Als de kreig ausbrach" ("When the War Broke Out") and "As the War Ended," though published years after the events that they chronicle, are more successful than some much earlier efforts.

The war, whether still raging or just concluded, is a palpable presence in many of Böll's most successful stories. Just as in the pages of Hemingway, it reduces men—often boys in Böll's case—to their most fallible selves, and while it seldom brings out the best in human beings, it frequently makes their behavior understandable and sometimes excusable. "Die botschaft" ("Breaking the News") tells of a former soldier's arrival by train in a dreary village to inform a woman that he has seen her husband die, not even in combat but in an overcrowded prisoner-of-war camp. Though he finds her with another man, her grief is genuine, and he acknowledges to himself that life must go on and that she is not to be judged. "Grün ist die heide" ("Green Are the Meadows") introduces another *Heimkehrer* (returning veteran) on a similar mission that fails, leaving him to conclude that the dead must bury the dead.

"Der mann mit den messern" ("The Men with the Knives"), published a year earlier, in 1948, and set again in a landscape of bombed-out buildings and rubble heaps, features a first-person narrator, a partially crippled former lieutenant, who succeeds in exorcising ghosts of the past. Hired as a partner by an enterprising former sergeant, now a knife-thrower on the vaudeville stage, the young veteran learns that his fear of knives whizzing by his head is conquerable

and that he can make a living at this dangerous game. Unlike wartime, when risking one's life was mere waste and when fear never left one, fear here is a step on the road to a more bearable future.

"MY EXPENSIVE LEG" AND "STRANGER, BEAR WORD TO THE SPARTANS WE . . ."

In "Mein teures bein" ("My Expensive Leg"), dating from these same postwar years, however, Böll rejects even the faint optimism of these other *Heimkehrer* stories in favor of gallows humor so bitter that it nearly backfires. In this story, an amputee "proves" to an uninterested bureaucrat at the employment office that his new wooden leg has cost the government thousands in pensions paid out to former officers, because he lost his leg while ensuring that these men could safely retreat before a Russian advance reached them.

When Benjamin Franklin leveled his sharpest satire against an England that had not only dispatched armies against her own people but also hired foreign mercenaries in the endeavor, he turned to the story of Leonidas and the Battle of Thermopylae. In "The Sale of the Hessians," published in 1777, Franklin compares the Americans struggling against hired Europeans to the small band of Spartans who died defending Greek freedom against Xerxes's brutish war machine. Böll draws on the same historical precedent in "Wanderer, kommst du nach spa . . ." (translated less enigmatically as "Stranger, Bear Word to the Spartans We . . ."). In Böll's story, however, it is the Nazi juggernaut that is equated with the Persian enemies of Greece, the Nazi forces that threaten their neighbors. Leonidas's words, meaning that the Spartans have preserved freedom at the cost of their lives, become an indictment of German authority, especially the teachers of the young, even those who taught Latin and Greek.

The story is richly symbolic, but the imagery is organic and unobtrusive and complements both the understated realism and the simplicity of prose style. When the first-person narrator, a feverish, wounded young soldier only three months out of school, notices in a classroom the shadow on the wall where the crucifix had stood for many years, the reader regards his observation as exactly the sort that one might make while waiting to be lifted onto the operating table, not as a statement about Catholicism's capitulation to the *Blut und boden* doctrines of National Socialism. The boy-soldier, drafted into the army from *Unterprima* (the second to last year in *Gymnasium*) and thus about eighteen, has been transported at night to a school now being used as a field hospital and morgue. He thinks that he recognizes it as the *Gymnasium* that he attended for eight long years, but he cannot be sure, since the light is dim and all schools look almost alike. Outside, the city is burning. In his disoriented state, it becomes important that he determine whether this is indeed his school.

Just as every former pupil longs masochistically to return to the site of his torment, the young soldier painstakingly examines the hallways and staircases through which he is carried. Gradually, he determines that the pictures, statues, and memorials to fallen classmates identify the building. It is not until he is taken into the art room, however, to await the surgeon's examination and knife that he is convinced. He recalls his authoritarian art teacher and the handwriting exercises that he was obliged to carry out in scripts such as gothic, Italianate, and cursive, when suddenly he sees still on the blackboard, in his own handwriting, the fragmentary sentence: "Stranger, Bear Word to the Spartans We . . . ." The rest has been rubbed out, but he knows he has returned. Minutes later a makeshift assistant, the school's kindly old janitor, and the doctor unwrap his bloody dressings in a dazzlingly lit alcove to reveal fatal wounds.

Although the plot is simplicity itself, the exquisite selection of descriptive details ironically comments on the betrayal not only of humanistic and Christian values but also of the young men by their elders. The portraits of German Electors end with Hitler's. The perversion of education is suggested by the pictures of "Germanic" types from the new class in "Race History," and the great philosopher Friedrich Wilhelm Nietzsche himself has become merely a Nazi stooge. As the broken POW, whose life has been ruined by the war, says to the reader in "In guter hut" ("The Waiting-Room")—and he speaks for Böll as well: "Perhaps you will understand that today I am very suspicious of these so-called sensible older people who after all . . . are also the voters of those earlier days."

OTHER MAJOR WORKS

LONG FICTION: *Der zug war pünktlich*, 1949 (*The Train Was on Time*, 1956); *Wo warst du, Adam?*, 1951 (*Adam, Where Art Thou?*, 1955); *Und sagte kein einziges wort*, 1953 (*Acquainted with the Night*, 1954); *Haus ohne hüter*, 1954 (*Tomorrow and Yesterday*, 1957); *Das brot der frühen jahre*, 1955 (*The Bread of Our Early Years*, 1957, also known as *The Bread of Those Early Years*, 1976); *Billard um halbzehn*, 1959 (*Billiards at Half-Past Nine*, 1961); *Ansichten eines clowns*, 1963 (*The Clown*, 1965); *Ende einer dienstfahrt*, 1966 (*End of a Mission*, 1967); *Gruppenbild mit dame*, 1971 (*Group Portrait with Lady*, 1973); *Die verlorene ehre der katharina blum: Oder, Wie gewalt entstehen und wohin sie führen kann*, 1974 (*The Lost Honor of Katharina Blum: Or, How Violence Develops and Where It Can Lead*, 1975); *Fürsorgliche belagerung*, 1979 (*The Safety Net*, 1982); *Der vermächtnis*, 1982 (*A Soldier's Legacy*, 1985); *Frauen vor flusslandschaft*, 1985 (*Women in a River Landscape*, 1988); *Der engel schwieg*, 1992 (wr. 1950; *The Silent Angel*, 1994).

PLAYS: *Ein schluck erde*, pb. 1962; *Aussatz*, pb. 1970.

SCREENPLAY: *Deutschland im herbst*, 1978.

POETRY: *Gedichte*, 1972; *Gedichte mit collagen von Klaus Staeck*, 1980.

NONFICTION: *Irisches tagebuch*, 1957 (*Irish Journal*, 1967); *Brief an einen jungen Katholiken*, 1961; *Frankfurter vorlesungen*, 1966; *Hierzulande*, 1967; *Aufsätze, kritiken, reden*, 1967; *Neue politische und literarische schriften*, 1973; *Schwierigkeiten mit der brüderlichkeit*, 1976; *Einmischung erwünscht*, 1977; *Missing Persons and Other Essays*, 1977; *Spuren der zeitgenossenschaft*, 1980; *Gefahren von falschen brüdern*, 1980; *Was soll aus dem jungen bloss werden? Oder, Irgendwas mit büchern*, 1981 (*What's to Become of the Boy? Or, Something to Do with Books*, 1984); *Vermintes gelände*, 1982; *Bild, Bonn, Boenisch*, 1984.

MISCELLANEOUS: *Heinrich Böll werke*, 1977-1979.

BIBLIOGRAPHY

Conard, Robert C. *Heinrich Böll*. Boston: Twayne, 1981. Written before Böll's death and thus incomplete in a number of respects, this book is nevertheless the best introduction to and study of Böll's work readily available to the general reader. Conard devotes three chapters to the short stories, examining them in chronological order. Includes the usual helpful bibliographies and chronologies of the Twayne series, though many sources are understandably in German.

_____. *Understanding Heinrich Böll*. Columbia: University of South Carolina Press, 1992. A general introduction to Böll's life and work, commenting on his major fiction.

Crampton, Patricia, trans. *Heinrich Böll, on His Death: Selected Obituaries and the Last Interview*. Bonn: Inter Nationes, 1985. This short volume is a collection of short elegiac essays, together with Böll's last interview. As such, no principle of organization is to be found, but it does offer many perceptive and impressionistic insights into both the man and the writer. Contains about a dozen photographs of Böll in his last years.

Macpherson, Enid. *A Student's Guide to Böll*. London: Heinemann Educational Books, 1972. A brief introduction intended for the student of German literature. In addition to devoting chapters to the novels and the short stories, Macpherson discusses Böll's critical writings and lectures for the light they throw on his narrative practice. The stories are placed in two basic categories: stories concerned with war and its aftermath and satiric stories commenting on postwar society. The chapter on Böll as a writer of short stories, a form he wanted to become the main vehicle of his work, is divided mainly into short sections on his major themes and character types.

Reed, Donna K. *The Novel and the Nazi Past*. New York: Peter Lang, 1985. A somewhat pedantic book concerned with the literature of *Vergangenheitsbewältigung* (coming to terms with the past), a jawbreaker that has resurfaced after the dissolution of the former German Democratic Republic. Thomas Mann and Günter Grass are discussed in addition to Böll, more specifically his novel *Billiards at Half-Past Nine*, as central to his political thought. Includes a bibliography on Nazism and the postwar period.

Reid, J. H. *Heinrich Böll: A German for His Time*. New York: Berg, 1988. Quoting Böll that writers must be understood as products of their time, Reid studies Böll as just that, tracing the political and social currents that shaped his work. Perceptive and evenhanded, this study is less concerned with belles lettres than ideologies and political history. The short stories find mention and commentary chiefly as expression of Böll's ideas. An excellent bibliography, largely in German, reflects the book's main concern.

Zachau, Reinhard K. *The Narrative Fiction of Heinrich Böll*. Cambridge, England: Cambridge University Press, 1997. A study of Böll's work in its social context in the second German Republic. The book includes several essays on Böll's major works, focusing on their literary traditions as well as the link in his work between moral/aesthetic issues and sociopolitical issues.

James E. Devlin

MARÍA LUISA BOMBAL

Born: Viña del Mar, Chile; June 8, 1910
Died: Santiago, Chile; May 6, 1980

PRINCIPAL SHORT FICTION
New Islands and Other Stories, 1982

OTHER LITERARY FORMS

María Luisa Bombal is the author of the following influential novels: *La última niebla*, 1934 (*The Final Mist*, 1982; previously revised and translated as *The House of Mist*, 1947); *La amortajada*, 1938 (translated as *The Shrouded Woman*, 1948); *La historia de María Griselda*, 1977.

ACHIEVEMENTS

María Luisa Bombal was the Chilean representative to the International PEN Conference in the United States in 1940; she received Chile's Academy of Arts and Letters Prize in 1977 for *The Story of María Griselda*.

BIOGRAPHY

María Luisa Bombal was born in Viña del Mar, Chile, on June 8, 1910. She moved to Paris in 1922 with her widowed mother and attended the Ecole Notre Dame de l'Assomption and the Lycée La Bruyère; she then studied philosophy and literature at the Sorbonne, University of Paris, where she became involved with the avant-garde movement in the arts. She returned to Chile in 1930 and became associated with a literary group that included Jorge Luis Borges, Victoria Ocampo, and Pablo Neruda. In 1935, her first work, *La última niebla* (*The Final Mist*), was enthusiastically received because of its narrative experimentalism.

In 1940, after she shot Eulogio Sanchez Errázuriz, either because of unrequited love or because she imagined him to represent all that was wrong with her life, Bombal moved to the United States and married. Her husband helped her begin writing screenplays. She continued to write and translate until her husband died, after which she moved back to Chile, where she lived until her death on May 6, 1980.

ANALYSIS

Although her output is relatively small, María Luisa Bombal has been hailed as one of the most important Latin American writers of the twentieth century. Part of the reason for this high praise is that she explored the inextricable mixture of fantasy and reality called Magical Realism before its more famous practitioners, Jorge Luis Borges, Julio Cortazar, Carlos Fuentes, and Gabriel García Márquez. The fact that she was female and wrote about the sexual liberation of women in a patriarchal culture that had long suppressed them has added to her fame in late twentieth century criticism.

Bombal more likely learned her narrative technique from the avant-garde of 1920's France than from her Latin American countrymen, for the European gothic tradition that inspired that literary trend is much in evidence in her fiction. The women in her stories, caught in a trap created for them by males, who force them to be either submissive wives or sexual objects, yearn to escape; however, the only means they have to do so is through dreams and fantasies, as they romantically yearn for dark, mysterious men, who turn out to be phantoms, or as they embody darkly mysterious sexual creatures, primevally as much animal as human.

"THE FINAL MIST"

A number of gothic romance conventions characterize "La última niebla" ("The Final Mist"). For example, the female protagonist marries a childhood friend who tells her he knows every inch of her body without her having to take her clothes off. Moreover, she feels she has to imitate his first wife, who, according to him, was a perfect woman before she died an untimely death, and, typical of such romances, the narrator, herself quite young, is unaware of her physicality, never having dared to look at her own breasts.

Throughout the story, a mist or fog hangs over everything, giving the external world the warm intimacy of a closed room, muffling all sound. This dreamlike real world is so permeated by the narrator's dreams and fantasies that when a young man of almost supernatural aspect appears and kisses her she feels she has been waiting for him and must surrender to his power; her sexual encounter with the stranger is described as an ultimate romantic fantasy in a single magical and dreamlike night.

As ten years go by, in typical romantic fashion, she never sees him again, does not know where he is, but feels that it is enough to know that somewhere he exists. However, when her sister-in-law shoots herself in her lover's house, she feels she is a "casualty" of her own invention, her life a "charade performed in shadows." The ultimate gothic fantasy element is played out in the story when the protagonist locates the house of her dream lover, only to discover that the man who lived there was blind and died of a fall fifteen years earlier. The story ends with her envy of her sister-in-law, who may have died for love; she considers suicide, but settles for living and dying correctly, while the mist settles over everything like a "shroud."

"THE TREE"

Bombal's best-known story is perhaps "El árbol" ("The Tree"), a self-conscious narrative manipulation of the interaction between past and present. The story begins in present tense as the protagonist, Brigida, who, while listening to an opening Wolfgang Amadeus Mozart piece at a concert, recalls allowing herself to be led into marrying a friend of her father. The second concert piece, by Beethoven, leads her back to her marriage and the tree outside her dressing room window, whose foliage reflected in her mirrors, creating the illusion of an infinite forest. As she listens to the third piece, by Frédéric Chopin, the music intermingles in her memory with rain hissing through the leaves of the rubber tree.

Brigida's husband Luis knows she does not love him, but says it is not convenient for them to separate. Although she realizes "that [i]s life," she feels that underneath the mediocrity of experience there is a melody of "grave and slow words that transfixed her." Just when she feels an unexpected sense of fulfillment and placidity, knowing she can live without hope or fear, she hears a thunderous noise. At this point the reader is made aware of the simultaneity of the past and present by the line "The Intermission? No. The rubber tree." The concert hall is ablaze with light and the audience files out, but she is imprisoned in the "web of her past," trapped in her dressing room, which has been flooded by a terrifying white light. Because her husband has had the rubber tree outside her window chopped down, the light reveals all the ugliness and shabbiness of things. Feeling he has stolen her intimacy, her secret, she leaves him.

The thematic focus of the story is a childlike mode of perception that is poetic and atemporal, lost in the shadows of desire and the imagination. Brigida's preference for the shadowy romantic world of her dressing room over the brightly lit external reality makes her unfit for practical experience. However, the story does not suggest that Brigida's obsession with the shadows made by the tree is an escape but rather that her desire for romantic love and loss of self in dream or passion is justifiable.

"BRAIDS" AND "THE UNKNOWN"

The two shortest stories in *New Islands and Other Stories* are similar in their essayistic and folklorish qualities. "Trenzas" ("Braids") begins like an essay on modern women, who cut off their braids and thus sever their ties with "magic currents that issue from the very heart of the earth." Examples of the supernatural power of woman's hair are cited from the stories of Tristram and Isolde, Queen Mélisande, and Bluebeard. After this essayistic preface, Bombal tells a fabulistic story of two sisters and the identification of braids with the primeval forest to illustrate why women, having renounced their braids, have lost their prophetic power and no longer have their old magnetism.

"Lo secreto" ("The Unknown") is a conventional fable about a pirate ship trapped centuries ago in a whirlpool and sent spinning to the bottom of the sea. When the pirate captain awakens, he thinks he has landed on a deserted island, but sees his sails billowing without wind and an inverted image of his beached ship above him. When he and his crew realize that their feet leave no tracks and their sails throw no shadow, they know they are a thousand fathoms beneath the sea and damned. The fable ends with the captain's terrifying moan—"a cry of affliction from someone desperate, burning with desire for something irrevocably lost."

"NEW ISLANDS"

"Las islas nuevas" ("New Islands"), the title story of Bombal's short fiction collection, climaxes the slender volume by making its heroine Yolanda not merely the psychologically desirous female figure but also the psychological archetype of desire itself. Imaged as a beautiful serpent and as a seagull, she is ageless, lost in a world of dreams, while at the same time the object of the dreams of others, particularly the male hunter Juan Manuel. Of the many metaphors that characterize the primitive nature of Yolanda, the central one is that of the new islands that have erupted in the lake, for just as the male hunter desires to explore and conquer the islands, so also does he wish to conquer Yolanda.

The magical nature of Yolanda is revealed most emphatically when Juan Manuel, in a typical romantic convention, peeks in her window and sees a "fairy tale unfold," for on her right shoulder he sees either the beginning of, or the atrophy of, a wing—an image Bombal uses to suggest that Yolanda, as magical female creature, is earth bound, with only vestigial remnants of her lost winged freedom—much like a mermaid who has lost her fish-like ability to live under the sea. Juan Manuel flees from the incomprehensible vision, "incapable of soaring into the intricate galleries of Nature in order to arrive at the mystery's origin."

OTHER MAJOR WORKS

LONG FICTION: *La última niebla*, 1934 (*The Final Mist*, 1982; previously trans. as *The House of Mist*, 1947); *La amortajada*, 1938 (*The Shrouded Woman*, 1948); *La historia de María Griselda*, 1977.

BIBLIOGRAPHY

Agosin, Marjorie. "María Luisa Bombal: *O el lenguaje alucinado*." *Symposium* 48 (Winter, 1995): 251-256. In this special issue on Latin American women writers, Agosin argues that Bombal challenged the conventional writing of her time by creating a language that moved back and forth between hallucination and daydream; says her female characters are marginalized women who seek the meaning of their lives through imagination and memory

Debicki, Andrew P. "Structure, Imagery, and Experience in María Luisa Bombal's 'The Tree'." *Studies in Short Fiction* 8 (Winter, 1971): 123-129. Discusses how Bombal uses imagery and descriptive detail to explore the theme of illusion and the conflict between illusory and matter-of-fact realities; argues that the patterns of the story heighten the reader's experience of the protagonist's plight while simultaneously placing that plight within a more universal scheme.

Diaz, Gwendolyn. "Desire and Discourse in María Luisa Bombal's *New Islands*." *Hispanofila* 112 (September, 1994): 51-62. Discusses the stories in *New Islands and Other Stories* as examples of Bombal's experimentation with a new language that reflects a woman's point of view and thought; argues that the heroine of the stories struggles to place her own perceptions in a world of phallocentric social structures; says Bombal wants to create a new rhythm that reflects a more complete view of a world previously divided by sexual hierarchies.

Kostopulos-Cooperman, Celeste. *The Lyrical Vision of María Luisa Bombal*. London: Tamesis Books, 1988. A brief monograph on the lyrical and poetic qualities of Bombal's fiction. Discusses Bombal's central thematic preoccupation of women in relationship to their surrounding worlds. Argues that both technically and thematically Bombal was clearly ahead of her time. Provides detailed discussions of "The New Islands" and "The Tree."

Long, William R. "Latina Writers Are Silent No Longer." *Los Angeles Times*, November 11, 1994, p. A1. Notes that books by Latin American women have become best-sellers in what many have called a new "boom" in Latin American literature, reminiscent of the explosion of talented male writers in the 1960's; quotes several writers, scholars, and critics who argue that the most original work being produced in the 1990's in Latin America is by women who are talking about themselves in an open and daring way, a trend that reflects the breaking down of gender bias throughout Latin America.

Mendez Rodenas, Adriana. "Narcissus in Bloom: The Desiring Subject in Modern Latin American Narrative: María Luisa Bombal and Juan Rulfo." In *Latin American Women's Writing: Feminist Readings in Theory in Crisis*, edited by Anny Brooksbank Jones. New York: Oxford University Press, 1996. Mendez Rodenas applies psychoanalytic theory and a feminist approach to Bombal's fiction, especially focusing on her novel *La*

amortajada, translated as *The Shrouded Woman* (1948); compares her use of the Narcissus theme with Juan Rulfo's use of the myth.

Rivero, Isel. "Among Generals, Bishops, and Guerillas." *Ms.* 1 (May/June, 1991): 70-72. An article on Latin American women writers, noting that while they still wrestle with the process of day-to-day living, their stories are breaking the silence their sisters have endured for so long; discusses the work of several writers, including Bombal, Isabel Allende, and Victoria Ocampo.

Charles E. May

ARNA BONTEMPS

Born: Alexandria, Louisiana; October 13, 1902
Died: Nashville, Tennessee; June 4, 1973

PRINCIPAL SHORT FICTION
The Old South, 1973

OTHER LITERARY FORMS

Arna Bontemps was a prolific writer of African American histories, biographies, and children's books, as well as an editor and anthologist. His best known adult novel is *Black Thunder* (1936). He and Countée Cullen adapted Bontemps's first novel, *God Sends Sunday* (1931), as a Broadway musical, *St. Louis Woman* (pr. 1946). His poetry collection, *Personals*, appeared in 1963.

ACHIEVEMENTS

Arna Bontemps was awarded prizes by *Opportunity* (*Journal of Negro Life*) for poetry and for his story "A Summer Tragedy." He was also granted two Rosenwald grants and two John Simon Guggenheim Memorial Foundation Fellowships for creative writing. In 1956 he received the Jane Addams Children's Book Award and was a finalist for the Newbery Medal. He was named Honorary Consultant to the Library of Congress in American Cultural History in 1972.

BIOGRAPHY

Arna Wendell Bontemps descended from a prosperous, light-complexioned family of "Creoles of Color" (French and African American heritage) in Louisiana; when he was a small child, he and his nuclear family and almost all of his mother's extended family migrated to California. After his mother's death, he lived on his grandmother's farm near Los Angeles until his father sent him away to boarding school to complete his secondary education. As Bontemps was leaving to enroll at Pacific Union College, his father commanded him to renounce his African American past, about which the boy learned a great deal from his Louisiana relatives, who were living in California or were visiting there. His appreciation of his racial past continued to grow.

After receiving his B.A. in English, Bontemps moved to New York, where he became a part of the Harlem Renaissance along with Zora Neale Hurston, Jean Toomer, and Langston Hughes, who became one of Bontemps's closest friends and his literary collaborator. In New York, Bontemps taught school and married Alberta Johnson in 1926. They had five children.

Bontemps taught for a year at Oakwood Academy in Huntsville, Alabama, and learned about racial oppression through the famous trials of the "Scottsville boys," which were being held nearby. He escaped to California, where he finished his second novel. Settling in Chicago, Bontemps received a master's degree in library science from the University of Chicago. He then returned to the South to accept a position as a full professor and head librarian at Fisk University in Nashville, where he remained until 1966 when he was named writer-in-residence at the University of Illinois at Chicago Circle. In 1969 he rejoined the Fisk faculty to serve as writer-in-residence. He died in Nashville in 1973.

ANALYSIS

The Old South, Arna Bontemps's collection of short stories, contains fourteen selections, the first of which is an important essay, "Why I Returned," an account of his early life in Louisiana and California and his later life in Alabama and Tennessee. All of the selections are set in the South of the 1930's (a time when this region was yet unchanged and thus "old") or concern characters from the South. Some of the stories are also autobiographical—"The Cure," "Three Pennies for Luck," "Saturday Night"—and some are sharply satirical portraits of influential white women: a wealthy patron of young black musicians in "A Woman with a Mission" and a principal of a black boarding school in "Heathens at Home." The titles of these latter stories are self-explanatory.

Bontemps was brought up in the Seventh-day Adventist church, for which his father had abandoned the Creoles' traditional Catholicism. The boarding school and college Bontemps attended as well as the academy where he taught in Alabama were sponsored by the Adventists. Though Bontemps did not remain active in this church, he was deeply religious all his life. Several of his stories thus have religious settings and themes, including "Let the Church Roll On," a study of a black congregation's lively charismatic church service. Bontemps was early influenced by music since his father and other relatives had been blues and jazz musicians in Louisiana. "Talk to the Music," "Lonesome Boy, Silver Trumpet," and "A Woman with a Mission" all concern young black musicians.

Arna Bontemps (Library of Congress)

Several selections concern black folk culture and folklore: "The Cure," "Lonesome Boy, Silver Trumpet," and "The Devil Is a Conjurer." The latter story reflects the human desire to invest nature with a sense of the mysterious, which unimaginative men find foolish and unprofitable. In addition, at least seven of Bontemps's stories, including the three named above, involve a young boy or man seeking or discovering meaning and worth in family and community, which some Bontemps scholars believe was a principal desire in the author's own life.

Bontemps's short stories treat sensitive political, economic, and social themes that are also employed in his two novels of slave revolts, *Black Thunder* (1936) and *Drums at Dusk* (1939).

"Blue Boy" in *The Old South* concerns an escaped black murderer who is hunted down and killed after he commits a second homicide. The action in this story is seen from two perspectives, that of a young child and of the criminal himself. Robert Bone argues that the criminal named Blue is in fact "Bontemps's apotheosis of the blues hero." In his best stories Bontemps achieves an aesthetic distance, mastery of literary form, and a belief in transcendence in spite of his characters' struggles in a world that often denies them human value. Though Bontemps's stories have been compared with those of Richard Wright, Bontemps's are less angry and acerbic.

"A SUMMER TRAGEDY"

"A Summer Tragedy," first published in *Opportunity* in 1935, is Bontemps's best-known, most frequently anthologized, and perhaps most successful short story because of its artistic interlacing of setting, symbolism, characterization, and folklore. As Bontemps's biographer, Kirkland C. Jones, has observed, this story is "to the Bontemps canon what 'Sonny's Blues' has become to Baldwin's short fiction efforts—outstanding."

An elderly black couple, Jennie and Jeff Patton, have for decades been tenant farmers on Greenbrier Plantation in an unnamed southern state. The Pattons are ill, frail, and barely ambulatory; Jennie is nearly blind. Their five adult children have all died in violent situations, none of which is specified, suggesting that life for blacks, particularly the young, was dangerous and uncertain in the South.

The opening scene reveals the old couple dressing in their clean but threadbare black "Sunday-best." Their actions are described, slowly and painfully, as they prepare for some great, momentous occasion. The story is set in the fullness of the green, fecund early summer fields; all of nature—plants, animals, and birds—seems to be celebrating life, youth, warmth, and procreation, as contrasted with the aging, pinched, wintry, weary, and deathlike lives of Jennie and Jeff. Nevertheless, they affirm their love for each other and resolve to persevere in their plans, which are not clear to the reader until late in the story. At first, Bontemps's narrative seems almost naturalistic in the tradition of Theodore Dreiser as the Pattons reflect upon their lives of hard, monotonous, futile labor that has left them only more debt-ridden. Their existence seems to be a cruel trap, a vicious, meaningless struggle. They own an old, battered, hard-to-crank Model-T Ford that will later serve a vital but ominous purpose.

Yet the story is not merely documentary with dreary details. Jeff and Jennie are presented as three-dimensional characters through a psychological point of view which allows the reader to share their thoughts, feelings, and memories. Bontemps had also skillfully used folk motifs to provide both verisimilitude and foreshadowing. For example, the Pattons' sickly "frizzly" chickens, which are supposed to protect the farm from evil spirits by devouring them, seem to be as death-doomed as their owners.

Jeff reflects on the many mules he has worn out in his years of plantation toil. His stingy employer has allowed him to have only one mule at a time; thus a long succession of mules has been killed by excessive and unremitting toil. Jeff is not aware that he is symbolically a mule for whom the callous old Major Stevenson has also had no sympathy. Moreover, Jeff himself has never felt pity for a man who is too weak to work.

Passing a neighbor's house on the journey through the countryside, Jennie is silently amused to think that their neighbor, Delia, who sees the Pattons' car drive past, is consumed with curiosity to know their destination. Delia, it seems, had once made passes at Jeff when he was a young married man. By refusing to supply Delia with any information, Jennie feels she is punishing her neighbor for her long-ago indiscretion. Such details as these help humanize and individualize Bontemps's characters, making them psychologically credible. The reader gradually becomes aware that because of the couple's love for one another and their fear that one may grow too weak to help the other, they are determined to perish together.

As the Pattons near the high banks of the river levee, they can hear the rushing water. They drive over the levee and into the dark, swirling water. (Some readers contend that the stream is Louisiana's Red River, which flows near Bontemps's birthplace.) In death, Jeff and Jennie have preserved their independence and dignity. As the car sinks, one wheel sticks up out of the mud in a shallow place—fate's ironical monument to the lives and courageous deaths of Jeff and Jennie Patton. Free of histrionics and sentimentality, this well-handled story is, as critic Robert Bone contends, truly "compelling."

"TALK TO THE MUSIC"

In the years just prior to World War I, young Norman Taylor leaves his home in Rapides Parish (where Bontemps himself was born) and travels two hundred miles to attend college in New Orleans. However, instead of enrolling in college as his parents expect, Norman informally enrolls in a real-life course in blues music, which he studies in the notorious Storyville area, where the inimitable blues singer Mayme Dupree performs in a night club. Apparently Norman has not been able to "study" the blues in Rapides Parish, where it may have been considered "the Devil's music" by good churchgoing folk. Norman pretends to be a waiter at the club and is finally able to hear the fabulous Mayme sing her own style of blues. Her singing moves the audience to look into their hearts and individual and collective pasts and thus both figuratively and literally "talk to" (communicate with) the music as it is performed. Later Norman confesses to Mayme that her blues touched him like Adam and Eve's wail over their innocence lost in Eden, but Mayme comments that he is "crazy." Nevertheless, "Talk to the Music" richly evokes scenes and senses in New Orleans and convincingly dramatizes the young man's struggles to hear Mayme's blues and to learn from her lips about her loves and losses—which are shared not only by African Americans but also by all humanity.

OTHER MAJOR WORKS

LONG FICTION: *God Sends Sunday*, 1931; *Black Thunder*, 1936; *Drums at Dusk*, 1939.

PLAY: *St. Louis Woman*, pr. 1946 (with Countée Cullen).

POETRY: *Personals*, 1963.

NONFICTION: *Father of the Blues*, 1941 (biography, with W. C. Handy); *They Seek a City*, 1945 (history, with Jack Conroy; revised as *Anyplace but Here*, 1966); *Frederick Douglass: Slave, Fighter, Freeman*, 1959; *One Hundred Years of Negro Freedom*, 1961 (history); *Free at Last: The Life of Frederick Douglass*, 1971.

CHILDREN'S LITERATURE: *Popo and Fifina: Children of Haiti* (with Langston Hughes) 1932; *You Can't Pet a Possum*, 1934; *Sad-Faced Boy*, 1937; *The*

Fast Sooner Hound, 1942 (with Conroy); *The Story of the Negro*, 1948; *Sam Patch*, 1951 (with Conroy); *Chariot in the Sky: A Story of the Jubilee Singers*, 1951; *The Story of George Washington Carver*, 1954; *Lonesome Boy*, 1955; *Frederick Douglass: Slave, Fighter, Freeman*, 1959; *Famous Negro Athletes*, 1964; *Mr. Kelso's Lion*, 1970; *Young Booker: Booker T. Washington's Early Days*, 1972; *The Pasteboard Bandit*, 1997 (with Langston Hughes); *Bubber Goes to Heaven*, 1998.

EDITED TEXTS: *The Poetry of the Negro*, 1949 (revised 1971, with Hughes); *The Book of Negro Folklore*, 1958 (with Hughes); *American Negro Poetry*, 1963; *Great Slave Narratives*, 1969; *Hold Fast to Dreams*, 1969; *The Harlem Renaissance Remembered*, 1972.

BIBLIOGRAPHY

Bone, Robert. "Arna Bontemps." *Down Home: A History of Afro-American Short Fiction From Its Beginnings to the End of the Harlem Renaissance.* New York: G. P. Putnam's Sons, 1975. 272-287. Brief but incisive analyses of four of the stories from *The Old South*: "Boy Blue," "A Summer Tragedy," "The Cure," and "Three Pennies for Luck." Notes the use of nature symbolism and folklore in Bontemps's short stories.

Canaday, Nicholas. "Arna Bontemps: The Louisiana Heritage." *Callaloo* 4 (October-February, 1981): 163-169. Traces the significant influence of Bontemps's Louisiana great-uncle, Buddy (Joe Ward), on the author's novel *God Sends Sunday* and on "The Cure" in *The Old South*.

Jones, Kirkland C. "Bontemps and the Old South." *African American Review* 27, no. 2 (1993): 179-185. Argues that the Old South is employed more greatly in Bontemps's fiction than in that of any other Harlem Renaissance writer. Brief but perceptive critiques of five of *The Old South* selections: "Summer Tragedy," "The Cure," "Talk to the Music," "Boy Blue," and "Why I Returned."

_____. *Renaissance Man from Louisiana, A Biography of Arna Wendell Bontemps.* Westport, Conn.: Greenwood Press, 1992. The first full-scale biography of Bontemps. Treats the author's life and career in detail but only cursorily analyzes or evaluates the writings.

Yardley, Jonathan. Review of *The Old South. New York Times Book Review* (December, 1973): 11. Comments on the impression of informality and chattiness the reader gets on a first reading of Bontemps's stories, but a second reading reveals the author's concern about race relations while avoiding bitterness.

Philip A. Tapley

JORGE LUIS BORGES

Born: Buenos Aires, Argentina; August 24, 1899
Died: Geneva, Switzerland; June 14, 1986

PRINCIPAL SHORT FICTION

Historia universal de la infamia, 1935 (*A Universal History of Infamy*, 1972)

El jardín de senderos que se bifurcan, 1941

Seis problemas para don Isidro Parodi, 1942 (with Bioy Casares, under joint pseudonym H. Bustos Domecq, *Six Problems for Don Isidro Parodi*, 1981)

Ficciones, 1935-1944, 1944 (English translation, 1962)

Dos fantasías memorables, 1946 (with Bioy Casares, under joint pseudonym H. Bustos Domecq)

El Aleph, 1949, 1952 (translated in *The Aleph and Other Stories, 1933-1969*, 1970)

La muerte y la brújula, 1951

La hermana de Eloísa, 1955 (with Luisa Mercedes Levinson)

Cuentos, 1958

Crónicas de H. Bustos Domecq, 1967 (with Bioy Casares, *Chronicles of Bustos Domecq*, 1976)

El informe de Brodie, 1970 (*Doctor Brodie's Report*, 1972)

El matreto, 1970

El congreso, 1971 (*The Congress*, 1974)

El libro de arena, 1975 (*The Book of Sand*, 1977)

Narraciones, 1980

OTHER LITERARY FORMS

Though most famous for his work in short fiction, Jorge Luis Borges also holds a significant place in Latino literature for his work in poetry and the essay. In fact, Borges would be considered a major writer in Latino letters for his work in these two genres (the vast majority of which was produced before the Argentine writer branched into short fiction) even had he never written a single short story. Borges's early poetry (that for which he earned his reputation as a poet) is of the ultraist school, an avant-grade brand of poetry influenced by expressionism and Dadaism and intended by its Latino practitioners as a reaction to Latino modernism. Borges's essays, as readers familiar with his fiction might expect, are imaginative and witty and usually deal with topics in literature or philosophy. Interestingly, because of the writer's playful imagination, many of his essays read more like fiction than essay, while, because of his propensity both for toying with philosophical concepts and for fusing the fictitious and the real, much of his fiction reads more like essay than fiction. It seems only fitting, however, that for a writer for whom the line between fiction and reality is almost nonexistent the line between fiction and essay should be almost nonexistent as well.

ACHIEVEMENTS

It is virtually impossible to overstate the importance of Jorge Luis Borges within the context of Latino fiction, for he is, quite simply, the single most important writer of short fiction in the history of Latino literature. This is true not only because of his stories themselves, and chiefly those published in *Ficciones, 1935-1944* and *El Aleph*, but also, just as important, because of how his stories contributed to the evolution of Latino fiction, both short and long, in the latter half of the twentieth century.

Borges was the father of Latino's "new narrative," the type of narrative practiced by the likes of Julio Cortázar, Gabriel García Márquez, Carlos Fuentes, Mario Vargas Llosa, and others. Latino fiction prior to Borges was chiefly concerned with painting a realistic and detailed picture of external Latino reality. Borges's imaginative *ficciones* (or fictions) almost single-handedly changed this, teaching Latino writers to be creative, to use their imagination, to treat fiction as fiction, to allow the fictional world to be just that: fictional. Borges's works also taught Latino writers to deal with universal themes and to write for an intellectual reader. Without Borges, not only would the literary world be without some superb stories, but also Latino narrative in the second half of the twentieth century would have been radically different from what it evolved to be.

BIOGRAPHY

Jorge Luis Borges was born on August 24, 1899, in Buenos Aires, Argentina, the first of two children born to Jorge Guillermo Borges and Leonor Acevedo de Borges. (His sister, Norah, was born in 1901.) Borges's ancestors included prominent Argentine military and historical figures on both sides of his family and an English grandmother on his father's.

"Georgie," as Borges's family called him, began reading very early, first in English, then in Spanish. Tutored first by his English grandmother and later by a private governess, and with access to his father's library (which contained numerous volumes in English), young Borges devoured a wide range of writings, among them those of Robert Louis Stevenson, Rudyard Kipling, and Mark Twain, as well as works of mythology, novels of chivalry, *The Thousand and One Nights* (c. 1450), and Miguel de Cervantes' *Don Quixote de la Mancha* (1605, 1615).

Borges finally entered school at age nine, and at age thirteen he published his first story, a dramatic sketch entitled "El rey de la selva" (the king of the jungle), about his favorite animal, the tiger. Borges and his family traveled to Europe in 1914. World War I broke out while they were visiting Geneva, Switzerland, and they remained there until 1918. During his time in Geneva, Borges began to take an

Jorge Luis Borges (©Washington Post; reprinted by permission of the D.C. Public Library)

interest in French poetry, particularly that of Victor Hugo and Charles Baudelaire, as well as the poetry of Heinrich Heine and the German expressionists. He also began to read the works of Walt Whitman, Arthur Schopenhauer, and G. K. Chesterton, and he maintained his literary connection to his native Argentina by reading *gauchesca* (gaucho) poetry.

In 1919 Borges and his family moved to Spain, living for various lengths of time in Barcelona, Majorca, Seville, and Madrid. While in Spain, Borges associated with a group of ultraist poets and published some poetry in an ultraist magazine. In 1921, Borges and his family returned to Buenos Aires. His return to his native city after a seven-year absence inspired him to write his first volume of poetry, entitled *Fervor de Buenos Aires* (fervor of Buenos Aires) and published in 1923. During this same period (in 1922), he collaborated on a "billboard review" entitled *Prisma* (prism) and edited the manifesto "Ultraísmo" (ultraism), published in the magazine *Nosotros* (us).

He also helped found a short-lived magazine entitled *Proa* (prow). Following a second trip with his family to Europe (1923-1924), Borges continued to write poetry during the 1920's, but he began to branch out into the essay genre as well, publishing three collections of essays during this period: *Inquisiciones* (inquisitions) in 1925, *El tamaño de mi esperanza* (the size of my hope) in 1926, and *El idioma de los argentinos* (the language of the Argentines) in 1928. One of his collections of poetry, *Cuaderno San Martín* (San Martín notebook), won for him second prize in the Municipal Literature Competition in 1929. The prize carried an award of three thousand pesos, which Borges used to buy an edition of the *Encyclopædia Britannica*.

Borges continued writing both poetry and essays in the 1930's, but this decade would also bring his first (though unconventional) steps into fiction. He began contributing to the magazine *Sur* (south) in 1931 (through which he met his friend and future literary collaborator Adolfo Bioy Casares); later, in 1933, he became the director of *Crítica* (criticism), a Saturday literary supplement for a Buenos Aires newspaper. As a contributor to the supplement, Borges began to rewrite stories that he took from various sources, adding his own personal touches and reworking them as he saw fit. He finally wrote, under a pen name, a wholly original piece entitled "Hombres de las orillas" (men from the outskirts), which appeared on September 16, 1933, in the supplement. This story and his other *Crítica* pieces were well received and published together in 1935 in a volume entitled *Historia universal de la infamia*.

Borges's foray into fiction writing continued to follow an unconventional path when in 1936 he began writing a book-review page for the magazine *El Hogar* (the home). Each entry carried a brief biography of the author whose work was being reviewed. Once again, Borges could not leave well enough alone. To the author's true biographical facts, Borges began to add his own "facts," even including apocryphal anecdotes from the author's life and supplementing the author's bibliography with false titles. This mix of fact and fiction, with no regard or concern for which was which, would come to be one of the trademarks of Borges's fiction.

Borges took a job as an assistant librarian in a suburban Buenos Aires library in 1937, a position whose work load and setting afforded the writer ample time and resources to read and write. In December of 1938, however, the Argentine writer suffered a near-fatal accident, slipping on a staircase and striking his head while returning to his apartment. The resulting head injury developed into septicemia, and Borges was hospitalized for more than two weeks. While still recovering in early 1939, Borges decided that he would abandon poetry and the essay (though he would later return to these genres) and dedicate his literary efforts to short fiction. Though it is somewhat unclear as to precisely why he made this decision (there are various accounts), it is speculated by some (and Borges's own comments have supported such speculation) that he did so because after his head injury he was not sure that he could write poetry and essays of the quality for which he had been known before the accident. Short stories, for which he was virtually unknown at this point, would not allow anyone to compare an old Borges with a new, and potentially inferior, Borges. Again, this is only one suggestion as to why the Argentine writer made the decision he did; what is most important, however, is that he made it, and this decision, and the accident that seems to have caused it, would change the face of Latino fiction of the twentieth century.

Almost immediately, Borges began to produce a series of short stories that would make him the most important writer in Latino fiction and that would eventually make him famous. The first of these stories was "Pierre Menard, autor del *Quijote*" ("Pierre Menard, Author of the *Quixote*"), which appeared in *Sur* in May of 1939. This story was followed in 1940 by "Tlön, Uqbar, Orbis Tertius" ("Tlön, Uqbar, Orbis Tertius") and the collection *El jardín de senderous que se bifurcan* (the garden of forking paths) in 1941. Six stories were added to the eight collected in *El jardín de senderos que se bifurcan*, and a new collection, entitled *Ficciones, 1935-1944*, one of the most important collections of short fiction in Latino literature, appeared in 1944. Another landmark collection, *El Aleph*, followed in 1949.

During this time, the height of his literary career up to this point, Borges, who was anti-Peronist, fell into disfavor with the government of Argentine president Juan Perón. He was dismissed from his position at the library in 1944 and appointed inspector of poultry and eggs in the municipal market. He resigned, but he did return to public service in 1955 when, following the fall of Perón, he was named the director of the National Library. Ironically, in the same year, he lost his sight, which had been declining for several years.

Despite the loss of his sight, Borges continued to write (through dictation), though less than before. At the same time, his two collections of stories from the 1940's had made him a household name among Latino literati. Worldwide recognition came in 1961, when he shared the Formentor Prize (worth ten thousand dollars) with Samuel Beckett. The fame that this award brought Borges changed his life. That fall, he traveled to the United States to lecture at the University of Texas, and between 1961 and his death in 1986, he would make numerous trips to the United States and elsewhere teaching and speaking at colleges and universities, attending literary conferences on his works, collecting literary awards, and otherwise serving as an international ambassador for Latino literature.

Borges married for the first time (at age sixty-eight) in 1967, the same year that he accepted an invitation to teach at Harvard University as a Charles Eliot Norton lecturer. The marriage dissolved in 1970, with Borges, according to one popular anecdote, leaving the home he shared with his wife and taking only his prized *Encyclopædia Britannica* with him. Perón returned to the Argentine presidency in 1973, and Borges resigned as director of the National Library. His mother died at age ninety-nine in 1975.

Borges continued to write during the 1970's and until his death, working in short fiction, poetry, and the essay (having returned to these last two genres in the 1950's). The bulk of his fame, however, and particularly that specifically related to short fiction, had come from his two collections of stories from the 1940's. He was nominated repeatedly for the Nobel Prize in Literature but never won it. In 1986, he mar-

ried his companion María Kodama and shortly thereafter died of cancer of the liver on June 14, 1986, in Geneva, Switzerland.

ANALYSIS

Jorge Luis Borges may be, quite simply, the single most important writer of short fiction in the history of Latino literature. The stories he published in his collections *Ficciones, 1935-1944* and *El Aleph*, particularly the former, not only gave Latino (and world) literature a body of remarkable stories but also opened the door to a whole new type of fiction that would be practiced by the likes of the above-mentioned Cortázar, García Márquez, Fuentes, and Vargas Llosa, and that, in the hands of these writers and others like them, would put Latino fiction on the world literary map in the 1960's.

Prior to Borges, and particularly between 1920 and 1940, Latino fiction, as stated previously, was concerned chiefly with painting a realistic and detailed picture of external Latino reality. Description frequently ruled over action, environment over character, and types over individuals. Social message, also, was often more important to the writer than was narrative artistry. Latino fiction after Borges (that is, after his landmark collections of stories of the 1940's) was decidedly different in that it was no longer documentary in nature, turned its focus toward the inner workings of its fully individualized human characters, presented various interpretations of reality, expressed universal as well as regional and national themes, invited reader participation, and emphasized the importance of artistic—and frequently unconventional—presentation of the story, particularly with respect to narrative voice, language, structure (and the closely related element of time), and characterization. This "new narrative," as it came to be called, would have been impossible without Borges's tradition-breaking fiction.

This is not to say that Borges's stories fully embody each of the characteristics of the Latino "new narrative" listed above. Ironically, they do not. For example, Borges's characters are often far more archetypal than individual, his presentation tends to be for the most part quite traditional, and reader participation (at least as compared to that required in the works of other "new narrativists") is frequently not a factor. The major contributions that Borges made to Latino narrative through his stories lie, first, in his use of imagination, second, in his focus on universal themes common to all human beings, and third, in the intellectual aspect of his works. In the 1940's, Borges, unlike most who were writing so-called Latino fiction, treated fiction as fiction. Rather than use fiction to document everyday reality, Borges used it to invent new realities, to toy with philosophical concepts, and in the process to create truly fictional worlds, governed by their own rules. He also chose to write chiefly about universal human beings rather than exclusively about Latinos. His characters are, for example, European, or Chinese, frequently of no discernible nationality, and only occasionally Latino. In most cases, even when a character's nationality is revealed, it is of no real importance, particularly with respect to theme. Almost all Borges's characters are important not because of the country from which they come but because they are human beings, faced not with situations and conflicts particular to their nationality but with situations and conflicts common to all human beings. Finally, unlike his predecessors and many of his contemporaries, Borges did not aim his fiction at the masses. He wrote instead, it seems, more for himself, and, by extension, for the intellectual reader. These three aspects of his fiction—treating fiction as fiction, placing universal characters in universal conflicts, and writing for a more intellectual audience—stand as the Argentine writer's three most important contributions to Latino fiction in the latter half of the twentieth century, and to one degree or another, virtually every one of the Latino "new narrativists," from Cortázar to García Márquez, followed Borges's lead in these areas.

Given the above, it is no surprise that Borges's *ficciones* (his stories are more aptly called "fictions" than "stories," for while all fit emphatically into the first category, since they contain fictitious elements, many do not fit nearly so well into a traditional definition of the second, since they read more like essays than stories) are sophisticated, compact, even mathematically precise narratives that range in type from

what might be called the "traditional" short story (a rarity) to fictionalized essay (neither pure story nor pure essay but instead a unique mix of the two, complete, oddly enough, with both fictitious characters and footnotes, both fictitious and factual) to detective story or spy thriller (though always with an unmistakably Borgesian touch) to fictional illustration of a philosophical concept (this last type being, perhaps, most common). Regardless of the specific category into which each story might fall, almost all, to one degree or another, touch on either what Borges viewed as the labyrinthine nature of the universe, irony (particularly with respect to human destiny), the concept of time, the hubris of those who believe they know all there is to know, or any combination of these elements.

As stated above, most of Borges's fame as a writer of fiction and virtually all of his considerable influence on Latino "new narrative" are derived from his two masterpiece collections, *Ficciones, 1935-1944* and *El Aleph*. Of these two, the first stands out as the more important and may be the single most important collection of short fiction in the history of Latino literature.

Ficciones, 1935-1944 contains fourteen stories (seventeen for editions published after 1956). Seven of the fourteen were written between 1939 and 1941 and, along with an eighth story, were originally collected in *El jardín de senderos que se bifurcan* (the garden of forking paths). The other six stories were added in 1944. Virtually every story in this collection has become a Latino classic, and together they reveal the variety of Borges's themes and story types.

"DEATH AND THE COMPASS"

"La muerte y la brújula" ("Death and the Compass") is one of the most popular of the stories found in *Ficciones, 1935-1944*. In it, detective Erik Lönnrot is faced with the task of solving three apparent murders that have taken place exactly one month apart at locations that form a geographical equilateral triangle. The overly rational Lönnrot, through elaborate reasoning, divines when and where the next murder is to take place. He goes there to prevent the murder and to capture the murderer, only to find himself captured, having been lured to the scene by his arch-enemy, Red Scharlach, so that he, Lönnrot, can be killed.

This story is a perfect example of Borges's ability to take a standard subgenre, in this case the detective story, and give it his own personal signature, as the story is replete with Borgesian trademarks. The most prominent of these concerns irony and hubris. Following the first murder and published reports of Lönnrot's line of investigation, Scharlach, who has sworn to kill Lönnrot, constructs the remainder of the murder scenario, knowing that Lönnrot will not rest until he deciphers the apparent patterns and then—believing he knows, by virtue of his reasoning, all there is to know—will blindly show up at the right spot at the right time for Scharlach to capture and kill him. Ironically, Lönnrot's intelligence and his reliance (or over-reliance) on reasoning, accompanied in no small measure by his self-assurance and intellectual vanity, which blind him to any potential danger, bring him to his death. Other trademark Borgesian elements in the story include the totally non-Latino content (from characters to setting), numerous references to Jews and things Jewish (a talmudic congress, rabbis, and Cabalistic studies, to name only a few), and an intellectual content and ambience throughout not typical of the traditional detective story. (Lönnrot figures out, for example, that the four points that indicate the four apparent murders—there are really only three—correspond to the Tetragrammaton, the four Hebrew letters that make up "the ineffable name of God.")

"THE GARDEN OF FORKING PATHS"

"The Garden of Forking Paths" is another story from *Ficciones, 1935-1944* which in the most general sense (but only in the most general sense) fits comfortably into a traditional category, that of spy thriller, but like "Death and the Compass," in Borges's hands it is anything but a story typical of its particular subgenre. In this story, Dr. Yu Tsun (once again, a non-Latino character), a Chinese professor of English, working in England (a non-Latino setting as well) as a spy for the Germans during World War I, has been captured and now dictates his story. Yu tells of how he had needed to transmit vital information to the Germans concerning the name of the town in which the British were massing artillery in preparation for an attack. Yu's superior, however, had been captured, thus severing Yu's normal lines of communication. Identified as a spy and pursued by the British, Yu tells how he had selected, from the phone directory, the only man he believed could help him communicate his message, one Stephen Albert (though the reader at this point is not aware of exactly how Albert could be of help to Yu). Yu tells of how he traveled to Albert's house, hotly pursued by a British agent. Yu had never met Albert, but Albert mistook him for someone else and invited Yu into the house. The two talked for a hour about Chinese astrologer and writer Ts'ui Pêen (who happened to be one of Yu's ancestors) and Ts'ui's labyrinthine book *The Garden of Forking Paths* (which, given its content, gives Borges's story a story-within-a-story element) as Yu stalled for time for the British agent to catch up with him. Yu says that as the agent approached the house, Yu killed Albert and then allowed himself to be captured by the agent. The final paragraph of the story reveals that Yu had chosen to kill Albert and then be arrested so that news of the incident would appear in the newspaper. He knew that his German colleagues would read the small news item and would divine Yu's intended message: that the British had been massing artillery near the French town of Albert—thus Yu's reason for having chosen Stephen Albert.

"THE CIRCULAR RUINS"

"Las ruinas circulares" ("The Circular Ruins") is one of a number of examples in *Ficciones, 1935-1944* of Borges's frequent practice of using a story to illustrate (or at least toy with) philosophical concepts, in this particular case, most notably, the Gnostic concept of one creator behind another creator. In this story, a mysterious man travels to an equally mysterious place with the intention of creating another person by dreaming him. The man experiences great difficulty in this at first, but eventually he is successful. The man instructs his creation and then sends him off. Before he does, however, the man erases his creation's knowledge of how he came to be, for the man does not wish him to know that he exists only as the dream of another. Soon after the man's creation has

left, fire breaks out and surrounds the man. He prepares for death, but as the flames begin to engulf him,
he cannot feel them. He realizes then that he too,
ironically, is but an illusion, not real at all but simply
the dream of another.

"PIERRE MENARD, AUTHOR OF THE *Quixote*"

"Pierre Menard, autor del *Quijote*" ("Pierre Menard, Author of the *Quixote*"), also from *Ficciones,
1935-1944*, is one of Borges's most famous stories
that may be classified as a fictionalized essay, for it is
clearly not a story: a fiction, yes, but a story (at least
by any traditional definition of the term), no. In it, a
pompous first-person narrator, a literary critic, in what
is presented as an essay of literary criticism, tells of
the writer Pierre Menard (fictional in the real world
but completely real in Borges's fictive universe). After considerable discussion of Menard's bibliography
(complete with titles and publication dates, all fictional but with titles of real literary journals—once
again, an example of Borges's practice of fusing the
fictive and the real), as well as other facts about the author, the critic discusses Menard's attempt to compose
a contemporary version of Cervantes' *Don Quixote de
la Mancha*. Menard accomplishes this not by writing
a new *Don Quixote de la Mancha* but simply by copy-
ing Cervantes' original text word for word. The critic
even examines identical passages from the two versions and declares that Menard's version, though identical to Cervantes', is actually richer. The critic pursues the reasons and ramifications of this fact further.
The result is, among other things, a tongue-in-cheek
send-up of scholars and literary critics and the snobbish and often ridiculous criticism that they publish.

"THE SOUTH"

Finally, "El Sur" ("The South"), from *Ficciones,
1935-1944* as well, is a classic Borges story that demonstrates the author's ability to mix reality (at best a
relative term in Borges's world and in Latino "new
narrative" as a whole) with fantasy and, more important, to show that the line between the two is not only
very subtle but also of no real importance, for fantasy
is just as much a part of the universe as so-called reality. This story, which Borges once said he considered
his best, concerns Johannes Dahlmann, a librarian in
Buenos Aires. Dahlmann, the reader is told, has sev-

eral heroic, military ancestors, and though he himself
is a city-dwelling intellectual, he prefers to identify
himself with his more romantic ancestors. In that
spirit, Dahlmann even maintains a family ranch in the
"South" (capitalized here and roughly the Argentine
equivalent, in history and image, to North America's
"Old West"). He is, however, an absentee landowner,
spending all of his time in Buenos Aires, keeping the
ranch only to maintain a connection, although a
chiefly symbolic one, with his family's more exciting
past. Entering his apartment one night, Dahlmann accidentally runs into a doorway (an accident very similar to that which Borges suffered in 1938). The resulting head injury develops into septicemia (as was
the case with Borges as well), and he is sent off to a
sanatorium. Finally, he recovers well enough to
travel, at his doctor's suggestion, to his ranch in the
South to convalesce. His train trip to the South is
vague to him at best, as he slips in and out of sleep.
Unfamiliar with the region, he disembarks one stop
too early and waits in a general store for transporta-
tion. While there, he is harassed by a group of ruffians. He accepts the challenge of one among them,
and as the story ends, he is about to step outside for a
knife fight he knows he cannot win.

If that were all there were to "The South," the
story would be interesting, perhaps, but certainly
nothing spectacular, and it would probably fit fairly
comfortably into the type of Latino narrative popular
before Borges. There is more, however, and it is this
"more" that places the story firmly within the param-
eters of Latino "new narrative." The story is, in fact,
the literary equivalent of an optical illusion. For those
who can perceive only one angle, the story is essentially that described above. For those who can make
out the other angle, however, the story is completely
different. There are numerous subtle though undeni-
ably present hints throughout the second half of the
story, after Dahlmann supposedly leaves the sanatorium, that suggest that the protagonist does not step
out to fight at the end of the story. In fact, he never
even leaves the sanatorium at all but instead dies
there. His trip to the South, his encounter with the
ruffians, and his acceptance of their challenge, which
will lead to certain death, are all nothing but a dream,

dreamt, it seems, in the sanatorium, for death in a knife fight is the death that he, Dahlmann—the librarian who likes to identify himself with his heroic and romantic ancestors—would have preferred compared to that of the sanatorium. This added dimension as well as the rather subtle manner in which it is suggested (an attentive reader is required) separates both the story and its author from the type of fiction and fiction writer that characterized Latino fiction before Borges. It is this type of added dimension that makes Borges's fiction "new" and makes him a truly fascinating writer to read.

Borges continued to write short fiction after *Ficciones, 1935-1944* and *El Aleph*, but the stories produced during this period never approached the popularity among readers nor the acclaim among critics associated with the two earlier collections. This is attributable in part to the fact that most of the stories the Argentine writer published in the 1960's, as well as the 1970's and 1980's, lack much of what makes Borges Borges. Most are decidedly more realistic, often more Argentine in focus, and in general less complex—all in all, less Borgesian and, according to critics, less impressive. Some of this, particularly the change in complexity, has been explained as attributable to the fact that because of his loss of sight, Borges turned to dictation, which made reediting and polishing more difficult. Regardless of the reason, most of Borges's fiction after his two landmark collections of the 1940's has been largely ignored.

OTHER MAJOR WORKS

LONG FICTION: *Un modelo para la muerte*, 1946 (with Adolfo Bioy Casares, under joint pseudonym B. Suárez Lynch).

SCREENPLAYS: *Los orilleros y El paraíso de los creyentes*, 1955 (with Bioy Casares); *Les Autres*, 1974 (with Bioy Casares and Hugo Santiago).

POETRY: *Fervor de Buenos Aires*, 1923, 1969; *Luna de enfrente*, 1925; *Cuaderno San Martín*, 1929; *Poemas, 1923-1943*, 1943; *Poemas, 1923-1953*, 1954; *Obra poética, 1923-1958*, 1958; *Obra poética, 1923-1964*, 1964; *Seis poemas escandinavos*, 1966; *Siete poemas*, 1967; *El otro, el mismo*, 1969; *Elogio de la sombra*, 1969 (*In Praise of Darkness*, 1974); *El*

oro de los tigres, 1972 (translated in *The Gold of Tigers: Selected Later Poems*, 1977); *La rosa profunda*, 1975 (translated in *The Gold of Tigers); La moneda de hierro*, 1976; *Historia de la noche*, 1977; *La cifra*, 1981; *Los conjurados*, 1986.

NONFICTION: *Inquisiciones*, 1925; *El tamaño de mi esperanza*, 1926; *El idioma de los argentinos*, 1928; *Evaristo Carriego*, 1930 (English translation, 1984); *Figari*, 1930; *Discusión*, 1932; *Las Kennigar*, 1933; *Historia de la eternidad*, 1936; *Nueva refutación del tiempo*, 1947; *Aspectos de la literatura gauchesca*, 1950; *Antiguas literaturas germánicas*, 1951 (with Delia Ingenieros; revised as *Literaturas germánicas medievales*, 1966, with Maria Esther Vásquez); *Otras Inquisiciones*, 1952 (*Other Inquisitions*, 1964); *El "Martin Fierro,"* 1953 (with Margarita Guerrero); *Leopoldo Lugones*, 1955 (with Betina Edelberg); *Manual de zoología fantástica*, 1957 (with Guerrero; *The Imaginary Zoo*, 1969, revised as *El libro de los seres imaginarios*, 1967, *The Book of Imaginary Beings*, 1969); *La poesía gauchesca*, 1960; *Introducción a la literatura norteamericana*, 1967 (with Esther Zemborain de Torres; *An Introduction to American Literature*, 1971); *Prólogos*, 1975; *¿ Qué es el budismo?*, 1976 (with Alicia Jurado); *Cosmogonías*, 1976; *Libro de sueños*, 1976; *Siete noches*, 1980 (*Seven Nights*, 1984); *Nueve ensayos dantescos*, 1982.

TRANSLATIONS: *Orlando*, 1937 (of Virginia Woolf's novel); *La metamórfosis*, 1938 (of Franz Kafka's novel *Die Verwandlung); Un bárbaro en Asia*, 1941 (of Henri Michaux's travel notes); *Los mejores cuentos policiales*, 1943 (with Bioy Casares, of detective stories by various authors); *Bartleby, el escribiente*, 1943 (trans. of Herman Melville's novella *Bartleby the Scrivener); Los mejores cuentos policiales, segunda serie*, 1951 (with Bioy Casares, of detective stories by various authors); *Cuentos breves y extraordinarios*, 1955, 1973 (with Bioy Casares, of short stories by various authors; *Extraordinary Tales*, 1973); *Las palmeras salvajes*, 1956 (of William Faulkner's novel *The Wild Palms); Hojas de hierba*, 1969 (of Walt Whitman's *Leaves of Grass*).

EDITED TEXT: *El compadrito: Su destino, sus barrios, su música*, 1945, 1968 (with Silvina Bullrich).

ANTHOLOGIES: *Antología clásica de la literatura argentina*, 1937; *Antología de la literatura fantástica*, 1940 (with Bioy Casares and Silvia Ocampo); *Antología poética argentina*, 1941 (with Bioy Casares and Ocampo); *Poesía gauchesca*, 1955 (2 volumes, with Bioy Casares); *Libro del cielo y del infierno*, 1960, 1975 (with Bioy Casares); *Versos*, by Evaristo Carriego, 1972; *Antología poética*, by Francisco de Quevedo, 1982; *Antología poética*, by Leopoldo Lugones, 1982; *El amigo de la muerte*, by Pedro Antonio de Alarcón, 1984.

MISCELLANEOUS: *Obras completas*, 1953-1967 (10 volumes); *Antología personal*, 1961 (*A Personal Anthology*, 1967); *Labyrinths: Selected Stories and Other Writings*, 1962, 1964; *Nueva antología personal*, 1968; *Selected Poems, 1923-1967*, 1972 (also includes prose); *Adrogue*, 1977; *Obras completas en colaboración*, 1979 (with others); *Borges: A Reader*, 1981; *Atlas*, 1984 (with María Kodama; English translation, 1985).

BIBLIOGRAPHY

Aizenberg, Edna, ed. *Borges and His Successors*. Columbia: University of Missouri Press, 1990. Collection of essays by various critics on Borges's relationship to such writers as Italo Calvino and Umberto Eco, his influence on such writers as Peter Carey and Salvador Elizondo, and his similarity to such thinkers as Michel Foucault, Paul de Man, and Jacques Derrida.

Bell-Villada, Gene H. *Borges and His Fiction: A Guide to His Mind and Art*. Chapel Hill: University of North Carolina Press, 1981. An excellent introduction to Borges and his works for North American readers. In lengthy sections entitled "Borges's Worlds," "Borges's Fiction," and "Borges's Place in Literature," Bell-Villada provides detailed and very readable commentary concerning Borges's background, his many stories, and his career, all the while downplaying the Argentine writer's role as a philosopher and intellectual and emphasizing his role as a storyteller. A superb study.

Christ, Ronald. *The Narrow Art: Borges' Art of Allusion*. New York: New York University Press, 1969. An important study of how Borges relinquishes circumstantial reality to reach the primordial world of myth. For Borges, the fantastic is not characteristic of another world, but rather is the covert essence of this world. Shows how Borges's fiction is intertextually related to the mythic, fantastic, literary tradition.

Harss, Luis, and Barbara Dohmann. "Jorge Luis Borges: Or, The Consolation by Philosophy." In *Into the Mainstream: Conversations with Latin American Writers*. New York: Harper & Row, 1967. This piece combines and intertwines personal biography, literary biography, critical commentary, and interview to produce a multifaceted look at Borges's life, his works, and his philosophical beliefs, and, most of all, how his philosophical beliefs are reflected in both his poetry and, more so here, his prose. A classic piece of the body of criticism written on Borges in spite of its publication date.

McMurray, George R. *Jorge Luis Borges*. New York: Frederick Ungar, 1980. Intended by the author as "an attempt to decipher the formal and thematic aspects of a synthetic universe that rivals reality in its almost overwhelming complexity," namely Borges's universe. A very good and well-organized study of Borges's dominant themes and narrative devices, with many specific references to the Argentine author's stories. Includes an informative introduction on Borges's life and a conclusion that coherently brings together the diverse elements discussed in the book.

Newman, Charles, and Mary Kinzie, eds. *Prose for Borges: TriQuarterly 25*. Evanston, Ill.: Northwestern University Press, 1972. A collection of tributes, critical essays, biographical reminiscences, and interviews by such Borges friends and critics as Adolfo Bioy Casares, Anthony Kerrigan, Robert Alter, Carter Wheelock, and Ronald Christ. Essays discuss Borges's relationship to Nathaniel Hawthorne, the fantastic, the Latin American novel, and American literature.

Nunez-Faraco, Humberto. "In Search of *The Aleph*: Memory, Truth, and Falsehood in Borges's Poetics." *The Modern Language Review* 92 (July, 1997): 613-629. Discusses autobiographical allusions, literary references to Dante, and cultural reality in the story "El Aleph." Argues that Borges's story uses cunning and deception to bring about its psychological and intellectual effect.

Rodríguez Monegal, Emir. *Jorge Luis Borges: A Literary Biography.* New York: E. P. Dutton, 1978. The definitive biography of Borges by one of the Argentine writer's (and contemporary Latin American literature's) most prominent critics. Particularly interesting for its constant blending of facts about Borges's life and literary text by him concerning or related to the events or personalities discussed. Detailed, lengthy, and highly informative. Very useful for anyone seeking a better understanding of Borges the writer.

Soud, Stephen E. "Borges the Golem-Maker: Intimations of 'Presence' in 'The Circular Ruins.'" *MLN* 110 (September, 1995): 739-754. Argues that Borges uses the legend of the golem to establish authorial presence in the story. Argues that Borges did not seek to deconstruct literature but to resacralize it and to salvage the power of the logos, the Divine Word.

Stabb, Martin S. *Borges Revisited.* Boston: Twayne, 1991. An update of Stabb's *Jorge Luis Borges*, published in 1970 and listed below. Though Borges's early works, including those from the 1940's and 1950's, are discussed and analyzed here, emphasis is on Borges's post-1970 writings, how the "canonical" (to use Stabb's term) Borges compares to the later Borges, and "a fresh assessment of the Argentine master's position as a major Western literary presence." An excellent study, particularly used in tandem with Stabb's earlier book on Borges.

_____. *Jorge Luis Borges.* New York: Twayne, 1970. An excellent study of Borges intended by its author "to introduce the work of this fascinating and complex writer to North American readers." Includes an opening chapter on Borges's life and career, followed by chapters on the Argentine writer's work in the genres of poetry, essay, and fiction, as well as a concluding chapter entitled "Borges and the Critics." A superb and very readable introduction to all aspects of Borges's literary production through 1968.

Wheelock, Carter. *The Mythmaker: A Study of Motif and Symbol in the Short Stories of Jorge Luis Borges.* Austin: University of Texas Press, 1969. Argues that Borges has a superb conceptual grasp of mythic reality as described by anthropologists and philosophers Mircea Eliade, Ernst Cassirer, and Sir James Frazier. Discusses Borges's stories as allegories of the construction of metaphor, the imaginative apprehension of reality, and the nature of thought.

Wreen, Michael J. "Don Quixote Rides Again." *Romanic Review* 86 (January, 1995): 141-163. Argues that Pierre Menard is not the new Cervantes in Borges's story "Pierre Menard, Author of the Quixote," but rather the new Quixote. Asserts that in the story Borges pokes fun at himself and that a proper interpretation of the story requires readers to understand that Menard's Quixote is simply Cervantes' Quixote, although Menard thinks it is a new and important work.

Yates, Donald A. *Jorge Luis Borges: Life, Work, and Criticism.* Fredericton, Canada: York Press, 1985. A brief sketch of, as the title indicates, Borges's life, work, and criticism. Chapters include "A Biography of Jorge Luis Borges," "A Chronological List of Borges's Major Works," "A Summary of Borges's Principal Writings," "An Evaluation of Borges's Achievements," and "Annotated Bibliography." Far more complete and information-filled than its length would suggest.

Zubizarreta, Armando F. "'Borges and I,' a Narrative Sleight of Hand." *Studies in 20th Century Literature* 22 (Summer, 1998): 371-381. Argues that the two characters in the sketch are involved in the implementation of vengeance. Argues that the character Borges, driven by a compulsive pattern of stealing, unsuspectingly takes over the I character's grievances against him through his own writing.

Keith H. Brower

TADEUSZ BOROWSKI

Born: Żhitomir, Ukraine, U.S.S.R. (now Zhytomyr, Ukraine); November 12, 1922
Died: Warsaw, Poland; July 3, 1951

PRINCIPAL SHORT FICTION

Pożegnanie z Marią, 1948
Kamienny świat, 1948
This Way for the Gas, Ladies and Gentlemen, and Other Stories, 1967

OTHER LITERARY FORMS

Tadeusz Borowski began his career by writing poetry, which first reflected life in Nazi-occupied Warsaw and later his experiences in concentration camps. He continued to compose poems during the year that he spent in Germany immediately following the war (when he also began to write short fiction), but then he gave up that form entirely. During the last several years of his life, he increasingly turned to nonfiction, which includes some autobiographical sketches but consists predominantly of often highly politicized journalistic writings.

ACHIEVEMENTS

From the start, Tadeusz Borowski's poetry indicated that he was a writer of rare talent. The piercing imagery, emotional intensity, and sheer lyrical power of his verses showed that there could be poetry not only after Auschwitz but also within Auschwitz. While his career as a poet was both short and not particularly prolific (for understandable reasons), his distinctive and despairing voice has caused his poetry not only to survive but also to grow in stature over the years.

Borowski's reputation, however, especially outside Poland, rests more on his short fiction. The two small collections of stories that appeared in 1948 convey both the concentration camps and the immediate postwar world in a wholly unexpected manner. They relate the horrors from the perspective of a prisoner who has learned to do what is necessary to survive and who does not attempt to impose any notions of right or wrong about the individual acts of those caught up within the system. The narrator's eerie emotional detachment does not soften the picture of the war and its aftermath, but instead conveys the brutality with an immediacy that makes the stories unforgettable.

BIOGRAPHY

The tragically short life of Tadeusz Borowski was intertwined with the totalitarian systems that ruled Eastern Europe for much of the twentieth century. He was born in Żhitomir, a city that had been part of Poland (and known as Żytomierz) until 1793, but that remained within the Ukrainian Republic when the boundaries of a new Poland were drawn after World War I. First Borowski's father and then his mother were arrested and sent off to distant parts of Russia while he was still a child; for some time, he was reared by an aunt. In 1932, as part of a prisoner exchange, the father was released to Poland; he arranged to have Tadeusz and his older brother brought out, and the mother rejoined the family in 1934.

Tadeusz then attended a Franciscan boarding school and completed his secondary education in Warsaw. By then, it was already May of 1940; the Nazis had occupied the city, and Poles had been forbidden to continue their education beyond elementary school. Borowski was graduated from one of the secret schools that had sprung up around the city, a period that he described in his memoir *Matura na Targowej* (1947; *Exams on Targowa*, 1960). He then entered the underground Warsaw University, where he studied Polish language and literature while supporting himself by working as a night watchman at a building firm. He became associated with other promising young writers, many of whom, like Borowski, made their literary debuts with illegal mimeographed publications; unlike most of the others, he was to survive the war. His first volume of poetry, *Gdziekolwiek ziemia* (wherever the earth), appeared in 1942, in an edition of 165 mimeographed copies. Meanwhile, he had also fallen in love with a young woman named Maria Rundo, who was subsequently arrested by the Gestapo. In February, 1943, while searching for her, Borowski fell into a trap set by the authorities and was himself arrested.

Borowski was sent to prison and from there to Auschwitz, where he learned that Rundo was being held in the women's zone. He survived illness and a variety of jobs at the camp; during one interval, he had the relatively good fortune to work as a hospital orderly and assisted Rundo by having medicine sent to her. When Auschwitz was being evacuated by the Germans in August of 1944 as Soviet troops advanced through Poland, he was sent to camps within Germany proper and was finally liberated from Dachau by American forces in May, 1945. He remained in Germany about a year, looking for his lost Maria, who had ended up in Sweden. As an unknown Polish writer, Borowski had no prospects in Germany, and that consideration, as much as any other, may have inspired his decision to return to Poland, where he was reunited with Maria Rundo.

While in Munich, Borowski had published a second volume of verse, *Imiona nurtu* (1945; the names of the current), and had written his most powerful stories about Auschwitz; these appeared in a book, *Byliśmy w Oświęcimiu* (1946; we were in Auschwitz), written jointly with two other survivors, and later formed the core of his first collection, *Pożegnanie z Maria* (farewell to Maria), published in 1948. That same year witnessed the publication of his second collection, *Kamienny świat* (world of stone). His reputation as a prose writer rests largely on only these two collections, parts of which were combined to form the one English collection of his stories, *This Way for the Gas, Ladies and Gentlemen, and Other Stories*. His other collections consist largely of feuilletons and memoirs, which in form and manner resemble his short fiction but are perhaps best categorized as journalism.

Borowski's activities during the final years of his life are not easy to comprehend. He gradually abandoned his promising literary career in order to write increasingly strident and barbed attacks on Western culture; from literature, he passed into political journalism. The change apparently did not occur only from external pressure but from some inner need as well: He had come to believe that capitalism and Western democracy had opened the way for Adolf Hitler and saw communism as a counter-force. Then, at age twenty-eight, only days after the birth of his daughter and having already achieved prominence in official circles, he took his own life by turning on the gas in his apartment. Several motives have been cited, ranging from an extramarital affair to a sense that he was burned out as a writer to disillusionment with the regime that he had supported. Whatever the true cause, or combination of causes, his suicide marked the final tragedy of an ill-starred life.

ANALYSIS

Tadeusz Borowski's best short fiction was written within a period of only two to three years, and therefore it may seem futile to speak of his "development." Virtually all the works in his two major collections reflect either directly or indirectly his experiences in Auschwitz and other camps; they are alike in expressing despair, a sense of being caught up in a world that has lost meaning, and a concern with what it means to continue living in such a world. Yet there are noteworthy differences between the earliest stories, which appeared in *Byliśmy w Oświęcimiu* (we were in Auschwitz) and then along with others, in *Pożegnanie z Maria* (farewell to Maria), as opposed to those in *Kamienny świat* (world of stone). The first works are among his longest and tend to be episodic, relying for their effect on chronicling the events of a night, a day, or a few weeks. The latter works are shorter, more concentrated; they describe a single incident or situation, and they sometimes deal with later experiences: the liberation from the camps, or the immediate postwar period.

"AUSCHWITZ, OUR HOME [A LETTER]"

"U nas, w Auschwitzu" ("Auschwitz, Our Home [A Letter]"), which tellingly employs the German rather than the Polish (*Oświęcim*) spelling for the camp, is perhaps the most clearly autobiographical of the early stories. It takes the form of a letter, or perhaps a series of letters, about his training as a medical orderly, and includes, particularly toward the end, details about his arrest and his being sent to Auschwitz, which is often used as the single name for what was actually a complex of camps: Auschwitz, Birkenau, Harmenz. The crematoriums were at Birkenau; when the narrator is transferred from there to Auschwitz, life improves for him. The title hints at the bitter irony that underlies the story, for to those who know Birkenau, Auschwitz is indeed a home, a kind of idyll. Here, those in training are relatively well dressed; there are many smiles and even a wedding.

Typically for Borowski, the story contains events but no plot as such; it relies for its effect on the accumulation of observations and incidents. The narrator frequently uses his precamp experiences and values in his effort to analyze the camps, but more effective are his glimpses into the everyday reality that he witnesses. Early in the story, he describes what passes for a cultural center at the Auschwitz camp: It contains a music room, a library, and a museum. The piano, however, cannot be played during work hours, the library is always locked, and the museum contains only photographs confiscated from prisoners' letters. Upstairs in this cultural center is a bordello, where female prisoners are kept for the pleasure of those in authority. The narrator then notes that women can also be found in the experimental section, where they may be operated on or are purposely infected. He later describes an incident in which several trucks pass by full of naked women; they scream to the men that they are being taken to the gas chambers and plead to be saved, but not a single person among the ten thousand or so looking on tries to help. The almost visceral effect of the story arises from the unexpected and almost casual intrusion of the horrors, the contrast between them and the ordinary life that seems only a step away, and perhaps worst of all the acceptance of this world on the part of all who are in it.

"DAY AT HARMENZ"

In "Dzień na Hermenzach" ("Day at Harmenz"), Borowski takes his readers more directly into the brutality of camp life. At first glance the story simply seems to chronicle a day at a work site, with each incident providing another glimpse into the hunger, fear, and exhaustion that formed the lot of prisoners. The individual scenes are sufficiently memorable that it is easy to lose sight of Borowski's artistry: He does

not merely pile up a number of unrelated incidents but in fact creates a series of leitmotifs and gives the entire piece a sense of both drama and structure. Thus, in the first scene, readers are introduced to Becker, who had been placed in charge of his fellow prisoners at a previous camp and hanged his own son for stealing bread. Becker, desperate for food, says that the sign of real hunger is when one person regards another as something to eat. In the final scene, this same Becker has been "selected" to be sent to the ovens; still hungry, he asks the narrator for a bit of food, and the narrator—in a noteworthy gesture—tells him to eat his fill. The true emphasis of the story, though, is on the narrator's survival. Danger is everywhere; he must use all his cunning to get food himself and to outwit the guards and fellow prisoners. Unstated but clearly implied is that his well-being may result in the suffering or deaths of others, but he accepts that necessity, just as Becker believes that he was right to hang his own son. In this world, a different morality prevails.

"THIS WAY FOR THE GAS, LADIES AND GENTLEMEN"

Nowhere are Borowski's chief themes presented more harrowingly than in the story that serves as the title piece for the English edition of his works, "Proszę państwa do gazu" ("This Way for the Gas, Ladies and Gentlemen"). It is the narrator's job to help unload the trains of newly arrived prisoners at Birkenau. Scene after scene describes the confusion, the violence, and the terror as people are loaded onto the trucks that will take them to the gas chambers. Meanwhile, the narrator seems to move about in a daze as he carries out of the railway cars the bodies of naked infants, holding several in each hand, as though they were chickens; gathers the clothing and valuables left behind, while an SS man collects the gold and currency; and witnesses instances in which tormented individuals emerge momentarily from the mass of victims.

Perhaps the most searing moment occurs when a young woman, desperate to live, tries to run away from her own child, who chases after her with his arms out. A Russian prisoner, also helping unload the transport, knocks the woman off her feet, swears foully at her, and heaves first her and then her child onto one of the trucks going to the gas chambers. The SS guard approves the prisoner's actions with a *gut gemacht* ("well done"). Borowski does not allow his readers the comfort of simply blaming the German guards for the horrors—what about the woman who tries to abandon her own child to the ovens, or the prisoner who knocks her down, or for that matter the narrator who does nothing to help? Borowski does not answer these questions; he merely presents them for his readers to ponder.

Yet the desire to live does not obliterate all sense of right and wrong. The narrator's companion, a Frenchman named Henri, constantly stuffs tomatoes, sardines, and other delicacies into his mouth; although he seems to care little for those whom he is leading to death, in fact he is trying to hide the truth from them to soften their last moments. The narrator, whose dulled perceptions fail to shield him from the horror, vomits during his night's work. No one survives without doing evil, but survival does not necessarily mean losing all awareness of right and wrong.

"THE SUPPER" AND "SILENCE"

The later stories, usually only three or four pages long and concentrating on a single incident or theme, can be equally disturbing. Thus "Kolacje" ("The Supper") describes in graphic detail the execution of some twenty Russian soldiers while the other prisoners, starving after a day's work, are forced to watch. Those ordered to shoot the Russians from behind at point-blank range have dressed for the occasion, but the only concern they show is not to get splattered by the shattered heads. Typically for these stories, "The Supper" depends on a single shock at the very end rather than on a litany of horrors. At first, it is not clear why the prisoners have swarmed over the execution site before heading off to supper, but in the last lines the narrator tells how a fellow prisoner tries to convince him that human brains are so tender that they can be eaten raw. With those few words the focus abruptly shifts from the execution to the inhuman suffering of the prisoners who are still alive.

When the stories deal with the end of the war or its aftermath, Borowski's emerging anti-Western feelings come to the fore. Thus in "Milczenie" ("Si-

lence"), a young American officer comes to a barracks housing former prisoners. Speaking through an interpreter, he promises them that those who committed crimes in the camp will be punished and asks them to refrain from any illegal acts. The former prisoners receive his remarks with applause and cheerful shouts; after he leaves, they drag out a hated tormentor, whom they had gagged and hidden, and beat him to death. The chief point, though, is less the surprise ending than the naïve good nature of the American, whose words betray a total inability to comprehend the perspective of those who had suffered in the camp.

"WORLD OF STONE"

The story that reveals the most about the effect that the camps had on Borowski may be the title story of his second collection, "Kamienny świat" ("World of Stone"). He tells of the way in which he has stopped caring for his appearance, of how he takes long walks through the city and feels only indifference. In the evening, he goes back to his apartment and attempts to discover within himself some kind of feeling toward the people he has seen, for he wants to write an immortal epic about this world that seems to be chiseled from stone. On that note the story ends, but it is clear that he has lost some vital connection with the world—people are only part of a whirling mass, and he can no longer perceive individual, human concerns. The emptiness that Borowski expresses foreshadows his suicide only a few years later; in the final analysis, Borowski was not able to outlive Auschwitz.

OTHER MAJOR WORKS

POETRY: *Gdziekolwiek ziemia*, 1942; *Imiona nurtu*, 1945; *Selected Poems*, 1990.

NONFICTION: *Pewien zolnierz*, 1947; *Matura na Targowej*, 1947 (*Exams on Targowa*, 1960); *Opowiadania z ksiazek i gazet*, 1949.

MISCELLANEOUS: *Utwory zebrane w pieciu tomach*, 1954 (5 volumes).

BIBLIOGRAPHY

Barańczak, Stanisław. Introduction to *Selected Poems*. Walnut Creek, Calif.: Hit & Run Press, 1990. Barańczak, himself a prominent critic and

Polish poet, concisely sketches Borowski's career. He points out that, while those familiar only with Borowski's stories sometimes accuse him of moral indifference or cynicism, the poems reveal him to have been a highly moral writer for whom the indifferent narrator was only a literary device.

Kuhiwczak, Piotr. "Beyond Self: A Lesson from the Concentration Camps." *Canadian Review of Comparative Literature* 19 (September, 1993): 395-405. Discusses Borowski's treatment of Nazi concentration camps; compares his work with that of Italian writer Primo Levi.

Kott, Jan. Introduction to *This Way for the Gas, Ladies and Gentlemen*. New York: Penguin Books, 1976. Kott's biographical section is both detailed and factual. In discussing the stories, he focuses on the manner in which "Borowski describes Auschwitz like an entomologist."

Miłosz, Czesław. *The Captive Mind*. New York: Alfred A. Knopf, 1953. The chapter "Beta, the Disappointed Lover" is devoted to Borowski. Miłosz provides a sensitive analysis of the manner in which the stories on the camps achieve their effect and also, taking advantage of his firsthand acquaintance with "Beta" (as Borowski is called throughout the chapter), tries to find the causes for his evolution from writer to journalist.

_____. *The History of Polish Literature*. New York: Macmillan, 1969. Miłosz condenses his assessment of Borowski as both a person and a writer. Writing some years after his first account, he concludes that Borowski's life and work, despite the contradictions, were motivated by a search for moral values.

Stylinski, Andrezej. "Auschwitz Horrors Shared in Polish Schools." *The Ottawa Citizen*, January 29, 1995, p. A2. Discusses the fact that Borowski's books are on the required reading lists of high school literature classes in Poland; comments briefly on Borowski's life and fiction.

Walc, Jan. "When the Earth Is No Longer a Dream and Cannot Be Dreamed Through to the End." *The Polish Review* 32 (1987): 181-194. The analytic sections are devoted to Borowski's poetry, but Walc discusses the manner in which Borowski's life before the war may have affected him as a writer and examines quotations from the late essays that are not otherwise available in English.

Wirth, Andrzej. "A Discovery of Tragedy: The Incomplete Account of Tadeusz Borowski." *The Polish Review* 12, no. 3 (1967): 43-52. Wirth examines the narrators in Borowski's concentration camp stories, emphasizing the disjunction between what is being described and the narrator's response. Borowski created a new type of tragedy, "a tragedy without alternative, without choice, without competing values."

Woroszylski, Wiktor. "The Prosecutor Within." *Polish Perspectives* 3, no. 6 (1960): 27-30. Woroszylski briefly discusses Borowski's career. He notes that Borowski stressed the necessity of prisoners to "adjust" to the unspeakable nightmare that surrounded them and thus raised uncomfortable questions about the morality of survival. Translations of three short works by Borowski follow this article.

Barry Scherr

ELIZABETH BOWEN

Born: Dublin, Ireland; June 7, 1899
Died: London, England; February 22, 1973

PRINCIPAL SHORT FICTION

Encounters, 1923
Ann Lee's and Other Stories, 1926
Joining Charles, 1929
The Cat Jumps and Other Stories, 1934
Look at All Those Roses, 1941
The Demon Lover, 1945 (pb. in U.S. as *Ivy Gripped the Steps and Other Stories*, 1946)
The Early Stories, 1951
Stories by Elizabeth Bowen, 1959
A Day in the Dark and Other Stories, 1965
Elizabeth Bowen's Irish Stories, 1978
The Collected Stories of Elizabeth Bowen, 1980

OTHER LITERARY FORMS

Elizabeth Bowen is as well known for her ten novels as she is for her short-story collections. She also wrote books of history, travel, literary essays, personal impressions, a play, and a children's book.

ACHIEVEMENTS

Elizabeth Bowen's career is distinguished by achievements on two separate, though related, fronts. On the one hand, she was among the most well-known and accomplished British women novelists of her generation, a generation which, in the period between the wars, did much to consolidate the distinctive existence of women's fiction. Bowen's work in this area is noteworthy for its psychological acuity, sense of atmosphere, and impassioned fastidiousness of style.

As an Anglo-Irish writer, on the other hand, she maintained more self-consciously than most of her predecessors an understanding of her class's destiny. Themes that are prevalent throughout her work—loss of innocence, decline of fortune, impoverishment of the will—gain an additional haunting quality from her sensitivity to the Irish context. Her awareness of the apparent historical irrelevance of the Anglo-Irish also gives her short stories in particular an important cultural resonance.

BIOGRAPHY

Elizabeth Dorothea Cole Bowen received her formal education at Downe House in Kent and at the London County Council School of Art. In 1923 she married Alan Charles Cameron and lived with him in Northampton and Old Headington, Oxford. In 1935 she and her husband moved to Regent's Park, London, where Bowen became a member of the Bloomsbury group. During World War II she stayed in London, where she worked for the Ministry of Information and as an air-raid warden. In 1948 she was made a Commander of the British Empire. She was awarded an honorary Doctor of Letters by Trinity College, Dublin, in 1949. After the death of her husband in 1952, Bowen returned to live at Bowen's Court in Ireland, her family estate. In 1957 she was awarded an honorary Doctor of Letters by the University of Oxford. In 1960 she sold Bowen's Court and returned to Old Headington, Oxford. After a final trip to Ireland, Elizabeth Bowen died in London on February 22, 1973.

ANALYSIS

Elizabeth Bowen's stories are set in the first half of the twentieth century in England and Ireland. Often the action takes place against a background of war. Taken together, her stories provide a chronicle of the social, political, and psychic life of England from the beginning of the century through World War II. Her characters are mainly drawn from the middle class, although upper- and lower-class characters appear as well. Although Bowen's protagonist is usually a woman, men also play important roles. By selecting significant detail and by utilizing mythic parallels, Bowen constructs stories whose settings, actions, and characters are simultaneously realistic and symbolic.

Bowen's characters exist in a world which has lost contact with meaning; traditional forms and ideas

Elizabeth Bowen (Library of Congress)

have lost meaning and vitality. Both identity and a sense of belonging are lost; "Who am I?" and "Where am I?" are typical questions asked by Bowen protagonists. Some characters merely go through the motions and rituals of daily life, experiencing pattern without meaning. Others have a vague consciousness that something is wrong; unfulfilled, they suffer from boredom, apathy, and confusion. Sometimes, such characters are driven to seek alternatives in their lives. In "Summer Night," while the Major, an example of the first type of character, goes about his evening routine, shutting up the house for the night, his wife, Emma, pretending to visit friends, leaves her traditional family for an assignation with Robinson, a man she hardly knows. He represents another type: the man who adapts to meaninglessness by utilizing power amorally to manipulate and control. Emma is disillusioned in her search for vitality and love when she discovers that Robinson wants sex and nothing else. Other characters, such as Justin, are fully con-

scious of the situation; they know that they "don't live" and conceive the need for a "new form" but are impotent to break through to achieve one.

"SUMMER NIGHT"

Although Bowen's stories focus on those characters who seek meaning or who are in the process of breaking through, they also represent a final type—one whose thinking and feeling are unified and in harmony with existence. An example from "Summer Night" is Justin's deaf sister, Queenie. While Robinson is left alone in his house, while Emma leans drunk and crying against a telegraph pole, and while Justin goes to mail an angry letter to Robinson, Queenie lies in bed remembering a time when she sat with a young man beside the lake below the ruin of the castle now on Robinson's land: "while her hand brushed the ferns in the cracks of the stone seat emanations of kindness passed from him to her. The subtle deaf girl had made the transposition of this nothing or everything into an everything." Queenie imagines: "Tonight it was Robinson who, guided by Queenie down leaf tunnels, took the place on the stone seat by the lake." It is Queenie's memory and imagination that creates, at least for herself, a world of love, unrealized, but realizable, by the others. Memory recalls the lost estate of human beings, represented here by the castle, its grounds, and its garden, as well as man's lost identity. Queenie *is* a queen. All human beings are rightfully queens and kings in Bowen's fiction. Queenie's memory reaches back to the archetypal roots of being, in harmony with life; her imagination projects this condition in the here and now and as a possibility for the future. Queenie's thinking is the true thinking Justin calls for, thinking that breaks through to a "new form," which is composed of archetypal truth transformed to suit the conditions of modern life. Throughout Bowen's fiction this kind of thought takes the form of fantasy, hallucination, and dream. Bowen's fiction itself, the expression of *her* imagination, also exemplifies this thinking.

"HER TABLE SPREAD"

Toward the end of "Summer Night" it occurs to Justin that possibly Emma should have come to him rather than Robinson. In "Her Table Spread" Bowen brings together two characters much like Emma and Justin. Valeria Cuff, heiress and owner of a castle in Ireland, situated on an estuary where English ships are allowed to anchor, invites Mr. Alban, a cynical and disillusioned young man from London, to a dinner party. These characters represent opposites which concern Bowen throughout her fiction: male and female, darkness and light, thought and feeling, physical and spiritual, rational and irrational. The separation or conflict of these opposites creates a world of war; their unification creates a world of love.

Valeria's orientation is romantic, "irrational," and optimistic: "Her mind was made up: she was a princess." She invites Alban to her castle, "excited" at the thought of marrying him. Alban is realistic, rational, and pessimistic: "He had failed to love. . . . He knew some spring had dried up at the root of the world." Alban is disconcerted by Valeria's erratic, impulsive behavior and by her apparent vulgarity. He has heard "she was abnormal—at twenty-five, of statuesque development, still detained in childhood." Ironically, as Alban realizes "his presence must constitute an occasion," he is "put out of" Valeria's mind when a destroyer anchors in the estuary. Valeria believes it is the same destroyer that had anchored there the previous spring at Easter when two officers, Mr. Graves and Mr. Garrett, came ashore and were entertained by friends. Valeria's expectation that the officers will come to dinner initially separates her from Alban. When the officers fail to arrive, she runs outside to signal them with a lantern. Old Mr. Rossiter, uncle to Mrs. Treye, Valeria's aunt, leads Alban to the boathouse to prevent Valeria from rowing out to the destroyer. When a bat flies against Alban's ear, he flees, and, ascending the steps back toward the castle, he hears Valeria sobbing in the dark. When he calls to her, expressing concern and sympathy, she mistakes him for Mr. Garrett. Her fantasy of love is realized as she and Alban stand together, unified in a field of light shining from the castle.

Symbolic details and analogies with pagan and Christian myth universalize the meaning of the story. Alban is associated with the destroyer, with Graves and Garrett, and with their emblems, statues of Mars and Mercury. Like the destroyer, Alban is "fixed in

the dark rain, by an indifferent shore." The officers represent aspects of Alban. The name Graves suggests death; and the statue associated with Graves is Mars, god of war. Garrett is a pun on *garret*, which derives from a word meaning to defend or protect. Garrett's statue is Mercury, a god associated by the Romans with peace. Alban's link with the destroyer, with death and war, threatens the destruction of Valeria's dreams of love and peace. The Garrett aspect of Alban, however, linked with protection and peace, offers the possibility of the realization of Valeria's dreams.

Valeria is associated with two symbolic items. Among the gifts she has to offer is a leopard skin, suggesting the animal and the sensual, and a statue of Venus, goddess of love. Valeria thus offers love in both its physical and spiritual aspects. Contained in her fantasies is the expectation that love will put an end to war. She thinks: "Invasions from the water would henceforth be social, perhaps amorous," and she imagines marrying Garrett and inviting "all the Navy up the estuary" for tea: "The Navy would be unable to tear itself away." As Valeria attempts to signal the destroyer with the lantern, she thinks that Graves and Garrett will have to fight for her; instead, the battle takes place within Alban.

The pagan symbolism in "Her Table Spread" is overlain and transformed by Christian symbolism. Valeria's castle and its grounds, like the ruins of the castle in "Summer Night," represent a lost Eden. Valeria *is* an heiress and a princess; she is an incarnation of Eve seeking her rightful role and place in a paradise of love and peace. Symbolically, she calls to Adam (Alban) to reclaim *his* inheritance—to join her in re-creating the garden. The way is expressed in Bowen's use of the second major Christian myth. Alban must undergo the experience of Christ, the second Adam, to redeem his "fallen" self; he must reject temptation and undergo crucifixion—sacrifice his ego. The trip to the boathouse is Alban's descent into hell. There he is tempted by Old Mr. Rossiter, the Devil. Rossiter offers Alban whiskey, which he refuses, and tempts him with Valeria: "She's a girl you could shape. She's got a nice income." Alban's rejection of this temptation, his refusal to *listen* to the

Devil, is signified by his flight from the boathouse when a bat flies against his ear.

As Alban ascends the steps, he recognizes where he is: "Hell." This recognition is the precondition for discovering where he belongs. At this point he undergoes a symbolic crucifixion. Hearing Valeria "sobbing" in "absolute desperation," Alban clings "to a creaking tree." The sympathy Alban feels for Valeria signifies the death of Graves within him and the resurrection of Garrett. Valeria has also experienced crucifixion. Graves and Garrett have not arrived and her lantern has gone out; she, too, is in hell. Humbled and in darkness, the two meet. Alban speaks with tenderness: "Quietly, my dear girl." Valeria speaks with concern. "Don't you remember the way?" The year before the destroyer had anchored "at Easter." Now Valeria is present at and participates in resurrection: *"Mr. Garrett has landed."* She laughs "like a princess, and magnificently justified." Standing with Valeria in the glow of light from the castle, observed by the two female guests, Alban experiences love: "Such a strong tenderness reached him that, standing there in full manhood, he was for a moment not exiled. For the moment, without moving or speaking, he stood, in the dark, in a flame, as though all three said: 'My darling.'"

"THE DEMON LOVER"

A world of love is achieved, if only momentarily, in "Her Table Spread." In "The Demon Lover" Bowen creates a story of love denied or repressed, and its power transformed into the demonic. The stories complement each other. The first takes place at a castle in Ireland in the spring and recalls the previous Easter; the second is set in an abandoned London flat in autumn during the bombing of London in World War II and recalls a previous autumn during World War I. The action of "Her Table Spread" concludes with the coming of night. The protagonists of the first story are a young woman in search of love and a young man associated with war; those of the second are a forty-year-old married woman who has denied love and her fiancé of twenty years before, a solider lost in action during World War I. Both female characters are "abnormal": Valeria of "Her Table Spread" caught up in fantasy, Kathleen of "The Demon

Lover" subject to hallucination. Bowen utilizes elements of the Eden myth to universalize the meaning of both stories.

In "The Demon Lover" Mrs. Kathleen Drover returns to her abandoned London flat to pick up some things she had left behind when her family moved to the country to escape the bombing. In the dark flat where everything is covered with a dustlike film, she opens a door, and reflected light reveals an unstamped letter recently placed on a hall table. Since the caretaker is away and the house has been locked, there is no logical explanation for the appearance of the letter. Unnerved, Mrs. Drover takes it upstairs to her bedroom, where she reads it. The letter reminds her that today is the anniversary of the day years before when she made a promise of fidelity to a young soldier on leave from France during World War I—and that they had agreed to meet on this day "at an hour arranged." Although her "fiancé was reported missing, presumed killed," he has apparently survived and awaits the meeting. When Kathleen hears the church clock strike six, she becomes terrified, but maintains enough control to gather the items she came for and to formulate a plan to leave the house, hire a taxi, and bring the driver back with her to pick up the bundles. Meanwhile, in the basement "a door or window was being opened by someone who chose this moment to leave the house."

This statement provides a realistic solution to the problem of the letter's appearance, but a psychological interpretation offers an alternative conclusion. The London flat symbolizes Kathleen's life as Mrs. Drover, and the shock of finding the letter reveals to Kathleen the meaninglessness of this life and the falseness of her identity as Mrs. Drover. By marrying Drover, Kathleen has been "unfaithful" not only to the soldier but also to herself. It is this self which emerges as a result of the "crisis"—actually the crisis of World War II—and which has unconsciously motivated Mrs. Drover's return to the house. The fact that the letter is signed K., Kathleen's initial, suggests that she wrote the letter, which is a sign of the reemergence of her lost self. The house represents not only Kathleen's life as Mrs. Drover but also the repressed-Kathleen aspect of her identity. The person in the basement who leaves the house at the same moment Mrs. Drover lets herself out the front door is a projection of this repressed self, the self Mrs. Drover now unknowingly goes to face.

Overlying the psychological meaning of the story are two additional levels of meaning, one allegorical, the other archetypal. The young Kathleen represents England, defended and protected by the soldier, who represents the generation of those who fought for the country during the first war. Kathleen's loveless and meaningless marriage to Drover represents England's betrayal of the values the war was fought to defend—a betrayal which has contributed to the creation of World War II. The letter writer asserts: "In view of the fact that nothing has changed, I shall rely upon you to keep your promise." Because Kathleen and England have betrayed themselves, because love has failed, war continues, and both the individual and the country must suffer destructive consequences.

On the archetypal level, Kathleen and the soldier are incarnations of Eve and Adam, although the soldier is an Adam transformed by war into a devil who coerces Eve to "fall," forces her to make the "sinister truth." The soldier's uniform is the sign of his transformation. His true nature, his Adamic self, is covered and denied by the clothes of war. Kathleen is unable to touch the true self of the soldier, and he is unable to reach out to her. The scene takes place at night in a garden beneath a tree. Intimidated by not being kissed, Kathleen imagines "spectral glitters in the place" of the soldier's eyes. To "verify his presence," she puts out a hand, which he takes and presses "painfully, onto one of the breast buttons of his uniform." In this way he forces her to make a vow of fidelity—a pact with the Devil. He says, "I shall be with you . . . sooner or later. You won't forget that. You need do nothing but wait." Kathleen suffers the fate of Eve, feels that unnatural promise drive down between her and the rest of all humankind. When the soldier, her "fiancé," is reported "missing, presumed killed," she experiences "a complete dislocation from everything."

Compelled now to confront her fate, she gets into a taxi, which seems to be awaiting her. When the driver turns in the direction of her house without being told where to drive, Kathleen leans "forward to scratch at the glass panel that divided the driver's head from her own . . . driver and passenger, not six inches between them, remained for an eternity eye to eye." Reunited with her demon lover, Kathleen screams "freely" as the taxi accelerates "without mercy" into the "hinterland of deserted streets." The failure of love condemns Kathleen—and by implication humankind—to insanity and damnation in the modern wasteland.

In spite of the pessimistic conclusion of "The Demon Lover," Bowen's short fiction is ultimately affirmative. In a 1970 *McCall's* essay she lamented that many people, especially the young, are "adrift, psychologically . . . homeless, lost in a void." She expresses her desire to "do something that would arrest the drift, fill up the vacuum, convey the sense that there is, after all, SOMETHING. . . . (For I know that there is.)" Bowen's fiction conveys the existence of this something, which some would call God, others simply the source of being. Whatever it is called, it exists within each individual and in the natural world. Its primary nature is love, expressed in acts of kindness, sympathy, understanding, and tolerance. It is the potential for unity among people and harmony with the world. This potential is mirrored in the unity and harmony of Bowen's stories. The lyric descriptive passages, the coherence of matter and form, the intense visual images, and the emotional force of her stories demonstrate Bowen's mastery of the short-story form. Her stories deserve to be recognized as among the best written in the twentieth century.

OTHER MAJOR WORKS

LONG FICTION: *The Hotel*, 1927; *The Last September*, 1929; *Friends and Relations*, 1931; *To the North*, 1932; *The House in Paris*, 1935; *The Death of the Heart*, 1938; *The Heat of the Day*, 1949; *A World of Love*, 1955; *The Little Girls*, 1964; *Eva Trout*, 1968.

PLAY: *Castle Anna*, pr. 1948 (with John Perry).

NONFICTION: *Bowen's Court*, 1942; *Seven Winters*, 1942; *English Novelists*, 1942; *Collected Impressions*, 1950; *The Shelbourne: A Center of Dublin Life for More than a Century*, 1951; *A Time in Rome*, 1960; *Afterthought: Pieces About Writing*, 1962;

Pictures and Conversations, 1975; *The Mulberry Tree: Writings of Elizabeth Bowen*, 1986.

CHILDREN'S LITERATURE: *The Good Tiger*, 1965.

BIBLIOGRAPHY

Austin, Allan E. *Elizabeth Bowen*. Rev. ed. New York: Twayne, 1989. Austin contends Bowen's better stories investigate psychological states that are more unusual than those in her novels. He calls "The Demon Lover" a ghost story that builds up and culminates like an Alfred Hitchcock movie.

Bloom, Harold, ed. *Elizabeth Bowen: Modern Critical Views*. New York: Chelsea House, 1987. A collection of eleven essays, surveying the range of Bowen criticism. Excerpts from the main book-length critical works on Bowen are included. The volume also contains some comparatively inaccessible articles on Bowen's short fiction, and essays on her work by the poets Mona Van Duyn and Alfred Corn. Supplemented by an extensive bibliography.

Craig, Patricia. *Elizabeth Bowen*. Harmondsworth, Middlesex, England: Penguin Books, 1986. A short biographical study. Indebted to Victoria Glendinning's work (below), though drawing on later research, particularly on Bowen's Irish connections. The work also contains perceptive readings of Bowen's stories and novels. Includes a useful chronology.

Glendinning, Victoria. *Elizabeth Bowen*. New York: Alfred A. Knopf, 1977. A comprehensive biography. The author is well versed in the complexities of Bowen's Irish context and details them informatively. Bowen's standing as an eminent English novelist of the 1930's is also established and assessed. Full use is made of Bowen's numerous autobiographical essays, and her private life is also candidly discussed.

Jarrett, Mary. "Ambiguous Ghosts: The Short Stories of Elizabeth Bowen." *Journal of the Short Story in English*, no. 8 (Spring, 1987): 71-79. A discussion of the themes of alienation, imprisonment, loss of identity, and the conflict of fiction and reality in Bowen's stories, focusing primarily on the so-called ghost stories.

Jordan, Heather Bryant. *How Will the Heart Endure: Elizabeth Bowen and the Landscape of War*. Ann Arbor: The University of Michigan Press, 1992. Although this book focuses primarily on Bowen's novels, chapter 8 focuses on the stories she wrote during the war years between 1939 and 1945. Suggests that war was the most important influence of Bowen's life and art, that two of her most common fictional motifs of houses and ghosts reflect war's threat to cultural values and its blurring of the lines between reality and fantasy.

Kenney, Edward J. *Elizabeth Bowen*. Lewisburg, Pa.: Bucknell University Press, 1977. A brief survey of Bowen's life and works. Drawing on Bowen's autobiographical writings, this study opens with a sketch of her background. This leads to a discussion of the theme of identity problems in her fiction. The study's main concern is then developed. This concern is with Bowen's use of the illusory, its nature, its necessity, and its frailty.

Lassner, Phyllis. *Elizabeth Bowen: A Study of the Short Fiction*. New York: Twayne, 1991. An introduction to Bowen's short fiction focusing on its unique characteristics. Deals with the basic conflicts in the stories between the present and the past, often embodied in female ghosts and ancestral homes. Interprets many of her stories in terms of women's struggle with a patriarchal society that stands in the way of their pursuit for a creative life. Includes essays on short fiction by Bowen and discussions of her stories by William Trevor and Eudora Welty.

Lee, Hermione. *Elizabeth Bowen: An Estimation*. London: Vision Press, 1981. A comprehensive and sophisticated study. Large claims are made for Bowen's work. She is said to be both the equal of her Bloomsbury contemporaries and an important exponent of the European modernism deriving from Gustave Flaubert and Henry James. Bowen's concentration on the intersection of the cultural and the psychological is also incisively analyzed.

Partridge, A. C. "Language and Identity in the Shorter Fiction of Elizabeth Bowen." In *Irish Writers and Society at Large*, edited by Masaru Sekine. Totowa, N.J.: Barnes and Noble, 1985. An overview of Bowen's short stories that focuses on her impressionism, her economy, and her Jamesian approach to narrative. Illustrates that style is Bowen's overriding preoccupation.

Rubens, Robert. "Elizabeth Bowen: A Woman of Wisdom." *Contemporary Review* 268 (June, 1996): 304-307. Examines the complex style of Bowen's work as a reflection of her personality and background; discusses her romanticism and her rejection of the dehumanization of the twentieth century.

James L. Green, updated by George O'Brien

JANE BOWLES
Jane Auer

Born: New York, New York; February 22, 1917
Died: Málaga, Spain; May 4, 1973

PRINCIPAL SHORT FICTION

Plain Pleasures, 1966

OTHER LITERARY FORMS

In addition to her short stories, Jane Bowles wrote a novel and a play. She began several other works of fiction (including another novel) in her notebooks, selections from which have been published in various collections of her work. Her letters have been collected by Millicent Dillon in *Out in the World: Selected Letters of Jane Bowles, 1935-1970* (1985).

ACHIEVEMENTS

Jane Bowles's literary output, though small in quantity, has received accolades for its originality and experimentation. Her unique use of language and nontraditional narrative techniques has led to stories that are as unsettling in their form as they are in their content. Her characters are often drawn as both grotesque and comic, yet Bowles maintains a compassionate stance toward them—a technique that is usually absent in more experimental contemporary writing. The characters themselves can be seen as experimental: they are mostly women, either strong-willed and assertive or curiously passive, yet they behave in ways that surprise and shock the reader. Her works operate on a series of contrasts or opposing tensions; like Bowles herself, her fiction is an enigma

and a delight, challenging the reader with its puzzling obscurity and its compelling humanity.

BIOGRAPHY

Jane Auer Bowles was born in New York City in 1917, the only child of Sidney and Claire Auer. In 1927, her family moved to Woodmere, Long Island. Jane was thirteen years old and away at summer camp when her father died unexpectedly; she and her mother moved back to New York soon thereafter. As a child, Bowles had a French governess and learned to speak French before English. Later, she attended boarding school but left after less than a year, having fallen from a horse and broken her leg. She developed tuberculosis of the knee and went to Switzerland for treatment. She remained there for two years, studying with a French tutor and spending most of her convalescence confined to bed. From these early experiences, she learned to use her imagination to escape the physical pain and emotional isolation that she felt, developing a captivating wit and charm to deflect attention from her physical disabilities.

She left Switzerland in 1934 and met the writer Louis-Ferdinand Céline on board the ship to New York. They visited frequently during the voyage, and by the time Bowles returned to New York, she had decided to become a writer. In 1935, she began a novel in French, "Le Phaéton Hypocrite" (the hypocritical Phaéton), the manuscript of which has not survived. From 1935 on, Bowles began frequenting nightclubs in Greenwich Village and meeting other young people with literary and artistic interests. At this point, she set the pattern for years to come: frequent partying, relationships with both men and women, heavy drinking, and occasional depressions brought on, it seemed, by her inability to settle down to writing.

In 1937, she was introduced to Paul Bowles, who was at the time a composer and poet. They were married February 21, 1938. Their marriage was unusual, in that they maintained very separate personal lives and often lived apart, yet they were devoted to each other. Paul Bowles was very encouraging of Jane's work, even when she went through long periods of writer's block. In fact, he credits her writing with his own beginning as a writer of fiction.

She began her novel *Two Serious Ladies* (1943) in 1938. Like much of her fiction, it is partly autobiographical, although not in any traditional sense. She wrote most of her short stories and a play, *In the Summer House* (1954), in the 1940's. Although most of her work was published in magazines during that decade, her collection of short stories, *Plain Pleasures*, did not appear until 1966. In 1948, she moved to Morocco, where Paul had been living since 1947. From the 1950's on, Bowles continued to live in Tangier and traveled often. Her complicated personal relationships with women and a busy social life often took precedence over her writing, a discipline that she found increasingly difficult. Writing had always been a struggle but also something that she felt compelled to do; she was envious of those who wrote easily. In 1957, she suffered a stroke, after which her health steadily declined. She spent the last years of her life in a hospital in Málaga, Spain, where she died in 1973.

ANALYSIS

Jane Bowles's short stories deal with personal relationships between characters who behave in bizarre and unpredictable ways. The stories contain an undercurrent of fear or foreboding, the cause of which is only sometimes revealed. Characters leave their usual environments and must then cope with new, often hostile ones. Portrayals of women predominate; family relationships—especially mothers and daugh-

ters, and sisters—form the core of ever-shifting narratives of emotional betrayal and psychological trauma. Despite the serious and even grim nature of the stories, they are also filled with humor and tenderness. Bowles's wit shines through in amusing dialogues (or, more often, monologues) and comic juxtapositions of characters' reactions to their situations. The settings for the stories are places Bowles knew from her travels: Central America, North Africa, and the northeast United States.

"A GUATEMALAN IDYLL" AND "A DAY IN THE OPEN"

"A Guatemalan Idyll" and "A Day in the Open" were Bowles's first published stories. They were originally conceived as part of her novel, *Two Serious Ladies*, but at the advice of her husband, Paul, these pieces were edited from the novel and published separately. "A Guatemalan Idyll" interweaves several plots. In one, an unnamed male traveler, in Guatemala on business, has an affair with Señora Ramirez, who is staying at the same pension. In another plot, Lilina Ramirez, her younger daughter, buys a snake from some boys on the street and then later lets it loose in the middle of town, where it is squashed by a bus. Accompanying Lilina at this moment is Enrique, a young boy whose head is bandaged as the result of falling on a rusty nail. Later in the story, Señora Ramirez takes a walk out of town, toward a volcano in the distance, and falls asleep in a little kiosk near a convent. A boy wakes her and then she seduces him. Consuelo Ramirez (Lilina's older sister) and Señorita Córdoba (a beautiful and well-bred young lady) are both secretly in love with the American traveler. The story ends with the traveler's departure.

The juxtaposition of these several plots, together with the strange events and their symbolic details, forms a richly compelling and multilayered narrative. The opposing tensions of sin and pleasure, guilt and justification, and remorse and indifference are common to Bowles's fiction. Another subplot involves Señora Ramirez's corset, which—like Lilina's snake and the half-ruined convent—symbolizes the oppression of religion, with its doctrine of original sin. Ultimately, the title of the story is ironic: What appears on the surface to be a pleasant vacation in the country for the various characters turns out to be fraught with guilt, disgust, and a lack of emotional tenderness.

"A Day in the Open" can be read as a companion piece to "A Guatemalan Idyll." Señor Ramirez, whose wife and two daughters are staying at a pension in a small town, hires two prostitutes to accompany him and a business associate on a picnic out in the country. Inez, one of the prostitutes, is straightforward and businesslike, more concerned with the financial aspects of their transaction. In contrast, her colleague, Julia, who is physically more delicate and suffering from an undiagnosed pain in her side, expresses genuine tenderness and love for Señor Ramirez. Alfredo, the business associate, remains aloof throughout the story, more interested in the numbers in a ledger than in the naked women at the picnic. Toward the end of the story, Señor Ramirez proves his physical strength by carrying Julia toward a waterfall (which, like the volcano in Señora Ramirez's landscape, seems to symbolize dangerous passion). He suddenly slips and drops Julia, who cuts her head on the rocks. They all leave the picnic site abruptly, Julia with her profusely bleeding head bandaged in a shawl.

A condensed and less complex version of "A Guatemalan Idyll," "A Day in the Open" deals similarly with sin and its effects: here, Julia's injury. The four characters suggest several combinations of opposites (strength and weakness, vitality and disinterest, cunning and stupidity), yet Bowles manages to transcend their being mere abstractions by giving them humane qualities, too. This story, like much of Bowles's work, casts the landscape in a vaguely sinister light, delightful in its natural beauty but also threatening in its power for destruction.

"CAMP CATARACT"

The physical setting of "Camp Cataract" involves such a contrast: The camp is located near a spectacular waterfall, which turns out to be the site of a character's death at the end of the story. Harriet, a self-described nature lover, has gone to Camp Cataract for her nerves. She enjoys being there and away from home, where she lives with her sister Sadie, who like Harriet is not married, and another sister, Evelyn, and her husband, Bert Hoffer. Sadie, who fears that Har-

riet might one day leave them for good, goes to Camp Cataract to convince Harriet to come home. Harriet, by no means pleased with Sadie's surprise visit (according to her doctor, Harriet is to have no family visitors), avoids her as much as possible.

"Camp Cataract" is the most elaborate and longest of Bowles's short stories, involving many of her recurrent thematic elements: troubled individuals trapped in troubling relationships, unattached middle-aged women, physical and psychological disabilities, emotionally upsetting incidents, and a violent, unexpected ending. The plot suddenly turns on itself: the reader believes that Sadie and Harriet have met for lunch and had a conversation in the woods, when in actuality, Sadie has imagined it all. Harriet later goes to meet her near the waterfall and finds that Sadie has disappeared; and although it is not explicitly stated, the reader can assume that Sadie has committed suicide by jumping off the bridge that goes behind the cataract. Bowles often wrote unsettling endings to her stories, endings that have both a grim finality and a troubling lack of closure.

"PLAIN PLEASURES"

"Plain Pleasures" differs from many of Bowles's stories in that its protagonists are a man and a woman, rather than two women. Alva Perry is a reserved widow in her early forties; her neighbor of many years, John Drake, is also middle-aged and painfully shy. One night, Mrs. Perry invites Mr. Drake (whom she barely knows) to a potato bake—one of life's "plain pleasures"—outside their tenement, and in turn, he invites her out to dinner the next night. She is angry and inimical throughout the meal. She has too much to drink and goes upstairs, looking for a rest room but ending up in what turns out to be the proprietor's bedroom. She passes out; the proprietor discovers her there and explains the situation to Mr. Drake, who leaves the restaurant, disconsolate.

The story ends with Mrs. Perry awakening in the strange room, then going down into the dining room, whispering "My sweet John Drake." Her comment is puzzling, given her harsh treatment of him during dinner the night before. Millicent Dillon, in her biography of Jane Bowles, explains that "In fact what has happened, but is not explicitly stated in the story, is that in the night she has been raped by the proprietor. Only after this violation is she able to feel tenderness for John Drake." "Plain Pleasures" is another ironic title, for although the story begins with a rather sweet encounter between two lonely people, it ends up with a typically Bowlesian undercurrent of violence—in this case, the leering and unsavory proprietor.

"EVERYTHING IS NICE"

"Everything Is Nice" was originally published as a nonfiction article entitled "East Side: North Africa." Paul Bowles later edited it, changed the narrator to third person, and included it in the collection *Plain Pleasures*. In the story, Jeanie, an American woman, and Zodelia, a Muslim woman, go together to a house where other Muslim women are gathered. They ask Jeanie questions about her life and her curious behavior: They want to know why she spends half her time with Muslims and half her time with Nazarenes (a term for Christians or Westerners in general). Jeanie soon tires of their questions and leaves abruptly, promising Zodelia that she will see her the next day.

Like Jeanie, Bowles divided her time in Tangier between her community of Moroccan friends and a group of expatriate Westerners. The tension that Bowles felt between the two cultures is evident in this story when the Muslim women ask Jeanie—partly out of polite interest but also with a tone of accusation—about her mother, her husband, and the Nazarene hotel where she lives part of the time. Jeanie's ambivalent position is symbolized at the end of the story by the powdery blue whitewash that rubs off on her finger when she touches a wall. It reminds her of a time when she once reached out to touch the face of a clown. While the Muslim women at the house insist that "everything is nice," Jeanie feels uncomfortable in her roles; she is caught between two different worlds, an anomaly in both, an amusing oddity to be observed but one who ultimately presents a false face to the outside world.

"A STICK OF GREEN CANDY"

The interior world of a solitary little girl predominates in "A Stick of Green Candy." Mary plays extensive imaginative games (she is the head of a regiment) in a clay pit near her house, avoiding the public playground full of other children. One day a boy from

a house nearby infiltrates her hideout, and she follows him home. She meets his mother, who chats amiably with Mary, but Mary instead seeks "the dark gulf that always had separated her from the adult world." She leaves the house suddenly, taking with her a stick of green candy, which the boy's mother had offered her. After the boy's intrusion into her private space of imagination, however, Mary loses the ability to continue her games with the pretend regiment. Mary's abrupt entrance into a more sociable interaction creates an ambivalent ending, with Mary turning a "cold face" away from the clay pit and creeping back home.

The stories discussed above are all included in *Plain Pleasures*. In the expanded edition of Bowles's collected works, *My Sister's Hand in Mine* (1978), several other stories appear that were not included in the 1966 collection. Three of these—"Andrew," "Emmy Moore's Journal," and "Going to Massachusetts"—were written as part of longer, unfinished works. They all deal with characters who are trying to escape their current existence for a new life in a new location: Andrew simply wants to get away and ends up being inducted into the Army; Emmy Moore leaves Paul, her husband of sixteen years, for the Hotel Henry, where she begins to write her journal; and Bozoe Flanner is supposed to go to Massachusetts but gets only as far as the next town up the road. A common thread in these and other stories by Bowles is the feeling of being trapped in a stagnating situation, with only partial success in getting away from it The three other pieces in *My Sister's Hand in Mine*—"The Iron Table," "Lila and Frank," and "Friday"—were selected from Bowles's notebooks. These fragments involve Hemingwayesque conversations between couples, usually in restaurants, on topics ranging from the decline of Western civilization to a small-town stranger's lack of appetite.

The fiction of Bowles is by no means conventional or predictable. Her characters shift from one topic to another in a single sentence; they behave erratically and often suffer extreme mood changes; they remain in difficult and unproductive relationships. Yet for Bowles, a sense of community—even a gathering of unpleasant eccentrics—seems preferable to isolation.

Those characters who do choose to be alone engage in an alternative world of imagination. Whether deliberately and playfully obscure or rife with layers of symbols and intentional multiple meanings, the fiction of Jane Bowles always manages to captivate.

OTHER MAJOR WORKS

LONG FICTION: *Two Serious Ladies*, 1943.

PLAY: *In the Summer House*, pr. 1953.

NONFICTION: *Out in the World: Selected Letters of Jane Bowles, 1935-1970*, 1985 (Millicent Dillon, editor).

MISCELLANEOUS: *The Collected Works of Jane Bowles*, 1966; *Feminine Wiles*, 1976; *My Sister's Hand in Mine*, 1978.

BIBLIOGRAPHY

Ashbery, John. "Up from the Underground." Review of *The Collected Works of Jane Bowles. The New York Times Book Review*, February 29, 1967, 5. In this oft-quoted review, Ashbery calls Bowles "one of the finest modern writers of fiction, in any language." He observes that Bowles's work often involves a conflict between weak and strong characters; he also praises her use of local color in dialogue and details.

Dillon, Millicent. "Jane Bowles: Experiment as Character." In *Breaking the Sequence: Women's Experimental Fiction*, edited by Ellen G. Friedman and Miriam Fuchs. Princeton, N.J.: Princeton University Press, 1989. This essay revises Dillon's comments (in the 1981 biography, below) about Bowles's writer's block. Dillon asserts that the fragments that characterized Bowles's writing (which Bowles saw as artistic failures) can instead be seen as "a valid expression of her own narrative vision." She adds that the sudden shifts in plot and narrative voice, which marked Bowles's work as eccentric when it first appeared, can be appreciated in a critical climate forty years later, which takes a more accepting attitude toward experimental forms.

_____. "Keeper of the Flame." *The New Yorker* 72 (January 27, 1997): 27-28. Discusses the efforts of an eighteen-year-old Spanish high school student to have Bowles's remains exhumed from a cemetery of San Miguel in Malaga (which is to make way for a freeway) and reburied in Marbella.

_____. *A Little Original Sin: The Life and Work of Jane Bowles*. New York: Holt, Rinehart and Winston, 1981. This illuminating and thoroughly researched biography gives full coverage of Jane Bowles's life and offers insightful commentary on her work. Dillon suggests that much of Bowles's work (and in turn, her life) was concerned with the notion of sin and its absolution, with imagination as another powerful force in her writing.

Gentile, Kathy Justice. "'The Dreaded Voyage into the World': Jane Bowles and Her Serious Ladies." *Studies in American Fiction* 22 (Spring, 1994): 47-60. Discusses the concept of dread in Bowles's short fiction and her novel. Argues that her work has been neglected because of her avant-garde reputation and because of the subject of dread. Claims that her heroine in the story "Camp Cataract" confronts dread from a perspective of existential freedom.

Green, Michelle. *The Dream at the End of the World: Paul Bowles and the Literary Renegades in Tangier*. New York: HarperCollins, 1991. Green provides a fascinating portrait of the exotic "outpost" of Tangier in the decades after World War II. She gives additional biographical information about Jane and Paul Bowles, plus factual information about Jane Bowles's works and their publication history.

Lougy, Robert E. "The World and Art of Jane Bowles, 1917-1973." *CEA Critic*, no. 49 (1987): 157-173. Lougy explores the major themes and forms of Bowles's work: isolation, fragmentation, guilt, and eccentricity. He often provides biographical background for aspects of her fiction and labels her a much more contemporary author than many other writers of her time.

Skerl, Jennie, ed. *A Tawdry Place of Salvation: The Art of Jane Bowles*. Carbondale: Southern Illinois University Press, 1997. A good interpretation of Bowles's characters, settings, and themes. Includes bibliographical references and an index.

Ann A. Merrill

PAUL BOWLES

Born: New York, New York; December 30, 1910

Died: Tangiers, Morocco; November 18, 1999

PRINCIPAL SHORT FICTION
The Delicate Prey and Other Stories, 1950
A Little Stone: Stories, 1950
The Hours After Noon, 1959
A Hundred Camels in the Courtyard, 1962
The Time of Friendship, 1967
Pages from Cold Point and Other Stories, 1968
Three Tales, 1975
Things Gone and Things Still Here, 1977
Collected Stories of Paul Bowles, 1939-1976, 1979
Midnight Mass, 1981
In the Red Room, 1982
Unwelcome Words, 1988
Call at Corazón and Other Stories, 1988
A Distant Episode: The Selected Stories, 1988
A Thousand Days for Mokhtar, and Other Stories, 1989
Too Far from Home, 1993 (novella)

OTHER LITERARY FORMS
Though he began his literary career relatively late, Paul Bowles produced a significant body of work in a variety of forms, including the novel (his most famous is *The Sheltering Sky*, 1949), travel essays, poetry, and an autobiography (*Without Stopping*, 1972). Bowles also translated the work of some Moroccan writers and published the collection *Too Far from Home: The Selected Writings of Paul Bowles* in 1993. Before turning to writing, Bowles won fame as a composer.

ACHIEVEMENTS
Paul Bowles won the Rea Award in 1991, and his first novel, *The Sheltering Sky*, was widely acclaimed as an existential masterpiece. *Esquire* magazine called the creative nonfiction work *Points in Time* (1982) a "brilliant achievement, innovative in form."

BIOGRAPHY
Paul Frederick Bowles's life spans much of the twentieth century, but the events that dominated the lives of his contemporaries in the United States had little effect on him. After attending the University of Virginia, Bowles went to Europe, where his literary career began with the publication of some youthful poems in the journal *Transitions*. During the 1930's, Bowles drifted from New York to Berlin, Paris, and Mexico. In New York and Berlin, he studied music with Aaron Copland. His musical career was furthered in Paris, where he studied with Virgil Thomson. Also in Paris, Bowles met Gertrude Stein, to whom he attributed the initial impetus for his subsequent writing career. Stein criticized his poetry and suggested that he devote himself to music instead, but she also urged him to go to Morocco. He took her advice, and eventually Morocco became his permanent home.

In 1938, Bowles married Jane Auer, a playwright and novelist. They traveled to diverse places such as Mexico, Central America, and Ceylon (modern Sri Lanka), journeys that Bowles recalls in his travel essays, collected in *Their Heads Are Green and Their Hands Are Blue* (1963). During the 1940's, Bowles composed music for ballet and opera (*The Wind Remains*), as well as incidental music for drama, including Tennessee Williams's *The Glass Menagerie* (pr. 1944). When Jane Bowles was working on her novel *Two Serious Ladies* (1943), Paul Bowles decided to try his hand at a novel as well. The result was *The Sheltering Sky*, published in 1949, a year after the Bowleses made Tangier their permanent residence. The novel, with its stark existentialism, was a critical success and reached *The New York Times* best-seller list. While *The Sheltering Sky* would remain his most popular and critically acclaimed work, Bowles continued to produce a steady stream of highly crafted stories, novels, and works of nonfiction. He also translated the tales of Moroccan oral storytellers, as well as the published work of North African authors.

As Paul Bowles's literary output flourished, Jane Bowles, suffering a stroke, ended her writing career in 1957. Although she survived the illness, her health and emotional outlook declined so badly that she would never again compose fiction. In 1967 she was committed to a Spanish psychiatric hospital, and she died in 1973. Bowles, devastated by his wife's death, wrote little original material for nearly a decade. Then, in 1982, he broke his silence with *Points in Time*. This avant-garde work of creative nonfiction received strong critical praise and proved that Bowles's literary energies were still powerful.

Public interest in Bowles reached a new height with the 1990 release of Bernardo Bertolucci's film version of *The Sheltering Sky*, in which Bowles had a minor role, and with the 1995 Paul Bowles symposium and celebration at the Lincoln Center. A sharp increase in critical and biographical studies of Paul Bowles occurred in the 1990's as well. Bowles died of a heart attack in Tangiers in 1999.

ANALYSIS

Paul Bowles is best placed in a category by himself. Though his work is tangentially related to that of other writers—the southern gothic of William Faulkner and Flannery O'Connor, the sexual primitivism of D. H. Lawrence, and the neocolonial meditations of Graham Greene and E. M. Forster, all of which suggest themselves as influences—Bowles occupies a unique place in literature. No other writer has produced a body of work that so consistently rejects the culture that has given birth to it. The intensity with which Bowles and his principal characters spurn the Western world and all it stands for distinguishes his stories even from other literature of exile.

Bowles's work has received only scattered critical acclaim. Perhaps because he lived most of his life in Morocco and because most of his work is set outside the United States, he remains outside the American literary scene and has not been the focus of considerable critical attention. Nevertheless, Bowles has been acclaimed by important writers, such as Gore Vidal and Tennessee Williams. Bowles's affinity for the grotesque and lurid has led some reviewers to dismiss his work as gratuitously violent. Indeed, the pessi-

Paul Bowles (Cherie Nutting)

mism and nihilism that dominate his stories can be overwhelming. Beneath the surface violence, however, the reader finds a consistent, thoughtful, and chilling vision of life.

His clear style presents readers with a very real world, yet the reality readers so palpably experience in reading Bowles is ultimately a hallucination. His stories concentrate on the ambiguity of human morality. Order is only superficial in this world; readers sense its inevitable dissolution at every turn. The jungle and the desert reside within every human situation, and the rationality with which readers attempt to suppress them proves to be their greatest self-delusion.

Bowles's stories are generally set in exotic locations, North Africa and Latin America being his favorite landscapes. Physical setting is crucial in his work. It is more than backdrop; often it becomes a modulating force, regulating and tempering the characters who wander into its domain. These characters are often visiting Westerners, who—spiritually empty themselves—come with a superficial craving for new experiences. Beneath the surface, however, these lost ciphers have no truly purposeful quest. They are merely fleeing the vacuity of their Western world; they seek nothing except escape.

Many of Bowles's stories have no Western characters at all. Even then, the alienation inherent in the landscape is evident and, indeed, prominent. No facile primitivism surfaces in Bowles's world. The non-Westerners are not noble savages; they are isolated and displaced persons as well, brutalized by the landscape and compelled to see into the heart of darkness beating there. This is the world Bowles explores. It is a brutal world, both nightmarish and stark in its features. Bowles's style matches the landscape: He writes without adornment or prettiness. This clear and honest style is not without grace, but it is the grace of the desert about which he so often writes, a grace many find too austere.

"A DISTANT EPISODE"

One of Bowles's first stories, and one of his finest, is the macabre "A Distant Episode," which first appeared in *The Delicate Prey and Other Stories*. Several writers and critics, including Williams, hailed this as one of the finest American short stories. A nameless American professor of linguistics visits a small town in the Sahara, where he tries to strike up a conversation with a surly waiter. The waiter reluctantly promises to help the professor purchase some boxes made from camel udders. They walk by moonlight through a dangerous part of town, encountering corpses and wild dogs, until the waiter abandons the professor on a cliff. The hostile nomadic group that makes the boxes is encamped somewhere beneath the cliff, and despite all foreboding, the professor descends to find them. There, he is robbed and beaten. In the morning, the nomads cut out his tongue and depart into the desert. The professor lives among them for months; dressed in a rattling suit of smashed tin cans, he is brought out as a sort of clown and made to entertain the community. "A Distant Episode" is the quintessential Bowles story. All his principal themes

are starkly set forth in the account of the professor's transformation from curiosity-seeker to curiosity. Something takes hold of him in this foreign setting, something over which he has no control, and the civilized veneer of the Westerner is easily wiped away. Significantly, the linguist loses his tongue, and thus the apparent gratuitousness of the violence becomes psychologically telling. He loses not only his tongue but also his mind and spirit.

"THE ECHO"

Another early story, "The Echo," also from *The Delicate Prey and Other Stories*, extends Bowles's obsession with inhospitable landscapes. Aileen, a college-age woman from the United States, has come to live with her expatriate mother in Colombia. The mother lives in an impressive house perched near a cliff with a woman named Prue. Prue is an artist, quite masculine in both appearance and attitude, who seems to be the lover of Aileen's mother. The antagonism between lover and daughter builds to the point that Aileen's mother asks Aileen to leave. On the day of Aileen's departure, in a final encounter, Prue taunts Aileen until the girl explodes and viciously attacks her. In this story, the daughter's estrangement from her mother is reflected in the alien landscape, so that it is the place itself that first prompts Aileen's primal scream and then literally echoes it from the black walls of the gorge. Once again, Bowles's character is stripped of her superficial civility and forced to confront the dark stranger within.

"PAGES FROM COLD POINT"

Mr. Norton, in the story "Pages from Cold Point," is the Bowles character which most embodies the extremity of Western nihilism. A clever, if blighted, cynic, Norton undertakes the journey so typical of Bowles's characters—the journey from civilization (in this case, civilization at its most refined: the university campus) to a primitive land in the Third World where Western certainties have a way of dissolving. Norton leaves the university after the death of his wife (her name, Hope, is significant) and goes to a tropical island with his teenage son, Racky. Bit by bit, Norton learns that the attention his son is paying to the young boys of the island town has stirred up trouble. Shockingly, in the scene when father confronts son, an incestuous affair begins. Racky's hopelessness and corruption are the disturbing by-products of a society gone haywire. The seduction proves easy and even appears "natural" to Norton, who feels that nothing drastic has happened. His description is so understated as to be disturbing. Readers are reminded that in Bowles's world, corruption is insidious and pervasive.

"AT PASO ROJO"

Bowles is fascinated by what happens to people when their civilized notions are suddenly disturbed by some encounter with primitive people or a foreboding landscape. In the story "At Paso Rojo," first appearing in *The Delicate Prey and Other Stories*, the drama is played out in the psychological terrain of sexual repression and maladjustment. The story is set in Central America. It concerns the visit of two sisters, both middle-aged spinsters, to the ranch of their brother following the death of their mother. One of the sisters, Chalia, disturbed and vulnerable after the loss of her mother, begins behaving oddly. There seems little doubt that the brutal landscape has some bearing on her crack-up. After a ride in the country, Chalia finds herself alone with one of the ranch hands, a young and virile mestizo. She makes advances but is rejected. Chalia exacts revenge by stealing money from her brother and then giving the money to the mestizo. Later, Chalia encounters the drunk boy on the road and pushes him over a small cliff. When he is found, still a bit drunk and with a large amount of money in his pocket, the theft is revealed. Chalia denies having given him the money, and the ranch hand is dismissed. This unpredictable eruption of violent, even sadistic, behavior in a normally "civilized" character is fascinating to Bowles. Again and again in his fiction, the characters fall prey to violent urges that they do not understand. Ultimately, these urges lead to a masochistic desire for annihilation.

"THE DELICATE PREY"

One of Bowles's most acclaimed stories is "The Delicate Prey," a stunning story of three Arab merchants who undertake a perilous journey across remote regions of the Sahara desert. Several days into the journey, the three merchants encounter a solitary

traveler. Although wary, they allow the stranger to travel with them since he is alone and not of the barbaric nomadic group known as the Reguiba (the same bunch that captured the professor in "A Distant Episode"). The stranger claims to be a good shot and promises to supply the traveling party with gazelle meat. A few days later, the stranger goes off to shoot gazelles. Upon hearing gun shots, the elder merchant, hoping to join in the shooting, pursues the stranger. After more shots, a second merchant departs in pursuit, leaving the youngest of the party alone. Eventually, the stranger returns alone, and the boy is easily captured. The stranger mutilates, rapes, and murders the boy, all without the slightest compunction. The stranger later arrives at a trading town and tries to sell the merchants' leather, a type of leather that is unique to the merchants' band. Thus he is discovered, and some travelers from the merchants' town capture him and bury him in the sand of the desert, leaving only his head exposed.

"The Delicate Prey" is a demanding story. Bowles insists that readers look inside themselves and account for the cruelty that they find there. There is nothing noble about the characters, and certainly the story presents the reader with a world devoid of altruism. A first encounter with the story produces a feeling of strangeness and terror. To examine it more closely, however, is to uncover something familiar and haunting in this simple tale. The reader knows what is going to happen and yet is still horrified. The retribution exacted in the story's conclusion is severe and grotesque, and yet, in a strange way, gratifying. Bowles wants to direct readers' attention to the darkness present not only in their gratuitously violent actions but also in their sense of justice. The queasiness they experience is in part attributable to the fact that they recognize the ineluctable pattern of the action. The characters are not monsters. They are acting, if anything, all too humanly.

"TAPIAMA"

A predominant theme in Bowles's stories is the encounter of spiritually bankrupt Americans with alien cultures. In the story "Tapiama," which first appeared in *The Time of Friendship*, this theme is amply articulated. It is a story that reminds the reader of

Samuel Beckett or Jean-Paul Sartre. Nothing seems to happen in the story, certainly nothing like the shocking events upon which Bowles's stories so often turn. Still, an unnerving suspense is created by the constant threat of such an event. In the end, though the conclusion is shadowy and uncertain, "Tapiama" is a story that resonates with revelation.

In the story, an American photographer in a Latin American country goes for a midnight walk along the beach. He is puzzled by a light on the water and, upon hailing it, is asked by a boatman if he wishes to go to Tapiama. It is all quite mysterious to him, yet he agrees to go on the boat. He has no idea why he goes. This is a typical moment in a Bowles story: The protagonist seems to suffer a sudden loss of will, a Westernized version of accidie. He recognizes the absurdity of it all, yet he feels compelled to let events run their course: He will not assert himself. The boat arrives in Tapiama, which appears to be a factory town run by a sugar concern. The protagonist drifts into a seedy bar. He is accosted by a prostitute and by a belligerent gendarme. Ants crawl on the beams, a dead snake hangs from the rafters, and a monkey dances. In this bizarre setting, the American gets drunk on the local brew. When he finally manages to escape, the effort exhausts him, and he lies in the bottom of a boat, content to drift where the current takes him. Finally, the boat is discovered by some men who begin poling it upriver into the jungle and some unknown fate.

The theme of "Tapiama"—and, in fact, of many of Bowles's stories—is neatly captured in the closing pages. The American, drunk and nearly unconscious, hears the sound of a bird calling from the jungle. When he imitates the call, the strangers in the boat with him explode with laughter. This is a bird, they explain to him, that tries to sit in the nests of other birds and fights with them until it is driven off. Its call means "Nobody wants me." This is the condition of the photographer and all Bowles's Westerners. Slumming their way through other cultures, they fight and are driven off by the "natives." Nobody likes them, and indeed there is little to like. Their homelessness is indicative of their spiritual emptiness.

TOO FAR FROM HOME

Another alienated American appears in *Too Far from Home*, set in the Niger River Valley, a Bowles novella which appeared in the collection *Too Far from Home: The Selected Writings* (1993). Anita, fleeing New York City and a painful divorce, arrives in North Africa to live with her brother Tom, an artist who revels in exotic desert landscapes. From the moment she arrives, Anita feels out of place in the vast, hot, African spaces, and she takes out her tensions on Tom and the household staff. She is particularly uncomfortable with Sekou, a local chieftain who acts as head of the household.

One morning, Tom asks Anita to purchase film from his friend Mme Massot, the French woman who owns the camera shop in the nearby village. Tom sends Sekou to act as Anita's guide. On the way, two young Americans on a motorcycle collide with Sekou, wounding him in the leg. Incensed, Anita shouts dire warnings at the motorcyclists. A few days later, Anita, walking amid the high dunes, discovers the Americans, their motorcycle wrecked, their bodies splattered with blood. She assumes they are dead and leaves the scene, telling no one. Soon after, she has nightmares about consuming a headless man's flesh, a dream she claims Sekou has willed upon her.

Just before she leaves Africa, Anita hears that the motorcyclists did not die from their injuries; they perished from exposure. Therefore, she may have been able to save their lives if she had reported the accident. She also learns that Sekou claims she cursed the motorcyclists when she screamed abuse at them, thus causing their death through magic. Sekou believes that his leg will not improve until Anita withdraws her curse and forgives the young men. He has dreamed of visiting her in her sleep to beg her to forgive the young men, but she has always refused. Anita, hearing this tale, forgives them out loud before Sekou, who approves. The next morning, when Anita leaves the Niger River, she feels healed and realizes she will miss the North African landscape, the adobe village, and most of all Sekou.

While this story possesses many key Bowles motifs, its conclusion possesses an ambivalence out of character for the usually uncompromisingly grim author. Like *The Sheltering Sky*, *Too Far from Home* portrays a dysfunctional artistic couple in a foreign country, although in this story they are brother and sister. Still, there are unconscious incestuous connections between Tom and Anita, who often act like a married couple. Anita even becomes jealous of Mme Massot's interest in Tom and his artwork. Also, *Too Far from Home* contains spiritually empty Westerners in an alien landscape, as well as sudden and brutal violence. However, while Anita's failure to understand the Niger River realm and its culture result in her passionately violent curse and the tragic death of two young men, the curse and Sekou's forgiveness lead Anita to reconcile with North Africa, its people, and her emotional being.

OTHER MAJOR WORKS

LONG FICTION: *The Sheltering Sky*, 1949; *Let It Come Down*, 1952; *The Spider's House*, 1955; *Up Above the World*, 1966.

NONFICTION: *Yallah*, 1957; *Their Heads Are Green and Their Hands Are Blue*, 1963; *Without Stopping*, 1972; *Points in Time*, 1982; *Days: Tangier Journal, 1987-1989*, 1991; *In Touch: The Letters of Paul Bowles*, 1994 (Jeffrey Miller, editor).

POETRY: *Scenes*, 1968; *The Thicket of Spring: Poems, 1926-1969*, 1972; *Next to Nothing*, 1976; *Next to Nothing: Collected Poems, 1926-1977*, 1981.

TRANSLATIONS: *The Lost Trail of the Sahara*, 1951 (of R. Frison-Roche's novel); *No Exit*, 1958 (of Jean-Paul Sartre's play); *A Life Full of Holes*, 1964 (of Driss ben Hamed Charhadi's autobiography); *Love with a Few Hairs*, 1967 (of Mohammed Mrabet's fiction); *The Lemon*, 1969 (of Mrabet's fiction); *M'Hashish*, 1969 (of Mrabet's fiction); *For Bread Alone*, 1973 (of Mohamed Choukri's fiction); *Jean Genet in Tangier*, 1974 (of Choukri's nonfiction); *The Boy Who Set the Fire*, 1974 (of Mrabet's fiction); *The Oblivion Seekers*, 1975 (of Isabelle Eberhardt's fiction); *Look and Move On*, 1976 (of Mrabet's fiction); *Harmless Poisons, Blameless Sins*, 1976 (of Mrabet's fiction); *The Big Mirror*, 1977 (of Mrabet's fiction); *The Beach Café*, 1980 (of Mrabet's fiction); *The Chest*, 1983 (of Mrabet's fiction); *The Beg-*

gar's Knife, 1985 (of Rodrigo Rey Rosa's fiction); *Chocolate Creams and Dollars*, 1992 (of Mrabet's fiction).

MISCELLANEOUS: *Too Far from Home: The Selected Writings of Paul Bowles*, 1993.

BIBLIOGRAPHY

Caponi, Gena Dagel. *Paul Bowles: Romantic Savage*. Carbondale: Southern Illinois University Press, 1994. A biographical/critical study of Bowles's life and art that examines the sources of his fiction, his major themes and techniques, and his methods of story composition.

_____, ed. *Conversations with Paul Bowles*. Jackson: University Press of Mississippi, 1993. In this collection of reprinted and unpublished interviews, Bowles talks about his life and art, even though he claims that the man who wrote his books does not exist except in the books. Bowles has a penchant for perverse responses to interview questions but still communicates a great deal about the relationship between himself and his work.

Dillon, Millicent. "Tracing Paul Bowles." *Raritan* 17 (Winter, 1998): 47-63. In these excerpts from her biography of Bowles, *You Are Not I*, Dillon traces the relationship between Bowles and his wife Jane Auer Bowles, reevaluates earlier views in her biography of Jane Bowles, and recounts her own speculations on his life and work.

Green, Michelle. *The Dream at the End of the World: Paul Bowles and the Literary Renegades in Tangier*. New York: HarperCollins, 1991. A lively account of the artistic and socialite sets that congregated in Tangier in the 1940's and 1950's. Investigates the life of Bowles and those who came to stay with him in Morocco. Green gives some interesting background details for readers of Bowles's fiction. Includes an index and photographs.

Hibbard, Allen. *Paul Bowles: A Study of the Short Fiction*. New York: Twayne, 1993. This introduction to Bowles's short fiction discusses his debt to Edgar Allan Poe's theories of formal unity and analyzes his short-story collections as carefully organized wholes. Also includes material from Bowles's notebooks and previously published critical essays by other critics.

Patterson, Richard. *A World Outside: The Fiction of Paul Bowles*. Austin: University of Texas Press, 1987. This scholarly examination of Bowles's work is comprehensive in its analysis. *The Sheltering Sky* is given much attention. Patterson's notes and index are quite good.

Pounds, Wayne. *Paul Bowles: The Inner Geography*. New York: Peter Lang, 1985. A good introduction to Bowles and his use of landscape. Demonstrates the connection between setting and the spiritual states of Bowles's characters.

Sawyer-Laucanno, Christopher. *An Invisible Spectator: A Biography of Paul Bowles*. New York: Weidenfeld & Nicolson, 1989. Sawyer-Laucanno presents a very readable account of the writer's life and offers some intriguing speculation on the connection between the events of Bowles's life and the plots of his stories. The index and notes are useful, and a select bibliography lists Bowles's major works in literature and music.

Stephen Benz, updated by John Nizalowski

KAY BOYLE

Born: St. Paul, Minnesota; February 19, 1902
Died: Mill Valley, California; December 27, 1992

PRINCIPAL SHORT FICTION
Short Stories, 1929
Wedding Day and Other Stories, 1930
The First Lover and Other Stories, 1933
The White Horses of Vienna and Other Stories, 1936
The Crazy Hunter and Other Stories, 1940
Thirty Stories, 1946
The Smoking Mountain: Stories of Postwar Germany, 1951
Three Short Novels, 1958
Nothing Ever Breaks Except the Heart, 1966
Fifty Stories, 1980
Life Being the Best and Other Stories, 1988

OTHER LITERARY FORMS

In addition to her short stories, Kay Boyle published several novels, volumes of poetry, children's books, essay collections, and a book of memoirs. *Breaking the Silence: Why a Mother Tells Her Son About the Nazi Era* (1962) is her personal account, written for adolescents, of Europe during the Nazi regime. Boyle also ghostwrote, translated, and edited many other books. Hundreds of her stories, poems, and articles have appeared in periodicals ranging from the "little magazines" published in Paris in the 1920's to *The Saturday Evening Post* and *The New Yorker*, for which she was a correspondent from 1946 to 1953.

ACHIEVEMENTS

Both prolific and versatile, Kay Boyle has been respected during her long career for her exquisite technical style and her ardent political activism. She was very much a part of the expatriate group of writers living in Paris in the 1920's, and her work appeared in the avant-garde magazines alongside that of James Joyce, Gertrude Stein, Ernest Hemingway, and others. Her work is in many ways typical of the period, stylistically terse, carefully crafted, displaying keen psychological insight through the use of stream of consciousness and complex interior monologues. That her work was highly regarded is evidenced by her many awards: two John Simon Guggenheim Memorial Foundation Fellowships; O. Henry Awards in both 1935 and 1961; an honorary doctorate from Columbia College, Chicago; and membership in the National Institute of Arts and Letters. She taught at San Francisco State University and Eastern Washington University.

BIOGRAPHY

Born into an affluent family in St. Paul, Minnesota, in 1902, Kay Boyle moved and traveled frequently and extensively with her family during her childhood. After studying architecture for two years in Cincinnati, Boyle married Robert Brault, whose family never accepted her or the marriage. What was to have been a summer trip to France in 1923 became an eighteen-year expatriation, during which Boyle continued to write poetry and fiction. Boyle left her husband to live with editor Ernest Walsh until his death from tuberculosis in 1926. Boyle later returned to Brault with Walsh's child. They divorced in 1932, when she married Laurence Vail, a fellow American expatriate. After her marriage to Vail also ended in divorce, Boyle married Joseph von Franckenstein, an Austrian baron who had been forced out of his homeland during the Nazi invasion. She lived much of the time in Europe and was a correspondent for *The New Yorker.* She returned to the United States in 1953; Franckenstein died in 1963. Boyle taught at San Francisco State University from 1963 to 1979 and at Eastern Washington University in 1982. Her arrest and imprisonment following an anti-Vietnam War demonstration is the basis of her novel *The Underground Woman* (1975). She would remain actively involved in movements protesting social injustices and violations of human rights.

ANALYSIS

In a 1963 article Kay Boyle defines what she saw as the role of the serious writer: to be "the spokesman for those who remain inarticulate . . . an aeolian harp whose sensitive strings respond to the whispers of the concerned people of his time." The short-story writer, she believed, is "a moralist in the highest sense of the word"; the role of the short-story writer has always been "to speak briefly and clearly of the dignity and integrity of [the] individual." Perhaps it is through this definition that the reader may distinguish the central threads that run through the variegated fabric of Boyle's fiction and bind it into a single piece.

In the 1920's, when the young expatriate artists she knew in Paris were struggling to cast off the yokes of literary convention, Boyle championed the

Kay Boyle (Library of Congress)

bold and experimental in language, and her own early stories are intensely individual explorations of private experiences. Yet when the pressures of the social world came to bear so heavily on private lives in the twentieth century that they could not be ignored, Boyle began to expand the scope of her vision and vibrate to the note of the *new* times to affirm on a broader scale the same basic values—the "dignity and integrity" of the individual. Beginning in the 1930's, her subject matter encompassed the rise of Nazism, the French resistance, the Allied occupation of postwar Germany, and the civil rights and anti-Vietnam War movements in the United States, yet she never lost sight of the individual dramas acted out against these panoramic backdrops.

In the same article Boyle also quotes Albert Camus's statement that "a man's work is nothing but a long journey to recover through the detours of art, the two or three simple and great images which first gained access to his heart." In Boyle's journey of more than fifty years, a few central themes remained constant: a belief in the absolute essentiality of love to human well-being—whether on a personal or a global level; an awareness of the many obstacles to its attainment; and a tragic sense of loss when it fails and the gulfs between human beings stand unbridged.

"WEDDING DAY"

"Wedding Day," the title story of her first widely circulated volume of short stories, published in 1930, is typical of her early works. It is an intense exploration of a unique private experience written in an experimental style. The action is primarily psychological, and outward events are described as they reflect states of consciousness. Yet it is representative of Boyle's best work for decades to come, both in its central concern with the failure of love and in its bold and brilliant use of language.

"The red carpet that was to spurt like a hemorrhage from pillar to post was stacked in the corner," the story begins. From the first sentence the reader senses that things are out of joint. The wedding cake is ignored as it is carried into the pantry "with its beard lying white as hoarfrost on its bosom." "This was the last lunch," Boyle writes, and the brother and sister "came in with their buttonholes drooping with violets and sat sadly down, sat down to eat." To the funereal atmosphere of this wedding day, Boyle injects tension and bitterness. The son and mother argue as to whether the daughter will be given the family's prized copper saucepans, and he mocks the decorum his mother cherishes when he commands her not to cry, pointing his finger directly at her nose "so that when she looked at him with dignity her eyes wavered and crossed" and "she sat looking proudly at him, erect as a needle staring through its one open eye." As the mother and son bicker over who wanted the wedding in the first place, the bride-to-be is conspicuously silent. Finally, as the son snatches away each slice of roast beef his mother carves until she whimpers her fear of getting none herself, he and his sister burst into laughter. He tosses his napkin over the chandelier, and she follows him out of the room, leaving their mother alone "praying that this occasion at least pass off with dignity, with her heart not in her mouth but beating away in peace in its own bosom."

With the tension between children and mother clearly delineated and the exclusive camaraderie between brother and sister suggested, Boyle shifts both mood and scene and describes in almost incantatory prose the pair's idyllic jaunt through the spring afternoon in the hours remaining before the wedding:

> The sun was an imposition, an imposition, for they were another race stamping an easy trail through the wilderness of Paris, possessed of the same people, but of themselves like another race. No one else could by lifting of the head only be starting life over again, and it was a wonder the whole city of Paris did not hold its breath for them, for if anyone could have begun a new race, it was these two.

The incestuous overtones are strong. "It isn't too late yet, you know," the brother repeatedly insists as they stride through the streets, take a train into the *bois*, and row to the middle of a pond. "Over them was the sky set like a tomb," and as tears flow down their cheeks, the slow rain begins to fall. There is perfect correspondence between landscape and emotion, external objects mirroring the characters' internal states. The rain underscores the pair's frustration and despair as they realize the intensity of their love and the impossibility of its fulfillment:

> Everywhere, everywhere there were other countries to go to. And how were they to get from the boat with the chains that were on them, how uproot the willowing trees from their hearts, how strike the irons of spring that shackled them? What shame and shame that scorched a burning pathway to their dressing rooms! Their hearts were mourning for every Paris night and its half-hours before lunch when two straws crossed on the round table top on the marble anywhere meant I had a drink here and went on.

The inevitable wedding itself forms the final segment of the story, and the lyrical spell binding the pair is broken the instant they set foot in the house again to find their mother "tying white satin bows under the chins of the potted plants." The boy kicks down the hall the silver tray that will collect the guests' calling cards, and his mother is wearily certain "that this outburst presaged a thousand mishaps that were yet to come." The irony of the story lies not only in the reversal of expectations the title may have aroused in the reader but also in the discrepancy between different characters' perceptions of the same situation. The self-pitying matron worries only about the thousand little mishaps possible when a major disaster—the wedding itself—is imminent; but the guests arrive "in peace" and the brother delivers his sister to the altar. Boyle captures magnificently the enormous gulf between the placid surface appearance and the tumultuous inner reality of the situation as she takes the reader inside the bride's consciousness:

> This was the end, the end, they thought. She turned her face to her brother and suddenly their hearts fled together and sobbed like ringdoves in their bosoms. This was the end, the end, the end, this was the end.
>
> Down the room their feet fled in various ways, seeking an escape. To the edge of the carpet fled her feet, returned and followed reluctantly upon her brother's heels. Every piped note of the organ insisted that she go on. It isn't too late, he said. Too late, too late. The ring was given, the book was closed. The desolate, the barren sky continued to fling down dripping handfuls of fresh rain.

The mindless repetition of the phrase "the end" and the blind panic of the bride's imaginary flight have an intense psychological authenticity, and the recurrence of the brother's phrase "It isn't too late" and its perversion in "Too late, too late," along with the continuing rain, are evidence of the skill with which Boyle has woven motifs into the fabric of her story.

"Wedding Day" ends with dancing, but in an ironic counterpoint to the flight she had imagined at the altar, the bride's feet "were fleeing in a hundred ways throughout the rooms, fluttering from the punch bowl to her bedroom and back again." Through repetition and transformation of the image, Boyle underscores the fact that her path is now circumscribed. While the brother, limbered by the punch, dances about scattering calling cards, the mother, "in triumph on the arm of the General, danced lightly by" rejoicing that "no glass had yet been broken." "What a real success, what a *real* success," is her only thought as her feet float "Over the oriental prayer rugs, through the Persian forests of hemp, away and

away" in another absurdly circumscribed "escape" that is yet another mockery of the escape to "other countries" that the pair had dreamed of that afternoon on the lake.

Ironies and incongruities are hallmarks of Kay Boyle's fiction. For Boyle, reality depends on perception, and the fact that different perceptions of the same situation result in disparate and often conflicting "realities" creates a disturbing world in which individuals badly in need of contact and connection collide and bounce off one another like atoms. In "Wedding Day" Boyle juxtaposes a *real* loss of love with the surface gaiety of a wedding that celebrates no love at all, but which the mother terms "a *real* success." She exposes the painful isolation of each individual and the tragedy that the only remedy—a bonding through love—is so often thwarted or destroyed.

The barriers to love are many, both natural and man-made. In some of Boyle's stories those who would love are severed by death. Sometimes, as in the case of the brother and sister in "Wedding Day," love's fulfillment is simply made impossible by the facts of life in this imperfect world, and although readers can mourn for what has been lost, they can hardly argue about the obstacle itself—the incest taboo is nearly universal. Yet in many of her works Boyle presents a more assailable villain. In "Wedding Day" she treats unsympathetically the mother, who stands for all the petty proprieties that so often separate people. Boyle finds many barriers to human contact to be as arbitrary and immoral as the social conventions which cause Huck Finn's "conscience" to torment him as he helps his friend Jim to escape slavery, and in her fiction she quietly unleashes her fury against them. An obstacle she attacks repeatedly is a narrow-mindedness which blinds individuals to the inherent dignity and integrity of others, an egotism which in the plural becomes bigotry and chauvinism.

"THE WHITE HORSES OF VIENNA"

While Boyle and her family were living in Austria in the 1930's, she was an eyewitness as the social world began to impose itself on private lives, and she began to widen the scope of her artistic vision; yet her "political" stories have as their central concern the ways in which external events affect the individual. In one of her best-known stories, "The White Horses of Vienna," which won the O. Henry Award for best story of 1935, Boyle exposes the artificial barricades to human understanding and connection. The story explores the relationship between a Tyrolean doctor, who has injured his leg coming down the mountain after lighting a swastika fire in rebellion against the current government, and Dr. Heine, the young assistant sent from Vienna to take over his patients while he recovers. The Tyrolean doctor and his wife see immediately that Dr. Heine is a Jew.

The Tyrolean doctor is a clean-living, respected man. He had been a prisoner of war in Siberia and had studied abroad, but the many places in which he had been "had never left an evil mark." Boyle writes: "His face was as strong as rock, but it had seen so much of suffering that it had the look of being scarred, it seemed to be split in two, with one side of it given to resolve and the other to compassion." In his personal dealings it is the compassionate side that dominates. When his wife asks in a desperate whisper what they will do with "*him*," the Tyrolean doctor replies simply that they will send for his bag at the station and give him some *Apfelsaft* if he is thirsty. "It's harder on him than us," he tells her. Neither has the wife's own humanity been extinguished entirely by institutionalized bigotry, for when Dr. Heine's coat catches fire from a sterilizing lamp on the table, she wraps a piece of rug around him immediately and holds him tightly to smother the flames. Almost instinctively, she offers to try patching the burned-out place, but then she suddenly bites her lip and stands back "as if she had remembered the evil thing that stood between them."

The situation of the Tyrolean doctor, described as a "great, golden, wounded bird," is counterpointed in a story Dr. Heine tells at dinner one evening about the famous Lipizzaner horses of the Spanish Riding School in Vienna, still royal, "without any royalty left to bow their heads to, still shouldering into the arena with spirits a man would give his soul for, bending their knees in homage to the empty, canopied loge where royalty no longer sat." He tells of a particular horse that the government, badly in need of money,

had sold to an Indian maharaja. When the time had come for the horse to be taken away, a wound was discovered cut in his leg. After it had healed and it was again time for the horse to leave, another wound was found on its other leg. Finally the horse's blood was so poisoned that it had to be destroyed. No one knew who had caused the wounds until the horse's devoted little groom committed suicide that same day. When the after-dinner conversation is interrupted by the knocking of Heimwehr troops at the door, "men brought in from other parts of the country, billeted there to subdue the native people," the identification between the doctor and the steed is underscored. He cannot guide the troops up the mountain in search of those who have lit that evening's swastika fires because of his wounded leg.

Dr. Heine is relieved that the rest of the evening will be spent with family and friends watching one of the Tyrolean doctor's locally renowned marionette shows. After staring out the window at the burning swastikas, the "marvelously living flowers of fire springing out of the arid darkness," the "inexplicable signals given from one mountain to another in some secret gathering of power that cast him and his people out, forever out upon the waters of despair," Dr. Heine turns back, suddenly angry, and proclaims that the whole country is being ruined by politics, that it is impossible to have friends or even casual conversations on any other basis these days. "You're much wiser to make your puppets, *Herr Doktor*," he says.

Even the marionette show is political. The characters are a clown who explains he is carrying artificial flowers because he is on his way to his own funeral and wants them to be fresh when he gets there, and a handsome grasshopper, "a great, gleaming beauty" who prances about the stage with delicacy and wit to the music of Mozart. "It's really marvellous! He's as graceful as the white horses at Vienna, *Herr Doktor*," Dr. Heine calls out in delight. As the conversation continues between the clown, called "Chancellor," and the grasshopper addressed as "The Leader," Dr. Heine is not laughing so loudly. The Chancellor has a "ludicrous faith in the power of the Church" to support him; the Leader proclaims that the cities are full of churches, but "the country is full of God." The

Leader speaks with "a wild and stirring power that sent the cold of wonder up and down one's spine," and he seems "ready to waltz away at any moment with the power of stallion life that was leaping in his limbs." As the Chancellor proclaims, "I believe in the independence of the individual," he promptly trips over his own sword and falls flat among the daisies.

At the story's conclusion, Dr. Heine is standing alone on the cold mountainside, longing to be "indoors, with the warmth of his own people, and the intellect speaking." When he sees "a small necklace of men coming to him" up the mountain, the lights they bear "coming like little beacons of hope carried to him," Dr. Heine thinks,

> Come to me . . . come to me. I am a young man alone on a mountain. I am a young man alone, as my race is alone, lost here amongst them all.

Yet ironically, what Dr. Heine views as "beacons of hope" are carried by the Heimwehr troops, the Tyrolean doctor's enemies. As in "Wedding Day," Boyle presents a single situation and plays off the characters' reactions to it against one another to illustrate the gaps between individuals and the relativity of truth and reality in the world.

His personal loyalties transcending his politics, Dr. Heine rushes to warn the family of the Heimwehr's approach. When the troops arrive they announce that the Austrian chancellor, Dollfuss, had been assassinated in Vienna that afternoon. They have come to arrest the doctor, whose rebel sympathies are known. "Ah, politics, politics again!" cries Dr. Heine, wringing his hands "like a woman about to cry." He runs outdoors and takes the doctor's hand as he is being carried away on a stretcher, asking what he can do to help. "You can throw me peaches and chocolate from the street," replies the Tyrolean doctor, smiling, "his cheeks scarred with the marks of laughter in the light from the hurricane lamps that the men were carrying down." His wife is not a good shot, he adds, and he missed all the oranges she had thrown him after the February slaughter. At this image of the Tyrolean doctor caged like an animal but still noble, with his spirit still unbroken, Dr. Heine is left "thinking in anguish of the snow-white horses,

the Lipizzaners, the relics of pride, the still unbroken vestiges of beauty bending their knees to the empty loge of royalty where there was no royalty any more."

In "The White Horses of Vienna," Boyle expresses hope, if not faith, that even in the face of divisive social forces, the basic connections of compassion between individuals might survive. In a work that is a testament to her humanity, she presents the Tyrolean doctor's plight with such sensitivity that readers, like the Jewish assistant, are forced to view with understanding and empathy this proud man's search for a cause that will redeem the dignity and honor of his wounded people while at the same time abhorring the cause itself. Boyle sees and presents in all its human complexity what at first glance seems a black-and-white political issue. Boyle, however, was no Pollyanna. As the social conflict that motivates this story snowballed into world war and mass genocide, she saw with a cold, realistic eye how little survived of the goodwill among human beings she had hoped for. In many of her stories written in the 1940's and to the present day, she has examined unflinchingly and sometimes bitterly the individual tragedies played out in the shadow of the global one.

"WINTER NIGHT"

In "Winter Night," published in 1946, she draws a delicate portrait of a little girl named Felicia and a woman sent by a "sitting parent" agency to spend the evening with her in a New York apartment. The woman, in her strange accent, tells Felicia that today is an anniversary, that three years ago that night she had begun to care for another little girl who also studied ballet and whose mother, like Felicia's, had had to go away. The difference was that the other girl's mother had been sent away on a train car in which there were no seats, and she never came back, but she was able to write a short letter on a smuggled scrap of paper and slip it through the cracks on the floor of the moving train in the hope that some kind stranger would send it to its destination. The woman can only comfort herself with the thought that "They must be quietly asleep somewhere, and not crying all night because they are hungry and because they are cold."

"There is a time of apprehension which begins with the beginning of darkness, and to which only the speech of love can lend security," the story begins, as Boyle describes the dying light of a January afternoon in New York City. Felicia and the "sitting parent," both left alone, have found that security in each other. When, after midnight, Felicia's mother tiptoes in the front door, slipping the three blue foxskins from her shoulder and dropping the velvet bag on a chair, she hears only the sound of breathing in the dark living room, and no one speaks to her in greeting as she crosses to the bedroom: "And then, as startling as a slap across her delicately tinted face, she saw the woman lying sleeping on the divan, and Felicia, in her school dress still, asleep within the woman's arms." The story is not baldly didactic, but Boyle *is* moralizing. By juxtaposing the cases of the two little girls left alone by their mothers and cared for by a stranger, she shows that the failure of love is a tragic loss on an individual as well as on a global scale. Again, personal concerns merge with political and social ones, and readers find the failure of love on any level to be the fundamental tragedy of life.

Some of the stories Boyle has written about the war and its aftermath are less subtle, "artistic" explorations of individual struggles as they are frankly moralistic adventure stories written for commercial magazines, and they were more popular with the public than with the critics. Yet one of her finest works was also a product of her war experiences. *The Smoking Mountain: Stories of Postwar Germany* (1951) consists of eleven stories, several originally published by *The New Yorker*, which had employed Boyle as a correspondent for the express purpose of sending "fiction out of Germany." It is prefaced by seventy-seven-page nonfiction account of a de-Nazification trial Boyle witnessed in Frankfurt in 1948, which reveals her immense skill as a reporter as well. The book presents a painful vision. Any hope that a renewed understanding among peoples might result from the catastrophic "lesson" of the war is dashed, for the point of many of the stories and certainly of the introduction is how little difference the war has made in the fundamental attitudes of the defeated but silently defiant Germans who can still say of 1943 and 1944— "the years when the gas chambers burned the brightest. . . .Those were the good years for everyone."

In 1929, Boyle, with writers Hart Crane, Vail, and others, signed Eugene Jolas's manifesto, "Revolution of the Word," condemning literary pretentiousness and outdated literary conventions. The goal, then, was to make literature at once fresh and experimental and at the same time accessible to the reader. Boyle would remain politically involved and productive as a writer, publishing collections of poetry, short stories, and essays in the 1980's. She would continue in her work to test the individual against events of historical significance, such as the threat of Nazism or the war in Vietnam. Although critics have accused her later works of selling out to popular taste, and her style of losing its innovative edge, Boyle remained steadfast in defining her artistic purpose as a moral responsibility to defend the integrity of the individual and human rights. To do so, Boyle argued, she must be accessible to the public.

OTHER MAJOR WORKS

LONG FICTION: *Plagued by the Nightingale*, 1931; *Year Before Last*, 1932; *Gentlemen, I Address You Privately*, 1933; *My Next Bride*, 1934; *Death of a Man*, 1936; *Monday Night*, 1938; *Primer for Combat*, 1942; *Avalanche*, 1944; *A Frenchman Must Die*, 1946; *1939*, 1948; *His Human Majesty*, 1949; *The Seagull on the Step*, 1955; *Generation Without Farewell*, 1960; *The Underground Woman*, 1975.

POETRY: *A Glad Day*, 1938; *American Citizen Naturalized in Leadville, Colorado*, 1944; *Collected Poems*, 1962; *Testament for My Students and Other Poems*, 1970; *This Is Not a Letter and Other Poems*, 1985; *Collected Poems of Kay Boyle*, 1991.

NONFICTION: *Breaking the Silence: Why a Mother Tells Her Son About the Nazi Era*, 1962; *The Autobiography of Emanuel Carnevali*, 1967; *Being Geniuses Together, 1920-1930*, 1968 (with Robert McAlmon); *The Long Walk at San Francisco State and Other Essays*, 1970; *Enough of Dying! An Anthology of Peace Writings*, 1972; *Words That Must Somehow Be Said: The Selected Essays of Kay Boyle, 1927-1984*, 1985.

CHILDREN'S LITERATURE: *The Youngest Camel*, 1939, 1959; *Pinky, the Cat Who Liked to Sleep*, 1966; *Pinky in Persia*, 1968.

EDITED TEXT: *365 Days*, 1936 (with others).

BIBLIOGRAPHY

Bell, Elizabeth S. *Kay Boyle: A Study of the Short Fiction.* New York: Twayne, 1992. An excellent introduction to Boyle's short stories. Includes bibliographical references and an index.

Boyle, Kay. "Kay Boyle: An Eightieth Birthday Interview." Interview by David R. Mesher. *The Malahat Review* 65 (July, 1983): 82-95. As the title suggests, this interview with Boyle was conducted on the occasion of her eightieth birthday. In it, she discusses her life and her work.

Carpenter, Richard C. "Kay Boyle." *English Journal* 42 (November, 1953): 425-430. This volume provides a helpful and general look at Boyle's early novels and short fiction.

_____. "Kay Boyle: The Figure in the Carpet." *Critique: Studies in Modern Fiction* 7 (Winter, 1964-1965): 65-78. Carpenter rejects the common complaint that Boyle is a mere "stylist," discussing her thematic depth, particularly in "The Bridegroom's Body" and "The Crazy Hunter."

Elkins, Marilyn, ed. *Critical Essays on Kay Boyle.* New York: G. K. Hall, 1997. A collection of reviews and critical essays on Boyle's work by various critics, reviewers, and commentators.

Hollenberg, Donna. "Abortion, Identity Formation, and the Expatriate Woman Writer: H.D. and Kay Boyle in the Twenties." *Twentieth Century Literature* 40 (Winter, 1994): 499-517. Discusses the theme of self-loss through the roles of marriage and motherhood in Boyle's early works. Shows how expatriation allowed some psychic space to explore the effect of gender roles on her aspirations. Discusses the effect of inadequate maternal role models upon her identity as an artist.

Mellen, Joan. *Kay Boyle: Author of Herself.* New York: Farrar, Straus and Giroux, 1994. Drawing on personal conversations with Boyle and her family, Mellen discusses the autobiographical nature of Boyle's writing and lays bare much of Boyle's own mythologizing of her life in her autobiographical writing.

Moore, Harry T. "Kay Boyle's Fiction." In *The Age of the Modern and Other Literary Essays.* Carbondale: Southern Illinois University Press, 1971. Moore attributes Boyle's lack of success, despite her supreme talent, to timing. He examines *Generation Without Farewell*, arguing that it far surpasses other contemporary novels about postwar Germany.

Porter, Katherine Anne. "Kay Boyle: Example to the Young." In *The Critic as Artist: Essays on Books, 1920-1970*, edited by Gilbert A. Harrison. New York: Liveright, 1972. This essay examines Boyle as she fits in the literary movement of her time. Focuses on some of her stories, as well as on the novel *Plagued by the Nightingale*.

Spanier, Sandra Whipple. *Kay Boyle: Artist and Activist.* Carbondale: Southern Illinois University Press, 1986. Heavily annotated, thorough, and the first critical biography and major work on Boyle. Supplemented by select but extensive primary and secondary bibliographies. Illustrated.

Twentieth-Century Literature 34 (Fall, 1988). A special issue on Kay Boyle, with personal reminiscences by Malcolm Cowley, Jessica Mitford, Howard Nemerov, and Studs Terkel, among others. Also contains several critical essays on Boyle's work.

Sandra Whipple Spanier, updated by Lou Thompson

T. CORAGHESSAN BOYLE
Thomas John Boyle

Born: Peekskill, New York; 1948

PRINCIPAL SHORT FICTION

Descent of Man, 1979

Greasy Lake and Other Stories, 1985

If the River Was Whiskey, 1989

The Collected Stories of T. Coraghessan Boyle, 1993

Without a Hero, 1994

T. C. Boyle Stories: The Collected Stories of T. Coraghessan Boyle, 1998

OTHER LITERARY FORMS

T. Coraghessan Boyle's novels, which explore many of the same subjects and themes as his short fiction, have received popular attention and critical praise. *The Road to Wellville* (1993) was made into a motion picture in 1994.

ACHIEVEMENTS

T. Coraghessan Boyle received a National Endowment for the Arts Fellowship in 1977. *Descent of Man*, his first collection of stories, won the St. Lawrence Award for Short Fiction. His novel *Water Music* (1981) received the Aga Khan Award, and another novel, *World's End* (1987), was awarded the PEN/Faulkner Award for Fiction.

BIOGRAPHY

Born into a lower-middle-class family in Peekskill, New York, in 1948, Thomas John Boyle was a rebellious youth who performed in a rock-and-roll band, committed acts of vandalism, and drank heavily. He did not get along with his father, a school-bus driver whose alcoholism killed him at fifty-four, in 1972. Boyle's mother, a secretary, was also an alcoholic and died of liver failure. Assuming the name T. Coraghessan Boyle at the State University of New York at Potsdam, he studied saxophone and clarinet until he realized that he lacked the necessary discipline for music. He then drifted into literature. After college, to avoid military service during the Vietnam War, he taught English for two years at his alma mater, Lakeland High School, in Shrub Oak, New York, while indulging in heroin on weekends.

In 1972, Boyle entered the creative writing program at the University of Iowa, where he studied under Vance Bourjaily, John Cheever, and John Irving, earning a Ph.D. in 1977, with a short-story collection, later published as *Descent of Man*, serving as his dissertation. Such academic achievement is ironic for someone placed in a class for slow learners in the second grade. Boyle became a teacher at the University of Southern California, where he founded an undergraduate creative writing program, and settled in Woodland Hills with his wife, Karen Kvashay, and their children, Kerrie, Milo, and Spencer. One of the most public and flamboyant writers of his time, Boyle delighted in performing public and recorded readings.

ANALYSIS

During a time when the majority of serious American writers have been concerned with the minutiae of everyday life, T. Coraghessan Boyle has stood out by exploring a wide range of subjects, locales, periods, and strata of society. Distinctive as a stylist, storyteller, and satirist, Boyle enthusiastically encompasses numerous literary conventions into his fiction, turning them into something fresh and often humorous. He examines both the detritus and the silliness of the world, exulting in its absurdities.

His short fiction is most notable for its extraordinary range of subjects, which include a chimpanzee who has translated Charles Darwin, Friedrich Wilhelm Nietzsche, and Noam Chomsky into Yerkish; the final performance of blues musician Robert Johnson; the importation of starlings into the United States; an attempt to improve the public image of the Ayatollah Ruhollah Khomeini; and a statue of the Virgin Mary that re-creates a man's sins for all the world to see. Boyle's stories delve into such topics as violence, sexuality, paranoia, guilt, and the clichés of popular culture. While some of his stories are realistic, most exaggerate the world's absurdities for comic effect. His tone is predominantly satirical but rarely angry.

"BLOODFALL"

"Bloodfall" depicts the effects of an apparently endless rainfall of blood on seven young adults who live together. Although they smoke marijuana, burn incense, and listen to thunderously loud rock and roll, they are not hippies but well-to-do materialists who use electric toothbrushes and drive BMWs. They sleep together in a bed that they appropriately think of as "the nest," since they have attempted to withdraw from the often disconcerting realities of the outside world, seeking comfortable refuge in their home.

The inexplicable rain of blood cuts them off completely from the rest of the world by knocking out their telephone and television. They cannot drive for food since they cannot see through a blood-smeared windshield. Their response to this terrifying situation is to ignore it: "Isabelle said it would be better if we all went to bed. She expressed a hope that after a long nap things would somehow come to their senses." The blood begins to stain everything about their antiseptic existence: their white clothing when they venture outside, their white carpet when the flood begins to seep under their door. They are confident that the bloodfall will stop, since logic demands that it will, and it does. Since such an event is illogical to begin with, however, "Bloodfall" ends with the start of a new downpour, this time consisting of "heavy, feculent, and wet" fecal matter.

Boyle often satirizes modern human beings' feeble efforts to protect themselves from outside forces, as in "Peace of Mind," an attack on home security systems, but the image of the blood invading the white world of these smug materialists is his strongest statement on this theme. Boyle's vividly contrasting images of red and white and his telling accumulation of the trite details of the lives of contemporary American consumers contribute to the story's effectiveness. As throughout his fiction, Boyle borrows from the conventions of popular culture, in this case horror fiction and films, to create a compelling vision of modern alienation.

T. Coraghessan Boyle in 1990 (AP/Wide World Photos)

"THE BIG GARAGE"

"The Big Garage" is an equally frightening but more comic horror story. When the Audi belonging to B. breaks down, a tow truck mysteriously appears and takes it to Tegeler's Big Garage, an enormous service center in the middle of nowhere. Because it is late at night and no mechanics are available, B. is forced to sleep on a cot in a storage closet where other customers are also waiting for their vehicles to be repaired. B. discovers that he must go through a complicated maze to the appointment office and fill out a seven-page application for an appointment to have his car serviced. Fed up with this nonsense, B. confronts a team of German mechanics who taunt him and throw him down a chute into the car wash, where he is washed and waxed. After trying and failing to escape by hitchhiking, B. gives in and goes across the street to Tegeler's Big Lot, where the owner of the Big Garage sells his broken customers Tegelers, his own inferior make.

B. is caught up in a bureaucratic nightmare out of a Franz Kafka novel, such as *Der Prozess* (1925; *The Trial*, 1937). Boyle takes a familiar situation and exaggerates it to show how everyday life can become an impersonal, nerve-racking, humiliating experience. He makes a serious statement about alienation and the often vicious insensitivity of a consumer culture while also having fun through slapstick and literary parody.

"THE OVERCOAT II"

Boyle combines homage to a favorite work of literature with political satire in "The Overcoat II," an updating of Nikolai Gogol's "Shinel" (1839; in *The Overcoat and Other Stories*, 1923) to the Moscow of the 1980's. Akaky Akakievich Bashmachkin, a devoted clerk in the Soviet bureaucracy, has no interests outside his work, no time for anything but waiting in endless queues for scarce goods. Yet the only blemish on his party-line life is the cheap, tattered overcoat he has bought because a central department store clerk, attacking the quality of Soviet-made products, tried to sell him a black-market overcoat.

Akaky is ridiculed by his unpatriotic coworkers because he appears to use the coat to give himself the aura of a Marxist saint. Old Studniuk, one of the fourteen residents who share his apartment, tells Akaky he must use the black market to get everything he can: "There ain't no comrade commissioner going to come round and give it to you." Akaky sells his television set and exhausts his savings to spend three months' salary on a camel's hair overcoat with a fox collar. His fellow clerks are impressed, and one, Mishkin, invites Akaky to his home. After leaving Mishkin's house, where he had one of the best times of his life, he is beaten and his coat stolen. The police recover the coat but keep it and fine Akaky for receiving stolen goods. Feeling betrayed by all he has believed in, Akaky develops pneumonia, dies, and is soon forgotten. The police inspector who has interrogated him wears the coat proudly.

Like "Ike and Nina," in which President Dwight David Eisenhower and Premier Nikita S. Khrushchev's wife have an affair in 1959, "The Overcoat II" satirizes Soviet life. Gogol's Akaky dies from the despair of losing his beloved coat, Boyle's from losing his belief in the Soviet system, something even more

irreplaceable. Gogol ends his story with Akaky's ghost seeking revenge against those who have wronged him, Boyle's with an enemy profiting from the clerk's naïve belief in a system that exploits him. The happiness that Akaky experiences at Mishkin's party must be short-lived, for in Boyle's paranoid universe, some unexpected, uncontrollable force is out to get the individual. Only those as cynical as the society in which they live can survive.

"TWO SHIPS"

The uncontrollable force confronting the protagonist of "Two Ships" is his childhood best friend. The teenage Jack and Casper are rebels together, assaulting symbols of wealth and religion. They run away from home, but Jack gives up two weeks before Casper. During this experience, Jack recognizes the streak of madness in his friend and is both repelled by and attracted to it: "He was serious, he was committed, his was the rapture of saints and martyrs, both feet over the line." Casper's passion leads him to convert fervently to Marxism. When he is drafted during the Vietnam War, he deserts the army.

Jack does not see Casper for several years after he goes into the army, but he receives several packages containing lengthy, incoherent poems expressing Casper's political views. Jack then goes to law school, marries, and settles down. After he receives a telephone call from Casper asking him to stick up for his friend, Jack tells an agent at the Federal Bureau of Investigation (FBI) that Casper is "seriously impaired." Following eleven months in a mental institution, Casper returns to his hometown, and Jack is frightened. Casper finally visits him but terrifies Jack even further by saying little. Jack begins packing.

More than guilt about betraying his friend to the FBI, Jack experiences shame over how their lives have diverged: "I'd become what we'd reacted against together, what he'd devoted his mad, misguided life to subverting." Jack is disturbed by Casper's reminding him how he has failed himself through his willingness to play society's game by its rules, his becoming a corporate attorney who defends polluters, his lack of passion for and commitment to anything but his family, and his failure to accept any responsibility for the state of the world. "Two Ships" effectively blends such major Boyle subjects as paranoia, friendship, and betrayal. His characters are constantly betraying each other and themselves.

"THE HECTOR QUESADILLA STORY"

While generally satirical and often condemnatory, Boyle's fiction is not always cynical and unforgiving. "The Hector Quesadilla Story," one of the best baseball stories ever written, demonstrates the possibility of getting a chance to overcome failure. The title character plays for the Los Angeles Dodgers but only pinch-hits, because he is too old, too fat, and too slow to perform well in the field. (Boyle has loosely based this character on Manny Mota, the legendary pinch hitter for the Dodgers in the 1970's.) A grandfather whose official baseball age is several years short of actuality, Hector lives only to eat the spicy Mexican food that he passionately loves and to play the game that he loves even more. He keeps telling his wife he will play one more season but secretly has no intention of quitting. Meanwhile, he waits patiently at the end of the bench to prove himself again, to come alive in the only way he knows how.

Hector is convinced that something special will happen during a game with the Atlanta Braves, whom the Dodgers are battling for first place, because it falls on his birthday. With the score tied in the ninth inning, he is denied his "moment of catharsis," his chance to win the game. As the contest drags on into extra innings, the manager refuses to let him bat because the Dodgers have run out of players and Hector would have to play in the field if the score remained tied. With his team trailing by one run in the bottom of the thirty-first inning in the longest game in major league history, Hector finally gets his chance but is foolishly thrown out trying to stretch a double into a triple. When the next batter hits a home run, Hector is forced to pitch for the first time because no one else is available. All seems lost when the Braves score four runs off him in the next inning, but Hector redeems himself with a bases-loaded home run to tie the score once again. The game then "goes on forever."

"The Hector Quesadilla Story" works on two levels. On one, it is about the most magical quality of baseball: "How can he get old?" Hector asks himself.

"The grass is always green, the lights always shining, no clocks or periods or halves or quarters, no punch-in and punch-out: this is the game that never ends." Without the restraints of time seen in such games as football and basketball, a baseball game could theoretically last forever. On the second level, the story deals with how the individual feels the limitations that time imposes upon him and how he fights against them. Hector tries to ignore what his body, his family, and common sense tell him. Because a baseball game can go on forever, so can he. He appropriates the magic of the game for himself: "it's a game of infinite surprises." Boyle makes baseball a metaphor for life itself.

"SORRY FUGU"

The tone of most of Boyle's stories is primarily comic, and in one of the best, "Sorry Fugu," he also displays the gentler side of his satire. Albert D'Angelo, owner and chef of D'Angelo's, wants his new restaurant to be both good and successful. He wants it to meet the challenge of Willa Frank, the restaurant critic who always gives negative reviews, even to those places that Albert reveres. He fears and longs for the day when she and her companion, known only as "the Palate," will enter his establishment. Luckily, Albert knows when the great moment has arrived, since one of his employees knows Willa and her boyfriend, Jock McNamee. Unfortunately, she has come on one of those nights when all goes wrong, and Albert knows he has failed on the first of her three visits. They arrive the second time with an older couple. Albert is prepared this time, only to see each of them pass the dishes to Jock, who is not interested in any of them.

Albert understands what to do on the third visit after his employee tells him that what Jock really likes is the "shanty Irish" food his mother used to make. Albert then ignores what the couple orders and serves the Palate peas, boiled potatoes, a slab of cheap, overcooked meat, and catsup. When the outraged Willa charges into the kitchen, Albert seduces her with squid rings in aioli sauce, lobster tortellini, *taglierini alla pizzaiola*, Russian *coulibiac* of salmon, and fugu, a Japanese blowfish. Willa confesses that she relies on Jock's crude judgment, since at least he is consistent in disliking everything, and that she is afraid to risk a positive review.

While other American writers of Boyle's generation fill their fiction with brand names and trendy antiques as a means of delineating their characters, Boyle uses food to explore their social status and individuality. What is most important about "Sorry Fugu," however, is its depiction of the roles of the critic and the artist. Boyle satirizes the superficiality of many critics through Willa's uncertainty about her tastes and dishonesty in relying on Jock's lack of taste. Albert is an artist in the care he takes in creating his dishes: "Albert put his soul into each dish, arranged and garnished the plates with all the patient care and shimmering inspiration of a Toulouse-Lautrec bent over a canvas." Boyle takes the same care as a stylist, as when Albert contemplates Willa's name: "It was a bony name, scant and lean, stripped of sensuality, the antithesis of the round, full-bodied Leonora. It spoke of a knotty Puritan toughness, a denying of the flesh, no compromise in the face of temptation." Since Boyle has said in interviews that he wants to be both popular and critically praised, Albert appears to be a self-portrait of an artist who needs to be judged by the highest standards.

WITHOUT A HERO

Boyle continued his eclectic exploration of the absurdities of the world in his short-story collection *Without a Hero*. "Filthy with Things" tells the humorous yet oddly disturbing story of a married couple suffocating in a world of suburban materialism that has advanced so far beyond their control that they must hire an organizing specialist to kick them out of their own house and take possession of their belongings. As the narrator watches the workers sort through and catalog everything he owns, he feels "as if he doesn't exist, as if he's already become an irrelevance in the face of the terrible weight of his possessions," or, more broadly, of a late twentieth century American culture in which materiality often defines the person.

One of the most prominent of Boyle's many recurring obsessions is his interest in the influence that animals have on human behavior, and vice versa. The narrator of "Carnal Knowledge" gets involved with a group of animal-rights activists when he falls in love with Alena, a militant vegetarian whose crippled dog urinates on him at the beach. After quitting his job to take part in antifur demonstrations in Beverly Hills, the narrator is coerced into taking part in a plot to "liberate" thousands of turkeys from a poultry farm a few weeks before Thanksgiving. The raid does more harm than good, however, when large numbers of turkeys wander onto a fog-enshrouded freeway and cause a truck to jackknife. After being spurned by Alena, who travels north with another man to defend grizzly bears, the protagonist drives by the accident scene, where the road is "coated in feathers, turkey feathers" and where there is "a red pulp ground into the surface of road." He promptly returns to eating the Big Macs that he has been subconsciously craving for days. Beneath the humor of such stories lies a message to which Boyle often returns: The universe is an ambiguous, unpredictable place, and each person must find his or her own solitary way to negotiate its absurdities.

T. C. BOYLE STORIES

T. C. Boyle Stories: The Collected Stories of T. Coraghessan Boyle is a 691-page volume which includes all the tales from the author's previous short-story collections, plus four stories previously unpublished in book form and three previously unpublished anywhere, an impressive sixty-eight over a twenty-five-year period. Although reading a complete collection of an author's work often means plowing through the mediocre to get to the good (and this book is no exception), one benefit is the opportunity to see the development of the writer over time. In Boyle's case, there is a clear tendency for early stories to be driven more by premise than by character. In stories such as "Bloodfall," characterization tends to be subordinate to the idea. In subsequent stories, Boyle began demonstrating a willingness to invest more time and effort into exploring the multiple dimensions of his characters, and by the 1980's, a clear preference for dwelling on the subtleties of the human condition had emerged.

In the midst of this development, several common threads tie most, if not all, of Boyle's stories together, most notably his use of humor of all types—parody, slapstick, satire, wit, and irony—and his dedication to keen observation rendered through bold, colorful language. This latter quality, which seems to be missing from a large portion of contemporary American fiction, is a clear reflection of Boyle's belief that it is possible for fiction to possess the same vitality as rock-and-roll music.

OTHER MAJOR WORKS

LONG FICTION: *Water Music*, 1981; *Budding Prospects: A Pastoral*, 1984; *World's End*, 1987; *East Is East*, 1990; *The Road to Wellville*, 1993; *The Tortilla Curtain*, 1995; *Riven Rock*, 1998; *A Friend of the Earth*, 2000.

BIBLIOGRAPHY

Boyle, T. Coraghessan. Interview by David Stanton. *Poets & Writers* 18 (January/February, 1990): 29-34. Boyle explains his need to promote himself through readings and interviews, his strong self-confidence in his abilities, his doubts about creative-writing programs, and the positive effect that writing novels has had on his short fiction. He believes that his earlier stories call attention to themselves too much.

_____. "The Maximalist Novelist." Interview by Helen Dudar. *The Wall Street Journal*, November 5, 1990, p. A13. This interview discusses Boyle's work habits; his attitudes toward his art, teaching, and success; and his fear of running out of material.

_____. "A Punk's Past Recaptured." Interview by Anthony DeCurtis. *Rolling Stone*, January 14, 1988, 54-57. In his most revealing interview, Boyle talks about his drug use, the importance of understanding history, and the autobiographical element in his fiction. He expresses the desire to be like Kurt Vonnegut, in showing that literature can be both serious and entertaining, and like John Updike, in constantly changing his approach to fiction and improving as an artist.

_____. "Rolling Boyle." Interview by Tad Friend. *The New York Times Magazine*, December 9, 1990, 50, 64, 66, 68. Boyle portrays himself as a missionary for literature who promotes himself to ensure that he is read. He comments on the new maturity and reality in some of his fiction but admits that the absurd and bizarre are more natural for him. Boyle also expresses pessimism about the future of the human race.

Chase, Brennan. "Like, Chill!" *Los Angeles* 38 (April, 1993): 80-82. A biographical sketch, focusing on Boyle's successful literary career and celebrity status in Hollywood. Boyle maintains that he is an academic whose purpose is to write.

Friend, Tad. "Rolling Boyle." *The New York Times Magazine*, December 9, 1990, 50. Discusses Boyle's critical success but notes that the glowing reviews he has received are not enough for Boyle, who tells friends that he wants to be the most famous writer alive and the greatest writer ever.

Vaid, Krishna Baldev. "Franz Kafka Writes to T. Coraghessan Boyle." *Michigan Quarterly Review* 35 (Summer, 1996): 533-549. As if writing a letter from Franz Kafka, Vaid discusses the work of Boyle, investigates the similarity between the two writers, and argues that the reader could grow as tired of Kafka's logic as of Boyle's broad panoramas.

Walker, Michael. "Boyle's Greasy Lake and the Moral Failure of Postmodernism." *Studies in Short Fiction* 31 (Spring, 1994): 247-255. Argues that because postmodernism lacks moral standards, such exaggerations and self-absorption as can be seen in Boyle's story are but substitutes for a moral point of view. Claims that Boyle's story is a parody of the story of revelation. Compares the story to John Updike's "A&P," insisting that Boyle denies his protagonist any possibility of learning anything from his experience.

Michael Adams, updated by Douglas Long

RAY BRADBURY

Born: Waukegan, Illinois; August 22, 1920

PRINCIPAL SHORT FICTION

Dark Carnival, 1947

The Martian Chronicles, 1950

The Illustrated Man, 1951

The Golden Apples of the Sun, 1953

The October Country, 1955

A Medicine for Melancholy, 1959

Twice Twenty-two, 1959

The Machineries of Joy, 1964

Autumn People, 1965

Vintage Bradbury, 1965

Tomorrow Midnight, 1966

I Sing the Body Electric!, 1969

Long After Midnight, 1976

The Stories of Ray Bradbury, 1980

The Last Circus and The Electrocution, 1980

Dinosaur Tales, 1983

A Memory of Murder, 1984

The Toynbee Convector, 1988

Quicker than the Eye, 1996

Driving Blind, 1997

OTHER LITERARY FORMS

Although Ray Bradbury described himself as essentially a short-story writer, his contributions to a wide variety of other genres have been substantial. Indeed, he has intentionally sought to compose successfully in virtually every literary form. His best-known novels are *Fahrenheit 451* (1953), *Dandelion Wine* (1957), and *Something Wicked This Way Comes* (1962), the last being his favorite of all of his works. Among his screenplays, the most successful have been *Moby Dick* (1956), written in collaboration with filmmaker John Huston, and *Icarus Montgolfier Wright* (1961) with George C. Johnson, which was nominated for an Academy Award. Bradbury had his stage plays produced in Los Angeles and New York City, and several of them have been published, representative samples of which are *The Anthem Sprinters and Other Antics* (1963) and *The Pedestrian* (1966).

He also wrote many plays for radio and television. Some of the most important of the several volumes of poetry that he published were collected in *The Complete Poems of Ray Bradbury* (1982). He also wrote books for children and adolescents, including *Ahmed and the Oblivion Machines: A Fable* (1998); compiled anthologies of fantasy and science-fiction stories, such as *The Circus of Dr. Lao and Other Improbable Stories* (1956); and published nonfiction works dealing with his interests in creativity and the future, such as *Yestermorrow: Obvious Answers to Impossible Futures* (1991).

ACHIEVEMENTS

Despite Bradbury's once being named the United States' best-known science-fiction writer in a poll, his actual literary accomplishments are based on an oeuvre whose vast variety and deeply humanistic themes transcend science fiction as it is commonly understood. His many stories, from gothic horror to social criticism, from playful fantasies to nostalgic accounts of midwestern American life, have been anthologized in several hundred collections, in English as well as many foreign languages, and several of the stories that he published early in his career now occupy a distinguished niche in twentieth century American literature.

Some of his early tales were recognized with O. Henry Prizes in 1947 and 1948, and in 1949 he was voted Best Author by the National Fantasy Fan Federation. Bradbury's "Sun and Shadow" won the Benjamin Franklin Magazine Award as the best story of 1953-1954, and in 1954 he received a National Institute of Arts and Letters Award in Literature. His novel *Fahrenheit 451* won a gold medal from the Commonwealth Club of California, and his book *Switch on the Night* (1955) was honored with a Boy's Club of America Junior Book Award in 1956. He received the Mrs. Ann Radcliffe Award of the Count Dracula Society in 1965 and 1971, the Writers' Guild of America West Valentine Davies Award in 1974, and the World Fantasy Award for Life Achievement in 1977. Whittier College gave him an honorary doctor of literature degree in 1979. PEN, an international writers' organization of poets, playwrights, editors, essayists, and novelists, gave Bradbury its Body of Work Award in 1985. In 1988 Bradbury won the Nebula Award, and in 1995 he was named Los Angeles Citizen of the Year.

BIOGRAPHY

Ray Douglas Bradbury often makes use of his own life in his writings, and he insisted that he had total recall of the myriad experiences of his life through his photographic—some would say eidetic—memory: He stated that he always had vivid recollections of the day of his birth, August 22, 1920, in Waukegan, Illinois. Leonard Spaulding Bradbury, his father, was a lineman with the Bureau of Power and Light (his distant ancestor Mary Bradbury was among those tried for witchcraft in Salem, Massachusetts); Esther Marie (née Moberg) Bradbury, his mother, had emigrated from Sweden to the United States when she was very young. A child with an exceptionally lively imagination, Ray Bradbury amused himself with his fantasies but experienced anguish from his nightmares. His mother took him to his first film, *The Hunchback of Notre Dame* (1923), when he was three years old, and he was both frightened and entranced by Lon Chaney's performance. This experience originated his lifelong love affair with motion pictures, and he wrote that he could remember the scenes and plots of all the films that he ever attended.

As he grew up, Bradbury passed through a series of passions that included circuses, dinosaurs, and Mars (the latter via the writings of Edgar Rice Burroughs). Neva Bradbury, an aunt, assisted his maturation as a person and writer by introducing him to the joys of fairy tales, L. Frank Baum's *Oz* books, live theater, and the stories of Edgar Allan Poe. In Bradbury's own view, the most important event in his childhood occurred in 1932 when a carnival came to town. He attended the performance of a magician, Mr. Electrico, whose spellbinding act involved electrifying himself to such an extent that sparks jumped between his teeth and every white hair on his head stood erect. Bradbury and the magician became

Ray Bradbury (Thomas Victor)

friends, and their walks and talks along the Lake Michigan shore behind the carnival so energized his imagination that, a few weeks after this encounter, he began to compose stories for several hours a day. One of his first efforts was a sequel to a Martian novel of Burroughs.

During the Depression, Bradbury's father had difficulty finding work, and in 1932 the family moved to Arizona, where they had previously spent some time in the mid-1920's. Still in search of steady work, his father moved the family to Los Angeles, which was where Ray Bradbury attended high school and which became his permanent home. His formal education ended with his graduation from Los Angeles High School, but his education as a writer continued through his extensive reading and his participation in theater groups (one of which was sponsored by the actress Laraine Day). To support his writing, he worked as a newsboy in downtown Los Angeles for several years.

In World War II, Bradbury's poor eyesight prevented him from serving in the army, but this disappointment gave him the freedom to pursue his career as a writer, and his stories began to be published in such pulp magazines as *Weird Tales* and Hugo Gernsback's *Amazing Stories*. The high quality of Bradbury's stories was quickly recognized, and he was able to get his new stories published in such mass-circulation magazines as *Collier's, The Saturday Evening Post, Harper's Magazine*, and *Mademoiselle*. Because of his success as a writer, he had the financial security to marry Marguerite Susan McClure in 1947 (they had met when she, a book clerk, had waited on him). The marriage produced four daughters.

By the early 1950's, Bradbury, now recognized as an accomplished science-fiction and fantasy writer, began his involvement with Hollywood through an original screenplay that would eventually be released as *It Came from Outer Space* (1952). In the mid-1950's, he traveled to Ireland in connection with a screenplay of *Moby Dick* that he wrote with John Huston (he later drew on his experiences with the Irish for several stories and plays that took his work in a new direction). Upon his return to the United States, Bradbury composed a large number of television scripts for such shows as *Alfred Hitchcock Presents, Suspense*, and *The Twilight Zone*.

During the late 1950's and early 1960's, Bradbury moved away from science fiction, and his stories and novels increasingly focused on humanistic themes and his midwestern childhood. In the late 1960's and throughout the 1970's and 1980's, Bradbury's output of short and long fiction decreased, and his ideas found outlets in such literary forms as poems, plays, and essays. He also participated in a number of projects, such as "A Journey Through United States History," the exhibit that occupied the upper floor of the United States Pavilion for the New York World's Fair in 1964. Because of this display's success, the Walt Disney organization hired him to help develop the exhibit Spaceship Earth for the Epcot Center at Disney World in Florida. He continued to diversify his activities during the 1980's by collaborating on projects to turn his novel *Fahrenheit 451* into an opera and his novel *Dandelion Wine* into a musical. In the late 1980's and early 1990's, he returned to some of the subjects and themes that had earlier established his reputation with the publication of short-story collections *The Toynbee Convector, Quicker than the Eye*, and *Driving Blind*, and the novels *A Graveyard for Lunatics: Another Tale of Two Cities* (1990) and *Green Shadows, White Whale* (1992).

ANALYSIS

Ray Bradbury once said that he had not so much thought his way through life as he had done things and discovered what those things meant and who he was after the doing. This metamorphosis of experience under the aegis of memory also characterizes many of his stories, which are often transmogrifications of his personal experiences. He therefore used his stories as ways of hiding and finding himself, a self whose constant changes interested, amused, and sometimes frightened him. He believed that human beings are composed of time, and in many of his science-fiction stories, a frequent theme is the dialectic between the past and the future. For example, in several of his Martian stories, the invaders of the Red Planet have to come to terms with their transformation into Martians, since survival in an alien world necessitates the invader's union with the invaded. Aggression and submission might represent the initial dialectic, but survival or death becomes the most determinative.

Even in stories where Bradbury's characters and settings seem ordinary, this theme of metamorphosis is nevertheless present, because these stories often show ordinary people being transformed by extraordinary, sometimes bizarre situations. Sometimes Bradbury's purpose is to point out the enlightening power of the abnormal; sometimes he wants to reveal the limitations of the everyday and ordinary. His best works are often wrenching indictments of the dangers of unrestrained scientific and technical progress, though his work also encourages the hope that humanity will deal creatively with the new worlds it seems driven to make. His characters are changed by their experiences, particularly when they encounter great evil beneath the surface of seemingly normal life, but in other stories Bradbury gives the reader a window through which to see the positive meaning of life (these stories, usually sentimental, are life-affirming, permitting readers to believe that human dreams can be fulfilled). By helping readers to imagine the unimaginable, he helps them to think about the unthinkable. He speaks of his tales as "idea fiction," and he prefers to call himself a magical realist. He casts magic spells through his poetic words and highly imaginative visions, and because of this aura of enchantment, some critics have seen his chief subject as childhood or the child hidden in the adult unconscious.

A danger exists, however, in treating Bradbury as a writer of fantasy suitable only for adolescents. This may be true for some of his works, but many of his stories exhibit emotional depths and logical complexities that call for a sophisticated dialectic between the adult and his buried childhood. The difference between fantasy and reality is not strongly developed in the child, whose experience of the world is minimal. Bradbury often plays with this tension between fantasy and reality in dealing with his principal themes—the power of the past, the freedom of the present, and the temptations and traps of the future. In the world of Bradbury's stories, fantasy becomes essential for a person existing in an increasingly technological era or with experiences that, like an iceberg, are nine-tenths buried below the surface. In these cases, the abilities to fantasize various alternatives or futures, and to choose the best among them, become necessary for survival.

Because of Bradbury's woefully inadequate knowledge of science and the lack of verisimilitude in the technological gadgetry of his science-fiction stories, many aficionados of the genre do not consider him a genuine science-fiction writer. He agrees. His science-fiction settings are backgrounds for characters with social, religious, and moral dilemmas. Like fellow science-fiction writer Isaac Asimov, Bradbury believes that science fiction's value lies in helping human beings to visualize and solve future problems before they actually occur, but unlike Asimov, he has a deep suspicion of the machine and a great faith in the human heart's capacity to perceive, do good, and

create beauty. Because of this attitude, many critics view Bradbury as essentially a romantic. Since F. L. Lucas once counted 11,396 definitions of "romanticism," however, perhaps Bradbury's brand of romanticism should be more fully articulated. He has expressed an attraction for spontaneity of thought and action, and he actively cultivates his own unconscious. He believes deeply in the power of the imagination, and he accepts Blaise Pascal's sentiment that the heart has reasons about which the reason knows nothing.

In making an assessment of Bradbury's contribution to modern American literature, one must come to terms with the role he played in popularizing science fiction and making it critically respectable. Bradbury himself once stated that, for him, science fiction is "the most important literature in the history of the world," since it tells the story of "civilization birthing itself." He has also said that he considers himself not a science-fiction writer but an "idea writer," someone who loves ideas and enjoys playing with them. Many of his science-fiction critics would concur in this characterization, since they have had problems categorizing this man who knows so little about science as a traditional science-fiction writer. When asked whether the Mariner mission's revelations about the inhospitability of Mars to humankind had invalidated his stories about the planet, Bradbury responded that these discoveries in no way affected them, because he had been composing poetic myths, not scientific forecasts.

In addition to their lack of scientific verisimilitude, his stories have other weaknesses. Few of his characters are memorable, and most are simply vehicles for his ideas. He has said frankly that he devises characters to personify his ideas and that all of his characters—youths, astronauts, and grotesques—are, in some way, variations on himself. Other critics have noticed failures in Bradbury's imaginative powers, particularly in his later stories. The settings and images that seemed fresh when first used in the early stories became stale as they continued to be used in the later ones. Disch complained that Bradbury's sentimental attachments to his past themes "have made him nearly oblivious to new data from any source."

Despite these criticisms, Bradbury's stories possess great strengths. If his characters are made negligible by the burden of the ideas that they are forced to carry, these same ideas can open readers to his enchanting sense of wonder. These readers can be inspired by his enthusiasm for new experiences and new worlds. They may also be uplifted by the underlying optimism present even in his most pessimistic work and come to share his belief that human beings will overcome materialism, avarice, and obsession with power to achieve the expansion of what is best in the human spirit that has been his principal theme.

DARK CARNIVAL

Many of these characteristics, along with Bradbury's penchant for the grotesque and macabre, can be seen in his first collection of stories, *Dark Carnival*. August Derleth, a Wisconsin writer who had established Arkham House to publish stories of fantasy and horror for a limited audience, had read Bradbury's stories in the pulp magazine *Weird Tales*, recognized their quality, and suggested that Bradbury collect them in a book. *Dark Carnival* was very successful with its specialized market, and its three thousand copies were quickly sold and soon become collectors' items. The book's title was aptly chosen, since the stories often deal with the dark and strange. Several stories make use, although in highly altered forms, of emotions and events in Bradbury's own life. For example, "The Small Assassin" depicts an infant, terrified at finding himself in a hostile world, taking revenge on his parents. Bradbury uses this metamorphosis of a supposedly innocent newborn into an assassin to explore some of the feelings he had as a very young child.

Death is a motif that appears often in these tales, but unlike Poe, whom he admired, Bradbury uses the morbid not for its macabre fascination, as Poe did, but to shift readers onto a different level from which they can see reality in a new and enlightening way. In most of these tales, more happens in the imaginations of Bradbury's characters than happens in their lives. He has the ability to reach down into the labyrinthine unconscious of his characters and pull out odd desires, strange dreams, and horrendous fears. For example, in "The Next in Line," a story that grew out of

his own experience on a trip to Guanajuato, northwest of Mexico City, a young American wife is simultaneously frightened and fascinated by the rows of propped-up mummified bodies in a Guanajuato catacomb. After her traumatic ordeal, she finds herself increasingly immobilized by her alienation from the death-haunted Mexican society and by her fear that her own body is a potential mummy. Another story, "Skeleton," has a similar theme. A man is obsessed by the horrible bones that he carries within him, but when a strange creature crawls down his throat and consumes the bones that were the source of his obsession, he is transformed into a human jellyfish. These and other fantasies and horrors serve as exorcisms through which the devils of one's unconscious are expelled. The best of these stories leave the reader cleansed and transformed, with an expanded consciousness and control of the fears that can make people prisoners of their own hidden emotions.

THE MARTIAN CHRONICLES

Some critics see the twenty-six stories collected in *The Martian Chronicles* as the beginning of the most prolific and productive phase of Bradbury's career. Like *Dark Carnival*, this collection resulted from the suggestion of an editor, but in this case Bradbury added passages to link together his stories about Mars. These bridge passages help to interrelate the stories but they do not make them into a unified novel. This places *The Martian Chronicles* into a peculiar literary category—less than a novel but more than a collection of short stories. Despite difficulties in categorizing this book, it is commonly recognized as Bradbury's most outstanding work. When it was first published, it was widely reviewed and read by people who did not ordinarily read science fiction. The poet Christopher Isherwood, for example, praised the book for its poetic language and its penetrating analysis of human beings forced to function on the frontier of an alien world. Within twenty years of its publication, *The Martian Chronicles* sold more than three million copies and was translated into more than thirty languages.

The Martian Chronicles is not totally unrelated to *Dark Carnival*, since Bradbury's Mars is a fantasy world, a creation not of a highly trained scientific imagination but of a mythmaker and an explorer of the unconscious. Within the time frame of 1999 to 2026, Bradbury orders his stories to give the reader a sense of the coherent evolution of the settling of Mars by Earthlings. The early stories deal with the difficulties the emigrants from Earth have in establishing successful colonies on Mars. The fifteen stories of the middle section explore the rise and fall of these colonies. The stories in the final section are concerned with the possible renovation of the human race on Mars after an annihilative nuclear war on Earth.

In several of the stories in *The Martian Chronicles*, Bradbury is once again fascinated by the subject of death. Earthlings who make the mistake of trying to duplicate Earth's culture on Mars meet difficulties and death. This theme is particularly clear in "The Third Expedition," a story that was originally titled "Mars Is Heaven" and that deeply impressed the critic and writer Jorge Luis Borges. In "The Third Expedition," Captain John Black and his crew constitute a third attempt by Earthlings to create a successful settlement on Mars, this time in a town that bears a striking resemblance to traditional midwestern American towns of the 1920's. It turns out that the Martians have deceived the Earthlings by using telepathic powers to manufacture this counterfeit town in their receptive imaginations. Captain Black and his crew have such a deep desire to believe in what they think they see that they delude themselves into seeing what the Martians want them to see. This mass hypnosis produced by the Martians capitalizes on the crew's self-delusion and on its members' need to re-create their past. When each Earthling is securely locked within what he believes is his home, he is murdered by the Martians. Trapped by their past and unable to resist, they are destroyed. Illusion and reality, time and identity, change and stability are the themes that intertwine in Bradbury's treatment of this story (one can understand why Borges liked it so much, since his own work dwells on the theme of the Other as an inextricable element in one's own identity).

THE ILLUSTRATED MAN

Soon after *The Martian Chronicles* appeared, Bradbury published another book of interlinked stories, *The Illustrated Man*. Most of its eighteen stories

had been published in various magazines between 1947 and 1951, but some had been written specifically for this book. The framing device, which is neither as consistent nor as unifying as the bridge passages in *The Martian Chronicles*, derives from tattoos that completely cover the skin of a running character. The tattoos, however, do not grow out of the personality of this character, as would be expected for a real tattooed man whose likes and dislikes would be represented in the permanent images he chooses to decorate his body. Instead, each tattoo embodies a Bradburian idea that comes alive in a particular story. The otherwise unrelated stories fall into several categories—tales of robots and space travel as well as stories of Mexicans and Martians. Four of the stories are set on Bradbury's Mars, and two of these are closely related to *The Martian Chronicles*. Some of the stories have themes related to those initially developed in *Dark Carnival*. For example, like "The Small Assassin," "The Veldt" concerns the revenge of children against their parents, this time in a futuristic setting. The children, who are obsessed with a room-filling television device that can depict scenes with three-dimensional realism, choose to watch an African veldt inhabited by lions gorging themselves on carcasses. The parents, who try to get their children to control their television addiction, end up as food for the lions. In this story, Bradbury makes use of a favorite theme—the blurred distinction between illusion and reality. Other stories in *The Illustrated Man* are animated by such social concerns as racism and with ethical and religious dilemmas derived from modern science and technology. For example, "The Fire Balloons" focuses on a religious missionary's discovery that the only surviving Martians have metamorphosed from human forms to floating balls of blue flame (reminiscent of the fire balloons in Earth's Fourth of July celebrations). After undergoing this transformation, these Martian flames are no longer capable of sin. Bradbury implies that a new planet means a new theology, the fall is reversible, and a state of innocence can be regained.

THE GOLDEN APPLES OF THE SUN

Bradbury's fourth collection, *The Golden Apples of the Sun*, used neither linking passages nor a frame narrative to interrelate the twenty-two stories. Instead, this book initiated the Bradburian potpourri of stories that would characterize most of his later collections: nostalgic, satiric, and humorous stories whose settings could be Mars, Mexico, or the Midwest and whose genre could be fantasy, science fiction, crime, or horror. He would use this variety of approach, setting, and genre to cast a revelatory light on aspects of modern life that conventional fiction was avoiding. Although the critical reception of *The Golden Apples of the Sun* was largely favorable, some critics found several of the stories disappointing and noted a falling-off from the high level of quality of *The Martian Chronicles* and *The Illustrated Man*. Despite the divided opinions, general agreement existed on the success of several of the stories, for example, "Sun and Shadow," which was set in Mexico and which won both praise and awards. Another story, "The Fog Horn," became the basis of a film, *The Beast from Twenty Thousand Fathoms* (1953). It is about a lonely dinosaur who is attracted by the sound of a fog horn, interpreting it as the mating call of a potential companion (he dies of a broken heart when he swims to shore and discovers his error). The story "A Sound of Thunder" develops a favorite Bradburian theme of the profound effect of the past on the future. It depicts what happens when a time traveler steps on a butterfly in the past and inadvertently changes the future (this will remind modern readers of the "butterfly effect" in chaos theory, in which the beating of a butterfly's wings in a Brazilian rain forest may cause a tornado in Kansas via a long chain of cause and effect).

THE OCTOBER COUNTRY

The October Country, a collection that has as its core the stories of *Dark Carnival* along with four new stories, appeared appropriately in October of 1955. Bradbury described the country of the title as a place "whose people are autumn people, thinking only autumn thoughts" and whose steps "at night on the empty walks sound like rain." In the light of the earlier success of *Dark Carnival*, it is surprising that several critics were not as kind to this collection as they had been to Bradbury's earlier ones. For example, Carlos Baker, Ernest Hemingway's biographer,

predicted in his review that the only route that Bradbury's writings could follow if he continued in the direction that he had chosen was down. Some critics did see him trying, in this and later collections, to develop new subjects, themes, and approaches. For them, his imagination was still nimble, his mind adventurous, and his heart sensitive. They also noticed his increased emphasis on social issues and his desire to treat the joyous side of human nature. For most critics, however, Bradbury's later collections of stories were repetitive mixes of ideas, themes, and treatments that he had used many times before.

A MEDICINE FOR MELANCHOLY

The problems sensed by these critics can be seen in the collection of twenty-two stories titled *A Medicine for Melancholy*. In addition to the expected stories of fantasy and science fiction, *A Medicine for Melancholy* includes tales from the lives of the Irish, Mexicans, and Mexican Americans. The title story explores the awakening womanhood of an eighteenth century London girl who is cured of melancholia by the visit of what she interprets as Saint Bosco but who is in reality a dustman. Two of the stories in this collection, "Icarus Montgolfier Wright" and "In a Season of Calm Weather," led to films, and others, "A Fever Dream" for example, are reminiscent of films. In "A Fever Dream," aliens invade Earth not externally but by taking over the minds and hearts of their Earth victims (the film analogue is the 1956 *The Invasion of the Body Snatchers*). Derivative, too, seems the story "All Summer in a Day," about a group of children on cloud-enshrouded Venus who get to see the sun only once every seven years (the analogue here is Asimov's classic story "Nightfall").

THE MACHINERIES OF JOY

In the 1960's and 1970's, Bradbury's career entered a new phase characterized by a decreasing output of short stories and novels and an increasing output of plays and poetry. When he did bring out short-story collections, the majority of critics saw little suggesting artistic growth, though a minority actually preferred his new stories, interpreting them as examples of a mature writer whose stories had acquired humanity, depth, and polish. These latter critics are also the ones who were not attracted to his tales about corpses, vampires, and cemeteries and who preferred his new optimism and his emphasis on civil rights, religion, and morality. Many of the stories in *The Machineries of Joy* provide good examples of these new tendencies. There are still stories characteristic of the old Bradbury—a science-fiction tale in which the explorers of a new planet find themselves possessed by a resident intelligence, and a horror story in which raising giant mushrooms gets out of hand. Many of the stories, however, contain the epiphanic appearance of human warmth in unexpected situations. For example, in "Almost the End of the World," when sunspots destroy television reception, a world addicted to this opiate of the mind and heart is forced to rediscover the forgotten joys of interpersonal communication.

I SING THE BODY ELECTRIC!

Bradbury's next collection, *I Sing the Body Electric!* also met with a mixed critical response. Academic critics and readers who had formed their taste for Bradbury on his early works found this potpourri of seventeen stories pretentious and a decline from his best science-fiction, fantasy, and horror stories. Some stories are slight—indeed, little more than anecdotes: In "The Women," for example, a man experiences the sea as a woman and his wife as her rival. On the other hand, some critics found Bradbury's new stories enthralling and insightful, with the unexpected—a robot Abraham Lincoln, Ernest Hemingway's spirit, and an automated Martian city—confronting the reader at every turn of the page. The stories of *I Sing the Body Electric!* certainly contain some of Bradbury's favorite themes—the dialectic between past and future, reality and illusion. For example, the title story concerns a robot grandmother ideally programmed to meet the needs of the children of a recently motherless family. This electrical grandmother embodies the past (she has all the sentiment humans conventionally associate with this figure) and the future (she is a rechargeable AC-DC Mark V model and can never die). Another story that deals with the presentness of the past is "Night Call, Collect." In this tale, an old man alone on a deserted Mars receives a telephone call from himself when he was much younger (he has forgotten that he devised

this plan many years earlier in order to assuage the loneliness of his old age). His young self battles with his old self, and as the old man dies, past, present, and future commingle in an odd but somehow enlightening amalgam.

LONG AFTER MIDNIGHT

Long After Midnight contained twenty-two stories, several of which had been written in the late 1940's and early 1950's but never anthologized. Some critics found the new stories aimless, uninspired, and self-indulgent, but others felt that many of them were poignant, sensitive, and touching. These latter critics thought that several of these stories represented Bradbury's new grasp of the power of love to overcome evil and to make permanent valued moments from the past. A few of the stories broke new ground in terms of subject matter: "The Better Part of Wisdom" is a compassionate and restrained treatment of homosexuality and "Have I Got a Chocolate Bar for You!" deals gracefully with a relationship between a priest and a penitent.

THE STORIES OF RAY BRADBURY

In 1980, Bradbury selected one hundred stories from three decades of his work in *The Stories of Ray Bradbury*. Many reviewers treated this book's publication as an opportunity to analyze Bradbury's lifetime achievement as a short-story writer. Some found much to praise, comparing his body of work to Poe's, O. Henry's, and Guy de Maupassant's. Thomas M. Disch, however, in an influential essay in *The New York Times Book Review*, denigrated Bradbury's stories as "schmaltzy" and "more often meretricious than not." Unlike those critics who praised Bradbury's early work and saw a decline in the quality of his later stories, Disch stated that early and late are "meaningless distinctions" in Bradbury's output. He criticized Bradbury condescendingly as a child manqué, attributing his success to the fact that "like Peter Pan, he won't grow up."

THE TOYNBEE CONVECTOR

To those who thought that Bradbury was using *The Stories of Ray Bradbury* to bid farewell to the form that had been his home for most of his life as a writer, another collection, *The Toynbee Convector*, showed that they were mistaken. As with his other late collections, this, too, contained the familiar blend of science fiction and gothic horror as well as sentimental tales of Ireland and Middle America, but it broke little new ground.

QUICKER THAN THE EYE

Most of the twenty-one stories in *Quicker than the Eye* are loaded with symbols and metaphors about look-alikes, death, doors that open to the unknown, revelations from the unconscious mind, and psychic connections to the past and future. Magicians always fascinated Bradbury. They pretend to do something, the audience blinks, and "quicker than the eye, silks fall out of a hat." Bradbury performs magic with words, and stories "fall out" of his imagination.

In "Quicker than the Eye," the narrator and his wife watch a magician saw a woman in half and make her disappear. Men in the audience laugh. Then, Miss Quick, a pickpocket, nimbly removes wallets and other personal items from ten unsuspecting male volunteers. Miss Quick particularly humiliates one volunteer, who looks exactly like the narrator, by stripping him "quicker than the eye." The angry narrator identifies with his "double's" vulnerability, but his wife laughs.

Several stories have themes of revenge and death. In "The Electrocution," carnival worker Johnny straps Electra in the Death Chair, blindfolds her, and pulls the switch. Blue flames shoot from her body, and, with a sword, she touches and "connects" with a fascinated youth in the crowd. After Electra and her lover meet secretly, Johnny, in a jealous rage, beats him up. The next time he "electrocutes" Electra, he turns up the voltage and says, "You're dead!" She replies, "Yes, I am."

Some doors that open to the unknown are better left closed. The title "Dorian in Excelsus" is wordplay on the liturgical phrase *Gloria in excelis* and refers to Oscar Wilde's *The Picture of Dorian Gray* (1890 serial, 1891 expanded). A handsome youth invites the aging, dissipated narrator to become a Friend of Dorian at a spa. Behind golden doors, the narrator discovers how Friends of Dorian shed age and become physically beautiful. To regain youth, he must wrestle in Dorian's gym with hundreds of lustful men. Dorian is a "gelatinous, undulant jellyfish,

the sponge of men's depravity and guilt, a pustule, bacteria, priapic jelly." He lives by breathing the sweaty stench of human passion and sin. The horrified narrator refuses Dorian's offer and scratches him with a fingernail. Dorian screams as noxious gases escape, and he and his Friends die.

Psychic connections to the past and future are recurring themes in *Quicker than the Eye*. The title character in "That Woman on the Lawn" awakens a teenage boy with her crying. Her picture is in his family album. He directs her to an address down the street, and they agree to meet in three years; he is her future baby.

OTHER MAJOR WORKS

LONG FICTION: *Fahrenheit 451*, 1953; *Dandelion Wine*, 1957; *Something Wicked This Way Comes*, 1962; *Death Is a Lonely Business*, 1985; *A Graveyard for Lunatics: Another Tale of Two Cities*, 1990; *Green Shadows, White Whale*, 1992.

PLAYS: *The Anthem Sprinters and Other Antics*, pb. 1963; *The World of Ray Bradbury: Three Fables of the Future*, pr. 1964; *The Day It Rained Forever*, pb. 1966; *The Pedestrian*, pb. 1966; *Dandelion Wine*, pr. 1967; *The Wonderful Ice Cream Suit and Other Plays*, pb. 1972; *Madrigals for the Space Age*, pb. 1972; *Pillar of Fire and Other Plays for Today, Tomorrow, and Beyond Tomorrow*, pb. 1975; *That Ghost, That Bride of Time: Excerpts from a Play-in-Progress*, pb. 1976; *The Martian Chronicles*, pr. 1977; *Fahrenheit 451*, pr. 1979 (musical); *A Device Out of Time*, pb. 1986.

SCREENPLAYS: *It Came from Outer Space*, 1952 (with David Schwartz); *Moby Dick*, 1956 (with John Huston); *Icarus Montgolfier Wright*, 1961 (with George C. Johnson); *The Picasso Summer*, 1969 (with Ed Weinberger).

POETRY: *Old Ahab's Friend, and Friend to Noah, Speaks His Piece: A Celebration*, 1971; *When Elephants Last in the Dooryard Bloomed: Celebrations for Almost Any Day in the Year*, 1973; *Where Robot Mice and Robot Men Run Round in Robot Towns: New Poems, Both Light and Dark*, 1977; *Twin Hieroglyphs That Swim the River Dust*, 1978; *The Bike Repairman*, 1978; *The Aqueduct*, 1979; *The Haunted*

Computer and the Android Pope, 1981; *The Complete Poems of Ray Bradbury*, 1982; *Forever and the Earth*, 1984; *Death Has Lost Its Charm for Me*, 1987; *With Cat for Comforter*, 1997 (with Louise Max); *Dogs Think That Every Day Is Christmas*, 1997.

NONFICTION: *Teacher's Guide to Science Fiction*, 1968 (with Lewy Olfson); *Mars and the Mind of Man*, 1973; *Zen and the Art of Writing*, 1973; *The Mummies of Guanajuato*, 1978; *The Art of Playboy*, 1985; *Zen in the Art of Writing: Essays on Creativity*, 1989; *Yestermorrow: Obvious Answers to Impossible Futures*, 1991.

CHILDREN'S LITERATURE: *Switch on the Night*, 1955; *R Is for Rocket*, 1962; *S Is for Space*, 1966; *The Halloween Tree*, 1972; *Fever Dream*, 1987; *Ahmed and the Oblivion Machines: A Fable*, 1998.

EDITED TEXTS: *Timeless Stories for Today and Tomorrow*, 1952; *The Circus of Dr. Lao and Other Improbable Stories*, 1956.

BIBLIOGRAPHY

Bolhafner, J. Stephen. "The Ray Bradbury Chronicles." *St. Louis Post-Dispatch*, December 1, 1996. An interview with Bradbury on the occasion of the publication of his collection of short stories *Quicker than the Eye*. Bradbury reminisces about the beginnings of his career, talks about getting over his fear of flying, and discusses *The Martian Chronicles* as fantasy, mythology, and magical realism.

Bradbury, Ray. "Sci-fi for Your D: Drive." *Newsweek* 126 (November 13, 1995): 89. In this interview-story, Bradbury discusses why he is putting his most widely acclaimed short-story collection, *The Martian Chronicles*, on CD-ROM. Bradbury also discusses the role of imagination in technology, the space program, and his favorite literary figures.

Greenberg, Martin Henry, and Joseph D. Olander, eds. *Ray Bradbury*. New York: Taplinger, 1980. This anthology of Bradbury criticism is part of the Writers of the Twenty-first Century series. Some of the articles defend Bradbury against the charge that he is not really a science-fiction writer but an opponent of science and technology; other articles defend him against the charge that he is mawkish. Includes an extensive Bradbury bibliography compiled by Marshall B. Tymn and an index.

Johnson, Wayne L. *Ray Bradbury*. New York: Frederick Ungar, 1980. Although this volume is the work of a fan rather than a critic, it provides a good general introduction to Bradbury's stories of fantasy and science fiction. Johnson's approach is thematic rather than chronological (he uses the categories of magic, monsters, and machines to facilitate his discussion of Bradbury's principal approaches, ideas, and themes). Index.

Mogen, David. *Ray Bradbury*. Boston: Twayne, 1986. This brief introduction to Bradbury's career centers on analyses of the literary influences that shaped the development of his style and the themes whose successful embodiment in his short stories and novels shaped his reputation. The detailed notes at the end of the book contain many useful references. Bibliography and index.

Nolan, William F. *The Ray Bradbury Companion: A Life and Career History, Photolog, and Comprehensive Checklist of Writings with Facsimiles from Ray Bradbury's Unpublished and Uncollected Work in All Media*. Detroit: Gale Research, 1975. The ample subtitle gives a good idea of this book's contents. After its publication, its information on Bradbury has been updated by Donn Albright, in "The Ray Bradbury Index," in several issues of *Xenophile* (May, 1975; September, 1976; and November, 1977).

Slusser, George Edgar. *The Bradbury Chronicles*. San Bernardino, Calif.: Borgo Press, 1977. This booklet is part of a series, Popular Writers of Today. Intended for young students and general audiences, this brief work discusses summarily some of Bradbury's most important writings. Bibliography.

Touponce, William F. *Naming the Unnameable: Ray Bradbury and the Fantastic After Freud*. Mercer Island, Wash.: Starmont House, 1997. Touponce finds the psychoanalytic ideas of Sigmund Freud and Carl Jung helpful in plumbing the effectiveness of much of Bradbury's work (though in a letter to the author, Bradbury himself denies any direct influence, since he has "read little Freud or Jung"). Nevertheless, Touponce believes that Bradbury has given us stories of a modern con-

sciousness that often forgets its debt to the unconscious.

Robert J. Paradowski,
updated by Martha E. Rhynes

RICHARD BRAUTIGAN

Born: Tacoma, Washington; January 30, 1935
Died: Bolinas, California; September, 1984

PRINCIPAL SHORT FICTION
Trout Fishing in America, 1967
Revenge of the Lawn: Stories, 1962-1970, 1971
The Tokyo-Montana Express, 1980

OTHER LITERARY FORMS

Richard Brautigan's fragmented prose style makes any effort to classify his work into long and short fiction difficult and somewhat arbitrary. Brautigan himself called all of his prose works novels, with the single exception of *Revenge of the Lawn*, but critics have understandably referred to his books as "un-novels" or "Brautigans," works that seem approachable only on their own terms because they deliberately confront the realistic tradition of the novel by disregarding causality and character development.

Nevertheless, *Trout Fishing in America* and *The Tokyo-Montana Express* can be grouped with *Revenge of the Lawn* as examples of Brautigan's short fiction. Although arguably unified by point of view, setting, theme, and recurrent characters, *Trout Fishing in America* and *The Tokyo-Montana Express* lack any semblance of coherent plot, and many of the individual selections which compose each book possess an integrity independent of context. Brautigan's other novels are distinguished by at least a thin strand of continuous narrative. The most important of these longer fictions are *A Confederate General from Big Sur* (1964), *In Watermelon Sugar* (1968), and *The Abortion: An Historical Romance* (1971). The best known of his poetry collections are *The Pill Versus the Springhill Mine Disaster* (1968), *Rommel Drives*

On Deep into Egypt (1970), and *June 30th, June 30th* (1978).

ACHIEVEMENTS

When Don Allen's Four Season Foundation published *Trout Fishing in America* in 1967, it became a favorite of the counterculture movement that was peaking that year during the "summer of love." In the following year, Richard Brautigan was awarded a grant from the National Endowment for the Arts, and *Trout Fishing in America* became a best-seller, eventually selling more than two million copies in twelve languages.

Trout Fishing in America was Brautigan's first fictional work and established his success and reputation. In a sense, it became the standard against which his later works would be judged. Unfortunately, it associated him closely with the counterculture movement, giving rise to popular and even critical misconceptions. Brautigan was not (as some supposed) a spokesman for the hippie movement; rather, the counterculture simply became his first sizable audience. In actuality, Brautigan's roots were more in the Beat poetry movement (which influenced his prose style), and he has even been considered a precursor to the metafictionalists of the 1970's.

In any case, Brautigan brought a special quality to his fiction, a style of expression which, though deceptively simple and direct, teems with figures of speech that often seem to defy the bounds of language. Early critics seemed to miss, ignore, or disparage exactly these distinctive formal qualities. Often, Brautigan's subject matter—the dead-end fixity of materialism, outworn myths, or the decay of the American dream—places him at home in the tradition of twentieth century American writers. What made Brautigan's fiction attractive to his early psychedelic audience, however, was something new: implicit in his nontraditional structure and distended metaphors was the suggestion that experience could be transformed by imagination. The pursuit of shimmering, elusive instances of imaginative insight might possibly offer a personal alternative to the stultification of culture amid the grotesque remnants of American myth. Many postmodern writers have read Brautigan; W. P. Kinsella has referred to some of his own short works as "Brautigans." At the very least, these writers have been alerted to the possibilities suggested by Brautigan's work. His influence may be greater than anyone could have guessed.

BIOGRAPHY

Richard Brautigan was born in Tacoma, Washington, in the midst of the Great Depression. Very little is known about his early life. Although Brautigan apparently drew on his childhood experiences in his fiction, his idiosyncratic attitude toward his past made him reluctant to discuss actual details with anyone. From anecdotal fragments confided to a few persons

Richard Brautigan (Library of Congress)

close to him, a far less than idyllic picture emerges that includes a pattern of abandonment and mistreatment at the hands of stepfathers. Deprivation seems to have been a part of his heritage, and Brautigan would claim throughout his life that he never graduated from high school.

In 1956, Brautigan moved to San Francisco and became peripherally aligned with the Beat poets. He wrote and published several volumes of poetry, but none sold well. He also met an educated young woman, Virginia Adler, who became his first wife and the mother of Ianthe, their daughter. Adler supported the family by doing secretarial work. Problems arose when Brautigan continued his bachelor habits of haunting bars and bringing his friends home for further revels. In time, Virginia became involved with one of Brautigan's drinking friends and ran away with him to live in Salt Lake City in 1963. Although he was devastated, Brautigan wrote one of his best novels, *In Watermelon Sugar*, in 1964.

Success showered on Brautigan with the publication of *Trout Fishing in America* in 1967. Fame and money afforded him opportunity for a period of more or less unbridled hedonism. After purchasing a ranch in Montana, Brautigan spent portions of the year entertaining friends, and, perhaps, cultivating a lifestyle that quickly became an unfortunate blend of egoism and dissipation. Although his friends would fondly recall their early days with Brautigan, heavy drinking and a mordant sense of paranoia began to estrange most of them. Brautigan's later work was beginning to suffer at the hands of critics, his counterculture audience was dispersing, and sales in the United States were down. In Japan, however, his translated work was creating a wave of interest. In 1977, he married one of his Japanese admirers, Akiko. There was a brief period of happiness while they lived together in San Francisco, and Brautigan began to write *The Tokyo-Montana Express* in 1978. Unfortunately, Akiko, like so many others, was unable to cope with the peculiar stresses of a relationship with Brautigan; she left him. Brautigan tried the lecture circuit in 1980, but it was an unhappy venture. Sometime near the end of September, 1984, Richard Brautigan shut himself up in his house in Bolinas,

California, and took his own life with a handgun. His body was discovered on October 25, 1984.

ANALYSIS

Richard Brautigan's short fiction explores the imagination's power to transform reality. In some stories, this means contrasting a gritty, naturalistic portrait of cheap materialism, personal defeat, and latent violence with a vision of the lost American Eden or a nostalgic remembrance of childhood's innocence. Collectively, the stories describe a search for good in contemporary America, but because they sympathize with the defeated, they suggest that such a search is futile. Brautigan's stories stoically accept the conditions of existence, withholding judgment while suggesting that the imagination holds the only possible hope for transcendence.

The stories are self-consciously artificial, continually calling attention to the process of their creation. The typographical experimentation, outrageous figures of speech, extreme compression, and deceptively simplistic syntax work through a disengaged narrative voice to create prose that has been compared to skywriting. The conscious artificiality of Brautigan's stylistic mannerisms has led some critics to dismiss his work as whimsical, coy, naïve, and self-indulgent.

TROUT FISHING IN AMERICA

Although *Trout Fishing in America* became popular as a counterculture book during the late 1960's, it was written in 1961 as a late expression of the San Francisco Beat movement. Brautigan, like other Beats, had been conditioned by the experience of the Great Depression and World War II, historical examples of deprivation and violence, and he saw in these experiences deep truths that belied America's complacent prosperity. In contrast to the radicals of the 1930's and the New Left of the 1960's, Brautigan and other Beats sought social change not through collective action but through personal transformation.

Thus, *Trout Fishing in America* is an antididactic book, an effort to document America from a disengaged, thoroughly nonpolitical point of view. Although the America it documents is spiritually decayed, the forty-seven stories that compose *Trout Fishing in America* do not promote a program of so-

cial reform. Instead, the book's underlying philosophy, derived from Zen Buddhist belief, assumes that life is essentially determined and that social progress is an illusion. Brautigan expounds a politics of the imagination in which social activism is supplanted by the individual imagination's ability to create a vision of freedom, a vision of an America that is "often only a place in the mind." To this extent, the explicit theme of Kurt Vonnegut's *Mother Night*, which was published in 1961, as *Trout Fishing in America* was being written, suits Brautigan's book: "We are what we pretend to be, so we must be careful what we pretend to be." Brautigan's unnamed narrator uses his imagination to "fish" for something of value in the stream of contemporary America, but like his comically failed fisherman Alonso Hagen in "Fishing on the Streets of Eternity," his effort becomes "an interesting experiment in total loss."

Stylistically, *Trout Fishing in America* seems without literary precedent, a documentary collage of prose poems and cultural allusions that exhibits no interest in character, plot development, or psychological motivation. Literary parodies (of Ernest Hemingway, John Steinbeck, Henry David Thoreau) are juxtaposed to references to historical figures (Richard Nixon, "Pretty Boy" Floyd, Andrew Carnegie, Caryl Chessman, Deanna Durbin) and the signatures of popular culture (bumper stickers, diaries, tombstone engravings, recipes, warning signs). Woven through this cultural stew is the protean phrase "Trout Fishing in America," which is applied to people, places, a hotel, a pen nib, a state of mind, and the book itself.

"The Cover for Trout Fishing in America," the opening piece, exemplifies the book's self-consciousness and introduces Brautigan's ironic view of America. By describing the book's cover photograph, Brautigan reminds his reader that *Trout Fishing in America* is itself an artifact, a component of the society he is documenting. He then juxtaposes a statue of Benjamin Franklin, the prototypical American optimist, to the derelicts who sadly wait in the park hoping for a handout. Although the concluding quotation from Franz Kafka, "I like the Americans because they are healthy and optimistic," is ironic, Brautigan's matter-of-fact presentation prevents the piece from being read as social protest. Instead, the book implies that optimism, no matter how ill-founded, is a part of the American condition.

"THE KOOL-AID WINO" AND "TROUT FISHING ON THE BEVEL"

In a complementary way, "The Kool-Aid Wino" demonstrates the imagination's power to overcome the limitations of existence. The Kool-Aid Wino is a child who is restricted from picking beans or engaging in active play by a hernia. His family is too poor to afford an operation or even a truss, so the Kool-Aid Wino spends his days lovingly preparing a watered-down, sugarless version of Kool-Aid "like a famous brain surgeon removing a disordered portion of the imagination." Through his ceremonious preparation and consumption he creates "his own Kool-Aid reality" and is "able to illuminate himself by it." The story celebrates the human capacity to transcend reality while simultaneously portraying the sad deprivations that make such imaginative escape necessary.

In "Trout Fishing on the Bevel," Brautigan's narrator describes fishing a stream that runs past two graveyards, one for the rich and one for the poor. Like many of Brautigan's short fictions, "Trout Fishing on the Bevel" meditates on loneliness, poverty, death, and the desire to transcend them. The narrator describes the weathered boards, "like heels of stale bread," that mark the graves of the poor and imagines darkly humorous inscriptions ("Beloved Worked-to-Death Mother Of") that disclose the painful reality usually disguised by euphemisms. In contrast, the graves of the rich are marked with "marble hors d'oeuvres like horses trotting up the fancy paths to the sky." Admittedly "bothered" by "the poverty of the dead," the narrator has "a vision of going over to the poor graveyard and gathering up grass and fruit jars and tin cans and markers and wilted flowers and bugs and weeds and clods and going home and putting a hook in the vise and tying a fly with all that stuff and then going outside and casting it up into the sky, watching it float over clouds and then into the evening star." It is one of Brautigan's clearest statements of his artistic purpose, expressing his desire to construct from the forgotten or overlooked bits of life

an art that can imaginatively free his narrator and his reader from the particular loneliness of existence.

"THE CLEVELAND WRECKING YARD"

"The Cleveland Wrecking Yard" is placed near the end of *Trout Fishing in America*, and it provides a caricature of America's obsessive materialism. At the Cleveland Wrecking Yard, a microcosm of America, the narrator finds a trout stream for sale, stacked up in lengths beside toilets and other used plumbing supplies, but he does not condemn this outrageous "commodification" of nature; instead, he sees the Cleveland Wrecking Yard as a repository for tarnished dreams that can only be revitalized with imagination. Indeed, the process by which discarded items can be recycled parallels the way in which Brautigan salvages the scraps of American culture to construct *Trout Fishing in America*.

"REVENGE OF THE LAWN"

Many of the stories collected in *Revenge of the Lawn* deal with childhood, portraying it as a fragile refuge, a time when people are more open to the transforming power of imagination. The stories contrast this freedom with the crippling disillusionments that accompany maturation and the sadder ways adults use imagination to escape reality.

The title story, however, shows Brautigan at his most playful, demonstrating an ability to use comic misdirection and a deadpan narrative voice in the manner of Mark Twain. This rambling, autobiographical remembrance focuses on his grandmother, his grandfather, and a man named Jack. The grandfather, "a minor Washington mystic," went mad after he correctly "prophesied the exact date when World War I would start." In his madness he returns to an eternal childhood in which he is six years old. He is replaced by Jack, an itinerant salesman of lots in Florida, who hawks "a vision of eternal oranges and sunshine." These contrasting visionaries are set against the grandmother, a bootlegger, who sells a utilitarian sort of bottled vision. The action of the story revolves around Jack's relationship to nature, specifically the lawn which he has destroyed by driving on it, a pear tree which grows in the yard, the bees that are attracted to the pears, and the grandmother's geese. The geese eat some fermenting mash and pass out in the yard. The grandmother, comically assuming that the geese are dead, plucks them. They recover and are standing about "like some helpless, primitive American advertisement for aspirin," when Jack, distracted by the sight, drives into the house. In a concluding note, the narrator writes that his earliest memory is an image of Jack setting fire to the tree "while the fruit was still green on the branches." "Revenge of the Lawn" demonstrates Brautigan's ability to write comic narrative while satirizing man's foolish attempts to manage nature.

"CORPORAL"

"Corporal" is a bittersweet inverted Horatio Alger story in which the narrator recounts his wartime involvement in a paper drive. The young patriots were to earn military ranks according to the amount of paper they collected. The narrator's initial eagerness was thwarted, however, when he realized that "the kids who wore the best clothes and had lots of spending money and got to eat hot lunch every day" had an unfair advantage, for these kids "were already generals," and "they strutted their military airs around the playground." Like so many of Brautigan's characters, the narrator admitted defeat and entered "the disenchanted paper shadows of America where failure is a bounced check or a bad report card or a letter ending a love affair and all the words that hurt people when they read them." "Corporal" evokes the opposing worlds of good and bad paper, the childlike creative dream and the stifling economic and social reality. The story painfully portrays the disappointments that constitute so much of life, and emphasizes, in a manner that is particularly relevant for an author who places imaginative creation at the center of life, the precariousness of a life lived in the mind.

"THE WORLD WAR I LOS ANGELES AIRPLANE"

The last piece in *Revenge of the Lawn* is one of the most openly autobiographical. "The World War I Los Angeles Airplane" is Brautigan's response to the death of his father-in-law, but this piece, despite its specificity, effectively communicates Brautigan's general sense of life as a process of attrition. "The World War I Los Angeles Airplane" exemplifies Brautigan's disregard for traditional narrative method and his love of lists, for after a brief introduction, the

story presents a numbered catalog of thirty-three separate thoughts. In an elliptical manner, these distinct statements chronicle the life of a defeated man. Most suggestive is the contrast between his father-in-law's experience as a pilot in World War I, when "he had been followed by a rainbow across the skies of France," and the quiet alcoholism of his final years of inactivity, when he watched daytime television and "used sweet wine in place of life because he didn't have any more life to use." The father-in-law's retreat from life parallels the Kool-Aid Wino's, except that in "The World War I Los Angeles Airplane" there is no intimation that the escape is illuminating.

During the 1970's, Brautigan announced his intention to write a novel parodying a popular genre each year. *The Hawkline Monster: A Gothic Western* (1974), *Willard and His Bowling Trophies: A Perverse Mystery* (1975), *Sombrero Fallout: A Japanese Novel* (1976), and *Dreaming of Babylon: A Private Eye Novel, 1942* (1977) were critical disasters for Brautigan. By the time he published *The Tokyo-Montana Express* in 1980, his literary reputation had been ruined, and he had been deserted by most of his readers. His status as a counterculture hero, which was always based on a misunderstanding of his work, had become irrelevant, except as another barrier standing between him and the readers of the 1980's. Although Brautigan resumed lecturing to promote *The Tokyo-Montana Express*, he was unable to recapture the broad acceptance that had made him a best-selling author a decade before. Nevertheless, *The Tokyo-Montana Express*, for all of its unevenness, marked a healthy return to the effective short fiction evident in *Trout Fishing in America* and *Revenge of the Lawn*.

THE TOKYO-MONTANA EXPRESS

The Tokyo-Montana Express contains 131 individual prose pieces. A few of these approximate the traditional form of the short story, but most would more accurately be called anecdotes, vignettes, or prose poems. Overall, Brautigan's tendency toward compression is more evident in *The Tokyo-Montana Express* than in his earlier work. He is also more restrained in his use of bizarre figures of speech, and the disengaged flatness of his prose is more consistent.

As in all of his short fiction, Brautigan's primary concern in *The Tokyo-Montana Express* is the imagination. In *Trout Fishing in America*, he figuratively "fishes" for a vision of America; in *The Tokyo-Montana Express*, he travels an imaginary trans-Pacific railroad, a vehicle for the metaphysical commutation of ideas between East and West. Written after a period during which he spent most of his time either in Japan or on his farm in Montana, Brautigan's collection examines the cultures of East and West, repeatedly showing the ironic similarities and in the end suggesting that Montana's big sky country may be a geographically appropriate setting for the philosophy of Japan.

In *The Tokyo-Montana Express*, Brautigan's involvement with Zen Buddhist thought is more explicit than in his earlier work, expressing itself in the stoic attitude of the narrative voice he employs. One paradox expressed in the collection is that while all experiences are equally worthy of examination, all experiences are also ultimately insignificant. The narrator's emotional disengagement cannot disguise a sadness that is much more prevalent here than in Brautigan's earlier work. Indeed, the narrator in *The Tokyo-Montana Express* expects very little of life, accepts the inevitable process of attrition, assumes that any meaning must originate in the individual imagination, and exhibits great faith in the integrity of that imagination.

"ANOTHER TEXAS GHOST STORY" AND "WEREWOLF RASPBERRIES"

"Another Texas Ghost Story" recounts the life of a man who, while growing up on a remote Texas ranch, is visited at night by a ghost. Forty years later at a family reunion, he accidentally admits his childhood experience to his brother and two sisters only to discover that they too had seen the apparition when they were children. They were all afraid to mention it at the time because they were afraid they would be thought crazy. In "Another Texas Ghost Story," Brautigan connects childhood and imagination and implies that societal pressure makes people less receptive to the wonder around them.

"Werewolf Raspberries" is an example of the extreme compression of many pieces in *The Tokyo-*

Montana Express. Its seventy-nine words, interrupted by ellipses, seem like the fragmented remains of a more complete narrative, yet this abbreviated prose poem manages to communicate a complex story. Set in the spring of 1940 with a Glenn Miller recording playing in the background, the narrative voice in "Werewolf Raspberries" addresses a young man whose single-minded romantic desire to give his girl "a great big kiss" has been inexplicably thwarted by the raspberries' "little teeth shining in the moonlight." The piece concludes with the ironic remonstrance that "If you had played your cards right, you could have been killed at Pearl Harbor instead." On one level, this brief prose poem expresses a nostalgic feel for dreams lost to the inevitable imperfections and accidents of existence, but the final comment ironically compares the harmless adolescent dream of romance with the lethal, but equally adolescent, dream of glory.

"THE MENU/1965"

"The Menu/1965" is the longest piece in *The Tokyo-Montana Express*, and it shows Brautigan extracting significance from a strange but mundane object, in this case the monthly menu prepared for residents of San Quentin's Death Row. The narrator resists judging the significance of this artifact; instead, he reports several other people's reactions to this strange juxtaposition of dining and death. At the end, the narrator and the intellectual father of a friend become entranced in "a long conversation where the menu became a kind of thought diving bell going deeper and deeper, deeper and deeper until we were at the cold flat bottom of the sea, staring fish-like at the colored Easter eggs that were going to be served next Sunday on Death Row." The allusion to Easter portrays the condemned prisoners as Christlike sacrifices, but the primary focus of the story is the fascination of the object and the manner in which it triggers the imagination.

All of Brautigan's short fictions are meant to become "thought diving bells" for the reader, and often, as in "The Menu/1965," the process of mental exploration begins with the contemplation of a simple object or event. In the end, Brautigan's creative process stands as an exemplum of a method for confronting life's attrition.

OTHER MAJOR WORKS

LONG FICTION: *A Confederate General from Big Sur*, 1964; *In Watermelon Sugar*, 1968; *The Abortion: An Historical Romance*, 1971; *The Hawkline Monster: A Gothic Western*, 1974; *Willard and His Bowling Trophies: A Perverse Mystery*, 1975; *Sombrero Fallout: A Japanese Novel*, 1976; *Dreaming of Babylon: A Private Eye Novel, 1942*, 1977; *So the Wind Won't Blow It All Away*, 1982.

POETRY: *The Return of the Rivers*, 1957; *The Galilee Hitch-Hiker*, 1958; *Lay the Marble Tea: Twenty-four Poems*, 1959; *The Octopus Frontier*, 1960; *All Watched Over by Machines of Loving Grace*, 1967; *The Pill Versus the Springhill Mine Disaster*, 1968; *Please Plant This Book*, 1968; *Rommel Drives on Deep into Egypt*, 1970; *Loading Mercury with a Pitchfork*, 1976; *June Thirtieth, June Thirtieth*, 1978.

BIBLIOGRAPHY

Abbott, Keith. *Downstream from "Trout Fishing in America."* Santa Barbara, Calif.: Capra Press, 1989. Abbott recounts his memories of Brautigan from their first meeting in San Francisco in 1966, through the Montana years, and back to 1982 in San Francisco. Abbott's last chapter, "Shadows and Marble," is a critical essay devoted to Brautigan's language and strategy of fiction.

Barber, John F. *Richard Brautigan: An Annotated Bibliography*. Jefferson, N.C.: McFarland, 1990. A good source for students of Brautigan.

Chénetier, Marc. *Richard Brautigan*. New York: Methuen, 1983. A semiotic examination of Brautigan's approach to structure and elements of style that generate meaning. This slender volume touches on several works, with particular attention to *Trout Fishing in America*.

Foster, Edward Halsey. *Richard Brautigan*. Boston: Twayne, 1983. This blend of biography and criticism deals primarily with Brautigan's work within his own cultural ambience, referring to other contemporary fiction, the Beat movement, and Zen Buddhism as an overall influence. Not always flattering, Foster discusses most of Brautigan's short fiction and novels.

Horvath, Brooke. "Richard Brautigan's Search for Control Over Death." *American Literature* 57 (October, 1985): 435-455. Horvath explores possible limits to Brautigan's response of imagination as a strategy for countering the basic issue of death in his four early novels and one of the stories in *The Tokyo-Montana Express*.

Kaylor, Noel Harold, ed. *Creative and Critical Approaches to the Short Story*. Lewiston: The Edwin Mellen Press, 1997. Farhat Iftekharuddin's essay, "The New Aesthetics in Brautigan's *Revenge of the Lawn: Stories 1962-1970*," deals primarily with Brautigan's short stories. Iftekharuddin's discussion of literary innovation and his treatment of other Brautigan critics make this an important contribution.

Seymore, James. "Author Richard Brautigan Apparently Takes His Own Life, But He Leaves a Rich Legacy." *People Weekly* 22 (November 12, 1984): 40-41. Provides a biographical background leading up to Brautigan's suicide, including his heavy drinking and depression at the loss of his readers.

Stull, William L. "Richard Brautigan's *Trout Fishing in America:* Notes of a Native Son." *American Literature* 56 (March, 1984): 69-80. Stull approaches general themes in *Trout Fishing in America* by examining some of the book's many allusions to other literature and Americana. A good get-acquainted piece.

Wright, Lawrence. "The Life and Death of Richard Brautigan." *Rolling Stone*, April 11, 1985, 29. A biographical sketch, noting Brautigan's early fame and cult following and the fading of his reputation and his suicide. Notes that when friends describe him, he seems two different people; at one point he was diagnosed as a paranoid schizophrenic.

Carl Brucker, updated by Mary Rohrberger

BERTOLT BRECHT

Born: Augsburg, Germany; February 10, 1898
Died: East Berlin, East Germany; August 14, 1956

Kalendergeschichten, 1948 (*Tales from the Calendar*, 1961)
Geschichten vom Herrn Keuner, 1958
Me-ti: Buch der Wendungen, 1965
Prosa, 1965 (5 volumes)

OTHER LITERARY FORMS

Bertolt Brecht is best known as a dramatist, but he also wrote poetry, novels, screenplays, dramatic theory, and essays on politics and society, as well as short fiction.

ACHIEVEMENTS

Although of necessity outside Germany in exile for sixteen years, it was in Germany, not Scandinavia or the United States, that Bertolt Brecht was best received. In 1922, at the beginning of his career as a writer, he received the Kleist Prize for literature for his drama *Trommeln in der Nacht* (1922; *Drums in the Night*, 1961). Later, when he had made his home in what was then East Germany, he received the National Prize of East Germany, First Class, in 1951. His work was recognized again in 1954, when he became a member of the Artistic Advisory Committee of the East German Ministry of Culture. At the same time, he was also vice president of the German Academy of the Arts. In 1954-1955, he was awarded the International Stalin Peace Prize.

Brecht's contribution as a dramatist has been compared to William Shakespeare's. In all of his works, he was a master stylist with a socialist vision, who encouraged his readers and audiences to think with critical distance.

BIOGRAPHY

Bertolt Brecht began studying medicine at the University of Munich in 1917, but a year later he was called up for military service as a medical orderly. He married Marianne Zoff in 1922, but they were divorced in 1927. Brecht left Munich for Berlin in 1924 and began an intensive study of economics and Marxism in 1926. After his divorce, he married the actress Helene Weigel, one of the best interpreters of his plays. Because of Nazi resentment against him and his work, Brecht and his family had to leave Germany in 1933, and they lived mostly in Scandinavia until they came to California in 1941. On October 30, 1947, Brecht was called before the House Committee on Un-American Activities and left the United States for Europe the next day. He settled in East Berlin in 1949 and formed the Berliner Ensemble acting company. Brecht died on August 14, 1956, of coronary thrombosis.

ANALYSIS

Although primarily known for his dramas and theoretical writings, Bertolt Brecht also wrote many short stories which have been unjustly neglected. He began writing stories while still at school and experimented with this genre all of his life. In 1928, he won first prize for "The Beast" in the *Berliner Illustrierte* short-story competition. Brecht's early stories are nihilistic, often with exotic settings and scoundrels as protagonists. The later stories criticize society and expose social injustice; the protagonists are either ordinary people or great historical figures whom Brecht cuts down to size.

Brecht theorized less about the short story than he did about the drama, but he did make important contributions to the short-story form, and his stories show a stylistic mastery of the genre. In his later stories, he uses alienation effects to ensure that the reader does not identify with the protagonists. In "On Reading Books" in *Me-ti: Buch der Wendungen* (me-ti: book of twists and turns), Brecht criticizes fiction that makes the reader forget the real world and become engrossed in the work. The reader, he believed, should not be caught up in the action but should view each event in the plot critically and differentiate between appearances and facts. Books should be read

Bertolt Brecht, testifying before the House Un-American Activities Committee in 1947 (AP/Wide World Photos)

so that they can be put aside from time to time for reflection. For this reason, Brecht praises the detective story since it is constructed logically and demands logical thought from the reader. Such a form is scientific, in Brecht's view: It presents readers with facts and problems to be solved and it challenges them to think, question, and learn—the goals of all Brecht's later works.

"THE BEAST"

"The Beast" is an example of how Brecht uses elements from the detective story to provoke his reader to think and observe facts, rather than be misled by appearances. The story's opening sentence states that a person's behavior is ambiguous and that this story, which has something shocking about it, will demonstrate this idea. Brecht, therefore, gives the reader clues at the outset as to how the story should be interpreted. At the beginning, a down-and-out old man comes to a film studio where a film about pogroms in

southern Russia is being made. Because he looks like the historical governor Muratow, who incited the pogroms, he is hired and plays a scene in which Muratow receives a delegation of Jews coming to beg him to end the murders. The director criticizes the old man for playing the role like a petty official rather than like a beast, yet two Jews who were part of the real delegation are impressed because the old man's acting corresponds to what actually took place. The director, however, refuses to believe the two eyewitnesses because they cannot recall a habit the historical Muratow had, which was, according to the director, constantly eating apples. After trying the scene again unsuccessfully, the old man is replaced by a real actor. Before leaving, however, he suggests sadistically that, instead of Muratow eating an apple, the leader of the Jews should be forced to eat one, which will stick in his throat from fear upon seeing Muratow signing the Jews' death warrant. The suggestion is immediately accepted, and the story ends with the actor plying his role to the hilt. Similarity to the historical Muratow is clearly insufficient; art is needed to portray real bestiality. At the close, it turns out that the old man really is Muratow, which the reader should have guessed since the story can be shocking only if this is the case.

One major theme presented in this story is that of role playing. At first the old man appears to be a shy, lonely outsider with whom one should sympathize. Gradually Brecht peels away this mask, exposing the cruelty beneath, seen particularly in the suggestion about the apples which shows that the old man, far from feeling remorse for his deeds, is just as cruel as ever. More important is Brecht's attitude toward art and reality. Brecht shows ironically how art distorts reality; as the scene is rehearsed, it moves further and further away from the real historical event and becomes more dramatic and emotional. This is precisely the kind of art which Brecht criticized in his theoretical writings. Art should appeal to reason, he believed, yet the public prefers art that captivates the emotions, and this is the art that sells.

The next stories are taken from *Tales from the Calendar*, which are counted among Brecht's best and are the ones which he himself prized most highly.

He was greatly influenced here by almanacs, which were widely read by the lower classes and whose stories combined popular appeal with practical moral lessons. Brecht learned from Johann Peter Hebel, who wrote for almanacs, but whereas the usual almanac story tended to teach people to be satisfied with their fate, Brecht gives his stories a radical political purpose; his goal is to unmask corruption and make people indignant at social injustice.

"CAESAR AND HIS LEGIONNAIRE"

"Caesar and His Legionnaire," an offshoot of Brecht's Caesar novel, uses history as an alienation effect. In his depiction of Roman society, Brecht gives the reader a yardstick by which to measure contemporary society, thus forcing the reader into a critical stance. The story's tone is dry and unemotional, and Brecht demythologizes Caesar by showing his death from a dual perspective. The first part of the story describes the last days of Caesar's life from his own perspective. Although he is at the height of his power, Caesar knows that his days are numbered. In an unsuccessful attempt to save his dictatorship, he tries to introduce democracy, but the people are too suspicious and fearful of him for it to succeed. He knows from a dream that he will be killed, but he is resigned to his death and goes to the senate, where the conspirators fall upon him—a laconic description of one of the most famous assassinations in history. Caesar is portrayed not as a great tragic figure but rather as a ruthless dictator, one who has put many people in prison and who has profited financially from his own rule. He is accused of having put money into Spanish banks under false names. The story also shows the ephemeral nature and corrupting influence of power.

The second part of the story deals with the same events but from the point of view of Terentius Scaper, a veteran who comes to Rome with his family because he has been evicted for not paying his rent. There are ironic parallels between Scaper's attempts to save himself from financial ruin and Caesar's attempts to save his dictatorship. The veteran's daughter raises money from an old admirer, who demands favors in return; but Rarus, Caesar's secretary and the daughter's fiancé, indignantly takes this money, intending to return it. Instead, he uses the money to bribe the guards to help Caesar escape in Scaper's ox cart. Before the escape can take place, however, Rarus is murdered, and Caesar dies, unwittingly owing Scaper the three hundred sesterces.

Brecht is especially concerned here with the effect of history on the common person. Caesar has brought his downfall on himself and is resigned to his death, refusing to flee. Rarus, however, has no such choice but is murdered because he is too close to Caesar. As for Scaper, Caesar's death means financial disaster, which was also true of Caesar's reign. Although Rome is flourishing, Scaper is poor and has not benefited at all from Rome's conquests. The difference between what history means to the rich and powerful and what it means to the common human being is a typical theme in Brecht's works.

"THE WOUNDED SOCRATES"

"The Wounded Socrates" describes Socrates' "heroic" deeds in the battle of Delion (424 B.C.E.), and here Brecht, who was strongly averse to conventional forms of heroism, differentiates between real and false courage. Socrates is a teacher famous for his dialectical irony. Like many of Brecht's characters, he is a man of the people who is against speculation and for practical experience, and the story is told with a great deal of humor and irony. Against his will, Socrates has to fight in the battle which is supposedly to defend his city, but in reality, according to Brecht's Marxist theory, is a continuation of business by other means. The aristocrats and the business people profit from the war, but the ordinary people fight and suffer yet reap no rewards. Socrates wishes only to get out of the battle safely, and his fear shows his common sense, since Brecht always regards the instinct to survive as being sensible. At the outset of the fighting, Socrates runs away, inadvertently straying into a thorn field where he gets a thorn in his foot. In pain, unable to run, and with the fighting dangerously close, he begins to yell and also encourages other soldiers to yell, which makes the Persians so afraid that they retreat and the battle is won. Socrates, trying to save himself, thus becomes a hero.

When he is brought home in triumph, his suspicious wife is skeptical of his heroism, thinking that he must have been drunk. Socrates tries to hide his wounded foot for fear of ridicule. For this one act of "heroism" he has become famous, but as one of his students sourly remarks, he had been making valuable contributions to intellectual thought for years and had been ignored. Socrates refuses to be honored, partly because the thorn in his foot will show the real reason why he yelled, but partly because he has always preached pacifism and this new heroic role embarrasses him. Finally, refusing to lie, he confesses to his friend Alcibiades who honors him for his real courage in telling the truth in such an awkward situation. Socrates, with all his weaknesses, emerges as a great man since he has the courage to tell the truth, and he gains dignity because he has the courage to uphold his values. Marxist notions of war as business and the destructive nature of capitalism are also stressed in this story.

"THE AUGSBURG CHALK CIRCLE"

The theme of the chalk circle is used not only in "The Augsburg Chalk Circle" but also in the plays *Mann ist Mann* (1926; *A Man's a Man*, 1961) and *Der Kaukasische Kreidekreis* (1948; *The Caucasian Chalk Circle*, 1948). Brecht learned about the chalk circle from a play by his friend Klabund, who adapted a drama of the same name by Li Hsing-dao, who lived in thirteenth century China. Brecht also drew on the biblical story of Solomon's wisdom in dealing with the two women who both claimed to be the mother of the same child.

In a sober and factual tone, Brecht begins in the style of a chronicler. The historical setting is the Thirty Years' War, and the geographical setting is Augsburg. It is a period of religious strife, yet religion appears in the story to be more concerned with plunder than with ideals. When the Catholic forces seize the city, Zingli, a rich Protestant, is murdered because he will not leave his profitable tannery. His wife is so preoccupied with saving her material things that she abandons her small child. Even later, when Anna, the maid, tells her that the child is safe, she refuses to acknowledge the child. Brecht focuses on the contrast between the rich capitalists represented by the Zinglis and Anna the proletarian maid. Anna, who has been badly treated by the Zinglis, is

humane; even in this time of danger and panic, she looks at the child too long and is seduced by the dangerous temptation in this world to goodness, and she rescues the child.

In the second part of the story, the reader sees the sacrifices that Anna makes for the child. She takes him to her brother in the country, but the brother's position on the farm is not secure. He has married his wife, of whom he is afraid, only because she will inherit the farm, but the wife has typically petit bourgeois values, formed by religion and public opinion. Anna immediately sees that she must say that the child is hers, for her sister-in-law is not charitable. The sister-in-law becomes suspicious when Anna's husband does not come, and she taunts Anna. Anna's brother arranges a marriage for her with a deathly ill cottager named Otterer who suddenly recovers and takes Anna to live with him. Although Anna finds him repulsive, for the child's sake she endures the poverty and the loveless marriage, and the child thrives. One day, years later, a fine lady takes the child away.

In the third part, Anna returns to Augsburg to sue for the return of "her" child. Court scenes, with their dialectical structure, are favorites with Brecht and also show his concern with justice. The judge is Ignaz Dollinger, a man of the people, known for his coarseness and learning, his wisdom and folk cunning. Playing the role of a distraught mother, Mrs. Zingli accuses Anna of taking the child for money, a reflection of Mrs. Zingli's own motives, for she has only been prompted to look for the child because he will inherit the tannery and thus provide her with a good standard of living. Anna, however, cares deeply for both the child's physical and mental development. Clearly, Dollinger favors Anna, although he knows she is lying. To solve the case, he tells his clerk to draw a circle on the floor and put the child in the middle. Dollinger says that the woman with the strongest love will be able to pull the child out of the circle, demonstrating that she is the true mother. Mrs. Zingli pulls with all her might, but Anna lets go for fear of hurting the child. Contrary to the sources, it is not the real mother who gets the child but she who best represents his interests—Anna who has sacrificed everything for his sake. Brecht thus upholds justice by abusing the actual law. The story shows a Marxian idea of the importance of social bonds rather than ties of blood, and it pits a positive heroine of the people against the materialistic bourgeoisie.

The stories discussed in this essay typify themes in many of Brecht's works. Social criticism, an interest in the common person, the fight against injustice, a demythologization of famous historical figures, and the use of alienation effects were concerns of Brecht all of his life. The early nihilist turned into the committed Marxist who looked toward the future to bring a Utopia in which all social ills would be righted. A faint hint of Utopia is suggested in his last story—justice is done, unlike in most of Brecht's works. Although skeptical of actually reaching Utopia, Brecht nevertheless held it up as a measure to see the shortcomings of the world.

OTHER MAJOR WORKS

LONG FICTION: *Der Dreigroschenroman*, 1934 (*The Three Penny Novel*, 1937, 1956); *Die Geschäfte des Herrn Julius Caesar*, 1956.

PLAYS: *Baal*, pb. 1922 (English translation, 1963); *Trommeln in der Nacht*, pr., pb. 1922 (*Drums in the Night*, 1961); *Im Dickicht der Städte*, pr. 1923 (*In the Jungle of Cities*, 1961); *Leben Eduards des Zweiten von England*, pr., pb. 1924 (with Lion Feuchtwanger, based on Christopher Marlowe's play *Edward II*; *Edward II*, 1966); *Die Hochzeit*, pr. 1926 (*The Wedding*, 1970; published as *Die Keinbürgerhochzeit*); *Mann ist Mann*, pr. 1926 (*A Man's a Man*, 1961); *Die Dreigroschenoper*, pr. 1928 (libretto; based on John Gay's play *The Beggar's Opera*; *The Threepenny Opera*, 1949); *Aufstieg und Fall der Stadt Mahagony*, pb. 1929 (libretto; *Rise and Fall of the City of Mahagonny*, 1957); *Das Badener Lehrstück vom Einverständnis*, pr. 1929 (*The Didactic Play of Baden: On Consent*, 1960); *Happy End*, pb. 1929 (lyrics with Elisabeth Hauptmann); *Der Ozeanflug*, pr., pb. 1929 (radio play; *The Flight of the Lindberghs*, 1930); *Der Jasager*, pr. 1930 (based on the Japanese Nō play *Taniko*; *He Who Said Yes*, 1946); *Die Massnahme*, pr. 1930 (libretto; *The Measures Taken*, 1960); *Die heilige Johanna der Schlachthöfe*, pb. 1931 (*St. Joan of the Stockyards*, 1956); *Der Neinsager*, pb. 1931 (*He Who Said No*, 1946); *Die Mutter*, pr., pb. 1932 (based on Maxim Gorky's novel *Mat*; *The Mother*, 1965); *Die Sieben Todsünden der Kleinbürger*, pr. 1933 (cantata; *The Seven Deadly Sins*, 1961); *Die Rundköpfe und die Spitzköpfe*, pr. 1935 (based on William Shakespeare's play *Measure for Measure*; *The Roundheads and the Peakheads*, 1937); *Die Ausnahme und die Regel*, pb. 1937 (*The Exception and the Rule*, 1954); *Die Gewehre der Frau Carrar*, pr., pb. 1937 (*Señora Carrar's Rifles*, 1938); *Die Horatier und die Kuriatier*, pb. 1938 (*The Horatians and the Curatians*, 1947); *Furcht und Elend des dritten Reiches*, pr. 1938 (*The Private Life of the Master Race*, 1944); *Das Verhör des Lukullus*, pb. 1940 (libretto; *The Trial of Lucullus*, 1943); *Mutter Courage und ihre Kinder*, pr. 1941 (based on Hans Jakob Christoffel von Grimmelshausen's *Der abenteuerliche Simplicissimus*; *Mother Courage and Her Children*, 1941); *Leben des Galilei*, pr. 1943 (*Life of Galileo*, 1947); *Der gute Mensch von Sezuan*, pr. 1943 (*The Good Woman of Setzuan*, 1948); *Herr Puntila und sein Knecht Matti*, pr. 1948 (*Mr. Puntila and His Hired Man, Matti*, 1976); *Der kaukasische Kreidekreis*, pr. 1948 (based on Li Hsing-dao's play *The Circle of Chalk*; *The Caucasian Chalk Circle*, 1948); *Die Antigone des Sophokles*, pr., pb. 1948; *Der Hofmeister*, pr. 1950 (adaptation of Jacob Lenz's *Der Hofmeister*; *The Tutor*, 1972); *Der Prozess der Jeanne d'Arc zu Rouen, 1431*, pr. 1952 (based on Anna Seghers's radio play; *The Trial of Jeanne d'Arc at Rouen, 1431*, 1972); *Don Juan*, pr. 1953 (based on Molière's *Don Juan*; English translation, 1972); *Die Gesichte der Simone Machard*, pb. 1956 (with Feuchtwanger; *The Visions of Simone Machard*, 1961); *Die Tage der Commune*, pr. 1956 (based on Nordahl Grieg's *Nederlaget*; *The Days of the Commune*, 1971); *Pauken und Trompeten*, pb. 1956 (adaptation of George Farquhar's *The Recruiting Officer*; *Trumpets and Drums*, 1972); *Der aufhaltsame Aufstieg des Arturo Ui*, pb. 1957 (*The Resistible Rise of Arturo Ui*, 1972); *Schweyk im zweiten Weltkrieg*, pb. 1957 (based on Jaroslav Hašsek's novel *Osudy dobrého vojáka Švejka ve svetove války*; *Schweyk in the Second World War*, 1975); *Coriolan*, pb. 1959 (adaptation of William Shakespeare's play *Coriolanus*; *Coriolanus*, 1972); *Turandot: Oder, Der Kongress der Weisswascher*, pr. 1970.

SCREENPLAYS: *Kuhle Wampe*, 1932 (English translation, 1933); *Hangmen Also Die*, 1943; *Das Lied der Ströme*, 1954; *Herr Puntila und sein Knecht Matti*, 1955.

POETRY: *Hauspostille*, 1972, 1951 (*Manual of Piety*, 1966); *Lieder, Gedichte, Chöre*, 1934 (*Songs, Poems, Choruses*, 1976); *Svendborger Gedichte*, 1939 (*Svendborg Poems*, 1976); *Selected Poems*, 1947; *Hundert Gedichte*, 1951 (*A Hundred Poems*, 1976); *Gedichte und Lieder*, 1956 (*Poems and Songs*, 1976); *Gedichte*, 1960-1965 (nine volumes); *Bertolt Brecht: Poems, 1913-1956*, 1976.

NONFICTION: *Der Messingkauf*, 1937-1951 (*The Messingkauf Dialogues*, 1965); *Arbeitsjournal*, 1938-1955, 1973 (three volumes); *Kleines Organon für das Theater*, 1948 (*A Little Organum for the Theater*, 1951); *Brecht on Theater*, 1964 (edited by John Willett); *Schriften zum Theater*, 1964-1967 (seven volumes); *Autobiographische Aufzeichnungen, 1920-1954*, 1975 (*Diaries, 1920-1922*, 1979).

BIBLIOGRAPHY

Bartram, Graham, and Anthony Waine, eds. *Brecht in Perspective*. London: Longman, 1982. Thirteen excellent essays by highly qualified scholars. The topics range from German drama before Brecht through Brecht's manifold innovations to Brecht's legacy for German and English playwrights. Indispensable reading for understanding the broader context of his works.

Cook, Bruce. *Brecht in Exile*. New York: Holt, Rinehart and Winston, 1982. A series of essays that covers Brecht's life in exile in America from 1933 until 1956. Briefly mentions that although Brecht had become quite skilled in the short story, he never mastered the novel. Discusses the story "The Augsburg Chalk Circle" as the source for the play *The Caucasian Chalk Circle*.

Dickson, Keith A. *Towards Utopia: A Study of Brecht*. Oxford, England: Clarendon Press, 1978. Contains a nine-range discussion of the short fiction, with analyses of three stories from *Tales from the Calendar*: "The Experiment," "The Heretic's Coat," and "Caesar and His Legionary." Places Brecht's works in the context of literary, philosophical, social, and political history. German quotations are translated at the end of the book.

Esslin, Martin. *Brecht: The Man and His Work*. 1960. Rev. ed. Garden City, N. Y.: Doubleday, 1971. A lucidly written biography. Emphasizes that Brecht's lasting fame is mainly attributable to his masterful use of language, not to the intended message of the works, which often has the opposite of the desired effect. The reference section includes a useful descriptive list of Brecht's principal works.

Fuegi, John. *Bertolt Brecht: Chaos, According to Plan*. Cambridge, England: Cambridge University Press, 1987. While concentrating on the dramatic works, Fuegi stresses the enormous contribution made by Brecht's loyal collaborators, including Elizabeth Hauptmann, who may actually have written most of "The Beast." Contains a detailed chronology in the appendix.

Hayman, Ronald. *Brecht: A Biography*. London: Weidenfeld & Nicolson, 1983. A lengthy, dispassionately objective biography with many interesting details. Hayman skillfully integrates the facts of Brecht's private life with the discussion of his works. Opens with a chronology and a list of performances.

Hill, Claude. *Bertolt Brecht*. Boston: Twayne, 1975. An overall introduction to Brecht's life and work. The only references to the short fiction are brief mentions of the Keuner stories and of the story "The Augsburg Chalk Circle" as the source for *The Caucasian Chalk Circle*. However, this is a good introduction to Brecht's work written for the general reader.

Jameson, Frederic. *Brecht and Method*. New York: Verso, 1998. A challenging study of Brecht as a modernist and postmodernist thinker by a noted neo-Marxist critic and theorist. Jameson discusses Brecht's dialectical method, his relationship to the montage theory of filmmaker Sergei Eisenstein, and the relationship between his theory and his practice.

Mews, Siegfried, ed. *A Bertolt Brecht Reference Companion*. Westport, Conn.: Greenwood Press, 1997. An indispensable guide for the student of Brecht. Includes bibliographical references and an index.

Völker, Klaus. *Brecht: A Biography*. Translated by John Nowell. New York: Seabury Press, 1978. Translation of *Bertolt Brecht: Eine Biographie*. Munich: Carl Hanser, 1976. A positive portrait of Brecht, with emphasis not necessarily on the major works. Interspersed with appropriate lines of Brecht's poetry. Good photo section, name index, and title index.

Walker, John. "City Jungles and Expressionist Reifications from Brecht to Hammett." *Twentieth Century Literature* 44 (Spring, 1998): 119-133.

Discusses how the fiction of Brecht and Dashiell Hammett presents the urban landscape as technological anti-utopia and primeval jungle. Discusses the urban jungle metaphor as background for both expressionism and noir. Argues that Hammett reproduces the model of human relations in Brecht's fiction.

Weideli, Walter. *The Art of Bertolt Brecht*. Translated by Daniel Russell. New York: New York University Press, 1963. One of the few studies of Brecht to mention his short stories. Suggests that the stories in *Calendar Tales* constitute a kind of popular almanac containing Brecht's rules of conduct. Contends Brecht reduces various heroes of history to a common denominator in the collection.

Jennifer Michaels, updated by Jean M. Snook

HAROLD BRODKEY

Born: Alton, Illinois; October 25, 1930
Died: New York, New York; January 26, 1996

PRINCIPAL SHORT FICTION

First Love and Other Sorrows, 1957, 1986
Women and Angels, 1985
Stories in an Almost Classical Mode, 1988
The World Is the Home of Love and Death: Stories, 1997

OTHER LITERARY FORMS

For more than three decades, Harold Brodkey worked on a sprawling, Proustian novel with a working title of "A Party of Animals," based on his life from birth to the end of college. Portions of the novel, under contract to Farrar, Straus and Giroux since 1961, appeared first in *The New Yorker, Esquire*, and *New American Review*. Two of the three segments of *Women and Angels*, "Ceil" and "Angel," were taken from this projected novel, which ran to more than two thousand pages in length. The novel was finally published in 1991 as *The Runaway Soul*. A volume of his

essays, *Sea Battles on Dry Land: Essays*, was published in 1999.

ACHIEVEMENTS

Harold Brodkey is best appreciated as a writer who produced three dozen stories that are so intricately presented as to make readers experience the smallest details. His greatest strength lay neither in plot construction nor in thematic development but in his ability to capture and report authentically the exact, second-by-second occurrences about which he writes.

Brodkey received both the Prix de Rome (Magazine Award) and the Brandeis Creative Arts Award in 1974. He received first prize in the O. Henry short-story awards in 1975 and again in 1976. Brodkey has been a fellow of the American Academy in Rome, of the John Simon Guggenheim Memorial Foundation, and of the National Endowment for the Arts.

BIOGRAPHY

Harold Roy Brodkey was born Aaron Roy Weintraub

Harold Brodkey (©Jerry Bauer)

across the Mississippi River and slightly to the northeast of St. Louis, Missouri, in Alton, Illinois, in 1930. His father, a junk man, was illiterate. Brodkey's mother—who was bright, bookish, and fluent in five or six languages—died when Harold was an infant, and the father, unable to care for the child, allowed Joseph and Doris Brodkey to adopt him. They changed his name to Harold and gave him their surname.

In Brodkey's fiction, Joseph and Doris Brodkey become Leila and S. L. (perhaps to suggest St. Louis) Cohn. Their daughter, somewhat older than Harold, is Nonie in Brodkey's stories. Brodkey has kept the details of his personal life private except as they are revealed in his stories.

When he was six, Brodkey's high intelligence quotient was recognized, and special training was recommended for him. His birth father took him from his adoptive parents when he learned this but could not cope with the boy and returned him the next day. Having lost his real mother so early that he could not

remember her, Brodkey created the mother he dreamed she was, reconstructing her from scraps of information gleaned from her acquaintances. By inventing her in his own imagination, Brodkey unleashed the earliest stirrings of his ability to create credible characters and situations.

Brodkey lost his adoptive parents when he was a teenager. Joseph Brodkey had a stroke when Harold was nine and was an invalid thereafter. He lived for five years, requiring constant attention. One year before her husband died, Doris Brodkey developed cancer and died during Harold's early days at Harvard University.

His Harvard scholarship and a small inheritance enabled Brodkey to live outside the Midwest. His first collection of stories, *First Love and Other Sorrows*, became an alternate selection of the Book-of-the-Month Club. The three segments of *Women and Angels*, published in 1985, were taken from *A Runaway Soul*, as were many of the stories found in *Stories in an Almost Classical Mode*. This book was also a Book-of-the-Month Club alternate selection.

Brodkey married Joanne Brown in 1952, and they had a daughter, Amma Emily, in 1953; the couple divorced in 1962. He married novelist Ellen Schwamm in 1980, and they settled in New York City. He has taught writing and literature at Cornell University and at the City College of the City University of New York. Harold Brodkey died in New York City on January 26, 1996.

ANALYSIS

Harold Brodkey writes about people and places that most readers recognize and consider unexceptional. It is attention to detail, to the slow, agonizingly detailed unfolding of the commonplace that has distinguished Brodkey as a chronicler of what it is like to grow up—Jewish and adopted—in the Midwest. In the early stories, the cast of characters is identical: an adoptive mother and father, an older sister given to tormenting, and her younger brother, the autobiographical character, the first-person and occasionally third-person narrator.

The first three stories of *First Love and Other Sorrows* are really the beginning of what seems to be an embryonic *Bildungsroman*. They detail the childhood of the first-person narrator, a child who longs for love but cannot attract it. The narrator was adopted by his foster parents in part because he was very attractive, but in "The State of Grace," the first story in the volume, he is thirteen years old, six feet tall, 125 pounds, and his ears stick out. He is displeased with the way he looks, extremely conscious of being the gangly teenager new to adolescence.

The first three stories in the first collection reveal the themes that his later work pursued and presage the focus of *A Runaway Soul*. A recurrent theme in Brodkey's work is that true selflessness as such does not exist. In his stories, as presumably in his early life, all Brodkey's characters have self-serving motives. This attitude may seem cynical, but in Brodkey's work it emerges as realistic. Sometimes Brodkey confuses reciprocity with selfishness, as, for example, in "Innocence," one of the later stories in *Stories in an Almost Classical Mode*, in which the first-person narrator is determined to give Orra Perkins her first orgasm, not so much to provide her with pleasure as to get a stronger hold on her and increase the intensity of his own sexual pleasure with her. It is difficult in this story to determine the line between selfishness and selflessness.

Brodkey's stories are essentially concerned with providing descriptive details about places and emotions. His prose style has been shaped considerably by the style of *The New Yorker*, in which many of his stories appeared. The prose is unadorned, lean and direct, carefully calculated, and assiduously polished. Brodkey succeeds best when he writes about his midwestern childhood in University City, Missouri, in an uncomplicated way, in a style that reports commonplaces.

FIRST LOVE AND OTHER SORROWS

The title story of *First Love and Other Sorrows* takes place in the springtime, when its narrator is sixteen years old and confronts a budding sexuality that raises many questions within him. He lives with his adoptive mother and his twenty-two-year-old sister, who seems no more pleased with herself physically than the narrator is with himself. The adoptive father is dead.

The boy's mother warns him against playing too hard and getting overheated. This admonition is a veiled warning that the heat of youthful sexuality can be as dangerous as the heat of April. The boy feels that such is the case, as a subplot that can be interpreted in a homosexual context makes clear. The sister dates Sonny Bruster, son of the town banker. The romance between them is not free of hazards. At one point, they stop seeing each other, but they reconcile and, before the story ends, are engaged. The boy feels like an intruder in the house of his mother, who makes it clear that she cooks only because he is there. The family situation is not hostile so much as vacant. The mother, a controlling woman, is vitally concerned with having her daughter marry someone prosperous. She, somewhat like Amanda Wingfield in Tennessee Williams's *The Glass Menagerie* (1944), had experienced genteel living but has been reduced to living more humbly.

The story ends with the narrator's sister engaged to Sonny Bruster. Her mother is composing letters at night to inform all her relatives of the engagement. The boy and his sister come into the kitchen, and the mother offers to heat up some soup for them. Her eyes fill with tears of emotion, and the three embrace and kiss. This story is typical of Brodkey's early work and gives a strong indication of the course of his succeeding work. Nothing much happens in the story except that an adolescent boy makes tentative moves toward growing into manhood. He is uncertain and fearful of rejection. The story deals with situations and emotions but has little plot. It is filled with the carefully observed, well-presented sights, sounds, and textures that characterize Brodkey's writing.

"SENTIMENTAL EDUCATION"

"Sentimental Education," included in *First Love and Other Sorrows*, was first published in *The New Yorker* only one month after "First Love and Other Sorrows" appeared in the same magazine. It marks a tentative step toward "Innocence," which it predates by sixteen years. Set in Cambridge, Massachusetts, where the nineteen-year-old protagonist, Elgin Smith, is an undergraduate at Harvard, the story's only other character is Caroline Hedges, a freshman at Radcliffe College. Both are virgins. As the story progresses, they have a passionate affair.

The action takes place within an academic year, during which Elgin and Caroline are forced to reassess their values. They are caught in a paradoxical situation, never fully resolved because, at school year's end, they part, although they do not break up decisively. They agree to meet again in the fall, but platonically. During their last five weeks before summer, the two abjure sex. They kiss, they touch, but they hold back. Finally, Caroline catches the night train to Baltimore and later goes to Europe for the summer. This story is different from the others in the collection. It is, unlike the first three, a third-person, author-omniscient narrative. It is the only story in the collection not directly related to any of the others and perhaps the most delicately presented story in *First Love and Other Sorrows*.

"INNOCENCE"

"Innocence," unlike many of Brodkey's stories in *Stories in an Almost Classical Mode*, was not first published in *The New Yorker* but appeared in *American Review*, presumably because of *The New Yorker*'s reluctance to publish the four-letter word used vulgarly to indicate copulation. "Innocence" is a story of young lust—as opposed to young love—in which the protagonist, a Harvard undergraduate, achieves what he feared was the unachievable, a sexual encounter with a much sought-after Radcliffe nymphet, Orra Perkins.

Orra has never achieved an orgasm because, according to her, she is too sexual to have orgasms. She is not distressed by this omission and strenuously discourages the narrator from trying to give her the orgasm that he wants her to experience. His motive is twofold: He thinks that he will, in a way, own Orra if he achieves his end. He also thinks that his own sexual pleasure with her will be enhanced if she can respond fully.

This story, generally considered to be among Brodkey's best, is some thirty pages long, twenty pages of it devoted to presenting a highly detailed account of how Orra is brought to the pinnacle of passion that the narrator wants for her. Before the story is over, Orra not only has her long-awaited orgasm but also, mulling it over, has another, multiple orgasm. Despite all the explicit physical detail that the story contains, the result is not prurient, but neither is it clinical. Rather it is realistic, direct, and detailed—detailed, indeed, to the point that the reader longs for Orra to climax.

This longing is part of Brodkey's technique. He does not seek to titillate his readers but to walk them through the experience, to exhaust them as Orra becomes exhausted. As the two participants in the event strain through what seems an endless encounter to achieve orgasm, readers are dragged along, worn down by the detailed narration of the event, to the point that they feel as physically spent as the perspiring participants when the moment of ecstasy finally arrives. Brodkey's theme concerns dependency and achieving union through weakness—in this case, Orra's previous lack of sexual fulfillment. The narrator's ability to bring her to the point of climax makes her dependent upon him in ways that she has never been before.

"CEIL"

It is difficult to say definitively whether "Ceil," one of the three stories in *Women and Angels*, is a success. Some would question whether it is a story or merely a musing, a recollection, a jotting of fragments. "Lila" and "Largely an Oral History of My Mother," both depictions of Brodkey's mother by adoption, are more complete works and provide a more coherent picture of their subject than "Ceil" does.

Despite this caveat, "Ceil" is among Brodkey's most important works. It reveals more than any other story the inner Brodkey, the Brodkey yearning to establish a link with his past, the Brodkey searching for home, straining to walk behind the curtain that separates him from his shadowy heritage. Although the writing in "Ceil" is uneven, it contains some of Brodkey's best images, particularly his writing about the great plains of the Midwest near Staunton, where his mother lived.

Ceil, the youngest of what Brodkey vaguely refers to as twenty or twenty-five children, was the offspring of a charismatic, brilliant rabbi and his long-suffering, remarkably fertile wife. Born near Odessa, Ceil was her father's favorite. He arranged a marriage for her, but she refused. She was a bright, independent girl who, when her father simultaneously forgave and put a curse upon her, left Russia for the United States.

Ceil disembarks from the ship and goes directly to a beauty shop. She does not like the way her hair looks afterward, and, within an hour, she is in a beauty salon having it redone. Not only do appearances matter to Ceil, often described by Lila as queenlike, but also she values success. She moves quickly from being a waitress to being a housemaid to being a successful business woman. She marries Max, a man much beneath her, originally from around Odessa. She is his superior in every way. Her success becomes legendary. Her self-satisfaction culminates with the birth of her son. Then, Ceil dies after an abortion, leaving Lila to become surrogate mother to two-year-old Wiley.

THE WORLD IS THE HOME OF LOVE AND DEATH

Published a year after his death, *The World Is the Home of Love and Death* is an unfortunate epitaph to the work of Harold Brodkey. Blasted by reviewers for its careless pretentiousness—several stories so loose and rambling that they seem like unedited rejects from his novel *The Runaway Soul*—the book's eleven stories are an uneven testimony to Brodkey's brilliance. Brodkey's self-proclaimed brilliance is just one of the reasons this final collection of stories was met with hostility by some reviewers and caution by others; even Brodkey's admirers warned Brodkey newcomers that this was not the place to begin. As one critic said, the book is for hardened Brodkey veterans.

Most of the stories focus on Brodkey's childhood persona Wiley Silenowicz (a central character in *The Runaway Soul*) growing up in Missouri during the Depression. Other members of the Silenowicz family featured in these loosely related stories are Wiley's adoptive mother, Lila, and her husband, S. L. Arrogantly intelligent, Wiley is not always an easy character to tolerate. His sense that he had been "a phenomenally pretty child" recalls Brodkey's own immodest admission once of being the "best living writer in English . . . the equivalent of a Wordsworth or a Milton."

In one of the most self-indulgent stories in the collection, "Waking," the young Wiley, mute and ill with shock after the death of his mother, confronts a new life with Lila, his adoptive mother. The only event in this long story is a bath Lila gives the boy as she tries to heal him by gentleness and coy wooing. Lila's theatrics and flirtation with the child are bound up with her genuine effort to rescue him from his grief and enable him to function in the world.

Most reviewers have singled out "Bullies" as the most subtle and sustained performance in the book. Although the story is forty pages long and primarily depends on reported dialogue between Lila and a neighbor named Ida, Brodkey manages to create a sensitive account of a long conversation filled with the nuances of forbidden flirtation between the two women. Wiley marvels at their ability to balance their talk in such a way as never to step over the taboo line: "Both women are controlled—and full of signals—so many that I don't see how they can keep track of what they are doing in the world. . . . "

As one reviewer has noted about this collection, Brodkey can seem needlessly self-indulgent and downright dull to any reader still interested in the old-fashioned pleasures of plot. Indeed here style, rather than mere event, is the heart of the matter. However, as it always was with Oscar Wilde, that most famous proponent of the superiority of style over mundane everyday reality, with Brodkey one is never quite sure if one is in the presence of genius or the consummate con man.

OTHER MAJOR WORKS

LONG FICTION: *The Runaway Soul*, 1991; *Profane Friendship*, 1994.

NONFICTION: *Avedon: Photographs, 1947-1977*, 1978 (with Richard Avedon); *This Wild Darkness: The Story of My Death*, 1996; *Sea Battles on Dry Land: Essays*, 1999.

BIBLIOGRAPHY

Bawer, Bruce. "A Genius for Publicity." *The New Criterion* 7 (December, 1988): 58-69. Bawer comments on how well known Brodkey has become even though his major work, *A Party of Animals*, has not appeared.

Bidney, Martin. "A Song of Innocence and of Experience: Rewriting Blake in Brodkey's 'Piping Down the Valleys Wild.'" *Studies in Short Fiction* 31 (Spring, 1994): 237-245. Argues that Brodkey's story is a reformulation of Blake's poem into a sophisticated study of innocence that is maintained because of experience. Maintains that, like Blake, Brodkey sees innocence as filled with tension that will be more fully revealed by experience.

_____. "An Unreliable Modern Mariner: Rewriting Coleridge in Harold Brodkey's 'The State of Grace.'" *Studies in Short Fiction* 31 (Winter, 1994): 47-55. Claims that Brodkey's story is a remaking of Samuel Taylor Coleridge's "The Rime of the Ancient Mariner." Asserts the story is balanced between witty takeoffs of Mariner themes and the seriousness of the protagonist's dilemma. Examines how in the story the Mariner motifs deflate the protagonist's self-deception.

Brodkey, Harold. "Harold Brodkey: The Art of Fiction." Interview by James Linville. *Paris Review* 33, no. 121. (Winter, 1991): 50. An insightful interview into Brodkey's style and methods.

_____. "In the Space of a Sentence." Interview by James Linville. *Harper's Magazine* 285 (August, 1992): 33. Discusses the ways in which good writing creates a unique perception in the reader's mind regarding public settings.

Garrison, Deborah Gottlieb. "The True Lover." *The New Yorker* 72 (October 7, 1996): 85. Notes that Brodkey often wrote about the problems associated with love during and after the sexual revolution; provides a biographical sketch leading up to Brodkey's announcement that he was infected with the virus that causes acquired immunodeficiency syndrome (AIDS).

Howard, Richard. "Almost Classic." *The New Republic* 209 (July 12, 1993): 10-11. Claims that Brodkey's AIDS disclosure constituted a blatant attempt to mythologize himself; calls the announcement a cruel and propagandistic assertion of artistic privilege, making death a matter of public relations; insists that his self-disclosure is obscene, for the cost of the publicity he seeks is paid for by millions of others who are suffering in dignity and silence.

Iannone, Carol. "The Brodkey Question." *Commentary* 87 (April, 1989): 58-61. Iannone questions why Brodkey has achieved the reputation that he has. Notes the lack of "artistic restraint" but credits him with sensitivity in his observations. She contends that he is "smashing the graven idol of aestheticism."

Kakutani, Michiko. "First-Person Stories, Tidy and Not." *The New York Times*, September 14, 1988, p. C25. Kakutani points to some unevenness in Brodkey's largely autobiographical stories.

Kermode, Frank. "I Am Only Equivocally Harold Brodkey." Review of *Stories in an Almost Classical Mode*, by Harold Brodkey. *The New York Times Book Review*, September 18, 1988, p. 3. In this review of *Stories in an Almost Classical Mode*, Kermode provides valuable observations about Brodkey's unique style.

Mano, D. Keith. "Harold Brodkey: The First Rave." *Esquire* 87 (January, 1977): 14-15. Mano is particularly compelling in his comments about Brodkey's "tyrannical use of punctuation," one of the writer's salient characteristics.

Shiras, Mary. "Accessible Dreams." *Commonweal* 67 (February 7, 1958): 493-494. This early assessment of Brodkey's *First Love and Other Sorrows* is essentially favorable. Comments on exceptional details that the author presents.

Smith, Denitia. "The Genius: Harold Brodkey and His Great (Unpublished) Novel." *New York* 21 (September 19, 1991): 54-66. The fullest and most important article on Brodkey. Smith provides illustrations and uncovers countless details of Brodkey's life available in no other source.

Weiseltier, Leon. "A Revelation." Review of *Women and Angels*, by Harold Brodkey. *The New Republic* 192 (May 20, 1985): 30-33. In one of the few reviews of *Women and Angels*, Weiseltier praises the new story, "Angel," but calls the other two stories "platitudinous."

R. Baird Shuman, updated by Charles E. May

LARRY BROWN

Born: Oxford, Mississippi; July 9, 1951

PRINCIPAL SHORT FICTION

Facing the Music, 1988
Big Bad Love, 1990

OTHER LITERARY FORMS

On Fire (1994) is a collection of autobiographical essays from Larry Brown's days as a firefighter in Oxford, Mississippi. The author of such novels as *Dirty Work* (1989), *Joe* (1991), *Father and Son* (1996), and *Billy Ray's Farm* (1997), Brown adapted *Dirty Work* for the prestigious *American Playhouse* series aired by the Public Broadcasting Service.

ACHIEVEMENTS

In 1990, Larry Brown received the Award for Literature from the Mississippi Institute of Arts and Letters for his story "Facing the Music." Brown has had stories anthologized in *The Best American Short Stories* in 1989 and 1992. The Southern Book Critics' Circle awarded Brown its 1991 award for fiction, and *Joe* was selected by the American Library Association as one of the twelve best fiction books of 1991.

BIOGRAPHY

Born in Oxford, Mississippi, on July 9, 1951, to Knox and Leona (Barlow) Brown, William Larry Brown has spent most of his life in that area. Brown was a Marine from 1970 until 1972 during the Vietnam conflict, but he remained stateside. On August 17, 1974, he married Mary Annie Coleman, and they have two sons, Billy Ray and Shane, and one daughter, LeAnne.

Brown did not attend college until 1982, when he took a class in creative writing at the University of Mississippi (Ole Miss) after years of writing convinced him that he still needed to find his voice. Author Ellen Douglas at Ole Miss more fully introduced him to the world of literature and simultaneously helped him forge that voice. In 1982, Brown's first short story was published in *Easyriders*, a magazine

for motorcyclists, but his short story "Facing the Music," published in 1987 in *The Mississippi Review*, captured the attention of Algonquin Books editor Shannon Ravenel and won national acclaim.

From the time he left the Marines, Brown held a variety of jobs, from his first job with a stove company to his final and most significant job as a firefighter with the Oxford Fire Department, from which he retired as captain in 1990 in order to spend all his energy on his writing.

ANALYSIS

When Algonquin Books was first marketing Larry Brown, it used his status as fireman-turned-writer to the firm's advantage, and, indeed, Brown's educational background is not the one usually associated with a writer. Brown's self-education has enabled him to stay true to himself and his art and follow his inclinations wherever they lead him. Where they lead him is into the same realm to which they led the major writer William Faulkner, who also came from Oxford, Mississippi, and into those "eternal verities of the human heart" of which Faulkner spoke so eloquently and which any enduring artist must plumb. Indeed, Brown denies the "Faulknerian" influence on his work, and it is not there in any but a superficial way. In an interview with *Publishers Weekly*, Brown, though flattered by the comparison with Faulkner, quite accurately pinpointed one of the major ways in which his work departs from Faulkner's when he said that Faulkner "wrote about so much that went back before his time. I don't get into that. I write about the here and now." In fact, stylistically, Brown is far afield from Faulkner and reads much more like minimalist writer Raymond Carver, whose influence Brown readily acknowledges.

Sometimes difficult to pigeonhole—ranging as they do from the realism of "Facing the Music" to the humor of "Waiting for the Ladies" to the absurdist satire of "Discipline"—Brown's stories nonetheless are of a piece when it comes to their clearheadedness and lack of sentimentality. Often criticized as bleak and violent, they mirror the isolation and lack of communication that characterize modern society. Despite the dark vision they frequently portray, Brown's works also show the possibility of redemption and hope. As he says in an interview in *The Southern Quarterly*, his "fiction is about people surviving, about people proceeding out from calamity."

Larry Brown (©Miriam Berkley)

FACING THE MUSIC

In an essay published in *Publishing Research Quarterly* and written with Brown and others, Shannon Ravenel notes that *Facing the Music*, Brown's first book-length publication, was a departure for the publishing company, as it was a collection of short stories rather than a novel. The strength of the title story alone, however, allowed the editors to ignore "conventional wisdom." Too harsh and biting to have been accepted by either *The New Yorker* or *Esquire*, the unconventional stories in the collection are varied, gritty, and, to use one of the terms most commonly associated with Brown's work, "honest." Spanning a number of voices—from that of an iso-

lated husband refusing to deal with his wife's mastectomy in "Facing the Music" to that of a young, African American, alcoholic mother in "Kubuku Rides (This Is It)" to that of Mr. Parker, jobless and friendless after his wife has him kill their dog in "Old Frank and Jesus" to that of a cynical (former) lover in "The End of Romance"—the stories all deal ultimately with what Brown, in an interview in *The Chattahoochee Review*, calls "the truths of the human heart."

The most poignant story of the collection, "Facing the Music" is the interior monologue of a husband who still loves his wife after her mastectomy yet detaches himself from her, choosing rather to watch old movies or even commit adultery rather than admit that he, too, has been hurt by her cancer. In the end, as she reaches for him in the dark, he recalls their honeymoon, the sweetness of their love for each other as he realizes, "your first love is your best love, that you'll never find any better." The story stops short of promising an easy healing of their relationship. The love for and of her family also encompasses but is unable to heal Kubuku in "Kubuku Rides (This Is It)." Still recovering from a drunk-driving accident, Kubuku rides into the dark at the end of the story to procure more alcohol as her husband turns out the porch light, which had always symbolically shone for her return. Pain is present throughout the collection, though frequently peppered with cynicism.

In "Samaritans" the narrator, a young, "white trash" woman, emerges from a Rambler filled with kids and her mother, uses a tale of woe to weasel thirty dollars from a man whose wife has left him, then spends it so she and her mother can get drunk. "Boy you a dumb sumbitch," her son tells her at the end of the story. "Leaving Town" presents a split narrative, focusing on an unhappily married carpenter and an older divorcé, who almost make a connection but are unable to because of her fears. "The End of Romance," the final story in the collection, is the most violent and darkest of all. In the midst of their breakup, the narrator and his girlfriend drive up to a convenience store and witness a shooting. When he returns to his girlfriend, who is waiting in the convertible outside, she screeches, distraught, "I WOULDN'T LEAVE YOU NOW FOR NOTHIN," as the wounded man flops on their car. She proceeds to tell him how they can heal their relationship ("maybe we should watch more TV together"), when the cops arrive and prepare to fire at the shooter. The narrator then calmly raises his hands, points to her, and says, "She did it."

BIG BAD LOVE

The three parts of *Big Bad Love* are linked by stories about writers, "The Apprentice," "Discipline," and *Ninety-two Days*. "The Apprentice" relates the story of a husband and wife who are almost driven apart by her need to write. His acceptance of her compulsion and his deep love for her keep their marriage intact. The satire "Discipline," quite different from Brown's other stories, is the mock-trial of a plagiarist, or at best, a literary imitator. Actually a novella, *Ninety-two Days* chronicles the stops and starts of the narrator as he attempts to write and publish and live something of a life in the meantime.

The other stories in the collection are more about the hits and misses of living itself. The narrator in "Big Bad Love" leaves his house to go drinking to avoid burying his dead dog, spends his time at the bar contemplating the fact that he is not sexually endowed enough to satisfy his wife, and returns to find she has left with a man who "has the equipment to take care" of her problem. Though he sees this as a possible new beginning, the loneliness sets in. "Old Soldiers" is a fond look at old soldiers who need one another to understand the horrors they have lived through, and "Sleep" traces the insomnia of an older couple who keep each other up at night with their fears. Perhaps the most interesting of the stories in the collection, "Waiting for the Ladies," highlights, in a rather unexpected manner, the need for connection and communication. When the narrator's wife tells her husband that someone exposed himself to her at the dumpster, he is incensed and goes to investigate the situation. Making a mental picture of the exhibitionist (fiftyish, living with his mother, on welfare, impotent), the narrator fails to note the similarity to himself, as he has quit his job and is suspicious of his wife's long lunches with her boss. After tracking down the exhibitionist, who is at home with his mother, the narrator enters, gun under his arm, and

then sits down with the terrified mother and son only to tell them "what my life then was like."

OTHER MAJOR WORKS

LONG FICTION: *Dirty Work*, 1989; *Joe*, 1991; *Father and Son*, 1996; *Billy Ray's Farm*, 1997; *Fay*, 2000.

NONFICTION: *On Fire*, 1994.

BIBLIOGRAPHY

Applebome, Peter. "Larry Brown's Long and Rough Road to Becoming a Writer." *The New York Times*, March 5, 1990, C11. Tracing what Barry Hannah called Brown's "miracle" in which "he became his own genius," the article examines Brown's apprenticeship, his numerous rejections, and the amazing determination that led him to publication and success.

Brown, Larry. "An Interview with Larry Brown." Interview by Kay Bonetti. *Missouri Review* 18 (1995): 79-107. This interview delves into Brown's background, the influences on his writing (Fyodor Dostoevski, Joseph Conrad, and Flannery O'Connor, as well as his days as a firefighter), his belief that writing is an acquired skill, and the darkness of his vision. It gives an overall perspective of the themes and motifs that pervade Brown's works, from his passion for the land and saving it from destruction to the importance of family and community and the tragedy of poverty.

Brown, Larry. "An Interview with Larry Brown." Interview by Susan Ketchin. *The Southern Quarterly* 32 (Winter, 1994): 95-109. This interview, centering on *Facing the Music*, emphasizes the philosophical underpinning of Brown's work. Revealing the significance of myths, dreams, and religion on his art, he pinpoints a common thread in his fiction as his characters, faced with seemingly unconquerable obstacles in the battle of good and evil, must decide to give in to despair or to continue the fight, no matter how hopeless.

Brown, Larry. "Interview with Larry Brown: Breadloaf '92." Interview by Dorie LaRue. *The Chattahoochee Review* 13 (Spring, 1993): 39-56. Brown traces his career as a writer to his love of reading as a child. Noting Homer and Mark Twain as early influences, he cites Raymond Carver, Lewis Nordan, and Paul MacCormac as current favorites. He discusses the stories in *Big Bad Love* in some detail, mentioning that he gave many of the characters his initials and, more significantly, that he attempted to make his characters memorable and potentially redeemable.

Brown, Larry. "Larry Brown: The Former Firefighter Talks About His Long Apprenticeship as a Writer." Interview by Bob Summer. *Publishers Weekly* 238 (October 11, 1991): 46-47. While discussing his journey from failing senior English to his successful publication of short-story collections and novels, Brown asserts that the ability to write is learned, not innate, and stresses the laborious nature of the act. In covering the influences on his writing, Brown denies much, if any, similarity to William Faulkner.

Farmer, Joy A. "The Sound and the Fury of Larry Brown's 'Waiting for the Ladies.'" *Studies in Short Fiction* 29 (Summer, 1992): 315-322. Examining the influence of structure and theme of Faulkner's *The Sound and the Fury* (1929), Farmer sees a correspondence between "N" in Brown's "Waiting for the Ladies" and the three Compson males of Faulkner's novel. Farmer makes her case that this story is a "reworking" of the novel, albeit a comic one.

Lyons, Paul. "Larry Brown's *Joe* and the Uses and Abuses of the 'Region' Concept." *Studies in American Fiction* 25 (Spring, 1997): 101-124. Although this essay deals with a novel, its placement of Brown's writing in a regional/cultural context is highly informative and applicable to his short fiction as well.

Jaquelyn W. Walsh

BLISS BROYARD

Born: Greenwich, Connecticut; September 5, 1966

PRINCIPAL SHORT FICTION
My Father, Dancing: Stories, 1999

OTHER LITERARY FORMS

Bliss Broyard has also written "My Father's Daughter," an essay appearing in *The Art of the Essay* (1999). In addition to her short stories, she has published essays and reviews in *The New York Times*, *The Washington Post*, and other periodicals. Broyard also produces and writes for "The Real World," a television series produced by Music Television (MTV).

ACHIEVEMENTS

My Father, Dancing was a *New York Times* Notable Book of 1999 and was listed as a *Boston Globe* Best Book of 1999. "Mr. Sweetly Indecent" was se-lected for *The Best American Short Stories 1998*. Her work has also been included in the 1994 edition of *The Pushcart Prize*.

BIOGRAPHY

Bliss Broyard's father was the late Anatole Broyard, the author and longtime literary critic and book review editor for *The New York Times*. Anatole Broyard exerted a profound influence on his daughter, and many of the stories in her first collection were inspired by her relationship with him.

An imaginative child and a voracious reader, who had been writing poems and stories for years, Bliss Broyard did not seriously consider becoming a writer herself until around the time her father was diagnosed with terminal prostate cancer. A friend from the elder Broyard's days in Greenwich Village, New York, came to visit him in the hospital and to pay an old debt, which was divided between Broyard's two children. With her share of the money ($250) Bliss Broyard enrolled in a fiction writing course at Harvard University. She eventually earned a master of fine arts in fiction writing, from University of Virginia, where she received a fellowship and where she subsequently also taught. In 1996, Broyard settled in Brooklyn, New York.

ANALYSIS

Bliss Broyard's first short-story collection generally garnered high praise as an auspicious debut. She is especially praised for her depiction of a young woman's coming-of-age and for her cool, economical style. Most important is her theme of a father's effect on a growing daughter, who sees him as the first and possibly the most important man in her life. Some of these father-daughter stories have their sources in Broyard's own life, particularly the title story "My Father, Dancing," which was based on Broyard's thoughts and feelings as her father lay dying in the hospital.

The voice and the perspective of each story are those of a young woman, and whether named Lily, Kate, Pilar, or Lucy, these young women are essentially the same woman with the same perspective. In addition, their situations, while sometimes comical, also provoke considerable apprehension. Furthermore, all the fathers in this collection share a close kinship—if not always famous, they are consistently handsome, suave, and overwhelming. Many of the stories feature fathers whose roguish, seductive sexuality has a powerful effect on their impressionable daughters. The bond between these often slick and breezy fathers and their adoring daughters is depicted in these stories as both a blessing and a curse, so that it is difficult to decide whether such a bond is an advantage or a catastrophe.

Many of her stories also depict the problems Broyard's young women have with men their own age, who often rate a poor second compared to the charming fathers of the previous generation. The psychological issues involving fathers and lovers are compounded by the difficulties involved in coming of age in a social world marked by permissive sexuality, divorce, blended families, and infidelity.

MY FATHER, DANCING

In *My Father, Dancing*, five of the eight stories concern a daughter's intense relationship with an adored, charming, and successful father. In the title story, a young woman named Kate reviews her life with her father as he lies dying from cancer. Central to these memories is her father's love of dancing with her to popular songs of the day at home or in clubs, even in preference to his dancer-wife, Kate's mother. There is considerable apprehension and genuine grief over the impending loss of her father, but when Kate returns to her family living room after her father dies and has a vision of her father as he was the first time he ever danced with her, when she was but a toddler, she realizes that their intense bond has, in an almost magical way, survived his death.

Kate's father is the first in a series of charismatic fathers in this collection. In the second story, "Mr. Sweetly Indecent," however, the charming father is associated with out-of-bounds sexual behavior. In this story, the daughter, while leaving a sexual liaison with a virtual stranger, spies her father kissing a woman with whom he has obviously also spent the night. The parallels between their behavior disturb her, but she also sees that her father, as a married family man, is the more culpable. Her father breezily alleviates his daughter's sense of betrayal, assuring her that this adulterous incident is superficial and will never endanger the love he has for her mother. His daughter is less mollified by these assurances than by her knowledge of the continued, mysterious bond between her mother and father, in which her mother appears as the stronger and wiser figure. However, she has also discerned a talent for deception in her womanizing father and is struck by the fact that she herself evinces promiscuous tendencies.

A beloved father also appears in "At the Bottom of the Lake" as the long-expected guest of a young woman named Lucy who has invited him to stay with her at the family cabin on a lake. When her father finally returns to the cabin for a visit accompanied by his alcoholic second wife Victoria, Lucy's hopes of a family reunion that would heal the pain of her parents' devastating divorce are dashed. The weekend is cut short by a quarrel between Lucy and the temperamental Victoria, but it is Victoria who wisely warns Lucy that her behavior is alienating her patient fiancé Sam. Although Lucy comes to realize she cannot bring back the past, Lucy's affection for the cabin indicates her longing for the kind of love and family life she enjoyed when she was her father's adored little girl.

Fathers are also central to the plot of "The Trouble with Mr. Leopold." Here, an insecure schoolgirl named Celia asks her talented and literary father to help her write one of her papers. Her suburban prep school's headmaster, detecting the deception, promptly gives a low grade. The rivalry between the headmaster, Mr. Leopold, and Celia's rather pompous father, both of whom come from similar working-class backgrounds in Brooklyn, and both of whom have risen in the world, seems to take precedence over Celia's own needs.

Inappropriate sexuality, a dominant theme in this collection, also surfaces in this story in the person of Mr. Leopold, whose interest in his female students concentrates as much on their bodies as on their minds.

Two other stories feature a young girl's attachment not to her father, but to an older and more successful man. In "Loose Talk," a girl named Pilar finds that her relationship with her devoted boyfriend is compromised by her infatuation with a famous musician, a magical, larger-than-life figure. In "Ugliest Faces," a college student named Bridget is in a relationship with one of her former teachers, who is eight years older than she is. His rival is Spike, a drunken fraternity boy whom Pilar accidentally runs down with her automobile, and who insists that Pilar compensate him for his injuries through sexual favors. Fearful of losing her pride of place with her older lover, Pilar finds herself building an ugly, secret life centering on the thuggish Spike and the debt she owes him.

A young girl's dissatisfaction with her peers is also a subject of the last two stories, "A Day in the Country" and "Snowed In," which both feature a young girl named Lily. In "A Day in the Country," the barely teenaged Lily is pressured by her best friend into an unwelcome sexual situation with a boy her own age. While the boy in question possesses little

charm, Lily's father, a well-known conductor, effortlessly draws women to him, including a neighboring mother and daughter as well as Lily's friend Kelly. Lily's father also seems to be casually seducing a woman who has arrived as the date of one of his house guests. "Snowed In," the last story, is once again set in Connecticut and also features Lily, who is now a young woman. Trapped by a snowstorm in an upscale suburban house with a party of her friends, Lily also seems trapped in a peer culture dominated by the preferences of the boys in the house for alcohol and a pornographic movie they find in the video collection of the parents who own the house. Lily is simultaneously repelled and attracted by the pornography, which leads to a joyless sexual episode with one of the boys, Bobby Callahan. Whether it is the insensitive Bobby, or the more devoted but dull boyfriends of other stories, these boys are devoid of the swashbuckling charm of the fathers of the previous generation. Whereas the first and title story in the collection concerns the exciting bond between a magical father and his captivated daughter, the final story in the collection, by way of contrast, gives the reader a portrait of a young girl utterly disappointed with the romantic prospects offered to her by the boys of her own generation.

BIBLIOGRAPHY

Bellafonte, Gina. "Windows into Life." *Time*, August 2, 1999, 91. Review of collections by four emerging short-story writers includes *My Father, Dancing*. Describes Broyard's writing as "spare and lovely," praises her for elegantly exploring the bond between father and daughter.

Goodman, Allegra. "I Remember Papa." *The New York Times Book Review*, August 15, 1999, 7. Review of *My Father, Dancing* praises the collection for its accurate documentation of the trials of girlhood and especially for the distinctive examination of fathers and daughters.

Grossinger, Harvey. "Bliss Broyard Debuts with Heartfelt Stories." Review of *My Father, Dancing*, by Bliss Broyard. *Houston Chronicle*, October 24, 1999, p. 14. Praises the stories as well-crafted and tautly paced; particularly singles out the father-daughter stories as most compelling. Especially praises the title story as the product of an overflow of genuine sorrow and loss but praises all the stories as "unaffected and heartfelt." Especially perceptive discussion of "The Trouble with Mr. Leopold" and "Loose Talk."

Lehmann-Haupt, Christopher. "Flawed Fathers, Daughters Who Love and Learn." Review of *My Father, Dancing*, by Bliss Broyard. *The New York Times*, July 29, 1999, p. E9. Describes the book as a sharply observed collection of stories and praises her prose as having considerable power but faults Broyard's dialogue as too stiff and lacking in variety. Also comments on the theme of the seductive and overwhelming father.

Lenhard, Elizabeth. "Bloodlines, not plot lines carry weight in 'Dancing'." *The Atlanta Journal-Constitution*, August 8, 1999, p. L11. Describes *My Father, Dancing* as awkward and unsophisticated and is critical of Broyard's dependence on her father both as subject and as an entree to the literary world. Notes what she describes as the distasteful "overindulged Electra complex" in many of the stories but does praise Broyard for occasionally creating a lovely episode.

Linfield, Susie. "Stories of Father Obsession and Betrayal." Review of *My Father, Dancing*, by Bliss Broyard. *The Los Angeles Times*, August 26, 1999, p. 5. Perceptively notes that these stories are essentially about one girl with one story to tell. Describes the young women narrators as obsessed with their fathers and as troublingly passive. Despite their many virtues, the stories suffer from a narrowness of vision.

Schillinger, Lizza. "Daughters and Rebels." Review of *My Father, Dancing*, by Bliss Broyard. *The Washington Post*, August 15, 1999, p. 5. Describes the collection as a coming-of-age collection that will particularly appeal to like-minded women. Discusses the dominant role of the father-daughter relationship in the stories, but notes that the young heroines have a worrisome combination of sexual precocity and emotional fragility. Praises the final story, "Snowed In," as the best of the collection because it is not dominated by a father figure and instead perceptively portrays a group of world-weary but emotionally vulnerable children of wealthy suburbanites who are going bad.

Margaret Boe Birns

PEARL S. BUCK
Pearl Sydenstricker

Born: Hillsboro, West Virginia; June 26, 1892
Died: Danby, Vermont; March 6, 1973

PRINCIPAL SHORT FICTION
The First Wife and Other Stories, 1933
Today and Forever, 1941
Twenty-seven Stories, 1943
Far and Near, Stories of Japan, China, and America, 1947
American Triptych, 1958
Fourteen Stories, 1961
Hearts Come Home and Other Stories, 1962

The Good Deed and Other Stories, 1969
Once Upon a Christmas, 1972
East and West, 1975
Secrets of the Heart, 1976
The Lovers and Other Stories, 1977
The Woman Who Was Changed and Other Stories, 1979

OTHER LITERARY FORMS
Pearl S. Buck's reputation rests primarily on her novels about China, most notably *The Good Earth* (1931), and on her biographical and autobiographical

writings. In awarding her the Nobel Prize in Literature in 1938, the selection committee singled out for special praise *The Exile* (1936) and *Fighting Angel: Portrait of a Soul* (1936), her biographies of her missionary parents. She also wrote a number of essays, plays, and children's books and translated a classic Chinese novel.

ACHIEVEMENTS

Pearl S.Buck's writings have indelibly shaped many Western readers' images of the Far East and especially of China, where she spent the first half of her life. Her portrayal of the life of the Chinese peasants in *The Good Earth* won her the Pulitzer Prize in 1932 and was a major factor in making her the first American woman to receive the Nobel Prize in Literature. Buck's best work provides a moving, realistic portrayal of her characters in their struggles to survive in the midst of natural disasters and social turmoil. Even when her fiction is slick and sentimental, she provides her readers with provocative themes to con-

Pearl S. Buck, Nobel Laureate for Literature in 1978
(©The Nobel Foundation)

sider. In both her books and her extensive humanitarian activities, her major concern was to improve understanding among those of different sexes, ages, races, and nationalities.

BIOGRAPHY

Pearl Sydenstricker Buck spent her childhood and young adult years in China with her missionary parents, where she attended mission schools and studied with a Confucian tutor. Then she attended Randolph-Macon Woman's College in Virginia before returning to China, where she married John Lossing Buck, an American agricultural expert. She received her M.A. in English literature from Cornell in 1926, and soon began publishing extensively. She divorced John Lossing Buck in 1935 and later that same year married Richard J. Walsh, president of the John Day publishing firm. Elected to the National Institute of Arts and Letters in 1936, she won the Nobel Prize in 1938. She founded the East and West Association, an organization working toward greater international understanding, and the Pearl Buck Foundation, an agency supporting homeless Amerasian children throughout Asia. Proceeds from her publications continued to fund the agency.

ANALYSIS

Pearl S. Buck's best-known stories were typically published first in large circulation magazines, then included in collections of her short fiction. "The Enemy," "Hearts Come Home," and "The Good Deed" are examples reflecting Buck's international themes. By depicting characters in exotic or potentially threatening surroundings, Buck heightens cultural contrasts and emphasizes common human characteristics. The outsiders she presents may meet a Good Samaritan figure, fall in love and marry, or achieve greater understanding of others and themselves as Buck foregrounds the power of human beings, however weak and short-sighted they may be, to transform one another intellectually and emotionally.

In her short fiction, as in her novel *The Good Earth*, universal human experiences dominate: love, marriage, birth of children, death of loved ones, threats of natural disaster, and the encroachment of new ways on old culture that creates major conflicts. The stories, however, often lack the realism of the novels, and occasionally they become sentimental and didactic. Still, their color and simplicity of style enabled Buck to succeed in reaching the wide audience she felt literature should serve.

"THE ENEMY"

In "The Enemy," a story set in Japan during World War II, a wounded American washes up on the beach near the home of a respected Japanese surgeon, who finds both his daily activities and traditional attitudes transformed by the encounter with the American. Before the American's appearance, Dr. Sadao Hoki and his family live according to the old Japanese ways despite his modern profession. Their home has the traditional inner and outer courts and gardens tended by servants; Dr. Hoki's father had lived with them until his death. The Hokis' marriage, too, is traditional, for although they met in America where both were students, they waited to fall in love until after their marriage had been parentally arranged in Japan. Mrs. Hoki remains respectfully silent much of the time she is in her husband's presence; she eats only after he has eaten his own meal. The narrative voice reveals that Dr. Hoki has many tender feelings for her because of her devotion to the old ways.

The exposition of the story is complete after the narrator describes Dr. Hoki's thoughts as he stands gazing at the islands beyond his home. These were, according to his old father, "stepping stones to the future for Japan," a future for which he prepared his son with the best American education available. When Mrs. Hoki arrives to tell her husband that the meal has been prepared, a figure appears in the mists along the rocky coast. As the man staggers, finally collapsing unconscious, they rush toward him, expecting to find an injured fisherman. With fear and horror, however, they discover that he is a white man, and they cannot decide at first what they should do with him.

They are unable to put the man back into the sea although they realize that for fear of the authorities they should do just that. When they move the injured man to safety, their servants leave for both political and superstitious reasons because they believe it is wrong to harbor an enemy. Only Mrs. Hoki remains to aid her husband when he discovers a bullet lodged near the wounded man's kidney. She washes the man's body, which she cannot bear for her husband to touch at first; then she manages to administer the anesthetic, although the sight of the man's wound sickens her. Her husband, on the other hand, marvels that the young man has survived this long and strives at length to remove the bullet without creating paralysis. Indeed, throughout the surgery Dr. Hoki cannot help speaking to the patient, addressing him as a friend despite his foreign appearance. They realize in the course of their ministrations that the man is an American, probably an escaped prisoner of war, for his body shows signs of abuse.

The surgery is successful, and the couple settle into a period of hope and fear as they await the patient's recovery. When soldiers appear with a summons, the doctor is terrified until he learns that he is needed to treat an ailing Japanese general. After the general begins to recover, the doctor confesses to him that he has helped a wounded American who would have surely died without his help and that now he cannot bear to execute the American after having spent so many years with Americans when he was in medical school. The general agrees to send assassins who will, within the next three days, murder the American even as he lies in the doctor's house.

Yet the days and nights pass, and the Hokis note only the American's recovery of strength and his deep gratitude toward them. Again they confront an opportunity to save him; the doctor gives him a boat, clothing, and food so that he may escape to a neighboring island and wait for a fishing boat. Days later, the doctor confesses to the general that the American has somehow escaped, and in a strange reversal, the general realizes with considerable anxiety that he has forgotten his promise to the doctor. The general then begs the doctor not to reveal their secret to the authorities, and the doctor willingly swears to the general's loyalty before returning home to discover his servants returned and peace restored.

Remaining somehow troubled, Dr. Hoki turns to face the island "steppingstones" of progress as he recalls the ugly faces of all the white people he has ever known and ponders why he could not kill the young white enemy. This resolution to the story suggests that although no dramatic change has occurred in the lives of the Japanese family, an awakening has perhaps been achieved as they discovered that they must for human reasons help the injured American.

"HEARTS COME HOME"

In "Hearts Come Home," a modern young businessman of China finally affirms the old ways of his culture. David Lin, a manager in a printing house, discovers to his surprise a young woman of simple beauty and individuality in the unlikely setting of a sophisticated modern dance in the home of a wealthy banker. The girl turns out to be the banker's daughter, visiting her father briefly before returning to school. Sensing in her a kindred spirit, Lin falls desperately in love with her because she is so different from the other sophisticated women of Shanghai.

Throughout David Lin's pursuit of Phyllis, the atmosphere, dialogue, and actions of their courtship heighten cultural contrasts between old and new in China. David spares no expense in treating her to the finest modern entertainment: They dance, drive about in the car, enjoy imported foods, and converse in a fashionable mixture of Chinese and American slang. Yet they grow distant rather than intimate; although they exchange kisses in the American fashion, David perceives Phyllis withdrawing from him, hiding her true personality more and more as the days pass.

He learns why one day when she suddenly asks him in Chinese whether he actually enjoys what they are doing, dancing in such a foreign and unrestrained style. Discovering that they share a dislike for dancing, she opens her heart to him, revealing to his pleased surprise that foreign things disgust her and that she does them only to please him.

The love for tradition that David and Phyllis share brings them close to each other in a new way. They exchange their traditional Chinese names, and before they know it they find themselves describing a Chinese marriage in which the old ways are celebrated. No longer will they kiss, wear foreign clothes, or eat foreign foods; their single-story house will have many courts and gardens filled with happy children. Yet David does not propose. He merely speaks of an arrangement which must soon be completed by their parents. Phyllis bids him a respectful goodbye according to the appropriate Chinese formula, and David leaves, peacefully contemplating their future.

"THE GOOD DEED"

"The Good Deed" portrays the impact of cultural changes on several generations, a common theme in Buck's work. Like "Hearts Come Home," this story suggests that the old ways can be valuable and satisfying. Mr. Pan, a Chinese emigrant to America, brings his aging mother to live with his wife and children in Chinatown in 1953. He discovers, however, that in saving her from the marauders destroying her native village, he has only brought her to another kind of suffering. For she sickens at the rebellion of his children, his wife's inability to speak her native tongue, and the loneliness of life in a busy city. Although Mr. Pan and his wife can supply the aged woman with excellent Chinese food and physical comforts, her spirit weakens daily.

The Pans decide in desperation that a visitor may help, and they invite Lili Yang, a young Chinese social worker, to visit old Mrs. Pan. Lili listens with interest as the old woman describes her native village, which lies in a wide valley from which the mountains rise as sharply as tigers' teeth. A gentle friendship develops between the two women, but a conflict emerges when old Mrs. Pan discovers that Lili, twenty-seven years old, remains unmarried. The aged one is shocked and troubled as she concludes that Lili's parents had been remiss in their duties by failing to arrange a satisfactory marriage for their daughter before their deaths. Lili weeps for the children she has always wanted, although she tries to hide her loneliness from old Mrs. Pan.

Once Lili has returned to her work, old Mrs. Pan presents her son with the responsibility of securing a husband for Lili. Indeed, the aged one decides that she herself will serve as Lili's parent, if her son will only supply her with a list of appropriate prospects. Such a good deed will be counted well in heaven for all concerned. Through the succeeding weeks old Mrs. Pan's life reflects her newfound purpose. With renewed energy she commands Mr. Pan to seek out unattached men of good character so that she may contact their parents, a project he finds most amusing as he recalls secretly that even he and his wife had fallen in love first, then allowed their parents to arrange a marriage later. He strives to explain to his mother that life in America is different, yet old Mrs. Pan remains determined.

Although she may do little else on her own, old Mrs. Pan stares daily out a window at the strangers passing along the street, hardly a suitable method of securing a mate for Lili, but at least a means of examining the young men of Chinatown. She develops an acquaintanceship with a young man who manages his father's pottery shop directly across the street. Learning from her son that this son of old Mr. Lim is wealthy and educated, she fixes upon him as an excellent prospect for Lili. Her son laughs at this possibility and tries to convince her that the young man will not submit to such an arrangement: He is handsome and educated, but Lili is plain and of simple virtue. At this argument, old Mrs. Pan becomes angry, reminding him that often women who lack beauty have much kinder hearts than their more attractive peers. She gives up her argument and makes plans of her own.

In order to meet the young man and perhaps at least introduce him to Lili, old Mrs. Pan waits until her son and his wife are gone and then asks one of the children to lead her across the street so that she may buy two bowls. The child dislikes her, however, and abandons her as soon as they reach the curb in front of the pottery shop. Fortunately, the young son of Mr. Lim rescues her, helping her into the shop and pleasantly conversing with her in excellent Chinese as she rests briefly. He then helps her find the bowls she seeks and they converse at greater length concerning the complexity of life in a large city. She finds herself confessing that if it had not been for Lili Yang, she would never have even looked out the window. When he asks who Lili Yang may be, she will not speak of her, for it would not be proper to discuss a virtuous young woman with a young man. Instead old Mrs. Pan goes into a lengthy speech on the virtues of women who are not beautiful. When he concludes that Lili must not be beautiful, old Mrs. Pan merely says that perhaps he will meet Lili some day and then they will discuss the matter of her beauty. Old Mrs.

Pan, satisfied that she has made a point, leaves with graciousness and dignity.

Returning home with the purchased bowls, she informs her son that she has spoken with old Mr. Lim's son and found him indeed pleasant. Her son realizes immediately what she has been doing and secretly cooperates by inviting Lili to visit them again, providing Mrs. Pan with an opportunity to introduce the young people. Old Mrs. Pan, however, achieves much more satisfaction than she expects, for in taking Lili with her to buy more pottery, old Mrs. Pan meets old Mr. Lim. While Lili and young James Lim are conversing in English, she and the aged father agree quietly that perhaps a match is possible and that certainly to arrange a marriage is the best of all good deeds under heaven. Observing the young people together, they set a date to have the horoscopes of the children read and to arrange the match; the date they choose, the reader learns, is the day of Lili and James's first American-style date.

A final theme appearing late in Pearl Buck's work is the search for female identity. In several early novels, including *East Wind: West Wind* (1930) and *This Proud Heart* (1938), she presents women struggling to fulfill their potential in antagonistic cultural settings. In the novella *The Woman Who Was Changed*, Buck depicts a woman who succeeds in expressing herself in the artistic and personal spheres. A particularly contemporary concern, women's struggles appear also in Buck's autobiography, *My Several Worlds* (1954).

OTHER MAJOR WORKS

LONG FICTION: *East Wind: West Wind*, 1930; *The Good Earth*, 1931; *Sons*, 1932; *The Mother*, 1934; *A House Divided*, 1935; *House of Earth*, 1935; *This Proud Heart*, 1938; *The Patriot*, 1939; *Other Gods: An American Legend*, 1940; *Dragon Seed*, 1942; *China Sky*, 1942; *The Promise*, 1943; *China Flight*, 1945; *Portrait of a Marriage*, 1945; *The Townsman*, 1945 (as John Sedges); *Pavilion of Women*, 1946; *The Angry Wife*, 1947 (as John Sedges); *Peony*, 1948; *Kinfolk*, 1949; *The Long Love*, 1949 (as John Sedges); *God's Men*, 1951; *The Hidden Flower*, 1952; *Bright Procession*, 1952 (as John Sedges);

Come, My Beloved, 1953; *Voices in the House*, 1953 (as John Sedges); *Imperial Woman*, 1956; *Letter from Peking*, 1957; *Command the Morning*, 1959; *Satan Never Sleeps*, 1962; *The Living Reed*, 1963; *Death in the Castle*, 1965; *The Time Is Noon*, 1967; *The New Year*, 1968; *The Three Daughters of Madame Liang*, 1969; *Mandala*, 1970; *The Goddess Abides*, 1972; *All Under Heaven*, 1973; *The Rainbow*, 1974.

NONFICTION: *East and West and the Novel*, 1932; *The Exile*, 1936; *Fighting Angel: Portrait of a Soul*, 1936; *The Chinese Novel*, 1939; *Of Men and Women*, 1941, expanded 1971; *American Unity and Asia*, 1942; *What America Means to Me*, 1943; *China in Black and White*, 1945; *Talk About Russia: With Masha Scott*, 1945; *Tell the People: Talks with James Yen About the Mass Education Movement*, 1945; *How It Happens: Talk About the German People, 1914-1933, with Erna von Pustau*, 1947; *American Argument: With Eslanda Goods*, 1949; *The Child Who Never Grew*, 1950; *My Several Worlds: A Personal Record*, 1954; *Friend to Friend: A Candid Exchange Between Pearl Buck and Carlos F. Romulo*, 1958; *A Bridge for Passing*, 1962; *The Joy of Children*, 1964; *Children for Adoption*, 1965; *The Gifts They Bring: Our Debt to the Mentally Retarded*, 1965; *The People of Japan*, 1966; *To My Daughters with Love*, 1967; *China as I See It*, 1970; *The Kennedy Women: A Personal Appraisal*, 1970; *The Story Bible*, 1971; *Pearl S. Buck's America*, 1971; *China: Past and Present*, 1972.

CHILDREN'S LITERATURE: *The Young Revolutionist*, 1932; *Stories for Little Children*, 1940; *The Chinese Children Next Door*, 1942; *The Water-Buffalo Children*, 1943; *The Dragon Fish*, 1944; *Yu Lan: Flying Boy of China*, 1945; *The Big Wave*, 1948; *One Bright Day and Other Stories for Children*, 1952; *The Man Who Changed China: The Story of Sun Yat-Sen*, 1953; *The Beech Tree*, 1954; *Johnny Jack and His Beginnings*, 1954; *Fourteen Stories*, 1961; *The Little Fox in the Middle*, 1966. *The Chinese Story Teller*, 1971.

TRANSLATION: *All Men Are Brothers*, 1933.

BIBLIOGRAPHY

Bentley, Phyllis. "The Art of Pearl S. Buck." *English Journal* 24 (December, 1935): 791-800. Analyzes Buck's early works from a technical perspective, focusing on setting, style, characterization, plot, and theme. Concludes that the great strength of Buck's fiction is its emphasis on the "continuity of life" from generation to generation.

Cevasco, George A. "Pearl Buck and the Chinese Novel." *Asian Studies* 5 (December, 1967): 437-450. Provides important insights into Buck's understanding of the novel as a form for the general public, not the scholar, and shows her debt to Chinese beliefs about the function of plot and characterization in fiction.

Conn, Peter. *Pearl S. Buck: A Cultural Biography*. Cambridge, England: Cambridge University Press, 1996. Attempts to revise the "smug literary consensus" that has relegated Pearl Buck to a "footnote" in literary history. Conn does not rehabilitate Buck as a great author but shows how her best work broke new ground in subject matter and is still vital to an understanding of American culture.

Dickstein, Lore. "Posthumous Stories." *The New York Times Book Review*, March 11, 1979, 20-21. Praises Buck's best work as having subject matter with a universal appeal and an easy, graceful style. Finds the late stories, however, to be excessively didactic and sentimental.

Doyle, Paul A. *Pearl S. Buck*. Boston: Twayne, 1980. A valuable survey of Buck's literary achievements, strengths, and weaknesses. Contains a biographical chapter and excellent bibliographies of both primary and secondary materials.

_____. "Pearl S. Buck's Short Stories: A Survey." *English Journal* 55 (January, 1966): 62-68. One of the few critical works devoted exclusively to Buck's short fiction. Her best stories, Doyle believes, contain realistic description, clearly delineated characters, and narrative interest. Too often, however, she wrote slick magazine fiction, excessively sentimental or filled with improbable incidents.

Liao, Kang. *Pearl S. Buck: A Cultural Bridge Across the Pacific*. Westport, Conn.: Greenwood Press, 1997. Examines Buck's political and social views and her means of expressing them. Studies the East-West cultural divide in the fiction.

Stirling, Nora. *Pearl Buck: A Woman in Conflict.* Piscataway, N.J.: New Century, 1983. A balanced, well-researched biography that provides impor-

tant insights into Buck's personality and the experiences that shaped her writings.

Chapel Louise Petty, updated by
Elizabeth Johnston Lipscomb

IVAN BUNIN

Born: Voronezh, Russia; October 22, 1870
Died: Paris, France; November 8, 1953

PRINCIPAL SHORT FICTION

"Na kray sveta" i drugiye rasskazy, 1897
Pereval: Rasskazy, 1892-1902, 1912
Sukhodol, 1912 (novella; *Dry Valley,* 1935)
Sukhodol: Povesti i rasskazy, 1911-1912, 1912
Izbrannyye rasskazy, 1914
Zolotoye dno: Rasskazy, 1903-1907, 1914
Chasha zhizni: Rasskazy, 1913-1914, 1915
The Gentleman from San Francisco and Other Stories, 1922
The Dreams of Chang and Other Stories, 1923
Fifteen Tales, 1924
Sny Changa: Izbrannyye rasskazy, 1927
Grammatika lyubvi: Izbrannyye rasskazy, 1929 (*The Grammar of Love,* 1934)
The Elaghin Affair and Other Stories, 1935
Tyomnyye allei, 1943, 1946 (*Dark Avenues and Other Stories,* 1949)
Petlistyye ushi i drugiye rasskazy, 1954
Rasskazy, 1955
The Gentleman from San Francisco and Other Stories, 1975
In a Far Distant Land, 1983

OTHER LITERARY FORMS

In addition to more than one hundred short stories, Ivan Bunin published in his sixty-six-year writing career several books of poetry, novels, memoirs, essays, travelogues, and translations. His collected and selected works have been published several times.

ACHIEVEMENTS

Ivan Bunin came on the literary scene in the 1890's, after the so-called Golden Age of Russian literature, dominated by the straightforward, realistic approach. Along with Maxim Gorky, Leonid Andreyev, and others, he wrote in the neorealistic vein, for which his poetically tinged prose was well suited. With his short stories, novels, and, to a lesser degree, poetry, he upheld the high standards of Russian literature as the world came to know it. It was therefore fitting that he would be the first Russian writer to receive the Nobel Prize, as "the incomparable painter of the vast and rich beauty of the Russian land." Despite his enmity toward the regime in the Soviet Union, his collected works have been published there twice posthumously (1956 and 1965-1967), and in 1973 two volumes of *Literaturnoe nasledstvo* (literary inheritance) were devoted to him.

BIOGRAPHY

Ivan Alexeyevich Bunin was born on October 22, 1870, in the central Russian town of Voronezh, in a cultured but impoverished family of landowning gentry. He grew up in rural Russia, and his love and understanding of it enabled him to write about the countryside with authority. He left school at the age of fifteen and never finished his formal education. He started writing and contributing to leading literary journals at an early age. His first book of poems was published in 1891 and his first collection of short stories in 1897. Bunin developed a yen for traveling and in 1900 began visiting many countries in Asia, Africa, and Europe, especially those along the Mediter-

Ivan Bunin, Nobel Laureate for Literature in 1933 (©The Nobel Foundation)

ranean. Many stories that came out of these travels were enriched by a peculiar exotic flavor. He was recognized early as one of the leading young writers in Russia, a reputation that remained relatively constant throughout his life. In fact, Gorky considered him in 1911 to be "the best contemporary writer."

The turning point in Bunin's life came during the revolution. Opposed to the Bolsheviks, he took part in the campaign against them, survived eight months of their rule, and in 1920 emigrated rather than live under them. After a brief stay in several countries, he settled in Paris in 1920, continuing to fight against the Bolsheviks. He also resumed his writing and published some of his best works. In 1933, he reached the pinnacle of his literary career as he received the Nobel Prize. As time passed, however, he withdrew increasingly from public life, cutting ties with fellow émigrés and living in poverty. During World War II,

yearning for his homeland, he rooted for the victory of the Soviet Union over its enemies, yet he refused to return afterward. He died in Paris on November 8, 1953, in poverty but writing to the very end.

ANALYSIS

Ivan Bunin wrote poetry, novels, and literary essays, but it was in short fiction that he was most successful. His stories employ a wide range of themes, but he returned to three themes time and again: the life of landed gentry and peasantry, love, and death. There are many other themes and subthemes, but those mentioned above constitute the main features of Bunin's profile as a writer.

In his early stories and novels, Bunin showed great interest in the fate of the landed gentry and peasantry and in their role in the society. His first novel, *Derevnya* (1910; *The Village*, 1923), depicts the anarchy, squalor, and drunkenness in Russian villages and the bleak prospects for the future. It is the gloomiest of Bunin's works. He continued in the same vein in his novella *Dry Valley*. Even though he subtitled it *A Poem*, it is quite naturalistic in tone. With its meager plot, the story is more of a chronicle of decay, moral degradation, spiritual emptiness, and even physical degeneration of the gentry and the peasants, both driven by irrational forces and equally doomed. The story also represents the author's vain attempt to recapture the glory of the old days, of the *temps perdu* of Russian rural life. In this sense, *Dry Valley* is a statement of Bunin's social philosophy of sorts and a revelation of his thinking about the state of both the gentry and the peasantry. His artistic acumen, especially the verbal mastery, lifts the story above the level of social tract, however, exemplified by the symbolism of the peasants dredging ponds in the bed of a river that has dried out.

Dry Valley is not the only work about the decay of Russian rural life. Stories such as "Nochnoi razgovor" ("A Nocturnal Conversation"), "Ermil," "Ignat," and "Vesennii vecher" ("A Spring Evening"), show similar features. A series of "mood paintings," "Antonovskie iabloki" ("Antonov's Apples"), more than any other story, conjures the nostalgic atmosphere of Bunin's world.

To be sure, not all the stories paint such bleak pictures of Russian life. Stories such as "Sverchok" ("Cricket") and "Veselyi dvor" ("A Gay Farmhouse") show that the peasants are capable of selfless love and that they possess spiritual values that might help them regenerate themselves. Still, the predominant effect in Bunin's early stories is bleakness and despair.

To escape such an atmosphere, Bunin undertook between 1900 and 1917 several journeys to the Mediterranean, the Middle East, and the Far East, out of which came some of his best stories: "Brat'ia" ("Brethren"), "Sny Changa" ("The Dreams of Chang"), "Syn" ("The Son"), and "Gospodin iz San Frantsisko" ("The Gentleman from San Francisco"). The changed mood of these stories, buoyed by the abundant life and exotic settings, could not fully repress Bunin's pessimistic outlook, but it sublimated it to artistic perfection. The stories with Asian settings manifest also his interest in the Buddhist tenet that suffering results from desire and that peace comes only when desire ceases.

For Bunin, love is one of the primary manifestations of human experience. He shows different types of love—love for the opposite sex, for one's family, and for other human beings—and various reactions to love. There is one constant in all these relationships: Love is basically an unhappy, even tragic experience. In "Brethren," for example, the father of the family, in his love and care for his dear ones, "was moved by earthly love, by that which, from the start of time, summons all creatures into being." Yet, by doing so, he was also bound to multiply his earthly sorrows. His beloved son, upon finding out that the woman he loved had betrayed him and run away to the city where she was giving pleasure to other men, allows a poisonous snake to bite him to death. A sudden death of a beloved woman in "Grammatika liubvi" ("Grammar of Love") forces her lover into total seclusion and degeneration because he is unable to cope with her death. In his virtual paralysis, all he hears and sees reminds him of her as he realizes that memories are all that is left to him. A young couple in the story "Meteor" ("Meteor") experiences only thirty minutes of amorous bliss before the inevitable return to harsh reality. In "Solnechny udar" ("Sunstroke"), a brief night of bliss is replaced by forlorn agony and despair after the parting. Thus, even though Bunin allows for the possibility of a true love, it almost invariably ends in unhappiness.

It is a harsh reality that dooms all these loves to unhappy endings. The presence of animalistic passion also contributes to degradation and eventual failure of erstwhile promising love relationships. A prince in "Gautami" takes advantage of a local beauty, who mistakes his passion for sincere love; when a child is born, he spurns her, relegating her to a distant corner on his estate. A young woman in "Lyogkoe dukhanie" ("Light Breathing") seduces an older man and promises to marry him, only to be murdered by him when she reneges. A tragic passion here is derived from both love and hatred. Ignat, a character in the story by the same title, resigns himself to a life with a half-witted woman because his love for his former wife was unfulfilled. He turns into a cruel man, capable of extreme violence. In perhaps the most dramatic illustration of love feelings gone astray, Mme Marot in "The Son" attempts to compensate for the vanished love of her husband with a love for her friend's young son, the physical consummation of which leads her to suicide and him to severe depression. Finally, in "Tyomnye allei" ("Dark Paths"), a man chances upon the woman he had abandoned long ago and realizes belatedly that he has squandered the opportunity for happiness. In all these stories, Bunin shows that unhappiness in love, no matter what the cause, changes the characters from sincere, well-meaning persons into bearers of unhappiness and tragedy.

The preponderance of such pessimistic attitudes toward love does not mean that Bunin denies the sublime nature of pure love and its fulfillment. Even in the death throes of the son in "Brethren," Bunin admits to "that ultimate, all-embracing thing which is called love, the yearning to encompass within one's heart all the universe, seen and unseen, and to bestow it anew upon some other." When pure, sincere love ceases to exist, be it because of harsh reality, impure passion, misunderstanding, or missed opportunity, unhappiness and sorrow invariably result, leading to degeneration. Thus, Bunin's lovers are capable of experiencing only fleeting moments of love. Bunin cannot seem to free himself from a belief that "all the torments of this universe, where everyone is either a slayer or slain, that all its sorrows and plaints, come from love."

"THE GENTLEMAN FROM SAN FRANCISCO"

The theme of death also plays a prominent—perhaps the most prominent—role in Bunin's opus. It is present in many stories, either as a primary objective or as a by-product. Nowhere is this theme more sharply focused than in his best story, "The Gentleman from San Francisco." It is a tale of a fifty-eight-year-old American millionaire who has worked hard all of his life and is now making a trip around the world with his unmarried daughter, in a belated attempt to make up for all the enjoyment that he has missed. They make a stop at Capri, the isle of beauty and joy, and while there, he is fatally stricken by a heart attack. The same ship that brought him to Capri takes him back home. The simple plot is fraught with philosophical and symbolic meanings. No one on the ship or at Capri remembered his name (he was known simply as the gentleman from San Francisco), as though he represented all humankind, making the story a morality play with the Everyman theme. There is an irony in the fact that, just as he was ready to enjoy the fruits of his labor for the first time, he meets death. The covert philosophical overtones compel the reader to think about the true meaning of life, and the horror of the gentleman's loneliness at the time of death, despite his daughter's presence, makes the thinking even more poignant. The transience of life devoid of a spiritual meaning is underscored by the sight of the casket in the boiler room of the ship, while on the way to Capri the gentleman enjoyed the journey on the deck.

A comparison with Leo Tolstoy's *Smert' Ivana Il'icha* (1886; *The Death of Ivan Ilyich*, 1887) imposes itself. Although the basic premises are the same, the difference lies in the approach to the principle of life and death. While Tolstoy muses over the moral question of death, Bunin refrains from overt philosophizing and from analyzing his characters beyond the artistic framework. He is interested primarily in the physical aspect of things and the emotional responses that they provoke. The Marxist interpretation of the story is even more out of place, for the fact that the gentleman is an American millionaire is a sheer coincidence; he could have been anyone else and the moral of the story would have been the same.

Death is depicted in many other stories, each time with a slightly different emphasis. In "Chasha zhizni" ("The Cup of Life"), death reveals the darker side of human nature. In "Petlistye ushi" ("Gnarled Ears"), it is tied directly to crime, and in "A Nocturnal Conversation" it comes as veritable horror visits upon the characters. Death is also often connected with love in Bunin's novellas, as in *Mitina lyubov'* (1925; *Mitya's Love*, 1926), where death comes from unrequited love, and in *Delo korneta Yelagina* (1927; *The Elaghin Affair*, 1935), where death is caused by jealousy. No matter what the reason is, Bunin's fascination with death is matched only by his preoccupation with the theme of love.

Among the chief characteristics of Bunin's style are economy of expression and full-bodied texture; a fine attention to detail; a leisurely pace and slow plot development; irony and understatement; "physical lyricism," rich imagery, and mood evocation; and a "classical," pure, precise, and concrete language. All these characteristics have made him one of the best writers in Russian literature.

OTHER MAJOR WORKS

LONG FICTION: *Derevnya*, 1910 (*The Village*, 1923); *Mitina lyubov'*, 1925 (*Mitya's Love*, 1926); *Delo korneta Yelagina*, 1927 (*The Elaghin Affair*, 1935); *Zhizn' Arsen'yeva: Istoki dney*, 1930 (*The Well of Days*, 1933); *Lika*, 1939; *Zhizn' Arsen'yeva: Yunost*, 1952.

POETRY: *Stikhotvoreniya: 1887-1891*, 1891; *Pod otkrytym nebom: Stikhotvoreniya*, 1898; *Listopad: Stikhotvoreniya*, 1901; *Stikhotvoreniya*, 1912; *Izbrannyye stikhi (1900-1925)*, 1929; *Stikhotvoreniya*, 1961.

NONFICTION: *Okayannyye dni*, 1935; *Osvobozhdeniye Tolstogo*, 1937; *Vospominaniya*, 1950 (*Memories and Portraits*, 1951); *O Chekhove: Nezakonchennaya rukopis'*, 1955; *Pod serpom i molotom*,

1975; *Ustami Buninykh*, 1977-1982 (3 volumes).

MISCELLANEOUS: *Stikhi i rasskazy*, 1900; *Sobran-iye sochineniy*, 1902-1909 (5 volumes); *Rasskazy i stikhotvoreniya, 1907-1910*, 1912; *Sukhodol: Povesti i rasskazy, 1911-1912*, 1912; *Ioann Rydalets: Rasskazy i stikhi, 1912-1913*, 1913; *Polnoye sobraniye sochineniy*, 1915 (6 volumes); *Gospodin iz San Frantsisko: Proizvedeniya, 1915-1916*, 1916; *Sobraniye sochineniy*, 1934-1939 (12 volumes); *Sobraniye sochineniy*, 1956 (5 volumes); *Sobraniye sochineniy*, 1965-1967 (9 volumes); *Sochineniya*, 1982 (3 volumes).

BIBLIOGRAPHY

Bayley, John. "The Backward Look." *The New York Review of Books* 42 (August 10, 1995): 31-33. Notes that Bunin expressed a genuine Russian sympathy and versatility in his writing; calls him a master of a detailed and pitiless realism, which he applied to the backwardness and barbarity of provincial Russia; provides a biographical background to Bunin's writing.

Connolly, Julian W. *Ivan Bunin*. Boston: Twayne, 1982. An introduction to Bunin's art for the general reader, focusing on his primary ideological positions and charting his evolution as an artist. The study includes a brief biographical sketch but is primarily organized around thematic discussions of Bunin's major prose works in chronological order.

Cravens, Gwyneth. "Past Present." *The Nation* 256 (February 8, 1993): 173-174. Claims Bunin's short stories are marked by acute and objective observations, surprising details caught by his artist's eye, and a crystalline style; notes that Bunin focused on the enigmas of nature, love, death, and the soul with a passion that would be unique among today's authors; discusses several of his works.

Gross, S. L. "Nature, Man, and God in Bunin's 'The Gentleman from San Francisco.'" *Modern Fiction Studies* 6, no. 2 (1960): 153-163. A perceptive analysis of "The Gentleman from San Francisco," focusing on its alleged pessimistic outlook. Gross takes exception to those critics who see it as a prevalently pessimistic story and counters with the image of two pipers from Abruzzi offering the vision of grace.

Kryzytski, Serge. *The Works of Ivan Bunin*. The Hague: Mouton, 1971. In this standard work on Bunin, Kryzytski combines biographical and critical approaches. He follows Bunin's career chronologically, commenting on each important work and its themes, influences, and overall significance. This valuable book concludes with a good bibliography.

Marullo, Thomas Gaiton. "Crime Without Punishment: Ivan Bunin's 'Loopy Ears.'" *Slavic Review* 40, no. 4 (1981): 614-624. Marullo compares "Loopy Ears" with *Crime and Punishment* of Fyodor Dostoevski, to whose works Bunin had a strong aversion. Sokolovsky of "Loopy Ears" experiences neither recrimination nor remorse for his crime. Marullo does not see Bunin as being in the "classical" tradition of Russian literature but as redirecting the Russian short story from the urban realism of the nineteenth century to the modernistic probing of the twentieth.

_____. *If You See the Buddha: Studies in the Fiction of Ivan Bunin*. Evanston, Ill.: Northwestern University Press, 1998. Part of the Studies in Russian Literature and Theory series, this is a good examination of Bunin's works. Includes bibliographical references and an index.

Minot, Susan. "Ivan Bunin." *The Paris Review* 37 (Winter, 1995): 152-153. A brief discussion of Bunin by a noted short-story writer, praising Bunin's short stories, commenting on his life and writing; asserts that Bunin's memoir of his friend Anton Chekhov is the most elegant tribute one writer has ever written about another.

Poggioli, Renato. "The Art of Ivan Bunin." In *Harvard Slavic Studies*. Vol. 1, edited by Horace G. Lunt et al. Cambridge, Mass.: Harvard University Press, 1953. An overall assessment of Bunin's short stories and novels. After discussing Bunin's relationship to Maxim Gorky, Poggioli touches upon the salient features of his main short stories, especially their poetic bent, and concludes with an in-depth examination of *The Village* and *Dry Valley*.

Struve, Gleb. "The Art of Ivan Bunin." *Slavonic and East European Review* 11, no. 32 (1933): 423-436. In this excellent introductory essay on Bunin, Struve, an expert on emigré Russian literature and a translator of Bunin's work, offers a cogent chronological analysis of the author's works, summarizing his most important features. Written two decades before Bunin's death, the essay could not assess his later works.

Woodward, James B. *Ivan Bunin: A Study of His Fiction*. Chapel Hill: University of North Carolina

Press, 1980. As the name implies, this study has a specific aim and scope, yet it is very thorough and scholarly; in fact, it is the most detailed and comprehensive study of Bunin's fiction. Woodward treats all important aspects of Bunin's fiction chronologically, combining critical examination and description and reevaluating earlier judgments on Bunin, which may be the book's most salient feature. An extensive bibliography and a thorough index make this book useful.

Vasa D. Mihailovich

ROBERT OLEN BUTLER

Born: Granite City, Illinois; January 20, 1945

PRINCIPAL SHORT FICTION
A Good Scent from a Strange Mountain, 1992
Tabloid Dreams, 1996

OTHER LITERARY FORMS

Although Robert Olen Butler has received particular praise for his short stories, his work has mostly been in the novel genre, where his special interest has been in the Vietnam experience. *The Alleys of Eden* (1981), *Sun Dogs* (1982), and *Deep Green Sea* (1997) all deal with this subject. His novel *They Whisper* (1994) has received substantial critical attention.

ACHIEVEMENTS

Several of Robert Olen Butler's stories have been selected for the annual publication *The Best American Short Stories*; he has also received a Rosenthal Foundation Award from the American Academy of Arts and Letters, a John Simon Guggenheim Memorial Foundation Fellowship in fiction, and a grant from the National Endowment for the Arts. In 1987, the Vietnam Veterans of America gave him the Tu Do Chinh Kien Award for outstanding contributions to American culture by a Vietnam veteran. In 1993, he

received the Pulitzer Prize for *A Good Scent from a Strange Mountain*.

BIOGRAPHY

Robert Olen Butler was born on January 20, 1945, in Granite City, Illinois; he received a bachelor's degree in theater from Northwestern University in 1967 and an M.A. in playwriting from the University of Iowa in 1969. He served with the U.S. Army in counterintelligence from 1969 to 1972, part of that time in Vietnam, where he also served as an interpreter.

Although Butler had begun writing plays during college, after his Vietnam experience he turned to narrative fiction, completing his first three novels during the hours he spent on a train commuting from his home to his editorial job for *Energy User News* in Manhattan. His experience in Vietnam furnished him with fertile subject matter and a desire to tell stories about it. However, his first published novel, *The Alleys of Eden* (1981), went through twenty-one rejections before it finally found a publisher. He has said of his earlier, unpublished fiction that it now serves as spare parts for his current work.

In 1985, Butler began teaching creative writing at McNeese State University, in Lake Charles, Louisiana (the setting for one of the stories from *A Good Scent from a Strange Mountain*), which he made his permanent home. Butler once said that he finds that much fiction about Vietnam fails to portray the Vietnamese people with sufficient depth, perhaps because it focuses primarily on military action. His task, he believes, is to write whatever books are given to him to write, regardless of their subjects or critical reception.

ANALYSIS

Robert Olen Butler's literary concerns have focused on human relationships, especially those between men and women, on American culture, and on Vietnam. Butler's Pulitzer Prize-winning collection *A Good Scent from a Strange Mountain* deals with the Vietnamese who came to America after the war: first with American attitudes toward the country's unsuccessful efforts to halt communism in Vietnam, next with the problems of people living in an alien culture and trying to adapt to their new country while maintaining their Vietnamese values and customs. Butler has great sympathy for these displaced persons—for their sensitivity, the rich culture they left behind, and their hardships in America. He treats all of them, from the Saigon "bar girl" to the newly successful businessman, with respect.

Tabloid Dreams uses the device of the shocking headlines often used by tabloids to lure readers: invasions from outer space, dead presidents found to be alive on desert islands, bizarre love relationships. Butler presents the bizarre claims literally; a *Titanic* victim is actually present as a spirit inhabiting a waterbed. The effects are sometimes comic—a dead husband returning as a parrot to spy on his wife—but often even the comedy has a serious edge as Butler views the American culture that takes such headlines seriously.

"CRICKETS"

"Crickets," from *A Good Scent from a Strange Mountain*, represents in miniature many of the themes of this collection. In the story, the narrator and his wife have escaped during Saigon's fall to the North Vietnamese. Now the family live in Lake Charles, Louisiana. Still the narrator feels like an outsider; he is smaller than most American men, and he dislikes his American name, Ted. Most worrisome,

Robert Olen Butler (Gray Little)

however, is his son's complete assimilation into American culture. Young Bill speaks no Vietnamese and acts like his American-born schoolmates. His father, eager to connect the boy with his cultural past, suggests a game he himself once played—cricket fighting. They spend a happy morning looking for the large crickets called charcoal crickets and for the small brown fire crickets. Bill, however, worries about getting his new Nike sneakers dirty and at last wanders off, bored. Moreover, they never find any fire crickets, the small, tenacious fighters most admired by children in Vietnam. The fire crickets not only suggest Ted's youth but also, in their willingness to battle the larger charcoal crickets, recall the outnumbered South Vietnamese army; they even suggest the comparatively small stature of the Vietnamese in America. Ted's final "See you later" to his son indicates his resigned acceptance of Bill's identity as an American boy.

"THE AMERICAN COUPLE"

The ironies of "The American Couple" are many layered; Butler examines the relationship between a Vietnam-born couple and their American-born counterparts who find themselves staying at the same resort hotel in Puerto Vallarta, Mexico. (The two wives have won their trips on that most American of television experiences, a game show.) Gabrielle Tran wishes to give her husband, Vinh, a successful entrepreneur in America, a restful vacation. Acutely sensitive to others' moods and attitudes, she makes a game of reading the subtexts of others' conversations, particularly those of their new acquaintances, Frank Davies and his wife Eileen. Like Vinh, Davies fought in Vietnam, an experience so crucial to him that he still talks about it constantly. When the couples explore the forest to see the abandoned movie set of *Night of the Iguana*, the two husbands end up in a sort of war game in which Vinh injures Frank. The backdrop of American culture—game shows, the Elizabeth Taylor/Richard Burton romance, the war in Vietnam—warns the reader that the Vietnamese couple may be at least as American as Frank and Eileen Davies. During the holiday, Gabrielle goes parasailing, rising above the resort and bay in a parachute, leaving behind all ties to earthly business. For a few moments, she is a soul freed from nationality. Significantly, Frank Davies plays no part in this freedom.

"A GOOD SCENT FROM A STRANGE MOUNTAIN"

In this title story from the collection, Đao, a hundred-year-old Vietnamese man now living with his children in Louisiana, is visited on several successive evenings by the spirit of Ho Chi Minh, the one-time leader of North Vietnam, whom he had met in 1917 in Paris, where Ho Chi Minh, long before he turned his attention to politics, was studying under a famous pastry chef. Now Ho visits his old friend with his hands still fragrant from handling sugar as in the old days. He seems to be marking the Vietnamese tradition that in the last days of one's life one receives friends and relatives. The fact that Ho Chi Minh is long dead makes no difference.

In their conversations, the two old men delicately discuss the different directions their lives have taken; Ho Chi Minh has chosen revolutionary politics and Đao has pursued the simplest form of Buddhism, the form represented by four Chinese characters which translate into the story's title: a good scent from a strange mountain—the key to the simple mystery of joy. The story's title contrasts with Ho, who confesses that he is not at peace in the afterlife. Now, in New Orleans, Đao's daughter and son-in-law murmur about the recent murder of a local Vietnamese journalist who, though still a patriot, has written that Vietnamese Americans should accept the reality of a communist Vietnam. The son-in-law's conversation implies that he and Đao's grandson were involved in the murder, a sour smell in the growing fragrance of the old man's impending peaceful death.

TABLOID DREAMS

In this collection, Butler uses tabloid-style titles—"Boy Born with Tattoo of Elvis," "Doomsday Meteor Is Coming"—as the premises for stories that take the titles' outlandish claims seriously. The results are sometimes humorous, sometimes serious. In the first story of the collection, "*Titanic* Victim Speaks Through Waterbed," the narrator has undergone a series of watery incarnations, the last one as part of a waterbed's filling. As he talks, he begins to sense how he wasted his life in pompous conformity and avoided all chances for love. An emblem of all he has missed, two people make love on the bed above him during this self-revealing narrative.

Most of the stories deal with human relationships, especially with love and marriage, fidelity and betrayal. In two stories—"Woman Uses Glass Eye to Spy on Philandering Husband" and "Jealous Husband Returns in Form of Parrot"—spouses find comic means of checking on their mates' love affairs. The parrot story makes particularly good use of its narrator's reincarnation as a parrot. Butler gives the angry bird a parrotlike point of view so that while he is outraged by his lover's new boyfriends, he also feels smug about the beauty of his plumage and frustrated by the limitations of his few words to communicate with the woman who has betrayed him.

One of the collection's strongest stories is "Help Me Find My Spaceman Lover," narrated by the naïvely folksy voice of Edna, who met her spaceman (she calls him "Desi" because he speaks with an accent) in the parking lot of the Bovary, Alabama, Wal Mart. As she describes their delicate courtship, the reader realizes that Edna is a sort of comic Madame Bovary, repressed by the conservative small-mindedness of her family and community. Desi, with no lips and with fingers that end in geckolike round pads, teaches her to see things from a wider point of view until, in the midst of the story's humor, the reader shares her sense of loss when they are parted. "How many chances do you have to be happy?" she asks.

OTHER MAJOR WORKS

LONG FICTION: *The Alleys of Eden*, 1981; *Sun Dogs*, 1982; *Countrymen of Bones*, 1983; *On Distant Ground*, 1985; *Wabash*, 1987; *The Deuce*, 1989; *They Whisper*, 1994; *The Deep Green Sea*, 1998; *Mr. Spaceman*, 2000.

BIBLIOGRAPHY

Butler, Robert Owen. "An Interview with Robert Olen Butler." Interview by Michael Kelsay. *Poets and Writers* (January/February, 1996): 40-49. A meaty interview in which Butler discusses his life and work. He talks about his distaste for being called a "Vietnam" novelist and describes how he came to write *A Good Scent from a Strange Mountain*. He discusses the importance of the concrete world to the novelist. Kelsay includes some brief analyses of Butler's themes.

Ewell, Barbara. "*Tabloid Dreams*." *America* 176 (May 17, 1997): 28-29. Ewell argues that a main theme of the collection considers the problem of determining what is fakery in a world like ours. She links the strangeness of these stories to the strangeness that the Vietnamese characters in *A Good Scent from a Strange Mountain* found in America.

Packer, George. "From the Mekong to the Bayous." *The New York Times Book Review* (June 7, 1992): 24. Packer discusses Butler's treatment of the Vietnamese in his stories, noting that for Butler, Vietnam was a place where Americans were improved and refined, learning to overcome their racism and cruelty. In contrast, Packer notes that Vietnamese Americans use their folklore to interpret their exile.

Ryan, Maureen. "Robert Olen Butler's Vietnam Veterans: Strangers in an Alien Home." *The Midwest Quarterly* (Spring, 1997): 274-295. Ryan discusses Butler's early Vietnam novels—*The Alleys of Eden*, *Sun Dogs*, and *On Distant Ground*. Ryan argues that the shared experiences of the novels' central characters make the works a trilogy. She also examines the theme of the difficulty of the veterans' reassimilation into American life.

Ann Davison Garbett

DINO BUZZATI
Dino Buzzati Traverso

Born: San Pellegrino, near Belluno, Italy; October 16, 1906
Died: Rome, Italy; January 28, 1972

PRINCIPAL SHORT FICTION
I sette messaggeri, 1942
Paura alla Scala, 1949
Il crollo della Baliverna, 1954
Esperimento di magia, 1958
Sessanta racconti, 1958
Egregio signore, siamo spiacenti di . . . , 1960
Catastrophe: The Strange Stories of Dino Buzzati, 1966
Il colombre, 1966
La boutique del mistero, 1968
Le notti difficili, 1971
180 racconti, 1982
Restless Nights, 1983
The Siren: A Selection from Dino Buzzati, 1984
Il meglio dei racconti di Dino Buzzati, 1989
Lo Strano Natale di Mr. Scrooge e altre storie, 1990
Bestiario, 1991

OTHER LITERARY FORMS

Dino Buzzati is best known as a novelist. His third novel, *Il deserto dei Tartari* (1940; *The Tartar Steppe*, 1952), critically acclaimed as his masterwork, has been translated into the major European languages as well as Japanese. Structured along the themes of time, obsession, solitude, waiting, and renunciation, it is set against the majestic beauty and mystery of rugged and timeless mountains. In *The Tartar Steppe*, these themes, present in the novella *Bàrnabo delle montagne* (1933; *Bàrnabo of the Mountains*, 1984), and the novel *Il segreto del Bosco Vecchio* (1935), become more existentialist. The protagonist's life, symbolic of life in general, is viewed as a perennial waiting, in which hope for heroic deeds results only in failure and final renunciation—for the inevitable destiny of all humans is death, symbolized in the novel by the Tartars.

Buzzati's *Il grande ritratto* (1960; *Larger than Life*, 1962) and *Un amore* (1963; *A Love Affair*, 1964) have different outward environments: The first has a science-fiction frame; the second is founded on erotic realism but is actually an artistic transposition of the author's painful personal experiences dating back to the 1940's. Inwardly, however, Buzzati's usual themes remain visible: solitude, anguish, and alienation, in a foreboding and mysterious atmosphere and ending in death.

Buzzati wrote fifteen plays. Twelve premiered in Milan; one in Naples, *L'uomo che andràa in America* (1962; the man who will go to America); one in Spoleto, *Le finestre* (1959; the windows); and one, *Una ragazza arrivò* (1959; a girl arrived), aired on Italian radio. Most of Buzzati's plays reflect the tormented, often nightmarish, atmosphere that characterizes his fiction. Perhaps the best known is *Un caso clinico* (1953; a clinical case), based on his story "Sette piani" ("Seven Floors"). After a successful run in Italy, it was staged in Berlin in 1954 and in Paris in 1955 by Albert Camus. His complete dramatic works were published together in the volume *Teatro* (1980; plays).

Buzzati's successful children's book *La famosa invasione degli orsi in Sicilia* (1945; *The Bears' Famous Invasion of Sicily*, 1947) contains the author's own drawings, originally created to entertain his sister's children.

Buzzati also wrote poetry that deals mainly with the absurdity of modern life. He produced a modern rendering of the Orpheus myth in *Poema a fumetti* (1969; comicstrip poem), in which the classic Greek poet Orpheus is transformed into Orfi, a rock-and-roll singer. It was awarded the Paese Sera Prize for best comic strip in 1969. Buzzati's interest in combining word and image is evident not only in this work but also in many of the numerous drawings and paintings he produced.

Buzzati's prose collection *In quel preciso momento* (1950; at that very moment) is difficult to define; it contains only a few stories, while the rest are notes or poignant reflections on his own actions and feelings as well as those of others, in which he captures all the themes found in his writings.

Buzzati's journalistic essays, written for the Milanese newspaper *Corriere della Sera*, subsequently were published in book form. They are original in style, with a marked tendency for the fantastic and bizarre.

ACHIEVEMENTS

Dino Buzzati's works, often taking a surrealistic and metaphysical turn, can be compared to the fantasies of Franz Kafka; in fact, he has frequently been referred to by literary critics as "the Italian Kafka." His closest affinity, however, is with the Romantic tradition of E. T. A. Hoffmann and Edgar Allan Poe. Through the themes and style of his short stories and novels—philosophical and symbolic tales of life's relentless passing, full of metaphysical allegories and strange events—his work can be related to that of other Italian authors such as Tommaso Landolfi and Italo Calvino; the extremism and pessimism of his narratives, however, are uniquely his own. Buzzati's characters, overwhelmed by cosmic fear, find themselves in a state of isolation and perpetual waiting. Buzzati's pessimism, however, is somewhat tempered by a vague Christian element, the hope of ultimate redemption from evil through the exercise of free will. Since death is viewed as the only possible conclusion to life, humans' ability to die with dignity constitutes the greatest heroic deed.

Some critics saw Buzzati's existentialism as a snobbish and egotistic attitude. Indeed, Buzzati's works are not easily appreciated by the unprepared reader, who will remain perplexed before the strange, often hidden and allegoric meaning of his prose. At the same time, however, the stories are captivating. He manages to maintain a sense of continuous suspense, capturing the reader's attention yet leaving him perplexed.

Translated into several languages, Buzzati's works became extremely popular in France, where a Buzzati society, Association Internationale des Amis de Dino Buzzati, was established in 1976. His masterpiece *The Tartar Steppe* influenced Julien Gracq's novel *Le Rivage des Syrtes* (1951; the shore of the Syrtes) and resulted in a French-Italian coproduction of a film directed by Valerio Zurlini in 1976. *The Tartar Steppe* won the Italian Academy Award.

Buzzati received the Gargano Prize in 1951 for *In quel preciso momento*, the Naples Prize in 1957 for *Il crollo della Baliverna*, the Strega Prize in 1958 for *Sessanta racconti*, and the All'Amalia Prize in 1970 for his narrative works in general. He is considered to be one of the most important writers of modern Italy.

BIOGRAPHY

Dino Buzzati Traverso was born at San Pellegrino, near Belluno, in the Dolomite Alps, where his family possessed a summerhouse. The mountains, to which he returned every summer, played an important part in his life (he became a passionate Alpine climber and skier) and influenced his narratives. He received all of his schooling, including a law degree, in Milan, where the Buzzati family resided even after the death, in 1920, of his father, Giulio Cesare Buzzati, a professor of international law. As a teenager, together with his friend Arturo Brambilla, Buzzati developed a passion for Egyptology and an intense interest in the designs of illustrator Arthur Rackham.

In 1928, Buzzati began a journalistic career for *Corriere della Sera*, the leading Italian newspaper, eventually becoming a chief editor. During World War II, he was a war correspondent with the Italian navy. Although he was only thirty-five years old, he feared that he was losing his youth and his strength, that he would no longer be able to climb his beloved mountains. Indeed, Buzzati would constantly measure his physical strength against the mountain: Every year the Dolomites seemed to him to become taller and more difficult to climb, while he worried over the slightest difficulty, and, like his characters, expected only catastrophes.

Buzzati was married late in life, at the age of sixty. His wife, Almerina Antoniazzi, became curator of his many papers, including sixty-three volumes of his diary, after he died of cancer in 1972.

ANALYSIS

Dino Buzzati's stories can be read on two levels: as strange tales, full of mysterious events, or as symbolic depictions of life's elusive reality. The period in which the action takes place is frequently vague; even when a precise date is given, there is a timeless quality about his stories. More important is the problem of existence itself, the inner torments that derive from the problem of facing reality.

"SEVEN MESSENGERS"

In "Seven Messengers" (included in *Restless Nights*), which gave the title to the first collection of Buzzati's short fiction, *I sette messaggeri*, a prince sets out to explore his father's kingdom in the company of seven knights, who serve him as messengers and links to his father, his capital, and his house. As the prince advances toward the frontier, however, the messengers take longer and longer to return, and the letters they bring him seem to recall distant things. One day, the prince realizes that the messenger about to depart for the capital will return only in thirty-four years, by which time the prince will be very old or even dead. Nevertheless, he continues his trip toward the border, with ever-increasing curiosity, to explore the unknown regions. Symbolically, the prince's trip is the journey of life. Day by day, one becomes more and more distant from one's parents and childhood sentiments, full of eagerness to discover what lies ahead, even if the ultimate goal is death.

"SEVEN FLOORS"

In "Seven Floors," from the same collection, a man with a minor illness is sent to a hospital, where he learns that the patients are housed on each of the seven floors according to the gravity of their state: The top floor, the seventh, is for mild cases; each lower floor is for increasingly severe cases; and the dying are moved to the first floor, where the blinds go down at the moment of death. The man, assigned to the seventh floor, is assured that he will be cured in two or three weeks. After ten days, however, he is asked, as a favor, to yield his room to a woman, who is arriving with two children who will be housed in the two adjacent rooms. He consents, only to discover that he is to be moved to the sixth floor—since no other rooms are available on the seventh floor—but is

assured that this is only a temporary arrangement. Gradually, however, he descends from floor to floor under different pretexts and with ever-increasing alarm, until he arrives on the first floor, where he watches the blinds go down in his room. Again, this man's strange adventure is symbolic of life: Each period brings one, often without awareness, closer to death.

"THE SCALA SCARE"

In "Paura alla Scala" ("The Scala Scare"), from the collection of that title, an old pianist who has trouble understanding his composer son and his new music goes to the Scala Theater for the premiere of a new opera. On his way, he finds the city strangely empty of people. He meets a former student, who makes an incomprehensible remark about the pianist's son and his friends. The opera, already polemical for its alleged political allusions, with its disturbing and violent music only increases the general tension among the audience. During intermission, a gentleman tries to warn the pianist about his son's impudence but does not finish his sentence. At the reception after the performance, there is much talk about a revolt in progress, and it is decided that it is unsafe to go home during the night. The fearful audience settles down to wait. Soon the audience splits into two groups: those favoring the rebellion and those condemning it, while some individuals oscillate between the two. Tension rises as the night progresses, and the old pianist, worried about his son, who is at home, decides to leave. Everyone watches him as he leaves on unsteady legs, the result of the generously flowing champagne at the reception. He reaches the center of the square in front of the Scala Theater, only to fall flat on his face with outstretched hands, as if felled by a machine gun. Everyone stares at him, but no one moves. When dawn finally arrives, a lone cyclist drives past; then, an old street sweeper starts sweeping the square; and later, more people begin appearing: The city is awakening to another day. The old pianist wakes up, full of amazement, gets on his feet, and trots home. An old flower-woman, dressed in black, enters the foyer, passing among the liverish-looking assembly and offering a gardenia. After establishing this mounting suspense, Buzzati ends the story abruptly, leaving the reader to wonder what, if anything, has happened.

"CATASTROPHE"

Similarly, in "Qualcosa era successo" ("Catastrophe"), from *Il crollo della Baliverna*, Buzzati describes, from a passenger's point of view, a ten-hour, nonstop journey by express train. Contact with the rest of the world is only indirect, through the view out the train windows. It soon becomes evident, however, that something unusual is happening out there, for all the people seem to communicate alarm to one another. Large crowds, as if in flight from danger, begin to move in the opposite direction from that in which the train is traveling. The stations which the train passes are crowded, yet none of the silent passengers manages to read the headline of the newspapers waved at them. A passenger grabs one, but it tears away, leaving in her hand only the letters -TION of the headline. When the train finally rolls into the station of the big city and comes to a stop, the passengers find a deserted place with no humans in sight.

This story was interpreted as symbolic of the fear of war or nuclear disaster. Buzzati, however, gives the reader a clue for an alternate interpretation when he makes his protagonist exclaim that trains are just like life itself.

"THE COLOMBER"

In "Il colombre" ("The Colomber"), from the collection of the same title, in spite of his father's warning to avoid the sea because of the mysterious and relentless fish the colomber, the young protagonist, Stefano, becomes a ship's captain. He knows that the colomber never abandons its chosen victim, but, nevertheless, fatefully attracted to seafaring, Stefano spends his entire life restlessly navigating the globe, the colomber always tantalizingly, ominously behind. Finally, old and disillusioned, never having enjoyed his riches or his travels, Stefano musters the courage to go out and face the enigmatic fish that has haunted his life. Only now as he stands before it does he discover that the colomber was in actuality only chasing after him to give him a pearl endowing its recipient with the gifts of luck, power, love, and peace of mind. Stefano has needlessly thrown away not only decades of his life but also the very essence of it.

"THE BEWITCHED JACKET"

In "La giacca stregata" ("The Bewitched Jacket"), from the same collection, a man discovers that every time he puts his hand into the pocket of his new suit, for which he has not yet paid, he finds a ten-thousand-lire bill. He starts extracting money only to realize that there is a direct relationship between this action and the tragic criminal events he reads about in the newspapers. Still he is unable to resist, until an old woman (who lives in the same apartment house as he) kills herself because she lost her only means of support, her monthly pension money, the sum of which corresponds exactly to the amount the man took from his magic pocket that day. Horrified, he drives to the mountains and burns the jacket but hears a voice saying, "Too late, too late," though no one is in sight. His car (bought with the mysterious money) is gone, as are his houses and savings in town. He is a ruined man; he also knows that one day the tailor who made that suit for him will demand payment. In this fantastic story, one sees that humans are responsible for their actions and will have to pay for them when the last rendering of accounts comes.

"SUICIDIO AL PARCO"

Particularly interesting are two surrealistic stories in which a metamorphosis occurs. Unlike Franz Kafka's novella *Die Verwandlung* (1915; *Metamorphosis*, 1936), which opens with a character already inexplicably transformed, Buzzati's stories show the transformations as they occur and offer reasons for them. In "Suicidio al parco" (suicide in the park), also from *Il colombre*, a young man's obsession with fancy cars reaches the point at which he speaks only of cars and ignores his loving, beautiful wife, Faustina. One day, a friend sees him in an unusual, fancy car, which he drives with passion. When asked about Faustina, he is vague, claiming that she has gone back to her parents. Some years later, the friend reads in the newspaper about a car that, driverless, drove through several street blocks, avoiding automobiles and pedestrians, and smashed itself against an old ruin in the park. Immediately, he thinks of Faustina and confronts her husband, who confesses that she, to make him happy, sacrificed herself by becoming a car. On the day of the accident, the thankless husband was on his way to sell the car, which had become old. Faustina, the car, therefore committed suicide. Employing the antique device of literalization—woman *as* object is transformed into woman *is* object—Buzzati deftly and economically criticizes a variety of modern ills: narcissism, chauvinism, dehumanization, and technological fetishism.

"THE COUNT'S WIFE"

A wife's metamorphosis is painfully observed by her husband in "La moglie conle ali" ("The Count's Wife"), from Buzzati's last collection published in his lifetime, *Le notti difficili*. The count is much older than his pretty wife, Lucina, and is very jealous of her. One day, he notices a strange growth on his wife's back, which becomes larger until it turns into full-fledged wings that reach the ground. Extremely worried and fearing scandal in his provincial town, he keeps her locked up and hidden at home. Upon the advice of his mother, a priest is consulted, who suggests that he test the wings: If Lucina can fly, the wings must be a gift of God rather than of the Devil. That night Lucina flies, joyful to be free, but she is locked up again so that she will not be seen. She resolves to continue her flights secretly. One autumn day, she is almost killed by a hunter. To save herself, she cries to the young hunter, whom she recognizes as a friend, not to shoot, and makes herself known. That evening, when the Count comes home, he finds the wings gone. Only the priest suspects that Lucina met the Devil and lost her wings.

Buzzati's stories are always original, even when based on old literary or pseudoreligious schemes, for he gives them his personal stamp. They are entertaining and at the same time extremely moral. Touching upon problems that are timeless, they are not restricted by national boundaries. Buzzati is, indeed, a master in the art of storytelling.

OTHER MAJOR WORKS

LONG FICTION: *Bàrnabo delle montagne*, 1933 (*Bàrnabo of the Mountains*, 1984); *Il segreto del Bosco Vecchio*, 1935; *Il deserto dei Tartari*, 1940 (*The Tartar Steppe*, 1952); *Il grande ritratto*, 1960 (*Larger than Life*, 1962); *Un amore*, 1963 (*A Love Affair*, 1964).

PLAYS: *Piccola passeggiata*, pb. 1942; *Un caso clinico*, pb. 1953; *Procedura penale*, pb. 1959 (libretto; music by Luciano Chailly); *Il mantello*, pb. 1960; (libretto; music by Chailly); *Battono alla porta*, pb. 1961 (libretto; based on Riccardo Malpiero's short story); *Era proibito*, pb. 1961 (libretto; music by Chailly); *L'uomo che andrà in America*, pb. 1968; *Una ragazza arrivò*, pb. 1968; *La fine del borghese*, pb. 1968; *Teatro*, pb. 1980.

POETRY: *Il capitano Pic ed altre poesie*, 1965; *Due poemetti*, 1967; *Poema a fumetti*, 1969; *Le Poesie*, 1982.

NONFICTION: *Cronache terrestri*, 1972; *Dino Buzzati al Giro d'Italia*, 1981; *Cronache nere*, 1984; *Lettere a Brambilla*, 1985; *Montagne di vetro: articoli e racconti dal 1932 al 1971*, 1989; *Il buttafuoco: Cronachediguerra sul mar*, 1992.

CHILDREN'S LITERATURE: *La famosa invasione degli orsi in Sicilia*, 1945 (*The Bears' Famous Invasion of Sicily*, 1947); *I dispiaceri del re*, 1980.

MISCELLANEOUS: *Il libro delle pipe*, 1945 (with Eppe Ramazzotti); *In quel preciso momento*, 1950 (includes stories and autobiographical sketches); *I miracoli di Val Morel*, 1971 (includes thirty-nine of Buzzati's paintings with his text); *Romanzi e racconti*, 1975; *Per grazia ricevuta*, 1983 (includes Buzzati's art); *Il reggimento parte all'alba*, 1985.

BIBLIOGRAPHY

Biasin, Gian-Paolo. "The Secret Fears of Man: Dino Buzzati." *Italian Quarterly* 6, no. 2 (1962): 78-93. Focusing on the magical rather than moral aspect of Buzzati's allegorical narratives, Biasin's well-presented article elucidates major elements—tensely brooding atmosphere, crystalline symbolism, journalistic technique or matter, and the themes of human fragility and the fear of death and the unforeseen—in Buzzati's fiction.

Cary, Joseph. *"Restless Nights: A Review."* Review of *Restless Nights*. *Parabola* 8, no. 4 (1983): 120-122. Opening the essay with Buzzati's definition of fantasy ("Things that do not exist, imagined by man for poetic ends"), Cary succinctly analyzes the talents—such as linguistic perception, economical but concrete expression, and perception of the incidents in an "as if" mode—that make Buzzati's fiction distinctive.

Fornacca, Daisy. "Dino Buzzati." *Books Abroad* 25, no. 1 (1951): 19-20. The Kafkian and fantastic elements in Buzzati's early stories are Fornacca's main concern in this short survey of Buzzati's preferred mechanisms of psychological autosuggestion and the ambiguous or precipitous ending. She correctly points out that Buzzati's intent is to illuminate, not solve or explain, the problems of existence.

Hyman, Stanley Edgar. "Fable Italian Style." *The New Yorker* 44 (June, 1968): 122-125. Hyman's identification of deficiencies in the novel *Larger than Life* sheds light on certain of Buzzati's stories as well. For Hyman, stereotypical characters, traditional plotting, and the dressing of ideas in science-fictional garb somewhat diminish Buzzati's paganistic affirmation of the human spirit.

Pacifici, Sergio. "Dino Buzzati: The Gothic Novel." In *The Modern Italian Novel: From Pea to Moravia*. Carbondale: Southern Illinois University Press, 1979. The concepts of fear (as theme, narrative strategy, and reader response), earthly pilgrimage, and loneliness as humanity's unalterable fate provide the basis for this essay, which concludes with the judgment that Buzzati's pervasive sense of religious resignation ultimately mars his work.

Rawson, Judy. "Dino Buzzati." In *Writers and Society in Contemporary Italy: A Collection of Essays*, edited by Michel Caesar and Peter Hainsworth. New York: St. Martin's Press, 1984. A well-balanced, comprehensive chronological survey of Buzzati's fiction and an excellent introduction for the non-Italian reading public. Analyzing individual stories, Rawson perceptively unites aspects of Buzzati's historical milieu, personal philosophy, and experience as both journalist and artist.

Siddell, Felix, ed. *Dino Buzzati*. Australia: Division of Italian Studies, La Trobe University, 1998. This volume offers criticism and interpretation of Buzzati's work.

Venuti, Lawrence. "Dino Buzzati's Fantastic Journalism." *Modern Fiction Studies* 28 (1982): 79-91. Discusses Buzzati's work from the point of view of the concept of "adaption," a narrative technique in which the author attempts to make the reader believe that the most fantastic actions can occur in his own world. Argues that Buzzati often exploits journalistic genres to give his fantasy an air of verisimilitude. Discusses several Buzzati stories which use this technique.

_____. Introduction to *Restless Nights: Selected Stories of Dino Buzzati*. San Francisco: North Point Press, 1983. The collection's translator provides a brief introduction to Buzzati's life, work, and the relationship of these to his European context and popularity. He also elucidates the contribution journalistic experience made to Buzzati's fantastic but convincing—and hauntingly memorable—narratives.

Winner, Anthony. "Authenticity, Authority, and Application: Buzzati, Kundera, Gordimer." *The Kenyon Review*, n.s. 20, nos. 3/4 (Summer/Fall, 1998): 94-120. Discusses concepts of authenticity and authority in Buzzati's fiction. Comments on Buzzati's attempt in one story to undermine a character's authenticity with the authority of fate, which introduces the terms of an impasse in the work of Milan Kundera and Nadine Gordimer.

Natalia Costa-Zalessow, updated by Terri Frongia

A. S. BYATT

Antonia Susan Drabble

Born: Sheffield, England; August 24, 1936

PRINCIPAL SHORT FICTION

Sugar and Other Stories, 1967

The Matisse Stories, 1993

The Djinn in the Nightingale's Eye: Five Fairy Stories, 1994

Elementals: Stories of Fire and Ice, 1998

OTHER LITERARY FORMS

A. S. Byatt began her career as a critic with *Degrees of Freedom: The Novels of Iris Murdoch* (1965) and has continued to produce occasional literary criticism. Her major work, however, has been in the novel; she has produced several novels and since the late 1980's has published a considerable amount of short fiction.

ACHIEVEMENTS

In 1986, A. S. Byatt received the Silver Pen Award for her novel *Still Life* (1985). She was made a Commander of the Order of the British Empire in 1959 and was awarded an English Speaking Union Fellowship in 1957-1958 and a Royal Society of Literature Fellowship in 1983 for her services to English literature. In 1990, Byatt was awarded the prestigious Booker McConnell Prize for her novel *Possession* (1990), which also received the *Irish Times*-Aer Lingus International Fiction Prize and the Best Book in Commonwealth Prize. She has become an international literary celebrity and is often asked for comment on artistic and social matters by British newspapers, journals, radio, and television.

BIOGRAPHY

Antonia Susan Byatt was born into the Drabble family in Sheffield, England, on August 24, 1936. Her parents were educated at Cambridge University, and she and her sister, Margaret Drabble (also a fiction writer and respected literary critic), were educated at Cambridge, where they had distinguished ca-

reers. Their father was a High Court judge and their mother a teacher. Part of Byatt's education took place in a boarding school, Mount School, a Quaker girls' school in York. Upon graduating from Cambridge in 1957, she spent a scholarship year at Bryn Mawr College, Pennsylvania, and did further study at Oxford in 1958-1959. In 1959, she married Ian Byatt, with whom she had two children. They divorced in 1969, and she married Peter Duffy, with whom she had two more children.

Her academic career began at the University of London, and she became a full-time member of the English Department in 1972. In 1964, her first novel, *The Shadow of the Sun*, appeared. She began to publish criticism in 1965 with her study of Iris Murdoch, *Degrees of Freedom: The Novels of Iris Murdoch*. In 1978, she offered a first volume of a set of four novels, *The Virgin in the Garden*. She continued her academic career until 1983, and a second novel in the tetralogy, *Still Life* (1985), added to her growing reputation. *Possession: A Romance* (1990) was both a critical and a popular success, and her career has flourished internationally ever since. In 1996, she published the third volume of the tetralogy, *Babel Tower*, and in the 1990's she added a considerable number of short stories to her bibliography.

ANALYSIS

A. S. Byatt's career as a fiction writer has always been on the move. She admits the influence of the French writer Marcel Proust and the English writer Iris Murdoch, both inclined to extending realistic fiction into areas which transcend simple tales of real life. Her short stories, like her novels, have always been stylistically and thematically dense. Her most successful stories often include an element of imaginative improvisation edging on Magic Realism, that late twentieth century movement in fiction which suffuses realistic fiction with incredible elements that, in the past, have been confined to fantasy literature. She is not satisfied with that; in *The Matisse Stories*, she develops tales that depend in subtle ways upon ambiguous connections with specific paintings by the French artist Henri Matisse. The reader does not have to know the paintings to appreciate the stories, but they are enriched by such knowledge. She takes another and different step into reshaping the short story in *The Djinn in the Nightingale's Eye*. The tales are stylistically and thematically incredible but are not for children. Intellectually and thematically, they are suitable only for adults.

Byatt is, despite her somewhat conservative moral attitudes, a part of the twentieth century movement in art that breaks the rules, thematically, structurally, psychologically, and aesthetically. Her stories are often a challenge to the reader's preconceptions about what is proper for certain kinds of literary art. However experimental Byatt's stories are, there is always a sense that she sees the form as capable not only of expansion and imaginative leaps but also of being used to examine the nature of the human predicament, if in a more ambiguous and less certain way than that of the tales of the late nineteenth and early twentieth century. Only the moral certainty of clever endings is missing.

"SUGAR"

This relatively early story is a good example of the way in which Byatt's themes are often connected with the problem of literary composition itself. On its face it is a simple tale of a woman attending at her father's deathbed in Amsterdam, where she chooses to tell the story of his life and that of her grandfather; this, in turn, leads her to think of her own life and her parents', which are complicated by the fact that her mother was prone to lying. What looks to be a simple moment of poignant recollection becomes an investigation of what is true. The conversations with her father lead to memories of her own experience of her grandfather, and she remembers, or thinks she remembers, incidents that begin to lose credibility when compared to her memories of her mother's tales of the family. Eventually she begins to realize that whether she likes it or not, the past is partly a fiction and she is not only a victim of it but also, like her mother, something of a perpetrator. There are, also, incidents in this story of a Yorkshire family which are

similar to certain facts in Byatt's own family history; she uses parts of her own experience with very little masking of their source. Byatt also has a strong affection for paintings by the great European artists, and she often brings them in to enrich her stories. In this tale, appropriately, she uses Vincent van Gogh and the museum in Amsterdam dedicated exclusively to his work.

"MEDUSA'S ANKLES"

Byatt will occasionally examine the world of middle-class, middle-aged, female angst which has been so successfully explored by Mavis Gallant and Alice Munro, but her use of this theme in "Medusa's Ankles," one of three stories in *The Matisse Stories*, shows how she can wed realistic material with a wider, aesthetic skein of associations. Sussanah, a successful academic with a bored husband, is regularly soothed by her visits to her hairdresser, Lucian, whose shop she chose originally because of a reproduction of Matisse's *Rosy Nude* which hangs in the salon. Its languor and overblown, richly hued voluptuousness give her some comfort, bothered as she is by middle age eroding her bodily charms.

One day, Lucian complains about his wife becoming less attractive as she ages; he is thinking of leaving her for a younger woman. On a later visit, he is still complaining about his wife; even her ankles are fat. What is most disturbing, however, for Sussanah, is the fact that the *Rosy Nude* has been replaced by a gray-and-black decor with photographs of thrusting, young, skinny models. The hair dressing goes badly, and Lucian, preoccupied and abrupt, makes a mess of her hair. Suddenly and surprisingly, Sussanah goes berserk and wrecks the salon. Lucian is understanding, admitting that he has often felt like doing the same. Sussanah goes home, washes the setting out of her hair, and oddly enough, is met by her husband with a show of affection and a compliment on her hair, worn, as he says, as he used to like it years ago.

This tale is sufficiently wry in itself but is best understood if the idea of Medusa, the mythological female monster, ugly and offensive, is seen as the middle-aged woman, and her attacks as a reasonable response to unfair treatment, rather than as a malignant act.

"A LAMIA IN THE CÉVENNES"

Byatt is often extravagant in description and lavish in eccentricity of style in many of her short stories. She is particularly so in her descriptions of colors and textures, sometimes beyond the textual relevance of the same. This story from *Elementals* provides her with the opportunity to revel in color and extend her imagination into the adult fairy tale.

Lycett-Kean, an English painter, disgusted with materialist London, goes to rural France, where he makes a living painting landscapes. He builds a swimming pool and is pleased, then artistically obsessed with the particularly blue color of the water, and he paints the color over and over. When he replenishes the pool from the local river, he discovers a serpent of wondrous colors in the pool. It speaks to him and tells him that it is a lamia, a beautiful woman trapped in a snake's body, although it has a human head that the painter finds repulsive. Nevertheless he is fascinated by the colors of the huge body, and he avidly produces paintings of it. She begs him to kiss her; if he does, she will become a woman and be his lover. He is reluctant, but she makes it clear that it would be unwise to betray her. The creature becomes restless and unhappy waiting for him to make up his mind.

Luckily, an English friend of vulgar character visits him, and suddenly, a blowsy, cheaply pretty woman joins him. The serpent has disappeared, and his friend and the flashy woman leave together. The painter goes on happily with his life, turning his painterly skills to a local butterfly. As in many fairy tales, all ends happily, if not quite in the way one would expect.

"THE GLASS COFFIN"

In *The Djinn in the Nightingale's Eye*, a volume of adult fairy tales, Byatt affects the singsong style of the fairy tale. The stories have plots similar to those of a child's tale, but they quickly involve adult problems and attitudes. Even the style, seemingly simplistic, is subtly changed by the use of an intellectually mature vocabulary and difficult ideas.

A tailor, wandering through a forest, comes upon a cottage and asks for shelter. A little gray man lets him in, in exchange for his labor. He so pleases the old man that he is offered his choice of one of three objects (a common motif in fairy tales). He chooses a glass key simply because he admires the workmanship. Following a series of complicated clues, he rescues a maiden from a golden coffin by using the key. She thinks that he is her Prince Charming and that they will live happily ever after. So they would in a child's tale.

The tailor suggests that he is no young lover but just an artisan trying to survive. The maiden assures him that he will be set for life if he helps her to escape from an evil suitor who immured her and turned her twin brother into a dog. The tailor kills the villain; the brother is restored to his natural state; all live happily together.

Of the tales in the collection, this one is the closest to a child's story. It might be readable by an older child. Its most obvious difference from an ordinary fairy tale lies in the extended conclusion and the refusal to bring on the happy ending with the rescue of the maiden. All ends in proper fairy-tale fashion, but as is often the case with the Byatt tales, the conclusion is a wry twist on the usual ending. Byatt takes the common fairy-tale motifs and pushes them slightly out of shape.

OTHER MAJOR WORKS

LONG FICTION: *Shadow of a Sun*, 1964; *The Game*, 1967; *The Virgin in the Garden*, 1978; *Still Life*, 1985; *Possession: A Romance*, 1990; *Angels and Insects*, 1992; *Babel Tower*, 1996.

NONFICTION: *Degrees of Freedom: The Novels of Iris Murdoch*, 1965; *Wordsworth and Coleridge in Their Time*, 1970 (republished as *Unruly Times*, 1989); *Iris Murdoch*, 1976; *Passions of the Mind: Selected Writings*, 1991; *Imagining Characters: Conversations About Women Writers, Jane Austen, Charlotte Brontë, George Eliot, Willa Cather, Iris Murdoch, and Toni Morrison*, 1997 (with Ignes Sodre).

EDITED TEXTS: *The Mill on the Floss*, 1979 (by George Eliot); *Selected Essays, Poems and Other Writings*, 1989 (by Eliot); *Dramatic Monologues*, 1990 (by Robert Browning); *The Oxford Book of English Short Stories*, 1998.

BIBLIOGRAPHY

Adil, Alev. "Obeying the Genie." *Times Literary Supplement* (January 6, 1995): 20. Discussion of the language in Byatt's short stories, with particular emphasis on the fairy stories.

Bawer, Bruce. "What We Do for Art." *New York Times Book Review*, April 30, 1995, p 9. It is often suggested that Byatt's world lacks realistic credibility. *The Matisse Stories* are discussed with that charge in mind.

Brookner, Anita, et al. "A. S. Byatt: *Possession: A Romance.*" *Contemporary Literary Critics Yearbook* 65 (1990): 121-133. Anita Brookner, the prominent British novelist and book reviewer, is joined by six other reviewers in commenting on the novel, but it is put in a context with her other works, including the short stories.

Kelly, Kathleen Coyne. *A. S. Byatt.* New York: Twayne, 1996. A general study of Byatt's career, with a chapter on the short stories. Short, clearly and simply written. Also provides an excellent bibliography of academic and general discussions of her work.

Spufford, Francis. "The Mantle of Jehovah." *London Review of Books* (June 25, 1987): 22-23. A review of *Sugar and Other Stories* put into the context of her other work, with special emphasis on the relation of her fiction to the genre of the British middle class novel.

Wood, James. "England." In *The Oxford Guide to Contemporary Writing.* New York: Oxford University Press, 1991. Byatt expects her readers to be well educated, and with that presumption in mind, she adds artistic and general intellectual allusions to enrich her themes. Wood suggests that much of the time such additions are unsuccessful and intrusive.

Charles Pullen

MICHAEL BYERS

Born: Seattle, Washington; 1971

PRINCIPAL SHORT FICTION

The Coast of Good Intentions: Stories, 1998

OTHER LITERARY FORMS

The Coast of Good Intentions is Michael Byers's first book.

ACHIEVEMENTS

Michael Byers was a Wallace Stegner Fellow at Stanford University between 1996 and 1998. His story "Settled on the Cranberry Coast" was selected for *Prize Stories: The O. Henry Awards* in 1995; "Shipmates Down Under" was selected for the annual publication *The Best American Short Stories* in 1997. *The Coast of Good Intentions* was a finalist for the Ernest Hemingway Foundation Award and in 1999 won the Whiting Writers Award, given to emerging writers of exceptional talent and promise.

BIOGRAPHY

Michael Byers was born and raised in Seattle, Washington, graduating from Garfield High School in 1987. He received his B.A. degree from Oberlin College in Ohio and taught elementary school in Louisiana for two years in the Teach for America program. He received a master of fine arts degree from the University of Michigan and enrolled in the writing program at Stanford University before moving back to Seattle.

ANALYSIS

The stories of Michael Byers belong to the contemporary short-story tradition represented by Ethan Canin's 1988 *Emperor of the Air* and Christopher Tilghman's 1990 *In a Father's Place*. Like Canin and Tilghman, Byers affirms, in a seemingly simple, matter-of-fact way, the solid, unsentimental values of family, commitment, and hope for the future. This is the kind of fiction that John Gardner urged in his book *Moral Fiction* (1978) and that Raymond Carver embodied in his 1983 collection *Cathedral*, hailed as mellower and more hopeful than his earlier, so-called minimalist stories.

Byers focuses primarily on men who, although certainly not simple, are simply trying hard to do their best. They are, like the retired schoolteacher in "Settled on the Cranberry Coast," still looking hopefully to the future, or, when they do look to the past, are like the elderly couple in "Dirigibles," reaffirmed rather than disappointed by where they have been. When Byers takes on the persona of a woman, as he does in "A Fair Trade," the past is perceived without regret, the present is accepted with equanimity, and the future is looked forward to with hope. Even the self-absorbed father in "Shipmates Down Under," who should take responsibility for his troubled marriage, and the young widower in "Spain, One Thousand and Three," who has, for ego's sake, treated women as conquests, ultimately are simply human with all the frailties to which humans are heir.

Such understanding, loving, and forgiving values are hard to resist, but they are also hard to present without either irony or sentimentality. Byers manages to avoid both, giving the reader characters who are neither perfect nor petulant, neither ironically bitter nor blissfully ignorant, but who are rather complex and believable human beings simply doing their best, which, Byers seems to suggest, is the most human thing anyone can do.

"SETTLED ON THE CRANBERRY COAST"

A satisfying story about second chances or the pleasant realization that it is never too late to live, "Settled on the Cranberry Coast" is narrated by Eddie, a bachelor who has just retired after teaching high school for twenty-seven years and has taken up part-time carpentry work. When Rosie, an old high school acquaintance who has also never married, hires him to repair an old house she has just bought, the story focuses quite comfortably on their inevitable gravitation toward each other. Rosie fills Eddie's need for a caring companion, while her six-year-old granddaughter Hannah, who lives with her, gives him the child he has never had.

As Eddie makes Rosie's house sturdier, their rela-

tionship grows as well, gradually affirming Eddie's opening sentence in the story: "This I know; our lives in these towns are slowly improving." Eddie can imagine moving in with Rosie and Hannah, thinking that we do not live our lives so much as come to them, as people and things "collect mysteriously" around us. At the end of the story, Eddie invites Hannah to go to the next town with him to buy radiators. In a simple scene handled perceptively and delicately by Byers, Eddie stands under a parking lot overhang in the rain, smoothing the sleeping child's hair, her head "perfectly round" on his shoulder. In a Carveresque final sentence, he thinks he is "on the verge of something" as he waits there, listening to Hannah's easy, settled breathing.

"DIRIGIBLES"

Because Byers was only in his twenties when he wrote these stories, reviewers have made much of his understanding of older characters, such as Eddie in "Settled on the Cranberry Coast." In "Dirigibles," Howard and Louise, in their late sixties and retired, are visited by James Couch, a friend from the old days, who is stopping on his way from Seattle to Montana. Couch talks about his daughter hang gliding in outer space, and Howard realizes that Couch has "gone a little way around the bend, and he [isn't] coming back." When Howard sets up a movie projector to show Couch old home movies from the time when they were friends, it turns out he has put in the wrong film; what they see instead is a very brief scene of Louise, young and thin and almost all legs, running naked from one doorway to another. Howard and Louise both laugh, remembering when he returned from service in the navy, and she came to the door nonchalantly nude.

After putting Couch to bed, the couple lie awake, and Howard says he played the greatest concert halls in Germany before the war, with ten thousand women waiting on his every need; he tells Louise to think of him like that, and she says, "Yes." He tells her he flew "great dirigibles of the age" over the "great nations of the earth," and she says, "Yes." In the last line, when he says "It's true. Everything is true," she says, "Oh, Howard. Howard." The conclusion is a great affirmative paean to love and union, much like the end of

Molly Bloom's famous soliloquy in James Joyce's *Ulysses* (1922).

"SHIPMATES DOWN UNDER"

This story focuses on the protagonist's relationship with his nine-year-old son, who seems principled and controlled; with his six-year-old daughter, who becomes mysteriously ill; and with his wife, who feels an outsider to his connection with the children. Because the daughter's illness threatens to dominate the story, the underlying marital conflict, which is its real subject, does not become apparent until the end when the child improves just as mysteriously as she fell ill.

The boy, who intuits the unspoken conflict between the parents, says he is writing a sequel to a boys' adventure book his father recommended and urges his father to take his mother on a vacation, as their planned vacation to Perth, Australia, the father's home, has been canceled because of the daughter's illness. When the protagonist talks to his wife about this, she calls him "Mister Distant, Mister Nowhere, Mr. Say Nothing," accusing him of living in his own little world with the children while pretending she does not exist. Although he denies this, when he sees the first sentence of his son's sequel—"My father and I live in Perth in a tiny white house with a wall around the garden"—he feels a "little bloom of secretive joy" in his heart. The story ends with his thinking that he will apologize to his wife and that they will overcome their difficulties. However, when he imagines them finally taking their disrupted trip to Australia, what he thinks of is the children remembering the experience, the hotel standing strong and unchanged, "the solid keeper of my precious cargo, these two damaged packages of my detailed dreams."

"IN SPAIN, ONE THOUSAND AND THREE"

The central character in this story, Martin Tuttleman, tries to cope with the loss of his wife at age twenty-five to cancer. A computer game designer, he has been away from work so long due to her illness that now, at least temporarily, he works in the support department, giving phone advice to kids playing the game he helped design. The primary focus of the story is Martin's constant sexual fantasies about women. Before his marriage, he slept with every

woman he could, and thinks of himself as having had more sex than anyone he knows. Now that his wife, who completely filled his sexual desire during their marriage, is dead, he has begun to fantasize about other women again.

The central crucial event in the story is an ambiguous encounter with his mother-in-law in his wife's old bedroom. When he takes one of his shirts out of her closet, the mother embraces him, and he compares the feel of her body to that of his wife. They begin rubbing against each other like "shy dancers" and then abruptly push apart. The story ends with his father-in-law angrily confronting him, demanding that he apologize. When he does so, he feels good, as if he were saying he is sorry to all the women he ever seduced.

"A FAIR TRADE"

This is the longest story in the collection, and it covers the longest span of time, nearly the whole life of the central character Andie, beginning at age fourteen with her trip to live with her aunt for a period after her father's death and her mother's emotional breakdown, and ending with a visit to her aunt some forty years later when she is in her fifties. However, most of the story focuses on the time Andie lived with her Aunt Maggie; the rest of her life is recounted in brief summary. During this period, Andie has fantasies about a mysterious European man who works for an elderly couple who live across the road. The only real plot complications occur when Maggie's unscrupulous boyfriend, who is trying to get the elderly couple's farm, threatens to tell the authorities that the man has made sexual advances toward Andie; when Maggie finds out, she sends the boyfriend packing.

The last part of the story covers Andie's life after she returns to her mother—summarizing her marriage, divorce, her daughter's going off to college, and finally her move back to Seattle when she is fiftyfive. Seeing her aunt's old boyfriend, now in his eighties, on television prompts a visit to her aunt, who has adopted a gay man, and who has a new boyfriend in his seventies. Although her aunt tells her she should have a man, Andie looks forward to twenty more years of being alone. She feels she has made a "fair trade," that her way is not a bad way to live. As she sits in a restaurant with her aunt and her adopted son, she shuffles her feet under the table, thinking that from other tables she may appear to be dancing.

BIBLIOGRAPHY

Dyer, Richard. "Short Stories Long on Empathy, Resonance." *The Boston Globe*, August 5, 1998, p. C5. Notes that although most of Byers's stories are direct and intimate, they are also technically accomplished, with complex patterns of mirrors and receding reverberations. Says Byers's writing is so good it is patronizing to call him promising, for he has already arrived.

Marshall, John. "Seattle's Michael Byers Wins Whiting Award." *Seattle Post-Intelligencer*, November 6, 1998, p. 21. A biographical sketch/interview story; Byers credits Charles Baxter, under whom he studied at the University of Michigan, as being one of his most important inspirations, saying he likes Baxter's scrupulousness and generosity and his moral approach to fiction.

"Michael Byers' *The Coast of Good Intentions*." *Kirkus Reviews* (May 11, 1998). Calls *The Coast of Good Intentions* a strong debut collection of graceful tales about unresolved lives; says that the crab factories, cranberry bogs, and fog-shrouded shores of the Pacific Northwest are the settings for quiet but astonishing emotional epiphanies.

Seligman, Craig. "Ordinary Beauty." *The New York Times*, May 10, 1998, p. 7, 19. Discusses how Byers's technically seamless prose depicts men for whom life has not worked out the way they would like; emphasizes that although Byers has some of the bleakness of the early Raymond Carver, his optimism shows though. Says his writing is both melancholy and hopeful, characterized by the unexpected beauty of the ordinary.

Smyth, Charles. "Byers' Pitch Is True." *January Magazine* (October, 1998). Praises Byers for his mature and tender compassion for his characters; says his stories are about people coming to terms with what life has dealt them. Claims that comparisons to Raymond Carver do not hold up, for Byers is less turbulent and more pensive; whereas Carver liked a spare, clean style, Byers likes longer, more leisurely sentences.

Wanner, Irene. "Byers Reveals Much About His Characters." *The Seattle Times*, May 10, 1998, p. M2. Praises Byers for his ability to portray older adults and small children with convincing detail and to reveal character through carefully controlled dialogue. Calls his stories carefully crafted examples of tight, modern American short stories.

Charles E. May

C

GEORGE WASHINGTON CABLE

Born: New Orleans, Louisiana; October 12, 1844
Died: St. Petersburg, Florida; January 31, 1925

PRINCIPAL SHORT FICTION

Old Creole Days, 1879
Madame Delphine, 1881
Strange True Stories of Louisiana, 1889
Strong Hearts, 1899
Posson Jone' and Père Raphaël, 1909
The Flower of the Chapdelaines, 1918

OTHER LITERARY FORMS

George Washington Cable's published books include several novels and collections of essays in addition to his short stories. His first novel, *The Grandissimes* (1880), captured national attention and widespread praise. His essays, although less popular, delineated and criticized social, economic, and political conditions in the South.

ACHIEVEMENTS

George Washington Cable achieved distinction for his realistic portrayal of New Orleans and Louisiana in his novels and short fiction. His Creole works abound with rich details of setting and character, and his attention to the varieties of dialect mark him as a brilliant local colorist. Yet his work also defies this narrow classification. His concern for the rights of African Americans and social conditions in general in the postbellum South inspired a number of essays. He also collaborated with Mark Twain on a series of lecture tours. His novels combine traditional forms such as romance and melodrama with the freshness of Creole detail and careful consideration of the looming social issues of the late nineteenth century. One of the finest regional writers of his day, Cable introduced the exotic Creole South to the rest of the country. He paved the way for later writers, such as William Faulkner, who likewise surpass mere regional identification to present intensely absorbing stories of the human condition.

BIOGRAPHY

After the death of his father, George Washington Cable left school at the age of twelve and worked in a warehouse. During the years he should have been in college he was a Confederate soldier. Ever eager to learn, he read incessantly while in the service. After the war he was a reporter for a short time, then a clerk for a cotton firm while continuing to publish personal essays signed "Drop Shot" for the New Orleans *Picayune*. In 1873, he met Edward King, who carried copies of his stories to the editors of *Scribner's Monthly*. In October of that year Cable's first story was published, and his first novel was published the following year. Desiring to be closer to literary circles, Cable left the South and settled with his family in Northampton, Massachusetts. He loved the energetic atmosphere of the North, and much of what he wrote about the South after the move lacked the clarity and fire of his earlier work. During a return trip to the South in 1925, Cable died, leaving stories of a period which would never be again.

ANALYSIS

By the 1880's, much of the passion that had divided the country during the Civil War had been displaced by a growing interest in life in other regions of the newly rejoined republic. No longer separated by political and economic differences, people began not only to accept cultural differences but also to express keen interest in them, and the fiction of local color was perfectly suited to these readers. Stories of the day tended to emphasize verisimilitude of detail within scenic elements: Settings were often colorful extravaganzas; characters were typically drawn to emphasize peculiarities of their region or culture yet were often poorly developed; and plots were often thin.

These characteristics are reflected in George Washington Cable's stories of New Orleans: Settings sparkle with picturesque detail and rich imagery, and character descriptions emphasize the cultural or regional peculiarities of speech, manner, and thought. Cable's characters are rarely developed beyond the superficial, being distanced by narrative perspective, vague in motivation, and frequently shrouded in mystery. Plots are sketchy events, lacking causal relationships and frequently relying on melodrama. Given these general characteristics, Cable's stories could be pigeonholed as merely more local color; but then much that is specifically Cable's richness would be lost. Deeper elements of Cable's unique literary perspective, however, play an important role in the total artistic impact of his stories. His New Orleans still retained much of her international flavor and embraced a unique mixture of races, clashing cultures, opposing values, old loyalties, and old hatreds; poverty and wealth coexisted; and caste systems were accepted and propagated. Cable's strongly developed social consciousness directed his writing talents to portray these elements sensitively. Thus, while preserving the picturesque, Cable probed the ramifications of racial juxtaposition and of social problems, capturing more completely the spirit of his literary domain. This added dimension of circumstantial reality, born out of Cable's personality and New Orleans's uniqueness, distinguishes Cable's powerful stories from the mass of local-color fiction of his day.

"'Sieur George"

Cable's first story, "'Sieur George," reflects characteristics typical both of local-color fiction and of Cable's fiction. The standard picturesque setting, in this case an old tenement building, rises before us as the narrator masterfully describes it: "With its gray stucco peeling off in broad patches, it has the solemn look of gentility in rags, and stands, or, as it were, hangs, about the corner of two ancient streets, like a faded fop who pretends to be looking for employment." The simile of inanimate object to animate one

George Washington Cable (Library of Congress)

is precise, and the images reinforce each other to create a subtle atmosphere of age and decay. Through its doors are seen "masses of cobwebbed iron . . . overhung by a creaking sign" into a courtyard "hung with many lines of wet clothes, its sides hugged by rotten staircases that seem vainly trying to clamber out of the rubbish." The neighborhood has been "long since given up to fifth-rate shops." The setting is thus vividly drawn by a composite of details each artistically contributing to a subtle atmosphere of time and ruin vital to the story's texture.

It is not unusual for Cable's characters to echo the atmosphere of the setting, giving it an organic quality that continues the link of inanimate to animate. When 'Sieur George first appeared, both he and the neighborhood were "fashionable." At the time of the story, some fifty years later, he is a reclusive "square small man" draped in a "newly repaired overcoat." No longer fashionable and usually drunk, 'Sieur George stumbles home never careening to right or left but now forcing himself slowly forward, as if there was a high gale in front, and now scudding briskly ahead at a ridiculous little dog-trot, as if there was a tornado behind.

The descriptive detail is visually vivid and continues the image of time and its erosion.

As is typical of local-color fiction, however, 'Sieur George is rather superficially portrayed, and this weakens the story. His actions are related to us by the omniscient narrator, whose detached perspective never allows us to experience any genuine sympathetic involvement with 'Sieur George. The reader hears about him but never knows his thoughts or feelings; consequently, he seems little more than a cardboard cutout. His motivations are vague, and his daily drunks continue only to be interrupted unexpectedly by surprising events. One day 'Sieur George shocks the neighborhood as he emerges from his apartment in full regimentals and marches off to the Mexican War, leaving his sister behind to become the new occupant of his rooms. Several years later, he suddenly reappears with battle scars and a tall dark companion. 'Sieur George and the stranger visit the sister weekly until her marriage to the stranger is announced by her appearance in bridal array. With the newlyweds gone, 'Sieur George returns to his rooms and drunken habits until the pattern is again interrupted when he returns home with the couple's infant. Since her mother had died and her drunken father had drowned in the river, 'Sieur George attentively raises the girl until it would violate proprieties for her to stay; finally, in a senseless moment, he blurts out that the only way for her to stay is for her to become his wife. She utters a mournful cry, runs to her room, and early the next morning leaves for a convent. 'Sieur George returns to drunkenness and finally becomes a penniless, homeless drifter searching the prairie "to find a night's rest in the high grass"—"and there's an end."

Not only are his motivations vague, but also he is shrouded in Cable's frequent cloak of mystery. After 'Sieur George has lived in the neighborhood for about a year, "something happened that greatly changed the tenor of his life." "Hints of a duel, of a reason warped, of disinheritance, and many other unauthorized rumors, fluttered up and floated off." Soon he begins to display the "symptoms of decay" stumbling home, and "whatever remuneration he received went its way for something that left him dingy and threadbare." The artistically interwoven pictures of him recycle the images of decay and ruin, but the only thing the reader knows that 'Sieur George cares about, and strongly so, is the mysterious small hair trunk he carefully guards. Even 'Sieur George's implied heroism is dubious and unconvincing. The reader hears about him marching off to war, returning with battle scars, and bravely directing the infant to womanhood; yet each admirable event on the one hand is treated only summarily, and on the other is undercut by his return to drunkenness. He is not a great man who, in a weak moment, has fallen prey to vicious evils; neither he nor his vices have any true tragic element. Finally, he is not a tragic man inspiring our sympathy but merely a man in a pathetic situation, and it is the feeling for his situation with which the reader is left.

It is 'Sieur George's landlord, Kookoo, who emerges most vividly from this story. Like his tenant and his building, Kookoo also shows the effects of time, for the "ancient Creole" has grown "old and wrinkled and brown." He is vividly sketched by three descriptive strokes: "He smokes cascarilla, wears velveteen and is as punctual as an executioner." Our perception of Kookoo is enhanced by the narrator's attitude toward him as a "periodically animate mummy" possessing "limited powers of conjecture." Kookoo's favorite pastimes are to eavesdrop on his tenants, watch the habits of 'Sieur George, and revel in the mystery of 'Sieur George's small hair trunk. His personality emerges through his actions, clearly motivated by nosiness and curiosity. Moreover, the reader becomes a partner to his consciousness as 'Sieur George leaves for war, taking the omniscient narrator with him. It is Kookoo, driven by a fifty-year-old curiosity and taking advantage of 'Sieur George's open door and drunken stupor, who leads the reader to the mysterious trunk and a final revelation about its owner: "The trunk was full, full, crowded down and running over full, of the tickets of the Havanna Lottery!"

The plot of "'Sieur George" is thin, often vague, and finally melodramatic; and the climax is less than satisfying because the ramifications of compulsive gambling have not been portrayed in 'Sieur George's superficial development. It is not uncommon for Cable, with his social consciousness, to give social problems an antagonistic role, but the problem here is that neither 'Sieur George nor his vices stand out clearly enough against the images of Kookoo and Creole life; thus, their possible impact is lost in the collage. What holds the reader's attention, however, is the sustained suspense created by the adroit changes in the angle of narration. The perspective shifts back and forth between the omniscient narrator and Kookoo: The narrator, who initially dominates the reader's perspective of 'Sieur George, demonstrates a vast knowledge with a detached precision; when 'Sieur George is absent, however, the reader becomes partner with Kookoo, whose perspective is limited but allows deeper involvement. When 'Sieur George returns, so does the perspective of the omniscient narrator. Not only does the reader know both "sides" of the story, but also the suspense of Kookoo's curiosity is sustained as the narrator continues. This technique and its adroit management create a sustained suspense that holds the reader to the end. Cable's changing angles of narration, along with the scenic setting and glimpses of Creole life, are the final salvation of the story. The reader may well be disappointed by the less than satisfying climax, but reaching it is a fine experience, and the final praise of the story is that it is so well told.

"JEAN-AH POQUELIN"

In a later story, "Jean-ah Poquelin," Cable uses basically the same techniques, but much more effectively. The story begins in a time when the "newly established American Government was the most hateful thing in Louisiana—when the Creoles were still kicking at such vile innovations as the trial by jury, American dances, antismuggling laws, and the printing of the Governor's proclamation in English." This atmosphere of conflict is quickly followed by a sense of impending doom as the narrator centers the reader's attention on the stark details of the old Poquelin plantation: standing above the marsh, "aloof from civili-

zation," "lifted up on pillars, grim, solid, and spiritless," "like a gigantic ammunition wagon stuck in the mud and abandoned by some retreating army." Two dead cypress trees "dotted with roosting vultures" and crawling waters filled with reptiles "to make one shudder to the ends of his days" create around the home an atmosphere of foreboding. This atmosphere is continued as the description of Jean Marie Poquelin unfolds. He was "once an opulent indigo planter, standing high in the esteem" of his friends but is "now a hermit, alike shunned by and shunning all who had ever known him." Typically reflecting the setting's atmosphere, Jean is yet somewhat unique among local-color characters because of his multifaceted and full development.

His personality is discovered through a series of flashbacks to happier times. Jean had been "a bold, frank, impetuous, chivalric adventurer," but there was no trait for which he was better known than "his apparent fondness" for his little brother, Jacques. Jacques, thirty years Jean's junior and really a half-brother, was "a gentle studious book-loving recluse." Together "they lived upon the ancestral estate like mated birds, one always on the wing, the other always in the nest." The brothers' tranquil relationship is abruptly interrupted when Jean returns from a two-year slaving expedition apparently without Jacques, who, unable to tolerate his brother's long absence, had begged to go along. Jean remained silent on this issue, but rumor was that Jacques had returned "but he had never been seen again," and "dark suspicion" fell upon Jean as his name "became a symbol of witchery, devilish crime, and hideous nursery fictions." Rumors of blood-red windows, owls with human voices, and the ghost of the departed brother keep the plantation and Jean shrouded in mystery while children viciously taunt him in the streets, calling names and throwing dirt clods with youthful expertise, as ignorant adults blame him for all their misfortunes. Old Jean betrays his silence as latent boldness responds to this ill treatment; "rolling up his brown fist" he would "pour forth such an unholy broadside of French imprecation and invective as would all but craze" the Creole children "with delight." His actions are justified, and readers cheer him on as they become personally involved in the story.

Time passes, and immigrants flood New Orleans, forcing growing pains on the city. Greedy non-Creole American land developers and displaced Creoles begin to encroach on Jean's lonely home. Through Jean's reaction to these forces, the reader learns more about him and becomes more deeply involved in his plight. Hoping to stop the invaders, Jean appeals to the Governor, and, in doing so, he projects much of his personality: He stands proudly with his large black eye "bold and open like that of a war horse, and his jaw shut together with the fierceness of iron." His open-neck shirt reveals "a herculean breast, hard and grizzled," yet there is "no fierceness of defiance in his look" but rather a "peaceful and peaceable fearlessness."

Jean's heroic stature is sensitively human, for on his face, "not marked in one or another feature, but as it were laid softly upon the countenance like an almost imperceptible veil, was the imprint of some great grief"—faint "but once seen, there it hung." In broken English, Jean protests the invasion of his privacy, but the reader senses the futility of his attempt as he is answered by questions about the wicked rumors. His temper flares as he declares, "I mine me hown bizniss." Jean's motivations may still be vague, but the strength of his convictions as to his rights and his powerful presence inspire the reader's respect.

Although he marches from the officials' rooms, Jean is kept ever present as he is discussed by the American and Creole developers. Old stories are retold, and Jean gains nobility as the greedy invaders callously plan how to oust him so that they can replace his home with a market. Their shallow commercialism and ignorant superstitions are illuminating foils to Jean's deep-seated desire to preserve his home. Jean's only champion, Little White, only temporarily stalls a mob determined to "chirivari" him, and ultimately they rush forward only to be met by Jean's only slave, an African mute, carting a draped coffin through the front gate. Old Jean is dead; and the crowd stands silent except for its unanimous gasp at seeing the white figure slowly walking behind the cart. The cause of so many rumors and cruelties is the "living remains—all that was left—of little Jacques

Poquelin, the long-hidden brother—a leper, as white as snow." The African adjusts the weight of the coffin on his shoulders, and "without one backward glance upon the unkind human world, turning their faces toward the ridge in the depth of the swamp known as Leper's Land, they stepped into the jungle, disappeared and were never seen again."

Melodramatic touches are frequent as the story turns on Jean's selfless devotion. The climax brings the reader's compassion to a peak well supported by all that has been learned about Jean: how his friends have spoken so well of him; the knowledge of his loving relationship with Jacques; and his justifiable responses to the jeering children, Creole cruelty, and non-Creole American aggression. Although his motivations are vague until the end, and he is shrouded in mystery, the rightness of his actions and speeches assures the reader of his innate goodness.

Cable again employs a changing angle of narration, but Jean is ever the subject of other characters' thoughts and actions; thus, he is ever kept before the reader. All the elements of the story are clearly aimed at telling the story of Jean and his doomed resistance. Compassion for Jean and his brother remains strong after the conclusion of the story, one of the few in which Cable beautifully balances his romantic fiction and social criticism. The story succeeds as both; it is a haunting "ghost" story while it attacks ignorant prejudice and makes a touching plea for human compassion.

Cable was the first literary voice of the New South. Writing within the realm of local-color fiction, he enriched his stories with the circumstantial reality of local history; he preserved the beautiful detail of colorful New Orleans in impressionistic backgrounds peopled by unique characters; and he was the first writer to bring the crude patois of the Creoles accurately to print. Cable's stories are a unique blend of romantic elements and circumstantial reality drawn from his literary domain. Although many of his stories are hampered by a lack of clear direction, the cluttering, often paragraphic glimpses of different cultures are rewarding reading; and where Cable achieved a precise utility of a story's elements, the total impact is unforgettable.

OTHER MAJOR WORKS

LONG FICTION: *The Grandissimes*, 1880; *Dr. Sevier*, 1884; *Bonaventure*, 1888; *John March, Southerner*, 1894; *The Cavalier*, 1901; *Bylow Hill*, 1902; *Kincaid's Battery*, 1908; *Gideon's Band*, 1914; *Lovers of Louisiana*, 1918.

NONFICTION: *The Creoles of Louisiana*, 1884; *The Silent South*, 1885; *The Negro Question*, 1890; *The Busy Man's Bible*, 1891; *A Memory of Roswell Smith*, 1892; *The Amateur Garden*, 1914.

MISCELLANEOUS: *The Cable Story Book: Selections for School Reading*, 1899.

BIBLIOGRAPHY

Bikle, Lucy Leffingwell Cable. *George W. Cable: His Life and Letters*. New York: Charles Scribner's Sons, 1928. This biography of Cable, written by his daughter, has the advantage of immediacy to, and intimacy with, the subject. Bikle covers the life of Cable primarily through the many letters that he wrote. The book is arranged chronologically, but the lack of an index makes finding specific information difficult at times.

Butcher, Philip. *George W. Cable*. New York: Twayne, 1962. This literary biography studies the life of Cable in the context of his work and vice versa. Like other biographies in the Twayne authors series, it provides a useful general introduction. Butcher covers the major phases of Cable's life—from New Orleans and *Old Creole Days* to the friendship with Mark Twain to his social and political involvement—in an honest, engaging fashion.

Cleman, John. *George Washington Cable Revisited*. New York: Twayne, 1996. A revision of an earlier critical introduction to Cable's life and work; discusses Cable's major work and the social context that frames it. Cleman also includes chapters devoted to Cable's advocacy of civil rights for African Americans, his political writing, and his later works of "pure fiction."

Ekstrom, Kjell. *George Washington Cable: A Study of His Early Life and Work*. New York: Haskell House, 1966. Ekstrom focuses on Cable's Creole fiction, giving much historical, literary, and cultural background to Cable's early work. In addition to the biographical information on Cable's early years, Ekstrom also discusses literary and nonliterary sources for the Creole short stories and novels.

Elfenbein, Anna Shannon. *Women on the Color Lines: Evolving Stereotypes and the Writings of George Washington Cable, Grace King, Kate Chopin*. Charlottesville: University Press of Virginia, 1989. Argues that Cable identified racism with sexism and classism and subverted the traditional literary categories that have segmented white women and women of color. Discusses how in the story "Tite Poulete" Cable moves beyond racism to a consideration of the shared oppression of all women.

Jones, Gavin. "Signifying Songs: The Double Meaning of Black Dialect in the Work of George Washington Cable." *American Literary History* 9 (Summer, 1997): 244-267. Discusses interaction of African American and French-Creole culture in Cable's works; argues that African American dialect, song, and satire were transmitted to the white community subversively.

Ladd, Barbara. *Nationalism and the Color Line in George W. Cable, Mark Twain, and William Faulkner*. Baton Rouge: Louisiana State University Press, 1996. Argues that racial thinking of the lower Mississippi River area, on which Cable focused, is colonialist and assimilationist.

Rubin, Louis D., Jr. *George W. Cable: The Life and Times of a Southern Heretic*. New York: Pegasus, 1969. This critical biography focuses on Cable's position within the tradition of southern writers, while also noting that Cable—atypically of other Southerners of the time—supported campaigns to give African Americans equal rights in the postbellum period. Rubin provides a number of excellent readings of, and insightful commentaries on, Cable's works, including a chapter on *Old Creole Days*. The select bibliography is useful for locating more information on Cable's fiction.

Turner, Arlin. *George W. Cable: A Biography*. Durham, N.C.: Duke University Press, 1956. Turner's thoroughly researched biography in many ways set the standard for further Cable studies. Turner discusses in great detail not only Cable's life but also his literary work, political involvement, geographical contexts, and the important historical events that affected Cable's life and work. As with the rest of this biography, the index and bibliography are extensive.

Kathy Ruth Frazier, updated by Ann A. Merrill

JAMES M. CAIN

Born: Annapolis, Maryland; July 1, 1892
Died: Hyattsville, Maryland; October 27, 1977

PRINCIPAL SHORT FICTION
"Pastorale," 1928
"The Taking of Monfaucon," 1929
"The Baby in the Icebox," 1933
"Come-Back," 1934
"Dead Man," 1936
"Hip, Hip, the Hippo," 1936
"The Birthday Party," 1936
"Brush Fire," 1936
"Coal Black," 1937
"Everything but the Truth," 1937
"The Girl in the Storm," 1940
"Payoff Girl," 1952
"Cigarette Girl," 1953
"Two O'Clock Blonde," 1953
"The Visitor," 1961
The Baby in the Icebox and Other Short Fiction,
    1981 (posthumous, edited by Roy Hoopes)
Career in C Major and Other Fiction, 1986 (edited
    by Roy Hoopes)

OTHER LITERARY FORMS
James M. Cain wrote novels, plays, screenplays, and magazine articles, in addition to short stories. The Mystery Writers of America designated him a Grand Master in 1970. His major novels include *The Postman Always Rings Twice* (1934), *Mildred Pierce* (1941), and *Double Indemnity* (1943). Earlier in his writing career, he was a reporter and an editorial writer.

ACHIEVEMENTS
Though sometimes included among the top writers of hard-boiled crime fiction, James M. Cain himself scorned this label. Critical opinion has swung around to his view that, indeed, he wrote about murders, from the criminal's point of view, but he did not write crime fiction. What makes his writing so gripping is not the typical pull to resolve a puzzle but the fascination of ordinary people suddenly finding themselves making a wish come true, a concept Cain described as terrifying and which he compared to opening Pandora's box. The influential existentialist writer Albert Camus claimed that his own novel *The Stranger* (1942) was influenced by Cain's *The Postman Always Rings Twice*.

BIOGRAPHY
James Mallahan Cain was the oldest of five children of Rose Mallahan, a singer, and James William Cain, a professor at St. John's College in Annapolis, Maryland. His grandparents were Irish immigrants who settled in New Haven, Connecticut, where his father attended Yale University. Cain was eleven when his father became the president of Washington College. Cain enrolled there at the age of fifteen, was graduated in 1910, received a master's degree in 1917, and taught math and English for a year after giving up his ambition to become an opera singer. He was a reporter for several newspapers and taught journalism at St. John's; then for seventeen years he wrote scripts in Hollywood. His fourth marriage, to opera singer Florence Macbeth Whitwell in 1947, was a happy one, which encouraged him to write about music in four of his novels. The literary figure who ex-

James M. Cain in 1946 (AP/Wide World Photos)

erted the single greatest influence on his career was H. L. Mencken, with whom he corresponded and who published his work in his periodical, the *American Mercury*.

ANALYSIS

James M. Cain's characters are ordinary people—capable of decency, passion, and crime—caught up in situations from which they seem incapable of extricating themselves. Cain valued the commonplace person and prided himself on writing the way people talk. In order to write accurately about the vagrants in *The Moth* (1948), for example, he visited the missions in Los Angeles where tramps gathered and interviewed many of them. He keeps up a relentless pace in his stories with a minimum of description and with blunt, brisk, and fast-paced dialogue.

Lack of exposition, typical of Cain's narrative style, also helps maintain the momentum. The reader is immediately confronted with an action in the present; in only one of Cain's twelve novels is there any flashback to explain the protagonist's background. What mattered to Cain's readers was not his characters' appearance. Cain's editors usually had to ask him to be more explicit about what his people looked like; the most he ever gave them was a movie-star approximation: "Like Clark Gable [or some other movie star]—fill it in yourself." What mattered to Cain was a character's "presence" as expressed in action. It was probably this virile approach to storytelling that endeared him to the French existentialists and the postwar Italians, who favored such a style.

"BRUSH FIRE"

The opening scene of "Brush Fire" depicts a group of men wielding shovels against a forest fire, coughing from the smoke and cursing. They have come up from the railroad yards on the promise of money to be made; they have been fed a ration of stew in army mess kits, outfitted in denims and shoes, and taken by truckloads from Los Angeles to the hills to fight this brush fire. We do not learn the protagonist's name until well into the story when the CCC man calls out the roll; we never learn the name of his girlfriend. The one introspective moment in the story expresses the protagonist's regret at leaving her:

> They parted—she to slip into the crowd unobtrusively; he to get his mess kit, for the supper line was already formed. As he watched the blue dress flit between the tents and disappear, a gulp came into his throat; it seemed to him that this girl he had held in his arms, whose name he hadn't even thought to inquire, was almost the sweetest human being he had ever met in his life.

By the end of the story he has committed murder for the sake of this nameless girl, and the man he kills in the evening is the same man whose life he had saved in the morning. The reporters who have covered both events are struck with the inherent ironies, but the protagonist, who moves unthinkingly from blind impulse, is unaware of ironies; such abstractions are foreign to him.

Cain keeps the story moving by not stopping to examine motivations; he simply carries the reader along in the rushing momentum of the story. The third shift is summoned for roll call and told to turn over their shovels to the fourth shift that is arriving. They assemble with singed hair, smoke-seared lungs, and burned feet. At the same moment that we learn the protagonist's name, we learn the antagonist's also.

> As each name was called there was a loud "Yo" so when his name, Paul Larkin, was called, he yelled "Yo" too. Then the foreman was calling a name and becoming annoyed because there was no answer. "Ike Pendleton! Ike Pendleton!"

Instantly Larkin races up the slope toward the fire where "a cloud of smoke doubled him back." He retreats, sucks in a lungful of air, then charges to where a body lay face down. The action is tersely rendered in taut, lean prose. "He tried to lift, but his lungful of air was spent: he had to breathe or die. He expelled it, inhaled, screamed at the pain of the smoke in his throat."

Critics complain that Cain's characters are so elemental that they seem stripped down to an animal vitality; in fact, it is precisely to this quality that Pendleton's survival is attributed. "He fought to his feet, reeled around with the hard, terrible vitality of some kind of animal." The men are fed and paid fifty cents an hour, and then the visitors, newspaper reporters, and photographers arrive. When they ask if there were any casualties, someone remembers that a man, whose name no one can remember, has been rescued. Paul is interviewed and has his picture taken as a crowd gathers. A girl, kicking a pebble, says, "Well, ain't *that* something to be getting his picture in the paper?" They talk, he buys her an ice-cream cone, they go for a walk, they embrace, and he brings her back to the camp without ever having exchanged names.

Later he sees Ike Pendleton, with doubled fists, cursing her, and the girl, backing away, crying. The explanation of the conflict is given by an anonymous choric figure. Cain claims that this technique of communicating information through dialogue—a mode of narration which effaces the narrator—which Ernest Hemingway is usually credited as having in-

vented, was his invention; he says that he arrived at this method of minimal exposition independently, before he had ever read any Hemingway. Its effectiveness can be judged by the shock with which the reader realizes that the girl is Mrs. Pendleton.

The fight accelerates; Paul intervenes and tension mounts toward the inevitable conclusion. That Cain can convince the reader that such an improbable event could seem inevitable is a mark of his storytelling skill. The reader is not given time to think about it as these characters act out their basest, most primitive impulses.

> He lunged at Ike with his fist—missed. Ike struck with the knife. He fended with his left arm, felt the steel cut in. With his other hand he struck, and Ike staggered back. There was a pile of shovels beside him, almost tripping him up. He grabbed one, swung, smashed it down on Ike's head. Ike went down. He stood there, waiting for Ike to get up, with that terrible vitality he had shown this morning. Ike didn't move.

This, then, is the meaning of death, that the animal motions cease, and this is the end of the story whose meaning is embodied in its action without any philosophic implications, without any cultural pretensions, a brutal depiction of sexual and aggressive drives in men too crude to sublimate them and too hungry to repress them.

OTHER MAJOR WORKS

LONG FICTION: *The Postman Always Rings Twice*, 1934; *Double Indemnity*, 1936; *Serenade*, 1937; *The Embezzler*, 1940; *Mildred Pierce*, 1941; *Love's Lovely Counterfeit*, 1942; *Three of a Kind (Double Indemnity, Career in C Major, The Embezzler)*, 1943; *Past All Dishonor*, 1946; *The Butterfly*, 1947; *Sinful Woman*, 1947; *The Moth*, 1948; *Three of Hearts*, 1949 (includes *Love's Lovely Counterfeit, Past All Dishonor*, and *The Butterfly*); *Jealous Woman*, 1950; *The Root of His Evil*, 1951 (as *Shameless*, 1979); *Galatea*, 1953; *Mignon*, 1963; *The Magician's Wife*, 1965; *Cain × 3*, 1969 (includes *The Postman Always Rings Twice, Double Indemnity*, and *Mildred Pierce*); *Rainbow's End*, 1975; *The Institute*, 1976; *Cloud Nine*, 1984; *The Enchanted Isle*, 1985.

PLAYS: *Crashing the Gates*, pr. 1926; *Trial by Jury*, pb. 1928 (dialogue); *Theological Interlude*, pb. 1928 (dialogue); *Will of the People*, pb. 1929 (dialogue); *Citizenship*, pb. 1929 (dialogue); *The Governor*, pb. 1930 (dialogue); *Don't Monkey with Uncle Sam*, pb. 1933 (dialogue).

SCREENPLAYS: *Algiers*, 1938; *Stand up and Fight*, 1939; *Gypsy Wildcat*, 1944.

NONFICTION: *Our Government*, 1930; *Sixty Years of Journalism*, 1985 (Roy Hoopes, editor).

BIBLIOGRAPHY

Cain, James M. "An Interview with James M. Cain." Interview by John Carr. *The Armchair Detective* 16, no. 1 (1973): 4-21. In this 1973 interview, Cain reveals interesting highlights of his career as a reporter and explains the influence of Vincent Sergeant Lawrence, a journalist and screenwriter, on his work. Cain's comments on his three major novels are particularly valuable. Contains an annotated list of people important in Cain's life and a bibliography of Cain's writings.

Forter, Gregory. "Double Cain." *Novel* 29 (Spring, 1996): 277-298. Argues that the primitive sense of smell is a powerful force in Cain's fiction; claims that for Cain smell overcomes resistance and enslaves one to the other.

Hoopes, Roy. *Cain*. New York; Holt, Rinehart and Winston, 1982. This comprehensive biography on Cain is divided into four chronological parts. Covers his years in Maryland and France, New York, Hollywood, and Hyattsville. Includes an afterword on Cain as newspaperman. Supplemented by extensive sources and notes, a list of Cain's publications, a filmography, and an index.

Madden, David. *James M. Cain*. New York: Twayne, 1970. An excellent introductory volume that accepts Cain's varied reputation as an excellent, a trashy, an important, and an always popular writer. Approaches every major aspect of his work on several levels, including his life in relation to his writing, analysis of his characters, and his technical expertise. Complemented by notes, a bibliography of primary and secondary sources, and an index.

Marling, William. *The American Roman Noir: Hammett, Cain, and Chandler*. Athens: University of Georgia Press, 1995. An intriguing exercise in literary criticism that links the hard-boiled writing of Dashiell Hammett, James M. Cain, and Raymond Chandler to contemporary economic and technological changes. Marling sees the authors as pioneers of an aesthetic for the postindustrial age.

Nyman, Jopi. *Hard-Boiled Fiction and Dark Romanticism*. New York: Peter Lang, 1998. Examines the fiction of Cain, Dashiell Hammett, Ernest Hemingway, and Horace McCoy.

Oates, Joyce Carol. "Man Under Sentence of Death: The Novels of James M. Cain." In *Tough Guy Writers of the Thirties*, edited by David Madden. Carbondale: Southern Illinois University Press, 1968. Approaches Cain's novels as significant for the light they throw on his relationship with the American audience of the 1930's and 1940's. A brief but broad-ranging essay.

Skenazy, Paul. *James M. Cain*. New York: Continuum, 1989. A comprehensive study of Cain's work. Skenazy is more critical of his subject's writing than is Madden but acknowledges Cain's importance and his continuing capacity to attract readers.

Wilson, Edmund. "The Boys in the Back Room." In *Classics and Commercials*. New York: Farrar, Straus & Giroux, 1950. A personal essay by an astute social and cultural commentator. This piece groups Cain with John Steinbeck, John O'Hara, and William Saroyan, and others in the 1930's and 1940's who were influenced by Ernest Hemingway. Considers Cain to be the best of these writers.

Ruth Rosenberg, updated by Shakuntala Jayaswal

ERSKINE CALDWELL

Born: White Oak, Georgia; December 17, 1903
Died: Paradise Valley, Arizona; April 11, 1987

PRINCIPAL SHORT FICTION

American Earth, 1931
Mama's Little Girl, 1932
Message for Genevieve, 1933
We Are the Living: Brief Stories, 1933
Kneel to the Rising Sun and Other Stories, 1935
Southways: Stories, 1938
Jackpot: The Short Stories of Erskine Caldwell, 1940
Georgia Boy, 1943
Stories by Erskine Caldwell: Twenty-four Representative Stories, 1944
Jackpot: Collected Short Stories, 1950
The Courting of Susie Brown, 1952
Complete Stories, 1953
Gulf Coast Stories, 1956
Certain Women, 1957
When You Think of Me, 1959
Men and Women: Twenty-two Stories, 1961
Stories of Life: North and South, 1983
The Black and White Stories of Erskine Caldwell, 1984

OTHER LITERARY FORMS

The corpus of Erskine Caldwell's work includes more than fifty-five volumes published in forty-three languages, with more than eighty million copies sold. Caldwell wrote approximately thirty novels, three books of social criticism and travel sketches, two autobiographies, two books for children, four "photo-text" coffee-table books, screenplays for Hollywood, and various pieces as a newspaper correspondent. His novel *Tobacco Road* (1932) was adapted to the stage by Jack Kirkland and ran for 3,182 performances.

ACHIEVEMENTS

Erskine Caldwell is finally regaining his place as one of the United States' important writers. In a remarkable literary career that covered more than six

decades, Caldwell gained fame in the early 1930's for his novels *Tobacco Road* and *God's Little Acre* (1933). He became one of the country's most controversial, banned, and censored authors, as well as one of the most financially successful. For some years it even became fashionable to denigrate his work, and he lapsed into relative obscurity for a time, but the 1980's witnessed a revival. Caldwell, who always preferred a quiet life, lived long enough to see the change in public opinion. He remains first and foremost a southern writer who belongs to the naturalistic tradition. He was instrumental in promoting a realistic portrayal of life in the United States, particularly the South. His style of writing has always been simple and direct. Caldwell often has been associated with Tennessee Williams and William Faulkner as one of the South's celebrated authors. In fact, Faulkner once praised the writer for his fiction. Caldwell's wide range of literary output is remarkable and encompasses short stories, novels and novellas, text-picture documentaries, and children's books. Throughout his life Caldwell received a number of awards ranging from the *Yale Review* award for fiction in 1933 to the Republic of Poland's Order of Cultural Merit in 1981. Two years later he was given the Republic of France's Commander of the Order of Arts and Letters and the following year was elevated to the select body of the American Academy of Arts and Letters.

BIOGRAPHY

The son of a well-known Presbyterian minister, Erskine Caldwell spent his boyhood in rural Georgia and South Carolina as his father moved from church to church. In 1920 he attended Erskine College for a year and a half; in 1923 he spent a year at the University of Virginia; and in 1924 he spent a summer at the University of Pennsylvania studying economics. After working for a brief time as a reporter for the Atlanta *Journal*, he left Georgia for Maine to devote his energies to full-time writing in 1926. Caldwell wrote nearly a hundred stories and novels before placing his first major publication with Maxwell Perkins and *Scribner's Magazine*. His novels in the 1930's, known primarily for their sexual suggestiveness and violence, firmly established him as a best-selling author. In 1937, in conjunction with the famous photographer Margaret Bourke-White, Caldwell published the remarkable *You Have Seen Their Faces*, a "phototext" depicting the plight of the southern poor that deserves to be ranked as one of the finest examples of

Erskine Caldwell (Library of Congress)

that genre. Caldwell was a war correspondent in Russia in 1942 and one of the few American journalists to cover the invasion of Russia. His later work is generally not as good as his early work (Faulkner once said that it "grew toward trash"), but the serious reader would do well to pay attention to *Call It Experience* (1951), his autobiography, and *Deep South: Memory and Observation* (1968), a nonfictional study of southern religion. In his later years, Caldwell turned more to nonfiction and autobiography. A lifelong smoker, he had two operations for lung cancer.

Caldwell finally succumbed to the disease in 1987 at the age of eighty-three.

ANALYSIS

Erskine Caldwell's reputation as a short-story writer rests mainly on the collections published in the 1930's: *American Earth*, *We Are the Living*, *Kneel to the Rising Sun and Other Stories*, and *Southways*. Most of these stories reflect a social protest against the racial and economic oppression in the South during the Great Depression. Along with writers such as John Steinbeck and James T. Farrell, Caldwell wrote of the struggles of the poor and is therefore a favorite of Marxist critics; he was also highly regarded in the Soviet Union. Although Caldwell's fiction deals with social injustice, he is not overtly didactic or doctrinaire. He may have written of the violence of racial prejudice, the hypocritical state of fundamentalist religion, or the economic agonies of sharecropping worn-out farmland, yet his first concern as a writer was always with the portrayal of individual characters rather than with lofty social issues. His ideology did not interfere with his art, and the result is a clean, stark narrative that often exhibits the ultrareal qualities of nightmare.

Good literature always bears the burden of altering the comfortable preconceptions of the world, and Caldwell's best fiction produces a disturbing effect on the reader. He is fond of placing his characters in complex situations, yet he has them react to these situations with the simple tropisms of instinct or the unthinking obedience to social custom. At the heart of one of his stories may be a profound moral point—such as a white dirt farmer's choice between defending his black friend or else permitting an unjust lynching—but Caldwell's characters face moral predicaments with the amoral reflexes of an automaton. There is rarely any evidence that Caldwell's characters grasp the seriousness of their situation. They do not experience epiphanies of self-redemption or rise to mythic patterns of suffering, but rather continue to submit, unaffected, to the agonies and absurdities of their world. For this reason, Caldwell's work was frequently banned in the 1930's as pornographic and for appearing to promote gratuitous violence.

"SATURDAY AFTERNOON"

"Saturday Afternoon," for example, is the story of an offhand killing, by a mob of whites, of a black man named Will Maxie for supposedly talking to a white girl. The fact that Will Maxie is innocent is never in question. Everyone admits that he is a "smart Negro," always properly deferential and a hard worker, but the whites hate him anyway because he makes too much money and has no vices. Will is chained to a sweet-gum tree and burned alive. Yet "Saturday Afternoon" is a compelling story, not because of its sensational violence, but rather because of the chilling indifference shown by the two central characters, Tom the town butcher and Jim his helper. The story opens in the back of the fly-ridden butcher shop as Tom is settling down for an afternoon nap on the butcher block, a slab of rump roast as a pillow. Jim bursts in and tells him that a lynching party is being formed, and they hurry out to join it. The two, however, are merely following the social instinct of herding animals rather than exercising any overt malice toward Will, and even the tone of the actual killing is casual, almost nonchalant: The local druggist sends his boy to sell sodas to the crowd, and Tom and Jim are as interested in swapping slugs of moonshine as they are in Will's death. Once the spectacle is over, they return to the butcher shop for the Saturday afternoon rush, business as usual. The violence may seem gratuitous, but Caldwell's carefully controlled tone undercuts its severity and reinforces the theme that mindless indifference to brutality can be more terrifying than purposeful evil. The moral impact of the story bypasses the consciousness of the characters but catches the reader between the eyes.

"KNEEL TO THE RISING SUN"

In "Kneel to the Rising Sun," the title story of Caldwell's 1935 collection, he shows that both racial oppression and economic oppression are closely linked. The central conflict in the story is between the white landowner Arch Gunnard and his two sharecroppers—Lonnie, a white, and Clem, a black. It is late afternoon and Lonnie has come to Arch's gas station to ask for extra food because he is being "short-rationed." The black tenant Clem has asked for extra rations and gotten them, but Lonnie cannot be so

bold. The unspoken rules of the caste system are strong, even between a white tenant and a white landowner. As Lonnie tries to make his request, Arch calmly takes out his jackknife and cuts the tail off Lonnie's dog. Lonnie leaves hungry and emasculated, his tailless dog following behind. In the second part of the story, Lonnie awakens in the night to find his old father gone from his bed. Clem helps him with the search, and they find his father trampled to death in Arch's hog pen where, in a fit of hunger, he went looking for food. As all three men view the torn body, Clem again shows the courage that Lonnie cannot by openly accusing Arch of starving his tenants. An argument ensues, and Arch leaves to drum up a lynching party. Lonnie is torn between loyalty to Clem as a friend and loyalty to his own race. He promises to lead the mob away from Clem's hiding place, but once Arch arrives, Lonnie leads him to Clem in stunned obedience. Clem dies in a hail of buckshot, and Lonnie returns home to his wife, who asks if he has brought extra food. "No," Lonnie quietly replies, "no, I ain't hungry."

The institutional enemy in Caldwell's fiction, as in much of his social criticism, is not so much racial bigotry as the economic system which fosters it, for bigotry is a by-product of an agrarian system which beats down the poor of both races. Like the plantation system it replaced, cotton sharecropping enriches the few at the expense of the many, and the violence of Clem's death in "Kneel to the Rising Sun" is no worse than the starvation leveled on Lonnie's family. Blacks are beaten into submission, and whites are evicted from the land. As one cotton-field boss says in *You Have Seen Their Faces*, "Folks here wouldn't give a dime a dozen for white tenants. They can get twice as much work out of blacks. But they need to be trained. Beat a dog and he'll obey you. They say it's the same with blacks." Caldwell treats the same issues, although in more melodramatic fashion, in the stories "Wild Flowers" and "A Knife to Cut the Cornbread With."

"THE GROWING SEASON"

Caldwell's prose style is plain and direct, and his method of narration depends entirely on concrete details and colloquial dialogue. It is not a method conducive to presenting symbolic import or psychological introspection, and Caldwell's critics often accuse him of creating flat characters. Yet Caldwell's carefully controlled manipulation of external descriptions can give rise to intense states of psychological unrest, as in one of his best stories, "The Growing Season." In the story, Jesse, a cotton farmer, has been working in the fields all morning trying to keep the wire grass away from his crop. He has made little headway because twelve acres of cotton is too much for one man to work. As he breaks at midday, his eyes burning bloodshot from the sun, Jesse hears "Fiddler" rattle his chain. Jesse cannot eat, and his attention repeatedly turns to the wire grass in his cotton and the rattling of Fiddler's chain. Unable to bear the heat and the weeds and the noise of the chain any longer, he herds Fiddler into a gully and brutally kills him with his shotgun and ax. The violence done, Jesse sharpens his hoe and returns to the fields, optimistic that he can save his crop. Caldwell never specifies what kind of creature "Fiddler" is, but after several close readings, it becomes clear that he is not a dog or a mule but a human being—perhaps a retarded child or a black.

Jesse's psychological state is externalized; he is what he sees and feels, and the surreal qualities of the outer world reflect his psychosis. He rubs his knuckles in his eye sockets as the sun blinds him, he cannot eat or sleep, and even Fiddler changes color. Caldwell's characters often experience a disruption of physical appetite and sensory perception as they engage in headlong pursuit of their bizarre idiosyncrasies. Furthermore, Fiddler's death produces a cathartic effect on Jesse. Caldwell implies that the choking circumstances that beat heavily on the poor require sure action to overcome them—even if that action is a violent one.

"CANDY-MAN BEECHUM"

Although Caldwell's plain prose style eschews most of the traditional literary devices, the rhetorical structure of his fiction utilizes the varied repetition of details and dialogue. In "Candy-Man Beechum," Caldwell incorporates the repetitions of colloquial black speech patterns to give the story the oral rhythms of a folk ballad in prose. The narrative line

of the story is simple and episodic: Candy-Man leaves the rural swamp where he works as a sawmill hand and heads for town on a Saturday night to see his gal. The language of "Candy-Man Beechum," however, is the language of the tall tale, and the opening of the story ascribes to Candy-Man the larger-than-life qualities of the folk hero: "It was ten miles out of the Ogeechee swamps, from the sawmill to the top of the ridge, but it was just one big step to Candy-Man." At each stop on his journey to town, someone asks the question, "Where you going, Candy-Man?" and he supplies various boastful answers. These questions and answers give structure to the story in much the same way that a verse and refrain give structure to a popular ballad, and, again like a popular ballad, they move toward a tragic end. As Candy-Man nears the white folks' town, the questions become more ominous until a white-boss policeman asks the final question, "What's your hurry, Candy-Man?" Candy-Man, however, will not compromise his vitality by acquiescing to his demands and is shot down in the street; even in death he maintains his own exuberant sense of identity. Caldwell uses similar kinds of repetition to heighten the erotic effect of other stories such as "August Afternoon" and "The Medicine Man."

Caldwell is often referred to as a local color writer of the "southern gothic" school, but the range of his work shows him to be one of the most diverse and voluminous (and neglected) writers of the twentieth century. If the subject matter of his short fiction seems somewhat limited, it is only because Caldwell insisted on writing about what he knew best by firsthand observation. He once said in an interview:

> I grew up in the Great Depression in Georgia. I know how poverty smells and feels. I was poor as to eating. Poor as to clothes. Poor as to housing. And nearly everybody else was too, and you can't know about poverty any better way. You don't like it and nobody else does but you can't help yourself. So you learn to live with it, and understand it and can appreciate how others feel about it.

It is this genuine "feel" of poverty and its accompanying themes of violence, bigotry, frustration, and absurd comedy that ensures a lengthy survival of Caldwell's best works.

OTHER MAJOR WORKS

LONG FICTION: *The Bastard*, 1929; *Poor Fool*, 1930; *Tobacco Road*, 1932; *God's Little Acre*, 1933; *Journeyman*, 1935; *Trouble in July*, 1940; *All Night Long: A Novel of Guerrilla Warfare in Russia*, 1942; *Tragic Ground*, 1944; *A House in the Uplands*, 1946; *The Sure Hand of God*, 1947; *This Very Earth*, 1948; *Place Called Estherville*, 1949; *Episode in Palmetto*, 1950; *A Lamp for Nightfall*, 1952; *Love and Money*, 1954; *Gretta*, 1955; *Claudelle Inglish*, 1958; *Jenny by Nature*; 1961; *Close to Home*, 1962; *The Last Night of Summer*, 1963; *Miss Mamma Aimee*, 1967; *Summertime Island*, 1968; *The Weather Shelter*, 1969; *The Earnshaw Neighborhood*, 1972; *Annette*, 1974.

NONFICTION: *Tenant Farmer*, 1935; *Some American People*, 1935; *You Have Seen Their Faces*, 1937 (with Margaret Bourke-White); *North of the Danube*, 1939 (with Margaret Bourke-White); *Say! Is This the U.S.A.?*, 1941 (with Margaret Bourke-White); *All-Out on the Road to Smolensk*, 1942 (with Margaret Bourke-White, also known as *Moscow Under Fire: A Wartime Diary*, 1941); *Russia at War*, 1942 (with Margaret Bourke-White); *The Humorous Side of Erskine Caldwell*, 1951; *Call It Experience: The Years of Learning How to Write*, 1951; *Around About America*, 1964; *In Search of Bisco*, 1965; *In the Shadow of the Steeple*, 1967; *Deep South: Memory and Observation*, 1968; *Writing in America*, 1968; *Afternoons in Mid-America*, 1976; *With All My Might*, 1987; *Conversations with Erskine Caldwell*, 1988.

CHILDREN'S LITERATURE: *Molly Cottontail*, 1958; *The Deer at Our House*, 1966.

MISCELLANEOUS: *The Caldwell Caravan: Novels and Stories*, 1946.

BIBLIOGRAPHY

Arnold, Edwin T., ed. *Conversations with Erskine Caldwell*. Jackson: University Press of Mississippi, 1988. This volume contains more than thirty articles and interviews with Caldwell on a wide range of subjects. Provides a good insight into the writer and the individual. Includes a useful intro-

duction, a chronology, and final thoughts.

Caldwell, Erskine. *With All My Might: An Autobiography*. Atlanta: Peachtree, 1987. Caldwell's second autobiography is his final work and was published a month before his death. A chatty and informative style suffuses the book and affords an interesting glimpse of Caldwell's remarkable career.

Devlin, James E. *Erskine Caldwell*. Boston: Twayne, 1984. Provides a good but limited introduction to Caldwell's literary career. Contains an interesting overview on the writer's career, five chapters covering individual works, and a final assessment. Supplemented by a chronology, notes and references, and a select bibliography.

Klevar, Harvey L. *Erskine Caldwell*. Knoxville: University of Tennessee Press, 1993. A detailed discussion of Caldwell's life, focusing on the South and Caldwell's relationship to it as reflected in his work.

Korges, James. *Erskine Caldwell*. Minneapolis: University of Minnesota Press, 1969. This short study of Caldwell examines his early work and asserts that he has a great comic vision and that he is one of the United States' most important writers. Augmented by a select bibliography.

McDonald, Robert L., ed. *The Critical Response to Erskine Caldwell*. Westport, Conn.: Greenwood Press, 1997. Includes reviews of Caldwell's major works, scholarly discussions of his themes and techniques, and academic analyses of the image of the South presented in his fiction.

MacDonald, Scott, ed. *Critical Essays on Erskine Caldwell*. Boston: G. K. Hall, 1981. An excellent collection of critical essays on Caldwell that spans almost fifty years of the writer's life. Arranged chronologically, the anthology constitutes a good introduction to Caldwell with seventy-five articles and more than thirty essays, including eight by the writer himself.

Miller, Dan B. *Erskine Caldwell*. New York: Alfred A. Knopf, 1995. A biography of Caldwell, focusing on his first forty years; details Caldwell's life and his growing up in the context of southern culture.

Silver, Andrew. "Laughing over Lost Causes: Erskine Caldwell's Quarrel with Southern Humor." *The Mississippi Quarterly* 50 (Winter, 1996/1997): 51-68. Discusses some of the characteristics of nineteenth century American frontier humor inherited by Caldwell, such as the narrator as cultured observer of frontier rustics; argues that Caldwell subverts southern humor and critiques Depression-era capitalism.

Roger J. McNutt, updated by Terry Theodore

HORTENSE CALISHER

Born: New York, New York; December 20, 1911

PRINCIPAL SHORT FICTION

In the Absence of Angels: Stories, 1951

Tale for the Mirror: A Novella and Other Stories, 1962

Extreme Magic: A Novella and Other Stories, 1964

"The Railway Police" and "The Last Trolley Ride," 1966

The Collected Stories of Hortense Calisher, 1975

Saratoga, Hot, 1985

The Novellas of Hortense Calisher, 1997

OTHER LITERARY FORMS

Although Hortense Calisher first became known as a short-story writer, she published several novels and novellas, including *False Entry* (1961) and *In the Slammer with Carol Smith* (1997), an autobiography, and articles and reviews for *The New Yorker*, *Harper's Magazine*, *Harper's Bazaar*, *Mademoiselle*, *The New York Times*, *The American Scholar*, *The New Criterion*, *Ladies' Home Journal*, *The Saturday Evening Post*, *The Kenyon Review*, and *The Nation*, among others.

ACHIEVEMENTS

Twice a John Simon Guggenheim Memorial Foundation Fellow and once a Hurst Fellow, Hortense Calisher also received an American Specialist's Grant from the U.S. Department of State, a National Council of the Arts Award, an Academy of Arts and Letters Award, four O. Henry Awards, and National Book Award nominations in 1962 for *False Entry* (1961), in 1973 for *Herself* (1972), and in 1976 for *The Collected Stories of Hortense Calisher*. She was president of the PEN Club and of the American Academy of Arts and Letters, and she won a Lifetime Achievement Award from the National Endowment for the Arts in 1989. The artistry of her prose has earned her standing as a "writer's writer," especially in the carefully structured novellas and short stories.

BIOGRAPHY

After graduating from Barnard College in 1932 with a B.A. in English, Hortense Calisher worked at a variety of jobs in New York, including sales clerk, model, and social worker for the Department of Public Welfare. In 1935, she married Heaton Bennet Heffelfinger, an engineer, and had two children. Her first marriage ended in divorce in 1958, and in 1959 Calisher married Curtis Harnack, a writer. Calisher's family history as a New York City native born of middle-class Jewish parents, a southern father and a German mother, provides the material for many of her stories; other stories are informed by her later life experiences as a suburban housewife. She taught creative writing and literature courses at a number of colleges and universities, including Barnard College, Iowa State University, Sarah Lawrence College, Brandeis University, the University of Pennsylvania, Columbia University, the State University of New York at Purchase, and the University of California at Irvine. She lectured in West Germany, Yugoslavia, Romania, and Hungary.

ANALYSIS

Hortense Calisher described the short story as "an apocalypse, served in a very small cup," thus indicating her Jamesian penchant for intense psychological portrayals presented within the aesthetic confines of brevity of style and economy of emotional impact. After "A Box of Ginger," her first published story, appeared in *The New Yorker* in 1948, critics praised Calisher's writings for their complexity of theme, verbal intricacy, and strength and multiplicity of evocation. She has been compared with Henry James and Gustave Flaubert in her passion for precision and craftsmanship and with Marcel Proust in her motifs of the many-sided psychological levels of human experience.

Calisher has been described as a spokesperson for the "middle ground" of the ordinary, rather than the extreme, the unusual, or the bizarre. Her most convincing characters are, by and large, observers of the mysteries of human existence, seeking viable modes of action and belief in their own individual progressions toward the development of self-identity. The existential themes of choice and commitment and the search for meaning through self-definition are pervasive in her writings, as is the influence of phenomenology. Her short stories, in fact, can be seen as exemplifications in art of Edmund Husserl's definition of the phenomenological *epoché* (suspension of judgment) as the capacity of a single moment of experience to unfold itself into endless perspectives of reality.

The themes of Calisher's stories focus upon bonding, the need for individual lives to merge in moments of appreciation, empathy, or love to assuage the emptiness, alienation, and apparent meaninglessness of much of human existence. The progression in her writings is generally outward, toward a merging or a reconciliation based upon understanding and new insight. Her stories also assert the power of illusions over everyday life and the reluctance with which fantasy is surrendered for the stark obduracy of reality. Primarily depictions of the complexity of human experience, Calisher's stories are presented via a poetic concern with language and imagery for communicating the subtleties of characters' insights

Hortense Calisher in 1967 (Library of Congress)

into their experience. She has been praised for the insights into the psychology of women in her works and for her own contributions to women's literature.

"IN GREENWICH THERE ARE MANY GRAVELLED WALKS"

"In Greenwich There Are Many Gravelled Walks," a story many critics consider a modern classic, is an example of Calisher's themes of bonding and insight, both often attained against a background of psychological suffering and a sense of the amorphous character of life in the modern world. On an afternoon in early August, Peter Birge returns to the small apartment he shares with his mother after taking her to the Greenwich sanatorium she had to frequent at intervals to discover that "his usually competent solitude had become more than he could bear." He is a victim of defeated plans; the money he had saved from his Army stint for a trip abroad will now have to be spent on his mother's psychiatric treatment. His mood is one of disheartenment and isolation. Recalling taking his mother to the sanatorium on this bright, clear summer day, he senses the irony of his own plight—anyone "might have thought the two of them were a couple, any couple, just off for a day in the country." He is aware that much insanity in the modern world passes for sanity and that beneath the seeming calm of most lives lie secrets and potential complexities known only to the participants themselves.

Peter's estrangement from his mother is complete; Greenwich has claimed her through the sanatorium as it had through the Village. In the Village, she had become a fixture, a "hanger-on" in the bars in the presence and superficial camaraderie of would-be painters, philosophers, and poets, until alcoholism and a steady routine of safe and predictable fantasy—"a buttery flow of harmless little lies and pretensions"—became all that she had subsisted on for more than twenty years. Arriving at the sanatorium was like playing out one more fantasy scene from the bars, a safe world of protection and illusion. For the son, however, no illusions are left to comfort him. "It was just that while others of his age still shared a communal wonder at what life might hold, he had long since been solitary in his knowledge of what life was."

Finding being alone unbearable, Peter is prompted by his loneliness to visit his friend, Robert Vielum, for the same reason that many others stopped by, "because there was likely to be somebody there." Robert is "a perennial taker of courses" who derives a "Ponce de Leon sustenance from the young." Buttressed by family fortunes, he has ambled his way through academics, gathering up a troupe of enchanted devotees fascinated by his adirectional philosophy of hedonism and apathy. Watching him closely, Peter discovers that Robert is very much like his mother; they are "charmers, who if they could not offer you the large strength, could still atone for the lack with so many small decencies." People are drawn to Robert as they are to Peter's mother, for the exhilarating excitement of "wearing one's newest façade, in the fit company of others similarly attired."

Peter discovers that he has arrived in the midst of a homosexual love triangle; Robert has abandoned his plans to go to Morocco with Vince in order to go to Italy with Mario Osti, a painter. Robert is charmingly aloof, totally insensitive and unresponsive to Vince's emotional sufferings over being abandoned and rejected. A fight ensues, and Vince retreats to the bedroom as Robert's daughter, Susan, arrives to spend the summer in her father's apartment. When Mario looks out the window into the courtyard and discovers that Vince has committed suicide, Robert's carefully poised game of façades and practiced indifference is shattered by the reality of human despair.

Mario's self-protecting "I'd better get out of here!" is in direct contrast to Peter's compassion and empathy for Susan, whom he feels to be a fellow survivor of the carelessness and emptiness of the chaos of other people's lives. "I don't care about any of it, really," Susan tells him, "my parents, or any of the people they tangle with." Peter finds this a feeling with which he can empathize, and he agrees even more fully with her statement: "I should think it would be the best privilege there is, though. To care, I mean." The bond of mutual understanding of what has been lost and what is missing and needed is established between Peter and Susan as he realizes that they are alike in their same disillusionment with the world. The story ends on a note of muted optimism as Peter tells himself that "tomorrow he would take her for a drive—whatever the weather. There were a lot of good roads around Greenwich." If one envisions Greenwich in the story, both the sanatorium and the Village, as symbols of the sterility and insanity of most modern existence, then the journey "around Greenwich" may well be an affirmation that the two young people can avoid the dissipation of their parents' lives through the bond of caring the couple has established.

"IF YOU DON'T WANT TO LIVE I CAN'T HELP YOU"

"In Greenwich There Are Many Gravelled Walks" is roundly critical of the self-destructive waste of emotional abilities most people's lives become, a viewpoint even more heavily endorsed in one of Calisher's more moralistic stories, "If You Don't Want to Live I Can't Help You." On the day that Professor Mary Ponthus, a teacher at a New England college and a scholar of some repute, is to receive an honorary doctorate of letters, she pays a visit to her nephew, Paul. Paul has lived off the trust fund that Mary has administered for twenty years, and his life has become cankered with dissipation. "Foredoomed to the dilettante," he has dabbled in painting, writing, and love affairs because "these were good ways to pass the time—and of time he had so much to pass."

Now, too, as Mary reflects, he is dabbling in disease. Suffering from tuberculosis, her death- and failure-obsessed nephew refuses to take care of himself. When Mary arrives, she finds him hung over and ill from a night of wild partying. Further, she discovers that Paul's lover of several years, Helen Bonner, has left him because of his manipulative and dissolute state. Mary wants to call the doctor, but Paul tells her that his doctor has given up on him because Paul refuses to enter a sanatorium and to care for himself properly. Paul pleads, instead, for Mary to call Helen and draw her back to him. "I can't manage," Paul says, seeing his own plight. "The best I can do is to cling to someone who can." Paul collapses, and Mary calls the doctor, who arrives to take Paul to the hospital. Paul tells the doctor, "I'm just like everyone else. I don't want to die." To which the doctor responds, "Maybe not. But if you don't want to live I can't help you." The thematic crux of the story is thus established. When it comes to life itself, the doctor tells Mary, there are "the ones who are willing, and the ones who will have to be dragged."

Attending the graduation ceremonies at which she will receive her honorary doctorate, Mary contemplates the doctor's words with a deep sense of despair. Surrounded by young college students with eager, bright views of their future, she feels her own age weighing upon her and feels suddenly out of place, useless, and defeated. At the reception later, she notices that her usual enthusiasm for the quick and keen intelligence of the young has waned. A phone call to Helen to ask her to return to Paul has failed, and Mary considers giving up her own plans to devote the rest of her life to Paul. "People like Paul can be looked after quite easily out of duty," she reflects, "the agony comes only when they are looked after with hope."

A young graduate student comes up to converse with Mary, and she feels a deep sense of his brilliance of mind and high ethical character. He stands in such marked contrast to Paul, who wasted all of his abilities, that Mary is drawn to the student and to unlocking his potential. "I can't help it," Mary reflects. "I'm of the breed that hopes. Maybe this one wants to live." Her resurgence of faith and her renewed energies for survival and purpose reveal to her that this is the crux of the human situation. "We are all in the dark together, but those are the ones who humanize the dark." The ending is existential in upholding the "dark" puzzle of existence but compassionate in asserting that those who will to live with strength and dignity humanize the darkness for us all.

"THE MIDDLE DRAWER"

The necessity for strengths of the heart is reiterated in "The Middle Drawer," a story of mother-daughter conflicts and their partial resolution through compassion. Published in a periodical in 1948, this is Calisher's first autobiographical story. After her mother's death from cancer, Hester is about to begin the process of going through her mother's most personal effects, locked in the middle drawer of her dresser. The gravity of exposing her mother's life to inspection for the final time causes Hester to reflect upon the course of their relationship and how flawed by failed communication their lives together had been.

Hester had come to know the drawer's contents gradually, through the course of a lifetime. She had begun peering over the drawer's edge as a baby, had played with the opera glasses and string of pearls she had found inside as a child, and had received from the drawer for her wedding the delicate diamond chain that had been her father's wedding gift to her mother. It is a small brown-toned photograph in the back of the drawer, however, that most held Hester's attention as she was growing up. The photograph was of her mother, Hedwig, as a child of two, bedecked in the garments of respectable poverty as she grew up in the small town of Oberelsbach, Germany, motherless since birth and stepmothered by a woman who had been "unloving, if not unkind." Hester senses that her mother was one of a legion of lonely children "who inhabited the familiar terror-struck dark that crouched under the lash of the adult."

Life "under the lash of the adult" had created in Hedwig an emotional reserve that precluded any open demonstration of love to Hester. Over the years, "the barrier of her mother's dissatisfaction with her had risen imperceptibly" until the two women stood as strangers, with bitter hurts and buried sorrows the only communion they had known. Hester's misery is that "she was forever impelled to earn her mother's approval at the expense of her own." Always, Hester had known, there had been buried the wish to find "the final barb, the homing shaft, that would maim her mother once and for all, as she felt herself to have been maimed."

The opportunity for the barb is given to Hester when she is called home to visit her mother after her mother's sudden operation for breast cancer. Hester discovers that her mother is suffering from a deep fear of the revulsion of others and a horror at what has been done to her. She has taken to sleeping alone at night and to eating from separate utensils from her family. It is clear to Hester that her father and her brother have not been successful in concealing their revulsion from Hedwig, thus contributing further to her isolation and anxiety.

One evening, when they are together in her mother's bedroom, Hedwig begins to discuss her operation with Hester and asks her if she would like to see the incision, which no one has seen since she left the hospital. Hester tells her mother that she would very much like to see it and recalls intensely the times that she had stood as a child before her mother, "vulnerable and bare, helplessly awaiting the cruel exactitude of her displeasure." Her mother reveals the mastectomy scar to Hester, and Hester, with infinite delicacy, draws her fingertips along the length of the scar "in a light, affirmative caress, and they stood eye to eye for an immeasurable second, on equal ground at last." Hester's discovery about her mother and herself in that moment of tender union is a freeing answer: "She was always vulnerable, Hester thought. As we all are. What she bequeathed me unwittingly, ironically, was fortitude—the fortitude of those who have had to live under the blow. But pity—that I

found for myself." The opportunity for the barb of hurt and rejection has been replaced by the empathy of understanding.

The story's ending blends poignancy with realism and psychological insight, for Hester knows that, however tender the moment of communion "on equal ground," her struggle to win her mother's approval would have continued and that the scars from their troubled relationship remain in Hester's psyche. Her own life is in the middle drawer she is about to open. She has been made who she is by her mother's influence and by the fact that her own grandmother died too soon to leave the imprint of love upon Hedwig. Like her mother, Hester has been scarred by an absence of love that worked its way through two generations and is, even now, affecting Hester's relationship with her own daughter. She realizes that the living carry "not one tangible wound but the burden of innumerable small cicatrices imposed upon us by our beginnings; we carry them with us always, and from these, from this agony, we are not absolved." With this recognition, Hester opens the middle drawer to face and absorb whatever truth her life and her mother's life might contain.

Like many of Calisher's short stories, "The Middle Drawer" builds to a phenomenological *epochē* which reveals numerous multifacted insights into the characters of the stories, the psychology of human motivations, and the metaphysics of human actions, especially actions springing from an ethical or a compassionate base. Calisher is not a facile optimist; she believes in strongly and portrays quite graphically the pain pervading most human lives. She does assert, however, an unwavering faith in the strength of the human will and in the necessity for commitment to ethical principles. Like Mary Ponthus in "If You Don't Want to Live I Can't Help You," Calisher affirms that we must "humanize the dark."

THE NOVELLAS OF HORTENSE CALISHER
Published in 1997, this collection contains seven stories, of which only one had been unpublished previously. In the book's introduction, Calisher defines a novella as being "not merely a shorter novel, of less wordage than commonly. It is a small one, tenaciously complete."

In order of publication, *Tale for the Mirror* (1962) is a gently ironic study of ethnic and cultural misunderstanding set in an old-money ingrown New York suburban community. The Hudson River setting is disturbed by the arrival of an eccentric Indian neurologist, Dr. Bhatta, who takes possession of a lavish estate and is viewed with suspicion by his neighbors. He is surrounded by an entourage of subservient females, client disciples, and an apparent madwoman living in his summer house. Whether Dr. Bhatta is a phony or merely a man who arranges the facts of his life into a story he can tell himself remains unresolved, for, in the last analysis, he too may be as much a victim seeking truth in the night as a criminal.

Extreme Magic (1964) revolves around Guy Callendar, who has lost his family in a house fire and tries to rebuild his life as a small-town antique dealer. He finally finds understanding with a battered wife whom he rescues from her alcoholic, suicidal, innkeeper husband through a miraculous intervention. *The Railway Police* (1966) is the story of an heiress and social worker to whom men are attracted by the colorful wigs she wears, only to be repelled by the discovery of her hereditary baldness. Seeing a vagrant being tossed off a train, she jettisons her fake hair and thus her life of pretense, gives all her money to needy clients, and goes off to live in the streets as an anonymous discard, a vagabond, obliterating all evidence of her place in the world.

Saratoga, Hot (1985) is about the fortunes and obsessions of a married couple in the upstate New York horse-racing resort of Saratoga Springs. The wife, a painter now healed from a crippling accident caused by the man who later married her, and her spouse encounter all types of characters, some sinister and some not, but all devoted to horses—gamblers, jockeys, aficionados, and mafiosi—who go with the territory. *The Man Who Spat Silver* (1986) is about a woman translator who escapes her daily solitude by taking long walks in the streets of New York City where she becomes obsessed with a salesman who intially attracts her attention by spitting on the sidewalk.

In all these stories, Calisher unfolds sagas of coming of age, infidelities, spousal abuse, mental illness,

alcoholism, money troubles, and especially loneliness. Still, they frequently celebrate mere existence through dedicated living and the inability of people to live in the present. Despite the frequent density of her prose, occasionally baffling plots, and too-intricate analyses of personality and motivation, a number of stories achieve Calisher's stated purpose of creating "an apocalypse in a very small cup."

OTHER MAJOR WORKS

LONG FICTION: *False Entry*, 1961; *Textures of Life*, 1963; *Journal from Ellipsia*, 1965; *The New Yorkers*, 1969; *Queenie*, 1971; *Standard Dreaming*, 1972; *Eagle Eye*, 1973; *On Keeping Women*, 1977; *Mysteries of Motion*, 1983; *The Bobby-Soxer*, 1986; *Age*, 1987; *The Small Bang*, 1992; *In the Palace of the Movie King*, 1993; *In the Slammer with Carol Smith*, 1997.

NONFICTION: *Herself*, 1972; *Kissing Cousins: A Memory*, 1988.

BIBLIOGRAPHY

Aarons, Victoria. "The Outsider Within: Women in Contemporary Jewish American Fiction." *Contemporary Literature* 28, no. 3 (1987): 378-393. This essay examines the ways in which women characters portrayed in fiction by Jewish American women reflect the position of women in a male-dominated tradition.

Calisher, Hortense. "The Art of Fiction: Hortense Calisher." Interview by Allen Gurganus, Pamela McCordick, and Mona Simpson. *The Paris Review* 29 (Winter, 1987): 157-187. This insightful interview with Calisher explores her various approaches to creative writing.

_____. Introduction to *The Novellas of Hortense Calisher*. New York: The Modern Library, 1997. The author explains how a novella differs from a novel.

Hahn, Emily. "In Appreciation of Hortense Calisher." *Wisconsin Studies in Contemporary Literature* 6 (Summer, 1965): 243-249. A close reading of the early fiction, identifying themes such as the friction between generations, which Calisher explores so sensitively in her stories.

"*Saturday Review* Talks to Hortense Calisher." *Saturday Review* 11 (July/August, 1985): 77. In this biographical sketch, based on an interview, Calisher says she considers the Bible a major influence on her style and the New York environment a major force in her artistic development.

Shinn, Thelma J. *Radiant Daughters: Fictional American Women*. Westport, Conn.: Greenwood Press, 1986. Includes an examination of the female characters in Calisher's fiction from the short stories collected since 1951 through *Mysteries of Motion* in 1983. Particularly relates her fiction to

contemporary American writers of the 1950's.

Snodgrass, Kathleen. *The Fiction of Hortense Calisher*. Newark: University of Delaware Press, 1993. Discusses the central dual theme of rites of passage and extradition in Calisher's fiction. Argues that her style is not something imposed on the subject matter, but the perfect embodiment of this dual theme. The first chapter discusses twelve autobiographical stories, mostly focused on the narrator and protagonist Hester Elkin.

Christina Murphy, updated by Thelma J. Shinn and Peter B. Heller

---

MORLEY CALLAGHAN

Born: Toronto, Canada; February 22, 1903
Died: Toronto, Canada; August 25, 1990

PRINCIPAL SHORT FICTION

A Native Argosy, 1929
No Man's Meat, 1931
Now That April's Here and Other Stories, 1936
Morley Callaghan's Stories, 1959
No Man's Meat, and The Enchanted Pimp, 1978
The Lost and Found Stories of Morley Callaghan, 1985

OTHER LITERARY FORMS

Although Morley Callaghan was a masterful short-story writer, he also won recognition for his many novels, the most highly regarded being *Such Is My Beloved* (1934), *More Joy in Heaven* (1937), *The Loved and the Lost* (1951), and *Close to the Sun Again* (1977). He is also the author of a novella (*No Man's Meat*), a children's book (*Luke Baldwin's Vow*, 1948), and three plays (*To Tell the Truth*, pr. 1949; *Turn Home Again*, pr. 1940; and *Season of the Witch*, pb. 1976). He recorded some of his stories for children, and others, such as *Luke Baldwin's Vow*, have been filmed. Starting his career as a journalist, Callaghan contributed articles and essays to newspapers and journals throughout his life. His nonfiction

works include the text for a book of John de Visser's photographs, entitled *Winter* (1974), and *That Summer in Paris: Memories of Tangled Friendships with Hemingway, Fitzgerald, and Some Others* (1963), an entertaining account of the heady days in Paris in 1929, when he socialized with Ernest Hemingway, F. Scott Fitzgerald, James Joyce, and other writers. Throughout his life, Callaghan continued to make significant contributions to Canadian cultural life as a book reviewer and essayist as well as a novelist.

ACHIEVEMENTS

In the 1920's, Morley Callaghan's stories impressed Hemingway, who introduced them to Ezra Pound. Pound subsequently printed them in his magazine, *The Exile*. The stories also impressed Fitzgerald, who presented them to Maxwell Perkins, his editor at Scribner's. Perkins later published Callaghan's stories as well as some of his novels. Although considered a highly promising writer in the 1920's and 1930's, Callaghan neither developed a large audience nor achieved the type of reputation that his works warrant. Edmund Wilson has commented that he is "perhaps the most unjustly neglected novelist in the English-speaking world." Even so, Callaghan was the recipient of several awards: Canada's Governor General's Literary Award (1951), the Gold Medal of the

Royal Society of Canada (1958), the Lorne Pierce Medal (1960), the Canada Council Molson Prize (1970), the Royal Bank of Canada Award (1970), and the Companion of the Order of Canada (1982). He was also nominated for a Nobel Prize. His fiction is praised for its direct, unornamented prose, though later criticism has suggested that his writing is wooden, with technical weaknesses. His fiction is also valued for its sympathetic portrayal of ordinary people and for its honest treatment of the problems of contemporary life. Callaghan's lifelong exploration of the conflict between spirituality and human weakness and alienation has illuminated the best of his writing.

Callaghan held a D.Litt. from the University of Western Ontario (1965), an LL.D. from the University of Toronto (1966), and a D.Litt. from the University of Windsor (1973). In 1989, the city of Toronto awarded him a Lifetime Achievement Award.

BIOGRAPHY

Born in Toronto, Canada, on September 22, 1903, Edward Morley Callaghan was reared by Roman Catholic parents of Irish descent. He grew up interested in sports, especially boxing and baseball, but at a young age he also displayed a talent for writing, selling at age seventeen his first article, a description of Yonge and Alberta streets in Toronto, to the *Star Weekly* for twelve dollars. In 1921, he entered St. Michael's College of the University of Toronto, and during the summers and part-time during the school year, he was a reporter for the Toronto *Daily Star*, the same newspaper that employed Ernest Hemingway, who encouraged him in his attempts at fiction writing. Morley received his B.A. in 1925, and enrolled in Osgoode Hall Law School in Toronto. He continued to write short stories, mailing them to Hemingway, who was then in Paris. Some of these stories, through Hemingway's assistance, appeared in various magazines, such as *This Quarter*, *Transition*, and *The Exile*. In 1928, the year that Callaghan finished law school and was admitted to the Ontario bar, Maxwell Perkins, of Scribner's, published several of his stories in *Scribner's Magazine* and agreed to print his first novel, *Strange Fugitive* (1928), as well as a collection

Morley Callaghan (John Martin)

of short stories, *A Native Argosy*. Forsaking law, Callaghan decided to be a writer. After marrying Loretto Florence Dee in 1929, he traveled to Paris, where he met with Hemingway and became acquainted with Fitzgerald and Joyce. He later recorded this volatile period in *That Summer in Paris*.

Leaving Paris in the autumn, Callaghan returned to Toronto, which became his home except for occasional stays in Pennsylvania and New York, where he socialized with Sherwood Anderson, Thomas Wolfe, James T. Farrell, Sinclair Lewis, and other writers. During this early period, from 1928 to 1937, he published a novel or a collection of short stories almost yearly. From 1937 to 1948, he neglected his fiction and devoted his time to radio programming and writing essays. It has been suggested that the events of that time—the rise of Nazism, the Spanish Civil War, the purges of Stalin, and World War II—contributed to his lack of interest in fiction. In 1948, he resumed writing novels and short stories, which appeared regularly in leading magazines. In his later years he devoted his energy to novels and nonfiction works. He also gained public recognition and respect in Canada as a radio broadcast personality and commentator on Canadian cultural life. Callaghan died on August 25, 1990, in Toronto.

ANALYSIS

Over his long career, Morley Callaghan published more than one hundred short stories, in such magazines as *The New Yorker, Scribner's Magazine*, and numerous other magazines. Many of these have been collected in his four volumes of short stories.

While there are variations and exceptions, Callaghan's stories generally have recognizable characteristics. Foremost of these is the style: Most noticeably in the early works, Callaghan employs short declarative sentences, colloquial dialogue, and plain, unadorned language. As he remarked in *That Summer in Paris*, he attempts to "tell the truth cleanly." This sparse, economical, straightforward style has been compared with Hemingway's. Perhaps Callaghan was influenced by Hemingway (he admired and respected the older author), but it is likely that Callaghan's work on a newspaper shaped his writing, just as Hemingway's style was honed by his years of reporting.

Like a journalist, Callaghan presented the events in his stories objectively, neither condemning nor praising his character. By precisely recording his observations, Callaghan allows his readers to form their own judgments. He strives "to strip the language, and make the style, the method, all the psychological ramifications, the ambience of the relationships, all the one thing, so the reader couldn't make separations. Cézanne's apples. The appleness of the apples. Yet just apples." In other words, he endeavored to capture the essence of the moment.

Although Callaghan's stories are often set in Canada, he should not be classified as a regional writer. His appeal ranges beyond the borders of his country. The themes he treats are universal and are not limited to Canadian issues; in fact, he has been criticized for not addressing Canadian problems more forcefully.

Many of his stories examine human relationships, and they therefore revolve around psychological issues rather than physical actions. They depict the ordinary person and his or her desire for happiness. This desire is often frustrated by environmental forces such as unemployment and injustice and by internal drives such as fear and sex. In the early stories, the characters, inarticulate and of less than normal intelligence, are on the edge of society: the poor, the disabled, the criminal, and the insane. The characters in Callaghan's later stories are more likely to be educated, but they still struggle in their quest for a better life. All Callaghan's characters reflect his concerns as a Roman Catholic, and a certain pessimism underlies their portrayals. Rarely in Callaghan's characters are innate spirituality and nobility of character allowed to triumph over the more ignoble of human instincts and behavior.

In 1928, Scribner's published Callaghan's first novel, *Strange Fugitive*, and followed this a year later with *A Native Argosy*, a collection of short fiction containing fourteen stories and two novellas. These stories are some of the most naturalistic produced by Callaghan, and the characters, themes, and style resemble that found in work by other naturalistic writers, such as Stephen Crane, Theodore Dreiser, and Frank Norris. Influenced by Charles Darwin, Karl Marx, and Sigmund Freud, these authors applied the principles of scientific determinism to their fiction. Humans are viewed as animals trapped in a constant struggle to survive. They are limited by forces that are beyond their control and even beyond their understanding. Callaghan, like the other naturalistic writers, presents the material in an objective and documentary manner, eschewing moral judgments and optimistic endings.

"A COUNTRY PASSION"

The first story in the collection, "A Country Passion," originally printed in *Transition*, portrays an inarticulate character who is ultimately destroyed by a combination of his instincts and society's strictures. Jim Cline loves Ettie Corley, a retarded girl twenty-nine years his junior, who will soon be sent to an asylum. He wants to marry the sixteen-year-old girl, but the minister forbids it because Jim has been in jail, as the reader learns later, for stealing chickens and for fighting. Although unable to marry, Jim nevertheless "had come to an agreement with her any way," and now he faces a charge of seduction which carries a life sentence. Jim's interest in Ettie is more than sexual. Out of concern for her, Jim has bought coal and food for Ettie's family in the winter and clothes for her. She needs him; as the minister comments, "she's had the worst home in town and something should have been done about it long ago." Nevertheless, the culture will not accept their union. After being arrested, Jim escapes from jail, harboring the vague notion that "if he could get out he could explain his idea to everybody and get people behind him" and his problem would be solved. Unable to concentrate, he cannot formulate his idea. He is caught and will presumably spend the rest of his life in jail, while Ettie will spend hers in an institution. Though Jim and Ettie struggle to attain happiness, they cannot overcome the forces that oppose them. The depressing outcome is relieved partly by their achieving, even for a brief moment, a sharing of their affection.

"AMUCK IN THE BUSH"

The naturalistic tone is found throughout the collection. In "Amuck in the Bush," Gus Rapp is portrayed as an animal, controlled by his instincts. Fired from his lumberyard job, he seeks revenge by attacking the boss's wife and five-year-old daughter. The attack is savage, and only because of his own awkwardness does he not kill them. After the attack, he appears as a mute and uncomprehending animal as he crashes through the forest. Eventually, he is drawn back to the town, where he is captured and roped to a lamppost.

"A WEDDING DRESS" AND "AN ESCAPADE"

Many of the characters in *A Native Argosy* are dissatisfied and troubled by vague, unarticulated desires. In "A Wedding Dress," Lena Schwartz has waited fifteen years to marry. Finally, when her fiancé has a good job, the wedding is scheduled. She longs for a dress that will show her to her advantage and make her desirable to her future husband. Unaware of her own actions, she steals an expensive dress from a store. Regretting the deed, she nevertheless tries on the fancy but ill-fitting dress. Still wearing it, she is

arrested. Her fiancé bails her out and takes her into his custody. In "An Escapade," a middle-aged woman is lonely and repressed. Because of the titillating gossip of her bridge-club friends, Rose Carew misses the service at her Catholic church in order to attend another service being held in a theater. During the service, she is sexually attracted to the man next to her. She does not, however, recognize the emotion; she only knows that she is uncomfortable. She hurriedly leaves, goes to her Catholic church, and prays until she recovers her equanimity. Both of these characters yearn for a change in their lives, but they cannot articulate their desires and are unable to initiate actions that might bring about the desired results.

"A PREDICAMENT"

Throughout Callaghan's work appear stories that contain characters, settings, and conflicts that are familiar to Catholics. In "A Predicament," a young priest hearing confessions must deal with a drunk who has wandered into the confessional booth. The man, thinking that he is on a streetcar, waits for his stop. The priest, ignoring him, hears confessions from the other booth, but it soon becomes apparent that the man will not go away and will probably cause a disturbance. The priest, young and somewhat insecure, is afraid of any embarrassment. To resolve the issue, the priest slips into the role of a streetcar conductor and announces to the man, "Step lively there; this is King and Young. Do you want to go past your stop?" The drunk quietly leaves. The priest is at first satisfied with his solution, but then his dishonesty bothers him. Earlier, he had chided a woman for telling lies, instructing her that lies lead to worse sins. Unsure of his position, he thinks that he should seek the bishop's advice but then decides to wait until he can consider his actions more closely. Thus, he postpones what might be a soul-searching encounter. Callaghan, gently and with humor, has shown that priests are no strangers to human weaknesses.

IN HIS OWN COUNTRY

In *A Native Argosy*, Callaghan included two novellas. One of these, *In His Own Country*, presents a man who attempts to find a synthesis between religion and science. Although Bill Lawson dreams of becoming a latter-day St. Thomas Aquinas, he is unsuited for the project because of his overwhelming ignorance. Indeed, the task throws him into a catatonic state. Flora, his wife, is concerned first with the income that the project might generate, then with his neglect of her, and finally with his well-being: He does not eat, shave, or take care of his clothes. She longs for the days when they would enjoy the evenings together. Eventually, he quits his job because the small hypocrisies associated with newspaper work taint him, or so he reasons, and render him unsuitable for his grand task. He grows increasingly bewildered as he tries to summarize what is known about geology, chemistry, and the other sciences. At one point, he argues that he can reduce all life to a simple chemical formula. He even converts to Catholicism in order to understand religion better. Finally, returning from a long walk, he discovers his wife with an old beau and dashes out of the house. Flora searches for him, but failing to find him, she retreats to her father's farm, a three-hour walk from town. Later, Bill is found incoherent on a bench. At first not expected to live, he is force-fed by his mother and eventually Flora returns to care for him. The town treats Bill as a marvel and admires him for the philosophical thoughts they assume that he is thinking. The ending is ambiguous. Is Bill a prophet, a saint, or a madman?

Flora as the point-of-view character is well chosen. Limited in intelligence, she makes no attempt to comprehend Bill's thoughts, which ultimately drive him to insanity. The sparse, economical prose style matches the limited perceptions of Flora. Bill and Flora belong to the roster of marginal characters in *A Native Argosy* who lack control over their own lives.

NOW THAT APRIL'S HERE AND OTHER STORIES

Callaghan's second collection of short stories, *Now That April's Here and Other Stories*, contains thirty-five stories that were published in magazines from 1929 to 1935. This later work shows the influence of Christian humanism, a belief in a Christian interpretation of the world coupled with a focus on humans' happiness and an emphasis on the realization of their potential. In 1933, Callaghan spent many hours with Jacques Maritain, the French theologican

and philosopher, who was then a visiting scholar at the University of Toronto. Maritain is credited with developing Christian existential thought as a response to Jean-Paul Sartre's essentially atheistic existentialism. His influence led Callaghan to moderate the strongly pessimistic tone of his fiction.

Less naturalistic in tone than the earlier tales, these stories present characters who, while they still cannot greatly alter the courses of their lives, can occasionally achieve a measure of peace, contentment, and dignity. Unlike the inarticulate characters of the previous volume, these later characters are more intelligent. Matching this change in the characterization, Callaghan's style is more complex; the sentences are longer and of greater variety as opposed to the pared-down style of the earlier volume. Yet while the style is more mature and the stories more optimistic, there is less variety than in the earlier volume. The stories presented in this collection for the most part follow a set pattern. The equilibrium of the opening is interrupted by a crisis; after the crisis is met, an equilibrium is again established, but some insight is achieved, all within the span of a few hours.

"THE BLUE KIMONO"

Many of the selections in *Now That April's Here and Other Stories* depict the struggles of young lovers to overcome the effects of the Depression. In "The Blue Kimono," George and his wife, Marthe, had come to the city for better opportunities, but since they have arrived in the city, their situation has worsened. Frustrated, George blames his wife for his unemployment. One night, he awakens and discovers Marthe tending their son. The woman is frightened, but George is too frustrated to notice his wife's concern; all he sees is her tattered blue kimono. He had bought it when they were first married, and now it seems to mock his attempts to secure a job. Gradually, his wife communicates her fears to him; the boy's symptoms resemble those of infantile paralysis. Immediately, the husband forgets his problems and tries to entertain the little boy. When the boy finally responds to the aspirin, the couple, who have weathered the crisis, are drawn closer. The wife thinks that she can mend the kimono so that it would not appear so ragged. Through their love for each other and for their son, the two have, for a moment, eliminated the tension caused by their poverty. In "The Blue Kimono" as in "A Wedding Dress," Callaghan uses clothing symbolically. These items suggest a happier moment and reveal the discrepancy between the characters' dreams and the reality that makes those dreams unattainable.

"A SICK CALL"

In this volume, as in *A Native Argosy*, Callaghan includes stories that utilize a situation that is familiar to Catholics. In "A Sick Call," Father Macdowell, an elderly priest, who is often chosen to hear confessions because nothing shocks him, is called to the bedside of a sick woman. Even though she has left the church, she, afraid of dying, wants to be absolved of her sins. Her husband, John, however, who rejects all religion, opposes the priest's visit. John is afraid that she will draw close to the church and thereby reject him, thus destroying the love they share. Yet the priest's advanced age, his gentleness, and his selective deafness secure for him a place at the side of the woman's bed. In order to hear her confession, Father Macdowell requests that John leave, but John refuses. Father Macdowell seemingly accepts defeat and in preparation for departing asks the husband for a glass of water. As John complies, the priest quickly hears the woman's confession and grants absolution. John, returning as the priest is making the sign of the Cross, knows that he has been tricked.

The priest leaves with a sense of satisfaction, yet gradually he grows concerned that he came between the wife and her husband. The priest recognizes John's love for her and remarks on the beauty of such strong love, but then he dismisses it, calling it pagan. He begins to doubt his convictions, however, and allows that perhaps the pagan love is valid. In "A Sick Call," Callaghan has again presented a priest with human failings; Father Macdowell relies on subterfuge in order to hear a confession. Yet the story is more than a character study of a priest; it is a discussion of what is sacred, and the answer is left ambiguous. Callaghan implies that sacredness is not the sole property of religion.

MORLEY CALLAGHAN'S STORIES

After a ten-year hiatus in writing fiction, Cal-

laghan resumed writing novels and short stories in the late 1940's. In 1959, he published his third collection of short stories, *Morley Callaghan's Stories*. For this, he selected his favorite stories from 1926 to 1953. Twelve had appeared earlier in *A Native Argosy*, thirty-two in *Now That April's Here and Other Stories*; the remaining thirteen, previously uncollected, had been written between 1936 and 1953. Callaghan in the prologue writes of the stories, "These are the ones that touch times and moods and people I like to remember now. Looking back on them I can see that I have been concerned with the problems of many kinds of people but I have neglected the very, very rich." These stories, as well as those in the other collections, show a sympathy for beleaguered ordinary human beings and an understanding of their problems.

"THE CHEAT'S REMORSE"

In "The Cheat's Remorse" (reprinted in the 1938 edition of Edward O'Brien's *Best Short Stories*), Callaghan focuses on people who have been adversely affected by the Depression. Phil, out of work, is drinking coffee in a diner. Although he has a possibility of a job, he needs a clean shirt before he can go for the interview. Yet his shirts are at the laundry, and he lacks the money to get them. At the diner, he notices a wealthy drunk drop a dollar when he pays the bill for a sandwich he did not even eat. Phil waits until the man leaves. As he stoops to pick up the money, however, a young woman places her foot on it. She, too, has been waiting for the drunk to leave, and she, too, needs the money. Phil offers to flip a coin to resolve the issue. The woman loses. Having used his trick coin, Phil cheated her. Yet immediately he regrets it, tries to give her the dollar, and even confesses his guilt, but she refuses. She argues perceptively that a single dollar could not begin to alleviate her problems but it might make some difference to him. He feels so bad that at the conclusion he is eyeing a tavern, planning to assuage his guilt with alcohol.

The characters are affected by economic forces over which they have little or no control. Thus the story has some affinities with the earlier naturalistic tales from *A Native Argosy*. In "The Cheat's Remorse," both the best and the worst are depicted. Phil, selfishly, willingly cheats the woman, but the woman, ignoring her need, offers to help Phil. So even though she is affected by the same forces, she maintains her humanity and dignity.

"A CAP FOR STEVE"

Callaghan effectively wrote stories from the point of view of characters who are limited in intelligence, and he was just as effectively able to employ a child's point of view. In "A Cap for Steve," Steve, a painfully shy young boy, is obsessed with baseball. His father belittles the sport, however, not realizing that baseball is Steve's only pleasure. Grudgingly, his father takes him to a baseball game during which Steve acquires the cap of one of the star players. The cap changes Steve into a leader. Yet he loses the cap and becomes despondent. Later he discovers another boy, a lawyer's son, wearing his cap, and he and his father call on the boy's father. The difference between the two families is apparent immediately. Steve's family is barely surviving, while the other boy's is wealthy. Since the lawyer's son bought the cap from another, the lawyer offers to sell it to Steve for the price he paid, five dollars. Even though five dollars represents a sacrifice for Steve and his father, they agree. Then the lawyer offers to buy back the cap because his son values it. At twenty dollars, Steve's father agrees. Stunned, Steve will not walk with his father on the return home. Steve's father realizes that he does not know his son and resolves to be more of a father. The boy accepts his father's apology and is willing to forget the cap as "the price [he] was willing to pay to be able to count on his father's admiration and approval."

Although the story is set in the Depression and illustrates class differences, the focus is on the father-and-son relationship. The father does not accept his son until he comes close to losing his love, but the boy is willing to forgive his father's indifference for the chance at a closer relationship. The emphasis is on the love that can survive under adverse conditions.

In 1985, Callaghan published a fourth volume of collected stories, *The Lost and Found Stories of Morley Callaghan*. The twenty-six stories in this volume were originally published in leading magazines in the 1930's, 1940's, and 1950's. During the prepa-

ration of *Morley Callaghan's Stories*, they had been overlooked, and in 1984, they were "found." The stories are similar in tone, style, and theme to the work that appears in the other collections.

In Callaghan, the inarticulate and the forgotten—the rural and urban poor, the insane, and the mentally weak—have found a voice. Throughout his career, in a straightforward narrative style, he told their story. Although Callaghan might not have received the recognition he deserves, he nevertheless should be studied. As one reviewer has written, Callaghan "sits across the path of Canadian literature like an old Labrador, you're not sure how to approach him, but you can't ignore him."

OTHER MAJOR WORKS

LONG FICTION: *Strange Fugitive*, 1928; *It's Never Over*, 1930; *A Broken Journey*, 1932; *Such Is My Beloved*, 1934; *They Shall Inherit the Earth*, 1935; *More Joy in Heaven*, 1937; *The Varsity Story*, 1948; *The Loved and the Lost*, 1951; *The Many Colored Coat*, 1960; *A Passion in Rome*, 1961; *A Fine and Private Place*, 1975; *Season of the Witch*, 1976; *Close to the Sun Again*, 1977; *A Time for Judas*, 1983; *Our Lady of the Snows*, 1985; *A Wild Old Man on the Road*, 1988.

PLAYS: *Turn Again Home*, pr. 1940 (also known as *Going Home*); *To Tell the Truth*, pr. 1949; *Season of the Witch*, pb. 1976.

NONFICTION: *That Summer in Paris: Memories of Tangled Friendships with Hemingway, Fitzgerald, and Some Others*, 1963; *Winter*, 1974.

CHILDREN'S LITERATURE: *Luke Baldwin's Vow*, 1948.

BIBLIOGRAPHY

Boire, Gary A. *Morley Callaghan: Literary Anarchist*. Toronto: ECW Press, 1994. A very good biography of Callaghan. Includes bibliographical references.

Conron, Brandon. *Morley Callaghan*. New York: Twayne, 1966. This volume is a comprehensive, carefully organized analysis of Callaghan's short fiction and novels to *A Passion in Rome*. Its straightforward style and format make it accessible to students. Besides its eight chapters, it includes a useful biographical chronology and a select bibliography.

Cude, Wilfred. "Morley Callaghan's Practical Monsters: Downhill from Where and When?" In *Modern Times*. Vol. 3 in *The Canadian Novel*, edited by John Moss. Toronto: NC Press, 1982. This florid essay treats the darker side of Callaghan's vision through a discussion of characterization in several of his short stories and in some of his novels such as *Luke Baldwin's Vow* and *A Passion in Rome*.

Gadpaille, Michelle. *The Canadian Short Story*. Toronto: Oxford University Press, 1988. Includes a brief discussion of Callaghan's short-story writing career, commenting on his working-class characters, the simplicity of his style, and his contribution to the development of the modern Canadian short story.

Hoar, Victor. *Morley Callaghan*. Toronto: Copp Clark, 1969. The style and thematic concerns in Callaghan's fiction to 1963 are treated in this book's two sections, "The Technique" and "The Themes." Hoar supports his commentary with plentiful quotations from Callaghan's works. A useful bibliography is included.

Kendle, Judith. "Morley Callaghan: An Annotated Bibliography." Vol. 5 in *The Annotated Bibliography of Canada's Major Authors*, edited by Robert Lecker and Jack David. Toronto: ECW Press, 1984. This volume contains the most exhaustive listing of primary sources ("Part I: Works by the Author") and secondary sources ("Part II: Works on the Author") on Callaghan's work up to 1984 that a student is likely to need. The categories cover the spectrum from books and articles through interviews to audiovisual material. A helpful "Index to Critics Listed in the Bibliography" is also included.

Marin, Rick. "Morley Callaghan." *The American Spectator* 24 (February, 1991): 36-37. A biographical sketch, noting that Callaghan was a famous literary figure in the 1920's when he was part of the Parisian expatriate set of Ernest Hemingway, James Joyce, and F. Scott Fitzgerald; asserts that Callaghan's decision to remain in his native Toronto affected his status in the literary world, but he accepted his relative obscurity with resignation rather than bitterness.

Morley, Patricia. *Morley Callaghan*. Toronto: McClelland and Stewart, 1978. This study considers Callaghan's fiction to the mid-1970's, including thorough, useful analysis of his short fiction.

Tracey, Grant. "One Great Way to Read Short Stories: Studying Character Deflection in Morley Callaghan's 'All the Years of Her Life.'" In *Short Stories in the Classroom*, edited by Carole L. Hamilton and Peter Kratzke. Urbana, Ill.: National Council of Teachers of English, 1999. An analysis of the story through the perspective of how events affect and change a single character.

Woodcock, George. "Possessing the Land: Notes on Canadian Fiction." In *The Canadian Imagination: Dimensions of a Literary Culture*, edited by David Staines. Cambridge, Mass.: Harvard University Press, 1977. Callaghan's fiction is discussed in the context of Canadian fiction and its development and direction since the nineteenth century. The student is provided with a valuable overview that underscores the significance of Callaghan's contribution to Canadian literature.

Barbara Wiedemann, updated by Jill Rollins

CRITICAL SURVEY
OF
SHORT FICTION

GEOGRAPHICAL INDEX

GEOGRAPHICAL INDEX

CATEGORY INDEX

ABSURDISM
Ilse Aichinger, 28
John Barth, 176
Donald Barthelme, 182
Samuel Beckett, 218
T. Coraghessan Boyle, 325
Albert Camus, 429
Robert Coover, 632
Thomas M. Disch, 745
Bruce Jay Friedman, 914
John L'Heureux, 1509
Jakov Lind, 1513
Jean-Paul Sartre, 2095

ADVENTURE. *See also* SCIENCE FICTION, SUSPENSE
H. E. Bates, 197
Saul Bellow, 233
T. Coraghessan Boyle, 325
Joseph Conrad, 620
Stephen Crane, 654
Arthur Conan Doyle, 775
Robert Greene, 1081
Jim Harrison, 1127
Bret Harte, 1133
Homer, 1222
Pam Houston, 1231
Samuel Johnson, 1314
Ursula K. Le Guin, 1476
Petronius, 1911
Robert Louis Stevenson, 2245
H. G. Wells, 2476

AFRICAN AMERICAN CULTURE
Maya Angelou, 83
James Baldwin, 135
Toni Cade Bambara, 152
Amiri Baraka, 165
Arna Bontemps, 281
Charles Waddell Chesnutt, 549
Samuel R. Delany, 709
Paul Laurence Dunbar, 793
Ralph Ellison, 837
Ernest J. Gaines, 930
Joel Chandler Harris, 1121

Chester Himes, 1204
Langston Hughes, 1238
Zora Neale Hurston, 1249
Charles Johnson, 1306
Jamaica Kincaid, 1362
Joaquim Maria Machado de
    Assis, 1569
Reginald McKnight, 1577
James Alan McPherson, 1581
Clarence Major, 1591
Paule Marshall, 1634
Ann Petry, 1916
Jean Toomer, 2335
Alice Walker, 2428
John Edgar Wideman, 2509
Richard Wright, 2560

AFRICAN CULTURE
Bessie Head, 1152
Margaret Laurence, 1438
Ben Okri, 1838
William Plomer, 1937

ALLEGORY
Joseph Addison, 14
Ilse Aichinger, 28
John Barth, 176
Dino Buzzati, 381
William Carleton, 455
Angela Carter, 469
Miguel de Cervantes, 491
John Cheever, 532
Anton Chekhov, 540
Robert Coover, 632
A. E. Coppard, 638
Dante, 670
E. M. Forster, 886
Johann Wolfgang von Goethe,
    1016
Thomas Hardy, 1112
John Hawkesworth, 1139
Nathaniel Hawthorne, 1143
Charles Johnson, 1306
Franz Kafka, 1328
Herman Melville, 1664
Rabbi Nahman of Bratslav,
    1745

Joyce Carol Oates, 1771
Thomas Pynchon, 2004
Leslie Marmon Silko, 2135
Susan Sontag, 2193
Richard Steele, 2213
Robert Louis Stevenson, 2245
Edith Wharton, 2500

ANTISTORY. *See also* IRREALISM, METAFICTION, POSTMODERNISM
Donald Barthelme, 182
Heinrich Böll, 272
Jorge Luis Borges, 285
Raymond Carver, 472
Robert Coover, 632
Stuart Dybek, 803
John Fowles, 891
Barry Hannah, 1108
Vladimir Nabokov, 1738

ASIAN AMERICAN CULTURE
Lan Samantha Chang, 511
Maxine Hong Kingston, 1378
Jhumpa Lahiri, 1424
Bharati Mukherjee, 1721
Amy Tan, 2279

ASIAN CULTURE
Ryūnosuke Akutagawa, 37
Pearl S. Buck, 366
Osamu Dazai, 699
Shūsaku Endō, 841
John Hawkesworth, 1139
Lafcadio Hearn, 1156
Ihara Saikaku, 1261
Maxine Hong Kingston, 1378
Lu Xun, 1541
Yukio Mishima, 1690
Tim O'Brien, 1790
Kenzaburō Ōe, 1809
Pu Songling, 1984
Jun'ichirō Tanizaki, 2283
Wang Anyi, 2443

CATEGORY INDEX